## THE SOCIAL ARCHAEOLOGY OF FOOD

This book offers a global perspective on the role food has played in shaping human societies, through both individual and collective identities. It integrates ethnographic and archaeological case studies from the European and Near Eastern Neolithic, Han China, ancient Cahokia, Classic Maya, the Andes, and many other periods and regions to ask how the meal in particular has acted as a social agent in the formation of society, economy, culture, and identity. Drawing on a range of social theorists, Hastorf provides a theoretical toolkit essential for any archaeologist interested in foodways. Studying the social life of food, this book engages with taste, practice, the meal, and the body to discuss power, identity, gender, and meaning that create our world as they created past societies.

Christine A. Hastorf is known for her contributions to palaeoethnobotany, agriculture, meaning in the everyday, food studies, political economy, and ritual in middle-range societies of the Andean region of South America. She has written and edited many articles and books. She has completed fieldwork in Mexico, California, New Mexico, Italy, Perú, Argentina, Bolivia, Turkey, and England. She oversees an archaeobotanical laboratory at UC Berkeley and directs an archaeological project in Bolivia. At the 2012 Society for American Archaeology meetings, she was awarded the Fryxell Award for Excellence in the Botanical Sciences in Archaeology.

# The Social Archaeology of Food

## Thinking about Eating from Prehistory to the Present

**CHRISTINE A. HASTORF**

University of California, Berkeley

CAMBRIDGE
UNIVERSITY PRESS

# CAMBRIDGE
## UNIVERSITY PRESS

University Printing House, Cambridge CB2 8BS, United Kingdom

One Liberty Plaza, 20th Floor, New York, NY 10006, USA

477 Williamstown Road, Port Melbourne, VIC 3207, Australia

4843/24, 2nd Floor, Ansari Road, Daryaganj, Delhi - 110002, India

79 Anson Road, #06-04/06, Singapore 079906

Cambridge University Press is part of the University of Cambridge.

It furthers the University's mission by disseminating knowledge in the pursuit of education, learning and research at the highest international levels of excellence.

www.cambridge.org
Information on this title: www.cambridge.org/9781107153363

First published 2017

*A catalogue record for this publication is available from the British Library*

*Library of Congress Cataloging in Publication data*
Names: Hastorf, Christine Ann, 1950– author.
Title: The social archaeology of food : thinking about eating from prehistory to the present / Christine A. Hastorf (University of California, Berkeley).
Description: New York, NY : Cambridge University Press, 2016. |
Includes bibliographical references and index.
Identifiers: LCCN 2016016037 | ISBN 9781107153363 (hardback)
Subjects: LCSH: Prehistoric peoples – Food. | Food habits – History – To 1500. | Diet – History – To 1500. | Excavations (Archaeology) | Social archaeology – Case studies. | Ethnology – Case studies.
Classification: LCC GN799.F6 H37 2016 | DDC 394.1/200901–dc23
LC record available at https://lccn.loc.gov/2016016037

ISBN 978-1-107-15336-3 Hardback
ISBN 978-1-316-60725-1 Paperback

*For my darling twins:*
*for life-loving Nick*
*and in loving memory of Kyle*

# Contents

*List of Figures*                                                      *page* x

*Preface*                                                              xiii

*Acknowledgments*                                                      xvii

1   Introduction: The Social Life of Food . . . . . . . . . . . . . . . . . . . . . . . .   1
    *The Place of Food in Archaeological Research*                       4
    *Five Themes in This Book*                                           7
        Materiality                                                     7
        Social Agency                                                   8
        The Senses                                                      9
        Economics                                                      10
        Taste                                                          10
    *The Centrality of Cultural Food Studies Today*                     12
    *Book Outline*                                                      13

PART I    LAYING THE GROUNDWORK                                         17

2   Framing Food Investigation . . . . . . . . . . . . . . . . . . . . . . . . . . . .   19
    *How People Choose the Food They Eat*                               20
        Rules of Edibility                                              22
        Omnivore's Paradox                                             24
        Nutrition                                                      25
    *The Gift of Food*                                                  27
    *The Crafting of Taste*                                             29
        Creating Civilized Taste in Europe                             32
        Creating Civilized Taste in China                              35
    *Taste, Emulation, and Social Position*                            39

|  | *Structuralism* | 42 |
|  | The Humoral Doctrine in Europe | 47 |
|  | The Humoral Structure in Asia | 49 |
|  | The Flavor Principle | 51 |
|  | *In Sum* | 53 |
| 3 | The Practices of a Meal in Society. . . . . . . . . . . . . . . . . . . . . . . . . | 55 |
|  | *What is a Meal?* | 59 |
|  | Archaeological Meals | 64 |
|  | *Cuisines and the Social Economies of Taste* | 67 |
|  | Archaeological Cuisines | 73 |
|  | *In Sum* | 79 |
|  | **PART II   FOOD STUDIES IN ARCHAEOLOGY** | 81 |
| 4 | The Archaeological Study of Food Activities. . . . . . . . . . . . . . . . . . | 83 |
|  | *Food Production and Procurement* | 84 |
|  | *Food Processing* | 91 |
|  | Drying, Pickling, and Rotting | 95 |
|  | Animal Processing | 98 |
|  | Plant Processing | 100 |
|  | *Food Storage* | 107 |
|  | *Food Preparation (Cooking)* | 117 |
|  | *Food Serving* | 129 |
|  | *Food Consumption (Eating)* | 134 |
|  | *Food Cleanup and Discard* | 138 |
|  | *In Sum* | 140 |
| 5 | Food Economics . . . . . . . . . . . . . . . . . . . . . . . . . . . . . . . . . . . . . . | 142 |
|  | *Food Production Models* | 144 |
|  | *Emulation and Inequality: Economics of Desire* | 146 |
|  | *Emulation and Inequality: Control over Production and Access* | 153 |
|  | *Staple and Wealth Finance* | 157 |
|  | *Provisioning* | 163 |
|  | *The Moral Economy* | 169 |
|  | *Euergetism* | 174 |
|  | *In Sum* | 176 |
| 6 | Food Politics: Power and Status . . . . . . . . . . . . . . . . . . . . . . . . . . | 179 |
|  | *The Gastropolitics of Daily Life: Gender Status* | 183 |
|  | *The Feast* | 194 |
|  | Celebratory Feasts | 197 |
|  | Potluck Feasts | 198 |

Contents

Alliance Building Feasts | 199
Competitive Feasts | 203
*Eating and Drinking in the Mississippian World* | 204
*Archaeological Food Politics* | 214
*In Sum* | 216

PART III   FOOD AND IDENTITY: THE POTENTIALS OF
FOOD ARCHAEOLOGY | 219

7   Food in the Construction of Group Identity.................... 223
*Boundedness, Food, and Community* | 228
*Defining Community* | 230
Signature Foods and Identity | 232
Food Nationalism | 237
Food at the Boundary: Culture Contact | 245
*Colonial Encounters* | 246
*Immigration* | 253
Family and Household Identity | 255
*The Maya Culinary Tradition through Family Meals and Feasts* | 260
*In Sum* | 271

8   The Creation of Personal Identity: Food, Body,
and Personhood........................................ 273
*Body Concepts* | 275
*The Open Body* | 282
The Permeable Body | 282
The Partible Body | 283
*Embodiment, Corporeality, and the Senses* | 287
*Relational Personhood, Gender, and Age* | 290
*The Individual: Techniques of the Body, Food Consumption,*
*and Gender Identity at a Neolithic Anatolian Village* | 296
*In Sum* | 307

9   Food Creates Society ................................. 309

*References* | 325
*Index* | 385

# Figures

| | | |
|---|---|---|
| 2.1 | A European medieval meal | *page* 33 |
| 2.2 | A Chinese Han Period meal | 36 |
| 2.3 | Lévi-Straus's food triangle | 43 |
| 3.1 | An English meal | 62 |
| 4.1 | Map of the Upper Mantaro Valley Region | 87 |
| 4.2 | Changes in the relative percentages and ubiquity crop yields in the Paca and Yanamarca Valleys | 89 |
| 4.3 a and b | Steps in bread making from grain cleaning through baking | 94 |
| 4.4 | Dried fish stacked in Norwegian storage room | 111 |
| 4.5 | Basket evidence and Building 5 at Çatalhöyük, showing basket locations | 114 |
| 4.6 | Preparation sequence of maize *chicha* | 126 |
| 4.7 | Artifactual and ecofactual evidence of *chicha* processing from the Upper Mantaro Archaeological Project | 127 |
| 4.8 | A Late Intermediate Andean meal | 134 |
| 5.1 | Changes in European use of sugar over time | 149 |
| 5.2 | Pacatnamu food densities | 155 |
| 5.3 | Sausa food, presented in standardized densities | 159 |
| 6.1 | Image of a Kwakwaka'wakw potlatch vessel from British Columbia, 80 by 70 cm | 201 |
| 6.2 | Map of the Mississippian complex at its greatest extent | 206 |
| 6.3 | Still life of a sumptuous meal 1597–1660, Pieter Claesz | 215 |
| 7.1 | Two images of a Thanksgiving meal. Note the iconic foods: the turkey and the seating arrangements. (a) The painting is of an archetypical American Thanksgiving by Norman Rockwell (1943), Freedom from want; (b) A U.S. Thanksgiving family dinner photograph | 226 |

7.2   Food pyramids from the United States, Asia, and
      Switzerland. (a) USDA 1992 food pyramid; (b) Asian food
      pyramid; (c) Swiss food pyramid                                         239
7.3   Plan of Household 1 with the two ceremonial-civic structures
      at Joya de Cerén, El Salvador                                           263
7.4   Household 1 Joya de Cerén, El Salvador, with ceramic vessel
      sizes plotted                                                          264
7.5   Structure 6 at household 1, Joya de Cerén nearest neighbor
      artifact distribution                                                  266
7.6   Joya de Cerén, El Salvador household 1, Structure 11                   267
7.7   A meal at Joya de Cerén, El Salvador                                   268
8.1   Building 5 at Çatalhöyük. (a) Isometric drawing; (b) plan of
      phase B5.B                                                             298
8.2   Adult collagen $\partial^{13}C$ and $\partial^{15}N$ values from the east mound at
      Çatalhöyük                                                            302

# Preface

Food creates people
The meal is a rich study
Every person's world

It is ironic that archaeologists, who spend time every day thinking about procuring their own food through breakfast, hot drinks in the morning, lunches on the run or with friends, as well as having enough food in the house for dinner, often shift away from the rhythm and meaning of these core parts of the every day to focus on distant words, concepts, and especially long-term trends and expansive forces when they turn to their material concerning the past. It is not often that we can archaeologically "see," let alone know, the significance of chipping stone around the fire hearth before the harvest, or smoking salmon after a big catch, let alone the centrality of the endless discussions about the condition of the stored food in the corner against the wall, the mix of herbs hanging from the rafters, or that beehive over the hill toward the mountain. Yet similar daily discussions and their webs of meanings occurred in every home we uncover in our work. The satisfaction of the meal and the looming tidying afterwards are ever present in most lives. Traces of activities are what we dig up, and it is through these acts that we generate statistical data to address our social and cultural questions. Cooking, availability of plants, hunks of animal meat, amount of fuel, and the sociality of the meal would be what was on the majority of people's minds over the millennia as they kept daily hunger at bay. Sometimes this took most of the waking hours, making it even more prominent both discursively and non-discursively. Other times it was a passing event, as larders were full or trees were ripe. Perhaps focusing on those daily activities can bring the past to life and enable us to review the larger questions of cultural change, political systems, and ritual structures with a more humane eye; it certainly will bring us closer to the people and their daily lives.

I began my archaeological career studying agriculture and human-plant interaction. I looked for evidence of production in a landscape through site excavations and agricultural field interviews. As I pursued this strategy I found I wanted to know why people changed their crop regimes when we uncovered evidence of demographic and political change. The data did not always suggest an economic answer. I was therefore led by the data from the Upper Mantaro Valley, Perú, to seek historical, cultural, and symbolic reasons for the crop changes in addition to the forceful environmental and economic data at hand. I also very much enjoyed talking with the farmers to register not only the knowledge they had of each field but also their nurturing of these fields, as they did for their animals.

As the palaeoethnobotanical methods were actively being critiqued, I also began to question the interpretations more than I had anticipated at the beginning of my entry into this craft. It was important to seek the locus of likely past activities. At first I thought I was studying the macrobotanical remains to look for evidence of consumption. With the help of Robin Dennell and Debby Pearsall, who visited UCLA in 1981 before I finished analyzing my Perúvian samples, I realized that these samples reflected production more than they did consumption. Now it is clear these data reflect processing. As I worked through that data, it began to dawn on me that each stage of the activity sequence was potentially visible in the archaeological record if we could tighten up our collection strategies, methods of inference, data recording, and data analysis. We had to try to separate, if possible, the various food activities: processing, preparation for storage or for consumption, cooking, presentation, cleanup, and so on. Both the location of the deposit and the content of the sample are important in interpretation. At the same time I began to study meal preparation and diet through stable isotope analysis, which added to my understanding of these different activity steps. I realized that we could recognize the different stages of the sequence from planting or gathering to meal creation and consumption. I had investigated the charred crust inside pots to learn about not only what was being cooked but also what was consumed over a lifetime in the human bone analysis. It was a natural step to think about consumption and food. The study of diet is important, and stable isotopes and organic compound analysis have certainly revolutionized our understanding of the past. But where were the people? That issue kept coming back to me as I thought about the people with whom I spoke in the Andes as well as about the people of the past. There was a large gap between the data and the lived lives of the people. At that time I was just beginning to cook real dinners for my own family, and thus I was confronted daily with issues of what to make with what I had in the house, how to plan for the week's meals, and so on. This daily preoccupation increasingly clarified the disjuncture growing in my palaeoethnobotanical thoughts. It required a change of orientation.

At about this time Sissel Johannessen started her work as a research fellow in my laboratory, and we both had this fascination with studying food via palaeoethnobotany. We organized a symposium at the Society for American Archaeology meetings in 1990 and then another at the American Anthropological Association meetings in 1991. Our hope was to get people to look at the past foodways more culturally, by thinking about eating, and so we titled the symposia that – a phrase that came from Heidi Lennstrom. The idea was to move beyond the items that were harvested and collected to cuisine, menus, recipes, ingredients, meals, the social contexts of meals, and the meanings of meals. We began writing about these topics in our research. Over the years I have thought, read, and taught about this subject; setting some of this approach down would be useful.

We were after the past, the invisible past, and that required imagination, just as the past people also used their imagination to live in their world. And so this book is a meditation on thinking about eating. Understanding is always a cultural act. This process of understanding is the cultural situation of humankind, for the struggle to understand is the work of imagination. This is what I have tried to do in this book.

# Acknowledgments

Many people have provided engaging discussion, references, data, interactions, and support. Foremost are the three archaeological projects that I have been involved with during my career. First is the Upper Mantaro Archaeological Project, directed by Tim Earle, Terry D'Altroy, Cathy Scott, and myself, with Cathy Costin, Glenn Russell, Elsie Sandefur, Heidi Lennstrom, Bruce Owen, Lisa LeCount, Marilyn Norconk, Andy Christenson, and Terry LeVine who were instrumental in this project. The Taraco Archaeological Project has also been an important part of my archaeological life, with Matt Bandy, Lee Steadman, Bill Whitehead, Kate Moore, José Luis Paz Soria, Maria Bruno, Ruth Fontenla, Emily Dean, David Kojan, Andy Roddick, José Capriles, Eduardo Machicado, Soledad Fernandez, Melissa Goodman-Elgar, Amanda Logan, Eduardo Pareja, Ron Davis, Diane Bellomy, Elsa Choque, Franz Choque, Facundo Llusco, and Silverio Choquehuanca participating, in addition to many others, creating a wonderful research environment. The Çatalhöyük Archaeological Project was also in my intellectual development. I especially want to thank Wendy Matthews, Sonya Atalay, Shahina Farid, Nerissa Russell, Kathy Twiss, Arlene Rosen, Meltem Açabay, Louise Martin, Theya Molleson, Bašak Bos, and Jonathan Last for their discussions, data, and ideas.

Many other colleagues and friends have provided useful insights and information over the years discussing food, including Debby Pearsall, Sissel Johannessen, Mary Weismantel, Alejandra Korstanje, Dolores Piperno, Roger Anyon, Peter Garnsey, Stephen Hugh-Jones, Martin Carver, Peggy Nelson, Ben Nelson, Mike Blake, Anita Cook, Tamara Bray, Wolf Gumerman, Marie-Louise Sørensen, Catherine Hills, Chris Evans, Marlene Suano, Joan Carothers, Stella Souvatzi, John Robb, Laura Gilliam, Margie Scarry, Kirsten Tripplett, Karen Wise, John Giorgi,

Ann Davis, Allan Hall, James Greig, Yong Ha Jeong, Laurie Wilkie, Steve Shackley, Ruth Tringham, Stanley Brandes, Pat Kirch, Junko Habu, Mike Richards, Stella Nair, Richard Bradley, Jerry Moore, Alistair Whittle, Diane Gifford-Gonzalez, Raquel Piqué, Emma Styles-Swaim, Katie Chiou, Rob Cuthrell, Alan Farahani, Anna Harkey, Brian Boyd, Ericka Engelstadt, James Coil, Steve Archer, Sonia Archila M., David Lentz, and Payson Sheets. The students in my food classes have been very active in opening up discussion on many issues, both at Berkeley and at the Universidad Autònoma de Barcelona. The Institute of International Studies book manuscript mini-grant graciously provided funds to bring together a wonderful group of social food scholars to discuss the issues raised in this book, which helped me finish the manuscript. These bright food scholars are Maria Bruno, Melanie Miller, Amanda Logan, Stacie King, Meg Conkey, Elizabeth Napier, and Jun Sunseri. Four manuscript reviewers were exceptionally perceptive, providing superb, challenging comments. Mary June-el Piper helped with editing the manuscript.

I also want to thank many institutions. The National Science Foundation (BNS 84-51369; BNS 84-11738, BCS-0234011), while not funding the writing of this work directly, did fund much of the archaeological work that I have been able to complete and thus gave me a sense of the possibilities and constraints in paleoethnobotanical data. The American Philosophical Society did provide support for writing time, which I am grateful for. I wrote major parts of this book while I was a bi-fellow at Newnham College in Cambridge. Stacy Kozakavich, Shanti Morell-Hart, Anna Harkey, Katie Chiou, Alan Farahani, and Melanie Miller crafted the figures elegantly and efficiently. Other agencies also have provided support for this book. The Abigail Hogden Publication Fund issued by deans Breslauer and Hesse at the University of California-Berkeley also supported writing. Most of all I would like to thank my family – Al, Barbara, and Betsey Hastorf, and Kyle, Nick, Chris, Greg, Sarah, Jacob, Ezra, Sophie, Tia Maye, Isabelle, Liz Hodder, Louise Quirke, and Anna Hills – for being in my life.

# CHAPTER 1

# Introduction: The Social Life of Food

*Food must not only be good to eat, but also good to think.*
Claude Lévi-Strauss 1968a

The wonderful thing about studying food is that one cannot unravel the biological aspects of food use and traditions without considering the cultural aspects as well. Food is a principal medium for social interaction, for human comfort and reassurance, for anxieties and fear; it is at the heart of ideological construction. It is difficult to separate the economic uses of food from the political or individual customs from those of one group. The study of food production, of cuisine, and of meals, of preparation and presentation, gives rise to grand views of regional economic production or intimate portraits of families sitting around hearths. Food, curiously, also brings into focus the hidden aspects of power relations and social life, as well as the production of social facts and people. These are just some of the reasons anthropologists are drawn to the study of food – it is indeed the definitive anthropological topic reflecting our fundamental natures, those of sociality, transformation, and sharing.

Although there are many ways in which one can study the past, in this book I explore the past using social and cultural approaches to food traditions. One of the goals of this book is to unravel the way food creates identity. I want to explore how food traditions energize and naturalize power differences, what roles cuisine plays in social discourse, and the signification of food in social contexts, reflexively creating the person, the family, and the group. I attempt to do this by focusing on what food activities look like today as well as what they looked like in the past.

How does archaeology participate in food history and social theory? Traditionally archaeologists have theorized about food in terms of its use to stave off hunger, by studying calories, effort, and carrying capacities or land and technological productivity. Social anthropologists and sociologists, on the other hand, tend to theorize about food by considering health, consumption, social practice, personhood creation including the desire for and valuation of food, and its contexts and meanings. I want to bring this theorizing into archaeological inquiry while also opening up food theory to include archaeology. Throughout this book I make what might be called sweeping statements about cultural manifestations. These ideas might at first appear to belong to one specific time or place, but I expressly leave these statements open, hoping that readers will decide for themselves if they fit in other settings, allowing us to make them "good to think with."

How do we begin to think about eating in the past? We know that food and shelter are necessary for humans to stay alive. Eating, in fact, is so basic to life that we at times overlook its centrality in our studies of the past. We often enter the past through plant and animal taxa lists, both of which provide substantial information and represent much work. But as the British archaeologist Andrew Sherratt aptly noted, "we do not eat species, we eat meals" (1991:50). The creation of food is an act of cognitive as well as physical transformation, signaling many layers of meaning while being an agent in our lives. We must recognize the powerful forces of production operating before food gets to the table, as well as the significance of food's capacity to create culture in such a mundane act. Eating is both banal and fraught with emotional consequences (Fishler 1988:279; Rozin 1976).

Emotions around food can run high, as one person's aphrodisiac gourmet meal of raw oysters is another's horror of incorporation. As do all animals, we assign categories to food options that identify what is edible and what is not, making some perfectly edible food items unacceptable for consumption while other, even poisonous foods are sought after. Food does not exist without classification and identification, like all of our symbols and things that receive meaning. Ingredients must be identified as edible before they are consumed or cooked. This requires a cognitive transformation. This categorization process engages with the agency of food, as food alters our bodies and experiences. Food therefore reflects embodied practical knowledge of people engaging with their environment. In the archaeological record, food remains have a materiality that archaeologists harness to gain an understanding about the past. Tracking abstract cultural concepts that are made visible through storage, preparation, and eating practices brings the web of meaning and signification into the realm of interpretation through this materiality of food remains.

I begin with the concept that food is a social fact. I assume that it is a transformative agent operating in all societal processes, both materially and psychologically (Gell 1998; Latour 1993). Looking at food this way, in modern and in past settings on group, family, and individual scales, heightens one's sense of the active role food has in creating, enacting, and sustaining cultural and social processes. It highlights food's agency – not only with the possibility of being entrapped by and even addicted to some foods but also being enchanted by them. Equally important is the active role of the associated objects within these processes. People express their agency through food as the cultural act of eating brings the diverse material and social aspects of life together in a unified framework, as cultural worlds are reconstructed through material spaces, architecture, and the consumption of new objects. A meal condenses social life, which is then amplified outward. Thus we engage with practice and agency when we study meals. In fact, one of the main tensions in this discussion is whether food reflects social life or are foods active agents in social life. This tension is present throughout this book, as we tack between different theoretical approaches to the past. I side with food being an agent in social life, as you will see, but you will find places where the other dynamic also operates.

Food is also engaged with identity. It is ultimately social, the first and most quintessential gift, and the glue that forms interpersonal relations: mothers feeding children, families eating together, communities gathering to celebrate or mourn (Mauss 1980 [1925]). Food sharing is therefore a nexus for giving; the locale where social life is formed and renegotiated, where inequalities are materialized and persons are formed. Societies are made manifest in their food traditions, recipes, and the daily cycles that meals create, formed in the sharing of meals and dishes. These actions create society, which in turn becomes the milieu of identity formation (Simmel 1992 [1910]). It is this dense web of social life and agency that we delve into.

Food cultures are created through memories. Recipes and cooking methods passed down from grandparents, parents, and other relatives evoke and maintain the memory of the family, with cooking becoming an identity-making experience whatever the emotional associations (Sutton 2001). There is a cultural importance to food that participates in creating the largest society as well as the individual. Eating is associated with evocative and emotional experiences and memories, but constructed appetites are what drive people to complete tasks that will result in a particular taste and sensation. Proust's memory of the smell and taste of the *madeleine* cookie in tea evoked such an emotive memory of his childhood that it formed the core of his four-volume *Remembrance of Things Past* (1934) and launched modern social theory disciplines.

Food sharing is probably the most common social act in human history. "... those who eat and drink together are by this very act tied to one another by a bond of friendship and mutual obligation ... We are to remember that the act of eating and drinking together is the solemn and stated expression of the fact that all those who share the meal are brethren (Robertson Smith 1889:247). In some societies eating alone is considered inappropriate, even sinister; in others, it is a requirement. Identifying eating habits can convey views about social interaction as well as personhood. How one shares food speaks about the place of the participants in society, their age, status, and situation.

The Classical Greeks called food *trophe*. The same word root is in their concept of nurturing people, *anatrepho*, which includes raising children and making kin through feeding, but also teaching them manners and enculturing them into society (Stella Souvatzi 2003, pers. comm.). Commensal or communal sharing and eating therefore intimately interweaves the individual into society at all levels. Many archaeologists have begun to use the term *commensal* to mean communal eating, especially eating at feasts, after Dietler's important 1996 article on political food. In Middle English it means sharing a meal at a table, from the Medieval Latin *commnslis* (*com*, "with," and *mnsa*, "table"). Commensality therefore infers eating together. The word also has a second meaning, as an unequal symbiotic relationship of two species that is beneficial to one party while the other remains unharmed and unaffected. This might be a concept to think about in some social settings.

## The Place of Food in Archaeological Research

Food-related archaeological studies have tended to emphasize diet, efficiency, and production rather than food and its expansive social field. Diet and subsistence questions, plant and animal husbandry, and evolutionary modeling have been core topics in processual and environmental archaeological approaches, to great effect (e.g., Gremillion 2011; Khare 1980; LaBianca 1991). These studies concentrate on where edibles were procured, their health benefits, eating costs, and what was consumed. We will spend some time looking at what such studies have brought to our understanding of the past, especially the particular success of the newer, microanalytical work of organic molecules, phytoliths, isotopes, pollen, starches, stable isotopes, bones, and parasites. These remains and the methods to identify them can enable us to direct archaeological inquiry toward the social questions of people and their lived values. This trajectory is complex and requires the weaving together of data and perspectives, perhaps in a more multifaceted manner than that with which most archaeologists are comfortable. Working with these approaches and data sets precludes focusing on one thing, for as you pull at one data thread you unravel others. This exercise is messy, rich, and complex, like a dense midden.

The materiality of food allows us to complete an archaeology of human experience, as both material and emotional aspects of a lived life surround food. What are the materialities of meals, food traditions, and cuisines? Our word for "meal" comes from the Old English for ground cereal grains, but its meaning has been transformed to an eating occasion, at a specific time and place. A meal can be composed of several dishes, but it need not be. How do the different parts of a meal, currently called "dishes," something prepared to be eaten, link people to ingredients and ingredients to society? How many linking arguments are sufficient for the identification of a social trend in the material data? Vestiges of past repasts are present in the archaeological record and can be investigated, but we are on slippery ground if we want the full picture. Food traditions are repeated ingredient combinations of meals. Cuisines are styles of cooking and preparing food, their temporal and contextual placements. Can we study food traditions and cuisines, especially their social dimensions, without a full range of the material correlates in the archaeological record? The objects that we dig up are part of a larger system of cultural entanglements. We can make these links between object and meaning because of the embodied practical knowledge that food activities encompass. Whereas social relationships are not always recoverable from archaeological data, human experience can be materialized. Given our expanding research capabilities and an emphasis on the new results that can be gained, these networks of interaction deserve to be explored.

A social approach to studying past culinary traditions should be able to incorporate all of these approaches while offering insights into past cultural and political dimensions of social life. Food's capacity to order experience and to direct courses of action grows out of its ubiquitous presence in social life as much as its materiality. The most prominent archaeological hesitation to incorporating a social approach has been the lack of tight correlates between the social aspects of food traditions and the material record; archaeologists can never watch people of the past cooking or eating. It is through our own food experiences that we can begin to trace food culture as it permeates social life in the past.

*Feasts: Archaeological and Ethnographic Perspectives on Food, Politics and Power* (Dietler and Hayden 2001) framed the debate between ecological functional approaches and the culturally constructed meanings of large meals and their contexts. As this debate gathered momentum in archaeology, archaeological examples on the study of past foodways present issues of cultural identity, cultural change, and meaning (Gerritsen 2000; Gosden and Hather 1999; Hagen 1992, 1995; Hamilakis 1999; Jones 2007; Miracle and Milner 2002; Parker Pearson 2003; Stroeckx 2005; Twiss 2007; van der Veen 2003, 2008; Wright 2004). In these works we can see the value in how archaeologists are opening up cultural vistas about the past through food archaeology. These publications illustrate how humanistic archaeology can be while applying rigorous scientific methodologies. Food has become a point where archaeologists can cross over into other disciplines because it is a quintessential interdisciplinary topic, harnessing many disciplines while also requiring multiple data sets and scales of analysis. We increasingly see articles that address values at the same time as they apply molecular or isotopic data.

Do we accept that studying food and cuisines moves us closer to lived lives and that studying eating in archaeological settings can provide insights into the past? The subdiscipline of food archaeology is not yet ubiquitous in current archaeological practice, although it is increasingly becoming so. It is exciting to read articles in which the authors use food to think critically about the past (e.g., Dietler 1996; Hard et al. 1996; Haaland 2007, Hastorf and Johannessen 1993; Hayden 1996; Jones 1999; Klarich 2010a; LeCount 2008; Lightfoot et al. 1997; Mills 2004; Potter and Ortman 2004; Scott 2001; Thomas 2007; Twiss 2012a; Wright 2000). Topics such as cuisine, appetite, taste, food preferences, and disgust have been harnessed to study identity in the past, as in the studies about group identity by Gasser and Kwaitkowski (1991), Johannessen et al. (2002), and Smith (2006), senses and taste by Hamilakis (2004), or cuisine by Atalay and Hastorf (2006) and Stahl (2002, 2014). Some ask whether these topics can be addressed in archaeology. In this book I propose that these avenues of inquiry can indeed be pursued in archaeology.

This accent on the social aspects of food is channeled by our sister disciplines in which food is an increasingly important investigatory lens. In addition, the social theory momentum in archaeology opens space for theorizing about food in past social formations. Although the ecological constraints on what people ate are significant and form the basis of our investigations on food, there are also strong sensory traditions and symbolic codes that influenced eating habits. Highlighting these social, cultural, and historical aspects of the past can open up questions about our hard-won material evidence. Through daily food activities people not only stay alive;

they remake themselves mentally, psychologically, and physically. In these practices the actions and material remnants connect to unlock the past, as we increasingly link the small bits of data together into a picture of seasonal cuisines and cultural preferences such as that presented about the Neolithic world by Atalay and Hastorf (2006).

Many aspects of past food activities are not visible. The actions themselves are gone: the stirring of the pot, people's conversations, the sounds and smells of cooking, savoring the taste as the cook checks the sauce, the anxious hunger of the onlookers, the sated feeling after eating, or the sequence of courses consumed. Our work here requires an acknowledgment of these invisible practices. Nevertheless, food archaeology begins with specific contexts of food remains, the meals, the kitchens, the technologies harnessed, and the rubbish left over. Studying the procedures linked to this evidence enables us to learn more about how people acted out their social and cultural dynamics through their food habits and styles.

## Five Themes in This Book

This book builds on a series of tenets. In addition to the fundamental premise of the agency of food in creating our identities, done so through memory, I build on five related concepts that thread throughout my presentations. The first premise is materially driven, another one is social, the third is sensory, the fourth economic, and the fifth cultural. All are framed by the belief that meals are not just cultural events, they are also agents; they are techniques of the body and exist through meaningful practices that get carried along through bodily repetition and memory. Based on these notions, the study of food allows us to investigate many issues of interest to archaeologists.

### Materiality

The first theme derives from the disciplines of materiality and identity and how artifacts reflexively and actively influence social worlds (DeMarrais et al. 2004; Dietler and Herbich 1998; Gosden 2005; Miller 1998a, 2005). The material culture of food creates as well as reflects social relations. In the following chapters I examine how food actively renews society and engages the participants through the *things* that are involved in food creation. Food – the material and the idea – is an ethnic marker, a group identifier, and a medium for exclusion and inclusion. In Barthes's (1979) study of French and U.S. eating habits, for example, we learn how the way of eating fish, meat, and salad communicates the identity of the individual as well as their social class. The French, Barthes noted, eat by class and gender; men eat meat in large bites, women nibble at salads. There is little snacking. In the United States, on the other hand, snacks are common and iconic foods are traditionally shared between genders. Barbequed meat is the core meal on the Fourth of July in the United States; unleavened bread must be served at a Jewish Passover *Seder* feast; and a baked cake, preferably layered and white, is essential at a wedding. Ingredients and their preparation signal and define activities and events. This premise of the material links to societal formation can help focus our application of plant taxa, ceramic wares, and animal bone frequencies to gatherings, ceremonies, differential power at social events, and social relations within communities. These interrelationships help us sense the material agency of things in the manner that Alfred Gell (1998) proposed.

*Social Agency*

The second tenet engages with and reflects the social world and therefore entails social agency – how a meal can be a political, social agent, reaffirming, transforming, or realigning relations among the participants (Appadurai 1981; Fajans 1988:145; Gell 1998). Eating partners exist in many societies, forming special bonds of trust and support in a fictive kinship that operates beyond dinner. The social world never operates far from food that people share. Acquaintances reach a different relationship if they eat together. People clearly manipulate food presentation to channel social outcomes (Appadurai 1981; Klarich 2010a:2; Weismantel 1988). Reflect on an important family meal at which someone wants to make an impression. The agency of the dishes, their presentation and flavors, are there to enchant the guests. All participants consume the meal, but each person is entrapped in a different social position; those that helped prepare the meal have a different social outcome than those that are invited. Food can be shared evenly or selectively, eaten quickly or slowly, left on the dish to signal satiation or fed to the dog under the table. The end result realigns the participants. Each of these acts is a construction of the social relationships that are played out around the table.

Identity is created through these acts of social eating. The restaurant is a benign example in which people are generally allowed to choose what they want to consume, communicating their personality and mood to others at the table. Power relations can be enacted behind the scenes. We hear of the power of chefs over their subordinates in professional kitchens, with scenes of melodramatic power displays during food preparation. There are evocative ethnographic examples of power relations seen in feasting and presentation too, with aggressive serving to neighboring communities on the Goodenough Islands presented by Young (1971) or the elegant wedding feasts of India, famously described as gastropolitics by Appadurai (1981).

A good meal and its setting enliven conversation and create consensus and social cohesion. Meals do this by resonating with past meals and the people who prepared and ate them, by evoking food memories through the sensory tastes and displays. Satiation – the sense of physical well-being, transformation, and communion – becomes the collective memory of a meal that can be called up in the future. This transformative experience resonates long after the meal is over, in the corporeal sensation of the meal and the affirmation of social relations, tucked away in memories. Like material heirlooms, past food experiences can evoke strong emotions and even sustain people when there is little else (Sutton 2001). Thinking about eating leads to thinking about people in their social world. *In Memory's Kitchen* records recipes remembered by women who were in the Terezín concentration camp during World War II, written down as these women tried to retain their sense of identity and community through remembered recipes and meals (De Silva 1996). Food heirlooms such as written-down recipes illustrate the active power of social memory and enchantment. By talking about and remembering past foods and recipes people connect to their past social worlds and to themselves. This is a common activity for those away from home.

### The Senses

The third, related premise of this book concerns sensory and physical engagement with food. Eating is a sensual act, since each meal physically transforms mood and energy levels. Anticipation occurs throughout the production, collection, storing, and processing of the ingredients as the remembrance of smells, tastes, and feelings resonates with the meals to come. Disgust as well as desire can be aroused by these sensations (Jones 2000). Food transforms each person's body through their eating and drinking; we can get ill from poor diet, or regain health through a good one. Corporeal transformations ensue with fermented beverages, poisons, or excessive calories; change can also come from hunger. All the senses are engaged in meal preparation and consumption; taste, smell, touch, hearing, and sight (Lalonde 1992). The pot bubbles as the cook tastes the stew with a wooden spoon. The senses are activated, physically transforming mood and bombarding the body with an increase in serotonin and insulin. Socially acquired tastes such as spicy or bitter foods are constructed, as seen in the cult-like engagement with chile peppers (*Capsicum*) that "chile heads" have, now around the world (www.chileheads.com/; Nabhan 2005; Weismantel 2004). Given that food preparation and the produced meals are physical, interactive events, we can track how corporeal transformations locate the participants in their social world through such sensory actions. This perspective leads us into the realms of identity, since archaeologists are increasingly realizing that certain foods, their production, preparation, and accompanying sensations create individuals and communities over thousands of years (Fuller and Rowlands 2009). This is what Elizabeth Rozin (1973) called core flavors.

## Economics

The fourth premise to be discussed is how food engages with cultural economics – the economics of value, access, desire, and control. This standpoint asserts that caloric efficiency and "energetic practicalities" do not guide everyone's actions with regard to food choice, but that people do include some economic constraints, costs, inputs, and outputs and production styles in their decision making. A strong component of cultural tradition – affective feelings, familiarity, and the understanding of what food is acceptable – enters into food consumption decisions. Further, the notion of power and control of production and access can never be removed from food. Who has the right or agency to harvest a crop or hunt an animal, procure a rare mushroom or bake a specific recipe? Part of this economic equation of food acquisition is the history and memory of tactics and practices. Some food ingredients are passed over while others are sought out. These actions are not based solely on cost and availability, although such criteria play a role in crafting cuisines. Organic matter becomes edible when it embodies desirability within an historical food tradition – what constitutes good food or proper eating situations is defined within a network of economic and historical influences (Logan 2012; Logan and Cruz 2014; Wilk 2006).

## Taste

Taste, the fifth theme, is an important cultural force that weaves through every example in this book, being both enabling and constraining (Bourdieu 1984; Elias 1939; Falk 1991; Giddens 1979; Warde 1997). Taste is not only one of the five senses, the sensory impression of food or other substances on the tongue and body; it is also an awareness of subtle differentiation, in value and quality. This cultural valuation carries embodied preferences and emulations, manifested in practices through unconscious and conscious regular encounters with the material world, responding to the memories of past meals. What is the relationship between disgust and good taste, and how do they interact with tradition, emulation, and individual taste (Jones 2000:62)? Bad taste and good taste are created through sensory experiences that are culturally filtered, feeding back onto the individual's perception (Jones 2000; Rozin and Fallon 1987). Personal taste is especially active at the point of refusal, when people do not readily adopt foreign foods or when disgust is stimulated. This action (disgust and/or refusal) can appear to be passive or unconscious, but it is active, based on meanings that have been incorporated into the mind and body through memories and cultural constructs. These taste traditions may seem conservative, but they are scalar – that is, taste continuities and change have to do with embodied forms of practical knowledge and cultural settings. People do not add new ingredients or techniques into their cuisine or preparation technology randomly, but in structured, historically contextualized ways (Bourdieu 1984; Fajans 1988; Farb and Armelagos 1980; Lyons and D'Andrea 2003; Roddick and Hastorf 2010). The North American Thanksgiving meal is a good example of embodied taste preferences. Reenacting grandma's preparations in the kitchen, gathering the ingredients, following the old recipe sequence, presenting food on the same or similar platters – these acts embody both conscious and unconscious actions, created through repetitive, meaningful practices recalled from the past in this community of Thanksgiving practice (further discussed in Chapter 7). Such sedimented embodiments shape every Thanksgiving meal. Preferences are not fixed but are reframed continuously. These canons of taste operate in food choice and commodity consumption in our own lives. When taste is added to the mix, it reminds us of how food economics of convenience and price are only two of the many components that go into our decision making concerning what we eat and drink (Jackson and Moores 1995; Krondl and Lau 1982; Miller 1998b; Sahlins 1976). Added to the economic realities in food consumption – what can grow where, transport costs, weather patterns, access – are practices of taste and valuation that frame the reception or rejection of food selection, including beliefs, health, flavors, emotions, desires, hedonism, self-esteem, memory, tradition, political implications, social position, capacity to make decisions, and even fame.

### The Centrality of Cultural Food Studies Today

> It (food) can instill power, prestige, substantiate kinship, create social relations, effect social control … participate in formation of person or aspects of identity, an operator in rites of passage, feasts, myths.
>
> Fajans 1988:143

The disciplines of sociology and history have placed food centrally in their intellectual agendas. Long-term histories have highlighted the cultures of food in historical change (Drummond and Wilbraham 1994; Forster and Ranum 1979; Mennell 1985; Mennell et al. 1992; Mintz 1996; Ramírez 2005; Scholliers 2001). Sociologists discuss how the generative structures of food are a critical and productive entry into the investigation of social classes as well as ethnicity (Barthes 1979; deCerteau 1989; deCerteau et al. 1998; McIntosh 1994; Warde 1997). Anthropology also has joined in with edited volumes by Counihan and Van Esterik (2013) and Forson and Counihan (2013). These disciplines note how food is constituted by historical conditions as it participates in and reflects long-term social change. The authors discuss how food reflects both large- and small-scale cultural processes. The number of wonderful historical and sociological publications relevant to food archaeology makes this a rich moment to address this issue in archaeology as well as to contribute to the greater discussion in food studies.

To gain a sense of the recent explosion of food studies in many disciplines, one need only visit the food section of a library and see the new shelves that have been added, with huge compendia such as *The Oxford Companion to Food* (Davidson 1999) and the two-volume *Cambridge World History of Food* (Kiple and Ornelas 2000). These books cover the gamut of approaches and cultures. The Oxford book is more a food preparation and processing volume, whereas the Cambridge set focuses on the study of society, history, and culture through food. Not only are many foods (raw and prepared) discussed but also attitudes, national trends, food policies, food disorders, and prehistoric diets. Methany and Beaudry (2015) have recently mimicked this in archaeology with their *Archaeology of Food Encyclopedia*. The vast quantity of recipe books and shows on television, often with a twist of cultural context or Braudelian long-term history, spans virtually every area of the world and group. Some television channels are now completely devoted to food programs. These presentations suggest that food will be tastier (and also more meaningful) if consumers know more about the history of what is about to go into their mouths. This plethora of recipes and preparations has led some commentators to critique this obsession in scholarship as a fad. Many are equally vehement about its centrality to our understanding of human existence (Counihan 1999; Counihan and Van Esterik 2013; Lupton 1996). Food scholars wax eloquent about food as a nexus in society. "Understanding people through their food, or satisfying curiosity about individuals' eating habits, is an activity which certain puritanically minded scholars claim to despise. If however we associated food with generosity, pleasure, and the basic texture of life itself, it becomes a matter of more than simply ephemeral interest" (Allen 1994:viii).

Why exactly has food studies burgeoned across so many disciplines? As we learn in Barthes's (1979) food analysis, emulation is central in food traditions. But more central to my mind is the universal appeal of food. Daily life is signposted by food preparation and consumption, by meal times, by gaining foodstuffs, by making dates to eat together. This attention to food results from concerns about the body, existence, and identity, which are directly related to incorporation and corporeality. But this interest also engages with satiation and sensation. We enjoy feeling good, and eating helps us feel good.

Thinking about eating is reflective. One can learn about oneself and others through the foods being consumed and what people think about those ingredients. Vestiges of past repasts are still with us in our own meals. Some food habits are long-lived. We still consume what can be called Neolithic foods, such as muesli and hummus, or Paleolithic foods, such as raw nuts and berries. Combinations of flavors and local specialties can be traced over many generations. Cooking equipment has not changed all that much. A container to hold liquid and a spoon are required for soup preparation, with a bowl to drink it from; these too are Paleolithic tools.

## Book Outline

In this book I propose food archaeology as a subdiscipline in its own right, moving it into a more central position in our discipline's and research projects' goals. Many of the artifacts we excavate and study are associated with food. Why not let food studies open up our views of the past? Likewise, food scholars also need to bring archaeology into their agendas as a serious contributor to the discipline.

Archaeology is a preeminently material endeavor, and fortunately for archaeologists, many artifacts are material correlates of past foodways: plant and animal remains are central, but so are ceramics, chipped and ground stone, organic residues, architectural layout, hearths, baskets, human bone,

stable isotopes, molecules, storage pits, middens, and environmental indicators also directly speak to foodways. Many current archaeological research
projects are multidisciplinary, incorporating methodologies that integrate
multiple data sets. A surprising range of historical records, storage tallies,
shipping orders, menus, shopping lists, stock inventories, cookbooks, health
treatises, and diaries provides information, adding strength to our interpretations of the excavated material.

The study of foodways is "the whole interrelated system of food con-
ceptualization, procurement, distribution, preservation, preparation, and
consumption" (Anderson 1971:2). Foodways allows for broad trends and
tropes. But such an approach suggests a sweeping view of long-term food
cultures, and archaeologists know that we in fact study individual deposits
and events in archaeological analysis, making us tack between the individual and the group. As we pursue the agency of food – that is, the relationships of identity and food in specific sites or lived lives – we can focus
on food events, food activities, and food practices of both the small and the
large temporal scope.

Rather than focusing on a world filled with symbolism, signs, discourses,
and meanings, or one based on economically driven efficiency, I hope
include the spectra of the pressures we experience in daily life when thinking about the past, delving into what was occupying people's minds, hands,
and stomachs, filling their workdays, carried around the countryside, and
prepared at their hearths. Foods are well suited to serve as metaphors for
understanding less well-understood but equally important aspects of social
life, be it human solidarity, loneliness, or engagement with the divine. Food,
including processed and prepared foods, as with all objects made or modified by people, are metaphorical expressions of culture and therefore link to
the identity of the maker, producer, and consumer.

In this book I present several avenues of study that can be applied to
archaeological settings, but I do not systematically cover all possible archaeological approaches to food studies. For example, I do not deal with caloric
constraints, seasonality patterns, or dietary reconstruction (see Pearsall 2015
chapter 7 and Gremillion 2011 for a good explanation). I do not cover food as
it relates to healing, chemical nutrition, or other biocultural aspects important to human existence (see Etkin 2006). Instead, my aim is to pursue past
social life through the study of food and cuisine. I discuss the cultural, economic, political, social, and symbolic aspects of cuisines, corporeal experiences, tastes, smells, and meanings surrounding food, and at the political
relations and social identities that are expressed and created in food activities. My strategy is to investigate these approaches to the past through both

ethnographic and archaeological examples, interweaving them within each topic. By juxtaposing modern examples with archaeological food studies drawn from a wide literature I try to bring our inquiry into sharper focus through the lens of food.

I wrote this book to focus on the agency of food in ideological formation, social identity, and personhood, to engage with the critical work of food in society, as well as to show the potential of these trajectories to help in understanding the human past. Building on the five premises outlined here, the following chapters concentrate on some of the classic archaeological questions while folding in new perspectives and methods. The cultural examples I use throughout the book are introduced in the early chapters and will be seen again in later chapters, highlighting different issues in the same material. Other examples are only used for specific subjects. My mixing of ethnographic and archaeological examples was done purposively to help disrupt our usual thought patterns and to seek the past in new ways.

The three parts of the book follow a vaguely temporal intellectual path. The first part, consisting of Chapters 2 and 3, lays the groundwork with foundational themes and scales of study. Frameworks in this study of food are outlined in Chapter 2. This chapter begins with food as the quintessential gift. Foods are infused with values, built on a full range of beliefs, rules, and experiences, which is addressed in this chapter. The crafting of taste and emulation are traced through two histories of taste in Europe and China. This leads to how food systems are created and classified. There are many analytical scales in the study of food, from landscape and climate to biochemistry; Chapter 3 covers the smallest – the meal. I focus on this analytical level not only because it is the moment of incorporation and satiation but also because the actions surrounding the preparation of the meal have material correlates and are often found in the archaeological record. From the meal we can follow many cultural dimensions of identity and society.

Part II's three chapters present what archaeology scholarship has been engaging with, the many steps and activities in food provisioning. By unpacking the *chaîne opératoire* of food preparation options (the sequence of practices in food preparation), the techniques of the body in Chapter 4, as well as food activities across the landscape, we begin to envision the possibilities of food-work in the past (Dobres 2000; Ingold 2000). These activities are self-creative dimensions of mundane tasks, bodily memories clearly leading to a range of past meals. The obligation is on us to remember and engage with this triangle of technology, knowledge, and agency when we deliberate about cuisines in the past. Chapter 5 turns to one of the more common themes in food studies – food economics. Food production models have contributed much to our longer views of societies. Food is often considered a mere staple in economic discussions, yet it also is and has been the basis for wealth and the focus of state power. The potential for inequality is ever present in ownership and access and that includes food, making this a common and important strand of food studies, as is so clear in today's current pressing issues in many urban settings. Chapter 6 presents the political side of food, where the gastropolitical ideas of Appadurai (1981) are the focus. While issues of gender roles and social positions stream throughout this book, they are directly discussed in this chapter. All meals have a political edge to them, but the overt power operating at feasts makes it an obvious meal to discuss. These orientations clearly lead to the other axes of social life, issues of community and identity, which are brought to the fore in the next part of the book.

Part III turns to the potential of food studies, mainly focusing on identity formation. In the two chapters comprising it the creation of identity at different scales of inquiry is addressed. Chapter 7 begins with the larger social entities. Here we look at community foods and how food creates group identities. Tracking food indigenization and assimilation helps us see how ingredients and dishes participate in the nuanced recreation of social identities, especially in the confusing environment of colonialism (Dietler 2007; Wilk 2006). This social creation is accessed through thinking about boundaries and bounded actions. In most settings, not just what communities produced on their own land – and therefore had access to – but also how they prepared their food is created by the boundaries of a group (Adapon 2008; Young, 1971). We look at household creation and identity through food sharing, with all of its tensions and solidity. In Chapter 8 the scale is the individual, and the creation of personhood through food and its incorporation into the body. This theme includes concepts about the body, embodiment, and personhood. Corporeality and the power of the senses are important in individuation or lack thereof. Identity formation is relational and bounded, not only with other people, plants and animals but also with things – and what is more common than interacting with things to eat? Chapter 8 does not contain as many examples as the earlier chapters do; my goal is to think about these concepts as we push ourselves farther along this trajectory. Chapter 9 assesses the study of food in a social context, bringing together the themes of the earlier chapters to see where food studies can guide us as we look into the past. Ultimately food keeps us alive, and in turn making us invested in it.

# PART I

# *Laying the Groundwork*

Food is the meeting place of nature and culture. One cannot unravel one side from the other, making food and all its components engagingly cultural while being driven by the biological need to stay alive. In many groups, food is the principal medium of social relations, both for self-identity as well as for satiation. Commensal studies, the study of eating together and foodways (like social memory), helps archaeological investigators recover the humanity of the past through the study of this daily, enjoyable act that garners meaning with each bite as it stimulates the memories of past meals. Through the study of past food we gain knowledge about parts of past cultures that have been less available through other approaches. By discussing key theoretical perspectives in sociology, history, and anthropology that speak to the archaeological investigation of food, I turn to archaeological examples to look for insights about the past. Through these perspectives, food analysis, ethnographies, and archaeological examples all provide ways to move us closer to past people and the influences that shaped their daily lives. One main tenet is that food is a transformative agent. People have constructed their worlds, ontologies, desires, and belief systems in ways that can carry us closer into the past. The social theories presented here are perspectives that I think need to be considered when addressing food and its meanings. By trying to apply these notions at the group, family, and individual levels we can see the agency of food in creating, enacting, and sustaining social processes, meaning constructs, and society. This section presents basic tenets in food anthropology and their approaches to societal construction and maintenance.

# CHAPTER 2

# Framing Food Investigation

Many ethnographers have ventured out to study kinship, economics, politics, gender relations, ritual, or trade, only to find that their informants channeled their interactions toward the food they eat. These experiences often redirected the anthropologists' investigations and also their theoretical approaches (Descola 1994; Hugh-Jones 1979; Kahn 1986; March 1987; Meigs 1984; Richards 1939; Weismantel 1988). One poignant example is that of Anna Meigs (1984), who went to Highland New Guinea to study divorce and its place in intergroup alliances. She found, however, that no one wanted to discuss it: "instead they wanted to tell me about what they were and were not allowed to eat. Doggedly I persisted in my attempts to unravel the intricacies of divorce and alliance: my attempts were met with good-natured indifference. Finally I gave up and decided to go with the flow" (Meigs 1984:ix). She proceeded to study the daily food practices and beliefs of the Hua. In so doing she uncovered a richly subtle world of social meaning, bodily identity, and social interaction that opened up the Hua existence to her, from kinship to personhood to politics and, in the end, to social alliances and divorce. This also is our goal in archaeological food studies: to use food as a portal to larger social worlds.

As an introduction to food archaeology, I will discuss a range of ideas about how people conceive of and decide upon what they eat. This chapter is not all encompassing, in part because of the topics that will be covered in the remaining chapters. Here I review some salient models with regard to food selection and food classification. I begin with a brief introduction to food selection models, noting some of the longer-lived principles in food choice traditions. To help us understand foods and how they might have been conceived in the past, I look at a range of ways societies have classified food, including how food is determined to be edible. Clarifying these conventions, concepts, and building blocks provides a structure and vocabulary for the issues and questions presented in the subsequent chapters.

## How People Choose the Food They Eat

Food choice is not as clear-cut as it seems. Choice is at the core of the modern global consumer economy, making people feel as though they have choice while hoodwinking them into consuming more. How do we choose which foods to buy or to grow? Today's urban grocery store is bursting with choice. The main choices in today's markets seem to be driven by chemistry. The same taxa are presented in various ways, differing by production methods and packaging. This is most striking in the vegetable section. The same pea and bean varieties can be purchased in several ways, one is "conventionally" grown and the other is "organically" grown. As an archaeologist who is always on alert for classification systems, this choice puzzles me. The U.S. store offers fresh vegetable choices based on production method and chemical history, not on size, color, smell, flavor, maturity, shape, or even harvest location– the categories anthropologists think foragers use to choose their food, and certainly the way other primates do. We are not given the opportunity to choose our peas based on the place of origin, who grew them, the political situation of the farmer, or the travel distance, let alone the carbon footprint! (In English stores the country of origin is listed.) Our choice is whether chemical fertilizers and pesticides were used on the crop or not. Even the word "conventional" is obfuscating. Since its origins in the Neolithic, all farming was what we call "organic." The "conventional" category refers to the system less than a hundred years old of adding nitrogen-rich chemical fertilizers and animal-killing poisons to fields. Then there is the category of prepared foods (ready meals), which opens up another range of food choice: whether, for example, to buy potatoes au gratin, French fries, dehydrated mashed potatoes, or fresh potatoes. Again it is the processing technique and list of chemicals on the package that helps us make our choice. Would that every artifact we excavate came with a processing and an ingredients label. Archaeological science is moving quickly toward this goal with genetic microprobes and portable XRF machines, but we are not there yet. To help us understand the foods we excavate as well as eat, we need to be aware of what scheme we are applying to past food choices and how it links to our own. There is a true disjuncture between food choice today and how archaeologists envision food choice in the past.

It is unprecedented in the history of human society that food ingredients are available all the time and that people can consume what they want, when they want. The culture of 24/7 access that has spread across the globe has begun to tatter some of the long-lived food selection models, unharnessing the traditional seasonal selectivity that drove food choice and constraint making for an unprecedented scale of decision making (Canclini 2001; Goldfrank 2005). Many people in First World countries are paying the health price for this liberation in food selection, as Schlosser (2001) points out in *Fast Food Nation*, his riveting book on the outcome of increasingly depending on heavily processed food. The question of food choice has been unleashed, ripped out of traditional regional, seasonal, or cost limitations through economics-of-scale production and subverting labor laws. Our food system represents a very different concept of how to assume people thought about their food choices in the past, informing us that we must think differently about eating in the past.

There are many approaches to studying how people decide what to eat. Social scientists concur that people's food choices usually operate within a specific range of situated options, based on conscious and unconscious cultural rules of practice, personal histories, and habits that somehow define and perpetuate food cultures, one's food *habitus* (Bourdieu 1984; Counihan 1997 [1984]; Krondl and Lau 1982; Mauss 1980 [1925]; Miller 1998). Consumption research has found that both economical and "uneconomical" principles operate in modern "foraging" in grocery stores, where actual production cost is only one element in decision making (Sigurdsson et al. 2010). These projects make us aware that many criteria are operating in food choice today and therefore in the past as well.

People can be acculturated to eat almost anything (Mintz 1996:35). However, people become selective in their food choices. Food choice depends on a combination of economic, cultural, physiological, and psychological factors (Huss-Ashmore and Johnston 1997; Rozin 1987). Choice, in other words, is built into our biological makeup, our situational economics, our experiences, family history, and the corporeal sensations we have when we eat. All the senses participate in our eventual choices of what we put in our mouths, including odor, texture, sensation after eating, flavor, as well as personal and cultural memories of consumed food (Beidler 1982:7; Sutton 2001).

Food scholars agree that human food choice is learned and is not wholly dependent on the biological or chemical nature of the foods themselves. But those few biological predispositions that humans have, such as a desire for sweetness, salt, and fat, can be unlearned and rechanneled (Fiddes 1991). As a child grows up surrounded by specific culinary preferences, s/he learns what items are desirable along with the subtle, appropriate combinations and quantities in varying situations. This complex web of cultural learning through practice, exchange, and boundaries is the subject of the renowned British anthropologist Mary Douglas (1966), whose work is presented in Chapters 3 and 7. Douglas is considered by some to be a structuralist in her investigations of food. More than any other anthropologist, she made us aware that food is central to the social endeavor. Her focus revolves around the symbolism inherent in the social relations manifested and reflected in the daily practice of meals, as the embodiment writers have done. Her analysis allows us to place "peoples' beliefs back into the social context of their lives" and materialize abstractions of belief (Douglas 1966, 1982:9). Unlike economically oriented food anthropologists, Mary Douglas views economy and society holistically. For her, the economy, like other parts of social life, is activated by the cultural values that influence decisions as much as it is by yields and costs –practice is activated by one's *habitus*.

This chapter visits a series of models that have been applied in food studies. The economics of food choice has been a strong component of how archaeologists see food choice developing and how decisions about food are made. But here I focus on other food choice models that revolve around the participation of symbolic structures and various ways people construct what is edible. Finally, nutrition and the body is discussed. In some ways these models are a microcosm of anthropology, setting the stage for further investigations in food archaeology.

### Rules of Edibility

The first criterion that defines food is whether something is edible. This is not a fixed category; many edible foods are not consumed and some poisonous items are. Edible classification decisions range from what the items look like, smell like, feel like in the mouth, how they impact the body, where they grow or are encountered, and their availability (cost), in addition to the many historical habits and beliefs that have been built up around them over the years (Rozin 1987; Simoons 1994). Although we must consider edibility when we study specific food from the past, core food preferences and/or regular taboos are more visible in the archaeological record based on relative frequency. The more relational consumption is, as with the intergenerational food rules of the Papua New Guinea Hua discussed in Chapter 8 (Meigs 1984), the harder it will be to uncover eating patterns in the archaeological record. What we cannot assume is that people will always eat the most efficiently procured foods.

Ingredients have to be considered edible to be eaten. Edmund Leach identified three food categories: edible and consumed, edible but tabooed, and edible but not recognized as food (Leach 1964; see also Falk 1991:764). These categories are constructed and physiologically arbitrary. The rules can be transgressed; for example, when people are starving they become cannibals, consuming edible but tabooed meat. Such actions are accept-able because of the context. The recent outcry about perfectly edible horse-meat (*Equus ferus caballus* L.) found in English prepared meals shows that breaking cultural taboos is not always acceptable. How do food classifica-tions change and new foods become identified?

We have historic examples of plants that shift from nonedible to edible, such as the tomato after it was brought to Europe from Mesoamerica. In Europe in the sixteenth century, the tomato (*Solanum lycopersicum*) was initially considered a dangerous food, being identified as the forbidden fruit from Eden (and therefore called the "love apple"). When first pre-sented as a food it was considered an aphrodisiac. Eventually (in Italy) it was used as a bright garnish but was not put into the mouth, being consid-ered too succulent and red. Despite centuries of censure, by the nineteenth century it was a core element in Italian cuisine and had spread throughout Europe as a garnish (Allen 2002; Wheaton 1983). Could this same tempo of long-term auxiliary use before regular consumption have occurred for a range of prehistoric plants, such as chile peppers (*Capsicum* spp.) or maize (*Zea mays*), which spread slowly along the western coast of South America (Hastorf 1999)?

Some poisonous items have become edible. Activating the cognitive dis-sonance of eating, people are attracted by the thrill of low-level danger. Both Japanese and East Indians add metal fragments into special drinks and onto their most elegant dishes (Falk 1991). The Japanese eat the poisonous puffer fish (*Tetraodontidae fugu*) as a special treat (Grivetti 1978:176). Consuming these fish slices gives a warm-to-numbing sensation in the mouth along with a sense of euphoria. Poisons tend to be piquant and bitter as well as neurologically stimulating, such as the chile pepper compound *capsaicin* (which is not dangerous but tastes as if it should be). Chile peppers have even received a heat ranking, the Scoville scale, an organoleptic ranking system applied to measure the amount of pain-stimulating molecules.

Frogs, puffer fish, and coffee all fall into this strong-flavored, slightly dangerous food category for which the act of eating is often considered slightly risqué, as certain foods go from being an acquired to a sought-after taste. These items can be ingested only if consumed in small doses, after being prepared in appropriate ways. People could have learned about these substances by placing small bits of the item on the tongue to taste for alkaloids or by giving portions to dogs, as is done today.

Many initiation rites include strong-flavored foods that children do not usually prefer on first taste (chile peppers in Native American Southwest, meat in China, coffee in the United States, and alcohol in Europe), which makes the eating experience unforgettable. Powerful emotive events such as life stage rites can then convert an aversion to an acceptance and new personhood (Fiddes 1995).

How do Western scholars explain food selection differences among members of the same group? Psychologist Paul Rozin concluded that the rules of food selection are primarily based on an individual's eating experiences (Rozin 1987). Gender, age, and biological factors do not determine food choice. Even parental influences on children's tastes have little impact. Preferences tend to be mediated through long-term socialization and personal experience. "For example, mother-father correlations in preferences or attitudes are equal to or higher than parent-child correlations" (Rozin 1987:196). His research suggests that daily food practices and aesthetics are inherited through repetitive (and recursive) eating patterns. These results are helpful in archaeological interpretation because we can identify regular, long-term food patterns in archaeological data.

Along with food preferences, taste aversions are also learned. People associate recently eaten foods with bad digestion, influencing future food choices (Garb and Stunkard 1974). Eating something that causes nausea can strongly enforce a future distaste for that substance, which can last a lifetime (Beidler 1982; Jones 2000; Rozin 1987:184–185). The psychology of food selection clearly has an impact on modern food traditions within communities and most probably did in the past as well.

### Omnivore's Paradox

Biology affects food preferences (Rozin 1987). Sweetness is the earliest and most innately sought taste that humans share with other primates (Beidler 1982:5). This desire for sweet foods has been linked to the desire for mother's milk and ripened fruit (Dudley 2000, 2014; Falk 1991:763). Although all people may begin their lives desiring sweet food, this preference does not necessarily continue throughout life. A craving for sweetness can be modulated culturally, as seen in the overpowering demand for sugar products in the English and American diets when compared with that of the French palette (Barthes 1979; Sahlins 1976). In foraging societies, the preferred tastes are sweet and fatty. These flavors are associated with well-being and confer superiority to the consumers in foraging societies who acquire them (Wiessner 1996:6).

Although people need to eat new foods to maintain a broad and healthy diet given seasonal variability, especially if they are foraging across a landscape, many people are nervous about ingesting unknown or new foods. These activities stimulate tensions at deep psychological levels. This is the Omnivore's Paradox, first spelled out by food sociologist Fischler (1980, 1988), and is a form of cognitive dissonance. People are basically conservative in their consumption patterns, repeating preferences and avoiding new foods. How do people make new dishes palatable? A common strategy for accepting new foods is to add common flavors to the new food, masking the newness, such as roasted horsemeat in place of roasted beef during World War II in northern Europe (Fiddes 1991). This strategy activates the power of the Flavor Principle, in which new ingredients are added to signature dishes to make them more familiar. This is the tenet of fast food outlets across the United States, and increasingly the world, providing the same taste and texture everywhere. For a new food to be considered edible, it must first be positively linked to other valued substances or be associated with significant events, places, or persons (Falk 1991:773).

People consume a range of ingredients to attain a balanced diet. And yet, people can tire of the sameness and out of curiosity desire to experience new tastes and textures (Rozin 1976, 1982). This taste dilemma has developed throughout mammalian history, as humans evolved to adapt to many habitats. Humans are omnivores. Being omnivorous requires exploration and innovation (Milton 1987). Yet, as Paul Rozin (1976) sees it, exploration and testing can lead to anxiety because of a fear of ingesting new, foreign food, not knowing whether it will be repugnant or tasty. Rozin has written about this hypothesis of food selection that humans (and rats!) have an aversion to consuming new foods yet at the same time have a drive to do so. He proposes that there is a paradox surrounding our food choice habits, a form of cognitive dissonance. This dilemma drives humans to eat beyond our biological imperative as we eat more and more variety than is needed for survival.

## Nutrition

When the anthropologist Audrey Richards set off in the 1930s to study the nutrition and food consumption practices of the Bemba in Zambia, she, like Anna Meigs years later did with the Hua, encountered unresponsive informants (A. Richards 1932, 1939). She shifted her topic to social organization.

In the end she tracked the food supply of a herding group by following their food system, eventually producing a richly detailed economic volume that discusses many aspects of Bemba society while illustrating the central role of food. This study is unique in its exhaustive reporting and attention to detail of Bemba foodways with specific detail of their nutritional consumption patterns. Based on her insights regarding food and the social and psychological impacts of differential access, she noted that nutritional needs always operate in food choice and consumption patterns. Richards found, however, that functional nutrition values are not by any means the only criteria operating in food choice.

The literature on human nutrition is vast (see Wilson 1979 or Briggs and Collaway 1984 for details). For several reasons, focusing primarily on nutrients in food choice is not the central aim of her book, although it might be easier for us to use this approach (but see Cordian et al. 2002). Animals, including human infants, select food not just to meet bodily requirements (Davis 1928, 1939; Milton 1987; Susanne et al. 1987). There is bioanthropological and textual evidence that periodic or even life-long deficiencies and famines have forced humans to alter their consumption practices. Evidence of various ailments tied to diet, such as caries, anemia, Harris lines (from periodic stress), and worse, indicates that people did not or could not always sustain well-rounded diets. Food rules often provide additional food for nutritionally vulnerable individuals, new mothers, children, or the ill (Huss-Ashmore and Glantz 1993; Shack 1969). People often had quite marked seasonal differences in their dietary intake, seen most clearly in hunter-gatherers. Grivetti (1978) and other nutrition scholars have noted that activities such as geophagy (consuming earth or minerals) were probably widespread and may have been a strategy by which people were able to gain a more complete complement of minerals and vitamins. Grivetti (1978:175) also points out that fermented beverages aid health through the production of safe drinking water and added nutrients, opening up a range of unconventional ideas about what constitutes food (see also Van Veen and Steinkraus 1970).

One major nutritive debate concerns the universality of meat craving (Abrams 1987). Nutritional and anthropological studies have focused on this issue. Some groups obsess about meat consumption, as in herding countries such as Argentina and Kenya. In those societies, when people suggest that they are starving they are really saying that they lack meat, though they have plenty of other calories and protein to eat (Holtzman 2009; Neitschmann 1973; Richards 1939). This "meat hunger" is primarily a psychological phenomenon (Simoons 1994). The ample examples of vegetarian societies that have survived for centuries further suggest that meat is not a biochemical requirement for human health.

Archaeologists assume that past societies were able to feed their members adequately most of the time. We know that people must meet basic caloric requirements to stay alive. Most archaeologists assume that people in the past consumed around 2,500 kcals a day. When calorie minima were erratic, pregnancies were not successful, and people died or migrated. Evidence of long-term stress is laid down on human bone and can be studied. To pursue the history of the general nutrition of a group, we can track a range of evidence such as Harris lines, broken bones, and tooth disorders in order to add that dimension to the other aspects in food investigations (Cohen and Crane-Kramer 2007; Huss-Ashmore and Goodman et al. 1982; Larsen 1997; Robb 1998).

## The Gift of Food

The essence of social life is exchange, binding people together through sharing with inferred obligation in a sequence of reciprocal acts (Mauss 1980 [1925]). Food is the earliest and most frequent gift as well as the most universally traded commodity (Mauss 1973 [1934]). Gifting is transferring something voluntarily by one person to another without compensation. Gift theory forms the basis for most anthropological studies of exchange, with its de-emphasis on supply and surplus economics and accent on social capital through honoring, shame, and obligation. Non-market societies differentiate between exchange values and use values. Sahlins (1972:178) calls reciprocity a "primitive mode of peace making," because gifting and sharing reduce social conflict. Mauss wrote that a gift is a social phenomenon, imbued with meanings and histories of a relationship, reformed with each new encounter. Gift exchange is the materialization of continuing relationships, especially remembered through the web of historical signification that accompanies the gift itself (Wiener 1992). Objects that are given carry a different meaning than those that are inherited or purchased. They gain their significance through the memories of the gifting events, with the recipients recalling the event and the gifter from every occurrence. A gift therefore is a thing *and* an act. Gifts have agency that continues via the memory of the gift-giving act as well as in the materialization of the gift itself. The most common gift is food. Social networks are built between individuals through food gifts that branch out into larger social alliances.

Although there is no guarantee that a gift will result in a reciprocal return or initiate a cycle of giving, inherent in a presentation is the hope of a return if not an increase in that return (Johnson 1982). Sherpa women in highland Nepal, for example, give food to visitors, a strongly held tradition and one within their household powers (March 1987:358). Much economic and social stability depends on continuing ties between people. Families need to maintain social exchange webs as individuals travel through the Himalayan Mountains. Yet there are difficulties in sustaining such exchanges over the long term, owing to the potential of escalatory gifting with each visit. The Sherpa women interviewed by Kathryn March claim that these food offerings are only proper when there are no motivating strings attached. They mask their food gifts as kindness and ethical propriety rather than claiming that the gifts link them into economic and social networks. Women therefore become the mediators within and between households, placing food and women at the center of this entangled social web.

As with the Sherpa gift network, the Trobriand Islands are linked through a trading network that sustains discrepancies in production as it engages families (Uberoi 1962; Weiner 1992). One can see food and supplies moving around the circle of islands in periodic exchanges. But what grabs the attention and leads the conversation during these interactions are the crafted wearables – armbands and other items made of shell. These items come from specific locations and have long, well-known histories. What makes these shell bands significant to the islanders are the memories attached to them. The days of exchange that follow the arrival of boats on an island focus on these heirlooms, although large amounts of food are brought to the exchange as well. Annette Weiner (1992) notes that these few, flashy, and well-discussed exchanges are accompanied by the bulk of what is traded – cloth and food. These ritualized exchanges are the "glue" of the social network, while it is the exchange of supplies and food that is the heart of these encounters. The trade of these historical decorations prompts more discussion in the anthropological literature than the food does because of their materiality and memory. As archaeologists we know that symbolic and economic capital are both important parts of such exchanges, but we might only identify the shell armbands. The bulk of the exchanges might not be visible in the archaeological record, especially if, as in this case, they are gifts of plants, food, drink, animals, dances, songs, stories, cloth, or woodcarvings.

Exchange is a common theme in archaeological study, but the interdigitating aspects of gifting and the intimately tied social indebtedness that accompanies all nonmonetary trade are less often recognized (but see Bender 1978; Blitz 1993; Dietler 1996, 2007; Hastorf and Johannessen

1993; Hayden 1992, 1996; Sherratt 1991). Long-distance exchange is most often identified archaeologically when foreign goods (obsidian), unusual concentrations (caches), or highly valued items (metal) are found. Food gifts are not as visible archaeologically if the food is not deposited in a special context, associated with containers, such as amphora outside the Mediterranean, or exotics, such as figs in England or coca leaves in the high Andes. Occasionally, one can see the act of food exchange, especially when long-distance movement of food occurred in containers. The Etruscan urns filled with wine that made their way up to the Celtic drinking feasts reflect ancient colonial trade as well as the agency of emulation (Dietler 1998, 1999, 2010). It is likely that these urns carried wine along these European Iron Age trade routes, used to toast those who engaged in trade while bringing news and unique social habits. Through such examples we can track colonial encounters that are identified by food exchanges.

Because of the recent shift in research interest toward smaller-scale activities, feasting has become increasingly prominent in archaeological discussions (Dietler and Hayden 2001; Jones 2007; Mills, 2004; Wills and Crown 2004). A feast is a social event that includes an abundance of prepared food and drink gifted to guests. This form of food gifting and its social power is increasingly visible archaeologically, especially as more sensitive analytical techniques become accessible. The work of feasts in human experience will be discussed further in Chapter 6.

## The Crafting of Taste

Taste is a preference, an experience, a judging, a sense by which the flavor or quality of a substance is detected by the tongue, and a style (Collins 1986). Taste sits between reality and desire (González Turmo 1997:125). Taste is culturally formed. Pliny the Elder noted that nearly fifty flavors of pork were recognized within Roman cuisine (D'Arms 2004:432). Taste preferences and appetite are formed by objective nutrition, symbolic principles, and embodied principles (Bourdieu 1984; Falk 1991:257). Two perspectives on taste are relevant to us here. The first orientation is the gustatory one, linked to sensations in the mouth. This activity distinguishes sweet, salty, sour, bitter, and *umami* (savory) on the tongue. Touching the food contributes to the reaction through texture and smell, as this adds to the sensation of the food experience. Taste has been studied widely, as the modern food industry tries to mimic nature's flavors for mass-produced, synthesized food ingredients. Taste tests demonstrate, however, that few people enjoy the same flavors similarly, making this a difficult science. While tastes clearly vary, social groups tend to value certain taste palettes similarly.

The second perspective of taste concerns aesthetics: the discernment, affectation, judgment, and opinion about something; the embodied preferences that influence opinion (Bourdieu 1984; Meredith 1990). Particular styles are favored based on aesthetics, emotions, values, memories, and moralities (Lupton 1996:95). Bourdieu defines taste as a product of the encounter between the object and the preference. Taste operated in the past as it does in the present (Stahl 2002). Taste practices define appropriateness and acceptability versus inappropriateness or even offensiveness, as when something is "in bad taste." Here we are more concerned with this second definition: the cultural construction of taste and its embodied forms of practical knowledge. Taste participates in the formation of the self and the creation of the group through shared preferences for certain foods and food combinations. This identity is personal, even though it is shaped by experiences within a cultural tradition.

Sociological historians have focused on the history of aesthetics and its role in changing cuisine and culinary styles in the European psyche. Shifts in taste reflect not only societal trends but also the power that desire and preference wield on society's beliefs (Bourdieu 1984; Elias [1939] 1978; Mennell 1985; Veblen 1899). Today we live within our own current taste sensibility. It has transformed over the past thousands of years along with personhood and place. I will return to this issue of personhood and its creation through cuisine and taste at length in Chapter 8, but here I want to turn to the concept of taste as a *distinctive authority* and how that participates in culinary formation (Stahl 2002). Whereas many have tracked food economics through the historical sea changes of moral and political events, scholars engaged with taste and practical knowledge focus more on emulation, desire, and choice as agents that direct social position and power in the everyday. The colonial historical encounter and conquest, in both Europe and Imperial China, demonstrate the rise of more sophisticated culinary rules accompanying multiple entanglements, power aggrandizement, and increasing expenditures on food and its accouterments (Goody 1981).

Controlling societal taste is a subtle yet profound form of political control, expressed through exclusion and specialized knowledge, corporeal actions, comportment, and advertising (Appadurai 1986). Distinction and controlling stylistic change is completed not just through controlling economic access but also by amplifying political differences, psychological inclinations, and cultural affiliations (Braudel 1973). In Europe, the aristocracy was desperately engaged in these practices, with only some styles filtering down to the masses through imitation. In fact, this is how many define elite: by their active, directed engagement in developing different tastes from the populace (Miller 1985). By tracking the etiquette of spitting, blowing one's nose, urination, and table manners, Norbert Elias (1978 [1939]) has established that the codes of proper behavior for these bodily functions were linked to other domains the European state tried to control, such as access to wealth, political decision making, and status. He surmised that the increasing concern for codifying how food was eaten was initiated by rulers well before today's hygienic justifications were put forward, concluding that broader, socially charged "canons of taste" were the sources of change that operated at all levels of society, and eventually were implemented in private, daily practices. These rules of comportment are tied to the concepts of cleanliness and dirt, eliciting disgust when matter or actions are out of place, as expressed in Mary Douglas's (1966) concepts of purity and danger. Every group has a concept of dirty food.

Etiquette, forms of consumption, and appetite derive from political traditions as well as social realities. Cultivating desire explains a lot of what occurred in European aesthetics over the past thousand years as table manners became more codified, as discussed by Elias. Conquest was in part implemented through a series of culinary encounters. Accompanying the rise of capitalism and increased inter-community trade was the development of an aesthetic of power over economic access that enabled an elite class to form. Noble classes began to have a range of new values. This constellation of activities they called *civilized*, the pinnacle of good taste. Core in this assemblage was the "civilizing of the appetite," which reflexively participated in the maintenance of class through selectively different culinary habits and embodied tastes. The *civilizing* process is the act of controlling one's instincts mentally, emotionally, and physically. Comportment and bodily control were important qualities of this trend, which still operate in Western society; the media is often pointing out the limits of current good taste.

Appetite is a state of mind that can be reflected and reaffirmed in a range of daily tasks (Bourdieu 1979). Because food tastes are formed through daily practice and learned cultural values, food consumption reflects the psychology *and* the standing of a person within society. People can change their taste and manners and thus attempt to alter their position. Norbert Elias and Stephen Mennell have both examined the psychological development of European taste and manners, from around AD 800 up to the nineteenth century. Mennell (1985, 1997) tracks this European history through eating habits and attitudes about how food should be consumed.

Elias (1978 [1939]) goes further, linking food access and consumption patterns to psychological states. These scholars find that an increasing concern with bodily self-control paralleled increasing stability in food resources. Attitudes to food therefore reflect not just the economic situation but also the social and political practices of control (Dietler 2007). Political control of an increasingly dense and hierarchical populace also placed pressure on personal embodiment, as these civilizing rules entered houses, bodies, and minds.

## Creating Civilized Taste in Europe

The civilizing story of Europe is one of increasing individuation and increasing individualism. Over time, table manners shifted such that food was increasingly distanced from the consumer. This process began in the noble and ruling classes and filtered down to the peasantry by the eighteenth century. Eating rules began to be recorded sometime in the fifteenth century in Europe (Black 1985). From Chaucer (1340–1400) we learn what were considered elite table manners – mainly, not dripping grease or food from the mouth or fingers while eating:

> At mete wel y-taught was she with-alle;
> She leet no morsel from hir lippes falle,
> Ne wette hir fingres in hir sauce depe.
> Wel coude she carie a morsel, and wel kepe,
> That no drope ne fille up-on hir brest.
> In curteisye was set ful moche hir lest.
> Hir over lippe wyped she so clene,
> That in hir coppe was no ferthing sene
> Of grece, whan she dronken hadde hir draughte.
> – Chaucer, Canterbury Tales, The Prologue
> (www.bartleby.com/40/0101.html)

The medieval culinary tradition included quite simple eating equipment accompanying complex food-processing beliefs. There were few presentation or serving containers. The early medieval table included serving platters and personal knives, with a shared goblet (Figure 2.1). Food containers were made of large slabs of bread, cut into bowl-like shapes, called "trenchers." Knives and chunks of bread were used to take up meat and soups, respectively. The peasants used all of their fingers to put food in their mouths, grabbing it out of the common bowl or receiving chunks of meat from a carver (Wilson 2012). Instead, the European elite began to use three fingers to pick up food (Goody 1982).

FIGURE 2.1. A European medieval meal (by Anna Harkey)

It was not just in English society that laboriously cooked foods set the rich apart (van der Veen 2003). Between AD 1150 and 1600 in Europe, a well-provisioned feast could only be hosted by the rich, for only they could amass enough high-quality food for this type of meal (Braudel 1973; Goody 1982:133). Elegantly presenting large pieces of cooked meat, if not whole animals, was *deregeure*. In fact, meat presentation became so ostentatious that King Edward I (1239–1307) reinforced the sumptuary laws in 1283, requesting restraint in the number of courses and the amount of meat served at a meal (Goody 1982).

During the 1400s, even important families experienced times of want. Despite this, by the 1500s, the more powerful families were increasingly bound socially and politically by both secular and religious etiquette, making culinary decisions no longer based solely on environmental constraints. Episodes of poor harvests continued to have a real impact in rural areas into the sixteenth century, however. Between 1500 and 1660 in England, one harvest in six failed. This led to occasional widespread famine, killing some members of the population and often triggering epidemics. In times of dearth, people ate bark, acorns, wild roots, nettles, chestnuts, hazelnuts, bracken, almond shells, and even brick mixed with barley. Bread often included offal and wild grass when yields were poor (Mennell 1985; Wilson 2012).

In the seventeenth century the hand of the state was entering European households as it never had before. New laws to control ostentatious gluttony took the form of rules regarding table manners, "proper" foods were promoted for certain occasions, more intricate preparations of less food, with the idea that moderation was a good thing (does this sound like today?). This was slowly being internalized from the top down in society, as these rules created new food traditions and sets of taste values than what had been operating earlier. This new food culture was in direct contradiction to the desire to eat whenever there was food at hand, as had been the norm for centuries in the feast-or-famine culture. Elias (1978) suggests that the insecurities and anxieties about famines, ingrained in people's psyches, were why people were so emotional about food and eating.

Bread trenchers began to be abandoned at the end of the 1600s as the nobility introduced individual wooden or pewter plates (Black 1985). Eventually everyone at a feast received their own drinking goblets, which allowed differences between the attendees to be noted based on their goblet types. Spoons, napkins, and then forks were introduced slowly, as eating increasingly separated the consumer from direct contact with their food.

By the end of the seventeenth century, European social and political class differences were clearly accentuated through selective cuisines and associated table manners. Elites began to desire delicate dishes that required increasingly complex preparation. Intricate sauces were developed in France, often with exotic spices. This shift from quantity to quality has continued up to today, seen recently in "nouvelle cuisines." This *civilizing* trajectory increasingly separated people from nature – they no longer touched the food they ate – as well as putting distance between each other, seen in the place settings that blossomed into a series of plates and cutlery for each person (Deetz 1977). This individuation was also enacted in the simultaneous adoption of separate sleeping rooms (Johnson 1993). Once harvests became more stable and movement of yields easier, after the sixteenth century, worry about famine as well as the potency of food superstitions slowly declined (Elias 1978; Mennell 1985:23). This stability reformed the feast-or-famine mode into the moderation-in-everything mode that accompanied the spread of Protestantism (Elias 1978).

By the 1800s, in "good" society, people were now removed from any contact with their food until it entered their mouth (Mennell 1985). As part of this European refinement, the elite also distanced themselves from the animals they were eating by having the meat cut into pieces before it was served on their individual plates, rather than the whole carcass being carved at the hearth or table as was common earlier. Throughout this history, food stability as well as growing international trade enabled the rich of Northern Europe to use food differently, marking their difference from the masses through new trajectories of taste, which they picked up from Southern European and foreign culinary traditions. This individualization not only created a European class structure in deed and mind; it also created individual bodies that were separated from the world around them. This topic will be further considered in Chapter 8 in the discussion of personhood and the body.

## Creating Civilized Taste in China

This same civilizing social trajectory of embodied taste occurred in China, creating distinct cultural groups across the continent through the vehicle of channeled preferences, tastes, and desires. Chinese definitions of properness and refinement were different from those in Europe. Studies have found these trends in China began earlier than in Europe, with widespread civilizing processes evident in the Zhou period (1200–221 BC) and solidifying in the Han period (206 BC–AD 220) (Figure 2.2). It is not just the intricate flavorings and their accompanying social values that make the various Chinese cuisines civilized and complex; it is also the complex etiquette and politicized actions that accompanied a meal. The seating arrangement, the order of serving, the balance of grains, vegetables, fruits, and meat all framed the political meal (Sterckx 2005). The longevity, complexity, and centrality of these cuisines make this region the most complex constellation of cuisines in the world.

Zhou military rulers attempted to conquer their enemies not only by war but also by social eating encounters in which the conquered people came in contact with and developed a craving for Zhou food. The Zhou leadership had developed a unifying elite cuisine, while the masses continued their varied and rich range of local cooking traditions across the regions (Katz 1982). This elite Zhou cuisine is evident in texts and painted murals that depict cooked rice Zhou style with the *keng* stew pot of roasted meats and wine (really rice ale), objects that are visible in art and the archaeological record in elite settings (Sterckx 2005:35; Ying-shih Yü 1977:66). These Zhou initiated political cuisines spread slowly across the Chinese continent by the end of the Han dynasty, AD 220.

Flavors, recipes, and the mastery of cooking have been recorded about Chinese daily life for more than 4,000 years. Bone engravings and texts provide information on the changing foodways of various dynasties. Beginning in the Zhou Dynasty, the sacred seed, soybean (*Glycine max* (L.) Merr.),

FIGURE 2.2. A Chinese Han Period meal (by Anna Harkey)

spread across all regions of China and became an important staple food along with rice, barley, wheat, and millet (Anderson 1988:24; Sterckx 2005). Chinese royal houses were noted for their unique cuisines, with hundreds if not thousands of people involved in feeding each noble household (Simoons 1991:14). These houses had chefs for specific food types: one had 342 fish specialists, 62 people overseeing pickles, and 342 wine servers. In AD 1425, for example, the royal court employed 6,300 cooks who fed 10,000 people a day (Huang 1969:90). These numbers and the intensity of special-ized preparation are unequaled to this day.

The Chinese had at least four 'haute cuisine' traditions: north and south of the Yangtze River, Sichuan (Szechwan) to the west, and the lower Yangtze River valley (Yüeh) to the east (Anderson 1988; Chang 1977; Sabban 2000; Simoons 1991). Each of these cuisines had its own flavor regime. North of the Yellow River, garlic, onions, duck, mutton, millet, and sweet balsamic vinegar sauce dominated, whereas fish, rice, and gin-ger were more common in the south (Rozin and Rozin 1981). In the west the *fagara* (*Zanthoxylum piperitum* (L.) DC) spicy pepper signified this cuisine. As discussed later in this chapter (The Flavor Principle), liquor, grain, and cooked meat were core in all four cuisines, but their flavoring and emphases differed, based on the varied spices and condiments present in the different regions. During the Five Dynasties phase (AD 907–960), for example, the competition between these northern and southern cuisines was also recorded at the imperial table, as power shifted from north to south during these fifty years. The cuisines were so codified that different classes ate different rice varieties (Freeman 1977:151). Once power shifted to the south at the end of this phase, the imperial cuisine became a mix of northern and southern flavors, which evolved into the Cantonese cuisine of today (Sabban 2000).

I focus especially on the Han dynasty (206 BC–AD 220) because of the excellent artifactual and textual evidence about meals and manners from this time period. Across the empire, a series of painted murals in noble tombs depicts the specific feast serving sequence, beginning with wine, then *keng* meat stew, grain dishes, and finally dessert, with fruit or fruit-based custards, almond custard, sweet locust soup, and so on, presented in specific types of bowls (Freeman 1977:69; Sterckx 2005). The number and variety of these dishes in a single meal denote the elegance of the meal and the household that produced it. Broiled and roasted meat was the most prized dish for the Han elite. Meat portioning occurred in China centuries before it did in Europe. In Han China, meat was cut into bite-sized pieces for ease in the delicate (and civilized) process of eating with chopsticks (Anderson 1988; Chang 1977b; Sabban 1986). Meat roasting and presentation is the most prominent event portrayed in the Han feasting murals that adorn noble tombs, illustrating meat's elevated culinary status. The painted Han feast scenes include beef flank, fatted dog, bear paw, panther breast, suckling pig, deer meat, and lamb shoulder (Ying-shih Yü 1977:67). Meat presentation was a form of political jockeying among the elite at banquets, since the types and number of meat dishes reflected the status of the host.

This prized meat grown for the elite was rarely consumed by the masses, who were vegetarians by lot. They lived on vegetable and starch-based stews that were drunk directly from bowls. Ying-shih Yü (1977:75) notes that the typical Han farming family would kill and roast a pig only once a year, for the New Year celebration. Rice, millet, and grain stews were ubiquitous, as was wine. These core foods are less commonly found in the archaeological record, but in tombs we find them ubiquitously, especially wine jars, labeled as rice, sweet, and wheat wines (ibid.:69).

"'Noodle foods' initially entered Chinese cuisine during Han times, having developed after the introduction of wheat grinding, traded in from the Near East" (Ying-shih Yü 1977:81). Boiling noodles gained popularity in the second century AD. The aristocracy liked these noodles along with mutton and milk products, bringing a new texture and flavor to northern meals

(Sabban 2000:1167). Noodles required bowls and spoons to eat, introducing particular cooking equipment along with the noodles. By the T'ang Dynasty (AD 618–907), the core dishes of the northern regions were based on wheat. These breads, steamed buns, cakes, and noodles, called *bing* or *ping* (which means "flour and water"), could be eaten with the fingers, but unlike in Europe, this eating style was not considered unrefined.

Rice remained the core starch staple in the south. There, the rice-based meal included pork, vegetables, or fish. Archaeological data show that fish was important early on, with pisciculture developing in ponds and rice paddies along the Yangtze River (Sabban 2000). In the Yangtze and Pearl River valleys, fish and rice dominated the cuisine, with vegetables, carp, and crabs flavored by ginger and wine. The southernmost region, around the Pearl River, is the Canton or Kwangtung region. Its cuisine developed later, differentiating only in the Ming Dynasty (AD 1368–1644) (Simoons 1991:55). A mix of exotic flavors was added to the rice, with an emphasis on fish and seafood, such as vinegar with crab or frog legs with winter melon and scallops. These were gentle, sophisticated flavors as opposed to the bolder flavor schemes to the north and west. Today some see this eastern region as having the most refined Chinese cuisine, it was a late development that grew out of prolonged trade, enabling the population to get to know and select from different tastes and culinary traditions from across the continent as well as by the sea.

The western Sichuan, like the two Yangtze cuisines, is an old food tradition, developing separately owing to its proximity to India and its moister climate. It is well known for its strong, spicy flavors, focusing on *fagara*, the Sichuan pepper, sesame oil, and bean paste, with the Western Hemisphere chile pepper (*Capsicum* spp.) entering in and in part replacing the indigenous pepper in the seventeenth century (Sabban 2000; Simoons 1991:52).

A rich archaeological example of a prehistoric haute cuisine comes from the southern area of China, south of the Yangtze River, during the Han Dynasty. These meals were rice-based, with a multitude of accompanying dishes. The famous Han tomb #1 of the wife of the Marquis Ma-wang-tui (Lady Dai), and its neighboring tomb #3, allow us to see, through their multifaceted, well-preserved evidence, how ingredients were combined into dishes, illustrating the subtlety of flavors that was valued in the Han cuisine (Pirazzoli-t'Serstevens 1991; Ying-shih Yü 1977:58). The bamboo slips that accompanied the food stores in Lady Dai's burial chamber describe the methods of cooking and preparation. The seasonings combined in Han dishes include salt, sugar, honey, soy sauce, *shih* (salted darkened beans), and leavening (Ying-shih Yü 1977:57). The most prominent dish was the *keng* stew, a seasoned, boiled meal based on grain or vegetables. The varied stew dishes deposited in the tomb included salted fish and bamboo shoots, deer meat and taro, chicken and squash, pork and turnip, fresh sturgeon, salted fish, and lotus root. Nine *keng* stew dishes are depicted on murals in Marquis Ma-wang-tui's tomb.

Documents suggest that the ancestor's required flavorless, pure meals sacrificed to them as offerings, whereas the living relished spicy dishes. The tomb's *keng* images fit this perfectly – pure meat with no flavoring. The painted bowls in the tomb hold ox, sheep, deer, pig, suckling pig, dog, wild duck, pheasant, and chicken. Ying-shih Yü notes that these dishes are especially remarkable because they are exactly the same as those discussed in the Zhou Dynasty Li chi Record of Rites (simplified Chinese: 礼记), a Confucian text from the same time period. This is a rare example of material conjuncture of food remains and their recipes, mural depictions, and texts (Ying-shih Yü 1977). We see here an archaeological example of a very elegant cuisine that stressed the local taste. These dishes do not include the spicy western *fagara*, nor the garlic and onions of the north, but stick to the southern cuisine, perhaps as an act of identity and regional affirmation. Such culinary traditions track the shifting manifestations of taste, but they also reflect the trade routes, the social valuation, and political emulation of elite cuisines.

## Taste, Emulation, and Social Position

Throughout the civilizing processes in both of these histories, we learn that the rich continued to expand their embodied differences through table manners and their palate by adding exotic flavors and then elaborating recipe preparations and presentation (Elias 1939; Mennell 1985; Simoons 1991). While the powerful continued to distinguish themselves through their new culinary traditions, some Europeans, as part of the incipient middle class, attempted to alter their stations by emulating the rich as they adopted new eating habits and tastes, adding plates and more meat to their meals. In this emulation process, tastes changed relatively quickly. Miller (1985) illustrates this societal dynamic in a modern Indian village. He charts the activities of lower castes who shift their daily and ritual use of food utensils, mimicking the upper castes. Adopting new tastes to alter one's social position is also exhibited in the United States, where less-well-off families try to eat like their better-off neighbors, purchasing archetypical foods such as steak with food stamps (Fitchen 1988). Whereas Miller (1985) discusses conscious mimicry of food activities that associate with other social castes,

Fitchen points out that the emulation noted in U.S. shopping styles is done not so much to mimic the higher class, but to join them. Here, class taste clearly channels food behaviors that have little to do with health or economics but much to do with identity and re-creation of self. Can we see this in the archaeological record?

The development of haute cuisine is based on status, emulation, and difference. *Haute cuisine* usually refers to intricate food rules that are selective and restrictive, with specially prepared, elegant, and expensive foodstuffs served in ornate surroundings, too complicated and expensive for the common person. These meals feed the top of the hierarchy. The social differentiation of an elite class is the goal. In societies with true haute cuisine recipes, accompanying cosmological and physiological systems are often materially recorded. The rich and elite expend much time and money maintaining their food aesthetics and rule-bound consumption patterns through complex recipes, ingredients, and codes of conduct surrounding the meal. The gulf between the masses and the elite is therefore experienced through food. Sumptuous meals with many dishes might have developed in many places, such as the Chinese and Zimbabwean courts or the Aztec and the Inka rulers' families. Historic cuisine writers tend to be selective about which cultures actually have such complex food practices. Goody claims that the qualities of haute cuisine only existed in Renaissance France, Rome, Egypt, Africa, the Middle East, Arabia, and China, preferring to use the terms "higher" and "lower" cuisines to describe the remaining cuisine spectra (Goody 1982:98). He does not mention any of the American cuisines, but I believe Mexican cuisine can easily be considered *alta* as well (Adapon 2008).

The essence of a haute cuisine is its selectivity, its ability to mark off a group of consumers from the masses through food incorporation and consumption etiquette. Selectivity can be constructed in a range of ways. The literature includes exotic and/or expensive ingredients, many steps in preparation, and the use of time-consuming and/or specialized equipment. Western European haute cuisine first coalesced in Italy in the second half of the sixteenth century, again, like in the Ming court, due to trade and movement of new flavors (Mennell 1985:69). Myth states that haute cuisine moved from Italy to France when Catherine de' Medici's cooks accompanied her to the French court in the middle of the sixteenth century, as dishes then slowly spread throughout the royal European courts. This new cultural style occurred in a range of material forms: architecture, art, furniture, and food. This haute cuisine is defined by its break from the medieval form of elite cooking that focused on roasts and exotic spices and fruits.

The new cuisine was based on preparation complexity and a new combination of ingredients. Basic to this new food trajectory was a shift from lard to butter, changing the foundational taste of the cuisine and therefore the palate of the consumers. The first French book that illustrated this split from medieval foodways was published in 1651 (Mennell 1985:71). It focuses on sauces, a characteristic that remains central to classical French haute cuisine today. Local fresh herbs later became important and in some ways represent a hearkening back to Iron Age cooking when the local kitchen gardens provided the spices (potherbs) and salad makings, before the long-distance trading networks brought in exotic edibles (Black 1985:14).

> Flandrin, Hyman and Hyman (1983) point to the cultural paradox that, just when the tastes and manners of the aristocracy were being strongly distanced from those of popular culture, aristocratic cooking was abandoning the spices which had hitherto been its most important distinguishing mark. The paradox was particularly apparent in the seventeenth century when Portuguese and Dutch merchants made spices more accessible to the bourgeoisie. At that time, what came to distinguish the aristocratic table was not the abundance and richness of dishes, but their delicacy. (Mennell 1985:73)

This emulatory race occurred just when English Christmas puddings entered the bourgeoisie British cuisines, filled with foreign fruit and spices. To maintain difference, the English nobility bought into the sauces of Italy and France and have not looked back. What we think of as modern French haute cuisine really became codified after the French Revolution, built on their local ingredients merging with the global Italian foodways (Freeman 1977:145).

Elegance and delicacy are crucial in haute cuisine, encouraging a new "good taste" that requires the converts to adopt new values. Luxury also is a concept that is associated with this food category (van der Veen 2003). Every group has luxury foods. Although the potentially Eurocentric definitions of delicacy and luxury will not suffice in archaeological settings, they do point out how we can begin to define haute cuisines in the contexts of our specific research settings.

Status-seeking emulation of shifting cuisines can be tracked by archaeologists. The adoption of a new glaze ware bowl at the New Mexico Salinas Pueblos registers how much effort people will expend to have unique, larger serving equipment at their feasts (Spielmann 2004). In her study of the Rio Grande Valley, Spielmann notes that these larger serving bowls were brought in from 100 km away for express use at communal meals. This effort was not necessary, since local black-on-white bowls could have been used at these meals. These objects carried value and "taste" across a broad region, reflecting their symbolically charged resonance and desire for these foreign bowls. This same Southwestern Native American practice is exactly what Veblen (1899) states as to why we purchase things today, not always because of their economical nature but because of our "canons of taste."

It is important for archaeologists to consider the power of preference and desire operating in eating habits and culinary activities. We are aware of some of the mechanisms that animate changes in cuisine. We can track small changes when new ingredients, utensils, or meal preparations enter the cuisine, as well as long-time trends of cuisine changes, and we should, because they recursively inform us about changing tastes and emulations. Every community's cuisine is rich enough to provide a ritual or a feast meal as well as an everyday meal, no matter how simple their range of ingredients (LeCount 2001). Studying the variability and changes in cuisines and their dishes is a productive starting place to track meaning and value in the past.

## Structuralism

Thus far in this chapter we have been skirting around one of the major contributors to the early study of food. "Structuralist analysis, though a bad master, can be a good servant; as a tactic of analysis it can afford an entrée into systems of meaning" (Robb 2007:154). Food anthropology cannot be investigated without consideration of the French anthropologist Claude Lévi-Strauss's concepts. His work in the Amazon region opened up a range of cross-referencing nature and culture relationships that highlighted the complex tensions of people within that world. One of these paths elucidated the centrality and potency of food in human society. In 1966 he focused his anthropological inquiry on food in his seminal work that included food classification, *The Culinary Triangle* (Figure 2.3), built on myths told by the people he studied. In that work his main premise was that the categories operating in the human mind are reflected in how people deal with food preparation. Lévi-Strauss proposed, as had Mary Douglas in *Purity and Danger* (1966), that the meal could be a metaphor of society, opening up many domains of social life through detailing food's participation in people's lives. What is good to eat is good to think.

Lévi-Strauss's (1968b) structural study of food beliefs found inspiration in Durkheim as well as Mauss. At that time Lévi-Strauss began to identify the structures of human thought, the deep structures present in all human

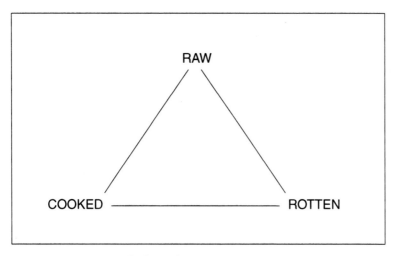

FIGURE 2.3. Lévi-Straus's food triangle

society, operating in daily life and exemplified in their foodways (Farb and Armelagos 1980; Goody 1982:17). Structuralism focuses on how underlying generative rules interconnect with observed behavior. He studied the way humans make their world meaningful through organizing the world around them, carried out in small, daily, recursive tasks. The social relationships with the world around them were most thoroughly reflected in cooking and food processing.

His premise was that by learning about people's food preparations we learn about people living in their world. Lévi-Strauss saw meals and their preparation as a kind of structuring structure, often organized in oppositions (and triads). His ingredients in these oppositions were "gustemes," a word derived from the smallest analytical category in structural linguistics, phonemes (Saussure 1966). He did not believe that culture operated exactly like a language, but he envisioned [food] classification as a form of social communication.

According to Lévi-Strauss, people use structures to organize their activities and engagement with the world around them. A social group's conceptual structure is made up of a large array of binary oppositions, creating a network of symbols that make up their culture. Lévi-Strauss sought underlying structures in the most fundamental actions of life, the transformation of animals and plants into food. He suggested that all food could be placed in one of three categories: raw, cooked, or rotten. Lévi-Strauss's now-famous culinary triangle embodies the transformations brought about by human effort through the mastery of fire, making food edible at the same time as it changed the food's meaning. These fundamental categories were clarified through the preparations of roasting (raw), boiling (cooked), and smoking (rotten) meat. These categories were more powerful than simply forms of cooking, however. They linked to the powers associated with the sources of and the relationships to meat (in the Amazon). This seemingly simple triangle was in fact constructed from the concepts held about meat's source animals, and their relationships to the essence of sentient (agentive) animals – that is, humans – and non-sentient (non-agentive) animals – that is, food. Raw meat is dangerous; eating it is appropriating the victims' animistic capacities (Fausto 2007). Raw meat or roasted/grilled meat is assumed to still hold the essence of the individual, that is, it still contains the powers (the animating essence) of the creature that was killed; thus eating it is like eating human flesh, like cannibalism, the eating of one's enemies. This eating act is dangerous and should include some appropriate actions in cooking, and only eaten by certain people. Boiling meat "de-agentivises" the animal's animating essence, making the meat just meat, and thus able to be eaten by all without fear, creating a space for commensalism. The raw meat of many Amazonian animals is considered to be essentially human flesh, dangerous to eat without some cultural transformation. This triangle, therefore, does not speak just to cooking procedures but to social relations across all living things, engaging with the transformations of beings people come in contact with as well as the intentionality of the consumers.

Lévi-Strauss later expanded this triangle to include other, more complex cooking styles, such as grilling, braising, and frying, that are applied throughout the world. This expanded model did not so effectively categorize the wider range of cooking activities within societies let alone their associated meanings. Placing these categories in a nested binary system based on the food's relationship with fire and water, which became cumbersome to think with and did not retain the elegance that his original food preparation structure did, which was built on a powerful worldview of human-animal relationships, as well as the construction of either making kin through eating together or destroying kin through eating someone.

This Amazonian food classification scheme was not defined by edibility, but by preparation, thus crafting levels of commensality and, through this, the making of kin who can eat together. This edibility-cooking organizing principle is significant for archaeologists, because with it we can identify processing activities, which are techniques of the body, and therefore have material correlates, traceable in the archaeological record. For Lévi-Strauss, the most common food-structuring principles gravitated around bipolar characteristics: edible vs. inedible (originally relating to eating someone vs. eating with someone) (Fausto 2007), strengthening vs. weakening foods, heating vs. cooling foods, wet vs. dry foods, hot vs. cold foods, soft and wet vs. hard and dry foods, and so on. Smell is also divided into five categories: rancid, scorched, putrid, fragrant, and rotten, which, in turn, are linked to five flavors: sour, bitter, sweet, pungent (piquant, hot), and salty. In China, for example, each flavor is equated with a cardinal direction (the simplified Chinese characters for the five cardinal points are east, south, west, north, and center, linking taste to place [Anderson 1988]). These structuring characteristics determine the qualities of dishes and also the social significance they carry (Brown 1985). These Chinese categories worked in Lévi-Strauss' structuralism.

The culinary triangle as it was originally proposed was operating in all societies, almost Freudian in nature. Lévi-Strauss saw the natural state of raw food as a deep organizing principle associated with danger. Cooking, transformation by fire, was linked to socialization and creating kin, an old and powerful force (Wrangham 2009). The third point of the triangle is "rotten," a decaying or fermenting that can occur naturally or culturally, making it more ambivalent than the other two points. Lévi-Strauss focused on the culturally created foods, the cooked food, as cooking morphed into the triangle of roasted, smoked, and boiled (Lévi-Strauss 1966:34). Boiling requires utensils that have been crafted by people, such as pots or baskets. Boiled food is therefore more cultural than roasted food is, which only requires heat, requiring a rack, stick, or string for the meat but clearly less human engagement than boiling requires. By thinking deeply about food processing, Lévi-Strauss inferred that culture equates with the process of transformation, which to him is the fundamental human endeavor, the act of engagement with the animate beings living around one. If Lévi-Strauss's valuation is transferred to past semiotic agentive situations in the Amazon, food boiled in pots would be edible and perhaps more highly valued than smoked food. This assumption can be sought.

Some of his cooking classifications are inconsistent, which has led to appropriate criticism (Lehrer 1972). The cultural metaphors of food preparation have been shown to be tautological and rigid when applied to specific examples and inflexible to changing cultural situations. As Goody (1982:30) points out, "social structures do not symbolize the acts of individuals." The main critique of this classification stems from structuralism's inability to address change, let alone human agency (Dobres and Robb 2000; Gell 1998). Lévi-Strauss's binary structures are meant to be universal and timeless. Because these criticisms do not refer to his original work on Amazonian worldviews, myths, and relationships with living things, we have lost some of the potency of Lévi-Strauss's original concepts.

Douglas (1966) also examines universal food issues of food taboos and boundary definitions created by incorporation. The agency in her social-order model is desire for membership. The bounded rules of practice to channel and control behavior are structured by and mediated through practice. One of the most important components in Douglas's corpus is her discussion of identity, which coalesced because communities need to create social and kin boundaries through categories and rules. These boundaries often mark the edibility-inedibility divide, defining moral and immoral people by their participation in specific cultural orders. Food rules grow out of the broader definitions of the social order. For Douglas, how a society determines what is edible reflects the essence of that society. Food rules derived from social morals operate at many levels. Certain foods can literally make people ill, not by poison or allergic reactions, but because of the moral or social associations of the specific items and their context of acquisition. As in Lévi-Strauss's work, that which is not edible or gained through dangerous or improper means, is impure and dangerous. One urban example of this is the disgust vegetarians feel for meat, even the sight or smell of it. These corporeal reactions to meat reflect the potent agency of Douglas's symbolic model of bounded categories. A criticism of structuralism is that culture can become a thing unto itself, detached from people and their everyday actions and thus not real. Pushing these structures and their relationships too far (out of context) is not effective, and I do not think that is what Douglas or Lévi-Strauss set out to propose.

For archaeologists, however, their approach holds promise. The important aspect of this work by Lévi-Strauss is the standpoint shift he provided through his links between contextual action, myth (concepts), and food. He takes us from thinking about plants, bones, and hearths to thinking about meals, cooking pots, heat sources, relationships to species, and who gained the food ingredients. Although universal models are easily open to criticism, archaeologists can gain insights with such *longue durée* structures, investigating societies through time as operational structures of engagement slowly shift.

Archaeologists have applied structures such as terrestrial-marine, above ground–below ground living things, inside-outside, or wild-domestic (*agrios-domus*) to past examples with some success (Hodder 1986, 1990; Hunn 1976). These types of classifications are not just ethnoscientific categories; they chart operationalized decision-making and category-defining trends across space and through time. Specific local values provide meaning to the skeleton of the categories. Such categories and their ramified meanings operate today. For example, roasting is symbolically significant in the Andes. It is reserved for special meals and thus is associated with and marks important events and ceremonial moments. Boiling in the Andes, on the other hand, is quotidian, a way to keep the meals ready throughout the workday. A proper meal for guests should be roasted, seen in today's *watia/pachamanca*/earth oven meals produced for special moments. The Andean take on the food triangle is not the same as Lévi-Strauss's Amazonian triangle. His was based on personal transformation, whereas the Andean world is based on the food transformation. Such cooking categories can link to other dualisms, such as profane-sacred and urban-rural. When we analyze charred plant remains from archaeological sites, we find it illustrative to record how the plants were charred and to look for patterns in cooking strategies and cultural settings, through the taphonomies of the plants.

McGhee's (1977) study of Arctic faunal remains and bone tools was enhanced by his structuralist approach. In his concise investigation of the prehistoric Thule culture, the ancestors of the Arctic Inuit, McGhee found that marine animal deposits were spatially separate from terrestrial animal bone deposits. Further, tool dichotomies made from antlers and ivory covaried with seasonality and gender. He makes a case that the categories *terrestrial* and *marine* were structuring structures within Thule society, channeling these two structures in their subsistence hunting as well as their societal categories of personhood. These structures braided a web of meanings among hunting activities, the animals that were hunted, and the seasons of the year. There is room to expand such structural analysis in food archaeology, with the caveat of careful, contextual interpretation.

## The Humoral Doctrine in Europe

Lévi-Strauss's original food triangle was based on the physical characteristics of ingredients and their heat treatments. The ingredients and the meal did not enter into Lévi-Strauss's model, but there are other structuralist models that direct people to choose the food they eat based on the food's characteristics. One widespread model operating in various places around the world is variously called the Law of Contagion, the Doctrine of Signatures, the Hippocratic doctrine of the four humors, or the Galenic Theory. The western European versions posit that health is determined by balancing bodily fluids (Frazer 1959[1890]; Meigs 1988; Visser 1991:196). While the concern is to maintain balance in the body, the active agent that brings the body into equilibrium is the food incorporated into the body.

This model determines food choice: what is consumed, when, and with what form of preparation. This incorporative orientation builds on the belief that the condition of the human body is directly forged by what is consumed. The shape, color, and taste determine the quality and form of the foods that are consumed. When a specific bodily condition has been identified – for example, the body is too dry and parched – moistness and moist food is required to bring the body back into balance. The appropriate plants or animals to be consumed are moist, such as peaches and pears, as other plants are avoided. According to this model, eating turnips can make you weak and act without force because of their nondescript shape and bland flavor. If you require more blood in your body, if you are feeling weak and out of balance, raw meat dripping with fresh blood should be consumed to regain vitality. If your fingers have been damaged, eating a seriated, fingerlike leaf will help them regain their original composition. This attributional concept is based on a sense of the broad interconnectedness and mimicry of living things, manifested in similar shapes and colors of objects. The physical quality of the ingredient is passed on to the consumer, adjusting the body's conditions.

A version of this long-lived and widespread maintenance of the human body through incorporation was recorded in the Classical Greek times linked to Hippocrates and his followers, passed through the Arabic medicinal tradition out into Mesopotamia and Egypt before resurfacing in Europe in the Middle Ages. It also has spread across the globe during the age of exploration, operating in many parts of Latin America and China (Mintz 1996). While this model has grown into a theory of personality types, temperaments, and attitudes, it is fundamentally a food classification system that dictates what should be eaten to balance and adjust one's mood.

The humoral doctrine is built on a hot-cold, moist-dry corporeal dichotomy. Essentially, the human body is made up of four substances, or humors, that form two bipolar, mutually exclusive qualities: blood is hot and moist, yellow bile is hot and dry, phlegm is cold and moist, and black bile is cold and dry. These fluids dictate a person's personality as well as bodily condition. These four essences have to be kept in balance to maintain health and good spirit. A person becomes ill when there is an imbalance in or an improper mix of these four essences (Farb and Armelagos 1980:118). Eating specific foods is the primary way to realign these humors. Since food consumption is actively involved in sustaining health, food ingredients have agency.

In contention with the interactiveness of the humoral system, the later European Cartesian and Platonic concept of body-mind separation created a boundary between the body and the mind, allowing food to influence but not integrate the two. Many scholars have pointed out that this less integrative tradition is still harbored in Western society, where food is not considered to participate in the creation of personhood (Curtin 1992). In the Cartesian ontology, food is fuel but does not actively form us. People of the Western scholarly tradition are unconsciously trained not to accept the humoral model of food and the body, although it lurks in the concept of the cold.

### The Humoral Structure in Asia

While the humoral model spread into the Americas during the early colonial period, it was fading in Europe. A version has remained active in Asian health and disease philosophies, meeting up again today across North America in the Chinese and Latin American urban neighborhoods.

Food, in this tradition, participates in the creation of the whole person. "As sustenance, food is mental as well as physical" (Curtin 1992:10). Specific ingested food combinations will integrate the mind and body differently. In this worldview, individuals have permeable bodies, ones that shift and connect to others through the food they eat. We will return to this embodiment at length in Chapter 8. This classification scheme builds on the Chinese principles of *yin* and *yang*, first recorded in the Shang Dynasty (1600–1100 BC). Yin and yang are primal, opposing but complementary principles. To maintain energy and health, these two energies should be in balance. Their balance is based on the person's temperament modulated by their sex, age, and body type, which are all regulated through substance intake. Males are primarily yang and therefore should consume more yin food to maintain their balance. Females are yin and should consume more yang food. Yin characteristics are cool, passive, calming, and associated with the feminine. Yin foods grow in the earth and include most of the plant kingdom. They are considered to be bland. Yang characteristics are spicy, active, excitable, and masculine, consisting primarily of meats, especially those rich in fat (Anderson 1988; Hubert 1997).

Over time, intricate, rule-bound dishes and cuisines developed throughout the Chinese subcontinent that began as medicinal constructs but were incorporated into culinary codes (Schafer 1997:87). This medically informed cuisine based on taste and mental balance was first recorded in the fourteenth century during Mongol rule. These early texts are recipe books based on the precepts of the dietician Hu Sihui, who lived between AD 1306 and 1368 (Sabban 1986). Not only do these recipes encourage

moderation and balance of yin and yang consumption; they include a recipe for immortality, which includes fruit and three types of water (Sabban
1986)! Yin and yang food categories are identifiable in the archaeological
record and can guide interpretation of what is found in Chinese archaeological settings.

To the west, Indian Ayurvedic medicine, which was first written down
around 500 BC, uses slightly different agents to maintain bodily balance.
In this philosophy, health is maintained through balancing three principles: energy production, sustenance transport, and excretion. The Hindu
Brahma Kumaris is a modern sect within this Vedic system, and its culinary
rules illustrate how these principles are operationalized. Like the Chinese
and Greek humoral systems, this view advocates that food influences our
thoughts and moods. Balance is achieved through food preparation and
consumption. Food's purpose, for the Brahma Kumaris, is to maintain
calm. This philosophy suggests that each person should learn what diet best
suits her- or himself to maintain personal calm. There are some credos that
guide the follower. Pure and calming foods are fruits, grains, beans, milk,
and vegetables. Stimulating foods that have a negative effect on stillness
include spices, coffee, vinegar, and watermelon. These two food groups are
eaten because they participate in balancing energy production. Ingredients
that are not beneficial to the mind in any way are meat, poultry, alcohol,
eggs, garlic, leeks, onions, and gelatin (Albion 1997:10). These last foods are
essentially forbidden in this culinary system.

This structural system has a very specific ingestion goal. Food values can
be modified; for example, chopping and preparing the fresh ingredients
impacts the release of nutrients. It is important to chop all ingredients that
will be cooked in the same dish identically. Followers of Brahma Kumaris
also believe that the moment of preparation influences the balance in the
prepared dish. Cooking with a clear and calm state of mind influences the
food's qualities and therefore its incorporation. Therefore, the same ingredients can affect bodies differently. Ingredients that are eaten raw, fried, or
boiled, or prepared by cooks in different moods, will have a different influence on the person's balance and calmness after the meal is consumed.

The anthropologist Eugene Anderson (1980) believes that the humoral,
Ayurvedic, and Chinese systems are related, thought to be underpinned by
the same structural opposition operating within the human body. He suggests that there was cross-pollination with the significant material and intellectual exchanges along the Silk Road, which intensified during the Han
dynasty (AD 25–220), suggesting that each structuring system influenced
the other. While that could be true, I see a fundamental difference in the

Chinese medicinal system and the Western humoral system, even if they were influencing each other over many centuries. In the Asian system, food literally forms an individual's essence, mood, and personality, similar to the permeable body concept of India, discussed in Chapter 8 (Busby 1997). In the European Galenic system, food's job is more engaged with maintaining and regaining bodily health, disarticulated from the emotions or the spirit. In medieval Europe, food improves one's mood and aligns one's body and mind, resonating with the permeable sense of self. This was lost in the Enlightenment with the growth of the Cartesian ontology (Thomas 2004). Mind-body unification was recently reintroduced into European intellectual traditions, coming from Eastern thought, but it is not yet fully operable in European daily food traditions.

## The Flavor Principle

Recent social scientific scholarship has unearthed the final food structuring principle I present in this chapter. In 1973 Elizabeth Rozin defined the flavor principle as a construct that crafts cuisines and how people decide what to eat. Flavor is a descriptive characteristic often determining edibility (Macbeth 1997). Specific flavors mark dishes, cuisines, and even cultural groups today, and I suggest this was so in the past. Cuisines are conservative because of taste – memory histories, accessible technologies, ingrained motor habits, and community-learned knowledge. Within food traditions, Rozin suggests that groups have a tendency to focus on a small number of seasonings and iconic ingredients and use them consistently, eventually making them a mnemonic of a group's identity. Repetitively adding combinations of ingredients associated with specific preparation techniques creates regional cuisines that build around specific core flavors. For example, core flavors in the southern Chinese cuisine are ginger and soy sauce; olive oil, garlic, and dried herbs are ubiquitous in Mediterranean food; and chile peppers and *tomatillos* (*Physalis philadelphica* Lam.) are common in Central American cuisines (Rozin 1973). Obviously, within each cuisine there are variations, dictated by plant varieties, cuisine histories, growing conditions, and preparation techniques that adjust the flavors and textures of each prepared dish. Within a modest range, however, people will reproduce what they regard as proper ("good") flavor combinations in their next meal (E. Rozin 1982:197). These core food ingredients entangle people in their cultural group, making both the meal and themselves recognizable and acceptable. The archetypal place we experience this core flavor enactment in 2016 is at the U.S. takeaway food court, where each food stand offers a different narrow range of meals, each based on core flavors iconic of a stereotypic, if unidentifiable, cultural group; Mexican, Chinese, Italian, to name some of the more ubiquitous stands at food courts.

This flavor principle becomes discursive when new items are introduced into a cuisine. Their success depends on how well the new flavor can blend with or be masked by the cuisine. For children in the United States and England, this is often accomplished by slathering a new dish with ketchup (Pliner and Stallberg-White 2000). The core flavors of this sweet tomato sauce helps children get over their food anxieties, making new items familiar and easier to eat. The tomato is a curious ingredient, as mentioned earlier. The *love apple* was rarely consumed in Europe for many years after it arrived from the Americas, and yet today it is definitely a core flavor in Italian cuisine (Allen 2002). The history of tomato's core flavor status is an interesting account of meaning, flavor, behavior, and identity in Europe.

Returning to where this chapter began, we can now see how Roland Barthes also drew on this concept of a cuisine signature flavor when he identified what he called the signifying units or unifying notions in Parisian foodways (Barthes 1979:169). These flavors, from clusters of ingredients, are highly valued and regularly consumed by its members. An evocative example in Greek cuisine is γανος. This important and highly valued flavor refers to a class of foods that are crispy, succulent, bright, and moist; sparkling. These characteristics are present in wine and honey, two iconic foods of the eastern Mediterranean. These γανος foods form the core of many Greek meals today and were important in the past (Homer 1935; Stella Souvatzi 2003 pers. comm.). Such core foods can communicate a shared past with every meal.

Some of the unifying notions surrounding core foods have almost magical qualities. We see this with the "chile heads" today, where different varieties, growing conditions, as well as amounts of water create a range of subtle, diverse chile pepper flavors for the connoisseur (Rozin 1987:190). Archaeobotanical research indicates that peppers were domesticated early, around 8000 BP, and then spread throughout most of the Americas quite early, later to Africa and Asia during the age of exploration, and only recently were accepted in Europe (Andrews 1993; Crosby 2003). The fruit adds a zesty taste to dishes, activates the digestive system, and is rich in vitamin A and C. After investigating all possible reasons for its positive valuation in a range of modern circumstances, Rozin concludes that its near ubiquitous adoption was due to the positive cultural values that initially defined it as a valued food, allied with sociability, spark, and sex. An item's popularity and longevity therefore depend on its flavor but also on its cultural classification (Fiddes 1991; Rozin 1987:191).

Flavors are rarely mentioned in archaeological publications. This is curious, since the Rozin's work clearly demonstrates its agency in many consumption decisions. Notable exceptions are Hamilakis's (2004) call for more incorporation of the senses in archaeological interpretation, illustrated by his investigation of a Bronze Age Cretan feast. He reminds us of the odor of the roasting meat and the tangy taste of the wine. Robb (2004) brings sensory aspects into his interpretation of Neolithic feasts by recognizing the importance of color and texture in Neolithic Italian Peninsula feast foods, especially when compared with the evidence of daily fare. Such notions should be essential in our research, with the help of the classification systems outlined here.

## In Sum

Using these models we can begin to think about how choice operated in the creation of good and bad food, in the rise of the pork prohibition of the Semitic peoples, or how choice might have influenced the spread of chile peppers in indigenous Central and South American cuisines. Why did certain physical characteristics of ingredients become salient, determining a core food's dominance within a dietary tradition, while others were prohibited or ignored?

This overview of several food selection models provides us with some frameworks to consider how people thought as well as ate in the past, how they chose their ingredients, and how daily meal activities constructed larger cuisine traditions that enveloped the group and shaped society. Tracking taste dispositions provides us with new perceptions and working hypotheses, which in turn can launch further, closer inquiries of the past. Although the chemistry and nutritional value of food ingredients operate in food choice, I do not propose that they are always *the* operative agent in food traditions and cuisines. Throughout the book, symbolic, structuralist approaches and rules of edibility lead us into a web of engaging approaches and questions concerning how people make sense of the organic material they encounter, and about the symbolic capital of their daily lives. Many studies build upon Lévi-Strauss' and Mary Douglas' food structures, classification, meaning, and cultural construction (Jones 2007), to which I will return in subsequent chapters. Marx's fetishism of production model, presented in Chapter 5, is the intellectual foundation for most economic food investigations and interestingly also explains some of the obsessions we see in modern food consumption. The stereotype that fear of new flavors, textures, and tastes makes cuisines conservatively persistent is both true and false. The speed and scope of culinary stasis and change is therefore an important way we can harness archaeological food studies to follow the meaning behind specific cuisines and their activities. Applying long-lived classification models such as the quadripartite humoral model or the Vedic principle of peaceful meals can help us not only build new, meaningful frameworks with which to address our data but also understand how differing views about food developed and existed across time. These models have material correlates that can be investigated in archaeological settings, expanding our arenas of study into different worldviews of the past.

We might not be able to identify the cultural or even ecological model operating in every archaeological setting, as food rules are relational and fluid, often bringing conflicting symbolic systems into play, but core flavors can be sought, and specific long-used preparation technologies can be identified that will help us glean social meaning from food-related artifacts.

The food classification principles outlined here contain food grammars and structuring arguments that were as active and agentive in the past as they are today (Gell 1998). Food is an agent because people create it. Food choice models discussed here operated in the past, defining groups, channeling and impacting identities, enchanting taste buds, and determining daily decisions. How conservative were food selection models? Can we uncover the choices made in the past, and can this lead us into richer understandings of how people thought about their food, their tasks, their landscape, and their neighbors? I think we can. But we have to activate the interaction of the material, the nonmaterial and the individual. What were the potential meanings of the food items, and how did the meal structures create the eaters, as the cooks recreated them? To do so we turn to the meal as a microcosm of food's agency in society.

# CHAPTER 3

# The Practices of a Meal in Society

*A meal is an eating occasion that takes place at a certain time and
includes specific, prepared food, or the food eaten on that occasion.*
(https://en.wikipedia.org/wiki/Meal)

Why did people create meals? Was it the desire for certain flavor and texture combinations; eating until one was sated, or being together? Meals are
often the place for illustrating proper social behavior to the young. They
are also the social interaction nexus for a group and of hospitality for guests.
Why did this entity develop as a daily practice? Was it part of the hominid
way of life, or did meals begin with humans? Was it all about fire and
the resulting expansion of edible foods as more plants and animals could
be detoxified? Or was having a mealtime with multiple ingredients simply the most powerful way to sustain social bonds and calm competition,
enabling the consumers to feel sated together at the same time as issues
were discussed? Some authors have suggested that communal eating is a
foundational attribute of being human. Others link meals to agriculture,
suggesting that foragers do not really eat meals but snacked throughout the
day. Mothers had to stop and feed their children; perhaps that was the time
to feed everyone.

   Why we eat meals opens up a range of questions: Why are clusters of
different ingredients, flavors, and textures eaten at once? Why is ingredient combination considered a good way to gain sustenance? Having a
range of foods ready to be consumed is not as easy as just eating one item
at a time. Why would it be better to prepare a mix of ingredients? Can we
study meals in the past to better understand some meanings behind their
development? Despite the definition of a meal having culturally and even
individually specific (emic) meanings, reflecting Mary Douglas's (1984)
suggestion that variations in meal structure and their content inform us

about not only daily life but also the larger society, we also consider these questions analytically (ethically) in this chapter. Can we uncover meals in archaeology?

This chapter has two goals. First I discuss the dynamic ingredients in this part of a food tradition, the meal, and how it has been identified in the archaeological record. Considering those questions posed previously: Is the essence of a meal to share food, to be communal, or are there other attributes that were important in creating a meal? Second, I focus on how meals work together to make up a cuisine. We can learn about society through the range of meal types people eat. Whether eaten on the go in the car, around a table at night, or for five days in a banquet hall, these different meal types immediately suggest different contexts and practices. Cuisines can be identified since they encompass sets of meals based on recurrent cooking practices, food traditions, and foodways. We address how thinking about meals and cuisines can give us new ways to investigate the past. Spending some time on this topic will heighten our awareness of the "virtuosity" of food (Appadurai 1981:495).

While a meal is so common to us that we don't think much about its existence, as archaeologists focusing on meals, we are confronted by a gap. There is a long way between the plant remains, animal bones, ceramic vessels, fire installations, middens, and past meals. Archeologists do not think about excavating meals; they think about seeking the practices that formed cuisines. A meal has not been a convenient frame of study. But in part this is exactly why I want to focus our thoughts on meals as we engage with this food topic. We assume that people did prepare and eat meals in the past (or is this again simply a Western perspective, having been raised with meals?), and just because people have not often left the plates and leftovers, archaeologists should not abandon the concept of a meal. While we dig up practices through the artifactual data patterns, lets consider how these link to meals, to actual past preparation and eating events. The meal is a practice for us to think about. We seek links between what we do and what people did in the past.

Although some of us snack, others eat the bulk of their food at meal-times, in packages of calories, flavors, and preparations. In fact, common wisdom in the popular press is that to maintain a proper body weight, one should not eat between meals; this is suggested to be how the French control obesity, despite their high-fat, high-calorie cuisine. Gatherers and hunters snack as they cut up a killed animal and nibble berries while collecting. With the arrival of cooking, as Lévi-Strauss noted, meals probably became more important, since the hearth fire creates a focal point for processing a range of foods at one time. Did regular use of fire create the meal?

The study of meal preparation begins with the structuralism of Lévi-Strauss and the symbolism of Mary Douglas for a good reason. While these food theorists provide definitions we can use to work on larger food issues, they also illustrate the stodgy reticence to change ones foodways. People necessarily act within a particular field of social performance constrained by boundaries, rules, strategies and habits (Robb 2007). The study of meals uncovers their agentive capacities, highlighting both the flexibility of the material involved and the actions of the cooks. Food preparation codes come to us from theories of practice, structuration, and agency (Bourdieu 1977; Gell 1998; Giddens and Cassell 1993). These agent-oriented, people-oriented theories have been applied in archaeological food studies, activating the meal and its symbolic content (Robb 2007). We visit these theories as we consider people transforming raw ingredients into meals.

Pierre Bourdieu discusses the creation of social meaning through daily acts of household maintenance that move beyond Lévi-Strauss and Douglas into the agency of both unconscious and conscious practices (Bourdieu 1984; Douglas 1971:69; Gose 1991). In discussing Kabyle residents of Algeria, Bourdieu (1977) integrates cuisine with architecture, physical sensations, and directional orientations in space and time. To assure that the relationship between meal format and social structure is not arbitrary (as signs can be), Bourdieu tracks the congruence between meal categories (breakfast, lunch, tea, etc.) and the larger symbolic, structural categories that persist throughout the social world: how people interact through their resource procurement practices, live their lives within their landscapes, and engage in their social relations in codified yet continuously new interactions. In other words, the rules for eating within a culture are followed in a reflexive manner, being part of the tacit knowledge of a group that holds the capacity to change with each new meal.

This embodied notion of practice is at the heart of Bourdieu's concept of *habitus*. He first illustrated this in the daily practices and structured meanings in Berber homes, where he learned the community's codes of behavior that enable people to act in new settings within their traditional fields of action. What was Bourdieu studying when he first outlined *habitus*? Kabyle family food activities-meals (1977). He describes women's food related tasks, preparing, serving, and eating food. He notes how their daily routines and personal comportment codes are structured by the actions of those around them, the patterns of daily life, including the topography's influence as people moved across the landscape. Routines are composed of monitoring and rationalizing expectations and motivations through the tensions of opposing pressures (Giddens and Cassell 1993:92). The concept of *habitus* echoes structuralist forms, yet within a flexible milieu that allows for slippage, contradictions, and creativity in people's lived lives. Meaning is the important ingredient that is often lost in a discussion of *habitus*, but it participates in actions, reproductions, and slippages, and therefore I include this meaning in with practice when I use the word *habitus* in this book. I do not want to only implicate the Marxist discussion of praxis with this joining of meaning and practice in *habitus*, but a fuller concept of action and value, more along the line of Arendt's (1998) theory of action.

*Habitus* and its imperfect reproduction of social life requires a link between routines, actors, dispositions, and activities – materiality. Latour (2005) tries to provide this link to materiality through objects' impacts on people. Objects continually intervene in human action, making them integral participants in people's activities and lives. Nowhere is this web of connections more evident than in culinary practices.

Giddens's (Giddens and Cassell 1993:89) structuration theory moves beyond the individual actor to the social practices of people and their things, creating A web of relationships. These fields of action are reproductive and recursive, not only re-creating edible meals for families day after day but also generating a meshwork of meanings with each meal (1993:91–93). The slippage makes each meal slightly different, as cooks throughout a community re-create their society through their meals. This is a community of eating practice, as a series of people learn how to prepare the same meal structures, by applying similar preparation technologies in different kitchens. These discrete, shared practices build larger communities and political entities. Social distinctions are produced and signified through these embodied practices and their associated technologies (Logan and Cruz 2014).

Ingold's *taskscapes* allows us to further envision these recursive activities and temporal rhythms of food gaining and preparation across a landscape (Ingold 2000). The notion of embedded practices in space and among people involves more than lifestyle and conditions of existence. This practical knowledge includes naturalized opinions generated over many years as well as the actual completion of tasks that over time become deeply embedded and made meaningful through repetition and successful outcomes. Meals are the most common outcome of food work and are charged with meaning, emulation, dissent, and creativity – and deserve our time as we seek them through the remains of those practices.

## What is a Meal?

As with all food issues, the definition of a meal is contextual and varies by group, continent, and family. Most people can define a meal for themselves, but it gets slippery when consensus is sought. To begin we will use the basal definition: an eating occasion that takes place at a certain time and/or includes specific prepared food – usually a social event. By focusing on the meal and its role in social discourse, this chapter visits the importance of context, taste, embodiment, and habitual practices surrounding food. Some meals are recognizable in the archaeological record, through deposits of co-occurring ingredients or in a combination of in situ artifacts. Must we encounter coprolites to be able to discuss meal practices and their meanings?

For those of us who are the cooks in our families, we can relate to Mary Douglas's attempts to periodically simplify the *chaîne opératoire* of a meal and lessen the workload. Her failed attempts with her family prompted her to ask, "What defines the category of a meal in our home?" (Douglas 1997 [1972]:36). The inexorable, ritualized reenactments of mealtimes instigated Douglas's attempt to understand the structure and meaning of this most daily of practices. Even in this age of casual eating and 24/7 access, most food events follow a sequence that connect the participants to a larger social meshwork of meaning. Meals constitute a set of culturally constructed rules about the food items, what can be eaten with what, when, and in what sequence. These rules are usually known to practitioners and recipients (Frake 1969; Giddens 1979). Although meals are diverse, they have a common theme – eating a balance of foods in sufficient quantity to be sated. This concept of satiation is not just an issue of nutrition, as suggested in the last chapter of Audrey Richards's (1932) study of Bemba meals, or in Katherine Milton's (1987) work on South American monkey diets. Sufficiency is also based on culturally determined values.

Meals usually involve serving food to a number of people. It is often awkward for an individual to eat alone. Sneaking food by oneself in some societies is considered suspicious and even sinister. How are the social patterns of meal forms maintained, and what causes them to change? One definition of a meal is an eating event that incorporates a number of food contrasts in a combination of ingredients. One eats more than one ingredient in a meal. Does that make a one-pot stew a meal? When we consider foraging societies, we often associate them with snacking. But there are many examples of foragers bringing food home, sharing and eating together around the hearth (Lee 1984). These look like meals because they have people eating together.

Meals often are described as foods being consumed in a series of dishes at one sitting, as with restaurant courses. This makes a meal diverse in flavor, texture, and color, adding a sense of performance. Meal types vary throughout the day, week, and season (Douglas 1997 [1972]). The modern urban work scene forces many to eat the same meal format five days a week, shifting meal times, types, and forms on the weekend. Seasonal cycles surely existed in the past as well.

Meal categories can be identified by their preparation and presentation (Conklin 1957). Connerton's work on bodily practices is helpful here; he invokes "incorporated practices" that link the body completing a task, an object, and the activity. For him, as for me, meals are habitual actions of daily subsistence that evoke the past with each reenactment. Incorporated actions allow for dishes and meal preparation to be more or less repeated, not just in ingredients but also postures, physical settings, as well as the range of senses that are engaged, recreating the recipe. Ingredients and anticipation work together in practice through the *chaîne opératoire* of the preparation and presentation to the consumers (Connerton 1989:72–73). Important here are the preparation acts that ramify throughout the rest of the day and year as people literally and mentally carry these meals with them after they leave the table, remembering them afterwards, and for the cook, envisioning the next meal's preparation, providing a rich palate of memory, the active agents of social life. Taskscape discussions highlight the dynamic importance of practice and memory in meals (Rowlands 1993).

Most people eat several meals a day. These meals can take place in a variety of formats, from standardized locations, such as in a kitchen or around a hearth, at a dining room table, or in an eating establishment. Meals can be eaten in cars, classrooms, or even while walking. Studying places specially designated for eating informs us about their valuation in the modern community. Having different locations for preparation, storage, and eating tells a different story than all of these located in one space. A fancy, expensive restaurant signifies that the meal is to be remembered, the occasion celebratory. We can also learn about the cultural context of the meal from its lavishness, the sequence of the dishes, the ingredients, as well as the number of flavor and texture contrasts, the preparation styles represented in the meal, the length of time people partake in the food, and the number of preparers.

Highly valued meals take more time to organize and prepare, taking place in special locations, often including more food or unusual ingredients.

These characteristics are what we associate with feasts. A modest case is seen in the Andes today, where helpers who assist in harvesting crops, must be fed cooked meals. Precooked potatoes with salsa will suffice for the family, but when additional people are there to help, hot soup, a meat or fish dish, boiled potatoes, and salsa are required to honor and repay their help, illustrated on the cover of this book.

Lavishness and ingredients determine feasts. Like the Andean farmers, the Bemba of Zambia ate porridge (starch) and relish (a savory sauce) daily, whereas a feast meal must include meat. A formal French feast is even more elaborate and must contain many courses, with a sequence of fish, eggs, and fowl. Mary Douglas (1975) explains the recursive links between daily meals and feasts. For the English, they are structurally similar, the feast simply being more sumptuously prepared and presented. In England, Sunday and Christmas dinners should have three courses, executed in a more intricate manner than daily meals, with more ingredients and more complex recipes (Douglas 1975). Dinner must be piping hot when placed on the table, the serving dishes warmed. The main course is always hot and savory, composed of meat, potato, and two vegetables (Figure 3.1); second comes a sweet, gooey pudding; and third, biscuits (cookies) and a hot drink.

Every society's meals have a complex grammar and syntax, built on habits and practices of cooks and consumers (Douglas and Nicod 1974; E. Rozin and P. Rozin 1981:243; Morell-Hart 2011). Molecular makeup, flavor, texture, and color combinations, as well as heating regimes, define courses and meals. The flavor principle, discussed in Chapter 2, frames specific combinations in dishes and meals, with specific flavors identifying specific meal (and dish) types.

Douglas (1997) deciphers meal structures from several cultures to illustrate how we can study meal structures. She codes dishes by their focal-ingredient-based dishes – A is for meat, stressing the place of meat as the focal ingredient in an English meal; B is the less stressed foods, vegetables; and I have added C for starch to open up her B category. In this way she describes the core English dinner as A+2B, one meat and two vegetables, whereas $C + B + 2A / 2A + 2B + 2C$ is a French meal, stressing starch, vegetable, and then two dishes that contain either meat or fish (Douglas 1997:43). State school lunches in the United States and England are required to have these three food categories from the modern concept of a food triangle: carbohydrates, vegetables, and proteins (except when Reagan was president). The onslaught of fast food being served at secondary schools has caused uproar among many parents, with the loss of hot dishes and milk in school lunches. The fast food suppliers retort

FIGURE 3.1. An English meal

that a hamburger with tomato ketchup and a bun is a full component of the food triangle, meeting USDA standards. I doubt Mary Douglas or Michael Pollan would agree.

Most of the world forms a meal around starch (C), served with a contrasting flavor (B). The starch can be cereal grain, bread, rice, or a tuber, accompanied by a flavorful set of ingredients: a vegetable dish in Asia, a relish in Africa, or tomato-based salsa in Latin America (Fiddes 1991). Often, the smaller dishes, the accents, are the more memorable parts of the meal, although archaeologists tend to focus on the staples, as spices and relishes are less easy to identify in the archaeological record.

Some meals are framed around a combination of items that work together in a catalytic manner, with blended flavors creating a certain effect on the body, such as the Barasana of Colombia's fish or game (A) and manioc bread (C) with a spicy chile pepper sauce (B) (Hugh-Jones 1995:59). The chile pepper aids in the digestion of the manioc. Other meals are sequences of food, to be consumed over time, as in the French meals. We can begin to look for meal grammars, core dishes, replacement options, and associated inscribed practices in the archaeological record.

Douglas's (1997) structural meal model places food items in a formal linguistic model using Sausserian semiotic structures for describing meals, applying the concepts of syntagm and paradigm. A *syntagmatic relationship* is one in which signs occur in sequence or parallel and operate together to create meaning, whereas a *paradigmatic relationship* is one in which an individual sign may be replaced by another sign. In Sausserian structuralism, "cuisine" is to a meal as "language" is to speech. Both contain the deep structuring structures that dictate acceptable cuisines and meals for a community.

Douglas (1997) applied this analysis to her family's meals. For her, the food paradigms are dishes that are relational to other dishes within a daily meal cycle, such as toast at breakfast or a potato at dinner. Linguistically, one noun replaces a different noun in a sentence, just as potato can replace toast as the starch (C). If tomato ketchup replaces green beans as the vegetable (B) in a meal, that is a paradigmatic food shift. Food syntagms are the dishes that make up the meal and are relational to each other; like beef and potatoes or llama meat and quinoa, they are the different word types in a sentence (Weismantel 1988). This can be illustrated by a Mexican meal with three components, A (meat and/or beans), C (maize tortilla), and B (salsa). If a dinner omelet made of eggs, potatoes, and spinach is served at 7 PM instead of beans, tortilla, and salsa, this is a syntagmatic replacement. Such categorizations of ingredients and meals can help clarify our understanding of meals and their content both today and in the past (Morell-Hart 2011).

Food archaeologists can identify the elements that make up a food category; for example, in the paradigmatic category of starch, will potatoes, rice, or pasta accompany lamb? What can these category options look like in specific archaeological settings, and how could they change in certain places and times? The syntagmatic structure would be the meal type. This is more difficult to assess by prehistoric archaeologists, except for the rare cases in which we find evidence for meals in burials or coprolites.

Some archaeological food scholars have begun to organize their food data to see what was eaten with what, tracing the syntagmatic structures of meals (Logan 2012; Morell-Hart 2011). Building on these structural rules of food replacement, Amanda Logan recently studied the changing food cuisine of the West African Banda throughout their colonial history over the past 600 years. By identifying how new foods were brought in, replacing others or blending into the diet, she traces the values and meaning of these new foodstuffs. She invokes Richard Wilk's work in Belize on how foods enter a cuisine: "[H]e sees new foods as being incorporated through blending, submersion (or hiding), substitution, and alternation/promotion, among others" (Wilk 2006:114–115). To these points I would add two mechanisms that emphasize the temporal dimension of crop adoption to meals: habituation (building on Appadurai 1986) and experimentation (Logan 2012:323).

Whether one uses Douglas's structure of paradigms and syntagms or describes the food item shifts as substitution, blending, and promotion, such meal documentation in archaeological investigation will be of great help in understanding past meals, as Logan (2012) demonstrates.

*Archaeological Meals*

The clearest evidence of past meals comes from the direct contexts of coprolites and preserved stomach contents (Glob 1969; Hillman 1986; Reinhard and Bryant 1992; Sobolik 1988; Sutton and Reinhard 1995; Williams-Dean 1986). Analysis of human feces or stomach contents, only rarely preserved or recovered, enables us to learn exactly what was consumed in meals or snacks (Reinhard 1993). Their preservation generally requires a dry, protected environment, although anaerobic wet privies can yield good evidence of consumption as well. Identification of the contents of meals enables us to learn about meal recipes and see the inscribed variety in their seasonality.

In one insightful study, Sutton and Reinhard (1995) investigated 115 coprolites from the Antelope House Pueblo II-III settlement in northern Arizona. Between AD 950 and 1300, thousands of coprolites were deposited and subsequently preserved in this Ancestral Puebloan cave/cliff dwelling settlement. These people lived in stonewalled rooms under an overhang above the valley, complete with storage and preparation/cooking areas. Sutton and Reinhard were able to identify the food combinations of individual meals and came up with three main meal types. The diet included both domestic and wild foods, with maize being the core food ingredient along with beans as well as a range of wild plants and animals. Ceramic storage vessels and grinding stones indicate that the most commonly eaten plants were stored and processed at the settlement for year-round consumption. A cluster analysis and selective immunoelectrophoresis study clarified that these meal types were built around whole maize kernels, ground or milled maize, and wild plant taxa (Sutton and Reinhard 1995:743). Products of the two maize food preparation strategies, whole and milled corn, were not consumed in the same meal, suggesting that one starch (C) was sufficient in their meals.

The most common meal was based on whole kernels, implying that this maize was eaten fresh in the summer when first harvested, as corn on the cob or in soup (C). A range of hearty stews filled with multiple textures and flavors were eaten in the late summer and autumn after the harvest, C + 2B. These summer whole-kernel (C) stews include a mix of wild herbaceous species, purslane (*Portulaca*), sumac (*Rhus*), beeweed (*Cleome*), prickly pear fruit (*Opuntia*), beans (*Phaseolus*) (B), and flavors such as groundcherry (*Physalis angulata*), along with small game (A) (Sutton and Reinhard 1995:746–747). Minnis (1989) found evidence of this same recipe in a coprolite from the Mesa Verde area from the same time (Pueblo II and III). Minnis concluded that maize constituted around 80 percent of their diet. These late-summer meals are the richest meals of the year, with the most diverse flavors and taxa, as many fresh ingredients were thrown into the pot.

A variant meal, more likely an autumnal soup, had fewer species but concentrated on whole maize kernels and a sweet fruit. One version was groundcherry fruit and maize. Another was whole kernel maize and sumac fruit (presumably dried). These maize-based meals have a structure similar to the early spring meals: a sweet or pungent flavor added to the maize staple, or C + B. They would have been flavorful, filling meals and suggest that the sweet flavor was a highly valued ingredient, is it is for the Bemba, discussed in Chapter 2.

A second meal type at Antelope House was derived from stored food. The core of this meal was milled maize from dried kernels. Ground meals are simpler dishes. These winter meals are primarily maize flour (C), at times mixed with ground *Chenopodium/Amaranthus* seeds (C). These gruels or cornhusk-wrapped gruels (*tamales*) did not contain the same variety of fresh, summer-ripened herbaceous plants, but they had the fineness of the ground ingredients in these winter preparations, suggesting a continued effort in preparation.

The third Antelope House meal recipe consists wholly of locally indigenous taxa (C + B), built around the milled *Chenopodium/Amaranthus* seed (C) accompanied by a range of wild species, such as yucca (*Yucca* spp.) and horsetail (*Equisetum* spp.) (B) (Sutton and Reinhard 1995:747). In these meals the starchy seeds replace maize. All of these "wild" meals were similar in that the ground starchy seeds that were the core of the gruel, are ancestral meals. What does this third, less common meal type tell us about life in the Southwest during that time? These meals could have been consumed at any time during the year since the thirteen most common wild plant taxa in these meals could have been collected in the summer and stored over the winter. These wild meals hearken to the past, representing recipes eaten before foreign domesticates came into their diet and tied them to farming. These older meals perhaps were preferred to the domestic flavors, at least seasonally. Alternatively they could have been starvation foods, eaten only after domestic stores ran out, retreating to the bounty of the landscape in the later winter and spring months. Whatever the circumstance of consumption, these wild meals must have had a special resonance for the residents. The first two meal types are different from this third recipe. The domesticate-based meal contains paradigmatic shifts from the original meal concept, but they keep the same general meal structure, demonstrating that maize entered into the cuisine as a starch.

Sutton and Reinhard completed a second study at neighboring sites in Canyon de Chelly, where they tracked a longer temporal span of meals. The residents at these sites were farmers who also continued to consume the foodstuffs and meals of their foraging ancestors. They ate a similar range of meals to those from Antelope House, with fewer ingredients in the winter months and more fresh greens and seeds in the summer months. Although meat was always present in these meals, it was much less abundant than the vegetable ingredients. This cuisine tradition continued as long as these settlements were occupied, reflecting the conservative nature of their meal culture and outlining a food tradition for this region and time. The one significant change through time in the Canyon de Chelly recipes was that the food was increasingly ground, perhaps a value that gained importance over time, although as it clearly took labor away from other tasks, it made the maize more digestible. What did this ground maize mean to the residents?

We see seasonality in these meals. The residents added seasonally available ingredients, with special meals of bighorn sheep (*Ovis canadensis*), pronghorn antelope (*Antilocapra americana*), rabbits/hares (*Sylvilagus* spp. and *Lepus californicus*), and deer (*Odocoileus hemionus*). Wild plant foods were part of most meals. Many of the wild plant field followers like purslane and beeweed were added for flavor to the summer and autumn meals, suggesting the acceptance of disturbed taxa maslin fields in farming and in recipes to spice up the steady maize-based meals. Notably, these data demonstrate that the meals were all stews and the portion sizes did not change over time (Douglas 1971). The cooks emulated their mothers' cooking for 400 years, again identifying the community of practice throughout these communities. Departure from these cliff dwellings has often been linked to drought and associated food production loss, which could be the case, but some also suggest that they migrated away to join others. I wonder what their meals looked like once living in the Rio Grande Pueblos?

These archaeological meals materialize Bourdieu's *habitus* of meal preparation and consumption, enabling archaeologists to get closer to people, their daily decisions, and how identity and social structure were embodied and enacted in the past (Mills 2007; Robb 2007). Having begun with meal structures, we can now consider constancy and change in meals. What do they say about these people's lives? Through the materialization of meals we can learn about a range of economic and social aspects that meals communicate about past societies. Whether we have coprolites, stable isotopes, faunal remains, plant remains, or only ceramic serving vessels, each of these data sets provides information about meals that can be placed into their social contexts. We turn to cuisine and place meals in a broader context.

## Cuisines and the Social Economies of Taste

*Cuisine* is the French word for "kitchen," brought into the English language with the Norman Conquest in AD 1066. A cuisine is a unique and consistent set of ingredients, cooking techniques, and flavor principles, carrying psychological, social, and religious attitudes toward food, eating practices, and meals (Barker 1982:154; Farb and Armelagos 1980:227). Aesthetic tastes, cultural attitudes, regional history, and personal predilections in addition to nutrition shape a cuisine (Ashkenazi 1991). Flavor is an important marker defining the aesthetic taste of a community (Rozin 1982).

We cannot understand the power of a meal without it being embedded in a culturally constituted cuisine. As style is a way of doing things, cuisine is the style of an eating tradition. It is the larger system of rules that weaves together foodstuffs, technologies, recipes, and table manners through time and space, but also moral, cosmological meanings and tastes of meals in a social milieu, making the combination of meals and their ingredients choreographed and stylized for the viewer (Appadurai 1981:496).

In her rural Ecuador food study, Mary Weismantel (1988) illustrates that everyone has a cuisine, however simple. Within each cuisine is a spectrum of eating styles, from the sumptuous dishes and meals to the mundane, daily meals and snacks. These meals each have their unique contextual meanings and values. In rural Africa, where everyone eats the same food items, the Ashanti define social classes by the amount of food people eat (Goody 1982:204). The leaders are allowed to eat the greatest amount in any one sitting, making a heavy person a person of renown, while the lowly person only gets small portions (Shack 1971). This cuisine of volume clearly contrasts with what is operating in Western society today, where it is not the portion size but the combinations of ingredients and preparations that designate a cuisine's class and economic standing, often with new additions to be trendy (Counihan and Van Esterik 2013; Paoli 1963; Pollan 2006). The newest version of this is Chef Watson, an online computer that works with the chemical ingredients of foods to create new recipes, as foodies seek out new taste sensations in what is called cognitive cooking (www.ibmchefwatson.com).

At its most basic, cuisine is a style of food preparation with specific ingredients. For the Rozins, cuisine is the culturally expounded and transmitted body of food-related practices of any given culture (E. Rozin and P. Rozin 1981:243). *Practice* is the operative word, also aiding archaeologists as we study past food practices through the different practices of growing, collecting, processing, and cooking food. For example, even identifying just one archaeological plant or processing technique can open up new ideas about past cuisines. Wheat processing is diverse, from finely ground and squeezed pasta, to cracked, to rough whole meal, to pounded muesli. Each of these forms of wheat is associated with specific cuisines – in this case, respectively, Italian, Turkish, English, and Alpen.

A cuisine transforms natural food stuffs into cultural entities, acculturating not only the food but also the diners. It is an expressive field of discourse, revealing the position of the consumers in their world and even directing their moral and religious beliefs (Appadurai 1981; Farb and Armelagos 1980:232). Cuisines are codes that channel the style of preparation and consumption, the sequence and flavors in dishes, and even the weekly cycles of meals. Cuisines tend to be conservative, as corporeal learning becomes habituated through repeated and passed-on acts (Farb and Armelagos 1980:190). These practices can be very long-lived: the Chinese imperial cuisine lasted for more than 3,000 years. These activities are driven by ideal, remembered tastes, textures, and flavors, by dish presentation, as well as by the overall moral correctness of the meal (Douglas 1997).

Culinary history is social history; when it shifts, we can be sure other parts of society are also changing. Bourdieu (1977) admits that cuisines change, but they do not do so randomly. Societies that produce their own food and have a fairly stable diet find solace and contentment in a steady, unchanging diet. They prefer their own staples and flavorings as opposed to taking up new items (Powers and Powers 1984). It is not a question of boredom, but rather reassurance, as familiarity is sought by having the next meal be similar to the preceding ones, both in foodstuffs and in preparation techniques (Macbeth and Lawry 1997:4). In my home these "comfort foods" are usually based on simple recipes that were eaten when young. Today's trend to eat new, unknown items, to expand one's cuisine, is particularly promoted by the modern, Western press as part of the food industry's strategy to expand the food market.

People have strong attachments to their cuisine, including aversions to the food cultures of others (Ohnuki-Tierney 1993). Societies use culturally important foods and associated culinary patterns as metaphors of themselves. Presentation of a particular meal or cuisine marks the boundary between the collective and the "other" (Ohnuki-Tierney 1993; Rovane 2006). The Japanese believe rice is more than the staple of their cuisine; it creates their identity as well as a sacred metaphor for the state. Long-lived flavor combinations and their tempos of change allow us to track aspects of social and cultural life that can be elusive in archaeological inquiry. Changing cuisines signal other changes throughout society. Cuisines can materialize social changes more subtly than other elements of society can, initiating a semiotic cultural study for archaeologists (Thomas 2004). Therefore, understanding a cuisine's components and tracking its history can be rewarding.

Culinary practices bring structure and meaning to daily life. Cuisines are filled with "typical" and "authentic" meals, providing a cocoon of identity. Daily cooking is recursive in that each time a cook uses familiar ingredients, the taste of the resulting dish will be acceptable to the local palate. This is a goal of the fast food industry around the world – to provide a meal with regular and consistent flavors, odors, and textures, providing a naturalized and familiar cuisine to those who consume them no matter where one is. Much expense goes into ensuring that the cheese, beef, and bread in a particular restaurant will taste the same in Russia as it does in Texas (Schlosser 2001). Goody (1982:189) described this creation of a global cuisine through the spread of Coca-Cola and supermarkets. Global food traditions seen in these widespread, uniform, globally shared meals begin to erode local cuisines.

At the opposite end of a shared eating tradition is *haute cuisine*, wherein chefs exert great effort to create new flavors and dishes. Concentrating on local ingredients and cuisine fusion, gourmet chefs emphasize uniqueness. Both extremes of this culinary spectrum – standardized fast food and unique haute cuisine – are products of our current social and economic global economy. Eating at either end of this spectrum gives an aura of new identity, place, and membership within an imagined community (Anderson and O'Gorman 1991).

Some have linked the creation of a special cuisine to a stratified political structure (Goody 1982; Mintz 1996). Arjun Appadurai (1981:496), for example, assumes that hierarchical political and economic conditions that build alliances participate in the development of a haute cuisine. He suggests that only unequal social and economic settings allow for the development of complicated dish variety. These inequalities translate through a naturalized morality that permeates society and creates differences recursively through eating habits. Appadurai posits that specific, unique dishes reinforce social differences when differential access to food is common, as in slavery or caste societies. In these hierarchical situations, intricate food practices take on cosmological and moral properties. This is the case, Appadurai notes, because in these societies people and gods produce food together, creating moral rights and obligations. These cosmological (yet veiled) influences on cuisine operate in all castes of India, his place of study, where there is a range of cuisines, each carrying complex and subtle social ramifications. This was also the case in the Mesopotamian past (Bottero 2004).

These socio-moral constraints of obligation operate in empires but also in the smallest communities, as Weismantel (1991) shows in a rural Andean farming family. There, children prefer bread, a foreign food that costs money, over the traditional potatoes, which are locally produced, in an attempt to reposition themselves out of poverty. If we restrict Appadurai's webs of meaning only to overtly complex meals or to large, class or state societies, we are leaving out the agency of every cook producing dinner. Although they are not necessarily equally ornate, all groups develop cuisine rules. As Bourdieu (1977, 1984) tells us, it is through daily practices that meanings are created and maintained. It is in these daily practices of breakfast and dinner that distinctive cuisines are forged.

I prefer the concept of cuisine in its more inclusive, Mintzean sense, as a constellation of cooking methods, dishes, ingredients, consumption etiquette, meal cycles, and tastes, regardless of the size or scope of a culture (Mintz 1996). The identification of "high" or "low" cuisines is artificial. Assigning these categories to specific cuisines leads to the same problems we have in archaeology when we try to define political categories within a community. Here I associate *haute* cuisine, defined by specific ingredients, preparations, and table manners, with groups that participate in the maintenance of a permanent elite class.

What makes a cuisine different from a diet is its prescriptive rules, meanings, and accompanying emotions that are activated in the production of acceptable foods. A diet is simply the calories and ingredients being consumed. Staples form the bulk of the calories in a diet; flavorings often make up the bulk of the psychological importance (Rozin 1987:197). Past cuisines have the potential to chart consensus, choice, and political trends through food preferences because they reflect the broader tastes of a culture. Although all people eat, they do not eat all of the items available to them. Changes in frequencies of plant and animal consumption have been studied in archaeology, but these dietary trends are not often discussed along with the meanings and psychologies of the populace. The concept of cuisine helps us do that.

Beliefs about the proper ways of preparing and eating food inform status and class in addition to access to ingredients. These norms are learned at home through daily practices. Some culinary identities are deep-seated and continue despite radical changes in other parts of society. For example, the cuisine of combining fruit and meat, so common in Middle Eastern dishes, can be traced back to pre-Islamic consumption styles in Mesopotamia, reaffirming links to this millennia-old meal *habitus* (Bottero 2004). Lynn Harbottle traces Iranian immigrants to London, where their use of certain combinations of core ingredients in their meal preparations, such as apricots and lamb, continues to affirm their Iranian cuisine identities, both physically and emotionally (Harbottle 1997:177). In rural Anatolia, the basic ingredients of the cuisine – bulgur wheat, chickpeas, and lentils – have remained the core of some of this population's cuisine for 8,000 years, since the Neolithic.

Major cuisine shifts usually correlate with social or political upheaval, illustrated when people are forced to eat from another group's food tradition (Holtzman 2009; Macbeth and Lawry 1997:4; Powers and Powers 1984; Vroom 2000). This rupture is registered in the Irish dietary change, when the potato replaced oats and barley 500 years ago, initially because of landowner demands (Messer 1997). Such rupture has occurred with the recent entry of maize in northern Kenyan Samburu pastoral societies (Holtzman 2009). Sunflowers and maize across northern China have now become common crops; how are they entering the cuisine? In the Native North American diet, which changed rapidly following constraints imposed by European settlers, William and Marla Powers (1984) stunningly outline one such devastating culinary rupture for the Oglala Lakota hunting groups, forced to change from a cuisine of hunted bison, maize, and wild herbs to bags of wheat, cows (beef), lard, and coffee.

In the seventeenth century, the Oglala shifted from a generalized hunting and gathering strategy to intensive buffalo hunting with the introduction of the horse on the central plains of North America, which became their staple as well as their most sacred food. With the European incursion into the Plains in the nineteenth century in search of farmland, the Oglala's access to their hunting territory and its animals was increasingly restricted, making their core food scarce and starvation common. As hunting territories were restricted for the Oglala and the military wantonly killed off the buffalo, the U.S. government encouraged the natives to "act like Europeans" and farm. The Oglala were not interested in farming. They were given cattle to herd and crops to grow, with little success. Not only was this a sweeping alteration to their relationship with their landscape; it also cut into the core of their cuisine morality. At first the Oglala found beef offensive and did not want to eat it. Cut off from their previous economic livelihoods, many starved, not being able to take up a completely new food tradition.

The Oglala, no longer economically self-sufficient, were given rations of flour, coffee, and bacon and were forced to change their diet *and* cuisine, or die. In desperation they began killing the cows in the same way they had killed the buffalo in the summer and fall, chasing them on horseback, preparing and feasting family and friends in the traditional way (Powers and Powers 1984:62). This cognitive transference of the cow into the "spotted buffalo" was essential for them to survive. The economics of staying alive within these new conditions demanded a shift in their cuisine. "Standing Bear noted that 'our buffalo' had perished and we were a meat eating people, so we succumbed to the habit which at first seemed so distasteful to us" (ibid:62). They not only had to shift to beef as their staple, they also had to reinvent their ritual feasting tradition around new preparations and ingredients. After years of being constrained on the reservations, the overexploited wild tubers (C) that were roasted in pits and consumed with buffalo meat (A) were lost, and the foods of their incarceration developed into their cuisine. Flour dumplings (C) fried in bacon grease, made from the rations during those early years, slowly evolved into the traditional ritual meal of fry bread (Adams 2011). This dish has remained particularly symbolic to the Oglala, but not from the old ways; rather it is a mnemonic of incarceration that nearly killed them.

Powers and Powers (1984:63) note that these rations, when distributed, were often spoiled or rotten, making them even more repugnant to the Oglala, increasing the irony that these very ingredients have become "Indian" or "native" foods today. The economics of conquest and starvation accelerated this cuisine transformation, which was completed by naming, processing, and then ritualizing these foods. Coffee (B) became a medicine, fry bread (C) the starch, and beef the sacred meat (A), referencing the syntagmatic form of the earlier cuisine. A defeated people were deprived of their traditional foods and procurement strategies, yet their cultural *habitus* was not completely extracted from them. This reformulation of their cuisine through paradigmatic ingredient replacement does not mask their economic inequality but is an example of how even the downtrodden will maintain their identity through whatever agency they have (Adams 2011).

Meanwhile, other North American European cuisines were also transformed. Cuisine histories register different immigrant histories. Most Italian immigrants to the United States, for example, moved to cities and actively maintained their Italian cuisine as they opened food stores and restaurants, producing sausages with the same spices they had used in Italy, canning tomatoes, and making pasta, as well as importing Italian cheeses when possible (this is still ongoing in 2015). In contrast, Scandinavian rural immigrants did not maintain their food traditions but shifted to eat the rapidly evolving North American farm cuisine, based on a mix of European and American farmed foodstuffs with meals famously culminating in apple pie. Most of the Scandinavians became farmers in the interior of the continent, shifting from a coastal diet of dried fish and barley to wheat, maize, and pork. These minor and major cuisine changes reflect the level of impact this move had on populations' identities, practices, and cuisine. While the Italians were able to keep much of their cuisine and their society, the Scandinavians mainly clung to their baking traditions while adopting the new American farm cuisine, as it was impossible to remain with fish as the staple.

*Archaeological Cuisines*

Following this discussion of the structuring structures that form cuisines and how they are actively created in people's lives, I turn to archaeological settings to see what can be identified of cuisines in the past. To understand how cuisines inform us about past societies, let us look at a radical cuisine shift identified in the archaeological record to trace what such a change might have produced and signified in the lives of the people who lived through it. As in many areas across the globe, the Mesolithic foragers of Northern Europe went through a far-reaching shift in their food traditions with the onset of the Neolithic complex arriving on the continent. This shift brought new foods and lifestyles along with grain farming and herding from Anatolia (Ammerman and Cavalli-Sforza 1971; Evershed et al. 2008; Özdogan 2002; Price 1989, 1996). Many Near Eastern and European

scholars have focused their research on this question of the Neolithic farming and herding complex in Europe. Rather that review this research,
I turn to what it imparts regarding how people interacted with their food,
landscape, and each other.

The archaeological evidence, especially the new syntheses of absolute
dates, genetics, and stable isotopes, reveal that some years after the onset
of the Neolithic, around 10,000 years ago, a mix of domestic grains, cow,
goat, sheep, and pig remains is found increasingly northwards out of the
Fertile Crescent, suggesting varying tempos, routes, and acceptances up
into eastern Europe (Bocquet-Appel 2009; Bocquet-Appel et al. 2012). It
turns out that not only new plants, animals, and an annual cycle focused
on planting and herding spread into this region; there is evidence for the
migration of Neolithic farmers up the major river valleys, settling across
Europe (Bentley et al. 2003a). Interaction with the indigenous Mesolithic
hunters is evident, with a break from some of the old cuisine and its ingredients. This interaction further suggests an eventual worldview shift, even a
transformation in the concept of time (Borić 2003).

Some of the clearest evidence of this interaction and cultural transition
comes from the Danube Gorges, where detailed site and burial interpretation have been re-studied (Borić et. al. 2012; Borić and Price 2013). At the
site of Lepinski Vir in Serbia, the recent analysis of the two dwelling phases,
before and after the evidence of Neolithic material culture and people, elu-
cidates the impact of the arrival of the newcomers in this region, reflected
in how the past was remembered, while the new world of the farmer was
being increasingly manifested. This history is noted in new burial forms,
houses, and personal adornment. There was exchange of artifact styles,
ideas, and also people, as women from indigenous communities clearly
moved, lived, and were buried in the newcomers communities. The strontium isotope data support intermarriage, with the women moving between
communities, allowing for worldview sharing, which eventually brought
about farming and the Neolithic worldview throughout all communities
in this Danube region by around 5900 BC (Borić and Price 2013). From
strontium and other stable isotope data, Borić and Price have been able to
identify people who did not grow up in the vicinity of their death, supporting this idea of intermarriage between the hunter-gatherers-fisherfolk and
the farmer-pastoralists. Another dataset that supports this idea is the genetic
and isotopic evidence from Germany, which documents the movement
of Near Eastern genetic stock into Europe as farming men migrated and
mated with indigenous women there as well (Bentley et al. 2003; Rasteiro
et al. 2012; Skoglund et al. 2012).

With such powerful data, archaeologists increasingly postulate that these crops, animals, and new ways of viewing the world moved north with the migrating immigrants, rather than just the idea of farming being transmitted and traded. The demographic and burial evidence from this southeastern European region suggests that farming communities settled in valleys while the Mesolithic folk lived in upland areas (Bocquet-Appel 2009; Borić and Price 2013). This process displays a history that occurred over several thousand years across Europe up to Sweden (Skoglund et al. 2012).

The indigenous people of Denmark and Britain before about 4000 BC (5950 BP) had been eating a wide range of wild animals and plants, including fish, shellfish, mollusks, crustaceans, fowl, red and roe deer, elk, aurochs, and wild boar along with aquatic plants, nuts, herbs, grains, fruits, and herbs including apple, sloe and garlic mustard (Craig et al. 2011; Price 1989; Richards 2000; Richards et al. 2003b; Saul et al. 2013; Tauber 1981, 1983; Zvelebil 1995). As people adopted the Neolithic domestic cuisine, they shifted to a narrower diet of emmer and einkorn wheat, naked and hulled barley, and oats, along with domesticated cattle, pig, sheep, and dog (Koch 1998). Their diet breadth did not expand again until many years later with the age of exploration and the initiation of the modern global economy (Crosby 2003). Some might say this Neolithic cuisine and lifestyle shift was not necessarily an optimal choice (Hillman et al. 1989; Jones 1977). There are many examples, especially in the north, of people moving away from the bountiful shoreline resources with this new focus on inland farming of carbohydrate-rich ingredients. This new cuisine not only usurped the earlier cuisine; it shifted the core ingredient (A) from marine fish and crustaceans to domestic meat and milk, and also the starch (C) from indigenous wild grains, rhizomes and roots to farmed grasses (Fischer et al. 2007). This change also involved a lot more work, not only in the fields but also in grinding to make gruel and bread.

As Alasdair Whittle (1996; Bickle and Whittle 2013) demonstrates in his central European Neolithic research, this Near Eastern food complex gradually (over millennia) increased across central Europe (in the LBK culture), as mixed foraging and farming was replaced by farming alone. His data suggest that in some areas plants and animals were being exchanged – for example, seen in a local increase of agriculture in the late Mesolithic of Hungary (Whittle 1996). Other regions seemed to take up these domestic taxa more abruptly, as in Denmark and Britain, although marine foods remained part of the coastal diet for some time (Milner et al. 2004; Richards 2000; Richards et al. 2003b:292). By the Bronze Age, with people settled on the landscape and the cuisine firmly built around cereal and legume gruels

and soups, the remnants of the diverse Paleolithic diet with its range of
wild herbs, roots, and fruit had almost disappeared, continuing only east in
modern-day Ukraine (Lillie and Richards 2000). The cultural reasons for
this shift have not been clarified by archaeological research.

What was the Neolithic grain based cuisine of the European farmer like
to live on? Why did people adopt this? How did it make people feel? Anni
Gamerith's (1981) historic study of nineteenth-century Austrian farm meals
illustrates a similar cuisine and might shed some light on why people took
up this foreign cuisine. She studied the weekly dinner menus of fourteen
central Austrian farming families (Gamerith 1981:86–87). These meals
display minor variations on wheat dumplings, what she calls farinaceous
dishes (ground grain), and soups with meat and cabbage, making a meal
of C with A+B. Meat was eaten daily, but meals were dominated by wheat-
based recipes. Much like the Ancestral Puebloan core meals of maize or
wild seeds, with some fruit added, this narrow range of preparations and flavorings made for a sustainable but extremely narrow cuisine for the farmers, whose Mesolithic ancestors had consumed diverse meals and cuisines
for thousands of years.

Why did this almost complete cuisine shift occur across Europe with the
coming of these domesticates? Scholars working on this issue have suggested
a range of reasons. From the vantage point of our modern cuisine, we have
to be impressed at such a major ingredient and cuisine shift across a continent, even if the process spanned several thousand years. The closest scale
of such a cuisine change is registered in the onslaught of the European diet
into North America in the 1600s, which was much more abrupt and rapid,
spanning only several centuries. Was this Neolithic cuisine tied to a conquest
shift, like which happened to the Oglala Lakota, who were forced to turn to
wheat, beef, and coffee, or the shift to potato consumption by the Irish with
the impact of the English landholders? The data do not suggest conquest.
Douglas Price (1996) ties this Northern European Mesolithic-to-Neolithic
cuisine change to intergroup competition and prestige models, which suggest that specific groups gained status when they adopted these new, foreign
people and their foods. This emulatory model would have had reverbera-
tions throughout the society, especially if these crops also offered the thrill
of new, even forbidden tastes. Although crops were taken up at varying rates
across Europe, there are now several examples that link this cuisine change
to the immigration of new people into regions and who interbred with the
local inhabitants (Bentley et al. 2003). It does not seem to have been physical
conquest, but it might have been psychological conquest, that is, so much
intermarriage occurred as to swamp out the local patterns.

Another possibility is that the interest in and uptake of these new plants and animals was a result of increasing pressure on local food sources, such as coastal fish and mollusks, linked to climate change. Peter Rowley-Conwy (1984) posits that environmental pressures on marine food sources emanated out of the post-Pleistocene climatic shift. This shift would have been severe and sufficiently sustained to have markedly diminished marine resources, causing people to move inland from the coast in search for new resources, including introduced crops. The ecological evidence for a diminution of marine resources is not strong, nor can environmental scholars link the uptake of these new foods with the timing of long-term climatic shifts.

Others propose that increased stress on wild resources owing to the influx of migrants encouraged farming, making the locally gathered food more difficult to acquire. This thesis supports a production intensification model, which should be evident in increased marine food extraction as well as evidence of farming. Again, this thesis is not supported by the archaeological record. Instead, a strong increase in the plant and animal frequencies (and a concomitant reduction in marine resources) is reflected in the human stable isotope data (Richards et al. 2003b). Richards's (2000) stable isotopic work on English human remains over this Mesolithic-Neolithic transition demonstrates a reduction in seafood consumption, which strongly supports an ontological shift in the populace. We do not yet have a clear idea about the relative availability of food over this transition, but the archaeological evidence to date suggests that the shifts in food consumption were not driven by food stress.

Why would this cuisine and its ideological shift have happened so thoroughly across such a broad region, albeit along different trajectories and with different tempos across the continent? Although the southern folk moved in with their own cuisine, what was so attractive about it for the locals to accept it? There must have been some ideological values tied to these crops and animals, even if initially these new ways of life were not always positively valued. Were people (women) forced to work on these new farms, learning about the techniques, foods, and beliefs dissonantly, as the California native women did at the Russian outpost of Fort Ross, California (Lightfoot et al. 1998)? Or did these new foods seem exotic and attractive and thus were sought after even though there was little contact between the two disparate populations in the early years?

In the conversion model a new cultural and symbolic world was introduced, such that the belief in the old ways diminished as new activities created new *habitus* and new *chaîne opératoire*, as seen again later with the spread of new religions across this same region in the Iron Age (Jones 1977; Politis and Saunders 2002). The new cuisines and the new activities that accompanied them eventually resulted in a cuisine replacement, not just ingredient substitutions. Interest in these new foodstuffs was part of a larger cultural sea change of socialization and identity transformation. Accompanying these new domestic foods was an increased emphasis on food sharing reflected in expanded storage and presentation, materialized in more complexly designed ceramic vessels and experienced in bread and beer gatherings. The continuation of female imagery throughout this cultural change implies that a lingering emphasis on abundance and fertility accompanied this new cuisine, as some of the ontological bits and pieces of the Mesolithic world remained (Borić 2003; Cauvin 2000; Whittle 1996:364).

These data suggest a complex interplay among cuisine, taste, and belief in this past as it occurs in the present. This example in part allows us to consider if ideological conversions can be reflected in food changes. Comparing this Mesolithic-Neolithic cuisine transition with the religious conversions that rippled across pagan Europe at the onset of Christianity, we see a much less rapid change in the cuisine evidence earlier on. Shifts from the past Mesolithic traditions seem to have been gradual and stepped, not radical like a mental and physical conquest that accompanies religious conversions, such as when Christians convert to Vedic Hinduism or to Islam, or when Jewish people were forced to convert to Christianity during the Spanish inquisition. This more radical speed of conversion is illustrated historically in the cuisine shifts in Boeotia, Greece over a series of three historic invasions. New foods often require new ways of cooking and therefore new vessels. Joaneta Vroom (2000) investigated 1,000 years of dining to track one region's cuisine changes over several different political regimes. She studied domestic ceramic use, food recipes, and images of communal eating during three political regimes – the Byzantine hegemony (seventh–twelfth centuries), the Frankish entrance (thirteenth–fifteenth centuries), and the Ottoman conquest (sixteenth–nineteenth centuries), providing examples of a political regime change, a demographic influence, and a religious conversion. These three political, economic, and cultural influences were substantial enough to alter the daily cuisine practices of the residents, seen in their dinner settings, ceramics and cutlery, ingredients, and also table manners. With each change came a shift in who could eat together, how the food was presented and consumed, and what core ingredients were highlighted. This Boeotian meal history illustrates how new policies and political pressures can bleed throughout lifestyles and dining habits (Vroom 2000:213). People do remember their past, and in Boeotia they returned to their earlier eating traditions when the Franks left. Such resonation in cuisine and worldview shifts are illustrated in Danish Meso-Neolithic stable isotope evidence of a new cuisine adoption in a very different setting (Richards et al. 2003b:292). Although many reasons have been proposed for this cultural adoption, I agree with scholars that the most viable reason for the Neolithihc foodway adoption was an ideological shift of ingredient and life style valuation, as the residents slowly interbred and indigenized the crops, animals, and lifestyles.

Archaeologists need to look for social impacts registered in their data, such as the cuisine sea change the Mesolithic inhabitants experienced. Such a sweeping change, the dropping out of the marine staple foods that had been the core flavor and base of the diet, is one of the more far-reaching expressions of societal and ideological change manifested in the past (Jones 1977). The Neolithic shifted daily practices to fields and pastures from boats and shorelines, as Danish peninsular dwellers turned their backs upon their former coastal foraging and fishing *habitus* (Richards et al. 2003b). Perhaps more important is that their taste palette had to have radically altered for them to believe that cereal gruel and beef was more flavorful than fish, nuts, and berries. Wheat, barley, pork, and beef must have seemed seductive, as these products have now virtually converted the globe's population to their taste.

## In Sum

People can be fickle when it comes to their cuisine. Some yearn for an unchanging world: the local cuisine is usually considered more than acceptable fare; it is preferred. To many their traditional dishes link them to hearth, home, and family memories, as illustrated in the animated motion picture *Ratatouille* in which a dour food critic is won over by his childhood "comfort food" meal (Brandes and Anderson 2011). People long for the seasonal cuisine of their childhoods, as memory actively aids connection with their landscape and community (Sutton 2001). This situation is true not just for us but also for subsistence farmers and fisher folk in the past (Counihan 1997 [1984]; Gamerith 1981; Richards 1939).

Yet we have archaeological and historical examples of active and rapid cuisine change. Some seek out new foods to re-create themselves and their social standing, as have been experienced in the past fifty years around the globe (Wilk 2006). In the archaeological record, studied changes are derived from either conquest or emulation, both ideological and cosmological.

How did people view new meals and ingredients during times of change? Why do some groups resist change and try to maintain their traditional meals and cuisines, while others take up and even seek out new foods, dishes, and cuisines? Responses vary, but this question applied to the past opens up pathways in our studies of meaning and experience. New opinions accompany changes in food preparation or ingredients. Europeans have been wheat eaters for 6,000 years now. Were they originally forced into eating bread like the Oglala (Powers and Powers 1984) and the California Pomo women of Fort Ross (Lightfoot et al. 1998), or did they rush to accept it, like the Celtic leaders with the foreign wine brought by Greek traders (Dietler 1990)? How do new foods become exciting? Do constrained circumstances always make new meals the only available option, or are new foods tied to new belief systems, crafting desire for new tastes? These questions are at the heart of the social and economic omnivore's paradox as we investigate the entry of new meals and cuisines in the archaeological record.

Both meals and cuisines are composites, providing a basis from which to investigate the active *habitus* that sits at the heart of daily practice, linking mundane tasks to belief systems and social taste – in other words, to people's way of life. By focusing here specifically on the meal and its role in food archaeology, we have unleashed a range of questions that can direct us in our studies of the past. The meal and how it is crafted by and crafts the individual, the family, and the group provides access into past social lives and traditions. Studying cuisine's meals and serving utensils not only unveils daily life, family structure, storage patterns, presentation and resource access; it also speaks about economic domains, ideology, and lifestyles.

# PART II

# Food Studies in Archaeology

Archaeologists track long-term structures, charting the spread of changes and continuities, speculating on what they reflect about society. Specific flavors, textures, forms of preparation, cuts of meat, or combinations of dishes – cuisine constituents – can be traceable in archaeological settings, but reflect the one time event, the small scale. These long processes are made up many daily *habitus* activities, annual production/gathering timing plans, and to the many opinions that form taste, especially in the long term. Before turning more specifically to how cuisines participated in the formation of social lives, this section focuses on how archaeologists study food practices – how we can identify preparation, storage, and presentation, and how we can seek the elusive eating in archaeology. This section presents specific food activities and the methods archaeologists use to investigate the *chaîne opératoire* of food archaeology.

CHAPTER 4

# The Archaeological Study of Food Activities

This chapter focuses on how archaeologists encounter food in the archaeological record. We need to consider the bodily practices and the meanings potentially associated with these daily, common acts – the elements of food preparation and consumption. Identifying these small but regular nutritive acts illuminates past social life. Many preparation and processing stages and methods have been addressed in the archaeological literature; all of them cannot be presented here. Here I select representatives of the major stages in food preparation. Covering all methods used to identify these actions is not the goal here, but many are mentioned as links to how we know what we know about these past activities and how we can get at cuisine in the past through approaching things we encounter.

Food preparation entails a sequence of activities, a *chaîne opératoire* of ingredient gathering, processing and mixing. These tasks contextualize and create food traditions that encompass a range of taskscapes (Ingold 2000; Jones 2002:157; Miracle 2002:67; Twiss 2012). By discussing each activity class – procurement-production, curation processing, storage, consumption processing, presentation, serving, eating, cleaning up, and rubbish disposal – using artifact distributions, depositional histories, and covariance, we can make past food practices more visible. Although researchers have modeled subsistence, production, and collection costs quite successfully (e.g., Earle and Christenson 1980; Jochim 1976; Keene 1981), this is not the only focus of archaeological food studies, nor is focusing on Lévi-Strauss's preparation triangle. These details of food activities allow us to get closer to the past. As Boyd (2001:138) notes, we should be able to use food-related data to address most archaeological interpretation.

Despite our patchy data, one of archaeology's strongest interpretive tools is comparison. Incorporating more and different data sets, such as plants, microorganisms, animal remains, teeth, bone tools, ceramics, textiles, metal, chipped and ground stone, and a range of microanalyses, we clarify food activities. In these tasks we look for the actors: female, male, children, adults, grandmothers and grandfathers, highlighting women's work as well as men's. Although it is not always easy to isolate specific acts within food preparation sequences, each section of this chapter emphasizes a stage in the practice of making foodstuffs edible. This chapter is presented to open deliberations and envisionings about food in the past.

## Food Production and Procurement

Food production is goal-directed, with a major goal being human sustenance. Production is the most commonly discussed food activity in the archaeological literature. There are many well-supported examples of past production and procurement, usually from an economic or subsistence orientation (but see Gumerman 1997). For archaeologists, production means the daily work of tending, planting, or nurturing plants and animals so they grow to maturity and can be harvested for consumption. Procurement activities include hunting, collecting (plants and animals, including bivalves, fungi, and algae), netting, tending (pruning, weeding and cleaning, and feeding), and collecting (harvesting, milking, butchering). These activities dominate the archaeological literature because the process of domestication is important, fascinating, and materialized. Subsistence is not food, however. Subsistence is the maintenance of life and growth, and reproduction; food is nourishment, both physical and mental. As we seek to understand how plants and animals have channeled and been channeled by the lives of humans, we must keep in mind that procurement is part of a web of social meanings (Balée 1994; Boyd 2001; Ingold 1986). In all aspects, production is a social act. People work together in fields and often hunt in groups. Harvesting is a joint effort. A person's intentions in these acts are multiple, engaging with material resources, a social process across a landscape of practice.

Domestication's major impact on human history makes it an engaging subject of study. Subsistence studies contribute substantive information to the study of food and therefore are so plentiful they are impossible to summarize. Many archaeological publications highlight the transition from foraging, gathering, and hunting to farming and herding, expanding our views of past productivity and the impacts these activities have had on food choices (Bogaard 2004; Fairbairn and Weiss 2009; Gebauer and Price 1992; Harris 1996; Harris and Hillman 1989; Piperno and Pearsall 1998; Smith

2007; Zeder et al. 2006). These publications span a range of theoretical viewpoints and are data rich, displaying the importance of the means of this aspect of our history. It continues to be debated as to the many mechanisms that encouraged plant and animal domestication, which allows us to bring the concepts of meaning into this debate.

Karl Wittfogel (1957), building on the Marxist perspective of the means of production, investigated Asian agriculture using historical data with lasting impact on archaeological agricultural interpretation. Tracking the control of the irrigation systems, he demonstrated the powerful relationship between irrigation farming technologies and political control in dry environments, where control of water was control of society. Based on Wittfogel's thesis, archaeologists have studied many agricultural production schemes, yields, environmental constraints, political strategies, and technological expertise, effectively applying macro and micro economic models to past situations.

Past production studies begin with studying the local environmental setting and the resources that would have been available. Environmental reconstruction harnesses a range of ecological research, including off-site sediment and stratigraphy, pollen, diatoms, and lake cores, along with on-site, micormorphological collections, macrobotanical and faunal remains. Often this approach takes a large-scale view of production, noting capital investments such as irrigation canals and terraces (*landesque capital*; Brookfield 1984; Widgren 2007), or how changing culling patterns in herd management impacted the yields and daily workloads of farmers (Zeder 1991). Bone and plant frequencies are the backbone of these studies, coupled with sediment and landscape analysis.

In 1976, Robin Dennell engaged archaeobotanical interests when he wrote that archaeobotanical remains could best tell us about production, not consumption. Some years later, I also made a case that macrobotanical remains studies from agricultural sites optimally provided evidence about crop production and processing, not consumption (Hastorf 1988). In production studies that apply plant remains, we can link shifts in taxa to farm decision making, but only indirectly. To study agricultural production directly requires work in the fields themselves. This research dichotomy between production and consumption is also seen in faunal data (Binford 1978). Animal bones reveal patterns in culling and hunting that inform us about management decisions in through meat resources. Katherine Moore's (1989) study of camelid hunting in the Junín Puna of highland Perú illustrates a shift in herd oversight by hunters, who focused on culling young males to maximize reproduction rates. Faunal remains also inform us about herding practices. Jessica Pearson and colleagues completed a study of stable isotopic analysis of goat, sheep, and cattle faunal remains at two Anatolian Neolithic sites (Pearson et al. 2007, 2015). Stable isotope data of the animal bones reflect an overall average of their life's diet focusing on differing levels of nitrogenous foods as well as ecozones in which they grazed. In these data she traced what the animals were consuming in the landscape and thus about herding strategies, especially foddering versus grazing. The stable carbon and nitrogen values at the earlier site of Aşıklıhöyük suggested a low level of herding, with the strategy of gleaning animals from near the settlement. The later and larger Çatalhöyük site's animal isotope data reflect a variety of animal herding strategies, with animals eating in different sectors of the environment. These two levels of herding intensity inform us about the position of animals in these groups' daily life, both in terms of valuation as well as in their cuisine. Animals clearly increased in importance through time in this central Anatolian region, not only for eating but also for feasting and exchange (Bogaard et al. 2009; Spielmann 2004; Twiss 2007).

Artifactual remains also speak to food production. Stone hoes and axes are indicative of field clearing and land use (Bandy 2001; McAnany 1992; Shafer 1983). Micromorphology, sediment analysis, and pollen from fields are used to verify levels of production intensity and yield (Edwards 1991, Fish 1994; Goodman 2003, Kirch et al. 2012; Matthews et al. 1997; Miller and Gleason 1994). From the relative yields and production styles we can learn about past decision making and therefore changing interests in crops and animal production.

For evidence of food production we turn to macrobotanical data, the visible plant remains that survive and are systematically collected from archaeological contexts. The Upper Mantaro Valley region of highland Perú provides an excellent place to investigate agricultural production over a span of years as the political context shifted (Hastorf 1993). The region was particularly appropriate for investigating agricultural production because of the environmental variability, resulting in different domesticates having distinct optimal elevation production zones (ibid.:110–117, Figure 4.1). Maize has discrete growing limits within frost-free zones. Potatoes (*Solanum* spp.) and the other tubers have overlapping but different optimal production elevations. Legumes (*Lupinus meyenii*) are restricted to the lower microzones, whereas the *Chenopodium* pseudo cereal grain is quite versatile in its production range. Production shifts within zones speak of farmer decisions given their range of crop choice available for each microzone. From ethno-agronomic studies, relative and

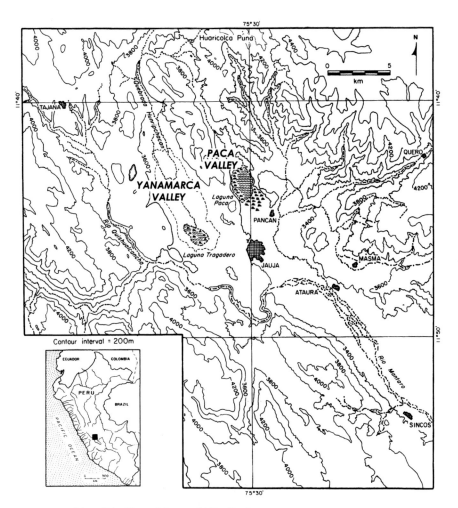

FIGURE 4.1. Map of the Upper Mantaro Valley Region

absolute yields have been discerned and a range of crop production mixes were proposed for each of the four major land-use zones near the settlements. These data were used to form models for the archaeobotanical remains that were systematically excavated, floated, and analyzed from a series of sites across the region, spanning four cultural phases. I organized the archaeobotanical evidence by density, percentage presence, and relative frequency. With these simple data manipulations I could track shifting plant production at each settlement, due in part to changing uses of the environmental zones but also to the political and demographic pressures seen in the settlement patterns. Of particular note was the impact of the Inka conquest on agricultural production, locally called the Wanka III phase (Hastorf 1991, 2001). The Inka relocated the local populace from their hilltop fortresses, where they lived during the Wanka II phase, into the warmer valley lands. Their ancestors had resided in the valleys 250 years previously, in the Wanka I phase. Although some returned to the locations of their previous settlements, they did not return to growing the same mix of valley (maize, legumes) and upland (potatoes and other tubers) crops that they had in the earlier times. Most notably, they were now growing more maize, the imperial crop of the Inka. I concluded this based on the maize's relative frequency within the assemblages, which changed from 4.3 to 3.5 to 9.3 across these three periods (Wanka I = 42% presence, 2.1 standardized density, Wanka II = 17% presence, 1.8 std. density; Wanka III = 63% presence, 17 std. density; Hastorf 2001a:164). The Inka demand for maize production in the region influenced the indigenous families' production regimes. During the Imperial decades, there was not only a shift in crop focus towards maize but also a new level of production intensity. The imperial pressures on Wanka household production economies are an example of situational political pressures on agricultural production decisions.

The influence of geography and social value on crop production is particularly apparent in the crop histories of two adjacent valleys in the Jauja region (Hastorf 1993:172). The Upper Mantaro study region consists of a series of small alluvial valleys that are tributaries of the main river valley (Figure 4.1). Environmentally, these small valleys appear to be the same, with roughly the same environmental conditions, elevation, and soils. But, as the data in Figure 4.2 demonstrate, the neighboring valleys, Paca and Yanamarca, have noticeably different production histories. Several sites in these valleys were sampled by excavation and their flotation samples analyzed for macrobotanical data. All of the local crops, including maize, can be grown in both valleys. Nevertheless, Figure 4.2 illustrates that the Paca Valley residents produced more maize than the Yanamarca Valley farmers did through all time periods studied, including today. This notable trend reflects historical traditions of different crop preferences in the two valleys. This example of local identity maintenance via specific crops and accompanying dishes will be discussed further in later chapters.

What is particularly intriguing is that when I spoke with the local farmers in these two valleys in 1980, they all said that the Paca Valley was known for its maize, while the Yanamarca Valley was not – it focused more on quinoa (*Chenopodium* sp.) production. These data present a long-term

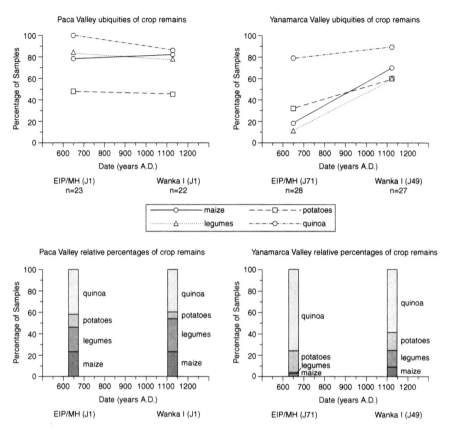

FIGURE 4.2. Changes in the relative percentages and ubiquity crop yields in the Paca and Yanamarca Valleys

stability in these valley production cultures that has persisted throughout the past 600 years, spanning a range of conquests and political pressures. This suggests quite strong and long-lived cultural focus of food crops in these two areas.

Changes in farming technology reflect changing social and economic goals of the residents. When people put more energy into farming, crop production intensification should be visible in the phytolith evidence. Phytoliths are small silica bodies that form between cells as water is taken into the cells. In a productive study, Arlene Rosen and Steve Weiner (1994) used phytolith architecture of cereals to identify irrigated and dry-farmed wheat production in the Levant. Large sheets of phytoliths occur when more water is given to grain crops, whereas these do not occur in dry farming. As a complement to studying internal plant morphology, Glynis Jones,

Mike Charles, and Amy Bogaard study wild seed macrobotanical analysis to identify crop production strategies. By focusing on the range of weed taxa that are associated with specific watering regimes, they link different seed taxa frequencies to specific growing conditions (Charles et al. 1997; G. Jones 1987).

Animal production regimes have been successfully investigated by a number of analysts interested in the production goals of herders. Different culling behaviors reflect distinct emphases on meat, milk, wool, or traction, each of which reflects different status (Clutton-Brock 1999; Crabtree 1990; Moore 1989; Wapnish and Hesse 1991; Zeder 1991). Wapnish and Hesse (1988), for example, investigated animal production at the Middle Bronze Age site of Tell Jemmeh in the Levant. Their economic argument proposed three herding models for the Middle Bronze Age II. In the first model, the occupants were self-sufficient, producing their own meat and/ or milk (and wool). In the second model, the residents consumed animal products but did not produce their own meat; they traded with others for the animal by-products they wanted to consume. And in the third model, they overproduced animals for product export, consuming the products themselves as well as exchanging meat and milk for other goods. Each of these strategies should have different pig, cattle, sheep, and goat faunal frequencies in the settlement's deposits. They tallied the faunal taxa in terms of skeletal and mortality counts (abundance and relative frequency) across domestic contexts to see which of the three models had the best fit. All body parts of the four taxa were present in the settlement, supporting the first, self-sufficient-producer hypothesis. Sheep and goats dominated the assemblage, representing 77% of the total sample (Wapnish and Hesse 1988:88). The few cattle bones found (10%) suggest that these animals were primarily produced for traction and milk, and were allowed to live to an old age. The pigs were killed before they were one year old, confirming they were only a meat source (12%). The sheep and goat data are more complex. Most (50–70%) of these animals were killed early, suggesting that they were raised for their meat. With the sex mortality data of the sheep and goats, Wapnish and Hesse propose that the residents were culling and eating young males, while they focused on milk production with the longer-lived females (ibid.:91). Their evidence supports a self-sufficient, generalist population producing and consuming their own food – the first model (ibid.:93). This economic food study effectively applied a series of bone element analyses and demonstrated that each animal had a different place within the resident's food activities.

## Food Processing

Fresh food has always been valued, but so has processed food that can be consumed at another time. Especially for communal meals and feasts but also for daily family meals, prior preparation is common. Food processing can delay microbial and enzymatic activity, extending the edibility of the ingredient. Today, refrigeration enables us to have fresh food on a regular basis (Goody 1982), but for millennia, dried, smoked, rotted, and cooked foods were the norm throughout most of the year (Lévi-Strauss 1966). "Nor is there any condition of pure rawness: only certain foods can really be eaten raw, and then only if they have been selected, washed, pared or cut or even seasoned" – in other words, before foods enter one's mouth, they are handled in some way to make them edible (Lévi-Strauss 1966:587). Once material is collected – killed, gathered in baskets, tied up in bundles, dug up from the earth, or speared on a stick – food is either consumed on the spot, stored as is, or processed for future use. Whether for immediate consumption or for storage, food processing is crucial to maintain a stable food supply (Goody 1982; Ingold 1986). Until quite recently, extending the longevity of food was a time-consuming activity in most households.

Processed food enables people to move into new regions, survive extreme weather conditions, eat a more balanced diet, feed their young more regularly, take care of the infirm, and gain a sense of safety and well-being. Food processing is part of the long cycle of control and domestication of the environment. Processing is intimately tied to storage, since much of what is processed is reserved for later use. The import of processing is registered in the recent history of canning, freezing, and freezer transport vehicles described by Jack Goody (1982:154), and of course this has expanded with today's routine air transport of fresh and freeze-dried food. The increasingly longer shelf lives of today's vegetables have altered the way the world eats, from dried and rehydrated foods to moist cans of salty beans, from ground corn to frozen, ready-to-heat-and-eat meals.

People spent a great deal of time processing their food stuffs in the past, as many of the tools and utensils found in the archaeological record were used for these tasks. Most lithic and bone tools, baskets, and ceramics were involved in food processing. Winnowing, shelling, cutting up, hanging, drying, smoking, cracking, parching, stewing, shredding, and pounding are just some of the activities that extend shelf life. These activities are time-consuming and must have kept people occupied throughout the year. Meal processing is required on a daily basis and is increasingly discussed in the archaeological literature (Klarich 2010b; Rodríguez-Alegría and Graff 2012), in part because of an increased interest in women's lives and work.

Elizabeth Brumfiel in Mexico and Patricia Crown in the American Southwest show how grinding and cooking took its toll on women as their daily workload was filled with processing (Brumfiel 1991; Crown 2000; Wright 2000). Musculoskeletal stress markers (MSM) and osteoarthritis (OA) identify types and amounts of labor and workload on the body, much of which can be linked to food production and preparation (Becker 2013). Stirring, grinding, load carrying, and farming can all be identified through a range of muscle attachments and bone wear. Given that food gathering and preparation were probably the most time-consuming activities in an individual's life, as cooks rallied those around them to help, their significance should move them to the forefront of our studies. These daily decisions have substantial implications too for personhood, identity, and one's place in society.

Some say that harnessing fire gave humans unprecedented control over food and environment (Gifford-Gonzalez 1993; Stahl 1984; Wandsnider 1997; Wrangham 2009; Wrangham et al. 1999). Lévi-Strauss placed fire's capacities to alter food at the center of his structural model: the raw and the cooked. The timing of people's controlled use of fire is still debated, whether around 1.9 million years ago, as Wrangham and colleagues suggest, or about 250,000 years ago, as Brace (1995, 1999:578) proposed. Why might this be important? Despite the debate over the timing, all human evolutionary scholars agree that this adoption was significant. Cooking broadened edible food availability and changed the hominoid diet sufficiently to enable more humanlike traits to be selected, especially those involved with social interaction. With more focus on preparation, people came together to eat, forming a place for interaction and society building. The timing and importance of cooking, especially carbohydrate cooking, is an important issue in human evolution that has many implications for people's agency.

Presenting a range of processing techniques illustrates their breadth as well as their material evidence in the archaeological record. Although the list of processing activities discussed here is not exhaustive, the important activities are demonstrated, guiding us to a deeper understanding of specific past societies and noting the economic, symbolic, and political implications of these activities. Turning to more specific animal- and then plant-processing methods will broaden our understanding of the visibility of processing in the archaeological record. Examples of meat butchery, fish drying, and grain processing, along with plant winnowing, parching (or blanching), and threshing, are included.

Although this section is descriptive and seemingly mundane in terms of theoretical significance, these activities had a powerful role on people's lives, not just in economic terms but in their symbolic significance and capacities to construct meaningful frames of social reference in a lived, Bourdieuan sense, through these habitual enactments as well as the time people spent thinking about and completing these tasks throughout their days. Food processing is probably the most fundamental structuring structure in human society. Prestigious foods may have required more processing time, as with hundred-year eggs in Chinese food culture (皮蛋), which are fermented in a detailed sequence and encased in clay to allow them to cure, preserving them almost indefinitely. With contextual analysis we can begin to identify the symbolic significance of different food-processing strategies. Some techniques, such as freeze-drying in the Andes (discussed later in the chapter), have special meanings linked to the ancestors, which gives the foods even greater value. The flavors of processed foods differ significantly in their valuation than the raw foods from which they are made, such as Kimchi pickling for the Koreans (Mintz 2011; di Schino 2011). This is especially important in seasonally marked environments, where high values are placed on processed foods that will be stored and used through the winter. But even in tropical regions, processing, such as manioc processing in the Amazon, makes plants edible for longer, expanding the larder tremendously. Archaeologists can identify processing sequences and perhaps uncover evidence of their valuations.

Most processing requires utensils. Even the simplest meal is made with utensils. The activities and associated material used to make bread include threshing, winnowing, drying, storing, grinding, mixing, kneading (some breads also include fermentation and rising), and baking; these procedures in turn require grain, water, possibly a leavening agent, sieves, grinding stones (querns), bowls, warm areas within the home, and a contained heat source. Each of these objects and their associated activities has a long history of development and use, linking all bread making to a range of tool use-lives and technical histories (Counihan 1997 [1984]). Detailing the processing and preparation steps with their material correlates, as illustrated in Figure 4.3, enables us to reflect on the combined ingredients, their associated actions, and the set of artifacts used to work with them.

Ingredient spatial distributions are not necessarily apparent in archaeological settings. Applying a task approach to any food practice helps archaeologists think about material correlates that would have been necessary to produce the end results, expanding our views about the activities, their required corporeal movements, and the time needed, in addition to

FIGURE 4.3. (a and b) Steps in bread making from grain cleaning through baking (drawn by Melanie Miller)

the objects involved – in other words, the *chaîne opératoire* of processed food (Conkey and Spector 1984). Archaeologists usually encounter only a small portion of the ingredients and associated artifacts from any processing sequence, requiring us to fill in the remaining activities and associated tools based on our knowledge, often unconsciously. It helps to be explicit (Figure 4.3). A partial view provided by artifacts and their spatial locations should not stop us from envisioning the fuller sequence, as illustrated for bread baking.

## Drying, Pickling, and Rotting

Notwithstanding the many caveats to (and critics of) his classification scheme, Lévi-Strauss opened us up to the structuring principles that have significance and influence about edibility beliefs (Lehrer 1972; Parker Pearson 2003:3). His raw, cooked, and rotted categories help us begin the study of food processing.

Goody (1982) reformulated Lévi-Strauss's raw vs. cooked classification scheme to raw vs. dried, labeling "dry" as an important form of processing. Drying is especially important because of its symbolic resonance. Most living things become drier as they age; many societies dry their dead as well as their food, seeing this as a natural stage for all things that hold power. Although I concentrate on the more material forms of food evidence in this chapter, the symbolic aspects of these transformations and their associated meanings have important connotations for other material as well (Campbell 2000; Hastorf 2003b; Jones 1999, 2002).

Heating organic matter makes it easier to digest. It breaks down toxic molecules, softens fibrous tissues, sweetens the flavor, and expands the range of edible foods (Wandsnider 1997). Many studies demonstrate that once the ripening season was over (late spring through autumn), desiccated foods were the mainstay of most terrestrial and even marine cuisines. Meat, fish, and bones were dried and stored (Henshilwood et al. 1994; Hoffman et al. 2000; Rowley-Conwy and Zvelebil 1989). In fact, dried meat "jerky," or *ch'arki* in Quechua, is a traditional food in many places throughout the Americas (White 1953). This treatment can be as simple as sun drying, or can include smoking, dry salting, or wet brining (Fisher 2011; Perry 2011; Stahl 1999:1359; Tomka 1994). No bones may be left at the place where meat jerky is consumed, but bones should look different if they have gone through this drying process, making them identifiable in the archaeological record (Stahl 1999). Goody focuses on canning and drying (1982), Wandsnider on roasting (1997).

Freezing, sun drying, and smoking were the first and most common procedures for prolonging the edibility of foodstuffs, keeping the micro-organisms at bay. Drying is a useful entry point in archaeological food-processing discussion because it requires the least effort and technology (Friesen 2001). We have a substantial amount of ethnographic evidence about how drying extends the edibility of moist foods for months, if not years: meat, fruit, nuts, seeds, bulbs, tubers, and fish have all been dried to prolong their shelf life. In the high-elevation mountains of South America, for example, where many foods are preserved by freeze-drying, this process has an almost sacred connotation. There is a parallel resonance in the Andes between food processing for storage longevity and the preparation of the dead to secure the longevity of the ancestors (Arriaza 1996; Arnold and Yapita 1996; Hastorf 2003b). In the Archaic phase, dead bodies were desiccated and sometimes mummified with salt, in the same manner as staple foods are: potatoes into *chuño, oca (Oxalis tuberosus)* into *calla*, and meat into *ch'arki*. Archaeological evidence of freeze-drying is registered in the cellular alteration in small, crushed tuber fragments and starch grains (Hastorf 1993; Rumold 2010:295). Highland residents only need sunny days, freezing nights, and a flat surface to make *chuño, calla*, and *ch'arki*. The symbolic links between the staple foodstuffs, the ancestors, and their guardianship of the landscape resources is clear in ethnography and is increasingly suggested in archaeological settings (Arnold and Hastorf 2008). In another example, Turkic steppe people preserve yogurt by sun-drying the whey into hard lumps (Perry 2011:242). These lumps are then ground and when needed, hydrated into a soup. Versions of these techniques are common throughout societies that live in cold climates, yet they are virtually never mentioned in archaeological discussions.

Three other drying techniques – smoking, parching, and blanching – require more equipment: a frame, a flat surface, or a vessel over a fire that provides direct or indirect heat to speed the drying process. Smoke frames, pits, or parching pans are visible in the archaeological record (Binford 1967). Hillman (1984) recorded parching at specific stages in traditional Turkish cereal grain processing and can be identifiable in the archaeological record. Blanching, which is putting food briefly into boiling water or steam to seal their surface, helps slow enzymatic activity and allows foodstuffs such as nuts, once dried, to be stored longer (Wandsnider 1997:5). We might be able to identify blanching in the archaeological record with further focused experimental research.

Salting, pickling, brining, marinating, and curdling are more complicated treatments. By replacing the water with acidic ingredients in both plants and meat (and thereby creating an anaerobic environment), decomposition is slowed. Common pickling examples are sauerkraut/kimchii, which is cabbage preserved in an acid bath (vinegar), or Roman *garum*, which is fish soaked in vinegar (Buccini 2011). Adding yeast agents consumes the sugars in many foodstuffs, also slowing organic activity. The reverse of this process is used to reconstitute foods, as with dried fish in the making of *lutefisk* (lyedfish in Norwegian) (Kurlansky 1997). In this reverse process dried fish is soaked in water and wood ashes until it regains a firm, edible consistency (Riddersvold 1990). Foods such as *lutefisk* and *chuño* are doubly processed, thereby increasing their value. Both are first dried for storage and then rehydrated (brought back to life) by soaking/cooking them in lie or water. They have value today because of this extra preparation, and I suggest that they did in the past as well.

Rotting can also preserve food, even though we tend to associate this process with food going off or spoiling (Perry 2011). Some people enjoy eating rotted food. Rotting is actually a form of fermentation. Fermenting agents speed up the process that naturally occurs after death in all organic matter. People intentionally add microorganisms that direct the type of rotting desired. For example, in the Andean highlands today, bags of tubers are left to rot in running water for two weeks, making *tunta*, which is considered a delicacy because of its tangy taste and unusual texture. Rotten meat was preferred over fresh meat by many North American Plains hunters, in part because of its more complex flavor. Making cheese requires lactic acid, a fermenting agent, and of course wine and beer also fit into this rotten/fermented category, emphasizing how popular these forms of rotting remain in today's processing techniques and cuisines. Although some of today's processed foods, such as a pop tart, with its fifty (!) ingredients, are a far cry from preindustrial food preservation focused on here, preservation has been a common form of food processing since humans began to retain food ingredients after a meal.

These examples are reminders that Lévi-Strauss's categories can be informative guideposts in our investigations about the past, if only by nudging us to look not just for food remains but also for signs of processing and preserving, which adds an informative dimension to our study of food ingredients. Processing techniques are not always easy to see archaeologically. Biomolecular, isotopes, lipids, and other geochemical analyses have begun to identify these processes and increasingly will be integrated into our projects. Identifying molecules such as diastase and lactic acid is crucial to recognize specific processing techniques. Such methods are currently being studied in several laboratories.

*Animal Processing*

Archaeologists identify animal species quite easily using complete bones or fish scales. It is not as easy to identify how they were processed, especially when dried, smoked, steamed, or salted. Butchering marks on bone, anatomical part frequencies, and utility indices are linked to meat-processing steps that inform us of the relative valuation of different animals in specific societies. Crader (1990), for example, presents detailed pig- and cow-butchering evidence from slave quarters at Thomas Jefferson's home in Monticello, tracking the different forms of meat processing and highlighting the differences in slave vs. master taskscapes. This study reveals social hierarchy through differential food access and processing. She outlines five butchering types: cutting, chopping, shearing, scraping, and sawing. Bone evidence can identify roasting and boiling frequencies. Crader points out that boiling meat in a single pot (stew, as she calls it) allows the meat to drop off the bone, leaving no cut mark evidence besides the initial butchering. Roasted meat, on the other hand, must be carved, leaving regular cut marks on the bones. Based on these correlates, she found that the slave quarter bone discard suggests 20 percent roasted and 80 percent boiled meat. Based on the bone distribution, she infers that the slaves ate higher-valued roasts as well as the pot-boiled meals. Alternatively, bone from the master's roasts could have been reused by the slaves for their own meals, after the meat was eaten at the main house, or perhaps rubbish from the main house had been discarded in their middens. The point here is that bone frequencies and processing styles are relevant not only to cuisine in a Douglasian symbolic sense but also to materially hidden but always active master-slave relations, as these power relationships were reflected in all of their daily activities. Given the value of roasted meat in that society, this evidence leads us to ask how closely the slaves were being monitored as they engaged in their masters' lives.

Other meat-processing examples in the archaeological literature are informative not only about food economics but also about culinary strategies and therefore food practices. In 1993, Diane Gifford-Gonzalez wrote an important article on the social implications of butchery patterns. From her African ethnographic study she learned that butchering, cooking, and storage decisions are primarily in the female domain. Further, how the food will be cooked dictates how the meat and bones are treated throughout the processing sequence. She stressed the importance of the kill itself for those attending the meal. The meal then reflects the hunting style as well as the butchering style at the kill site (Gifford-Gonzalez 1993:188).

Gifford-Gonzalez makes the case that butchery decisions are influenced by how the meat, marrow, and other useful parts of the animals will be stored and processed for consumption; future processing plans even influence the hunt and which animals are selected (Gifford-Gonzalez 1993:188). An animal will be butchered differently if it is to be made into jerky (dried meat), boiled in stew, or roasted in an oven (Albarella and Serjeantson 2002; Binford 1978; Russell and Martin 2005; O'Connell et al. 1988; Yellen 1977). If the meat is cut up at a mass kill site for a quick departure, only choice muscles will be stripped and perhaps a few bones taken (Frison 1970, 1974). If a single animal has been killed, the whole animal may be brought home for processing (O'Connell et al. 1988; Yellen 1977). Yellen (1977) discusses how the processing of meat, bones, marrow, and blood at the cooking location can be visible archaeologically through fragment distributions. Marrow processing is more widespread than perhaps archaeologists have recognized (Coy 1975; Leechman 1951; Mulville and Outram 2005; Outram 2001; Velik 1977). Grease extraction was an important activity, as Leechman points out for North American prairie animal processing. The extracted and refined marrow grease was used like oil and butter today, as it could be stored for two to three years in bags made from the animals' organs (Leechman 1951:356). People traveled with and traded this processed grease, which was highly prized and versatile. Grease processing enabled people to stay together and not have to always be hunting, making it truly a social glue. In settled communities, grease provided an essential ingredient in many soups and stews, as well as having uses beyond cooking, such as for tool manufacture and light.

To better identify meat processing in archaeological hunter-gatherer faunal assemblages, Friesen (2001) reformulates Binford's (1978) Drying Utility Index evidence with Alaskan and Canadian caribou hunting information. Binford's index calculates which carcass portions will be selected for drying meat. Friesen proposes an effective statistic that identifies meat drying in bone assemblages. He creates a more streamlined method of calculation called the Meat Drying Index, which he applies to a range of cache sites, determining the amount of meat that was dried from the bones found at the sites. Each major element has a meat weight equivalent, which can be studied individually. These meat-processing indicators are most useful in spatially discrete bone assemblages, clarifying the processing/storage activities rather than consumption events.

Fish processing leaves regular evidence (Coupland et al. 2010). Fish drying has been identified in Alaska on Unimak Island. By comparing fish head frequencies to vertebrae frequencies, Hoffman and colleagues (2000) have separated processing camps from consumption sites. Careful spatial study unpacks these different activities within an assemblage, enabling archaeologists to identify processing activity locations (Coy 1975).

Examples of preservation using water have also been identified. Henshilwood and colleagues (1994) found archaeological evidence of bivalve steaming on the west coast of the South African Cape. Inspired by the very large middens of mussel shells that date to between 3000 and 1800 BP, they experimented and found a simple, effective way that the inland dwellers dried and stored bivalve meat for later consumption. They concluded that these massive coastal middens were processing locations for seasonal, large-scale mussel harvesting. The harvested mollusks were steamed for four days on moist seaweed. Then for three days they were dried in the sun. Once dry, the mussels were transported inland and stored. This simple processing sequence explains not only these huge middens but also a stable food source of the interior inhabitants.

People foraged differently depending on how they planned to use the food, whether for a particular dish or for storage (Gifford-Gonzalez 1993). We recognize this today, for this is how we shop. A culinary approach to subsistence allows us to move past strict economics to study the hunting patterns and determine what the people wanted to do with their harvest. Meat storing requires different butchering practices than those used for fresh meat consumption (Cassoli and Tagliacozzo 1997; Friesen 2001; Kent 1999; Stokes 2000; Yellen 1977).

*Plant Processing*

As with meat, plant processing can entail a long sequence of activities, informing us about the social world of the participants. Although food is determined by what is in the environment, choice demonstrates the cultural concerns and social rules in food traditions. Fruit can be picked off a tree and eaten, entailing no work and no social engagement, but most plant consumption requires cooperation. People working together form a bond towards a common goal (having food to eat). Processing complexities speak to the value of the plant. Seed harvests require many more steps than most other foodstuffs to prepare them for dry storage (Caparelli et al. 2011; Yen 1980). Grains hold a central position of in societies that focus on grain harvests. This is evident in the high ubiquity of grain processing evidence around the world, of wheat, barley, rice, millet, amaranthus or quinoa. Two archaeobotanists, Gordon Hillman and Glynis Jones, first highlighted this sequence of cleaning Eurasian cereals and pulses ethnographically, documenting a *chaîne opératoire* of grain-processing activities (Hillman 1984; Jones 1983, 1984). They recorded at least fourteen steps between the field and the pot (Jones 1984:44) (or loaf of bread: Figure 4.3). This processing sequence transforms cereal and pulse plants to edible grain stores via threshing, winnowing, sieving, and finally hand-cleaning to extract the inedible impurities. These grains can then be stored for more than a year. There are usually at least two phases of threshing, two winnowings, a parching, and both coarse and fine sieving (Hillman 1984). Grain can be stored at any stage, but generally not before the first threshing, winnowing, and parching. Threshing and winnowing must take place off-site or at the edges of a settlement or field. Winnowing requires wind to separate the edible seed from the inedible chaff. The sieving and hand-cleaning stages focus on the wild seeds that grow among the domestic plants, which can also be identified archaeologically. Each stage leaves a botanical signature in chaff, grain, and wild seed frequencies. Only the charred remains of these actions are found in most excavations.

With careful study and decent preservation, we can identify processing sequences archaeologically, which in turn can inform us about crop valuation and the types of work that occurred in these settings (Valamoti 2004). The excavations at the Neolithic site of Çatalhöyük in western Turkey have uncovered evidence of several plant-processing stages (Atalay and Hastorf 2005, 2006; Fairbairn et al. 2005; Helbaek 1964). We have evidence of winnowing on the eastern side of the settlement in the KOPAL area. The nearby Küçükköy villagers, who take advantage of the lively spring winds from the southeast to complete this first phase of processing, use this same orientation today. Initial processing was completed with baskets and skin sieves, employing a tossing motion aided by the wind to remove the straw, little pebbles, and heavier wild seeds (Rosen 2005; Wendrich 2005, field notes). This initial crop processing is evident in the KOPAL archaeobotanical remains (Fairbairn et al. 2005; Matthews 2005; Roberts et al. 2006; Rosen 2005). Silicified awns, spines, hairs, and glume beaks, the results of threshing and winnowing, were densely distributed in this area. The early settlement, pre-level 12 deposits also have high densities of chaff, indicating that crop winnowing took place on this side of the settlement in the very early days of its existence (Farid 2007). Lower chaff and small wild seed densities are found within the structures and middens, where the final sieving and cleaning remains were dumped within the settlement.

Processing equipment for both seeds and roots has been analyzed in archaeological research. To highlight what we gain from studying processing tools and their reflection of social life, grain-processing examples from

Eurasia and from the Americas are presented and then contrasted with an Alpine example.

Pounding and grinding are important to access the grain. With the earliest focus on grains, the Neolithic social world was entwined with mortars, pestles, and stone bowls. Common food processing evidence suggests that these foods were consumed throughout the Levant. Small-scale grinding equipment found in the earliest Nautufian settlements (12650 to 11250 BC) informs how ground food and drink might have been prepared with wooden mortars, which are not often preserved (Capparelli et al. 2011; Valamoti 2004; Wright 2000:97). The pestles would not have ground the main food consumed but less common foods such as spices, infusions, ritual items and medicines. In the semi-sedentary Natufian communities, wild food remains as well as cereals, hearths, and stone bowls were found inside the shelters, where the meals were cooked and consumed (Wright 2000). Food storage pits were located outside the houses in sheltered locations. Utensils, used for wheat and barley grain processing, were decorated and movable, suggesting special and versatile symbolic values were associated with grain processing.

The pre-pottery Neolithic A (PPNA, 10450–8800 BC) houses exhibit less emphasis on cooking and cooks, as the ground stone tools are not as decorated. Interestingly, the storage bins became highly decorated, reflecting more power to the provider in these communities. Does this change reflect a shifting emphasis onto the stores themselves, rather than the preparer, grinding the food? We may never know who completed these tasks, but we can see that storage became increasingly symbolically important at this time. Ironically, more seclusion and separation of food preparation and consumption is also apparent inside the house walls in this phase, suggesting both more work and less social interaction for the cooks. Were they eating more ground food than earlier as well? In the PPNA houses, domestic cereals were increasingly harvested (Wright 2000:98). Processing became linked to cooking as the pestles were spatially associated with the interior hearths, placed in the center of the one-room houses (Wright 2000:101). Why did the location of food preparation shift at these settlements?

Later, in early pre-pottery Neolithic B times (PPNB 8800–7550 BC), a sea-change occurred in this Levantine society. Family identity and gendered tasks become even more demarcated, which perhaps was not in the best interests of the women of the group. The grinding stones become considerably larger, detailed, and immovable as the diet became increasingly cereal based (Wright 2000:103). Milling stations and storage were placed on the entrance porches of the smaller houses and in the courtyards of the larger, multi-roomed houses, suggesting increased centrality of food processing within the daily practices of the households (Wright 2000:107). These locations were between the interior and the exterior world, engaging with the community yet clearly linked to specific houses. Grinders had to spend more time grinding, which is reflected in women's bodies through bone wear and the larger stones. Although the cuisine was similar, the social context of its preparation and consumption shifted. Cooking and consumption was beginning to move into the privacy of individual homes. These working women, who no longer walked the landscape to gather food, had increasingly less interaction with their friends in the community and spent more time preparing meals, as processing food increasingly occurred indoors.

The late PPNB reflects the final change in this social trajectory. Eating was now separated from preparation. Houses were larger, with more people living together – perhaps extended families rather than nuclear families, as suggested for earlier times. Wright (2000:112) believes that interior locations became more specialized, as specific rooms were designated as kitchens. The storage areas were larger and clearly contained more food, becoming more important as banks for the family while expressing the increased focus on crop production. Cooking and eating occurred inside, even upstairs, where others could no longer see, hear, or even smell the prepared meals. The larger villages had more complex buildings that encouraged distance between the families. What did this mean to the inhabitants? More work, more grinding, less sharing, and more privatization. Marxist forces of controlling production were alive and well in this early Neolithic sequence, but why did these shifts in food preparation occur? I am guessing it was not the women grinders who suggested that they grind more. What about fuel? What about other foods in the cuisine? These could be linked to form a richer picture.

Grinding with increasingly larger stones suggests that flour-based foods became more important, transitioning from use as special food or drink into the daily meal. If women were responsible for the grinding, as Wright suggests, their food labor clearly intensified throughout this temporal sequence. The valuation placed on this labor, however, seemed to lessen. Grinding activities eventually became constrained and removed from the community to within the house – with a loss of sociality for those who spent their time grinding every day.

This same historical sequence is known for other places and times. Women were also the primary food processors in the American Southwest

(Crown 2000:221). As in the Levant, specialized stone processing tools increased with sedentism and farming. Tracking grinding stones in association with ceramics, one gets a fairly clear picture of how many people were fed and what the dishes in a meal were like. Patricia Crown proposes that increasing concern about fuel conservation impacted the grinding implements' size and shape over time. This preparation change suggests that women spent more time processing grains and inventing meals that could be cooked with less fuel, such as ground meal wrapped in maize leaves and piki bread. This same sequence is also true in Japanese cuisine history, in which considerable time is spent preparing the ingredients so the food can be cooked much faster, thereby saving fuel but placing a much higher labor burden on the cooks (Wilson 2012).

In the American Southwest grinding implement size increases in association with the maize evidence and stable isotope dietary data, tracked by Hard, Mauldin, and Raymond (1996). Grinding stone (*mano*) size correlates with the grinding surface area (*metate*) and therefore the amount of grain (maize) ground. Across sixteen temporal phases and several cultural areas there was a (nonlinear) increase in mano size. Maize consumption histories varied by region. The authors found three patterns in these data: an early and strong use of maize that continued to increase over time; a low level of maize consumption with intensification of maize grinding beginning late in the sequence; and an initial, intensive maize adoption that remained steady over time. While we don't see the exact meals, we do see the processing of them, with three different tempos of this food preparation.

Crown (2000) associates these work tools with women's work. In conjunction with the ground stone evidence she suggests a parallel social status shift within Southwestern societies, as women's grinding became not only more intensive but also more valued. These women put in long days of grinding to feed their families. The increasing shift to recipes requiring ground grain gave women a central position in the household linked to this specific food work, but in a manner different to that suggested by Wright. In the Levant, Wright sees more work in food processing linked to women's separation and removal from society, whereas in the American Southwest example Crown suggests that the grinding, located in the house, became more central and highly valued. What other data was added so that these two scholars came up with opposite valuations of the cooks in more or less the same situation? These two studies demonstrate why cultural context and associated artifacts are so crucial in our analyses and interpretations, as both scholars drew on their local archaeological data, yet come up with different conclusions about the cooks in their work rooms. We need more information to sort out the cooks, and the scholars need to provide these data to help us accept their valuations.

Grinding is not the only path to softer food. In the American Southwest, grinding tools are correlated with maize use and agricultural dependence. Southwestern scholars suggest that as maize production increased, it required a concomitant amount of processing. Like wheat and barley, maize does not have to be ground to be consumed. Gruels and soups of whole grains were consumed, requiring only winnowing and boiling, a common dish. Andean meals, for example, are often whole grain stews and are rarely ground. Ethnographic evidence of grain processing in the rural Austrian Alpine farming valleys, gathered by Anni Gamerith (1981), documents another form of cereal processing that was less time consuming than grinding. Informants told Gamerith that rolling or soft pounding with a wooden mallet makes the grain sweeter, easier to digest, quicker to cook, and more nutritious than stone ground methods (as with the rolled oat breakfast *muesli* cereals of today; Meyer-Renschhausen 1991:104). These Alpine data place the Natufian stone grinding evidence in a new light, indicating that time-consuming grinding was not essential or possibly even the optimal form of meal preparation. Alpine women have created a different processing history. They were not pulled into long hours of food processing through grinding. Flour is less easily stored than whole grain anyway, directing us to consider other reasons why some groups focused on grain grinding. Stone-ground grain releases nutrients, making the meal more versatile in that it is easier to carry, quicker to cook, and easier to digest, but it ruined the backs and arms of the grinders.

Cereals can be stored after any number of different processing regimes (Valamoti 2004). Why did stone grinding spread across greater Mesoamerica (including the Southwest) but not in other American areas where grains also became staple foods? A long-standing ecological explanation has to do with fuel requirements. Whole grain soups need to boil for quite a while, whereas tortilla or *masa* (ground maize) cooking requires much less time and fuel. Was fuel a continual problem in the greater Levant and the Southwest? Are we seeing fuel as the important limiting factor in these cuisines, such that the women of these regions had to spend much of their days grinding instead of collecting fuel? Might it have been related to protection, not being able to roam safely across the countryside to gather fuel? Could other processing traditions have been practiced? Was the tradition of ground grain and bread associated with other social valuations that were accepted early in these regions, such that only bread could define a proper meal? More consideration is needed about this issue of grain grinding and its associated meanings.

Turning to a different plant tissue processing history in the xerophytic American Southwest and northern Mexico, archaeological scholars have identified agave cactus and maguey processing areas near where these plants grow densely today (Bohrer 1991; Gentry 1882; Fish et al. 1985; Fish et al. 1990; Fowler 1995; Minnis 1991; Parsons and Parsons 1990; Reagan 1930). Suzanne Fish and her colleagues (1990) have plotted charred roasting agave pits identified by fire-cracked rock distribution across extensive areas, reflecting human agency in extending the plants' range. These plants thrive on dry hill slopes and in valleys. They have been partially domesticated in that people have transplanted them for centuries, encouraging them to spread outside of their native habitat (Fish et al. 1990; Gasser and Kwiatkowski 1991a). The roots are harvested for multiple uses. When the plants flower, the subterranean agave hearts are excavated and roasted for more than twenty hours in sealed earth pits. Once roasted and then dried, they can be transported, remaining edible and flavorful for months and even years. In addition to the use of the hearts as food, the maguey leaves are cut and pounded to release fibers and their sap is boiled and made into a fermented beverage (Parsons and Parsons 1990). We can see why the residents put effort into this plant; it was highly valued and versatile.

Root processing was extremely important in many food traditions. It is more difficult to identify in the archaeological record than seed processing because the remains tend to be very thin layers of cells, except the rare charred root or tuber. Microbotanical starch and phytolith research has recently begun to make tuber processing more visible archaeologically in a broad range of locations. Atchison and Fullagar (1998) in Australia, Piperno and Holst (1998) in Panama, and Pearsall and colleagues (Chandler Ezell et al. 2006) in Ecuador have all demonstrated evidence of food processing by identifying tuber starches on stone grinding tools. These analyses allow us to see not only the past use of these soft, moist tuber foods but also the shredding and pounding involved in their processing. From Real Alto Ecuador, Deborah Pearsall and her University of Missouri laboratory team have identified phytoliths and starches from roots, tubers, and rhizomes of manioc (*Manihot* spp.), *Calathea* spp., and arrowroot (*Maranta* spp.), in addition to squash, beans, and maize micro-remains dating to 2800–2400 BC. From Panama, Piperno and Holst have identified manioc, arrowroot, and maize starch grains on milling stones and pounding cobbles from a series of sites, the earliest dating to 10000 BP. The fact that we now have

concrete ways to identify soft tissues in the tropics is encouraging archaeologists to recognize the centrality of food processing.

Starch found on ceramic sieves, grinding stones, and cutting tools from
the Andean/Amazon region implicates food processing and beer making not only with manioc but also with maize (DeBoer 1975; Perry 2004;
Rumold 2010). We are at a threshold of much more plant food-processing
knowledge via micro remains and biomolecular identifications that were
unthinkable until recently.

Fuel use, scheduling, and cooking traditions influence processing, just
as processing impacts cultural values. Even disease histories are affected
by processing techniques. The spread of the *pellagra* disease (a B vitamin
niacin deficiency) across Europe might have been averted had Cortez
returned to Spain from Mexico with a native woman who could teach
European cooks how to process maize in order to maintain a balanced diet
(P. Rozin 1982; 1987:199; Roe and Beck 2000). In other words, if they had
gained the Mesoamerican contextual processing knowledge of adding lime
while soaking the corn kernels before grinding the maize and eating it with
beans, this fatal dietary deficiency would not have existed across northern
Italy and Spain. This final food-processing example illustrates one of the
many reasons for integrating contextual, social, and historical knowledge
in seemingly pure economic decisions, linking food back to the core of
society, communities of practice (Lave and Wegner 1991). Each processing
stage embodies multiple aspects of value and meaning (Lechtman 1977).

## Food Storage

Storage is based on the concept of delayed return. It holds significant clues
to social structure and political organization (Ingold 1983, 1986; O'Shea
1981; Rowley-Conwy and Zvelebil 1989; Thomas 1999). Territoriality, if not
sedentism, developed to protect stored foods. Storing food reserves was an
important part of family and lineage formation because stores sustained
them. Storage requires foresight; not only do people have to prepare storage locations, they also have to orient their lives to gather and process the
foods into a storable form. These acts provide a sense of food security and at
the same time create an imagined future of meals to come. Until recently
in archaeology, storage has been viewed economically, primarily as a risk
management strategy (Halstead and O'Shea 1989; Ingold 1983; Kent 1999;
O'Shea 1981) or linked to strategic aggrandizement (Hayden 1990, 1996).
But storage is an important hub of social memory and group formation
(Hendon 2000) as well as an avenue for wealth, status, and notoriety (Young

1971). Ingold (1983) points out other active dimensions of storage, involving not only the physical items that are stored but the social relationships that comes with having stores. Whether hidden or visible, storage is a nexus of subsistence, security, sociality, and self-definition.

Storage informs us about social dynamics, group size, and inclusion, especially through its spatial configuration. What is stored and how? Is it food, tools, or ritual paraphernalia? Are the items mixed or separated? Is it communal or at the family level? Are the storage places visible/invisible, outside, inside, in the front, or well hidden in the back (Wright 2000)? Is the storage permanent and fixed, in structures, bins, pits, rocks, or silos, or in portable containers such as baskets, ceramic vessels, wooden constructions, hanging twined bags, on strings, or in hides? What is the appropriate place for storage: by the hearth, in a side room or an outer building, in the rafters, in a corner, or in a pit? Each of these styles of storage has a symbolic connotation, in addition to its practicality. Storage varies for different foodstuffs. It can be short term, for milk in hides and processed fat in small ceramic jars, or storage can be longer term, as with dried seeds, grains, fruit, and meat; in bins, baskets, or strung and hung from roof beams for easy access. Storage can be as simple as a pile of potatoes in the corner of a dark, rarely used room or an intricate, visible corncrib with decorations, associated taboos, and closure.

Storage is a large part of processing, as seen with circumpolar fish fermentation (Riddervold 1990). In Norway and Iceland, fermented *gravloks* (salmon) and *rakefisk* (cod) should be buried for months in barrels that are placed in sand pits (ibid.:49–52). Nothing is required, not even salt, although some buried fish is salted. The coolness of the earth stops decomposition and the pressure of the sand pushes the excess liquid out. Some fish need several months to reach the right consistency, making these processing strategies interdigitate in a harvest, storing, and preserving cycle. These pits are also secure, as they are not visible.

Ingold (1983) explains three dimensions of delayed return that indicate its importance: ecological storage, practical storage, and social storage. *Ecological storage* describes the energy gleaned from the environment – in other words, the yield. This aspect of storage emphasizes how the food source can become more stable as people alter their environments to be more productive. Crop selection and irrigation are two examples of how yields and therefore storage can be stabilized. *Practical storage* refers to all of the activities required to store food. This aspect of storage includes the technologies mustered to increase longevity – for example, plastering the interior of storage bins keeps vermin out, elevated storehouses aid air circulation, and salt retards decomposition. Social activities and work contribute to storing edible food. This aspect of storage has timing constraints as well as technological requirements. *Social storage* focuses on the socially accepted way to create and use the stores, often for the greater good, in display, feasting, and trade, as social capital (Spielmann 2004). This aspect accentuates decisions about retention, exchange, delayed returns, and social networks.

Curated materials evoke the past and therefore display how storage continually activates memories (Hendon 2000). Stored items are usually considered things of beauty. Even a pile of rotting tubers can be beautiful (Young 1971). Stored food is a mnemonic, reminding people of the crop's harvest as well as its potency. It speaks to the time when food was harvested or gathered and placed in storage, linking the past year's work to the consumption in the future (Malinowski 1935). Hendon takes this idea further, positing that storage actively constructs families' identities as it channels the morals of the group, in large part through family traditions and histories surrounding their cuisine consisting of the stored goods (Hendon 2000:42). The shared knowledge that surrounds storage helps maintain a moral authority over it. Food is extracted from the stores on a regular basis between harvests, as it is cited in daily life and ever-present in the consciousness and discussions of a group, especially when food is exchanged or presented. Ingold (1983) provides a good example of this identity-forming dynamic of stored food from the Pacific Northwest, illustrating the material-memory dynamics of storage vessels. In that region, wooden storage boxes kept in houses are considered to be alive. Stored within view, the boxes full of ritual paraphernalia actively remind the inhabitants of their contents and those items' participation in their lives. The stored goods within the boxes are like family members who are being stored in the slightly larger boxes – the wooden buildings. These symbolic resonances place storage at the core of these family identities, making the moral and memory links between the storeé and the stored ever present (Ingold 1983). In other words, once it becomes part of a culture, storage is integral in the maintenance of social life, well beyond its ability to support survival or even rituals.

Like crops, fields, and animals, storage is a material manifestation of a farming group's placement on the landscape and the obligations of people to their household, eliciting links to their social memories as society is recreated in every storage event. Sharing food beyond the family, as at feasts, ultimately depends on the success of food storage. Food storage is essential in an economy in which prestige is expressed in the generosity of meals provided to visitors (institutional generosity via food sharing), just as it is for risk aversion (Dietler 1996; Dietler and Herbich 2001; Halstead and O'Shea 1989; Hayden 1990; discussed further in Chapter 6). It has become a tenet of archaeological interpretation that expanding social and political dynamics requires cyclical feasting, which is built on food stores (Bender 1978; Spielmann 2004). Storage is productive in that real stores of foodstuffs feed people and thereby maintain society. But it also has social power in that individuals can request food under obligation through family networks. Until recently in small-scale societies, food stores were like banks.

Different meanings are communicated whether one's food stores are visible or hidden. Some goods will be visible to the community, some to the family, and some will be hidden even from family members within the home. The visibility of stores reveals their role in the community. Michael Young (1971) highlights the social ramifications of storage when he discusses yam harvests on Goodenough Island. There, the main yam yield is stored inside the houses, but some yams are also piled outside the houses in plain sight. These yams are actually allowed to rot, communicating how productive the farmer's fields are and calibrating the stature of the family within the community. Some years this surplus is applied to inter-community feasts. The amount of food presented to the neighboring community is always more than what the guests could consume, accentuating the generosity of the gifting houses. This type of food sharing activates status enhancement. The visual display of productive potency in the yams piled outside a house as well as in overfeeding the guests heightens the community's position in the region; the gifted yams embody the farmer's social standing, as memory made visible (Weiner 1992). Yams are the ultimate giving-while-keeping item in Melanesia because they increase local status within the community when they are given to others.

Secret food stores tell a different story of potency. Food stored inside holds special meaning to the inhabitants. These items are hidden in hopes that no one knows about them, at times not even family members. They can be small, such as caches of obsidian or jade, often in small pits (Walker 1995), or large as with piles of tubers in the corner of sleeping rooms. While hidden stores often are special goods, they can be food, as seen in the European "stone soup" story in which farmers claimed they had no food in their storerooms so it would not be stolen by the passing military. A common reason for secrecy is the threat of tax collection or raiding by other groups, but there may be additional political, safety or spiritual reasons for hiding food stores.

FIGURE 4.4. Dried fish stacked in Norwegian storage room (Riddervold 1990:22)

We can infer that storage has been thought about, discussed, worried over, hidden, defended, and, most importantly, relied on since at least the Neolithic times. For those of us who have easy access to supermarkets, local markets, and banks, we forget what having six months of stored food in your house feels like; it must have been a constant focus of attention and discussion, a source of security and survival. Although some of this importance is apparent in the archaeological record, usually only fragments of baskets or pottery, traces of silos or granaries, pits, or bits of charred food are visible archaeologically; some food stores might not have left any traces. Figure 4.4 is a wooden house filled with dried fish in Norway, illustrating the storage of one community. In a wet environment such as Norway, these above-ground storage units might not survive in the archaeological record – only the fish bones would remain (Coupland et al. 2010). From such traces we must construct the broader and more meaningful place of storage in a society, beginning with recognizing its significance in the past.

Even without material evidence, archaeologists must acknowledge that storage existed in many settings, including among hunter-gatherers (Halstead and O'Shea 1989; Henshilwood et al. 1994; Hoffman et al. 2000; Jordan 2003; Rowley-Conwy and Zvelebil 1989). Ethnographic examples suggest that dried meat was regularly cached in various places (known as "landscape storage"). This banking for leaner times speaks to memory and continuity, past hunting successes, and hopes for the future (Friesen 2001). With careful study, likely cache locations are identifiable in landscapes. Max Friesen (2001:326) noted that dried meat caches were placed on elevated locations throughout a hunters' territory, secured with stones to protect the meat from predators. These cairns then become not only a food indicator but mnemonics of the hunters' presence on the land, marking their past labors, their future well being, as well as their connections to the landscape spirits (Jordan 2003).

Granaries and silos on poles, placing materials in roof beams or in hides, in twined or woven sacks, will be difficult to identify in the archaeological record. Storage is often identified by subterranean pits or large ceramic vessels because of their archaeological visibility (Christakis 1999; Johannessen 1993; Wesson 1999; Winter 1976; Wright 2000; Wright et al. 1989). Although archaeologists often label them as refuse pits, they were probably initially used for food storage. Pits that can be easily covered over give a sense of secret food caching even at permanent settlements, suggesting private capital (Frieson 2001; Hendon 2000; Johannessen 1993).

Feelings of security and wealth surround storage. Large, in situ ceramic vessels are versions of subterranean pits. In Neopalatial Crete, Christakis (1999) notes that all domestic houses, including the palaces have rooms full of *pithoi*, large ceramic vessels permanently embedded in the earth, that are excellent for storage of grains and legumes but also oil and wine, being able to be completely sealed. The ceramic barrier kept out rodents and insects. These large and highly visible containers held enough food to get through until the next harvest and then some, illustrating a households' level of economic independence from the palaces during the Bronze Age.

Glynis Jones and her colleagues (1986) excavated storage rooms at the Bronze Age community of Assiros, Greece. Jones suggests that these rooms represent community storage not individual storage. After careful excavation and analysis of a burnt room filled with dense ceramic and ecofact remains, including macrobotanical specimens, they were able to identify what crops were stored in which vessel. Specific plants were stored separately, unveiling a form of recordkeeping by container. Terry D'Altroy and I investigated larger-scale specialized storage facilities in the Mantaro Valley of Perú (D'Altroy and Hastorf 1984). We conducted excavations within several stone storage structures that were built by the Inka state. As part of the Inka imperial economic system, *qolqa* storage structures were placed prominently on the hillsides at every administrative fort throughout the empire. These tidy, eye-catching rows of identical buildings illustrated to all who passed not only the wealth of the Inka but also their power over the means of local production (D'Altroy 2001). Early Spanish records of *qolqa* storage contents in the Mantaro Valley, thirty years after the fall of the Inka hegemony, record what was still being stored in these structures, overseen by the local elite. A wide range of goods was stored in these structures, including firewood, sandals, and cloth, in addition to foodstuffs. We found evidence of edible remains in each structure we excavated, suggesting the predominance of foodstuffs in these storage units. This centralized food bank was reproduced throughout the realm, reflecting state power over people and land. Local families stored their own produce, apparently in a structure in their compound, most likely in piles or woven sacks, no longer visible to us (Hastorf 1991). At the state level, however, we see how the Inka used storage to generate awe and power through conspicuous display by putting the storage complexes on prominent, visible hillsides, not in hidden rooms in their administrative compounds as did the contemporary Chimur of the north coast of Perú (Moseley and Day 1982).

Food storage has been identified at the household level with both permanent and movable containers at the Neolithic Anatolian site of Çatalhöyük, as mentioned earlier in this chapter and in Chapter 8 (Atalay and Hastorf 2006; Bogaard et al. 2009; Wendrich 2005; Figure 4.5). Every excavated building contains mud plaster bins in small side rooms as well as evidence of portable baskets of wood, hide or reeds (Cessford 2007; Farid 2007; Mellaart 1963). The portable remains suggest that some of these small, organically rich storerooms were filled with portable storage containers, most likely made of baskets or hides, as well as a range of dried food hanging on twine from ceiling beams. A side room in Building 1 (space 186) had a wooden storage bin with dehusked lentil grains (Matthews 2005). Ismael Yaslı of the nearby village Küçükköy noted that there were two types of portable storage containers in his grandmother's house. One was a basket and the other was made of clay and wood (Küçükköy tapes 2001). The latter container had a wooden frame lined with unfired dried mud. At Çatalhöyük, Wendrich (2005) has identified basket fragments as well as circular phytolith traces of reed baskets. The baskets were made of local marsh plant stems (Rosen 2005; Wendrich 2005). Space 156 in Building 5 is a small side room with the densest phytolith evidence of these baskets. Arlene Rosen (2005) found wheat chaff in one of the baskets, suggesting that it was used for storing or winnowing. The evidence of baskets in Building 1 around the built-in plaster bin that contained semi-cleaned lentils suggest that this centrally located feature was used for short-term food

FIGURE 4.5. Basket evidence and Building 5 at Çatalhöyük, showing basket locations (courtesy of the Çatalhöyük Research Project)

storage. Space 93 in Building 52 has a row of mud bins adjoining two walls (Bogaard et al. 2009). Strings of hanging fruit are suggested in this storage space based on organic evidence found on the floor. The bins yielded evidence of barley, peas, almonds, and wheat in addition to bone and horn tools of boar, deer, and cattle.

A small side room in Building 5, space 157 (Figure 4.5), was lined with at least six bins (Cessford 2005). The bins have especially thick clay packing to keep out the mice and insects (Matthews 2005). Micromorphology and phytolith analysis reveals that the floor was covered with woven mats. Rosen found wheat phytoliths in front of one bin, illustrating spillage from storage or retrieval of the grain. From the floor in front of another bin barley phytoliths and organic chemical traces also were recovered (Middleton et al. 2005; Rosen 2005). The small sixth bin contained a mix of wheat and barley.

These hidden bins contained domesticate plants in addition to processing tools and female clay figurines (Atalay and Hastorf 2005, 2006; Bogaard et al. 2009). The focus on domesticates in these peripheral bins is intriguing. We know that the inhabitants collected and consumed wild plants as well, but the wild foods seem to have been stored in other places in Building 5, such as portable containers – perhaps a continuation of an older tradition. Bogaard and colleagues (2009:657) more recently identified wild mustard occurring in bins. Could this perhaps have been cultivated, since the seeds were placed in the bins with domesticates?

Meat stores are not evident at the settlement; perhaps dried and processed meat hung from the rafters in these rooms, stored in a different manner than the plant stores. Inedible animal parts were very visible, however: horns and crania were mounted on benches and walls. Lithic tools were hidden in the sand around the ovens. The dead, like the wild food stores, were placed in baskets under the floor, suggesting potent links between the stored dead and the stored wild foodstuffs. Although wild animals were highlighted and displayed, residents kept their plant food stores hidden within the household recesses, suggesting a sense of concern over sharing knowledge of the presence and size of these food banks. Resonating with cognitive dissonance, wild animals were lauded and performed on the walls and in the center room though rarely eaten, while daily meals were composed of the more humble, hidden crops, nuts, and fruit.

This rich vision of storage and its symbolic participation in Çatalhöyük life allows us to reexamine portable, short-term storage, most likely in ceramic vessels. The ceramic vessel is the ultimate portable container, a finding that has received much archaeological ink. Ironically, not all ceramics have been studied to answer questions about food (but see Blinman 1989; Blitz 1993; Christakis 1999; Hastorf and DeNiro 1985; Mills 1999; Parker Pearson 2003). Biomolecular and chemical research can identify what was stored in vessels: for example, infrared spectrometry, GC/MS (gas chromatography/mass spectrometry), ICP (inductively coupled plasma atomic emission spectrometry), and other organic chemical analyses (e.g., Biers and McGovern 1990; Evershed et al. 2008; Mulville and Outram 2005; White and Page 1992). These molecular analyses can identify archaeological organic residues, animal fats, plant oils, resins, waxes, complex carbohydrates, and proteins by electron separation of individual preserved compounds. Lipids, the most frequent class of medium-sized molecules produced by biological organisms, are more soluble in organic solvents than in water (Evershed 1993:75). In contrast to carbohydrates and proteins, they are the most stable components in foods because they are relatively resistant to decay, making them a key target of these microanalyses. Lipids preserve well in porous material such as ceramic vessels because they are absorbed into the pottery fabric (Rottländer and Schlichtherle 1979) and can be extracted by dissolution in a solvent. These techniques have thus far identified wine, oil, olives, fish, honey, acorns, maize, meat, grease, milk, and pine pitch, suggesting that both encrustations and molecular analyses of containers are important for identifying past mobile storage activities.

In Europe, molecular analysis has focused on the identification of milk in the Neolithic. Studies of milk and meat lipids and proteins have identified milk compounds in contexts that antedate the famous secondary products revolution that Andrew Sherratt (1983) proposed. Milk has been identified on a range of bowls across the British Isles and Northern Europe that are contemporaneous with the first evidence of cattle (Craig 2003; Dudd and Evershed 1998; Dudd et al.1999; Evershed 1993; Mulville and Outram 2005). We also have evidence of milk processing much earlier than before, in the seventh millennium in northwestern Anatolia (Evershed et al. 2008).

Andrew Jones (1996, 1999, 2002) applied these analytical techniques to study the social and metaphorical aspects of storage in Neolithic Orkney. The stone and sod houses at the site of Barnhill each contained ceramic storage vessels still in place. He found vessel residues that are Neolithic in character, dominated by cow's milk and barley but also including apples, beef, pork, venison, wheat, *Chenopodium* seeds, hazelnuts, and onion (Jones 2002:156–157). Storage of both barley and cow's milk grew in dietary importance over time (Jones 1996:296). Bins around the edge of the houses probably stored bulky grain harvests. Jones (2002) outlines the biographies of the ceramics and how they were produced, used, and disposed of, as well as their association with the foodstuffs. From GC/MS analysis of the large storage pots embedded in the interior floors of the houses ($n$=16) Jones (1996:132) found that they contained barley. Barley was thus stored both in chambers encircling the house and also in large, immobile vessels. The movable pots had a range of ingredients and were more likely used for cooking.

Barley, in contrast to other foodstuffs, such as wheat, wild fruit, seeds, or animals, is the only ingredient that was stored in pottery vessels. Jones identified a single large barley storage vessel in each house, planted in the floor. These vessels clearly did not contain the complete stores of barley, let alone all of the harvested and collected foods. These vessels, their placement, and the barley they contained must have had very specific, charged connotations for the household and the community, perhaps like the rotting yams in the front of houses on the Goodenough Islands. These grains would have been visible to household members and visitors. Perhaps the vessel was a mnemonic for storage, was involved in other social rituals and designated to be "consumed" by the ancestors, or was the current portion of food for the week. This well-placed vessel full of grain could have suggested the fullness of the harvest and was kept through the winter in the home as a reminder, consumed when all else was gone. Or perhaps this was the seed for the next year. Jones interpreted these vessel placements as commemorative acts, linking the stored resources to the stored ancestors.

Jones linked both the living and the dead to the barley storage at the periphery of the chambered houses on Orkney; a relationship between the dead and the living established through storing the grain, now dead, was curated for use by the living, just as the human bones of the ancestors were curated and most likely called upon when help was required. The stores were opened and used not only for the daily meals that were consumed around the interior hearths, but also at ritual feasts at the nearby standing stones (Jones 2002:166). Distinctive parallel spatial patterning occurs in the contemporaneous chambered tombs, which store human crania (Jones 1999). The dead are brought together in one place, the chambered tombs (the storage of ancestors), like the foodstuffs, which are stored around the edge of the houses (Jones 1999:72). The spatial storage patterns of food and the dead suggest that storage was an active and flexible structure in this Neolithic society, both nutritionally and socially.

## Food Preparation (Cooking)

> The white man's stove he found good for roasting and broiling as in his own earth oven or open-fire cooking, but he considered that the modern stove ruined boiled food. Said Ishi, "White man puts good food in pot full of boiling water. Leaves a long time. Food cooks too fast, too long. Meat spoiled. Vegetables spoiled. The right way is to cook like acorn mush. Put cold water in basket. Place hot rocks in water till it bubbles. Add acorn meal. It cooks *pukka-pukka*. Then it is done. Same way, make deer stew. Or rabbit stew. Cook *pukka-pukka*. Not too long. Meat firm, broth clear, vegetables good, not soft and coming apart." (transcribed in Kroeber 1967:168)

There are many ways to cook food, each one signifying a reenactment of long-developed traditions filled with intimate social interactions, past and present. How these meals are prepared and the associated feelings enacted carry personal histories. For Ishi, cooking with low heat was the ideal. Variations of what is considered proper cooking must be considered when we study food preparations in the past. "In any cuisine, nothing is simply cooked, but must be cooked in one fashion or another" (Lévi-Strauss 1966:587).

Cooking transforms food from a natural, raw state into the cultural domain (Fajans 1988:158; Jones 1996:296). Cooking expands our understanding of resource production and intensification (Hastorf 1991; Stahl 1989; Wandsnider 1997), fuel use (Goldstein 2007; Johannessen and Hastorf 1990); symbolic systems (Arnott 1975; Brumfiel 1991; Dietler 1999, 2001; Hastorf and Johannessen 1993; Russell 1999; Simoons 1994), cultural construction (Lyons and D'Andrea 2003; Taube 1985; Twiss 2007), the construction of political boundaries (Barthes 1979; Goody 1982; Johannessen et al. 2002; McIntosh 1994; Thomas 2007; Twiss 2012), and gender relations (Caplan 1993; Counihan and Kaplan 1998; Hastorf 1991; Moore 1999). Most cooking involves utensils, often durable, long-lived ones, such as ceramic pots and metal spits, but some are ephemeral, such as wooden spoons, leaves, and branch frames. Recognizing these activity correlates in the archaeological record makes the social act of food preparation more visible in archaeological interpretation. They illustrate the hours of work, the valuation of the cook's preparation and the eaters' experiences. Most cooking acts are missing in the archaeological record. Archaeologists have to consider food treatment, in the absence of material remains (DeBoer 1975). This section discusses meal preparation, with a focus on the heating of foods to make them ready for consumption. Through this thought experiment we learn about the material links of processing along with some of the potential meanings of such activities.

Cooking makes food more digestible, detoxifies poisonous compounds, predigests food, and kills microorganisms. It blends ingredients into new flavors and creates new tastes and textures. As cooking makes food more digestible, it also makes it more pleasing and edible. Meals are cooked with a cultural ideal in mind, using acceptable utensils and procedures developed over millennia. This web of utensil, ingredient, and preparer highlights the intricacies of creation and meaning. Because the transformations involved in meals are so central in daily practice, it is part of a very large web of meaning.

In May 2002 an article in the *New York Times* outlined the role of cooking in human social evolution (Angier 2002). The piece discussed the important role of cooking in human evolution. Cooking makes many organic substances edible. For example, twenty-one of the forty-eight main tuberous plants in Africa become edible when heated (Wrangham et al. 1999). When humans gained control of fire and began cooking food is still debated, but the impact on human evolution is not (Wrangham 2009; see especially Brace 1995).

There are a vast number of cooking strategies, as seen in the myriad cookbooks and cooking traditions followed today. Cookbook contents are actually quite narrow. Where are the rotted meat recipes? It took me five years to find a recipe about preparing fermented fish (lutefisk) written in English! Different meal preparations exist across the globe, yet, as with any cuisine, groups tend to stick to their familiar cooking styles. Daily meal preparation is a practical knowledge, repetitive, unconscious, and ingrained, but it is also intimately linked to bodily practices: chopping and stirring is often done without conscious thought (Hamilakis 2002; see Chapter 8). These strong links between cooking and society are being acknowledged in archaeology.

Cooking means more than heating; it involves many steps and can take many hours or even days of work (McGee 2004). A common activity is to reduce the food to bite-sized pieces (E. Rozin 1982:192). Some activities make a substance digestible by removing the less digestible parts. Other cooking acts increase the nutrient release by crushing or smashing over heat. More intricate cooking tends to be applied to flesh and fibrous plant foods. These processes have their own vocabulary within any cuisine. I discuss only a few of the main cooking activities and do not include the terms found in any one cuisine, such as sautéing in French or 炒 in Cantonese.

As discussed in Chapter 2, Lévi-Strauss expanded his culinary triangle of raw, cooked, and rotted to include types of heat treatment. One important triad is smoking, boiling, and roasting (Lévi-Strauss 1997 [1966]; 1972). Air, water, and (dry) heat are central in these three processes (Lévi-Strauss 1997:34). His triadic scheme breaks down when one considers the many variants (Lehrer 1972). Other preparation activities are increasingly difficult to place in neat dyadic relationships. These procedures include cutting (slicing, chipping, chopping, dicing, carving), reducing (pureeing, mashing, stewing, boiling, straining), incorporation of multiple substances (by mixing, stirring, beating, whipping, blending, folding), separation and extraction of water (squeezing, pressing, skimming, leaching), dry separation (grinding, milling, pounding, grating), introducing chemical or bacterial agents to soften the tissue (fermenting, curdling, marinating, pickling, molding), chemical reduction to detoxify or augment the makeup (soaking, leaching, rinsing), and cooking to improve digestibility, soften, and preserve (heating, dry-baking, toasting, moist-steaming, boiling, frying, indirect-smoking, direct-grilling, roasting) (E. Rozin 1982:194;

Meyer-Renschhausen 1991; Stahl 1989). These are only some of the activi-ties mentioned in the cooking literature. Once we leave the initial Lévi-Straussean triad, the dyadic symmetries become a maze unless they are specifically grounded in cultural settings. Daunting as this list of activities is, such charting of activities can be illuminating and informative, as we will see in later chapters.

Ann Stahl (1989) and Luann Wandsnider (1997) have studied archaeo-logical cooking, providing important linking arguments in food preparation and digestibility. From their experimental studies we gain concrete mate-rial links between cooking regimes and material remains. They explicitly emphasize the energetics of the prepared meals and the resulting nutritive values. Ann Stahl (1989) focused on the nutritional content of foods after they have been processed and cooked. She outlined the diverse possibilities of food processing by organizing them into four main results. First, heat can liberate nutrients for human digestion. This is the most common result of cooking. Second, food processing can decrease the original foods' nutri-tional value in some cases, as in overcooking vegetables. Third, making food units smaller often aids in digestibility and detoxification, increasing the surface area of the item. Fourth, heating and especially fermentation increase nutrients and digestibility. Stahl provides a general rationale as to why cooking is useful by outlining the links between the process and the evidence.

LuAnn Wandsnider (1997) builds on Stahl's work, expounding on the specifics of food chemistry and heating strategies. She discusses additional factors that influence cooking, the labor and time required in preparation, who will eat the food, and with what associated materials, especially with reference to fuel and utensils. She discusses the relationships between chemistry, heat sources, and edibility, explaining the influence of mois-ture levels, pH, kills irritating organisms, eliminates toxins, and denatures proteins to aid digestion (Wandsnider 1997:2). In their discussion of plant detoxification, Johns and Kubo (1988) note that heat treatment is not effec-tive for all toxins. In fact, potatoes do not lose their alkaloids through cook-ing; heat actually activates them. Heating, however, makes the starch in potatoes more digestible, so in the case of potatoes, cooking has multiple outcomes. Johns and Kubo note that scraping off or cutting out (avoidance) is at times the only way to deal with some alkaloids in foodstuffs. Therefore, when digestibility is considered, each specific plant and animal product must be investigated individually.

Which cooking techniques maximally release food energy in digestion? Results depend on the amount of fat and the type of starch, sugar, and protein in the plant or animal (e.g., inulin and fructan). Wandsnider's ethnographic analysis of North American meat cooking demonstrates that boiling, broiling, spit roasting, coal roasting, and pit roasting efficiencies are correlated with the amount of fat in the meat. She also rightly concentrates on roots and tubers, identifying them as less-well-known but early and important food sources. Archaeologists note these in the archaeological record but rarely discuss them (but see Kubiak-Martens 2002; Wollstonecroft and Erkal 1999; Wollstonecroft et al. 2008). By outlining the range of root preparation techniques, including moist and dry baking, boiling, drying, and consuming fresh, Wandsnider (1997:16) directs us to actively look for this processing in past diets. Archaeobotanists have been making headway in identifying these plant foods with starch analysis, as outlined earlier in this chapter (Henry et al. 2009; Perry 2004, Piperno and Holst 1998).

Baking pits or earth ovens, sometimes recorded in archaeology as rubbish pits or smudge pits (Binford 1967), were a common cooking strategy for larger meals. Pits cook fatty foods with little fuel (Frison 1983; Wandsnider 1997:33). Fire-cracked rock and blackened pits are the best indicators of pit ovens. Wandsnider compiles many pit cooking variants from Polynesia and the American Northwest and Southwest. In the Pacific Northwest, for example, pit roasting of the staple camas root (*Camassia* Lindl.) when it ripened, produced a moist syrupy mass (inulin rich) that could be stored and eaten throughout the year (Turner and Kuhnlein 1983), like the agave of the American southwest. Pit-roasting usually involves a mix of plant and animal foodstuffs. Wandsnider's discussion of these foods and how their heating relates to human physiology is applicable in many cultural settings. She suggests that certain products were cooked in specific ways and that the foodstuffs often accompanied the introduction of these cooking techniques. We can look for this in the archaeological record.

Lyons and D'Andrea (2003) see a long-lived relationship in the Ethiopian cuisine through a close analysis of cooking techniques, between griddle cooking (dry frying) and oven baking. They studied two main starch food complexes, finger millet (*Eleusine coracana*) and teff (*Eragrostis tef*) flour brought in from the south quite early, and wheat and barley traded in from the northeast much later. They track the adoption speed in Ethiopia of these different cooking techniques that traveled with these crops. In their wonderfully detailed historical study they discuss the chemical constituents of these plant staples and how different heat regimes affect the plants differently. They conclude that the heating technologies can tell us about the plants that were eaten in the various communities.

Cooking technology impacts food choice and is central to Marx's (1939 [1867]) view of the means of production, as food is an important item of production. How people can and will prepare their food influences what is eaten. Those who eat unprocessed, rolled wheat, for example, consume a very different diet than those who focus on ground and processed white bread. Lyons and D'Andrea's (2003) charting of the impact of technology on food selection in northern Africa, provide some insightful results. They find that the rapidity of food adoption there was based on how similar the new processing and cooking technologies were to traditional preparations. They suggest that when a newly introduced or encountered domestic plant or animal fits easily into ongoing storage, preparation, and cooking practices, that foodstuff is rapidly adopted. However, if there is no precedent for the form of growing, processing, or cooking required by a new product, the plant or animal ingredient is more slowly and less often adopted. This model is useful in archaeological settings to track the tempo of uptake and the levels of technological interest in foods and tools, especially with a focus on storage and cooking techniques. It links to women's work and the set of tasks she must complete to get food for her family.

To study the importance of identity and technology in food choice, Lyons and D'Andrea (2003) traced historical Middle Eastern and African food histories. They found that these new foods and processing technologies spread from northern Africa and the Arabian Peninsula at different tempos based on social tenets. Whereas Yemenis appear to have added sorghum (*Sorghum bicolor*), an African cereal, into their Middle Eastern grinding and *tannur* oven style of baking quite quickly, Ethiopians had the opposite reaction, adapting the Middle Eastern cereals, wheat and barley, much more slowly into their African griddle cooking technology. Does this reflect the strength of food traditions and flavors or a dislike of bread? No, with further thought, they suggest that it was the cooking technologies that were the sticking points. Middle Eastern starch processing is dominated by grain grinding and baking, with its long history of grain grinding and bread baking since the Neolithic. On the other hand, African small seeded starchy staples are cooked by grinding, toasting, and heating the grainy batter over a flat stone, dry frying/griddle cooking, as is done today with *teff*. Africans had to add a bread oven to their cooking toolkit before wheat and barley could become common staple foods, because these grains did not react well to toasting, unlike the African *teff*.

These Ethiopian and Yemeni cooking stories illustrate the technological hurdles of some nonindigenous food adoptions, but they also highlight the strength of identity and agency in kitchen utensils. Some foreign grains became part of their cuisine only after appropriate technologies had been added to their meal *chaíne opératoire*, which also requires emotional and corporeal acceptance. Bread-baking technologies were eventually established in Ethiopia, increasing the production and also consumption of wheat and barley. But bread has never taken over the role of *teff* griddle bread within their cuisine and identities.

Crop adoption histories demonstrate the psychological aspects of the technological-identity hurdle. Although forced planting of a new crop can alter production cycles and seasonal work, as with conquest or territory loss, farmers must still learn to cook the new foods. In the seventeenth century, Irish farmers were forced with some reluctance to plant the potato, a root crop, as they did not have the tradition of cultivating, cooking, or eating root crops, having been grain farmers since the Neolithic (Leach 1999). The Irish peasants forced to plant the crops in their landlord's fields slowly became familiar with their planting, harvesting, and cooking. Once cropping, harvesting, and eating was compulsorily learned, this new crop became a weapon of the weak against the landlords, as the peasants realized that potatoes did not have to be milled to be consumed but could simply be boiled or roasted. By avoiding the milling charges at the landlords' mills, the Irish began to accept the production and taste of the potato with more gusto. In fact, they began to love it, and it substantially aided an Irish population boom. Even with the forced technological change, this crop became indigenized. Many still believe the potato was actually domesticated on that island and not in the South American highlands (Messer 1997)!

Interestingly, the adoption of grains into a root-based food system in New Zealand, as studied by Helen Leach (1999), required even more time and adjustment to adopt than did the potato in Ireland. The Maori inhabitants did not have the capacity to grind the cereals they were required to produce for their colonial overlords. They had to exchange food for grinding implements before they could regularly consume the Middle Eastern cereals themselves. The more costly preparation time as well as the new technological requirements influenced their very slow uptake of grains in to their cuisine across the islands.

These varying acceptance histories of planting, processing, and cooking illustrate the significance of the technological hurdles involved in the food selection process that is linked to the tempo of cuisine change and the food path from field to mouth, as first laid out in Chapter 2.

As discussed in the food processing section earlier, fuel is an important limiting factor in many cooking technologies. Increased preparation steps and fuel conservation are correlated. Slowly roasting huge pieces of meat requires a lot of heat over several hours, whereas quick frying can cook finely chopped meat and vegetables in two to three minutes. Fuel therefore needs to be incorporated into the cooking discussion.

Although it is common for archaeologists to study one implement or ecofact type at a time, that is not the most informative approach to past practices and certainly not how we live our own lives (Bourdieu 1979). Wandsnider urges us to discuss multiple data sets when studying cooking. One way to elucidate meal preparation is to trace the steps that are needed to create a dish or a meal – again, a *chaîne opératoire* of a meal or dish (Atalay and Hastorf 2006; Hastorf and Johannessen 1993). Each of us who cooks dinner is intimately, practically, and usually implicitly aware of the many steps involved in cooking a meal. Yet, we rarely consider these activity sequences and their implications in our study of past daily life, let alone the long history of sequenced actions each meal implied (Farb and Armelagos 1980; Goody 1982). Pepper ground onto British meat, for example, links the cook to the Far Eastern trade of the seventeenth century as black pepper (*Piper nigrum* L.) became more common, replacing other Middle Eastern and African spices, such as grains of paradise (*Aframomum melegueta* K. Schum.).

Speth (2000) identifies boiling and baking in a late prehistoric New Mexico faunal assemblage while contextualizing these preparations. Applying taphonomic bone analyses, counts, and ethnographic evidence, he finds that rabbits were ground up and boiled, whereas gophers and prairie dogs were roasted or baked whole. He takes a further step, leaning heavily on historic and ethnographic accounts from the region, noting that women traditionally did the crushing and boiling of the rabbits, whereas men helped with the roasting when they were preparing for larger food-sharing events (Speth 2000:102). This is a concrete example of seeing gender in cooking, but it gains us little in the cultural meanings of rabbit and gopher meals in New Mexico.

Can we study the gendered social dynamics of cooking and the meanings of meals in the archaeological record? I weave together multiple lines of data here to illustrate that we can. A contextual study begins with the sequence of preparation steps and the associated artifacts in a recipe, dish, and meal, gathering data to identify and confirm the sequence. Sissel Johannessen and I (1993) attempted this in a series of drink and stew studies with central Andean archaeological data. First was the study of maize beer preparation stages. We began with the place of maize (*Zea mays* L.) in pre-Hispanic Andean society, focusing on its symbolic importance in Inka state-craft and also where it was prepared in the local households that had access to maize. To make maize beer (*chicha*), the maize must go through a series of steps before it becomes the sought-after sparkling beverage (Cutler and Cárdenas 1947; Jennings et al. 2005). In the Andes these tasks are usually women's work, strongly suggesting that women were responsible for this fermented beverage processing in the past as well. Figure 4.6 illustrates one processing sequence from the Cochabamba Valley of Bolivia. The kernels are kept moist for several days, until they sprout. Then they are ground and simmered in a pot of water. Some of this ground grain is chewed and spit back into the pot to add the fermenting agent diastase. This boiled liquid is covered and stored for several days to ferment, then reheated and skimmed. The clear liquid is ready for drinking. This sequence – sprouting, grinding, boiling, pouring, skimming, storing, boiling, and consumption – results in a range of material correlates for us to seek in the archaeological record.

We sought evidence of *chicha* brewing in the archaeological record by investigating fourteen associated attributes from ground stone, ceramics, and botanical remains in the intermontane Mantaro Valley of Perú (D'Altroy and Hastorf 2001). We plotted the data sets over four phases, each artifact type illustrating a different part of the processing (Figure 4.7). The botanical data include the relative amount of maize in the archaeobotanical samples; the number of maize types encountered based on morphological research, especially the large-grained varieties known to be used for *chicha* today (Johannessen and Hastorf 1989); the relative amount of maize in the diet, based on stable isotope data from the human skeletal material (Hastorf 1991); and the relative amounts of maize $C_4$ versus $C_3$ evidence that was boiled in pots, also based on stable isotope data of boiled foodstuffs (Hastorf and DeNiro 1985). The grinding implements included *chicha* processing stones (bases [*maran*] and upper rockers [*tunawa*]) versus pounding (pestles and mortars) (Russell 1988), and the ceramic vessel analysis tallied liquid cooking jars versus toasting containers, the amount of storage jars, and the amount of individual liquid ceramic drinking vessels (Costin 1986; Hagstrum 1989). All of these data reflect a part of the production of *chicha*.

These data create a three-dimensional picture of the preparation activities. Although there was less maize production during the pre-Inka political centralization era (Wanka II times), the archaeological data suggest that *chicha* processing was in fact relatively common, more common than in the previous phase. This Wanka II beer making increase is indicated in the higher number of maize varieties, more ground stone, and jars for holding liquids. Further, their spatial distribution shows that beer consumption was more common in the elite /larger households. With the Inka conquest and their pointed interest in *chicha* as a political state meal, maize beer was

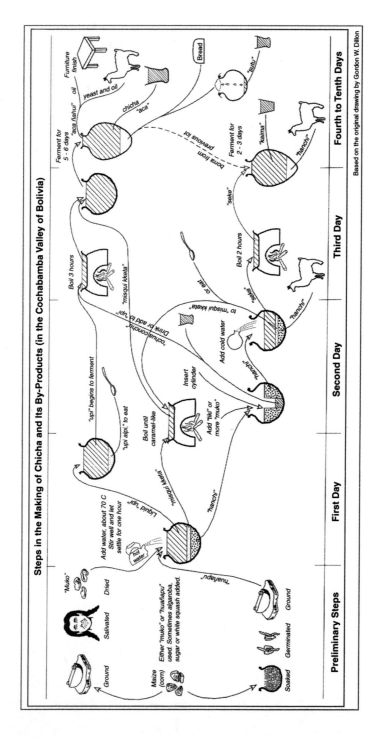

FIGURE 4.6. Preparation sequence of maize *chicha* (drawn by Melanie Miller based on Cutler and Cardenas 1947)

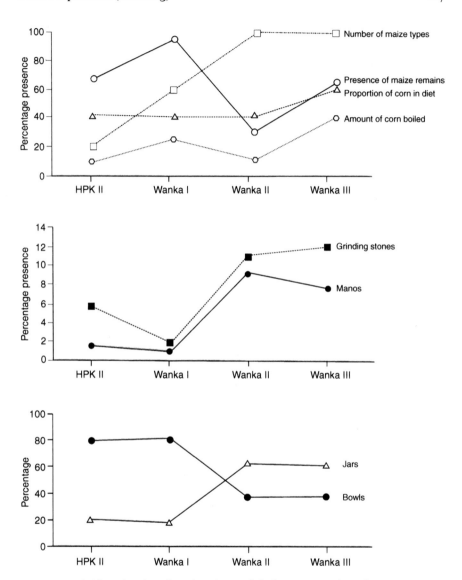

FIGURE 4.7. Artifactual and ecofactual evidence of *chicha* processing from the Upper Mantaro Archaeological Project

increasingly prepared in local homes, and its presentation shifted from the local ceramic vessels of the previous phase to the invisible wooden *kero* tumbler, associated with the Inka (Cummins 2002). In addition, some men consumed substantially more maize than their family members did, suggesting a dual place of maize beer in both the community domain and the

Inka state ceremonies (Hastorf 1991; Hastorf and Johannessen 1993). This history of *chicha* preparation infers both culturally derived appetites as well as political interests.

Boiling is the main source of heat in beer production. Boiling is a very common method of cooking today, but it is not easily identifiable in the archaeobotanical record because of the softening of plant tissues that occurs in during wet cooking. To identify how different preparation strategies would be reflected in the archaeological record, a group of eager archaeobotanists in my laboratory systematically processed and cooked fresh and dried maize kernels in a variety of ways and then charred them in a muffle furnace (Goette et al. 1994). We learned from these experiments that the archaeobotanical maize remains we were finding in the domestic samples from Perú were most like the boiled maize. This allowed us to register relative boiling frequencies throughout our samples. Ceramic pots were probably most often used for boiling, an assertion supported by the organic remains. Organic compounds extracted from ceramic or ground stone surfaces also reflect cooking practices (Bush and Zubrow 1986; Evershed 1990; Evershed et al. 1992; Evershed and Tuross 1996). In the Upper Mantaro region we collected and analyzed encrustations from ceramic vessels for their stable isotope components (DeNiro and Hastorf 1985). Stable isotopes are unchanging molecules that plants take up during life. Because they do not alter, they are passed along to the animals that eat them, thus enabling us to examine food consumption on the molecular level. Some plants, primarily the tropical grasses, take up carbon (C) differently than most other plants, they register a different carbon molecule and therefore weight, a four-carbon molecule. In the Mantaro region, maize was the only $C_4$ derived foodstuff that was consumed, allowing us to chart the relative amount of maize versus other staple plant foods, potatoes, quinoa, as well as camelid and *cuy* meat, all of which are $C_3$ or have a $C_3$ diet. With these data we could separate food preparation and cooking from consumption and production. Such techniques are increasingly common in archaeology, from the identification of starch grains in vesicles (Chandler-Ezell et al. 2006; Kealhofer et al. 1999; Logan et al. 2012; Piperno and Holst 1998;) to the lipids within ceramics via gas chromatography (Evershed 1990; Mukherjee et al. 2005; Mulville and Outram 2005) to stable isotopes in human bone (Knudson et al. 2001, 2007; Schoeninger 1979;). Combining methods enables us to learn about these intermediate food preparation activities, placing them in space and time while filling in the past food and consumption sequences.

## Food Serving

Food served at large, food-sharing meals (such as potluck dinners) or an intimate, home-cooked dinner for two conveys different information, not just about sustenance but also about the social relations of the participants. Plastic plates and forks versus matching china dishes on a white tablecloth speak about the level of formality and the specific value placed on the event by the preparers. How a meal is presented can reveal the scale of the meal, but more importantly it signifies the values of a particular cultural setting. These social acts of presentation are created by the embodied knowledge and traditions of a group. All preparation is a buildup to this presentation, in which the results are seen and consumed. Those who have worked hard, stored, and worried about the food finally present the food to gain or lose their social position. This event therefore holds the power of the discursive, overtly communicative, strategic presentation style as well as the nondiscursive, unconscious actions that emanate from it, even unintentionally. These performative gastropolitical acts are the locus of social tensions as well as of nurturance and sharing. The form and material used to serve the food recreates the community values nestled in the unspoken daily actions of eating (Sahlins 1976). DeCerteau (1989) highlights these tactics of presentation when he discusses what produce conflict or calmness in families. The dishes that are served and their qualities, the materials that are used to present the meals – these attributes have meanings that can defuse, hide, or highlight differences among the guests. An example from our society is when in-laws come for dinner and the cook is not sure what foods and what level of formality are considered appropriate. The choice of recipes and serving dishes are at the knife's edge of the social outcome.

In their work on table manners, presented in Chapter 2, Douglas (1997 [1972]), Elias (1978 [1939]), and Mennell (1985) illustrate the agency of food presentation, identifying and differentiating every level of society, channeled through the display of a meal, a banquet, or a ritual. The form of presentation outlines a social code identifying the event and its social value to the participants, as Appadurai (1981) illustrates at the Indian marriage feast. Some attendees gain prestige and even power through these large, performed food events; others are shuttled to the edges of society. No matter how small the meal, serving and its accompanying generosity always have the potential for social positioning. How this is modified and hidden or made overt informs us about the economics and politics of the situation. A feast, no matter how small, will still be considered a feast by those attending. Some examples demonstrate these capacities.

While focusing on the history of European table manners, Elias (1978) emphasizes that the *presentation* is the magnifying glass of consumptive behavior, which in turn is a microcosm of society. Every meal restates these eating behaviors while it reinterprets the associated social protocols of interaction, communalism, and social position. In ancient Syria, sacrificial offerings are placed in containers or at least in view, emitting their special value. Most prepared sacrificial foods are eventually consumed by the living, even if they are first presented in ritual offering to the dead, the spirits, or the deities (Lev-Tov and McGeough 2007; Sallaberger 2012).

Although not usually considered an important moment in the archaeological past, serving has become a worthy focus of study by ceramic archaeologists. Discussions of food display include work by Blitz (1993), Bray (2003a, 2003b), Mills (1999, 2007), Pirazzoli-t'Serstevens (1991), and Turner and Lofgren (1966). Barbara Mills (2007) takes a productive approach by focusing on the placement of designs and their potential to be seen or touched. Mills suggests a shifting entanglement in the American Southwest Ancestral Puebloan region as the ceramics became more decorative over time, eliciting more attention on the pots during the meal. With such studies we can begin to talk about the aesthetic experience of carrying or passing bowls of food in terms of both sight as well as the other senses – smell, taste, and touch. Serving vessel capacity and style speak to communal vs. individual meals and eating styles, as Vroom (2000) illustrates for historic Greece, presented earlier in the chapter.

When studying the visual performance of the serving vessels, it would be especially engaging to consider the sense of touch: How heavy were these vessels to carry when full? Could they be set down easily, or where they "tippy," fit only to be passed around? Were their surfaces rough or smooth? Could one feel the temperature of the ingredients through the vessel wall? Were there designs that could be seen only when holding the full bowl, when it is empty, or only by those across the way? Such sensory qualities during use expand the consideration of visual display into a broader, experiential discussion. Next would be to replicate the vessels and also potential recipes that would have been served in the past in such vessels. The smell of steaming food being passed around would make this a richer sensory understanding. Such close-up study would allow us to be there at the serving of the meal, giving us a greater understanding of the tacit, bodily sensations of the participants. Careful study of replicates and associated sensory experiences will add to the study of food presentation and serving vessels in the past (Cushing 1886; Hastorf 2001b). By revisiting ceramic studies and including these sensory qualities, we can combine the materialities with the social experience of giving, sharing, getting, and incorporation (Sillar 2009).

Adding lipid and other biomolecular analyses, discussed earlier in the storage section, we can identify the specific items that were served on plates and in bowls, whether passed around in single vessels or presented in redundant, matching table settings of individualized cutlery and dishes. As Glassie (1975) and Deetz (1977) have pointed out, the trend in modern Western eating habits is for increasingly individualized presentation. These artifacts and their frequencies inform us about both large and small social views of the individual within the community.

Neolithic Opovo in Vojvodina, Serbia, excavated by Ruth Tringham and her team (1992), provides archaeological evidence of such shifting food displays that correlate with a changing social life. At this Southeast European settlement located on the edge of a marsh, a series of houses were sequentially built and systematically burned down. Although the residents were regular hunters, domesticated plant foods were also found in the settlement's deposits. The three excavated houses spanned two time periods. House 5 was occupied first, with houses 2 and 3 built later. The team identified five ceramic vessel classes, placing them into four functional types; two were to store dry and moist foods and the other two were serving and cooking vessels. The earlier house (5) had more storage vessels of both types, with an equal number of serving/cooking and storage vessel types. Tringham proposed that the second story of the building held the stored food, which collapsed onto the floor in the burning, mixing the cooking and the storage assemblages. The later phase, represented by structures 2 and 3, had less evidence for second-story storage with fewer storage vessels. Houses 2 and 3 had five times more cooking and serving vessels than storage containers. The team members concluded that long-term storage was less important later at the settlement, based on the lack of second-story storage in addition to the evidence of possible storage pits associated with these two later houses. What did increase in this later time was the elaboration of meat and cereal service. These later houses contained not only more decorated serving vessels but also more nonlocal serving pottery types. What does this increased foodservice evidence connote: more socializing, more food sharing, more inter-family meals, more trade?

The archaeologists concluded that the earlier groups stayed in the houses permanently, storing their food for the whole year's consumption, whereas the later residents seemed to use their houses more as periodic meeting places, more during the hunting season when there was a concentration of food in and around the marsh. Especially in house 3, where there were multiple types of serving vessels, the authors suggest that meals became more signified as different group sizes were being served, requiring different sets of dishes (Tringham et al. 1992:377). The later vessel frequencies also suggest an increased group size at any one meal. This emphasis on eating together at Opovo reflects more intensive networking within the potentially larger group, reflected in more decorated serving vessels as well as increased diversity.

Returning to the Neolithic of eastern Scotland we see that Barnhill not only yielded rich storage evidence but also displays nuanced agency in the ceramic serving vessels (Jones 1999, 2002). Jones believes the medium and small ceramic grooved-ware vessels at Barnhill were used for presentation as well as for cooking. In the early phase of the settlement, ceramic vessels were made communally at one central place on the settlement, whereas later the individual households produced them. We do not learn from Jones how the meals were prepared except that each house had a hearth and an oven with some boiling pots, sooted on the exterior. From the GC/MS chemical analysis of these pot interiors he concludes that the mid-sized ceramics ($n=18$) were used for boiling milk (with some meat), and also for serving these soups. The smaller, hand-sized vessels ($n=3$) only served barley. He suggests that cooking styles diversified over time, evolving from the medium-sized vessels shared by all to larger boiling pots and small serving vessels. Did the later occupants have individual bowls of barley broth, gruel, fermented drink, or crushed barley suspended in hot water, different from the earlier communal meat dish that was shared at a meal? The data suggest this.

Given that the medium-sized vessels showed no evidence of barley being boiled in them, how did the residents prepare it? Did they toast the whole grains after winnowing, grind the grains, and throw that into mugs of hot water, or did they bake barley flour into griddlecakes on the hearth or in the oven and then dunk them in their steaming cups? An earlier meal could have been meat boiled in milk, consumed by all members straight from the pot. A typical later meal was oatcakes and a hot barley drink. The material evidence suggests a single locus of serving and intimate sharing of meals. Although Jones did not specifically discuss food presentation, these data embed the ceramic vessels' contextual life within the inhabitant's social lives through the action of serving, providing us with a potential vista of the social life as well as meals and their differences within these households, where people interacted during the sharing of a meal.

Jones focuses on cooking and presentation, and how these activities participate in the hamlet's shifting social identities. The acceptance of farming in the region impacted concepts of the local landscape as well as land use. At the same time, presentation shifts are suggested by increasing use of multiple cooking pots for serving food (Jones 2002:165). The layout of the living space supports attendance changes at the meals. Earlier, each house had several hearths and compartments, perhaps nuclear families sharing one roof and eating together. Remodeling resulted in a larger, more open house with individuality represented by the individual consumption vessels. These data unveil the development of a more unified community with stronger interpersonal ties in the later Neolithic (Thomas 1991). Food serving and its relationship to production and storage are essential in our understanding of the changes in Barnhill inhabitants' lives as seen through the treatment of both the living and the dead. Serving styles provide a sense of the social world and the interpersonal relations in a society. The ceramic pots reflect the grammar of food, with its storage, preparation, and presentation, localized around the oven.

As with this Neolithic meal example, we can at times approximate past dishes and their presentation, if not their fully nuanced meanings at the community level. Foss's (1994) study of dining rooms at Pompeii provides a view into another settlement's eating habits. He identifies dining rooms by the presence of couches. In the Roman world, proper meals were consumed lying down (Foss 1994:108). People in Pompeii ate in their household, at workshops, in elegant dining halls, on the street, and in large gathering places. There were street-side establishments where prepared food was purchased, similar to today's food trucks and fast food restaurants (Foss 1994:122). By plotting hearths, ovens, braziers, water heaters, tripods and other cooking items, counters, mortars, rooms, couches, cooking and serving wares (storage vessels, cauldrons, colanders, skillets, casseroles, bowls, plates, jugs, and cups), Foss was able to identify a range of serving locations in addition to the more "traditional" residential dining rooms. He provides a list of the utensils and their use locations, outlining the range of food consumption possibilities in this very well preserved settlement. A strong sense of political and economic difference is illustrated in Pompeii's serving spectra, from the equipment used to process and consume the food to the location and style of its consumption to the time it took people to consume it.

As exemplified by Blitz (1993) in "Big Pots for Big Shots," most archaeological food presentation studies focus on ceramics for a good reason. These artifacts are the most durable and are clearly linked to food, whether as offerings in royal tombs or smashed up in refuse middens. But many other items are used to serve food, such as leaves, mats, wooden bowls, gourds, baskets, textiles, glass, stone and metal bowls. Few of these items

FIGURE 4.8. A Late Intermediate Andean meal (by Anna Harkey)

are ever encountered in the archaeological record, but they were more common than ceramics in the past. Returning to the Upper Mantaro region again, we can envision meals being served in many organic items. Based on the range of archaeological data that has been investigated for these Late Intermediate Period houses, Figure 4.8 depicts an Andean Late Intermediate meal in the Yanamarka region. It would be fantastic to uncover such complete settings, but these are only rarely found (and usually in tombs), in historic settings, or depicted in drawings (Deetz 1977; Pirazzoli-t'Serstevens 1991). We have had to fill in the invisible hearth and the textiles that surely participated in every meal served in these Xauxa houses. Serving vessels do imply social relationships, as Mary Douglas tells us. Whether humble or elegant, the material evidence of food serving can teach us much about social and political settings.

## Food Consumption (Eating)

Food is the ultimate consumable commodity, making it well suited for tracking individual decisions and valuations (Lupton 1996; Miller 1998b:8). Eating is the final step in the transformation of foodstuffs. The sense of bodily change during a meal is the result of the body breaking down and taking up nutrients, energizing the body within a social milieu that colors the corporeal response to the consumed ingredients. Consumption practices participate in identity construction as well as maintaining healthy bodies (Orlove 1994:106; Miller 1998b). Very rarely do archaeologists encounter specific place settings and meals, such as Lady Dai's party meal in her burial chamber, complete with chopsticks ready for her guests' use (Pirazzoli-t'Serstevens 1991). Meals have also occasionally been encountered in Roman Iron Age Denmark, where tombs are lined with formal table settings, carving knives, and individual jugs accompanying the meal of porridge, meat, and beer served in pottery vessels (Glob 1969:146). Pumice-covered cities such as Pompeii also provide a close-up of individual meals on the verge of being consumed. Archaeologists must search for specific contexts, preservations, or technologies to study eating (Bush and Zubrow 1986).

Studying actual food that was eaten gets us closer to specific past decisions and acts. Actual individual meals are evocative and encourage a lot of research interest. The more common methods to study eating focus on food remains, either extracted from dirty preparation utensils or as part of a meal reflected in the bodily tissues. The surge in human bone chemistry and tooth analysis provides us with lifetimes of eating evidence, but not of an individual meal per se. Organic molecules, lipids, gut contents and coprolite research, trace element analysis (e.g., Ba, Pb, Zn, Sr), and stable isotopes (C, N, O, Sr, Pb) extracted from bone collagen and apatite have recently offered exciting insights into dietary histories, at times revealing actual consumed meals and dietary preferences (Froehle et al. 2010). This field is expanding. While this section's goal is not to cover all aspects of this exciting wing of archaeological methodology, I introduce a few examples that help dramatize the potential of our learning about eating.

From our own lives we know that eating is very personal and highly charged. "Picky," "discerning," "omnivorous," "junk" – all of these words describe different eating strategies today. The act of food incorporation is both banal and fraught with potentially irreversible consequences; it is the omnivore's paradox, discussed in Chapter 2 (Fischler 1988:279). What we choose to eat impacts how we see ourselves. The body and its sensory associations are central in our own lives as well as in our intellectual thinking about food and eating (Csodras 1990).

The clearest evidence of single meals comes from gut contents and coprolite analysis (e.g., Reinhard 1993; Reinhard and Bryant 1992; Reinhard et al. 1991; Robins et al. 1986; Sobolik 1988; Sutton and Reinhard 1995; Williams-Dean 1986; Williams-Dean and Bryant 1975). In Chapter 3

I presented unique archaeological evidence analyzed by Sutton and Reinhard, who identified several meal types. Actual digested meals have been studied using macroscopic analysis, accompanied by pollen, starch, electron spin resonance spectroscopy, DNA, and chemical analyses such as protein residue analysis. From Sutton and Reinhard's study we did not learn about the specific eating styles, we can ask if they did eat out of communal or individual bowls?

From a different gut content study, Glob (1969) reports that during the Iron Age in Northern Europe, 2,000 years ago, highborn people were sacrificed at the end of winter to aid in springtime renewal. The three people who were sacrificed and collected out of marshes well preserved ate domestic grain and wild seed gruels before they were ritually strangled (Glob 1969:33, 56, 91). The last meal of Ötze, the Bronze Age man killed at the pass of the southern Arlberg Alps, was toasted einkorn wheat cakes with wild greens and meat (A + B + C). We now know that this food came from the warmer valleys to the south in the spring (Fowler 2002; Spindler 1994). These meals from Arizona, Denmark, and Italy indicate that wild and domestic plants were eaten together in each setting, whether in the form of boiled gruel or toasted cake. These foods inform us about seasonality, location in the environment, and general social position.

Long-term consumption patterns can be approached via stable isotope and trace element analysis of human bones, teeth, and hair (Ambrose and Katzenberg 2000; Cadwallader 2013; DeNiro 1987; Hastorf and DeNiro 1985). From a wide range of studies over the past thirty years we have learned that what animals consume is taken up by different parts of the human body at different times and is partially retained within the soft and hard tissues of the body, recording what has been eaten over the individual's lifetime. Measuring body tissues for carbon $\delta^{13}C$, nitrogen $\delta^{15}N$, oxygen $\delta^{18}O$, and strontium $\delta^{88}Sr$ stable isotopes can indicate what foods predominated in an individual's meals over a lifetime (Ambrose 1993; Ambrose et al. 1997). These stable isotope signatures reflect the protein component of a diet in the bone collagen, and the whole dietary view is recorded in the apatite minerals of the bone. Refinements in the methods have led to more accurate interpretation of the results (e.g., Chisholm et al. 1982; DeNiro and Epstein 1978; Froehle et al. 2010; Heaton et al. 1986; Hedges and Reynard 2007; Richards et al. 2001; Schoeninger et al. 1983). Many studies now discuss diet and dietary change using stable isotope analysis (e.g., Finucane et al. 2006; Lambert and Grupe 1993, Murray and Schoeninger 1988; Price 1989; Richards and Hedges 1999; Tykot et al. 1996). One of the greatest hurdles has been to identify contamination and diagenesis of these isotope traces within the analyzed bone and plant matter (DeNiro and Hastorf 1985; DeNiro and Wiener 1988). We now have some clear ways to assess values.

As noted earlier, the use of mass-spectrometry (GC/MS) in archaeology has focused on lipid analysis because it is the most robust and reliable (Bethel et al. 1993; Charters et al. 1993; Copley et al. 2003; Dudd and Evershed 1998; Dudd et al. 1999; Dunne et al. 2012; Evershed 1993; Evershed and Tuross 1996). Some archaeological investigations have included protein residue analysis (Bethel et al. 1993; Dudd et al. 1999; Evershed and Tuross 1996; Mukherjee et al. 2005). One example is the nondestructive procedure Gerhardt and his colleagues (1990) applied to Greek vases. They were able to extract fatty acids, components of lipids, from Corinthian museum-curated figure vases from the sixth century BC by swirling and capturing chloroform and methanol solvents. After allowing the chemicals to permeate the pores, they gathered the prehistoric organic compounds in the liquid. This technique did not alter the integrity or appearance of the vessels, yet they learned that the vessels had previously held *wine*. Lipids are particularly informative extracts from coprolites as well; stanols, steroids, and fatty acids have been recovered and identified from Danish bog bodies (Bethel et al. 1993).

Ahead of its time, a study of coprolite, stable isotope, macro plant, and animal bone data yielded information on long-term dietary shifts in the Virú Valley of Perú (Ericson et al. 1989). Twenty-five coprolite-pollen samples and 50 carbon and nitrogen isotope samples from 22 sites spanning 1,500 years were analyzed. The results allowed the researchers to track maize farming as evidence of a major C4 intake signature would have signaled maize consumption. The nitrogen isotope values reflected a strong marine diet at the sites near the coast. A full range of plants and animals was uncovered in the trash middens, with a focus on camelids and marine life (ibid.:75). Through time, the domestic terrestrial animals dropped out as the diet became increasingly marine-oriented, with birds, fish, sea mammals, and mollusks. Beans, squash, maize, peanut, *lúcuma* fruit (*Pouteria lucuma*), manioc, avocado, and *algorrobo* fruit (*Prosopis* spp.) dominate the plant assemblage (ibid.:76–77). Squash, maize, and peanut occurred in both the middens and the coprolites, supporting their place as dietary staples. The coastal dwellers' diets remained steady. The authors identified two dining patterns, one on the coast and one inland. The coastal residents ate a lot of seafood with maize. At the inland settlements, maize consumption increased over time, becoming important in the diet by the Early Intermediate Period (AD 500). Animal

protein was consumed inland, but shifted from camelids to seafood by the
Middle Horizon occurred at these inland sites as well, suggesting more
trade with the coast over time. We see the impact of exchange and economic interconnectedness as the inland dwellers increasingly relied on
seafood for animal protein. Coprolite data provide meal evidence from
the twenty-four hours prior to deposition. Virú Valley coprolites contained
a range of non-food items, such as charcoal, bone fragments, shells, sand,
seeds, hair, and fish vertebrae, suggesting that some meals were served and
eaten rather haphazardly around a hearth relative to our ideas of food consumption. The most recent meals were a mix of cooked plants and either
meat or fish. As with Bronze Age meals, these data indicate that meals
contained both plant and animal ingredients, suggesting several dishes to
a meal (ibid.:72). The application of Douglas's definition of a meal, requiring multiple dishes, seems to be long-lived and widespread.

## Food Cleanup and Discard

Of all the activities discussed in this chapter, discard activities are by far
the most commonly encountered in archaeological settings. Ironically,
I have not read any publications describing archaeological evidence of
washing up after a meal. Food discard is the most commonly discussed
data in archaeological food studies; after all, that is what archaeologists
encounter – the leftovers. Food remains from cooking end up as cleaning
debris; spills in hearths, ovens, middens, pits, corners of rooms (presumably
having been swept there), or as sheet wash across exposed surfaces. Study of
unconsumed material should be the starting point for many of the previous
sections, working backwards from the discard event. Therefore, the taphonomic history of middens is important in the archaeological study of food
because it enables us to get a grip on the taphonomic history of every food-
related artifact. How a midden was deposited helps us interpret the material in it. Making these actions more accessible in our analysis would help
us recognize the agency of people tidying up after cooking and eating. Not
every community or culture can simply move on to a new campground.
Many groups are quite tidy, with evidence of cleaned floors and placing
items in storage locations. Other groups are quite happy to leave things
where they last used them. All of these actions, as well as what is done with
the rubbish, are informative about the values acted out through food. What
was clean? What was dirty? What level of post-use material was acceptable
inside vs. outside rooms, in corridors, against walls, and throughout enclosures? Such perspectives will help us include the other senses that must

have participated in these decisions: smell, size of remains, color, texture, level of degradation and desiccation of the rubbish, and so forth.

Hodder's (1982) revelation about the variation in the Nuba's pig and cattle bone discard activities is all about how people engage with their food refuse. Culturally meaningful insights regarding where refuse is placed and what is in it have significantly influenced our interpretation of archaeological sites (Hodder 1987; Moore 1986; Rathje 1977). Food discard practices tell us about a society's use of space and their meaning in the resident's lives, as well as about concepts of cleanliness and dirt, ritual and value, space and habitation (Hill 1995). Patterns uncovered in refuse can be informative about societal beliefs, rules, and norms of cleanliness, as seen in the discrete concentrations of deer remains stashed at the Caddo Crenshaw site in Arkansas, for example (Scott and Jackson 1998). Some rubbish is carefully disposed of, such as ceremonial or ritual rubbish that had completed its use life, requiring a meaningful discard: for example, unused Eucharist wafers and fermented, sanctified Catholic wine (Walker and Lucero 2000). Equally, some of these unearthed concentrations might have been caches that were being curated for future use, such as the deer meat deposits at the Crenshaw site (Walker 1995). Other deposits are unconscious dumps of everyday material as at Joya de Cerén in El Salvador, where stored foodstuffs, food in preparation, and discarded plants scattered across the floors and outer surfaces are visible and reflect daily behavior just before the volcanic explosion (Farahani et al 2017; Sheets 2002). As at Pompeii, we can identify the rubbish dumps at Joya de Cerén and compare their contents to what is in the storerooms and houses, getting a sense of plant and animal values and their use lives.

Taphonomic questions should not be far from our thoughts as we study discarded food remains: What food remains were rejected after preparation and consumption, where were they discarded, what are the accompanying materials, and how were these deposits treated after discard (Miller 1989)? Was the material dumped rapidly at one time and then covered over, not only sealing it but also protecting it from decomposition? Or was rubbish thrown across an open area, forming a mixed midden that was exposed to the elements, dog gnawing, animal scavenging, as well as human activities, such as digging for fill, building fires, and so on (Miksicek 1987).

A successful meal might leave little visible material besides fuel. To provide a picture of what was consumed, however, we can find the durable and inedible as with bones. Plant preservation is less likely, as archaeobotanists often do not identify any edible parts. Fortunately, archaeobotanists do encounter nutshells and other supportive tissues that people do not consume.

Utensils are also informative about past discard patterns. Broken tools and containers turn up regularly on settlements, especially ceramics. They are especially helpful in reconstructing cooking and processing. Lithic tools, more so than bone tools, are ubiquitous on archaeological sites but do not directly illustrate deposition. It is the sediment taphonomy that informs us most about discard patterns: how the material was deposited, how long it was exposed, and so forth. This is best studied through on-site micromorphological techniques (Courty et al. 1989; Matthews 2005; Matthews et al. 1997).

Some archaeologists have based their careers on the study of taphonomic principles to provide a better view of past behaviors. The substantial literature on taphonomy impacts all stages of interpretation, especially for bone (Gifford 1980; Gifford and Behrensmeyer 1977; Gifford-Gonzalez 1991; Moore et al. 2006), but also for plants (Miksicek 1987). Differential preservation must be present in our interpretations of food.

What seems to be left out completely is any substantive discussion of post-meal cleanup. We have dumps in middens, hearths, and oven areas, but it is rare that archaeologists discuss the clearing up – were pots cleared away, cleaned, and stored or left in and around the hearth? The activities of washing up and sweeping should receive more discursive discussion in archaeology, as it does in homes today.

## In Sum

Presenting the major steps in food procurement, creation, and deposition enables us to reiterate the many possible ways archaeology can identify past food activities, providing links between the material evidence and their political, symbolic, sensual meanings and economies of taste. The goal of this chapter is to understand the diversity of activities people complete along the path of getting food, the *chaîne opératoire* of preparation and eating. These activities entail substantial variation in different food traditions along with the material evidence that links directly to these actions. It is a rare archaeological site that has evidence for every part of this sequence, but this chapter has outlined the stages through a range of examples from the archaeological literature to show what might materialize at any one site.

Whether archaeological sites contain evidence for one or more of these stages in the sequence (the animal bone taxa frequencies from a range of sites in Palestine allow us to discuss the history of pork consumption) or a larger range of food activities at one site (as in the Upper Mantaro Valley sites, where flora, fauna, stable isotopes, ceramics, grinding stones, and human bones inform patterns of food production, cooking, and consumption), keeping in mind the processes involved is important. Each of the examples discussed in this chapter demonstrates how archaeological methodologies continue to progress so that, at most sites, we can say something about eating in the past. These examples highlight not only how important food is to our understanding of past social life, their technological possibilities, and daily practices, but also how food studies provide insights into the material world of other social milieu.

These issues can be addressed, even at sites with average preservation or incomplete artifactual coverage, given the right questions, assumptions, and linking arguments. In the next chapter we begin to do that with the economics of taste. We will ask whether food use is the basis for the development of difference or a reflection of difference.

# CHAPTER 5

# Food Economics

*In antiquity, food was power.*

Garnsey 1999:33

Human consciousness has always focused on the stomach, urging us to go out and find food (Gosden 1999:2). What is deemed proper to eat directs food procurement and production. Items must be accepted as food before they can be eaten, illustrating again the agency of foodstuffs (Dietler 2007; Robb 2007; Rozin 1976). This chapter focuses on the economic realities of gaining a full stomach, acknowledging the agency of meaning that engages with all aspects of food. Although in modern society the middle class has fairly easy access to daily food, year in and year out, such ease in provisioning is not effortless, nor without huge costs. Natural disasters, floods, droughts, hailstorms, and frosts can have serious impacts on the cost of dinner. In fact, specific food prices fluctuate annually owing to natural and cultural disasters, impacting what we purchase. When such vicissitudes occur, people go without, work much harder, eat different foods, live with relatives, move to another area, or perish. With lives at stake, it is a reasonable assumption that control of food is the basis of economies. In some dimensions of society, food scarcity and security are central. Is the statement at the beginning of this chapter true for other times, as it was for the Roman Empire about which Garnsey was writing – that controlling production of and access to food is the font of societal power? As noted in Chapter 3 and also suggested by Friedrich Engels (1942), food value is multifaceted, composed in part by the sociopolitical situation but also by economic access. Is food the basis for inequality, or does it merely reflect it? This chapter considers the role of food operating in economic inequality through several historical and prehistoric examples that illustrate a range of economic situations.

Economic analyses track the impacts of food production, distribution, and consumption (Goody 1982:14). Economic capital is potent because it can be converted into symbolic capital, augmenting prestige, authority, and status (Bourdieu 1977:171–183; Helms 1979). This idea is powerful because prestige and status can also be converted into economic capital through access and networking. How much can we learn about food in the past by studying such activities? Food studies build on a long history of economic analysis, explicitly since the eighteenth century when the Scottish philosopher Adam Smith (1999 [1776]) wrote the *Wealth of Nations*, influenced by the European Enlightenment philosophers who privileged economics over social or cultural dynamics (Thomas 2004). Building on these ideas, Marx 1939 [1867], Engels (1942), and others have shown that tracking food provisioning offers insights into long-term economic decisions and, in turn, power structures, and that food choice and value demonstrate people's economic position and aspirations. Recent scholars, including archaeologists, continue in this tradition, working with the idea that subsistence and food production have been a main motor of societal existence (Earle 1997).

Because food is essential, it is a target for control by political groups. Wittfogel's (1957) opus *Oriental Despotism* is a study of how state governments dominate societies by controlling their irrigation farming systems, illustrating how food can be the basis of unequal power in society. With many examples he demonstrates how, especially when food is scarce, overt political-economic power becomes overt in food production, clarifying the power that access to food holds within the economic system as well as the populace. But what does this system do when food is not scarce? How much control consumers have over the means of food production varies from complete equality of access with communal groups or self-sufficient farmers, to little control over access, for refugees or the landless. Provisioning and access might operate in an unacknowledged manner today, but they are always an active part of people's lives. Radically different outcomes emanate from different levels of control. Some food production situations create surplus, others scarcity. Identifying the difference is as important for studying the past as it is for us today. By investigating well-researched past economic examples we get a better sense of the dynamics operating in less-well-documented prehistoric settings.

Food inequalities are often naturalized in the name of different food traditions or taste preferences, as suggested in the Chimur case presented in this chapter, and seen in today's obesity epidemic and the advertised processed foods that drive it. Are these fattening foods consumed in large quantities by choice or by constraint, in an attempt to save on food costs or in the absence of other, healthier alternatives? In many settings, differential access becomes the focal point of control, as we learn in the Greek example discussed later in this chapter or with the Irish populace during the potato famine of 1845–1852. Tracking the economics of food production exposes the economic power network, as we see in today's globalism of food or in the colonial era in the past, helping us learn about the power and scale of economic differences.

## Food Production Models

We begin with models about food choice, on which economic anthropological approaches are built. These production and consumption models track supply and demand, input and output. Marx originated the concept of "commodity fetishism" to explain the alienated yet desired attachment to objects in situations where the consumer was not the producer. As a result of the distance between the production and the goods, the product becomes more valuable or "enhanced" by virtue of its detached, "mystical" existence, with people not knowing how or where the item came from (Marx 1973 [1894], Vol. 1:86–96). For Marx, this "fetishism" of the commodity disguises the potential monetary gain of this particular form of value enhancement. The stages of transformation between the original good and the final, higher-valued commodity are heavily manipulated by the cycles of supply, demand, and advertising. This augmentation is seen in manufactured items that have added layers of cost linked to advertising, name brands, and presentation. Although this fetishism has been used to explain why Westerners love to shop, it also explains the increased cost that people pay for processed food (ready-to-eat meals), and especially for out-of-season or otherwise exotic dishes (e.g., scallops from Perú, wine from France, apples from Chile). For Marx (1973 [1894], 1:93), produced goods become an "object" that is first alienated from the producer, both physically and cognitively, and then sold or traded at a much higher price. The engine of this "commodity fetishism" is people's desire and ability to purchase.

Since food is necessary to live, this requirement keeps the engine of desire tied to need. Food is a basic commodity that can be processed in a range of different ways, each with a different value-added cost. A fresh bunch of carrots costs less than a bag of washed carrots, and much less than a precooked meal with carrots in a sauce. The costs and benefits of food processing have long been at the core of commodity fetishism, increasingly so as food has become an international project. Economic thinking assumes that the manipulation of this desire for processed meals will increase the product value and therefore price. Consumption choice is driven by access but also by culturally defined desires.

A range of economic models has been used to study economic decision making in the past. In anthropology, this effort grew out of the functional orientation of Radcliffe-Brown (1922), who attempted to explain long-term dietary change. Ester Boserup (1965) opened up the energetics debate by studying production change through time. Archaeologists in the 1970s began asking these long-term questions and focused on energetics and scheduling (Brookfield 1972, 1984; Flannery 1973a, 1973b, 1974; Jochim 1976). In these models, input time-costs and output yields defined a range of economic food choices. Finding the least expensive foods that offered a balanced diet was assumed to be the goal of agro-pastoralism; however, none of these models explained most food choices studied ethnographically. Marvin Harris tried to explain food habits based on energetics, economics, and Western practicality, seen in his example of why cattle are not eaten in India. Harris's materialist rationality forced him to seek hidden, underlying costs to explain the seemingly illogical food selection (M. Harris 1985; Harris and Ross 1987). His cultural logic was contorted to me at least, which made many of his theories controversial, and in the end they lost much explanatory support.

Another energetics-derived model is that of diet breadth as applied to both foragers and farmers (Hawkes, Hill, and O'Connell 1982; Hawkes and O'Connell 1992; Stephens and Krebs 1986). This approach focuses on cost, measured as the cost of the time required acquiring food resources and their nutritional constraints. This decision-making model allows archaeologists to retrodict what activities maximized food yield. Tallying the input costs or time required to search, handle, and prepare food as well as the output or yields of calories and protein, anthropologists and archaeologists have made predictions about past economic food behavior (Earle and Christenson 1980; Keene 1981; Winterhalder 1986; Winterhalder and Goland 1993, 1997). Food preferences in this model are identified by ranked unit costs. Although these economic-energetics models are helpful in understanding the correspondence between costs and decisions in the past, in many archaeological examples the retrodicted economic decisions do not track with the evidence.

Such cost-based models allow us to track the web of food produce and labor, but not the unequal power that existed in these decisions, let alone different opinions about food values, which can influence not only what is grown but who has access to the produce. These approaches can provide an important starting point but not a satisfactory conclusion in food studies, being a good servant, like structuralism as described by Robb (2007).

### Emulation and Inequality: Economics of Desire

Based on a different economic logic than input cost, social value, like symbolic capital, contributes to many "economic" decisions. Not everyone seeks the least expensive foods. Some people actually choose foods because they are expensive and difficult to obtain. This is especially true when the fetishism of the commodity is operating. This "economic logic" is driven by emulation, value, desire, prestige, and restricted access. Certain foods are sought because of their cultural meanings (Graeber 2001; Miller 1985, 1998b). Cravings, associated with certain goods and culturally defined status, alter the energetically conceived commodity costs. This is most clearly displayed in wine sales. One can purchase a bottle of wine for one dollar in the United States, yet people will pay hundreds of dollars for specific wines. This is not cost-effective. These wine labels are imbued with other fetishized meanings that enhance the product's value to the beholder, in addition to its richer flavor.

Emulating other groups is often accomplished through purchasing goods that have specific associations. Mary Weismantel's work (1991) in rural highland Ecuador reveals the social enhancement when "store bought" versus locally produced food is consumed. She traces how expensive, foreign foods (*wanlla*), not part of the traditional Andean cuisine, become dishes cooked to display a heightened status, both internally in the consumer's sense of self in addition to externally by those who view this food event. Younger family members increasingly want to participate in the national and world culture through their food ways. They state this desire for bread (*pan*) and noodles (*fideos*), exotic products of city living that must be purchased. Mothers are pressured into buying bread and noodles to appease their children's longing. As with the desire of the American poor to eat like the middle class, familial tensions illustrated by Weismantel are expressed through their food desires (Fitchen 1988). Because store-bought bread requires cash and the ingredients cannot be grown locally, it has become a symbol and also an agent of a different way of life, an elite food, despite its not having much nutritional value. This is rural gastropolitics in a globalized world.

We might assume that expensive and rare foods marked wealth status differences in the past as well. When the Etruscan foods, bread and wine, were traded north into Europe, they were initially adopted only by Germanic leaders. North of the Mediterranean the Etruscans provided wine for large gatherings, enabling the purchasers (Celtic leaders) to gain social position over their contemporaries. Hosting allies to experience these high-status foods encouraged support as it highlighted their status. At these meals large cauldrons of food and drink were served along with roast meat. For generations the drink was beer made from locally grown grain, which the leaders sequestered for brewing. Throughout the Iron Age, as trade intensified with the Mediterranean, the Celtic hosts maintained their position by emulating the Etruscans, importing expensive wine and drinking paraphernalia as an indicator of globalized wealth and local political position (Dietler 1990; Elias 1978).

Both bread for the Ecuadorian rural farmer and wine for the Iron Age Celt signal people who were actively altering their social position by converting economic surplus into exotic food. The economic expense of these fetishized objects indicates new realms of status development channeled through the economics of inequality (Dietler 1996:98).

The arrival of foreign/expensive foods drives the display of munificence we associate with political foodways, but there is a clear economic cost to this activity. The Celtic leaders had to produce objects to trade with the Etruscans. As Marx predicted, people desire uneconomical foods and will work hard to get them, complicating the concept of cost and benefit in the macroeconomic models with which many archaeologists have worked (Earle and Christenson 1980). Social value and desire can initiate such emulative trade, which can eventually work into the masses' staple foods, seen in Indian black pepper's history in Europe and North America, now found on every table there. The price of such goods is high and can drive large parts of the economy (Mann 2011). Production and desire for the exotic run throughout European economic history.

Probably the most famous example of the dual forces of wealth and prestige driving a production system is the history of sugar cane (*Saccharum officinarum* L.). Economic inequality is at the core of this history, involving slavery and the global economic power of England in the sixteenth century (Mintz 1985). In his famous food anthropology work *Sweetness and Power* (1985), Sidney Mintz cunningly illustrates the workings of the Marxist economic engine of desire. Mintz traces the forces of profit coupled with aggressive encouragement of emulation, stoked by the human craving for sweetness. Mintz's thesis is that, over the past 500 years, this exotic commodity became a powerful economic force, directing modern European economic decisions in an expansionary system that was controlled by a few powerful people, riding on the back of desire, emulation, and colonialism.

This story takes place on three continents. English desire for sugar became intertwined with the expanding textile production in eastern North America, bolstered by the slave trade in Africa. While sugar cane was imported to the moist Caribbean islands from the Middle East, workers were brought in from Africa to produce it. This dual engine of desire, for money and for sweetness, bred stratified identities by controlling access to sugar through high prices, controlling human lives by adopting the African slaving tradition internationally, and encouraging the sweet tooth of Europe. Such was the global aspect of this economic system that even the English word for sugar was imported from the Arabic name for sugar cane, *al sukkar*.

Mintz tracks the desire for sugar, which was manipulated and fed by the drive for wealth and power. The craving for sweetness was encouraged by lowering sugar's price via increased production and international availability. Today, sugar is on every table and in every teacup in England. Michael Pollan (2006), the food journalist, picked up on this theme, noting its new iteration currently in full swing in the United States with the increasing use of corn syrup as a sweetener. In this modern version of international trade based on desire, sugar, along with pungent exotic spices, coffee, cocoa, and tobacco, went from being rare, elite, out-of-reach prestige exotics to essential, even staple commodities. This desire economy was completed by the manipulation of "objective" taste, reorienting not only dietary aesthetics but also state economies and political decisions (Mintz 1987:107). Slave trading and dreadful working conditions in England, the United States, and the Caribbean continued throughout this history, demonstrating the power of taste desires to maintain inequality within capitalist economies. Ever since this drastic inequality was initiated via the Columbian Exchange, the desire for sweetness has increased (Crosby 2003; Mann 2011). Just look at the amount of sweet drinks that are sold and consumed worldwide every year: on average, 89.9 liters per person per year over 18 countries studied, with 216 liters per capita per year in the United States (www.nationmaster.com/).

Before 1600 in England, sugar was not a food. It was a decoration, a medicine, and of course a status marker, as Etruscan wine had been for the Celts – exotic and expensive. The price was high, making it out of reach for most people. But over time the price came down (Figure 5.1). In 1400, 10 pounds of sugar cost 0.35 oz. of gold. By 1550, 10 pounds of sugar was worth only 0.08 oz. of gold – still expensive but getting within range for more people. By 1750, sugar was widely used by all classes, and by 1850 in England, it had become a staple food, consumed at a rate of 50 pounds per capita.

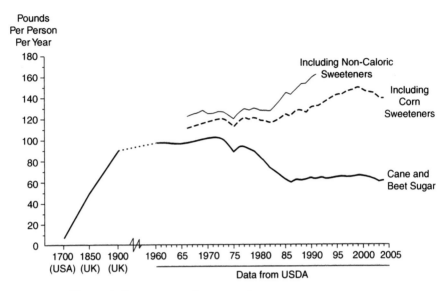

FIGURE 5.1. Changes in European use of sugar over time

In Europe today, the per capita sugar consumption is 84 pounds a year, but that is nothing compared to sugar consumption in the United States. The average American in 1967 consumed 114 pounds of sugar and sweeteners a year. By 2003, on average, each person ate 142 pounds of sugar per year, much of it in sweetened drinks (46 gallons per year, 174 liters even more than reported in the previous paragraph) (U.S. *News and World Report* 2005). Truly, the consumption of around 0.39 pounds of sugar *a day* has moved the innate interest in sweetness to within the edge of destruction for a human body. This is the economics of desire at an extreme.

The economics of desire explains other historical European foodways as well (Mann 2011). Exotic spices found in historic recipe books and in post-medieval European midden deposits portray a long history of the tensions between desire, exploitation, and the cost of highly valued foods. Was their use required (were they staples) or did they reflect affluent emulation? Although at nowhere near the same level of escalation as seen for sugar, the increased evidence of these piquant, flavorful items follows neither the diet breadth food choice model nor the least-cost model, but rather the value-laden, emulation model as well as the agency of these foodstuffs across Eurasia.

Spices that could not be grown in Europe were traded into Northern Europe intermittently throughout the early Middle Ages. First brought north with the Roman conquerors, these spices remained expensive, difficult to access, and steadily prized for centuries (Livarda 2011; Livarda and Orengo 2015; Livarda and van der Veen 2008; van der Veen 2014). Notwithstanding the Arab monopoly of long-distance spice routes into the port of Venice, European rulers used their money and their political networks to buy the spices, which furthered their own gastropolitical successes at banquets and state dinners with the fashionable impact of these new flavors (Küster 2000:436). Early on, Eastern spices were considered curatives as well as food by both merchants and consumers, yet the new flavors also made them exciting, even risqué. Archaeobotanical evidence of these taxa is rare across Europe, with the best preservation in waterlogged conditions. The scant archaeobotanical data, mainly from latrines and pits, confirm that it was the rich and the noble who bought, presented, and consumed these spices (Jones 2007; Livarda 2011; Livarda and van der Veen 2008; Lodwick 2013a, 2013b; van der Veen 2014).

Through the sixteenth century, English documents indicate that the noble and the religious (monasteries) purchased these spices, which they consumed in small quantities at special feasts and banquets. Only black pepper was priced within the purchasing power of freemen and merchants (Laurioux 1985). This commonly documented spice has also been identified from elite sixteenth- to seventeenth-century latrines and pits across Worcester, Shrewsbury, Oxford, London, and Taunton. It should be much more ubiquitous if the historic records are correct in noting the extent of its trade (Giorgi 1997:206; Greig 1990, 1996:228). In one pit, peppercorns were found with the African grains of paradise (mentioned earlier), suggesting that these deposits were the remains of a feast (or feasts). The importation of nutmeg (*Myristica fragrans* Houtt.) and its outer aril, mace, have been documented at a Scottish abbey by Dickson (1996). Somewhat ironically, by the seventeenth century, many of the African and Indian Ocean spices (via the Arabic traders' monopoly) were no longer purchased, as new trade routes from India opened up and a different set of spices became the darlings of the English elites (Dickson 1996:227).

The most common exotic spices encountered in English medieval archaeological settings are black pepper, nutmeg, and opium poppy (*Papaver somniferum* L.), providing new tastes and sensations. These spices were highly regarded across Europe and in English society, building on a historical tradition of privilege that grew out of their use by Romans centuries before. This emulative desire influenced the economics of long-distance trade, especially in England and France. Fourteenth-century texts note that French chefs became interested in ginger, whereas the English focused on saffron (*Crocus sativus*) (Laurioux 1985:46). Ginger root (*Zingiber officinale*) grew to dominate the European trade after the sixteenth century, going well with sugar (candied ginger holds a strong historical position in the European palette). The opium poppy seed increased in popularity over time as well. Unusually, the poppy is found quite commonly in medieval sewage locations in Norwich, suggesting that it might have been grown in southern England at the time (Greig 1988:115).

By no means have all foreign spices mentioned in historical texts been identified in the European archaeological record. There is enough evidence in the deposits, however, to accept their existence (Greig 1996:226). The important cardamom pod (*Elettaria cardamomum* and *E. major*) has not yet been identified in England but is identified in a range of sites in Germany from twelfth- to thirteenth-century contexts (Greig 1996:227; Hellwig 1997). The crocus stigma that defines saffron is often mentioned in documents as extremely important in aristocratic cuisine, but it has not yet been uncovered in the English archaeological record (pollen might be a help here). The galingale root (*Cyperus longus* L.) is mentioned as imported and consumed, being listed in recipes and even price lists, as was licorice (*Glycyrrhiza glabra* L.). Neither plant has been identified in the archaeological record. Records state that zedoary (*Curcuma zedoaria* (Christm.) Roscoe), turmeric (*Curcurma longa* L.), galangal (*Alpinia galanga* L. Willd.), and all of the ginger family were imported into England, but again, there is no material evidence yet for their arrival, spread, and use (Giorgi 1997; Greig 1983, 1988, 1996; Lautioux 1985; Simmoons 1991:374, 399; Wilson 1973:280). A taxon related to ginger, the melegueta pepper or grains of paradise, has been reported in thirteenth-century import inventories and identified in a fifteenth-century Worchester latrine (Greig 1996:226). Clove buds (*Syzygium aromaticum* (L.) Merrill & Perry), another of the relatively common spices, have only been identified in Britain and Europe by their pollen (Greig 1996:228).

The piquant Flavor Principle had been activated in England by the Romans, as these exotic flavors continued to be of interest especially to the rich and urban dwellers, even when they remained rare and expensive (Livarda 2011). As demand for these spices expanded after the seventeenth century and more traders transported them, they became more available to the masses. As this desire grew, so did merchants' wealth. Accompanying these cravings were sumptuary laws enacted by various governments across the globe to control the use of rare spices, foods, and courses at feasts. These sumptuary laws were enacted for many reasons, to control not only wealth concentration but also plant and animal extinction, which did happen. With this long history of desire, these spices are still the ubiquitous festival foods of Northern European winters, in mince pies, Christmas fruitcakes, and gingerbread. As is typical in moments of "emulatory" change, as trade opens up with its increased access among the less well-to-do, the nobility seeks other expensive foods while trying to maintain control over access by regulating consumption. When citrus fruits became the rage in England in the eighteenth century, the nobility propagated these exotics in protected environments constructing orangeries and enclosed gardens. These fruits must have been rarely eaten and were primarily for display, as orange pips are non-existent archaeobotanically until several centuries later.

This history and timing of the spice trade illustrates how social values and emulation dance with economics, driven by the inequalities of the time. Clearly, increasing spice and sugar consumption demonstrates how the English saw themselves in their world, increasingly conceiving of exotics as staples as they indigenized these foods. This flavor shift paralleled the conquests of the expansionary British Empire. While this might not seem odd to us today in the era of global food movement, these goods were precious luxury items, traveling over land and sea well before the combustion engine and the airplane, reminding us how strong such a desire was to maintain difference through an economic food system.

While least-cost models of food selection have had some success in answering questions about long-term production, other economic influences are also important when addressing how people choose what they eat; fashion and style are big business today and clearly impacted what was traded and eaten in the past as well. "It is well-established in anthropology that the value of things is based on several criteria: capital input, labor input, utility, abundance or scarcity, exchange rate and 'social' value, including religious and political significance" (Wiessner 2001:117).

Whereas Mintz makes a case that control over production drives social inequalities, the historians Braudel (1973) and Elias (1978) suggest that food desires reflect and manipulate economic life. As discussed in Chapter 2, these two historians track the history of European food traditions through increasing food security and desire that parallels the primacy of the self and how the individual *body* is crafted by the larger society's pressures (Gilchrist and Sloane 2005). In Chapter 8 we will focus on how the economies of desire intimately intertwine with the social body. Even in the face of grave economic pressures, English cuisine choices suggest that these foods continued to reflect the inequalities of the time, which were ultimately built on power, war, and conquest. We can sense how elites and economic leaders encouraged the trade of new products, as did the Celtic and English nobles, activating the omnivore's paradox in their use of their economic position, but how did they fund this desire? And how did such desires filter down to the rest of the population?

## Emulation and Inequality: Control over Production and Access

Not all citizens emulate elite food activities. Some people do not have the economic capacity or the desire, as I tried to demonstrate with the sugar and spice restrictions in medieval England. Others choose to stay with their own cuisines and not take on others', as the Oglala would have liked to do with their forced food shifts (Powers and Powers 1984), discussed in Chapter 3. Food is perhaps the most sensitive way by which we are controlled and can control others; thus it is one of the best reflections of social and economic status tensions (Fitchen 1988; Weismantel 1988). In fact, food choice can direct us to diverse levels of daily power over people. When people do not emulate the leadership or their national cuisines, other factors are at work, perhaps owing to long-lived local traditions, family histories, less empowerment or access, laws against such activities, or even active resistance, activating differences in food identity within society. Different food activities reflect group inequalities.

Differential access to food informs us about differential control over food production. Studying different eating patterns of distinct neighborhoods or classes illustrates differential control over staple food production within a hierarchical polity. Emulation is a continual force in societies. The sumptuary laws of England and France periodically tried to control the merchants from emulating the nobility, in clothing and food. George Gumerman IV has uncovered a prehistoric example of such emulation and control over classes in his study of archaeobotanical food evidence from four classes on the north coast of Perú (Gumerman 1991, 1994a, 1994b, 2002). Tracking their food patterns enables us to see variation in access to staples and the state control over labor and provisioning as well as the power to maintain one's identity through cuisine. Beginning in preceramic times, around 3000 BC, the people in this dry coastal region began to construct large, architecturally complex centers in the river valleys near the coast. Although political regimes tacked up and down the north coast over the millennia, cities controlled sophisticated irrigation systems in agriculturally fertile valleys. By AD 1100, labor projects had erected interconnecting field systems, reflecting a centralized food production system. The irrigated lands supported orchards of guava (*Psidium guajava* L.), avocado (*Persea americana* Mill.), *pacae* (*Inga feuilleei* DC.), and coca (*Erythroxylum coca* Lam.) as well as the annual staples maize (*Zea mays* L.), achira (*Canna edulis* Ker Gawl.), manioc (*Manihot esculenta* Crantz), beans (*Phaseolus* spp.), sweet potato (*Ipomoea batatas* (L.) Lam.), squash (*Cucurbita* spp.), and peanut (*Arachis hypogaea* L.). Gumerman studied food access at a series of households in and around Pacatnamu, a Chimur city in the Jequetepeque Valley, inhabited between AD 1100 and 1370 (Gumerman 1991, 1994a, 1994b, 2002). This large settlement had fifty ceremonial-civic *huaca* mounds with associated domestic precincts, illustrating the rich and powerful classes that lived in the city (Donnan and Cock 1986, 1997; Gumerman 1991, 1994a, b, 2002). Gumerman (1994b:84) studied floral and faunal evidence from four classes of people he called: nobility, attached textile specialists, farm laborers, and fisher folk.

To understand the nobles' cuisine, the Donnan project excavated middens from a series of central residential courtyards. These data were compared with information from nearby specialist producer homes, families who were economically attached to the nobles. Outside the city were a series of farmsteads which were also sampled, and finally houses of coastal fishermen provided unattached specialist dietary data. Figure 5.2 compares these four households' foodstuff densities, focusing on maize, chile peppers, fleshy fruit, wild herbs, coca, chile peppers, and camelid bones (in grams recovered per liter of bone recovered). While there was differential access to foodstuffs between the city dwellers and the rural food producers, we are also seeing differences in group preferences, cuisine traditions, and emulation, in part owing to power over production and distribution of staples.

The centrally located nobility at Pacatnamu procured their food from rural farms that they must have overseen. There is no evidence that they themselves farmed. Two nearby families were full-time textile workers, identified by the spinning and weaving artifacts found in their compounds. Their food remains suggest that they ate a diet similar to the nobility. Either they emulated the rich nobility or they received room and board from the state coffers. These attached specialists received pay in kind from the leaders (D'Altroy and Earle 1985). The central precinct inhabitants were not just elite but quite possibly nobility, with a host of slaves and servants to maintain their households and to produce goods that they could use while upholding the Chimur state. The other local workers studied by the Donnan project were fisher folk who lived close to the sea. These unattached economic specialists furnished the leadership with fish and traded their fish for other food. Gumerman notes that the fisher families had

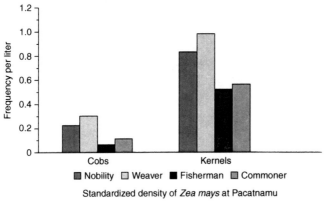

Standardized density of *Zea mays* at Pacatnamu

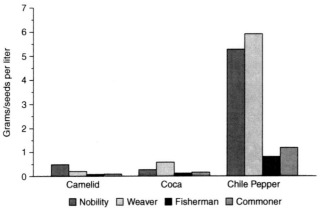

Standardized density of camelid (grams per liter), coca,
and chile pepper (seeds per liter) at Pacatnamu.

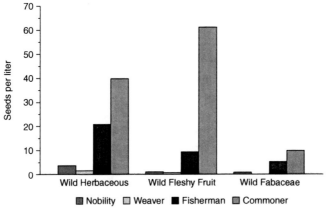

Standardized density distribution of wild plants at Pacatnamu

FIGURE 5.2. Pacatnamu food densities (redrawn from Gumerman 1994b)

trade beads and copper, suggesting that they had some control over their fish, trading it for what they desired. These data suggest that they were not "attached" in that they had some control over their own economics and therefore food access. The "commoners," as Gumerman calls them, were local people living across the valley that worked in the state-run farms that produced the vegetal staples. Since they conveyed their produce to the elite, how did they get their own food? Did they keep a portion of the produce? Did they have to fend for themselves, as did slaves in antebellum America? These farmers show no evidence of gaining access to elite goods, suggesting that they were unable to do what the fisherfolk did and have access to sumptuary goods.

Gumerman identifies maize, chile peppers, and coca as especially valuable food crops. The high kernel-to-cob values from the middens indicate that most of this staple food was distributed off the cob – that is, processed before distribution. Chile peppers are an important symbolic crop as well as a condiment (Hastorf 1998). A coca variety grown along the coast (*Erythroxylum novogranatense* var. *truxillense*) was considered a sacred plant, being food for deities brought out for ceremonies and rituals, whether family events or state functions. Although camelids (*Lama* spp.) were raised on the coast (Shimada and Shimada 1985), meat would have been costly and would have been consumed only at special events. Like coca, camelid remains reflect involvement in state ceremonies with their ideological traction. Wild plants are notable because these foods would have been the least likely to be monitored by the state, being collected throughout the countryside.

The differences are both qualitative and quantifiable between the food consumed in the city and in the country. The nobility had more camelid meat, maize, and chile peppers than the workers did; all of these items were products of the state system. The elite city household middens had five times more chile peppers than did those of the local laborers, suggesting that those connected to the state apparatus had more access and/or more funds to purchase them. The city dwellers also ate more of a maize-based cuisine.

The fisher folk and fieldworker data illustrate the lack of power over food that goes hand in hand with economic power. Both groups ate more wild herbaceous plants than did the nobility/city dwellers, as illustrated in the lowest group of densities, those of wild plants. The farmers' middens contained the densest evidence of wild herbs and fruits, presumably collecting them while working in the fields if not growing them in their kitchen gardens.

At Pacatnamu the different household ingredient patterns identify economic and political inequalities. The city dwellers could have procured wild herbs had they wanted to, but they did not. Emulation tends to look up. Most likely the nobility considered the wild taxa of little gustatory value. The Pacatnamu nobles consumed the highly valued cuisine of domesticates, in part because they could and also probably to differentiate themselves from the local workers. These four food cuisines accentuate diverse statuses, reflecting power and differential access. In contrast to the Sausa situation that I present next, these farmers did not emulate those in power through their food access.

## Staple and Wealth Finance

The Upper Mantaro Archaeological Project (UMARP) studied this issue of production expansion in a prehistoric setting through the impact of the Inka conquest, a pre-Columbian empire (AD 1450–1532), on local staple production in the indigenous Sausa economy (D'Altroy and Earle 1985; Earle 1987; Hastorf 1990, 2001a; Norconk 1987; Owen and Norconk 1987; Sandefur 2001). This central Andean valley had been occupied by agropastoral communities since Formative times, remaining autonomous until the Inka conquest around 1460. During the turbulent highland-wide post-Wari and Tiwanaku times, each valley, if not individual community, was an independent, self-identifying polity. The Inka, one of many highland groups, rapidly spread north and south from the Cusco region of the central Andean mountains after the 1400s, after consolidating the Cusco River Valley communities. Their conquest was extremely successful in large part because they managed to keep much of the local Andean economic and political system intact, replacing or rechanneling the local leaders to organize labor and report to them. The Inka, like other expanding polities, built their powerbase on labor mobilization (D'Altroy 2014; Dietler and Herbich 2001). But this came at a price. The Inka hosted many meals to keep the troops, the producers, and the local leaders within their purview, thus escalating crop production to feed the warriors and farmworkers, who in turn were pressed to produce higher yields. It was difficult to keep this new and very diverse populace together. In 1527, a civil war broke out after the untimely death of the emperor. This gave the Spanish easy access to the country and its leadership in 1532, and the Spanish quickly began reorienting production toward more mining (Cobo 1979; Garcilaso de la Vega 1966).

The Inka conquered the northern Upper Mantaro Valley populations in their early push north. This was a desirable conquest, as the valley is productive and the Inka were keen to expand their maize production base as well as gain the local mines. Although we do not have documents directly addressing the local production levels, we do have archaeological data. The region is agriculturally productive, with adequate rainfall, low valleys, gentle slopes, and extensive arable uplands. I have tracked the farming shifts between AD 500 and 1540 in order to address questions of staple production and its shifts over time (Hastorf 1988, 1990, 1993). From detailed paleoethnobotanical work we have learned that the local residents grew and ate a mixed diet of tubers (potatoes, oca, ulluco [*Ullucus tuberosa*], and mashua [*Tropaeolum tuberosum*]), *Chenopodium* spp. (quinoa, a pseudo-cereal), and maize with some legumes and meat. The meat was primarily camelid, with some deer, guinea pig, and dog, in addition to the occasional wild animal and bird (Sandefur 2001:184–186). The most common meals were mixed soups or stews (Hastorf and DeNiro 1985), made of potatoes, quinoa, and meat (Hastorf 2001a:169–171).

Even before the Inka conquest, the Sausa were engaged in long-distance trade of stone material, metal, and some highly valued plants. One foreign plant to enter the valley farms early was maize, before AD 200, but we also have evidence for coca and warm-valley spices at least by AD 1000 (Hastorf 1987; 1993). Locally grown maize increased in popularity through time. After the Wari and Tiwanaku dissolution at the end of the Middle Horizon, when all of the Andean groups were focusing inward (WI), the Sausa consolidated their population and moved to protected ridge tops (WII). This relocation phase spanned the period from 1350 to 1460. As Figure 5.3 shows, the WII relocation upslope impacted what people produced, as these upland settlements were farther from the warm valley maize fields. The same geographic impact is seen in production when, after the Inka arrived in 1460, the populace moved back downslope into the maize-growing lands. The staple production shifted again by this new political impact, and the WIII data display maize production at a more intensive level than even the WI levels, when the Sausa last lived in the valleys. Detailed and systematic collection of both plant and animals remains, along with the stable carbon and nitrogen isotope analysis of the human skeletons, indicate a marked dietary shift after the arrival of the Inka, especially for some young men, linked to the Inka's interest in serving maize and meat at their feasts (Figure 5.3). How was this shift in staple production funded?

While maize could be grown in the region, it could not be grown everywhere (Hastorf 1993). Maize also could have been traded from the more productive southern valley and from fields to the east. With imperial incorporation, the major local change in food consumption was increased use

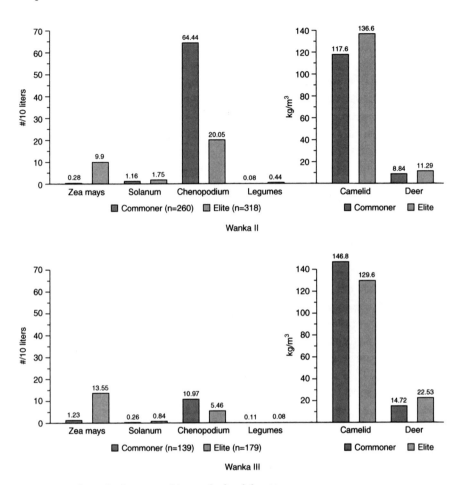

FIGURE 5.3. Sausa food, presented in standardized densities

of maize and meat in lieu of *Chenopodium*. It seems the local elites did not lack for food. During the WII phase, maize was clearly an expensive crop owing to increased transport costs. The increase in maize production in WIII was in part linked to the demographic shift back into the maize-growing zones, making it a less expensive and high-yielding crop (Hastorf 1993). But also, the Inka staple finance strategy focused the local production on maize. They built a state farm near the major local administrative center, Hatun Xauxa, reclaiming the warm-valley fields where the road and the river met (D'Altroy 2002:271). Along with increased WIII maize consumption, more meat was also consumed, especially deer hunted by the local elite (Sandefur 2001:184).

The increased meat and maize in Sausa homes illustrates that the Inka's economic policies directly impacted local food production and consumption. Some people ate more maize than others did, suggesting that local political stratification was realigned under the Inka conquest (Hastorf 1990, 2001a:174; Sandefur 2001:185). The agency of maize is evident in this sequence, influencing the farmer's own decisions. Local leaders had more access to trade goods, silver, exotic pottery, and lithic tools during the independent phase (WII). This continued under Inka domination, suggesting that the Sausa leaders chosen to oversee their populace for the state were likely to be the leaders from the pre-Inka times that continued to have a wider economic access than their neighbors did (Costin and Earle 1989).

Although the official Inka policy was to provide land for local farmers to produce their own sustenance, farming families shifted their staple production and consumption under the influence of the empire (Hastorf 1990). Did they develop new culinary desires, emulating the Inka's own interest in maize, meat, and coca, and thus produce more maize for their own larders, or did this shift in consumption occur because the Inka demand for staple production reoriented local production sufficiently to influence household production? Did the Sausa consume more of these high-value items because they in fact received them as pay in kind from the Inka out of the surplus distribution or at feasts at the Inka administrative centers?

What were the dynamics between local food production and Sausa elite surplus extraction during the Inka Empire? Terry D'Altroy and Tim Earle (1985) of the UMARP project have approached this question, outlining the mechanisms that funded both the local leaders and the Inka's commodity debt interactions. They identify two types of production: staple finance and wealth finance. Staple finance is the direct mobilization of subsistence and utilitarian goods, as in local subsistence farming to feed the population. Wealth finance is generated from transforming staple production into other goods and allows for the manufacture, procurement, and conversion of valuables. It focuses on the role of local food production in surplus economies, through which people in positions of power alienate staple produce to gain desired goods. These prestige goods could be local, highly valued produce such as meat and maize, in the case of the Inka, or they could be exotic goods, such as sugar and spices in England. Most scholars associate precious metals and gems with wealth finance, as we will see in the following example, but highly valued food can also operate as wealth goods.

In an attempt to determine how the Inka managed their resources to run their empire, D'Altroy and Earle (1985) track these two staples and discuss how wealth intertwined in the economic systems, each ostensibly operating with different goals. They begin with the premise that controlling staple food production is the basis of economic power and therefore of inequality. This economic sphere has the greatest impact on other domains of society, and thus if one controls food production, other domains can also be controlled, as Wittfogel theorized. The primary goal of staple production is to feed people, but it can also generate surplus that can be transformed into other economic domains. Stored surpluses can be used to pay (feed) specialists or other non-producers, or they can be traded for exotic items. The finance system therefore harnesses surplus produce to support the manufacture of or exchange for other goods, such as exotic foods. D'Altroy and Earle propose that differential access to food emanating from the mechanisms of the prestige economy is the basis for differential political power that breeds inequalities. Food wealth can support a range of non–food producers, specialists involved in other activities that construct and maintain the social, political, or religious structures, such as sophisticated architecture, decorative goods, clothing, codified cuisine, and trade (D'Altroy 2001). Having control over food surplus thus has the potential to create positions of unequal power, as was the case for the Inka and the Chimur. How does this dual economic system operate?

One way economic wealth feeds political power is through control over food, with authority over the production of and access to food. This production also has an accompanying web of meaning and signs that intertwine with the produce, giving it value that we cannot understand by studying the goods alone. These foods gain their symbolic capital from their constituents and contextual valuations. This symbolic capital generates prestige, acted out in the politics of the situation (Bourdieu 1977:171–183). Prestige and status drive the engine that provides meaning to society and its internal rankings, enacted within the economic system. Prestige is the reputation achieved within a system. Statuses are the relative positions within that social system. The fact that one's reputation is elastic, being convertible into economic goods or political acts, makes the study of prestige and status important for students of food because of the interdependencies of food valuation, status, and prestige. The meanings food engenders are not arbitrary; they develop out of the economics and the politics of the situation. "An expensive food stands for wealth, a cheap one for poverty" and all that those loaded terms imply (Weismantel 1989). These symbolic resonances are not divorced from economics.

Although prehispanic Andean polities varied greatly in size and organization, there seems to have been active reciprocity between local families with respect to farming aid. The archaeological evidence indicates that Sausa leaders might have initiated surplus production by harnessing agricultural help, but they still participated in food reciprocity, even if it was asymmetrical. Andean food provisioning functioned at the family and the community level. New patterns of provisioning have been suggested for the Andean populace during the Inka reign. The cycle of food distribution via seasonal state festivals (feasts) used centralized crop production and storage administration to support the conscripted labor through food and beer payments. The Inka staple finance system was essentially tripartite. One part of the land was given to state farms and production that went directly into the state's coffers (*qolqa* storage structures) (D'Altroy 2002). A second portion was allocated to maintaining the state religious sector, resulting in indirect yields for the state, probably also deposited into state coffers. A third portion of the land remained in the hands of the local population and would have been accessed by the people via the local leaders. Farmers probably could produce enough food to live on, as before, but with less margin of error, as much of the land's yields went into the state's storage facilities.

Several historical sources note that the Inka kept detailed records of the population and its activities, recorded on *quipu* (knotted string) and reported regularly to the Inka administrators (Betanzos 1996; D'Altroy 2002:235; Garcilaso de la Vega 1966; Murra 1980; Urton 2012). They recorded state farm yields. As part of this state apparatus, Garcilaso de la Vega claims that the Inka system of labor taxation operated within a nested kin-based system that resulted in parallel-stratified groups. The moral authority of this ideal included the goal that every member of society was to be fed if calamity befell them or they were too old to work (Garcilaso de la Vega 1966; Godelier 1974).

Both artifacts and texts suggest that the populace of the Upper Mantaro Valley was fed under such a kin-based system during the Inka regime. Was Garcilaso de la Vega correct about the socialistic food distribution of the Inka Empire? Were elders, widows and widowers provided for? The archaeological data suggest that food reciprocity and distribution did occur. Was this based on familial exchanges, or by decree and benevolence of the leaders? Probably a bit of both. How ubiquitous these types of community support throughout the Inka Empire were can be investigated.

At the same time, the Inka state was aggressive in its state farm and labor mobilization policies. We know that in a few highly productive valleys, the Inka cleared out the local populace and created new farms, bringing in other populations they could better control to work the fields, as in

Cochabamba, Urubamba, and Ayaviri. This intensive agricultural focus by the Inka rarely encroached completely on local farming production strategies (D'Altroy 2002:285). Instead, the Inka tended to build state farms in areas that had not previously been cultivated intensively. They built new canals and drainage systems in valleys and reclaimed hillsides with terraces. By emphasizing irrigation, they planted earlier than in the dry-farmed fields and were able to harvest before the rain-fed fields as well. These new farming systems were placed in areas that produced maize, the symbolic core of Inka cuisine. These additional agricultural fields extended the farmers' work year while producing higher yields in the mountain valleys. Thus the Inka state allowed household staple production in sufficient quantities to feed everyone through their own labor while also extracting labor to produce a surplus that financed the many state enterprises, the most important of which were to support the standing army and to build the road system, the pleasure palaces, and the ceremonial centers. These state operations were supported by this wealth finance system.

Although the Inka leadership produced and moved a range of prestige goods across their empire, including gold, silver, arsenical bronze, textiles, ceramics, and hallucinogenic plants, their economic engine was built on the staple foodstuffs that filled state storage. "Food made up the major part of surplus production [in Classical Greece] the land being the most important source of wealth, and food being the most significant produce of the land" (Garnsey 1999:23). We cannot measure the food yields that were transformed into prestige goods produced by the Inka state, but we can see the state's influence on local cuisines and diets, bringing local eating patterns more in line with state ideals. When the Sausa were in the Inka state, they had the capacity to emulate Inka state food ideals and acted on these emulative tendencies by consuming more maize beer and camelid meat.

## Provisioning

Periodic scarcity and starvation were (and still are) common in many parts of the world, where storing and preserving food occupy most waking hours. Control over food production can easily extend into control over access and distribution. Especially in larger, multi-sited polities, such as the Chimur in Perú or the Han in China, food-provisioning capabilities are crucial to the maintenance of society and can often form the basis of larger networks of political control, as in the greater Near East (Alcock et al. 2001; Marx 1939; Zeder 1991). How evident is food distribution in the past? To go one step further in our ruminating about staple finance, we look at how people gained their food if they did not produce it, and the implications these threads of control imply.

Gumerman's Chimur situation illustrates how disparities in food production and food access can be visible in the archaeological record. Did these working classes have any agency in their choice of cuisine? Were fish and wild plants perceived as lesser-quality foods and considered almost starvation foods by the ruling class? Clearly not just having enough food to eat but what kind was important, although such food insecurities have certainly been a preoccupation in the past. When food is an ever-present obsession, it can enlighten us about how it has been used to maintain economic difference and the relationship of food and status (Wiessner and Schiefenhövel 1996). Production of a more than adequate food supply is an indicator of access to resources, harnessing sufficient labor, or both (Dietler and Herbich 2001; Wiessner 1996:6). Food distribution is the final stage in the food sequence. Even today, when enough food is grown to feed the world, politically generated famines occur not because of the lack of available food, but because people or groups hinder the distribution of food to others (Mintz 1996:11). In the face of these famines, it is difficult to fathom how the current, economically expansive desires of agribusiness have pushed the modern food industry into producing too much food that is literally bad for us as well as ecologically damaging! I mention these situations to orient our economic discussion toward provisioning, to study the food of people whose access is controlled by others. Even during times of great constraint people retain some agency over the food they eat, if not receive (Powers and Powers 1984; Wilk 2006).

Discrepancies in food access are poignantly recorded in the history of slave diets. For Caribbean slave society, spanning the sixteenth to the nineteenth centuries, Sidney Mintz (1996) notes that some control over food provisioning, however humble, was at the heart of the agency of the enslaved. During the North American colonial era, Native Americans and African-American slaves were often close to starvation, which was accompanied by related diseases (Larsen 2001). Like the discussion of the Oglala food supply in Chapter 3, Mintz makes the case that the ability to distribute and cook one's own food was a step toward freedom. In those colonial American settings, the slaves produced the food for others as well as for themselves. As long as the owners controlled the production and distribution of food to the slaves, they retained substantial control over them, as did the elite over the farmers at Pacatnamu. But in some situations owners allowed the slaves to produce their own food on their own usufruct plots. This decision by the plantation owners may have been based on economics, but the lessening of oversight over daily tasks and food provisioning had huge social and political ramifications. In these situations the slave populations had a better diet and even developed an Afro-Caribbean cuisine (Wilkie 1996). Mintz (1996:41) speaks of their fields and their one-pot meals as the "training grounds for freedom." Increased control over food choice activated their taste of freedom.

Such small acts of empowerment in clearly unequal provisioning situations are registered in the French Louisiana plantations, reflecting economic differences in every meal (Scott 2001). Wild and domestic animal bone deposition shows the gradual evolution of two different cuisines in Louisiana. Ingredients provided to slaves were different from those consumed by the owners, as evidenced in the rubbish discarded outside the different cooking areas. We assume that the plantation owners could choose to eat whatever was available from their land and larder, whereas slaves were allocated what the owners did not want, and what the slaves caught themselves. Scott's faunal analysis suggests that slaves sought wild foods from the landscape, gaining diversity and nutrition from the land, at times resulting in a better diet than the landowners'.

We must suspend our own food valuations when studying what these two classes ate in Louisiana. In terms of beef, the French planters ate both high- and low-quality cuts whereas the slaves had access to only low-quality cuts of meat (Scott 2001:688). Based on evidence from the Rich Neck Plantation in Virginia, however, slave quarter middens contained more pork and wild species than the owner's middens (Franklin 2001:100), slaves occasionally gained access to whole animals, indicating that meat provisioning varied across the antebellum world.

Some cuisine histories illustrate the social and economic complexity of food provisioning for the disenfranchised. With self-provisioning, the slave diet included wild game such as opossum (*Didelphimorphia* sp.), squirrel (*Tamiasciurus hudsonicus*), and raccoon (*Procyon lotor*), whereas the British slave owners ate cattle, pig, and other domesticates, with less than 1 percent of their meat coming from wild taxa (Franklin 2001:99). In this North American colonial situation, wild meat consumption reflected lower-class cuisines. However, if these English plantation owners had actually been from the English landed gentry, with their history of privileged access to hunting in English forests, wild meat might have been considered the pinnacle of high status and absolutely forbidden to slaves (Grant 1988). With these different perspectives concerning wild foods existing in a single landscape, we can imagine the dissonant tensions of social memory concerning food traditions tugging at people's actual cuisines. The plantation owners were probably not from the English gentry, as they came from or created a cuisine that did not value wild game. Wild food therefore could have had two completely different meanings in the plantain setting, one of high prestige and one that was disdainful.

The noble English wild food tradition did migrate with some people to the Americas, as seen at early Annapolis. Lev-Tov (1998) compared the consumption of meat from a seventeenth-century middle-class family with that of a contemporaneous landed gentry migrant family. The gentry consumed wild game, whereas the middle-class Annapolis family ate domestic meat (Lev-Tov 1998:137). Meat valuation was in the eye of the beholder in the early North American colonial days.

After emancipation in 1863, Scott (2001) notes, the gentry and the slave cuisines gravitated toward each other, with more meat in both diets. This subsequent shift in provisioning was reflected in the foods consumed as well as in their preparation. The irony here is that the pre-emancipation slave meals and dishes, representing years of scrounging scraps and foraging in the wild, have become the more evocative cuisine of the American South and the Caribbean, especially when compared with the plantation owner's cuisine, which often had a very narrow palette of offerings despite their ostensibly having greater access to ingredients. That cuisine has faded along with their economic and political position.

These examples remind us that culturally dynamic worldviews and rapidly changing situations make interpretation of economic relationships particularly difficult to define via food systems (Lev-Tov 1998). Wild game on the table in a medieval English home represents the most elite of meals, banned for the peasants. Yet the fact that slaves could hunt and eat these very animals meant that a reorientation for some of America's elite emulation of previous high-status food had occurred. While these cuisines reflect the economic history of this time of great inequality, they also illustrate the importance of control over provisioning and the power of the meal (Allen 2002; Mintz 1996).

Despite state-level societies often having centralized economic controls, not every state had control over provisioning. This is most evident in how Mesopotamian cities were fed. By around 3000 BC, the Late Uruk, similar to that of the Chimur of coastal Perú, had been an empire for some years. This stratified polity exhibited complex food provisioning, with evidence of many different food inequalities. Overall, urban food provisioning was quite centrally organized and out of the hands of the individual, especially the staples – bread and beer. The rural producers, on the other hand, had control over staple meat production and even its distribution to the cities.

The urban elite controlled food provisioning in the cities through butchering markets.

Urban residents did not produce their own food. Rural nomadic herders provided meat to the city, mainly goats and sheep, represented in 98 percent of the bone evidence (Zeder 1991). The meat production evidence from the Kur River basin to the east of the Euphrates between 3200 and 1900 BC is fairly detailed. Melinda Zeder (1991) follows the provisioning of meat into the neighboring urban regional center of Tal-e Malyan, which eventually grew to 135 ha. She tracks the provisioning and management of meat over three phases of regional history: the Banesh, Kaftari, and Qaleh phases. As Malyan grew into a craft-producing, trade, and regional administrative center, staple distribution was increasingly regulated, as seen in the centralized meat-processing locales that were in the city.

In her meticulous faunal analysis Zeder identifies three urban provisioning patterns, registered in the meat cuts. Certain high-quality cuts of meat are restricted to public buildings, especially the temples, where special butchers worked on the sacrificial animals for offerings (Zeder 1991:250). In the craft-producing sectors, composed of specialists attached to the state, cost efficiency was more evident in the government meat provisioning, with lesser-quality meat being common. The third strategy was the unattached specialists, the city residents, who seemed to be able to choose meat for themselves. They gained meat from a range of sources, including relatives who brought in meat from the countryside, independent entrepreneurs, as well as the state-controlled centralized administration.

Governmental provisioning is evident, but the state did not control the meat production and distribution completely. Zeder's evidence suggests that the herders were in control of their herding practices, making slaughter and sale decisions themselves, rather than being driven by the urban consumers or dictated by those in political power. This meat was available to anyone who could afford it. Other data support the existence of middlemen between the nomadic herders and Malyan's administration, who regularly negotiated for the government's meat supply. The third meat path into the city was reserved for the religious elite. Specific cattle herds seem to have been kept near the city for the feasts and religious meals. Although some of the meat distribution was controlled by the state, especially that destined for the attached specialists and the temples, the bulk of the production was decentralized, left to the rural residents. The herders seem to have had substantial economic control. The animal frequencies from Malyan changed over time, suggesting that as regional demographic and political relationships shifted, meat sources did as well.

Some distance away, contemporaneous Uruk city residents had less control over their staple grain foods, as registered in the cuneiform texts. Around 3100 BC, one thousand years after this polity's founding, grain production was completely out of individual family's hands, relocated to state farms. This government ran a tight ship when it came to controlling the processing and distribution of grain, their medium of exchange. Uruk had a network of food processors, craftspeople, and religious temple associates, all attached to the state. Each sub-group had different access to the distributed grain. In this Mesopotamian hierarchical society, grain distribution was tied to the social control of people.

The early Sumerian cuneiform tablets document a complex situation of staple production, grain movement, and taxation. Texts provide a glimpse into how provisioning was organized at Uruk (Damerow 1996:151). There seems to have been centralized control over the provisioning once the foodstuffs arrived in the city's bakeries and breweries. Many worked in the state food industry, baking bread and brewing beer. Like the slaves in the English and French colonies, these indentured laborers worked twelve months a year in small workshops. The cuneiform texts discuss these food-processing jobs – not only milling wheat flour, the staple ingredient of the region, but also producing food, bread, and beer, for distribution.

In some of the Uruk clay tablets, Damerow (1996) found that state grain was rationed by rank, demonstrating that economic status determined access to food in Mesopotamian urban life. The tablets record exactly what foodstuffs an individual worker received in a month. Given the surplus of grain produced in this region at this time, it is interesting that some of the earliest tablets describe the rank of individuals by what they ate. In other words, each class was created and maintained through food provisioning; these people ate their economic position.

The slaves' daily pay was very small – under one liter of grain per day (Damerow 1996:164). These people were probably continuously vitamin deficient, unless they had access to other foodstuffs outside the purview of the state. Perhaps they collected or grew food themselves, as did the farmers of Pacatnamu, Perú. This was not recorded in the tablets, nor has such evidence been uncovered yet in the archaeological record. An osteological study would provide important data on the nutritional health of these different Sumerian classes. When food was scarce, did the different food resources actively promote inequalities or were they hidden from discussion? The provisioning of staple grain was increasingly monitored and controlled by the Uruk leaders. Were these differences in food access naturalized into acceptability without discussion? Were there revolts at Uruk over grain access?

More archaeological investigation needs to be done in Iran for us to learn about the likely inter-class tensions of Uruk over provisioning.

## The Moral Economy

Urbanism can develop only with adequate surplus food production to feed the non-farming population. Marx was concerned with the power that the masking of economic differences had on maintaining societal inequalities, specifically when it came to food provisioning. In parallel is the moral economy (Thompson 1971), where lived (unwritten) rules of moral obligations are called upon when these differences get out of hand. Here the "*sense of community* as the sense of the right and the general good that is acquired through living in a community" (Overing 1989:159) operates. Does every community mask their inequalities or try to alter them? Can groups reform their moral economy of the group consciousness and therefore reform their moral worldview? Can we see this in the archaeological record? Bender (1978) and Friedman and Rowlands (1977) suggest that the institution of feasting developed in part to help mask economic differences and encourage disgruntled people to remain within the group, by placating the group's differences and activating their moral commitments, at least periodically. The acceptance of these differences in hierarchical societies is an example of cognitive dissonance. These ideas have been discussed and reformulated many times, forming a core debate in economic and political anthropological and archaeological inquiry.

Although specialized, intensive production is only one part of the equation in the rise and the maintenance of large-scale societies where such scale and complexity allows for the manipulating of power over food access. Archaeological investigations of premodern societies have revealed a range of differences in control, regulation, and organization of food production but also in access.

Economic success has been defined as when people control their own production and distribution of food, clothing, and housing. In contrast, as with the Medieval estates, Uruk, or during the Inka imperial times, certain sectors of society controlled the food resources, which they periodically used to feed the less fortunate, thus keeping people fed (at least minimally) and lessening food insecurity overall, but still having control over food as well as the means of production (Thompson 1971). Is success defined when there is food surplus that can be displayed, shared so that everyone is fed? Or is economic success defined when some sector of society gains food wealth, which they hoard or use as a commodity in wealth finance and sell for other goods, including prestige goods to gain power over the populace, such as the Chimur? Which regime is more successful and/or ethical became a philosophical issue and is at the core of the English eighteenth-century moral economy issues (Thompson 1971), the current Democratic and Republican platforms in the United States, as well as the Tories versus Labour in England. Who has the moral authority to organize labor, to control production, to set pay scales and goods pricing, or to store food and release in times of need? Do the modern (Keynesian) economic strategies successfully feed the population or just manipulate the food resources for selected economic ends? There is no single template that is the model for a successful economic state. Some strategies are accepted over many years; other economic systems involve riot and instability. The definition of economic success in each society is therefore defined by what is acceptable to the group and its moral economy.

Historians document details that archaeologists can only infer concerning the economics of food supplies and access, as seen in the Malyan example. But what archaeologists provide for us is the reality of what happened to food access over the lifetime of a city or a state. Such documentation should not be treated lightly today, as today's governments manipulate these same commodities as Uruk did with grain. Economists and politicians can learn from archaeological food provisioning studies (Davidson 2015).

To conclude this discussion on the economics of food provisioning I turn to the Greek and Roman worlds (spanning approximately 500 BC to AD 300), whose diverse histories are particularly well documented. These Classical societies are considered the foundation of many European cultural practices. What were their food provisioning organizations and how well did they feed their populace? Did their moral policies and on-the-ground political actions create food security or insecurity?

A close read of the historical material demonstrates that food was central to the economic, political, and military activities of these two polities (Garnsey 1999; Sallares 1991). Feeding the populace was a central goal in the Classical moral economy. Production and provisioning were neither steady nor secure in either polity, however, and both polities maintained significant inequalities in access. It is somewhat shocking to learn how whimsical and disorganized food provisioning was in Athens. Grain was the core staple food crop. For several centuries after the Peloponnesian war (431–403 BC), Athens experienced frequent food crises that led to an aggressive expansion of its trading partners and the creation of colonies in grain-producing regions (such as the Black Sea and Egypt). The Romans too conquered many territories expressly to gain productive farmland.

Given that food crises were a regular occurrence throughout both polities, the economic activities that were initiated to gain food security for the urban centers directed these polities' histories.

Production is reflected in what was consumed, for which we have better data. Rome, at its height, ate broadly from the provisioning world, with dried fruit coming from Africa, grain from the east, and much fish and seafood from the west (Apicius 1958). But few members of the urban elite ate from the whole territory – mainly only the Roman city dwellers. Athenians and Attic Greeks ate a more local and humble fare of porridge and barley cakes with wine and olives as their dietary mainstay (Garnsey 1999:120; Garnsey and Morris 1989; Gozzini 1992; Sallares 1991:324; Wilkins 1995).[1]

Greek cuisine was based on a small number of core foods. Four staples were grown and traded around the Mediterranean: cereal grains (barley [Hordeum vulgare L.], durum wheat [Triticum durum Desf.], bread wheat [Triticum aestivum L.], spelt wheat [Triticum spelta L.], rye [Secale cereale L.], oats [Avena sativa L. (1753)], millet [Panicum]), legumes (chickpeas: Cicer arietinum L.; lentils: Lens culinaris Medikus; and broad beans: Vicia faba L.), olives (both fruit and oil; Olea europaea L.), and grapes (Vitus vinefera L.), transported and consumed most often as wine. Although the full range of cereals and pulses was planted across the eastern Mediterranean, throughout most of Greece, barley was the highest yielding and therefore the dominant cereal crop grown, especially in Attica (Garnsey 1988:91, 103). Durum wheat was the only wheat grown in Attica in substantive quantities until much later (Sallares 1991:335). Bread wheat was therefore traded in from the east, primarily from the Black Sea coast. Foodstuffs were dried, pressed, and stored for shipping – even fodder for domestic animals was regularly stored (Hesiod in Garnsey 1988; Galen in Garnsey 1999:40–41). In addition, historians report that Mediterranean people continued to collect and eat wild plants, especially in the spring, with bulbs and roots and of course the ubiquitous honey and herbs (Galen in Garnsey 1999:37). Some of the accessible wild "famine foods" were poisonous in their raw state and needed processing, adding to hunger stress when the Greeks had to resort to these plants. But local, wild foods, such as acorns and chestnuts, have been part of their diet into modern times.

---

[1] Curiously, there is no evidence for barley being made into beer in Classical Greece, which was being done at this time by the Celts to the north as well as the enemies of the Greeks, the Persians, to the northeast. The Greeks participated in cultural exchanges with the wine-growing regions to the north, but beer is a way to diversify one's diet in a grain-rich environment. This again illustrates the "emulatory" significance of cuisine, since they could have made beer but chose not to.

Seafood, fish, and meat were consumed in the more well-to-do homes, not commonly consumed in most homes and could never be considered a staple (Garnsey 1999:16). A typical Greek meal was porridge or soup made from ground cereals and pulses, diluted wine, and griddle-toasted "breads" (called "cakes") made of barley. Cakes made of wheat became common in the later Hellenistic Greek and Roman times.

Athenaeus recounts seventy-two different types of bread made in Greece during the second century AD (Goody 1982:103). These cereal "breads" contained a mixture of plants and were often not finely ground, making them coarse and hard. After the third century, increasingly adding wheat to these cakes made them more like the bread we know today. Cheese would have been a treat, and meat or fish very special, the meat being roasted rather than boiled. Wine was commonly consumed, but always mixed with water (Dietler 1990). Olive oil was also part of the meal. More elegant meals included a sauce, used as a relish to spice up the bland bread and porridge. The notorious Roman gourmand Apicius (1958) stressed the importance of sauces that must accompany every elite dish (see also Gozzini 1992:26). The most famous sauce in the Roman world was *garum*, a strong, fermented fish sauce requiring salt in its production. For the mainland Greeks, it was produced in Attica but also traded in from Spain, Libya, and Asia Minor (Garnsey 1999:16; Gozzini 1992:27; Grocock and Grainger 2006).

The early city-states produced most of their own food (Garnsey 1988:56–59, 1999:30). In both Athens and the early Roman Republic, food was produced on family farms, on small (1–4 ha) plots of land. In good years, these farms yielded a surplus. Except for some later Roman farms, with large slave populations, farms were family-run. Decisions about planting were decentralized and autonomous. Fields were mixed, having both trees and annuals, with animals grazing on the fallow patches. Kitchen gardens and storage were important. Successful olive harvests enabled farmers to store up to four years' supply of oil. Of course, elites and palaces had much larger storage facilities. Over time, fewer Greek family farmers owned their own land with increasing amounts of produce owned by off-site landowners. Landholders (citizens) had strong commitments to the cities, with regular trading ties, obligations, and requirements to sell their produce in urban markets (Gozzini 1992:17).

While famines were rare in Classical times, food crises were common, occurring many times during an individual's life. Drought was a common problem, lowering barley yields and resulting in the bread maslins filled with more field weed seeds than barley (Jones and Halstead 1995).

There are a number of well-reported droughts during Classical times: 428, 392, and 41–36 BC, as well as AD 5–9 (Garnsey 1988:173). Historian Peter Garnsey (1988:39) notes that in addition to these prolonged droughts, on the Greek mainland the barley crop failed on average one year in six, and other crops did not fare better. In Attica, the wheat crop failed one year in four. Even along the Black Sea, where colonies were set up to produce grain, 46 out of 100 years had deficient yields (ibid.:11). Although animals were kept at all farms, they did not often make it to the tables of the humble. The animals were most often taken to market for sale or given to the landowner for rent payments (ibid.:56). Animals were also required sacrifices for rituals such as life-course passages, life crises, and religious ceremonies. Piracy of shipped grain accentuated food stress in the cities, as precious loads were occasionally lost. In essence, food anxiety existed across Classical Greece.

Tactics to avoid food crises included intensifying local food production, hoarding, conquering more productive territory, emigration (colonization), trade, war, and infanticide (Garnsey 1988:69). These food maintenance strategies operated throughout the Greek and Roman world, but they were not adapted universally or systematically, creating a fairly unstable and inequitable food supply. A combination of regular trade and hoarding became central to the moral economy of these worlds.

Few but the largest city-states, such as Rome, were able to conquer and hold onto productive lands, due to the administrative costs of maintaining colonies. Instead, Greek families made contracts with families in other farming areas to gain produce. This included much gifting to guarantee being the first to receive grain, especially during lean years. A common response to Greek food shortages was to intensify trade in prestige goods, as seen also in the Micronesian exchange networks with the use of heirloom shells (Strathern 1971; Weiner 1992). These exchanges encouraged more movement of goods. Salt was the most prominent, *essential* trade item, with metals, tools, honey, and seeds following in importance. Trade partnerships between mainland farming areas and island populations were a common method of minimizing harvest risk and securing steady food supplies as well, mainly benefiting the farmer citizens – that is, the rich. Maintaining these special trading relationships meant that trade, gifting, and gracious hosting was continuous, whether harvests were good or bad, as expressed so clearly by Homer (Sherratt 2004). Most archaeologists focus on trade as a top-down elite strategy for economic gain, as it was for the Classical elite (Junker 2001). But trade and the liberality that it requires was clearly an important, ever-present strategy for all urban dwellers, being an important risk aversion strategy (Brumfiel and Earle 1987; Earle and Ericson 1977; Halstead and O'Shea 1989). Trade in food is more difficult to see in the archaeological record than trade in metal, stone, or ceramics, but foodstuffs were the most common trade items mentioned in the Classical (and Bronze Age) Greek texts as well as found on shipwrecks (Bass 1986; Gibbins 1991).

## Euergetism

Surprisingly, with the exception of this active trading culture, Athens had little in the way of governmental regulations about food supplies. Food distribution was left to the citizens (landholders) along with the responsibility to maintain the urban food supplies and provide protection against scarcity (Garnsey 1988:43). During the democratic era, the senate periodically proposed regulations to ensure access to food for the populace. Any ad hoc attempts at local control evaporated when yields were low; this was when hoarding was most apparent. Political power could not wrest the crops from their owners or gain control of production. The rich landholders decided for themselves when to open their storehouses. Reciprocity between neighbors, families, and farmers helped maintain rural food stability based on personal relationships, but urban food distribution did not occur in as equitable a manner. Landholders owned the grain, which was sold or stored as best benefited their families. In times of food stress, the Classical world mainly appealed to a moral notion of generosity, *euergetism*, to feed the masses.

In Classical Greece, food prices in the cities fluctuated seasonally. Garnsey notes that the leadership rarely stepped in to help with food distribution. During years of poor yields and shortages, political leaders generated rules and decrees meant to open grain stores, but they were not always effective (Garnsey pers. comm.). After a particularly poor harvest, Solon's rule was enacted in the sixth century BC to maximize food availability in Athens by forbidding the export of any food crop except olive oil.[2] Although landholders were not supposed to stockpile or sell locally produced grain elsewhere for higher prices when the food was needed locally, no law specifically required barley and wheat to be distributed to those in need until the fourth century.

According to Garnsey (1988:82), "After the virtual disappearance of democracy by the end of the fourth century BC, *euergetism* was the main

---

[2] This is exactly what occurred with rice in Japan in 2008.

safeguard of the common people of the towns against hunger and starvation." *Euergetism* is the Athenian concept of public generosity by the
rich – public gift giving – but it was triggered in Athens only under social
pressure, and the hoarders usually retained control of the food.[3]

Despite these public moral dicta, elites continued to manipulate the food
supply in urban settings, releasing minimal amounts of grain while attempting to extract higher prices from the vulnerable in the Greek populace. In
these settings, food really did increase inequality, especially in the absence
of a system of access or empowerment. The attempt by the moral economy
to alleviate food insecurity through *euergetics* only worked sporadically.

Eventually, Attic mainland farms were required to pay taxes in kind,
especially under the Roman Empire. The resulting food banks, like the
Inka *qolqa*, supported the government and made the farms less autonomous. Under Roman administration, the state's taxation apparatus fed
city residents through regulatory bodies and taxes. Trade, taxes, and the
asymmetrical relationships between the farmers and the landowners forced
intensification of staple production.

Even this administrative economy of feeding the masses was not stable.
In the later, more centralized, post-Augustinian Roman Empire (after AD
14), Roman citizens received food subsidies erratically, primarily when the
rulers feared rebellion (Garnsey 1988:196, 217). Food stress is indicated in
the osteological evidence from Roman burials, with stress-related Harris
lines ubiquitous in children and nursing women. Additional archaeological and biological anthropological analysis could reveal the periodicity
of the food stress. Although there was no stable, systematic form of food
distribution in the Roman Empire, the food laws did have some political
outcomes. For example, when the Roman magistrate Apollonius of Tyana
arrived at Aspendus on the Ionian coast sometime between AD 14 and 37,
he found a hungry population with only pulses to eat, while the rich owners stockpiled their cereals to export at a better price (Garnsey 1988:76).
"Consequently an excited crowd of all ages had set upon the chief magistrate, and were lighting a fire to burn him alive, although he was cling-
ing to the statues of the Emperor, which were more dreaded at that time
and more inviolable that the Zeus in Olympia" (Philostratus in Garnsey
1988:76). Worried for his life, Apollonius persuaded the hoarders to sell
their food stocks to their neighbors, albeit at high prices. We learn from
such stories that urban people did have problems with food supplies, as the
landowners continued to hoard for their own profit.

---

[3] Note that this word for local, altruistic gift giving has dropped out of our vocabulary today.

With food provisioning never centrally controlled accompanying unreliable yields, it is not surprising that food was the basis for much inequality in Classical times, with only erratic attempts to distribute food supplies. *Euergetics* is a noble concept, but the early Athenian government was not strong enough to make it operational. Even the Romans could not always enact it.

Erratic grain harvests were not the only pressure driving the Greeks to expand their trade and colonize. The Greeks wanted Black Sea wheat because they developed a taste for wheat bread over their lowly barley cakes (Dalby 1996). Throughout Classical times, and especially after 250 BC, Athenians and the greater Attic populace increasingly preferred wheat to the local barley. This was clearly a case of emulation driving economics and politics, as they adopted the cuisine of those who had wheat as their staple core food. The flavor and versatility of the wheat flour drew the elite to wheat-based meals, much as we saw with the northern Celts' interest in wine. Eventually the Greeks transformed this exotic good into a staple food, requiring the regular shipping of wheat to their ports. At first setting up trading partners, they later founded colonies along the Black Sea coast to increase protection and safety during transport. Thus a desire for an elite food led to new regional politics. Food provisioning was the basis of Greek inequality as that society was directly tied to land access, but it also led to colonization.

## In Sum

The moral economy of food is woven throughout this chapter's examples. Food economics operated along many different channels in premodern states. The Greco-Roman, Mesopotamian, Inka, Chimur, American South, and English examples each illustrate different forms of economic inequality and people's reactions, played out in food production and access. In the larger polities we can see how the power of the central authorities affected the daily lives of the residents through food access, scarcity, and security. Sometimes there was insufficient state power over production, as in the case of Attica; other times, too much, as at Uruk. Peter Garnsey suggests that most scholars had not looked for evidence of food crises in Classical Greece because that society created such beautiful works of art and architecture, as well as being successful traders. But food crises occurred regularly, almost every other year! An underlying food anxiety must have been present in the Classical Greek psyche, despite the Greeks' inward-oriented if somewhat disorganized approach to food provisioning. One's family came first, despite the moral calls for generosity affiliated with the concept of *euergetism*. Was *euergetism* operating within the Inka state, as reflected in the increase of maize in local Sausa diets under the Inka regime and the vast *qolqa* storage at every state facility? The *qolqa* system suggests that centralized food production included food support for the needy, as Godelier (1974) proposed.

Food provisioning went hand in hand with conquest and colonialism. Notwithstanding the authoritarian nature of the Inka regime, their strong food-sharing ethic seems to have led to a more stable food supply in some parts of the empire. The populace under the Inka had control over their own food production and provisioning, suggesting stable food access operating at all levels of the hierarchy. The people of Sumer, who had developed a successful urban lifestyle, lived in a state that created and maintained class differences through food rations. The grain allotments led to very real inequalities, again a clear example of food as agent.

Food provisioning can suggest economic inequality. Is it also indicative of other inequalities, such as lack of access to modes of production? Marx proposed that if staple production and provisioning was taken out of the hands of consumers, such as those at Uruk or the early North American slaves, inequalities would rise. Those who had control over most of their food production, such as the fisher folk of Pacatnamu or the farming Sausa, would have had less reason to fetishize their cuisine, even if their diet was different than that of other classes. The fisher folk clearly had control over some of their caught fish, and they acquired prestige goods with that surplus. Slaves who could produce their own food developed their own cuisines. Post-slavery dietary confluences further illustrate how increased equality in food promotes emulation.

The Classical examples of localized, personal control overriding state laws indicate that trade does not always increase food security or access, again demonstrating that food access closely reflects the politics as well as the economics of the time.

Who controls staple finance seems to be the key in these situations. Again, both Marx and Foucault have made this case clearly: having the power to produce and access one's own food, whether at an individual or a community level, results in a more equal society. Even in the Greek case, the citizens of Athens had a taste for the more prestigious wheat and thus redirected their trade, society, and even warfare to secure it. Sugar's legacy demonstrates the power that food has on global economics. Driving down the price of sugar made it affordable to the masses, which in turn increased its trade. We see globalism impacting our own cuisine, such as bananas and oranges grown thousands of miles away having become quotidian foods.

These archaeological and historical examples illustrate how the economic positions of all classes, including slaves and the poor, are reflected in their diet and cuisine. Despite economic differences and restricted access to some foods, taste traditions and even comfort foods develop, as with fry bread and coffee for the Oglala or grits for the Southern slaves. The humble fish and chips in England and the hamburger in the United States are inexpensive meals that have become the icon not only of a class but also of a nation. Although cheap calories often do not constitute a balanced diet, many times these meals transcend economics and gain a special place in a culture's consciousness. In the next chapter we turn to the political side of these interactions – how politics interacts with cuisine – and add another important dimension to thinking about eating.

# CHAPTER 6

# Food Politics: Power and Status

> *Given the diverse and powerful meanings related to the experience of food, it is hardly surprising that food is constantly used in the generation, maintenance, legitimation and deconstruction of authority and power.*
>
> Hamilakis 1999:40

Economic capital is potent because it can be converted into symbolic capital, augmenting one's prestige, honor, and status, which in turn hold great flexibility in bettering one's position in social life (Bourdieu 1977:171–183; Helms 1979). Further, symbolic capital is flexible because prestige and ranked status can often be converted back into economic capital, and always into political capital. The study of food therefore holds great analytical promise for archaeologists who want to study political negotiation. The advantage for archaeologists, as noted in the previous chapter, is having access to the material dimension of these political encounters and how ordinary people dealt with the situations (Dietler 2007). Introducing topics in the study of food requires attention to methodological rigor and new insights into the contextual framing of the practices of access and control. Daily food acts are best understood by studying them over time, as historians Mennell (1985), Drummond and Wilbraham (1994), Garnsey (1988), and others demonstrate, making archaeology a productive avenue for the study of food politics from any time period.

Although economics and politics are intimately intertwined, in this chapter I emphasize the political drives that influence and are influenced by cuisine choice. One of the greatest political differences worldwide is experienced along the gender divide, which I highlight in this chapter. I also turn to the archetypical political meal, the feast, to discuss the spectrum of political implications when performance and signification heighten certain political themes while masking others. Dietler (1990) reminds us that all meals are political, but some, such as the larger feasts, more overtly display control over the decisions of others.

Political differences exist in all human societies. Any time a group of people needs to make a decision, political influences are operating. John Stuart Mill, a liberal eighteenth-century British political economist, wrote that all political differences are initially accepted as natural – as assumed, unspoken conditions of life. These conditions must be made transparent, made discursive to be questioned and reformed. Because of this differential power and potential for control in all groups, we are interested in seeing how food activities participate in the political positioning of people, groups, and governments. Political decisions affect cuisines, not just in high-level decisions on tax and trade but also in daily, interpersonal lives, such as in family gatherings.

Politics participates in food traditions. The news media regularly reports on trade agreements crafted by national governments, forging stronger political friendships through the movement of foodstuffs. We read about the Americanization of other people's foodways and the mixed reaction to these changes (the acceptance of hamburger chains in the Far East at the same time as the rejection of American beef imports by Korea and Japan, for example). The Pizza Hut chain is found throughout England now; a MacDonald's restaurant has opened in the Forbidden City in Beijing (Watson 2005); and Japanese sushi restaurants are ubiquitous across the United States and Europe. These activities reveal the political aspirations of governments that assist these companies to open up new markets, and at the same time aiding and encouraging an interest in exotic prestige goods and status symbols in new markets (Dietler 2007).

In the previous chapter I presented how the desire for wheat helped drive territorial conquests by the Athenians and later by the Romans. The Romans used food to create citizens and classes throughout the empire by exotic ingredients and ornate banquet styles accompanying their conquests (Apicius 1958; Foss 1994; Garnsey 1999; van der Veen 2014). The ten-volume *De re coquinaria* associated with Apicius is a series of gourmand Roman cookbooks written in the late fourth and early fifth centuries AD. They cover a range of delicacies, including rare, expensive ingredients, providing a way for the creator and consumer to make a political statement through their meal. The forty-sixth entry in Apicius' second volume reads: "A Dish of Scallops – Lightly cook scallops or the firm part of oysters. Remove the hard and objectionable parts, mince the meat very fine, mix this with cooked spelt and eggs, season with pepper, shape into croquettes and wrap in caul, fry, underlay a rich fish sauce and serve as a delicious entrée" (Apicius 1958:64). Scallops (marine bivalve mollusk in the family Pectinidae) live in cold water, making this dish possible only for those who have access to boats and divers that can harvest the bivalves and transport them to the gourmand quickly. Gaining political clout through presenting such difficult-to-access ingredients requires substantial economic and political clout.

These elite Roman meals required considerable planning and financial expenditure; transporting food that spoiled quickly to the right venue, amassing ingredients, and taking the time to prepare the meal linked gourmand participants into a web of escalating prestige. Such desires spurred new production, trade, and conquest around the Mediterranean and beyond (Dietler 1999). Roman cookbooks called for the fish paste *garum* in almost every meal, spreading the exotic tastes of the Roman citizenry throughout the empire (Grainger 2006). To be Roman was to eat and drink the Roman way, with certain meals, dish sequences, and ingredients, forming an identity and a political position in the empire (M. Jones 2007). Such an explicitly political desire that linked to the economics of goods was the impetus of the Arab spice trade with Europe after all. We continue this today; when we travel, we want to eat local foods in a new place, to get a sense of the regional "flavor" of the culture, to "taste" the place and people who live there (Wilk 2006).

Changing one's political position can begin with altering one's eating habits. Political goals can lead to reevaluations of daily practices such as styles of eating, dress, comportment, speech, and housing. These play out not just in promotion and eventual acceptance of certain foods, as did growing and eating more maize in the Inka Empire or the ubiquity of fish paste across the Roman Mediterranean, but also in the political aspirations that are implied by newly adopted food traditions. Many have also tried to create new identities through intercultural flow when moving or starting a new job, just as the British elite adopted Roman cuisine and ingredients during the Roman conquest (M. Jones 2007:208) and the Belizeans worked to solidify an identity through a new cuisine (Wilk 1999, 2006).

To unveil political agendas portrayed at meals, food activities can be charted, gaining access to the existing, on-the-ground political situations. Food presentation is a tool for displaying asymmetrical ideologies, as feasts imbue differential power relations. Rules of etiquette dictate access, serving sequences, cuts of meat, ingredient combinations, and presentation, and in so doing imply the ability to act in other domains. The elegance and subtlety of some codes of meal conduct allows differences to be manifested while simultaneously constructing a sense of solidarity when dining together. These dissonant tensions lurk in every meal.

Class is one of the most common delimiters of culinary rules. In England at times, eating deer meat was treasonous. In medieval England, commoners were banned from hunting certain animals that were "owned" by the nobility, such as the king's deer or the queen's sturgeon (Stagg 1979 in Grant 2002:20). Elite classes have often had jurisdiction over specific animals and plants, such as the largest, the first of the season, or difficult-to-acquire food items. These prohibitions ripple throughout the population, creating rebels epitomized by Robin Hood, who became an outlaw by hunting the king's deer to feed starving villagers. In a way, this type of prohibition still exists; it has just been reformulated in our modern, over-extended world with bans on plants and animals that are threatened by extinction, such as whale hunting or the trapping of the highly prized ortolan bunting (*Emberiza hortulana* L. [1758]) in France as they fly south in September (especially Gascony) (watch this hunting on www.youtube.com/watch?v=GG65CecKSNc). Governments make these rules, but the populace must embrace them in order for them to work.

Arjun Appadurai (1981) calls the political discourse that encircles all things linked to eating *gastropolitics*, a useful concept because it invokes the charged meanings underlying all culinary events. Perhaps the most famous example of the political nature of food is the Indian wedding meal's political antics, described by Appadurai (1981). Food can "serve two diametrically opposed semiotic functions. It can serve to indicate and construct social relations characterized by equality, intimacy, or solidarity; and, it can serve to sustain relations characterized by rank, distance, or segmentation" (ibid.:496). Appadurai's political questions addressed by food highlight the powerful political dynamics at a meal, encouraging us to look for their ramifications in the larger society:

> To determine who in the gastro-political arena of a marriage ceremony has opted for what type of role, one has to pay attention to the following kinds of questions. Who is bearing the managerial burden of the purchase, storage, cooking, and serving of the food? Who are in places of priority in the eating space? Who is consigned to the Siberian regions furthest from these honored guests? Who is making real efforts to make others welcome and attending to their gastronomic satisfaction? Who walks up and down the aisles that separate the rows of eaters, coaxing them to eat more and urging the food-servers to be more prodigal, more

efficient, more insistent? Who are the typical targets of such attention? (Appadurai 1981:504)

These questions evoke levels of political discourse that are difficult, but not impossible, to recognize archaeologically. Certain foods and meals accentuate social exclusion. Other meals create cohesion and communal solidarity. Feasts especially can portray both these trajectories simultaneously, enforcing desired social hierarchies as well as reinforcing a sense of egalitarianism and communion (Lev-Tov 1998), all of which are topics of this chapter.

## The Gastropolitics of Daily Life: Gender Status

Along with class, gender is also a common definer of culinary rules. Mary Douglas and her successors remind us that food creates community through the daily enactment of mundane yet potent acts, uniting yet marking individuals as member, "other," or subaltern (Douglas 1966; Visser 1986; Weismantel 1988:18). In this section we follow the political ramifications in food politics as expressed along gender lines, with special regard to gender inequalities elicited in food acts. A great deal of evidence indicates that, throughout history, women have been responsible for most of the food processing. In cross-cultural studies of 185 societies, women completed most food preparation and cooking tasks, performing more than 80 percent of these tasks in any one group (Crown 2000; Murdock and Provost 1973). The only tasks that men tended to dominate in were hunting, butchering, generating fire, and farming (plowing). The importance and value of such activities varies within each society. Through these acts women acquire their own place and enablement, with their productive contributions being linked especially to familial prestige and position as well as training the next generations in these useful skills (Brumfiel 1991; Wiener 1992).

The double standard in gender inequality is especially evident at mealtimes. On the one hand, women are empowered through their control of the meal and its social milieu; on the other hand, we often see their disempowerment manifested in restrictive rules guiding when and what they can consume as well as how they can handle food. Ethnographic evidence provides us with a sensitive view of these negotiations that help us identify gender differences in the past.

One form of interpersonal inequality is materialized through food restrictions. These restrictions can be designated by age, sex, health, or other life situation (pregnancy, couvade, war, puberty). Although all societies have rules for what is edible, by whom, and when, this implicit political strategy becomes explicit when consumption prohibitions are made transparent, especially during status transitions such as coming of age, matrimony, pregnancy, situations of culture contact, or conquest. At these times "normal" foods are often not acceptable and special diets or taboos are enforced (Eichinger Ferro-Luzzi 1980; Kahn 1986; Moss 1993; Politis and Saunders 2002; Simoons 1994; Spielmann 1989:324–335). Such acts of food denial may have many rationales, including ideology and the belief that the foods are maladaptive, powerful, or dangerous (Jones 1977; Politis and Saunders 2002:126).

Can we identify and interpret such food choices in the archaeological record? Gustavo Politis and Nick Saunders (2002) sought confirmation of such associations in their detailed ethnoarchaeological study of Nukak hunters of the Colombian jungle. They provide examples of selective animal bone representation in the middens and link them to beliefs and behavior. The Nukak do not eat deer and tapir because of their beliefs about the human-animal relationships they have with these two creatures. Such ethnocosmology might be useful in our interpretation of the many Amazonian bone assemblages where few or no deer bones are encountered. Deer tibia used to make flutes for initiation rites are acquired by scavenging jaguar kill sites, not by hunting the animals themselves. The very selective deer bone patterns on sites can be related to the sacred association with jaguars and their prey, deer, providing archaeologists with meaningful interpretations of Amazonian faunal patterning.

Polynesians are the archetypical case in the study of food and gender, having originated the English word "taboo," derived from *kapu* or *tapu*. The English term typically does not have the sacred connotation of the original concept, which relates what individuals eat to their political position. Chiefs throughout Polynesia and Micronesia ate large quantities of food, including a great variety of fish, pig, and poi, eventually becoming huge. Their size reflected the well-being of the group. Their food consumption echoed the sacredness of their position. With standing came dietary restrictions. In pre-contact Hawai'i, pelagic fish could only be consumed by chiefs. Political power in this case was reflected in the body of the chief, making their cuisine of daily concern to the people. Politically influenced food selection operated not just for leaders but also in the humblest households. The Hawai'ian *kapu* system regulated everyone's food consumption. Women, for example, were generally not allowed to eat coconuts, pork, or certain varieties of fish and bananas (Daggett 1972; Jones O'Day and Kirch 2003; Kirch pers. comm. 2003).

The female food taboos had more than a nutritive impact; they reinforced the political positions of certain individuals, constantly reenstat-
ing their place within the political hierarchy. These taboos regulated the
female body as well as women's place in society. The prohibitions, while
ostensibly spiritual in origin and certainly naturalized within community
ontologies, perpetuated and naturalized gender inequalities and political
hierarchies, reflected especially in the hearths and ovens that separately
cooked male and female food within every household.

Hawai'i was not the only place where women got less protein than men
did. The Wamira on the coast of Papua New Guinea operate with a cultural logic that highlights female food taboos (Sahlins 1976). Their staple
foods are farmed taro (*Colocasia esculenta* L.), yams (*Dioscorea* spp.),
and pigs (*Sus* spp.). The Wamirians see themselves as innately selfish and
greedy, always desiring more food to eat. Therefore, prescriptions for food
intake and sharing are codified and strictly followed in an attempt to curb
this uncivilized and selfish desire. Public generosity is an important social
value and requires a great deal of secret hoarding. Any food that is visible
must be shared with all present. These actions produce a constant level of
anxiety about how much food can be seen or presented at any meal. The
Wamirian preoccupation with food and hunger has little basis in fact, as
they also have abundant sea resources as well as their farming.

Miriam Kahn (1986, 1988) claims that food is the vehicle through which
the Wamirians control the ambivalent relations between women and men
and manipulate political rivalries among families. These tensions are channeled through this preoccupation with the need to control one's body. Codes
of conduct include a range of food restrictions by status and gender. The
most restrictive food prohibitions are for pregnant and lactating women, who
cannot eat fish or fatty meat. Both men and women state this is because such
slippery food will make the fetus slip out early, reminiscent of the humoral
system described in Chapter 2, wherein greasy food makes the body slippery.

Marek Zvelibil (2000), in his ironically titled "Fat is a feminist issue,"
picks up this same theme in an archaeological study, noting that elder
men in foraging groups tend to support eating rules that restrict women's
access to fat, especially noted in Australian groups (ibid.:213). Along with
the desire for sweet foods, fat is a taste people crave. Why are women being
gastropolitically sidelined in these foraging societies (Moss 1993; Politis
1999:108)? Katherine Spielmann (1989) studied twenty-eight foraging
groups around the world that have different food taboos for women than
for men. Many groups, including the Wamira, restrict meat and especially
fat consumption for women who are menstruating, lactating, or pregnant,

creating longer birth spacing but also long-term, quotidian eating differences between males and females. This restriction seems to be long-lived in some societies, and should be visible in stable isotope indicators.

Mesolithic (9000 BP) diets recorded in the stable isotopes of human bones from the Danube Gorge sites of Vlasac and Lepinski Vir, as well as pre-contact Plains natives, reflect this dietary difference between men and women, recorded in the stable isotope nitrogen levels, as well as generally more food stress evident in females than males (Spielmann 1989, 2002; Zvelibil 2000). Discussed earlier, the Danube Gorge dwellers shifted from a diet based on fish to one based on terrestrial food with the coming of the Neolithic peoples and their lifeways (Bonsall et al. 2004; Borić and Price 2013). In that population, women ate less meat. Was this due to protein taboos, intended to extend birth spacing and lighten women's workload, or did they have more overtly political origins in these groups, with the intent of marginalizing women via their diet? Did the women themselves generate these dietary differences, as they made sure their children were fed first? Is the efficiency hypothesis a sufficient explanation for this difference occurring in groups? I do not think so. Is this long-term female health deficit part of the reason why women might have been particularly interested in domesticated carbohydrate plants at the transition to farming when the crops spread across Europe with farmers (Zvelibil 2000)? Did these non-tabooed foods mean that women could eat more, but only via the carbohydrates?

These gendered food taboos are closely allied to concepts of corporeal power. Kahn (1988) proposes that these taboos, reflecting less than the optimal health practices, are a result of male jealousy of women's innate procreative powers. This suggestion is partially supported by the focus on yam production enacted by Wamiran males, with the men even strutting around the community carrying their largest yams like newborn babies. These differential procreative powers are also being negotiated (and subverted) through food restrictions during a woman's fecund years. This illuminates the bifurcation in gender statuses in which women gain their place from childrearing and control of food practices, whereas Wamira men gain their position from gardening, warfare, and trade. Such long-lived food restrictions clearly make the female body more vulnerable to health issues over a life time, registered in the body and skeleton. The question remains, why do women allow, and in some cases enforce, these food differences that clearly are interconnected with other political domains?

What other explanations can be given for gender-based food taboos? Kahn's explanation for the Wamiran female food taboos is psychological, almost Freudian, highlighting anxieties over differential biological capabilities, whereby men are counteracting their lack of procreative powers by controlling what women eat. Another hypothesis is that food valuation is closely linked to gender, based on who produces the food. In some groups women's work is highly valued; in Andean farming families they control all stored foods (Hastorf 1991), and in the American Southwest they control meal preparation (Crown 2000). Patricia Crown suggests prehistoric Southwestern women had their own path to empowerment and position through increasingly complex food processing and in their cuisines. This contrasts with the Tlingit of the Pacific Northwest, who are foragers and fisher folk. Women's association with low-status shellfish collecting and consumption colors their inferior position within their community (Claasen 1991; Moss 1993:642). In many coastal groups shellfish were regularly consumed, yet they were seen as second-class foods linked to a range of symbolic, physical, and multifaceted status connotations.

Tlingit dietary rules and oral traditions reveal mixed feelings about shellfish. On the one hand, the Tlingit respect and value all foods, and shellfish are abundant and easy to procure. Many women, children, and elders appear to routinely gather shellfish during much of the year. On the other hand, the Tlingit believe that eating shellfish could risk one's physical health, ritual purity, and moral standing. Various members of society were restricted from eating shellfish at certain times in their lives. In general, people were discouraged from eating shellfish because it compromised one's purity and could lead to laziness and poverty (Moss 1993:644).

For the Tlingit, the social meaning of shellfish was that it was impure and thus it was not a high-status foodstuff, certainly not fit for chiefs to eat (Moss 1993). Is this a male conspiracy, or has Madonna Moss, like Miriam Kahn, opened up a political issue of ongoing tensions between the sexes, often resulting in women being politically sidelined through the food with which they were associated with, perhaps on purpose. Is this derived from concepts of brute strength is good and not using/having it is weak, like that often associated with male hunting? What about the poor shellfish: How did they get such a low status? What is problematic with accessible food? Clearly, no one can live on shellfish alone, but no coastal society survived without it. Large shell middens have been found along most coastlines, marking territory and residence longevity. These mounds could have even been status symbols. Why therefore is shellfish demoted to a lesser food?

In Mesolithic England and Denmark, as presented in Chapter 3, shellfish decrease radically as a percentage of the diet once farming arrives. Could this reduction in shellfish consumption be linked to Moss and Claasen's thesis of shellfish being less valued because of the ease of collecting (without skill tracking or fighting), making it less pure because it was associated with women's work, its periodic impurities from red tides, or the relatively little time expended to harvest enough for a meal? Or was it simply because it was not valued as highly as the exotic domesticates that were entering the region? This last idea seems the weakest of all. The Tlingit example would suggest it is not the efficiency of shellfish collecting that gave it lower esteem, but more likely the social value associated with the women who were gathering the shell resources. If so, this example is like the Wamira, a case of males manipulating food values because of what women do. Although health impacts on women living with these gendered food taboos have been discussed in the literature (Spielmann 1989), these differences also speak to differential political status, discursive in the daily meals while having real impacts on women's lives elsewhere, as they attempt to feed themselves and their children.

Food deprivation, fasting, or famine exposes other aspects of food politics. The Wamiran example illustrates how hunger can be manipulated politically through the creation of food anxieties that in turn can encourage certain codes of behavior. Seasons of hunger in the Goodenough Islands of Micronesia, for example, provoke anxiety among the residents (Young 1986). Hunger is a primary symbol of lack of resources and thus becomes a leitmotiv for loss of power. Obsession over food can become a driving political force in a family or a community, perhaps creating the unequal food rules we see in many foraging societies.

As among the Wamira and the Tlingit, the memory of hungry times and starvation can affect the valuation of these "starvation" foods, which is then reflected onto the status of people who are seen to eat those foods. At times such foods can be highly valued, harkening back to "purer" days, as we see today in the revaluation of homegrown food now promoted in Western urban society. Equally, it can signify when there was not enough food and therefore be a signal of poverty. The Tlingit clearly articulated this link between political status and food value, as did the chiefly societies of Polynesia, where hard to catch pelagic fish were reserved for the chief and common, easily gathered food was consumed by the lower classes and slaves. In these class-based societies, differing rules and consumption patterns for the rare and common foods defined and maintained political status. In addition to the food's physical traits, the characteristics of labor and access participated in these valuation schemes.[1] Such class and gender

---

[1] That cheap food (fast food) is typically lower-class food is a familiar adage in today's Western culinary traditions, but this is actually the opposite of how classic economic

schemes operated in many past societies and can be sought within the archaeological data.

How do women negotiate situations in which such practices of unequal access operate? In societies that place women in subaltern positions, are there ways for them to reclaim some power through their food practices? Can they have their own webs of social power that are generally invisible to outsiders? Can food be a weapon of the weak as well as a weapon of the dominant? Yes. We have several examples from historic analyses of women and food that reflect this possibility. Food definitely operated as a political weapon of the weak in the European Middle Ages. Women's status in late medieval European society was not unlike that of the foragers just discussed. Their lives were not their own; they lived as their fathers (and their husbands) dictated. One of the core foci in both family life and religious sainthood for these women was their food intake. The feminist historian Caroline Bynum (1987, 1997) points out that famine was on the increase during the thirteenth and fourteenth centuries in Europe. Due to this ubiquitous threat of starvation, access to food was correlated with political status and religion.

Medieval Christian religious behavior was obsessed with food, linking holiness to deprivation. By regularly doing without food, people prepared for future famines and lessened the potential for food riots when yields were down, as had occurred in the Roman world (Bynum 1997:139; also see Chapters 3 and 5). Holy day fasts and seasons of fasting were essential activities for all "good" (practicing) Christians. The focus was on consuming the body and blood of Christ, embodying and incorporating his saintliness and associated dogmas. Food consumption was a symbol of spirituality, both in Eucharistic 'feasting' and in austere fasting (Arnott 1991a, 1991b).

Food was the primary entrée to empowerment and political power for women in those times. "Food was not merely a resource women controlled; it was *the* resource women controlled" (emphasis in the original; Bynum 1997:146). Sigrid Arnott (1990) illustrates this through the life of a fifteenth-century woman, Margery Kempe of Bishop's Lynn, Norfolk, England. After a complex and controversial life, Kempe (2001) wrote about her married and spiritual life in the first English autobiography ever written, *The*

models define it. Their optimization models, used in processual archaeological studies, assume that people will attempt to gather or farm the least-expensive foods or the most easily acquired foods, only moving to the more-expensive ingredients when the less-expensive ones are exhausted. These political food examples should be a cautionary tale when applying such models, as we consider our interpretations of past food choice valuations, let alone when reflecting on the past in general [Cobb 2005].

*Book of Margery Kempe*, a carefully constructed social and political commentary of life in the 1400s. During her marriage to John Kempe she felt
increasingly enslaved by worldly things, including the "sexual favors" she
had to give her husband. After fourteen children, she activated the only
power in her possession and stopped eating with her husband. Arnott (1990,
1991a) suggests that Margery stopped eating because it was the only domain
in which she could make decisions about her life. Kempe wrote that John
considered her decision to be unacceptable because it jeopardized his
political standing in the community. They negotiated. Kempe's husband
allowed her to remain "chaste" on the condition that she ate with him
and paid his monetary debts! Margery accepted this deal. Sex and food
abstinence, especially from meat, is a tradition of medieval Christianity,
encouraged for all devout people but particularly powerful for female
saints during that time (Arnott 1991b).

Eating can be used to gain control over oneself and others, through
controlling food intake as well as giving food away (Bynum 1997:139). For
European women, control over consumption was a significant domain of
women's political actions between the thirteenth and sixteenth centuries.
Fasting was the way to saintliness, as is illustrated in the lives of ascetic
women and men. Through abstaining from all but the Eucharistic blood
and body of Christ, women felt closer to Jesus (Bynum 1987). The increase
in female saints during these centuries, some with quite overt mystical
leanings, suggests that this was one of the few paths to gain political independence within Christian church doctrines of the time (Arnott 1991a).
Within Christian norms, many of these women became renowned because
of their devotional fasting, visions, and practice of feeding others. Some of
these women were actually quite controversial, if not heretical. Because
they experienced direct visitations from Jesus, they said they no longer
needed priests and the church to receive communion. This was the case
for Lidwina from The Netherlands (Bynum 1997:143–145). While bedrid-
den with a broken rib she had received during ice-skating, Lidwina shed
skin, bones, and parts of her intestines while fasting, with no ill effects to
her health, eating only consecrated Eucharist. She was said to have healing
powers, as many came to visit her during her fifty-three years of life in bed.

These fasting women herald the reformation. In the 1400s, this was radical stuff, gaining a direct link to God through their focus on holy incorporation. Through their actions these women influenced not only their families
but also their society. Yet, these women lived in a circumscribed world.
Their food consumption was the fulcrum of their empowerment. By gravi-
tating to the corporeal and mystical extremes of Christianity, they gained

greater embodiment and even some political power as others recognized their actions. By abstaining from food, women's bodies could change – not only getting thinner but also diminishing their fertility. Arnott (1991b) makes a strong case that food abstention occurred not only among saints and in convents but also in households, where wives and marriageable girls tried to control their lives by controlling their food intake.

Catherine of Siena is perhaps the most renowned subaltern woman who used food to improve her political position in society, where she used starvation to lead to sainthood. Arnott (1991b) discussed her sainthood in the political context of the day. Her rich Sienese family was grooming Catherine for marriage, but being religious, she maintained early on that she was already married to Jesus. Catherine used the only legitimate means of power she had at the time – she starved herself to make herself unattractive to suitors. Holy fasting was a legitimate sacred act accepted by the society at large. When she began having associated visions, her family allowed her to move into a convent.

For women with little power over their lives, this was their only route to control within Christian mores. These women essentially trumped the clergy at their own sanctity status game. In that world, fasting woman became connected to Jesus through mutual suffering, using such phrases as "tasting the food of patience … pain is the refreshment … and the sighs are its food" (Bynum 1997:144). So constrained was their world that they had to suffer to have power.

These women tread a fine line between empowerment and burning at the stake. Popular support was required for them to be considered holy yet not be labeled as a heretic since they threatened the church doctrine of intercession. These young women found their political agency within a very limited domain by controlling food intake, an example of feminist politics lived very much through the body.

Providing faces and stories to complement Appadurai's Tamil wedding feasts and Bourdieu's Berber women's work, Weismantel's (1989, 1991) subtle interpretation of the rules of consumption operating within Ecuadorian family food culture demonstrates how gender politics are active in family meals. Unlike the Wamiran women of Papua New Guinea, Weismantel shows that women's agency can cut both ways, being circumscribed as well as activating empowerment. The farming families of Zumbagua, Ecuador, plant a range of Andean and Middle Eastern crops, primarily for their own consumption. With wages earned by family members away from the village, they also purchase foreign foods such as bread, rice, and noodles (Weismantel 1991). Despite a range of food options, all ingredients are usually prepared traditionally, whether as a formal hot meal of soup or gruel, a plate of potatoes and meat, or snacks of grains, beans, or potatoes. The men oversee the planting and harvest, but the women control the larder and food distribution (Hastorf 1991). Their power lies in cooking and distributing the daily meal. The humblest of daily meals contains agency and politics.

In Zumbagua, etiquette is highly valued. Even the simplest meal has strict codes of conduct for seating and serving: elders before youth, men before women, soup before drinks, and so forth (Weismantel 1988). "Decisions regarding this order belong to the woman doing the serving, normally the senior woman of the house. She herself merely ladles the food into bowls, remaining seated by the fire, while a child or younger women does the actual serving. But it is the woman at the hearth, as she hands over the bowl, who indicates to whom it will be served" (Weismantel 1988:179). This senior cook has an arsenal of behaviors she can use to manipulate the social scene of the family and guests. Her first tool is the size, quality, and design of the eating utensils. Bowls and spoons are handed out in order based on the rank of the people who are eating, while all watch and quietly accept their positions as dictated by their utensils. The differences allow status to be expressed, with the woman's favorites receiving newer or more ornate bowls and those in disfavor receiving smaller or older ones. The second tool is the contents of the bowl. The meal is constructed around soup, but different portions of meat and potatoes can be added to the broth while serving. The contents are carefully constructed, with specific quantities of each ingredient designed for each person (Weismantel 1988:180). This activity is done with care and thought. Each proffered foodstuff has social meaning, with the relationship between the servers and the served indicated by chunks of meat, potatoes, and beans. Important in this act is the agency of the gift. It is a grave offense to refuse any food that is offered at these meals, especially seconds. Even the simplest of meals recursively creates the shifting daily family politics.

Meals are the place of daily practice where women express opinions on current issues within the family and men let off steam, grumbling about the timing and content of the meal. A close reading of a meal can communicate the current status of family relations. One particular example displays the subtle levels of negotiation that occur within the realms of gender gastropolitics (Weismantel 1988:181). A young couple had gone to a village festival, but the woman, with two small, sleepy children, had tired of the event and wanted to return home with the children. The husband thought she was being ill tempered and went off with his friends. The woman walked home with great difficulty, carrying both sleeping children.

When her husband arrived home many hours later, drunk and sleepy and ready for bed, she informed him that he must be very hungry; as an obedient wife, she had prepared a nice dinner for him. Almost unconscious, he forced himself to sit upright long enough to eat two enormous bowls of soup under her reproachful eyes. The meal over, he crept off to bed, but his ordeal had only begun. The next day found him in an extremely delicate physical state, such that the three very substantial meals she prepared for him, which he dutifully consumed, resulted in several hasty exits from the kitchen to the bushes outside. She appeared to enjoy cooking for him very much that day, smugly playing the virtuous wife in front of her in-laws, who watched with some amusement and did not interfere. (Weismantel 1988:181)

We see the woman's hearth power at work here, as she uses the food rules to her advantage in this marital negotiation.

My 1991 article approached this issue of women and men's political positions in the family and society prehistorically via their diets. With the help of a geochemist, I applied stable isotope data to subfloor burials in highland Andean domestic architectural contexts from the pre-Inka, Late Intermediate (Wanka II) and from after the Inka conquest (Wanka III) in the same settlements. In brief, when the communities were independent, living in large hilltop clusters, everyone we studied – men and women, young and old – ate more or less the same diet, a mix of meat and domestic plants with a smattering of maize, but mainly potatoes and other tubers. As presented in Chapter 5, after the Inka conquered the region, people were required to complete a range of tasks for the Inka, including working in the state fields in the valley where maize was the focus, as well as young men forced to leave home for military service. What the stable isotope data told us about the impact of the Inka state on the family as well as gender relations had several facets. First, everyone ate more maize during the Inka phase; either they received maize from the Inka or they planted more themselves (it is not clear how much impact the state had in family production decisions). The more radical change was that a proportion of the local men had clearly consumed much more maize than the average resident. My conclusion was that these men had been sent off to work for the Inka, and during that time they received the state diet of meat and maize in the form of both food and drink. To me it clearly demonstrated the effect of the Inka Empire's political ideology on the lives of those under its jurisdiction. We could see the overarching Inka influence around the hearth, with the communities' dietary shift to more maize in their stews and tumblers. If that is not gastropolitics, I don't know what is.

Although a range of models has been proposed to explain how gendered differences develop within societies, rooted in the desire for political control over others. Two extremes are in the Hawai'ian and the European examples discussed in this chapter: overeating by certain males and undereating by some females. Both practices display an overt sense of creating political difference while acting within the food rules of their cultural worlds. This is agency at work. Can we approach gastropolitical meals archaeologically as we have approached them in history and ethnography? With the last example in this section I show that we can. It is difficult to identify individual meals and their settings in the archaeological record, such as an Indian wedding feast, a hung-over Ecuadorian husband, or the fasting women of Europe, except in rare circumstances of actual meals being uncovered (as at Antelope House, described in Chapter 3). But we can learn about small-scale gastropolitical events by studying the consumption setting in its historical context, using multiple data sets and bringing a range of data to bear on the politics of food. To continue on this journey, we turn to the most overt political meal of all, the feast.

## The Feast

When people think of a political meal, they usually turn to feasts. Feasts iconically manifest the political nature of a meal, making the non-discursive discursive. Feasts emphasize hierarchy through scale, serving sequence, plate content, and eating behavior, while ostensibly emphasizing communality during the event (Appadurai 1981:507; Douglas 1966; Lévi-Strauss 1966; Mennell 1985). These meals tell of long-lived food traditions, of the ingredients' valuations, of presentation to enhance memory, and of distinct groups identified through their different eating habits. They are polysemic, with the capacity to "unite and divide at the same time" (Dietler 2001:77).

Feasts have become a popular topic in archaeological discourse, as seen by the 2002 and 2003 plenary sessions at the Society for American Archaeology meetings and in numerous symposia and books in England, Germany, Greece, and Italy. Michael Dietler and Brian Hayden (2001a) promoted the importance of feasting in archaeological interpretation, placing meals prominently within political, economic, and ritual research. In their introduction, Dietler and Hayden ask whether a theory of feasting is possible. Their answer is yes, and it is central to an understanding of past political life, especially holding sway at the scale of households and communities (Dietler and Hayden 2001b:2). The study of past political economy, therefore, requires the study of feasts.

What is political about feasts? Although discarded leftovers provide archaeologists with evidence of meals, we usually see these past repasts through the tools that made them. The contexts, equipment, and settings can clarify the political goals of the meal. Their larger scale makes feasts more visible in the archaeological record. The potential to identify individual feasts or feasting traditions enables archaeologists to investigate the past on a smaller, more human scale through specific political events (e.g., Hendon 2000) rather than the broad sweep of societal change that usually is addressed in political studies (e.g., Wright 1977). It is this scale of the feast that helps us trace the negotiation of influence and authority, inspiring linking arguments between the largest political themes and daily domestic practices. "It is important to attempt to understand the practices by which individuals create, maintain and contest positions of power and authority within systems structured in these ways and, in pursuit of their conflicting interests, transform the structures of the systems themselves" (Dietler 2001:66).

Feasts can accomplish many goals, including increasing group solidarity, payment of debts, collection of tribute, recalling past glories, amassing labor surplus, promoting prestige, displaying opulence, soliciting allies, frightening enemies, equilibrating and exchanging valuables, seeking marriage partners, celebrating a life passage, arbitrating disputes, maintaining social control, making peace, instigating war, communicating with the deities, and honoring the dead (Dietler 2001:69; Rappaport 1968). Knowledge of these more specific goals can help direct our search for the links between culinary styles and political agendas. We hope that feast data can inform about past political negotiations.

Feasts are the material manifestation of political action. They are political because of the impact public food sharing and performance has on interpersonal and interfamilial relations, stoking gossip and discussion (Dietler 2001:71). Food and drink are the media that embody hospitality, largesse, and society as they harness real goods and labor, with the material control of decision making lurking throughout the event. They inculcate obligation, status, and competition. When there is more than one person at a meal, there is political intrigue (Appadurai 1981; Dietler 1996, 1999; Dietler and Hayden 2001; Hayden and Villeneuve, 2011; Wiessner and Schiefenhövel 1996).

Dietler and Hayden (2001b:3) define a feast as communal consumption of food and/or drink in an unusual event that bombards the senses. Other scholars add a more political edge to a feast, suggesting that feasts must include larger, supra-familial groups that honor someone or something while gaining prestige (Friedman and Rowlands 1978; Weismantel 1988). Each feast says something about the politics of the participants, their internal relations, levels of stratification, power dynamics, and concepts of sharing.

Feasts are performances that require unusual planning and preparation before the event, commentary and corporeal reactions during, and interpretation and deconstruction afterwards. Feasts often include explicit performances of singing, storytelling, toasting, music, and dancing. Musicians and jugglers were at ancient Chinese feasts (Ying-shih Yü 1977). In Amazonian feasts, participants share dances, myths, and ancestral stories and songs (Guss 1989). Political ramifications influence every stage of the event. Foodstuffs must be gathered, purchased, and stored, requiring the calling in of past obligations and the sale of surplus to acquire specific foods. Ingredients must be prepared by knowledgeable people who are willing to cook for the host. People who willingly consume become indebted to the host for future requests. All the tensions of gifting and obligation come to the fore at these events.

Dietler (2001:67) makes the case that there is always a ritual component to a feast, in that a known protocol with signified meanings and symbols is followed that differs from everyday activities. A feast is full of symbolic inequalities that hold both ambivalence and desire. The anxiety perhaps is due to the acknowledgment of ornate codes of behavior to be performed correctly as people are especially sensitive to being offended at these events. Special seating arrangements, food presentation, etiquette, sufficient and often unusual utensils, and appropriate mood setting all mark its distinctiveness, as well as the hope for political outcomes. People also feast with the deities and the dead. There are many examples, both past and present, of food offerings, including feasts conducted at shrines, sanctuaries, and temples (Fox 2012; Pollock 2012).

Essential to the experience are the heightened sensual and physical effects, impressive at the time but also in the memory. One does not just gain a full stomach at a feast; pleasurable sensations include heightened serotonin and glucose levels from the food, emotional transformation from the drink, and bodily pleasure from odors, views, touch, talk, music, and even sex. All of these promote synesthesia, an overloading of the senses: of sound, of taste, and of touch (Weismantel 2004). This haptic excess of sensual pleasure makes feasts stand out in our memories. Many people mark the past by the feasts they have attended. It is little wonder that people try to harness this sensual potency of a feast to political ends (Hamilakis 2002, 2004).

Rapapport (1968) found that feasts are the central cog in the political world of alliance building and warfare for the Papua New Guinean farmers and herders. It can take up to twenty years to prepare for one feast. Pigs are usually eaten only at feasts, making their maintenance not just surplus production but part of the political economy. Much energy and discussion revolves around the pig herd. Females raise the animals to be cashed in during marriage exchanges or as food gifts at feasts. Because of the pigs' great symbolic and economic value, the presentation of butchered pork at a feast straddles a thin line between amicable food sharing with one's friends and family in a gesture of largesse and the social one-upmanship and aggressive shaming of one's enemies through overfeeding and gifting (Young 1971). After Australian colonization of the Micronesian Goodenough Islands, internecine warfare was banned, and Michael Young describes how feasting then became the nexus for intercommunity prestige manipulation. Young shows that the male family heads began to display their surplus yields next to their homes, like fancy cars parked in Los Angeles driveways. Their neighbors are invited to a feast at which the hosts increase their fame by proffering food that exceeds what they received at a previous feast hosted by their neighbors. In this rich ethnography of shaming, status, and overt competition we note how feasting becomes a composite sociopolitical act that is embedded in their political culture.

Feasts occur within political contexts. Hayden (1996:128–129, 2001:38) and Dietler (1996, 2001:67–88) define feast types, each describing different political agendas, framing feasts around unequal status positions. Although I find the categories problematic for a number of reasons, because these terms are being applied throughout the literature, I will present their arguments here as I discuss four feast types. Importantly, these broad, stereotypic categories must be honed and redefined for each situation. Feasts range across a socially charged spectrum that can be identified archaeologically by the scale and diversity of cooked food, the range and size of the presentation technology, and also by their venue, the place of preparation, and their presentation and deposition (Hayden and Villeneuve 2011). Are these feast "types" materially distinct, and if so, how would we identify them in the archaeological record?

## Celebratory Feasts

The first type of feast is the celebratory, solidarity forming, empowering, minimally distinctive feast (Dietler's [2001] "entrepreneurial feast"). These meals have the least overt political agenda of their feast categories. Hayden's

(1996:128) celebratory feast is a gathering among equals. Although political maneuvering is not the explicit reason for the feast, "certain forms of symbolic capital" can be manipulated (Dietler 2001:76). In societies without hereditary status distinctions, hosting is the main way to gain or maintain any position of authority (Atkinson 1987; Dietler 2001:78). Memory can be important in such arenas, where equals come together, reminiscing over past get-togethers. The meal often remains potent by calling to mind past feasting events and the people who were present (Twiss 2012a). Wedding feasts, work feasts, and harvest festivals fit in this category, bringing communities of people together at periodic intervals. A small U.S. town's annual Fourth of July barbeque picnic manifests this genre; once people are sated, the mayor and other politicians give promotional speeches about the community, unifying the group while positioning themselves as the successful voice of the community.

Community feasts can be highly ritualized and structured in format, as at a barbeque picnic or wedding reception, each with their own material layout and sequence of events. In Chiripa, Bolivia, where I have worked for some years, the community hosts an annual feast to honor their schoolteachers. The residents responsible for the event rotate every year, but the food ingredients, the mode of preparation, and the rituals surrounding the honoring remain the same (this meal is illustrated on the front cover of this book). The teachers are clearly different from the community residents; each has a specific role, and they stick to it, repeating similar speeches every year. There are reciprocal aid feasts as well, which are work party feasts among people of approximately equal social standing, as when two families exchange harvest help, with the hosting family providing the cooked meal during the work day. These are called *ayni* in the Quechua language.

## Potluck Feasts

Potluck meals are not exactly as Dietler and Hayden define their solidarity feast, but they are similar to this politically covert feast category. Potluck meals are truly a feast among equals in which each participant brings a dish to share, in an ambience of equality. These meals can be very humble or large and abundant, giving the aura of a feast, with many different dishes. They tend to be meals shared by a group of self-identified members, but even these carry the potential for competition, as cooks quietly or not so quietly try to outdo each other by providing the best dish on the table. Potluck meals are inscribed with a sense of communality and democracy, being a meal that reaffirms membership through equal participation.

These meals are not usually considered highly charged political venues because they are associated with community building and integration, actively papering over any differences within the group. Can we draw any conclusions about their material composition? Archaeology does best with comparisons. These potluck get-togethers can be more diverse than other types of feasts, with a wide range of cooking and presentation equipment.

These meals can appear materially diverse, with various vessels that originate from different sources. The food might include many species, with many different preparation techniques. The utensils will probably be numerous and disorganized but may be similar; all of these traits will be familiar to those who have experienced a plethora of casserole dishes at Minnesota church potlucks (Blinman 1989; Johannessen 1993; Potter 2000).

Spatially, the general lack of organization or planned deposition could reflect the egalitarian nature of the meal, especially when compared with orchestrated feasts. These feasts may occur in specific locales, however, as can be seen in the Mississippian civic plazas discussed later in the chapter. Archaeologists Eric Blinman (1989) as well as James Potter and Scott Ortman (2004) study this feast type through analysis of ceramics across room blocks in the American Southwest. They suggest their data shows evidence of leveling within the small-scale farming communities. Blinman uses the differential distribution of cooking jar sizes in several feasting locales to identify communal feasting. Mixed vessel sizes found in what are labeled as feasting deposits suggest decentralized organization of meals, like the potluck meals of today.

These feasts afford a place to communicate a range of social relationships in small groups, from encouraging social cohesion to rectifying local disagreements. Archaeologists tend to identify potluck feasts when they encounter single-event mixed material associated with lower-status food remains (Blinman 1989). But archaeologists also have interpreted diversity of species and vessels at a meal dump as elite and elegant, when that diversity might just be communal. These labels must have accompanying data to support their interpretation.

## Alliance Building Feasts

The second Dietler and Hayden feast category has various names in the literature: patron-client, patron-role, promotional/alliance, and commensal feast. I choose the term *alliance building* for this feasting situation. These events emphasize the formal hospitality provided by those of superior status (Dietler 2001:82; Hayden 2001:55). Dietler's patron-client feast is similar to Hayden's

(1996:128–9) "commensal feast." These gatherings have an overt political
tinge and reflect asymmetrical positions. Reciprocation is not expected and
subordination and political and/or economic debt are renewed with each
feast. Generosity and gracious hospitality are important characteristics for the
host, as in the "good feasts" described in Homer's *Odyssey*, although they can
also carry dangerous outcomes (Bakker 2013:43; Fox 2012:101). Those Bronze
Age Greek feasts could get out of hand, but a good feast – that is, a proper
feast – is thoughtful, courteous, and fulfilling. Derrida (1999) discusses the
importance of hospitality and therefore of power and sovereignty. Pollock
(2012) attributes a top-down agency to these events, as the hosts are actively
gaining prestige from the attendees, and although feasts can be reciprocal
affairs, they often are not. Some level of exclusivity is always manifested.
Sallaberger (2012) calls this "vertical solidarity." These feasts may include
specialized equipment, which archaeologists often use to identify feasting,
such as the Vix krater found in a Celtic French grave.

An iconic example of an alliance-building feast is the potlatch feast of
the Pacific Northwest, where years of planning go into multi-day feast giveaways (Codere 1950). These targeted, large-scale meals gain their status
from an extravagant sequence of performances in honor of a specific cultural moment; celebrating births, puberty, weddings, funerals, or honoring the deceased. These events become a locus of prestige performance
through the presentation and sharing of large amounts of food and gifts,
supplied and prepared by the organizers' centrifugally gained resources.
The food ceremonies are elaborately prepared, drawing on resources well
beyond a single household. These feasts have an authorship that redefines
the host's position.

Serving vessels specifically made for these potlatch meals are highly decorated and especially large (Figure 6.1). These feasting bowls and spoons
are only used once every ten to fifteen years. Additional vessels are borrowed
from kin and friends, forming a potpourri of preparation vessels alongside
the specialized feasting presentation vessels (something to consider when
we consider Blinman's identification of the material remains of potlucks).
These meals are memorialized in their dramatic performances, the special
ingredients, and the rarely used presentation vessels. Their overt political
goal is to reaffirm or enhance the status of the hosting family, which aims
to host a distinctive, long-remembered event. The abundant giveaway leads
to a political repositioning of families and kin groups as debt and obligation
tilt to the receivers. These events ripple through the society for many years.

Hayden's term "commensal feast" hides these overt inequalities, although
he sees four domains at work: economic, redistributive, competitive, and the

FIGURE 6.1. Image of a Kwakwaka'wakw potlatch vessel from British Columbia, 80 by 70 cm
(Copyright © Phoebe A. Hearst Museum of Anthropology and the Regents of the University of California (cat. 2-19569))

essence - indebtedness. He stresses that the food gifts are really loans that the attendees know will have to be repaid with interest at another feast, through labor or in kind.

This indebtedness means that alliance feasts are common political devices used to firm up insecure positions and weave people together. While not hiding real differences, these feasts can veil status differences, allowing the indebted participants to act less trapped in their situation, and thus mute the cognitive dissonance of their unequal political relations (Wiessner 1996). These feast settings have a seductive quality, luring people into debt. The Austro-Hungarian Empire used dancing and drinking feasts to recruit soldiers. Once the men had begun drinking, the music would start. Any young man who joined in the dance was obliged to serve in the cavalry.

Kristina Kelertas (1997) claims that alliance-building feasts helped create and maintain Bronze Age chiefly families in northwestern Danish Jutland. From a detailed study at multiple sites in the Thy region she was able to reconstruct changing land use patterns involving cereal production and animal herding. She found that agricultural practices intensified at the end of the Late Neolithic and into the Early Bronze Age, with more cattle and field crop focus, specifically seeing denser fodder and wheat evidence. The archaeobotanical patterning suggests that the elite Bronze Age residences stored the bulk of the bread wheat, a highly valued crop new to the region. Access to wheat bread would have empowered these families at such feasts.

With data from a series of excavated houses she surmised that the local leaders initiated feasts to recruit labor for the more intensive farming needed to produce the surplus. In addition to feeding the workers, some of this surplus production was siphoned off for trade. Kelertas says these feasts developed out of the solidarity feasts that had been used to consolidate allegiances, spiraling into increasing inequality, which allowed the elite to extract more labor and eventually tribute as new goods and produce circulated in the region. For Kelertas the feast was the crucial act that enabled the concentration of power to emerge out of a more equal social network, accompanied by production intensification.

These first three feasting categories – celebratory, community, and alliance building – are not easily identified in the archaeological record, which makes the application of these labels problematic. Status differences may be seen in special, elite serving equipment or ingredients, yet these, like the accompanying rituals, are fluid and contextual, making blanket statements about the actual power differences activated at a feast difficult to pinpoint. In fact, the first type, the celebratory feast, has the potential to morph into the third type, the alliance-building feast (Atkinson 1987). The ethnographic literature provides many such examples.

Not only can a feast situation shift from one type of power dynamic to another, but also different feasting agendas can operate simultaneously at the same event. Participants often arrive with conflicting views about their position, and because feasts are fluid, held together by perspective, talk, and participation, different outcomes can be claimed for the same event (Hastorf 1959). Warren DeBoer (2001) engagingly shows how an Amazonian Conibo-Shipibo feast to honor young women's initiation rites escalated after several days into a concatenation of verbal aggression and drunken competition. In fact, there are many ethnographic and historical examples of attacks and even deaths at "alliance building" wedding feasts. Feasts are nexuses for the expression of political and social tensions as memories of past wrongs are brought to the fore once alcohol has begun to flow (Bakker 2013). After the first day of congeniality and pleasantries, the Conibo-Shipibo guests increasingly became hostile to the host community members, with fights breaking out and insults hurled. How these fights conclude determines the near future of regional political relations. This "festive revolution" attribute to feasts demonstrates how feasts can be a microcosm of the larger political situation. Even if these feasting categories may not have clear definitions with workable linking arguments in archaeological analysis, they guide us toward recognizing general political situations.

*Competitive Feasts*

The fourth category is the competitive, value-laden, or display feast. This type is more overt and more materially recognizable. Called "tournaments of value" by Appadurai (1986:21), "diacritical" by Dietler (1996:98–99), and *competitive* here, these meals are designed to promote status differences through differential access to ingredients and cuisines for select clientele, separating those who attend from those who do not (Dietler 2001:85; Hayden 1996:129, 2001:57). Exclusivity, taste, selective embodied practices, and manicured style actively craft specialized, high-status food manners, comportment, and cuisines, like Edwardian elite dinners (Bourdieu 1984; Goody 1982; Mennell 1985). Stylistic competition is active; emulation and sensitivity to style are mimicry tactics that drive the interaction dynamics. These feasts require unique, even remarkable items of rare, exotic, or new food ingredients and recipes, extra courses, or large quantities. Specialized gourmands are often involved in planning, preparation, and serving. Tantalizing, remarkable dishes are sought. Very expensive or even tabooed foods become edible in these situations. Appropriate taste and manners for these feasts must be learned because these meals have highly developed stylistic requirements and food rules. The ingredients, dishes, and actions reify political differences that are already operating in the larger society. While all feasts create differences, these diacritical, competitive feasts overtly display the differences among the elite since the hosts know all are judging their content and presentation.

Most archaeological feasting studies discuss these competitive feasts; exotic foods and unusual or very standardized utensils render them especially visible and allow the archaeologist to identify traces of the feast. Archaeologists tend to look for such unusual differences and hope that status-changing events were being registered in the past. Dietler (1990) compares the Hallstatt Iron Age competitive feast with the Rhône Valley Iron Age patron-client (alliance) feast to highlight their differing political trajectories. The Hallstatt leaders are believed to have held competitive feasts based on their use of noticeably foreign (Hellenistic) vessels and wine. Through the importation of costly, exotic goods hosts were trying to elevate their political standing by making these events out of the ordinary. Over time these Celtic leaders shifted from presenting beer in caldrons to imported wine in foreign metal vessels, re-choreographing the serving of the meal to carry more awe (Arnold 1999). While the Celts valued these events highly, the Greek traders thought these Gallic drinking feasts were barbaric, illustrating the contextual nature of feasts in specific groups

(Sallares 1991). To the south, in the Rhône Valley, feasts did not incorporate foreign artifacts, only wine, which they also seemed to lay on with gusto, suggesting to Dietler that these feasts exhibited less cost output and therefore less overt political pressure by the hosts. Can more cost and effort be equated with more political leverage in such presentations? This is something we need to think about.

Dietler (2001:70) notes that feasts are symbolically marked as being different from daily meals, which is a firm place to begin looking for evidence of feasting in the past, especially in prehistoric settings. Dietler and Hayden's (2001b) definitions of different types of feasts provided a starting place for archaeologists to structure their investigations of political meals, but we should remain vigilant about our need to explain contextual subtleties, operating assumptions, and local social meanings. Assumptions and definitions must be designed with care and used comparatively. Examples in this book illustrate that one group's highly valued food can be another's famine food.

The final example illustrating this contextual importance comes from the eastern U.S. and concerns lobster, my childhood feast food. According to historian Glenn Jones (2008, pers. comm. 2011), New England slave owners were only allowed to give lobster to their slaves a few days a week. Forcing the slaves to eat lobster more often was considered abusive. Lobster, a bottom feeder, held a very lowly place in the food constellation at that time and place, essentially starvation food barely fit for humans. Since the seventeenth century, however, the price of lobster along the eastern seaboard has risen substantially (Woodward 2004). In 1897, a whole lobster cost 40 cents in a restaurant; in 1920, it was 1.25 dollars, and in 2004, it was 30 dollars (Jones 2008). Today in the United States, a lobster dinner is a delicacy, being very expensive, and a feast in any setting. This lowly meal was reinvented over time, due to its political and social associations with leisure, coastal settings, and small-scale gathering. Over the past 400 years in New England, lobsters have been transformed from fertilizer and slave food to special, rare, expensive feast food, reminding us of how important historical context is when discussing archaeological evidence and assigning meanings.

## Eating and Drinking in the Mississippian World

In this final section on political food practices, I turn to a specific region and time for which there has been quite a bit of archaeological research, including evidence of food production and consumption, to see how the political world can be reflected in the archaeological evidence. Political meals operate at many levels within societies, and each genre can echo different meanings. The complication is that similar feast ingredients can portray quite different messages, determined by the political disposition of the event as well as the participants, as we learn from Appadurai (and the lobster story). This can make for obtuse interpretations in archaeology, requiring multiple data sets and a sensitive eye to gain confidence in interpretation. We turn our attention to what is called the Mississippian culture, which spanned much of temperate central and southeastern North America over a 700-year-long period. At its start, around AD 800, people were settled on the landscape, focusing on river valleys and building multi-community polities around ceremonial centers containing earthen mounds. Many scholars have described these palisaded centers as evidence of stratified hierarchies. The abandonment and disappearance of these centers was not uniform, and many reasons have been proposed for their demise. The earlier dissolutions could have resulted from localized overcrowding and poor diet, whereas the later collapses could have been from the early and rapid spread of European diseases. I focus on the central region in and around Cahokia, near present-day St. Louis, to trace the shifting valuation of maize and how this variability can alter the interpretation of the feasting evidence at these settlements.

The Mississippian cultural expansion grew out of the Woodland phase (1000 BC–AD 1000), which was a time of small, independent communities that increasingly focused on farming indigenous seed crops. During this gradual increase in agricultural production, squash (*Cucurbita* spp.), sunflower (*Helianthus annuus*), beans (*Phaseolus* spp.), tobacco (*Nicotiana tabacum*), and then maize (*Zea mays*) were slowly added to the fields of the locally domesticated indigenous plants called the Eastern agricultural complex: maygrass (*Phalaris caroliniana*), little barley (*Hordeum pusillum*), erect knotweed (*Polygonum erectum*), goosefoot (*Chenopodium berlandieri*), and sumpweed (*Iva annua*), grown for its oil (Johannessen 1988). These indigenous plants along with wild animals and hickory nuts, hazelnuts, and acorns constituted a healthy diet. In the early Mississippian era, political centers arose along the major rivers of central North America, identified by sprawling settlements with platform mounds, plazas, and clusters of houses that were eventually surrounded by wooden palisades, marking space and community while protecting stored food surplus. Later, radical cultural changes swept across a large area of the Midwest, with the spread of this Mississippian phenomenon beyond the river valleys. At its greatest extent, this style of living and belief system spanned west to the

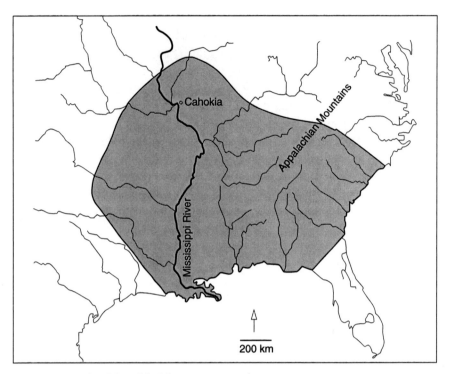

FIGURE 6.2. Map of the Mississippian complex at its greatest extent

Southern Plains, north to the Great Lakes, south to the Gulf of Mexico, and east to the Atlantic Ocean (Figure 6.2).

Rivers linked the dispersed population aggregations and facilitated trade in lithic materials, marine shell, copper, plants, iconography, and ideology. People were woven together throughout the settlement hierarchies in which smaller communities scattered across the landscape surrounded the populated centers with large earthen platform mounds. Excavations reveal that these mounds were renewed multiple times throughout their use lives, symptomatic of work groups periodically coalescing at these settlements, most likely for specific ceremonial occasions. This Mississippian complex has been described as an array of chiefly societies, the mounds and plazas being the foci for gatherings of a large number of people, including iconic paraphernalia linked to supernatural origin myths, ritual games (*chunky, or Tuchungkee* in Chowtaw), and communal feasting (Milner 1984; Pauketat 1994, 2002; Stepanaitis 1983).

Paleoethnobotanical analyses have identified regionally distinct large- and small-scale patterns, especially in the later Mississippian periods. The main early Mississippian plant foods were the small, indigenous, protein-rich grain crops mentioned earlier in this section. These seeds were planted extensively (as opposed to intensively), as most could be scattered in open patches in the forests and on floodplains. Throughout the Mississippian times, foreign, high-yielding cultigens – squash, corn, gourd, tobacco, and beans – slowly entered the agricultural systems, requiring formal fields and additional labor for their propagation (Johannessen 1988, 1993; Scarry 1993a, 1993b). These new crops resulted in expanded production as more land was cleared for agriculture. Work distribution therefore shifted from the mixed foraging-farming lifestyle of the Emergent Mississippian to one of increasing attention on agricultural fields. The faunal data suggest that more effort was needed to hunt local game animals with the advent of intensive farming, with the hunters still focusing on deer, fish, dog, reptiles, and small mammals. From this hard work the residents had a more diverse cuisine but also, perhaps more importantly, a food surplus. Early on, storage pits were found in the plazas of each community, these pits shifting into individual homes around AD 1000 (Johannessen 1993). Was this relocation of storage a result of decreased communal storage, a greater focus on trading and converting farm staples to surplus, and/or an increased sense of individual family identity?

The early spread of this ingredient complex coincided with agricultural intensification of both the indigenous starchy seeds and the Mesoamerican crops (Gremillion 1997; Johannessen 1988, 1993; Lopinot 1997; Scarry 1993a, 1993b, 1994; Simon 2000). Some Midwestern archaeologists claim that the foreign crops were introduced at a time of increasing control over staple and wealth resources, with the development of institutionalized social inequality evident in ritual and political leadership, played out in the fields.

From the historic accounts of the Mississippian descendants we learn that feasting and food gifting at periodic civic gatherings were highly valued (Bartram 1928; Cobb 2003; Swanton 1911; VanDerwarker 1999; Welch and Scarry 1995). Eighteenth-century eyewitnesses note that feasts were choreographed to designate political difference not only in the food dishes themselves but also in the food presentation. The men gathered in the plazas for ceremony and consumption, while the women prepared the unusual dishes at their residences, carried them into the plaza, and laid them out in specific arrangements. Venison, dog, and cornbread were the central display foods at these feasts (Swanton 1911; VanDerwarker 1999:26).

Mississippian archaeologists have used spatial distributions of artifacts to distinguish everyday meals from civic feasts. These suggested spatial,

gendered, and recipe differences have led VanDerwarker (1999) as well as
Pauketat and colleagues (2002) to assert that plaza rubbish will be different
than the quotidian meal remains found near the households. If the historic
reports are correct, we would expect that the plaza pits collected remains
of feast consumption and that the household pits, filled with leftovers from
daily meals, would not have the same food frequencies; things we can learn
from the archaeological evidence!

We need to consider the social context of the food remains further. How
much can the feasting evidence inform us about the political nature of this
society? How centralized or politically hierarchical these Mississippian centers were is still a matter of debate. Both household food practices and civic
rites participated in social identity formation. The public performances
need not have been a blatant appropriation of local traditions by the elite,
but they certainly could have included such political actions. Feasting can
be part of the rites surrounding community renewal festivals, ancestor wor-
ship, or other large gatherings in this civic feasting situation (McAnany
1998). Did leaders demand tribute of specific foods, such as wild meat,
engaging the regional population in surplus production, to be presented it
at the center's plazas during alliance-building feasts? Or did the leadership
only periodically receive foods from the surrounding populace at a festival similar to a potlatch, designed to clarify political relationships, focus
on mound renewal ceremonies, and general fecundity? Or does the plaza
feasting evidence reflect a potluck, communal gathering among equals to
solidify ties through meeting and materializing the group by renewing the
mounds, with much local food but not a lot of rare or highly valued food?
Interpretations of the remains will depend on the valuation of the regional
foods in a plaza setting and how we read the agency of the feasting food
evidence.

Because the Mississippian belief system is materialized across many
communities and regions, we assume that they shared tenets in their feasting enactments. Feasting remains could have been dumped in plaza pits
throughout the region. The local meanings of the foods, however, may
have varied. Johannessen and her colleagues (2002) suggest that at least
three long-lived, geographically distinct cuisines existed from the eighth
century AD through the Middle Mississippian (AD 1200–1400). One cuisine was in the north, into Wisconsin and around the Great Lakes; the second was in the upper Ohio Valley, Fort Ancient region; and the third zone
was along the Mississippi Valley, with Cahokia at its heart. The earlier Late
Woodland Wisconsin region shows a marginal reliance on indigenous cultivated crops, with a few of the small grains, especially little barley regularly

present, with meals dominated by wild foods. Later, in Mississippian times, the diet shifted to low row number corn, along with squash, sunflower, and tobacco (planted for ritual use), and indigenous grains, especially little barley and wild rice (*Zizania aquatica*) (Arzigian 1987). The Ohio region shifted from an early heavy use of the indigenous small grains in Late Woodland times to a predominance of maize, especially a large-grained eight-row variety, and beans, with steady contributions from local wild fruit, such as blackberry (*Rubus* spp.), peppergrass (*Lepidium* sp.), purslane (*Portulaca oleracea*), blueberry (*Vaccinium* spp.), and sumac (*Rhus* spp.) (Wagner 1987). Early on the diet in the Mississippi Valley had been quite similar to that in Ohio, with heavy use of small grains and oil-rich seeds, but later, corn with a high row number became of equal importance to the small grain and oil seed crops, with little use of wild plants (Johannessen 1988). These culinary geographies each had a different combination of arable crops and wild foods, reflecting local tastes, productivities, and values. These food traditions are the temporally sedimented preferences that were long-lasting even through political change, suggesting active, independent identities and political awareness of themselves vis-á-vis their neighbors over hundreds of years.

Can we decipher the political nature of these archaeological communities by taking a closer look at their feasts? We zoom in on the central Mississippian region to view the feasting evidence from two sectors of society, the rural communities and the center. We start along the Mississippi Valley and then turn to the center, Cahokia.

Sissel Johannessen (1993:184) has tracked plant production, ceramics, housing, and storage technologies at a series of settlements in the Cahokia hinterland beginning at the Mund site around AD 500. From her multiple data sets we learn how the local valuations of food altered as the larger, regional political pressures influenced the residents of the Mississippi Valley. Farming intensified beyond the indigenous plants, with the appearance of both squash and tobacco, informing us that the social worlds of these people were shifting. Only later, around AD 800, did high-row-number maize enter this region, adding a highly charged symbolic food to the rich local food base. The small grains and oil seed crops continued to be grown, but with less focus on nuts. Johannessen identified a shift in food storage location from communal pits in the plaza to individual household pits at this time. This change suggests that the intensified production might have yielded a surplus, controlled by individual families. The next century saw an elaboration in serving vessels, suggesting that even in the hinterlands people were increasingly conscious of how their meals were displayed, further suggesting the strengthening of individual family identity and position within a larger polity. At this same time Cahokia grew in size and visibility as construction of Monks Mound began. By AD 1000 Cahokia was clearly dominating the region. The inferred impact on the locals includes the loss of a village focus. Now people grew a mix of indigenous crops and the indigenized maize and squash.

During the Stirling phase (AD 1050–1150), this trend culminates across the countryside, with yet more design detail added to the ceramics, suggesting the importance of presentation. Families continued to live in a dispersed spatial pattern, with ever-larger storage pits within their homes (Johannessen 1993:199). This rural trend suggests an increasing sense of personhood within the large polity, as hoarding accompanied an almost Micronesian sense of one-upmanship in food presentation. People increasingly produced, stored, and ate maize owing to its potential for high yields, but also because of the highly charged symbolic baggage with which it had entered their cultural world. At the end of the Mississippian sequence maize was a common meal, with a 36 percent presence of $C_4$ maize residues boiled in Cahokia cooking pots (Beehr and Ambrose 2007). Were the regional farmers becoming more selfish, or were they buying into the widespread sense of individualism and display that was clearly growing at the political center of Cahokia? This trajectory is not the only one these folks could have taken. Why did they become more protective of their food stores and yet more complex in their meal presentation? Did families have to protect (hide) their yields because they were obliged to give their produce (pay taxes) to the center? Or did they guard their surplus to use in trade for the exotic items that were flooding into the region from the south?

Cahokia was occupied between AD 650 and 1200; its city center contained hundreds of platform mounds associated with intricate rituals. At its greatest extent, Cahokia, the largest of all Mississippian polities, extended for nearly 13 square kilometers along the rich Mississippi floodplain. Cahokia was a trade hub in the Mississippian system, receiving exotic items from far and wide, including seashells, chert, and copper. Some of the massive mounds, maintained and rebuilt throughout the center's history, were associated with plazas where large groups could meet for ceremonies, feasting, work, and exchange. With up to 15,000 people by AD 1000, Cahokia was probably stretched to the organizational and political limit in terms of farming, with distant settlements probably also provisioning the center (Pauketat and Lopinot 1997). This agribusiness caused cultural shifts across the region as well as political shifts at the center. New food values are also in evidence. In contrast to the other culinary traditions within the greater Mississippian world, at Cahokia maize became an industrial crop toward the end of the sequence, feeding the masses, as it did in the Valley of Mexico at Teotihuacán and in northern Spain in the seventeenth century.

That maize dominated the diet of the later Mississippian farmers is supported by bone collagen carbon and nitrogen isotope data that suggest most of their protein came from plants, whereas the higher-status individuals from the city consumed substantially more animal protein (Beehr and Ambrose 2007). Evidence from bone apatite and collagen suggests that some rural people's diet was up to 60 percent maize, whereas urban Cahokia maize consumption was in the area of 45 percent (Ambrose et al. 2003; Buikstra and Milner 1991;). The isotope evidence further supports the industrial nature of maize farming based on the archaeobotanical data from the American Bottom settlements at this time (post AD 1200); the poorest farmers in this intensive production zone lived on a diet of up to 80 percent maize with little animal protein. Three low-status women with this uniformly high maize diet (80 percent) exhibit diet-related pathogens, including high instances of caries and poor health. In contrast, the high-status residents buried at mound 72 at Cahokia consumed between 37 and 45 percent maize with substantially more animal protein in their diets (Ambrose et al. 2003:23). The evidence of decorative ceramics in the countryside supported by this rural maize diet reflects regular alliance-building feasts as well as the existence of elites who had better access to a well-rounded diet.

This Mississippian situation was much like the case in poor farming areas of Spain in the seventeenth century; the evidence of pellagra from high levels of maize in their diets indicates that they had little access to foods beyond the crops they tended either. These farmers were essentially indentured servants. In the Cahokia-dominated world, maize became a food of the masses, with high-quality foods such as wild nuts and indigenous grains being more expensive to procure. These nostalgic, greatly desired indigenous foods were brought into the center for some of the city dwellers to consume, as the locals could no longer afford to eat them. Does this sound familiar?

The political feast at Cahokia seems to have been different than its rural hinterland counterpart. The four-tier hierarchical settlement system, with Cahokia at the top, suggests more social inequality in this region than elsewhere in the Midwest. At the center we have evidence of very strong political rules operating, including power over life and death. The twenty-five burials at mound 72 that depict this power included sacrificial victims buried with many exotic goods. Is this a case of escalating centralized control by hereditary leaders or of competitive emulation and competition between local chiefly families? What did the feasts accompanying these sacrificial ceremonies look like?

Pauketat and his colleagues (2002) re-investigated remains from a feasting pit at the end of the Grand Plaza at Cahokia, east of the largest mound, which was thought to hold food from a sequence of large feasts. Although the food remains are not from primary deposits but from a midden (representing, at best, secondary deposition), the remains appear to be from seven consumption events that took place in this main plaza. Special dishes were brought into the center, especially apparent in the foods not found in the daily fare at contemporaneous Mississippian settlements. According to Lucretia Kelly (2001:257), select provisioning occurred at these seven feasts (Beehr and Ambrose 2007). The deposits contain a wide range of ingredients, with thirty edible plant taxa, including unusual species (Kelly 2001:265; Johannessen 1988:150). These summer feasts were rich in joints of deer, fish, and swan, along with quantities of richly flavored indigenous seed cakes. The plants were dominated by maygrass and sumpweed, with very few maize kernels. Since industrial maize production was just beginning throughout the region around AD 1000, why was less maize found at these Cahokia feasts than in the hinterlands? Is this because of the lower valuation of maize dishes at the center by this time? Or was it because of the recipes and how they were prepared for these feasts? Were these feasts so special that they were composed of very different ingredients than the average meal?

Dana Beehr and Stanley Ambrose (2007) add more insight into feasts in this polity. They propose that the maize included in Cahokia feasts was prepared in unusual ways in an attempt to make common food different. At mound 72, about 36 percent of the macrobotanical remains from the ceramic vessels uncovered from the feasting rubbish pits was maize, which was unexpected given the scarcity of macrobotanical evidence for maize in the remainder of the deposits (Beehr and Ambrose 2007). They surmised from this that the maize was eaten fresh, as corn on the cob, or perhaps in liquid form, like the *chicha* beer or *chicha morada* of the Andes, not common dishes of the mid-continent north America. The most common ceramic vessel, and the only one overrepresented in these plaza pits, is what Pauketat and his colleagues call seed jars – that is, small, neckless cups. These individual-sized vessels might have been used to consume liquid at feasts, perhaps maize beer (Pauketat et al. 2002:269). Whether or not maize was prepared as a drink at these festivities, drinking seems to have been an important feast component because of the concentration of these small vessels in this context.

Cahokia had more evidence of prepared dishes and diverse edibles than its hinterland (Kelly 2001; Pauketat et al. 2002). The seven feasts uncovered from the Grand Plaza near Monks Mound suggest a level of food diversity and richness that reflects the authority to gather an unusual range of ingredients, exemplified by the remains of a swan, signifying a very high-status feast. Pauketat and his colleagues suggest that the diverse pottery in the pit also reflects a broad range of people preparing and presenting the food, suggesting that many people were required to help with these large feasts.

There is no evidence of special serving dishes at these feasts (they could have been crafted from wood or grass), but the rich and diverse ingredients are reminiscent of medieval European feasts, with special dishes chosen to impress and delight. Were these potluck, alliance, or competitive feasts?

These examples illustrate that political feasts can have varying cultural undertones. Early on maize was high status in the countryside but had become a universal food later (Beehr and Ambrose 2007; Dietler 2001; Hayden 1996). At Cahokia we see no evidence of separate, centralized food storage. Rather, we see "barbeques" with heirloom foods. Could these feasts have been a planned version of a potluck to which people brought their most prized local specialties, masking any multiethnic differences and forming a feast among "equals," as recorded ethnohistorically for the feasts in the American Southeast (Swanton 1911)? Or were they more potent, still resembling food sharing but with the clear political overtones of the alliance-building feast, rallying families and lineages in the belief system through bringing a food tax, feasting together but also contributing labor to refurbish the mound?

These Midwestern data are not conclusive about the levels of power operating within these political feasts, but they do suggest that the different settlements within this region conceived of and organized their feasts differently, varying the quality and presentation but also control over the populace. The Cahokia evidence suggests large meals at which someone orchestrated a range of special foods to be brought in for sumptuous feasts. The burials at mound 72 also suggest that powerful men held sway over others. Perhaps some of the tasks that the leadership required in these civic districts were meted out to groups who completed their labor on the mound as part of a larger gathering that included feasts.

We can only guess at the recipes – how subtle the portions were and in what order the people were served. Given that the mounds were rebuilt several times over hundreds of years, a range of gastropolitical meals associated with this labor recruitment may have been organized in the guise of annual festivals. These meals could have been socially cohesive, pulled together quickly by a few families, or they could have been self-aggrandizing events by organizers, legitimizing their authority well beyond the requirements of mound renewal. Later historic documents of the descendants of these people suggest that summertime feasts involved the entire community, with each family providing what they could for these feasts, suggestive of a solidarity-building feast, a potluck meal. Although the political dynamics operating in these Mississippian feasts varied, they all portray wild game as a highly valued food. These encounters suggest that the post-Mississippian political system was not tightly centralized but that competing local leaders tried to keep the residents of the Mississippi Valley under some control, both forcing and encouraging them to join in. As with many archaeological examples, these midcontinental remains do not offer us that extra crispness that we gain with excellent preservation or documentation.

## Archaeological Food Politics

The faunal data from medieval English rubbish pits uncovered in Leicester provide a sharper snapshot of display feasts and elite control over food access than is available for the prehistoric U.S. Midwest, especially regarding exotic spices and wild foods (see Chapter 5). Excellent preservation at a series of middens in the medieval town center allows us to study meals from the sociopolitical vantage point of the elite. Working with medieval town maps, Lousia Gidney (2000) learned that the Earl of Huntingdon lived at the corner of Swinesmarket and Little Lane, Leicester, during the second half of the sixteenth century. Comparing this elite family's rubbish pits with contemporaneous middle-class domestic rubbish pits, she found that the nobility of the town were serving more wild food, deer, hare, and game birds, all high-status fare, whereas the more modest classes focused on cow, sheep, and pig at their feasts (Gidney 2000:170). These different culinary patterns reflect the high value the elite gave to wild game, a concept that had been escalating in England since the Norman Conquest, bringing more continental influences (Serjeantson 2000:182; Figure 6.3). The staple food in the sixteenth century was cereals, especially wheat, with meat and fish consumed periodically. This complex class-based medieval "foodscape" is revealed in the stable isotopic research of Muldner and Richards (2005). York monastery clergy ate more meat (beef, pork, mutton, and poultry) and fish (the fasting food) than did their neighboring lay-folk (Mays 1997; Muldner

FIGURE 6.3. Still life of a sumptuous meal 1597–1660, Pieter Claesz (Rijksmuseum, Amsterdam)

and Richards 2007:168). From a later, larger, and more contextualized study at Fishergate monastery we learn that the main variation in diet was consumed by the York laywomen, who ate less marine food than men, perhaps reflecting the Galenic form of dietary regulation determined by age and gender. Or it could be a monetary issue for the nunneries could not pay for meat and fish, as could their male counterpart institutions. Combining isotopic data with historic documents reveals multiple cuisines consuming the same food ingredients but in different frequencies, altered by social status, economic position, and political power, providing the crispness that we yearn for at Cahokia.

Across medieval England certain meat-rich cuts of deer and other game were more common in the Norman palaces and castles than in peasant households (Crabtree 1990:172; Figure 6.3). These cuts of meat often occurred with exotic spices (Goody 1982; Mennell 1985; Mintz 1985). Geese, swan, and eventually turkey became important aristocratic feast food, lasting into the Victorian era when they were paraded around at Christmas banquets. Through emulation, turkey has today become the common family's feast bird in England, replacing the local goose or pheasant (Serjeantson 2000:175; Thomas 2007). Medieval Leicester provides archaeological evidence for competitive, "emulatory" feasts, marked by expensive, highly valued and restricted ingredients, prepared and presented in memorable performances in the eating halls, when compared to the common table of the time.

## In Sum

The hidden, meaningful world of eating is cracked open at a feast, having the potential to yield data from which we can infer aspects of political society (Elias 1978). Ideological rules are reflected in the material practices of cooking and eating. The misguided assumption that feasts are only for the elite is a result of competitive, display feasts being the most clearly identifiable and thus the most commonly discussed in the archaeological literature, as is also mirrored in this chapter. Although elite feasts are easier to identify than other types, every self-identified group holds feasts, making it imperative in our food inquiries to consider a wide range of feasts through detailed contextual analyses. Including communal, potluck meals in the range of possibilities can open up feasting situations. Contextualizing and working with local values and shifting production will yield a better reading of the remains and thus enable assessment of the political dynamics as well as engagement with the food itself.

The agency of gastropolitics and its ubiquity is at the forefront here. Feasts illuminate political structure (Dietler 1990), gender relations (Crown 2000; Hastorf 1991; Mills 2004), foreign trade (Junker 2001), memories and identity (Twiss 2012a), sensual pleasures (Hamilakis 2004), and social stratification (Blitz 1993). As we learned from the Mississippian data, societies can have many variants of feasts, manifesting different political negotiations. "The 'festive landscape' in any given society will most likely be a palimpsest of several different modes of commensal politics operating in different contexts" (Dietler 2001:93). This makes our task more difficult, and yet also more likely to be successful as we seek out more data to unveil what the meal and the feast tell us about social status and political power in the past.

Political food studies are rich and deep. Culinary endeavors can teach us much more about political pasts, from staple finance to labor mobilization to status manipulation. Tracking women's workloads and contributions to food processing, presentation, and consumption will enable us to define the scale and axes of the relative status positions within communities, and also about the networks of decision making and empowerment (Brumfiel 1991; Crown 2000; Mills 2004). By learning about the preparation of foods, and the manner of serving dishes, we can retrace the steps from the cuisines to the values of certain foods to the desires of those who planned and prepared them.

This chapter has touched on only some of the issues of gastropolitics. This political perspective places food and its consumption at the heart of social life, identity, and politics, which is where it can best help us in our pursuit of past lifeways. Studying gastropolitics allows archaeologists to investigate the political actions of decision makers, food events, surplus production expenditures, and status enhancement through presentation and gifting. These actions contribute to the symbolic capital of political desire on which Bourdieu (1984) so often focused. The past value of the meal will never be calculable, nor can we identify the range of opinions about presentation and flavors from the participants. What we can learn is how the social and political dimensions intensified as both the hosts and the guests orchestrated these encounters, often through nuanced, codified acts of assistance and gracious generosity (Geertz 1973) or through fistfights (DeBoer 2001).

# PART III

# Food and Identity: The Potentials of Food Archaeology

With identity firmly at the center of food archaeology, webs of meaning play out in the body as well as in the *chaîne opératoire* of food creation, harnessing memory activation and new situations in the daily practices. The next two chapters focus on the practice and the structure of food in peoples lives, as well as thinking about where we can take archaeological food studies in the future. Although archaeologists study complexes of material, palimpsests of individual practices have formed them, making it complex to untangle individual acts. Change is rarely sudden; rather, it is a gradual blurring of imperfect reenactments, made up of individual strategies and choices within existing structures. Since handmade things are never replicated exactly, each handmade artifact and meal is unique, thus revealing the maker's praxis and agency in that formation. How can we investigate these identities through food?

While food practices are not the only activities that create society or shape one's self-perceptions, they are one of the major actions maintained and therefore transformed daily. Our vision of our communities and ourselves are constructed through these actions. When actions are condoned, collective esteem and solidarity are reinforced. Ohnuki-Tierney (1993) uses the phrase "metaphor of self" to express the link between rice and the Japanese self-identity, not just for the individual but also the group. A person within that society has a relationship with rice, as her/his body is maintained by it. We sense the multiple natures in this dynamic between rice, the individual, and the society. Self-identity situates the individual with respect to her/his place in the world, creating values, beliefs, and acceptable ways to act. "Identity contributes to how individuals and groups perceive and construct society, how they give meaning, and how they act, think, vote, socialize, buy, rejoice, perceive, work, eat, judge or relax. They do so by referring to economic, social, cultural, and political conditions, events and expectations, and while doing so, they affect the economics, the social the cultural and the political" (Scholliers 2001:5). People have many identities throughout their lives (Hall and DeGuay 1996). Some of these are fixed, such as land of birth, childhood family, ethnicity, or personality type. Other identities are flexible, as with occupation, political standing, hobbies, or religion – altered by circumstance or will, allowing for the forging of new identities and new cuisines. Identity provides meaning as well as flexibility in people's lives (Castells 1999).

People have strong feelings about their own cuisine, with accompanying aversions to foods of other cuisines (Ohnuki-Tierney 1993). The adage "you are what you eat" can operate at many levels. The study of food in context eventually returns to the social self and the way of being in the world. What we eat literally becomes intertwined with how we think about food and ourselves.

An explicitly social perspective allows us to study both the large scale of societal formation and maintenance as well as the small scale of human lives and the creation of personhood (Douglas 1984). Political and economic forces, as discussed in Part II, not only influence cuisines; they are also directed by strong social and cultural preferences that activate rules of propriety.

Focusing on this active yet unconscious side of identity construction, whether materially or psychologically, Scholliers suggests that we pursue *identification* as well as identity (2001:6). He urges us to give practice and corporeal language more of a role in the creation of self and of group, most active in memory, speech, learning, and participation, pushing us to study the construction of personhood. What better way to do this than through the study of daily practices, and what is more regularly recorded in the archaeological record than food practices? Some scholars promote the importance of *subjectivity* when studying societies foodways (Caplan 1997:15; Lupton 1996). They focus on selfhood in both its conscious and unconscious dimensions, the self as changeable and contextual. This places the individual at the center of the action in a reflexive, self-conscious world that often looks to be fragmented in its multiple components up close. But ironically that is what archaeology tends to deal with, the remains of individual actions collected together in clusters of material.

This part focuses on the social aspects of foodways in human society: first at the larger scale at the societal level and the group, then turning to the family and the individual. Recent studies concerning smaller-scale food consumption, eating practices, society, and manners allow us to see the closer workings of individual lives, which engagingly also reflect the larger-scale historical trends (Logan and Cruz 2014; Stahl 2014). The postmodern approaches to society introduced here are productive for archaeologists because they provide a new entry into the past. Through seeking daily practices, embodiment, and identity reflected in foodways we open up new ways of understanding the past.

CHAPTER 7

# Food in the Construction of Group Identity

> *Whether a food represents an individual self, a social group, or a people as a whole, this symbolic process renders foods as powerful not only conceptually but also psychologically. For this reason "our food" versus "their food" becomes a powerful way to express "we" versus "they."*
>
> Ohnuki-Tierney 1993:130

What is the relationship between identities and cultural practices? In this chapter we explore the relationship between social identities and food. Identity is nowhere and it is everywhere. Identity is an abstraction that permeates every human act and personal perception (Castells 1999; Insoll 2007). It constitutes the self and is recognized in embodied cultural practices. It continues in collective memories through recursive acts that situate individuals in their social worlds (Bourdieu 1984). Bodily practices reaffirm cultural memories shared within communities, making people members of groups through their bodily forms of memory (Connerton 1989). "Cultures are inherently relational in nature" (Dietler 2007:225). This relational abstraction of the group is manifested when we act and engage with things and with people. Material remains of past actions allow us to see group values and style preferences in production and consumption. The cultural embodied practices of *habitus* are keys to getting closer to the past.

What is shared most often in families? Meals. Culinary traditions are condensed social facts that reflect a group's dispositions and values. Because food is material, the actions and outcomes of food processing and consumption allow us to see wisps of these relational fields of community interest and therefore identity. This recursive construction of the self, of thoughts to materials and back, helps us render the invisible visible. The daily interactions that surround cooking and serving meals are thus

important contexts in which people's worldview is produced and materialized. A goal of this chapter is to ponder about how people saw themselves as
a group, which in turn speaks to how they created their identities through
the lens of choice and practice. I begin this exploration by asking a few
questions that structure this general approach. How is identity constructed
through daily practices? How does identity operate throughout all the
scales of social life, from the larger, collective memory of polities down to
individual practice? How do the common symbols of community identity,
such as recipes, eating comportment, meal size, and ingredients, come to
stand for the group? Here we are trying to harness practices that communicate affiliation and self to gain a fuller picture of society.

I begin by recounting some of the principles outlined in initial work
on identity formation within anthropology, primarily from the symbolic
and theory of practice literature. Regional food traditions have been the
subject of a number of anthropological, sociological, and historical studies, which provide archaeologists with effective vantage points for learning
about past identities (e.g., Bell and Valentine 1997; Brown and Mussell
1984; Caplan 1997; Macbeth 1997; Ohnuki-Tearney 1993; Scholliers 2001).
I turn to the construction of group identity in the past and look at several
of the approaches archaeologists have applied in their discussions of community. These topics include identity construction through symbolically
significant foods–signature foods, the nationalistic endeavor, how states
have used iconic foods in their construction, and how cultural boundaries
are formed through difference identities, most notably in colonial encounters. There is an inherent tension in archaeological studies between the
symbolic approaches introduced in Chapter 2 and the practice-based
approaches discussed here. I turn to smaller-scale studies and focus on
cultural contact and how encounters bring unconscious traditions into
sharp focus, highlighting the *chaîne opératoire* of daily practice. Finally,
at the heart of community, I look at the intense socialization that occurs at
the family level and how food participates in that strong identity creation.

This chapter approaches three social scales: the nation, the community, and the family, discussing the active dimensions of identity formation
through specific food practices at each scale. These nested social identities
clearly operate in one world, but for the purposes of my argument I have
divided these different aspects of the embodiment of identity based on
the different levels of precision. Embodiment is the process by which the
nonmaterial culture is transformed into visible personal practices, acted
out through the *chaîne opératoire* of food preparation. Culinary traditions
are active in all practices of identity formation, including gender, family,
age group, homeland, rank, occupation, and community (Sahlins 1976;

Stahl 2002; Sutton 2001). The pervasiveness of identity formation allows us to seek cultural understandings in the materiality of culinary memories, including competition, cooperation, social inclusion, and exclusion (Connerton 1989). Culinary practices participate in these affiliations through the remembrance and reenactment of past meals with each new created meal, seen in the images of an ideal and a real North American Thanksgiving meal in Figure 7.1. Cultural affiliation is particularly salient here because food practice materializes the abstractions of identity, political standing, authority, belief systems, and social history that have been difficult to grasp in archaeological research (Roddick and Hastorf 2010).

Nebulous concepts of identity formation become visible in shared practices and bodily actions. The symbolic and the material merge in these practices, even if their links are never made explicit. There is no one-to-one correspondence between food practices and identity, whatever the scale of analysis. Forms of membership and practical knowledge accessed in archaeological data will show selectively different views of the transmitted messages. These differences exist because of the unique memories created at each meal, building up to the collective world of a culinary tradition. Contemplating within this hermeneutic between the concrete food practices and the fluid frames of meaning that generate them is our goal.

Food traditions are materialized through habitual bodily techniques and remembered sensory clues that reengage us in our identities. These bodily practices encode habit-memory that can become subtlety specific, honing cultural boundaries through materialized differences, even between neighbors (Hamshaw-Thomas 2000; Hastorf 1998; Janik 2003; Johannessen et al. 2002). Basques are not unique in defining their cultural territory as "wherever there was good stuff to eat" (Bourdain 2001:68). "Good stuff," it turns out, can be a neighbor's food, even if it is not the same as your own. It is our job to identify these differences between good and bad "stuff" in the archaeological record. Recognizing and differentiating cuisines constructed of prescribed material expressions is an archaeological "portkey" to past memories and membership.

The bodily techniques involved in cooking and eating create membership through the embodied memories of repetition and form (Connerton 1989; Joyce 2003; LeCount 2008; Ortner 1973; Weismantel 1988). Our sense of self is embodied through these specific daily practices, expressing how we engage in our world. The capacity of food to express and create our identity is in part due to food's place in our lives. This daily, shared *habitus* of food traditions creates an impression of unity within and commitment to a larger community, if not the family, but it also provides a place for appropriation, rebellion, and resistance: not eating American french fries, I am thought of as odd.

(a)

(b)

FIGURE 7.1. Two images of a Thanksgiving meal. Note the iconic foods: the turkey and the seating arrangements. (a) The painting is of an archetypical American Thanksgiving by Norman Rockwell (1943), Freedom from want, printed by permission of the Norman Rockwell Family Agency, copyright 1943, the Norman Rockwell Family entities. (b) A U.S. Thanksgiving family dinner photograph, copyright istock 0000283094o6

The frontiers of food traditions are locations of crystallized difference and tension. Proposing the use of different ingredients or procedures causes a startled reaction if not dismay (Roddick and Hastorf 2010). For example, using new ingredients in the Thanksgiving turkey stuffing or gravy suddenly brings into focus just how one's food *habitus* is different from others who may be cooking with you. Participants stop to comment and ponder this rupture, often attempting to change it. In our archaeological data we can pursue how such boundaries came about, what tensions they held, and what the political ramifications were. Food identities harbor political discourse. Political situations are reflected in the inhabitants of a region, which is reproduced in their daily food habits. Political powers and authoritative individuals create and bend food boundaries in complex ways. Macbeth and Green (1997) trace such a national boundary through the differing food preferences recorded in the eastern Pyrenees. They interviewed Catalan teenagers who straddle the French-Spanish border in one valley. Their differing opinions about foods illustrate how the two nations have each crafted and imposed national identities and boundaries within a people who shared the same history until a century ago. Liver, spinach, greens, garlic, butter, and yogurt were preferred by the French teenagers, whereas the Spanish kids valued lamb and olives more than their French neighbors did. These preference disparities are recent, formed out of nationalistic endeavors, promoted through *national* dishes, food advertising, school cuisines, food pricing, and the entry of the state into local aesthetics (Moore 1994). Their long culinary heritage was etched in their foodways, however, as both groups appreciate many foods equally – both ate stews and bread eagerly. This study demonstrates how the covert powers of modern statecraft are actively bringing a long self-identified group, the mountain residents, into each nation by altering their food traditions (Macbeth and Green 1997).

This manipulation of food traditions does not always occur calmly or unconsciously. The European Renaissance court cuisine discussed in Chapter 2 added the sauce tradition that jumped from the Italian to the French and then to the English and Russian royal courts during a time when the populace was gaining access to foreign spices (Mennell 1985:60). This elite cuisine evolution promoted unity among the nobles while accentuating their differences from those who lived in the countryside. This class differentiation continued on many levels, and it actually led to ideological debates about bread recipes in the National Assembly during the French Revolution. The power of food habits and identity is enacted in people eating during times of political upheaval: each mouthful is a statement of position and identity.

### Boundedness, Food, and Community

Perhaps more than any other human dimension, food creates community through its web of symbolic meanings. This symbolic-moral potential is apparent, for example, in the dietary laws codified in the Buddhist texts (Sarvastivadavinaya) (Kieschnick 2005:188), Islamic sharia law, or the Hebrew Bible and kosher food rules (Douglas 1966). The explicit rules that define a community are based on long-held social mores, defining status, morals, values, and proper comportment. These rules become internalized in each participant as they are indigenized in the community. They channel practices, which in turn create boundaries around people – those who participate and those who do not. From her study of the biblical rules of conduct, practice, and incorporation Mary Douglas defined a major axis of community identity formation with the concepts of purity and contamination. These important operating principles in food practices determine what is edible and what is not, what is pure and what is impure, and what is contaminated and what is not. Ingredients must be made edible before they can be consumed; this can be done in many ways through producing, processing, and thinking food (Douglas 1966, 1972; Meigs 1988). In our global food world, many discursive and non-discursive rules operate, such as a food's sell-by date, after which the food is considered contaminated even if it is not. Raw food enthusiasts have specific heating temperatures that food is allowed to reach and still be raw. Although some are not long-lived dicta, they have wormed their way into our subconscious, directing our visceral reactions to food.

The rules about what is pure and how to handle food to make it pure can take many forms, both explicit and implicit. Let me illustrate how these codes define eating habits with several long-lived, religious examples. Edible or halal meat in the Islamic religion is not simply freshly butchered; it is meat slaughtered in a specific manner using specific tools. *Dhabīhah* (ذبح) slaughtered in a prescribed method, consisting of using a well-sharpened knife to make a swift, deep incision that severs the throat, the carotid artery, windpipe, and jugular vein ('Azzām 2004). This method is virtually the same for Hebraic kosher animal processing. Clean, uncontaminated tools must be used (e.g., the tools must never have been used on pigs). In the Biblical books of Leviticus and Deuteronomy, permissible foods are classified as "clean foods" and forbidden foods are "dirty" – matter out of place. Called Kashrut, these Jewish rules to live by are thought to have been written down around the sixth century BC. Buddhists, on the other hand, do not focus on the butchering style but on the animal and its cosmological place in the universe to determine edibility. They do not eat elephant or horsemeat because both animals are associated with ruling castes, being too pure to eat. Snakes are likewise classified as inedible, as eating them would offend the *naga* snake deities (Kieschnick 2005).

In many religions, meat must be offered to the deities before people can eat it; in some cases, such as described in the Torah, the offering may be in the form of smell – that is, a burnt offering. In the Islamic tradition, the consumption of blood is forbidden. But unique to the Jewish tradition, cooking a kid in its mother's milk, the fruit from the first three years of the fruit tree's yield, and all invertebrates, amphibians, or reptiles are forbidden. The rules for planting are particularly intriguing. The Jewish farmer may not mix crops in a field; that is, different plants must not be grown near each other. This of course is the opposite of traditional cropping strategies throughout Western Hemisphere indigenous farming.

Mary Douglas focused on the most famous and controversial Biblical rule, that of eating only cloven-hooved and ruminant mammals, thus forbidding consumption of pork, an animal that has long been domesticated and raised in the Levant. Many have tried to unravel the reason behind this rule. Douglas's reason was that these food dichotomies – edible versus inedible, good versus bad, clean versus polluted – reflect codes that delimit society and define cultural boundaries, and pig falls into the polluted matter-out-of-place category. Deborah Lupton (1996:27) also looks at ontological boundaries of what is considered edible, suggesting that people categorize food as good or bad based on cosmological and moral beliefs. Robertson Smith (1889), a nineteenth-century Scottish theologian, discussed how religious communities were formed through their defined codes of eating. Forbidden foods especially work to create these communities by highlighting the moral elements as they create the community's boundaries (Allen 2002). In any specific group, membership is defined by food choices that are commonly agreed on. This solidarity is enacted in ceremonial offerings and sacrifices, for which we have evidence well back in prehistory (Bianca D'Anna 2012). For Robertson Smith, the purpose of food offering and sacrifice is to share a meal with the deity, thereby creating unity between humans and gods. Gifting, as Mauss (1980 [1925]) explained, establishes obligations between participants. Eating together therefore activates a relationship that obliges the deity as well as the people. These sacred meals of food offerings have added resonance to create a particular space for moral definition, but also a place for testing and transgression. Hebrew texts note that the early Semitic rituals allowed certain "unclean" animals to be sacrificed, offered, and then eaten (Robertson Smith 1889:201). Pork was consumed at some of these early Hebraic sacred meals, although later the designated sacrificial animals shifted to quail, ox, sheep, and goat, with pig dropping out of both the sacred and the quotidian cuisine. Why did pork inhabit these moral boundaries and eventually move into the contaminated food category? How did rumination in animals become so crucial?

Why indeed were rules developed and written down to define such distinctions as pure and impure food? Douglas (1966) claims that such codes are harnessed to create a sense of community. The early Buddhist codes replicated the political caste structures later seen in China. In the Hebraic case, the Old Testament rules helped create a community identity for the scattered tribes who were experiencing endemic warfare on all sides. In the Levantine Bronze Age, the increasing political pressure from encroaching polities – the Philistines from the sea, the Egyptians from the south, and the Mesopotamians from the north – could have intensified the desire for community boundaries, accentuated through differing shared rules of practice, not just food practices.

Douglas (1966) found a connection between food-related rules and other rules of daily comportment. A meal decoded therefore symbolically summarizes a community. "Symbolic boundaries are necessary even for the private organizing of experience. But public rituals which perform this function are also necessary to the organizing of society" (Douglas 1970:50). Rules were sometimes written down to materialize membership, guiding members to live in a specific manner, making explicit the imagined communities as their boundaries were defined.

Religious texts note that society is maintained when food rules are known and properly followed. The tightening of social morality shifts to the political as pollution is linked to dangerous situations and even to social disorder. Transgressing food boundaries can be disruptive. Cooking certain foods can initiate social disarray, as white bread was banned by the French revolutionaries because of its association with the nobility (Allen 2002). Pork and horsemeat identified in processed food sales in 2013 caused riots in certain northern European communities (Reuters 2013; *Cambridge Evening News* 2013).

## Defining Community

Through food, status is negotiated and social boundaries are drawn (Jansen 2001:202). Group acceptance is a strong drive in a gregarious species like ours. People need to have friends. At the most basic level, how identities are created and maintained forges community membership. Many scholars note that food is a dense social fact imbued with codes of exclusion and inclusion (Caplan 1997; Douglas 1970; Goody 1982; Ohnuki-Tierney 1993). The foods that people eat reflect with whom they wish to identify (Fiddes 1991; Fitchen 1988). People work at defining their communities, with behaviors such as mimicry, sharing, and believing along similar lines. Retaining membership in a group requires active participation, including eating what that community deems acceptable. For example, teenage children know fatty foods will give them pimples (as their parents continually remind them), yet they eagerly eat them. They want to relax in the company of friends and so dive into burgers or chocolate when offered. Canadian teenagers label "junk food" such as candy bars as good food, forming a different food classification system than the one formed by their parents (Chapman and Maclean 1993). These rules distinguish the children from their parents, carving out a distinctive community membership by age. While a chocolate bar eaten with friends represents freedom from parents' rules and community acceptance within their gang, that same chocolate bar given by doting grandparents represents identity of another kind. Chocolate in both contexts remains a treat, one forbidden, one nurturing, in both settings it forges affiliations. This desire to belong through consumption is stronger than the nightmarish pimples of youth (Fitchen 1988). Yearning to participate in a community through emulation is why food advertising continues to be a multibillion-dollar industry (Schlosser 2001).

Many aspects of community life are expressed in nonverbal practices, with no marked labels or written rules, making them difficult to identify. We have to seek out their existence indirectly by tracking practices. This is the project of much anthropological research, and especially so for prehistoric archaeologists. Communities become more easily visible when members transgress the implicit and explicit codes of proper behavior, belief, and community *habitus*. When specific community members no longer abide by the accepted cultural rules, everyone becomes aware of that community's perimeter. Leaving a group's sphere of embodied practice suddenly makes the unspoken rules spoken, manifested in contrasting material practices, as when a Jewish person eats bacon (Bourdain 2001:68: Wiessner 1983). To define and then to realize the significance of these cultural codes – in our case, culinary communities – we need to identify the extent of this community and its stability. This can be done by investigating the food traditions of individual groups or subgroups (males versus females, farmers versus fisher folk), comparing their genealogies of practice, and how firm such rules seem to be. Gumerman's (2002) food study of coastal Perú society notes that crafts people and fisher folk, although distinct social groups, consumed very similar ingredients – it was the method of preparation that defined their distinct foodways.

When culinary cultures are spread across several communities, does this suggest unified culinary codes of practice and associated beliefs or simply parallel actions? Either pattern informs us about "canons of taste." We seek to answer the many questions about community identity. To see how this nebulous social phenomenon might be applied in archaeological research, in this chapter I present four scales of analysis, chosen for their potential to trace community identity formation. The first approach will be to trace specific, especially charged elements in a cuisine and how they activate community identities, looking at *signature foods*. This can be studied spatially and temporally by looking at recipes, meal structures, and individual foods, all of which are especially germane to archaeological inquiry (McIntosh 1994; Douglas 1966). A second strategy for visualizing community is to trace cuisines' explicit participation in politics and societal formation on a broad scale, through the creation of nations and other large communities such as religious groups – entities that are very aware of the need to maintain cohesive identities (Leone and Crosby 1987:409; MacBeth and Green 1997). A third approach builds on the previous one but focuses on the tensions that arise when two communities or culinary traditions come in direct contact with each other. Colonial encounters and immigration draw attention to this moment when identities are made explicit through the encounters of contrasting traditions. Communities are reified at these nexuses of encounter, forced adoption, or overt emulation. The fourth approach presented here is scalar, in which we move closer to the location of daily practice and look at how food traditions work to create the family, the core social unit.

### Signature Foods and Identity

I adopt Gasser and Kwaitkowski's (1991a) vocabulary for studying identity through food and call salient elements in a culinary tradition "signature foods." Signature foods are especially iconic within a community, often using the core flavors prominent in a food tradition (Rozin 1973). Many groups are identified by a signature staple food, such as the baguette in France, pasta in Italy, or tortillas in Mexico. Iconic, highly charged dishes can be a combination of ingredients that are associated with a group, such as apple pie or fish and chips. Signature dishes are often based on staples, such as boiled potatoes in the Andes or cabbage (stuffed cabbage or sauerkraut) in Eastern Europe. Wheat can be made into bread, pasta, or dumplings; maize can form tortillas or tamales. Some signature foods are not staples, such as a flavor or a seasonal food. These elements can range from being associated with a specific group or family to having a broad appeal across many different communities. Learning how iconic foods are negotiated in their social contexts helps us understand how food harnesses identity. Signature food distributions clarify cultural boundaries as well as compose the engine of community identity.

Signature foods are full of meaning and myth. They have personalities and receive nicknames, such as *la preciosa*, "the precious one," for potatoes in central Perú. Core foods are at the center of social life, if not actually living with the community, as do pigs in Highland New Guinea households. These foods are constantly tended, talked about, and even sung to, as yams are in the Trobriand Islands and cows are in English milking parlors (Malinowski 1935; BBC radio4 2005). Signature foods create community through the shared attention that they receive from community members. Foods that take on this role have a special resonance, for they provide a clear view of a food community. These foods and dishes bring the community together; non-members do not interact with the food in the same way (Adapon 2008). At times these signature foods become the focus of tourism – what one must experience when one visits a place, even if each dish tastes slightly different than the one previously eaten (Wilk 2006; Wilk and Barbasa 2012). These entities often have specific traction that we see by their distribution, range of preparations, longevity, advertising, and symbolic links to other domains within society.

Bread is an example of a signature staple food. By nature of its elemental position in many cuisines, bread has become one of the most potent symbols of cultural identity across the northern part of the globe. Bread is the most basic food across wheat-growing Europe, North Africa, and the Middle East, being found in many forms, with more than thirty distinct varieties in Europe alone. In Sardinian farming towns, until recently, women baked weekly at a communal oven using wheat harvested by men. It was through this recursive activity of bread baking that friendship and kinship were sustained. Baking bread together at community ovens meant women spent whole days working together, during which the social life of the village was recreated; while they baked bread, "they collectively reaffirmed local norms and morality" (Counihan 1997 [1984]:288).

The most common Christian prayer includes the following: "Give us this day our daily bread. And forgive us our trespasses, as we forgive those that trespass against us." In other words, a social contract is made with God to receive and eat bread (food) every day and in return get forgiveness. In the Jewish Passover feast, unleavened bread represents not only the first harvest of the year but also the purity of wheat on its own, before it is mixed with leavening agents. "Breaking bread" with others linguistically signifies sociality in the Western tradition, as demonstrated in the English word *companion*, which derives from the Latin for a person with whom (*com*) we share bread (*panis*; Visser 1991:2). The power of this signature food extends far back in time.

> Bread was of enormous symbolic importance to the ancient Egyptians, . . . they were said to bake about fifty different types. Sacred animals, even cats and wasps, were offered bread to eat. Graves were stocked with huge amounts of bread as food for the deceased; tombs were painted with bread baking scenes. Throughout the whole ritual life of the Egyptians, the stocking of tombs, the cults, and their endless offerings to the gods, bread was a central symbol. During certain festivals in which pigs were to be sacrificed, the poor, who could not afford living pigs, made models of them out of bread dough and offered these instead. (Farb and Armelagos 1980:130)

Archaeological evidence of bread making at the Amarna Egyptian worker's bakeries reveals that working classes ate different bread types than did the royalty (Samuel 1993, 1994). Through detailed archaeological analysis of the bread forms, ovens, and plant remains, Delwin Samuel uncovered how the wheat was processed and made into specific shapes, reflecting a material food boundary between the workers and the royalty (Samuel 1996b).

Although bread is a staple food throughout this broad region, it is also the locus of cultural distinctiveness. With the French baguette and brioche versus the Italian ciabatta and crostini, all contain almost the same ingredients, but the preparation techniques signal different culinary traditions. Bread has become a highly charged signifier that communities employ to mark their identities. Bread's power to define communities and their members is a result of both its widespread use as a staple food as well as its diverse forms of expression.

John Monaghan (1996) provides a similar potent example for the maize tortilla in Oaxaca Mexico. At the wedding ceremony, a single tortilla is split and consumed by the bride and groom to signify mutual respect for each other as well as for the maize (ibid.:184). During annual festivals, stacks of tortillas are distributed so all can eat "from the same tortilla," making this group consumption a metaphor of a unified community (Monaghan 1996; King 2007).

Signature foods can be salient indicators of community identity as well as a focus of competition. People try to accomplish this by making a similar event unique – baking a moister cake for a potluck dinner, for example, or providing more food at an annual dinner. Most neighboring communities participate in very similar cultural activities, mimicking acceptable rules of comportment. Let us consider an example of how this works in a community through their relationship with plants. Northwest Colombian Amazonian communities grow specific plant varieties (Hugh-Jones 1997, 2001). Barasana women inherit these specific varieties along family lines. Gourd plants, with their long vines, represent the lineage, whose daughters and sons are the fruit. Stephen Hugh-Jones notes that certain chile pepper shapes and flavors are associated with specific families as well. Peppers are the binding agent in fish and manioc dishes (Hugh-Jones 1995:231). With sexual connotations derived from their shape and spicy flavor, peppers operate at many metaphoric levels of meaning. The specific recipes based on these varieties embody the family. When women feed chile-pepper-flavored meals to their families, the members are rejoining their lineage as they incorporate their heritage into their bodies.

The Barasana culinary tradition operates at the regional level, with some aspects unifying the region while others denote differences throughout the communities. Plants such as manioc are individual community signature plants, passed down from mother to daughter at marriage, or coca, passed down from father to son at puberty. The food plants "are treated as integral parts of the group identities which endure through time and which are transferred and recombined on marriage" (Hugh-Jones 1995:63). At feasts, the Barasana transform their manioc into a fermented beverage, honoring the special value of the plant as well as incorporating the essence of the group. The Barasana's neighbors feast with beer made of a different plant, maize (Hugh-Jones 2001). These different plants therefore signify the different groups, denoting unique identities within a region, renewing their community ties, while differentiating themselves from their neighbors with each preparation and consumption event.

Signature plants distinguish neighboring communities, a fact that is especially useful in archaeological identity studies. The Ancestral Pueblo (Hohokam) people of the American Southwest were horticulturalists. They grew maize, beans, squash, cotton, and tobacco, as did those living across a wide region of the American continent. They also cultivated local indigenous plants, especially agave (*Agave americana*), *Chenopodium*, milk vetch (*Astragalus onobrychis* sp.), tansy mustard (*Descurainia* spp.), little barley (*Hordeum pusillum*), and maygrass. Wild taxa were also regularly collected and eaten, especially the *cholla* fruit (*Cylindropuntia*), *Amaranthus* seeds, and mesquite pods (*Prosopis* sp.). Based on archaeological research, it appears that the Hohokam culture area as it has been historically defined actually comprised a number of different, self-identifying groups who migrated into the region at different times (Gasser and Kwaitkowski 1991a). Once in close proximity, these different populations shared some material traits while maintaining their unique traditions and identities in other ways. Having new neighbors in fact seems to have sharpened their cultural differences.

Gasser and Kwiatkowski (1991a, 1991b) investigated two drainage basins during the Classic period, around AD 1000, within the Hohokam region of Arizona, identifying spatially discrete plant use patterns. Although this part of North America is very dry, irrigation is not always required. Slope wash farming can also be successful. The first group Gasser and Kwiatkowski discuss lived where the Gila and Salt River valleys meet; the second lived to the south, along the Santa Cruz River in the Tucson Basin (ibid. 1991a:209). These two communities ate different cuisines and farmed different crops, despite residing in the same region and undoubtedly communicating with each other regularly (ibid.:218). Some of the taxa were native cultivars and others were introduced domesticates. While some of the plant use differences can be correlated with micro-environmental variability, as certain taxa prosper in specific microclimates; the different plant densities found in the archaeological record point to divergent cultural decisions about what plant foods were proper to grow, collect, and eat.

Common plants along the Santa Cruz River in the southern Tucson Basin assemblages were tepary beans (*Phaseolus acutifolius*), tansy mustard, and plantain (*Plantago* sp.), the latter being rare at other Hohokam sites. The Tohono O'odam people still reside in this area and farm beans (Crosswhite 1981). To the north, along the lower Salt River, Gasser and Kwiatkowski (1991b:423) found agave to be ubiquitous in the assemblages (see also Fish et al. 1985). Large stands still grow on the hills in that area today. Little barley grass was abundant in the sites along the Gila River in the northern sector (ibid. 1991b:434), whereas mesquite and milk vetch were more common in the sites along the Agua Fria River. These different plant frequencies display long-term cuisine traditions in these different food patterns.

Based on a wide-ranging study of crop use throughout Eurasia, Fuller and Rowlands (2011) found persistent patterns of commensality and food preparation in different regions. They tie these different signature foods to differences in ritual practice, in particular sacrifice, the construction of bodily substances, and the ritualized reproduction of the social order. They studied Japanese steamed sticky rice, associated with food offerings to the ancestors as well as food shared within familial groups – the stickiness being salient as a metaphor for people "sticking" together. In contrast, in western Asia and northern India, deities received sacrifices of roasted and baked foods, focusing on the smoke constituting the offerings, with the actual food, the meat and bread, being consumed by the devotees (Fuller and Rowlands 2011).

Some of these trends, identifiable in the archaeological record, continue today, with agave still important in the northern Ancestral Pueblo area and beans dominant in the south. Archaeobotanical distributions show the durability of people's long-term aesthetic and culinary preferences as well as their cultural heritage, reflected in different harvest and consumption patterns. Signature foods such as bread in Europe and rice in Asia hold particular cultural significance, as does manioc for the Barasana (Gasser and Kwiatkowski 1991a:213–214, 1991b 447–449). Each population in the Colombian forest, in the Hohokam desert, or across Eurasia fashioned a slightly different cuisine based on their local culinary histories, built on repetitive actions in their collective memories and bodies. With new neighbors, such differences become discursive, and in some settings accentuated, identifying and at the same time defining or rupturing their geographical boundaries with conquest (Crosswhite 1981).

*Food Nationalism*

> Nationalism bordering on militancy is often accompanied by large numbers of proud cooks.
>
> Bourdain 2001:66

Communities are defined by shared cultural practices; cooking and consumption are at the heart of these practices (Barthes 1979; Miller 1988a; Wilk 1999). Community food identities can also engage with larger political entities, such as states, nations, and regions. Culinary traditions can be encouraged or even imposed by states. Nations, whether empires or modern states, consist of a series of self-identifying groups, at times awkwardly cobbled together as a result of some greater ambition. Government policies are continually attempting to create a sense of unity by generating a shared identity along as many channels as possible. This fostered unity has included language, religion, flags, colors, songs, and also cuisine. How do political leaders and larger communities harness this agency to expand control or solidify unity? Can polity leaders impact the daily practices on the ground, activated by imagined communities, to redirect domestic habits and social values? Leaders are continually trying to do this. One way, of course, is by way of the promotion of national culinary traditions.

In 2011, Michelle Obama, the wife of the then U.S. president, made a concerted effort to promote healthier eating habits at home and in schools through gardening, but the program had mixed results. Some small changes in diet are evident in the United States since this project began, but laws and value systems must change from the ground up as well as top down for such policies to enter each household. Through the dynamic of successful policy creation, joined with daily practices, cuisines are created and perpetuated in the image of the state (Wilk 1999, 2006). This goes beyond civilizing processes to the power of the government over people's lives, hearts, and minds, as discussed in the previous chapter. Some call this the agency of a nation; others call it meddling.

One potent example of food nationalism created by national policymakers is the ideal food pyramid, different versions of which are endorsed by the ministries of agriculture in various countries (Figure 7.2). When we compare the ideal food pyramids from several nations, we can see the historical and cultural variability among these regions in addition to their statecraft. Three examples from the United States, Switzerland, and Asia illustrate some of the similarities and differences. Shared ideas of good health include regular consumption of fruits and vegetables. The most striking difference is the place of red meat in these dietary ideals. It is rare in Asian cuisine, where it is eaten only once a month in the ideal diet, yet daily consumption is recommended in Switzerland and the United States. Water also plays different roles; some have water as a basic daily food whereas others do not even include it. Rehydration has become big business globally, with bottled water found in every country and even shipped around the world. These pyramids not only offer health advice to citizens, they also participate in the crafting of the nation-state identity in that they attempt to illustrate what every citizen should consume. The two pyramids for the United States, from 1992 and 2005, illustrate how this ideal diet has shifted. Exercise is stressed in the more recent chart, with less emphasis on sweets, fats, and grains. The 2005 Alpen pyramid emphasizes fruits and vegetables over grains, as well as exercise, and reflects that society's propensity for infusions and herbal teas, whereas the Asian chart emphasizes rice and other grains but not dairy products. These images reflect the regional and state cuisines with the overt goal of helping members of society, while also reinforcing these traditions.

As nations actively continue to maintain a sense of identity distinct from others, they accentuate unique food cultures, especially through regional

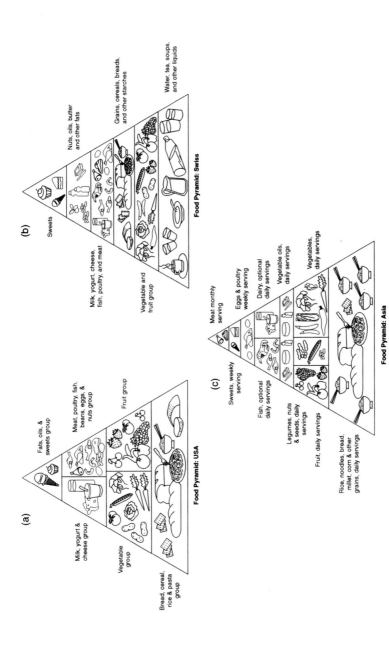

FIGURE 7.2. Food pyramids from the United States, Asia, and Switzerland.
(a) USDA 1992 food pyramid, based on http://en.wikipedia.org/wiki/File:USDA Food_Pyramid.gif, and USDA 2005 en.wikipedia.org/wiki/MyPyramid
(b) Swiss food pyramid, based on http://commons.wikimedia.org/wiki/File:Lebensmittelpyramide_der_sge_2005.svg
(c) Asian food pyramid, based on www.uofmhealth.org/health-library/hn-2026oo6

239

ingredients. Recipes and dishes are developed to assert cultural distinctiveness. The increasing globalization of food since the late twentieth century brings novel foods into everyday production, preparation, and consumption worldwide.

One sophisticated cuisine that was nearly destroyed by colonization is that of central Mexico. The Aztec haute cuisine encountered by the Spanish incorporated diverse and exotic meats and herbs prepared in myriad ways. The city's nobles had the most complex cuisine in Mesoamerica, with thirty different dishes presented to the emperor every day and detailed comportment and manners reflecting the extent of state control across a broad area. Although Tenochtitlan's markets had a range of fruits and animals for sale, the populace's staple food was maize tortillas or maize gruel with wild greens/herbs (*quelites*).

The farmers' households had much simpler cuisines and preparation techniques than were found at Tenochtitlan. Most houses had equipment to make tortillas as well as a range of pots for boiling soup. Brumfiel (1991) argues that as a result of its conquests, pre-Columbian Aztec society incorporated a range of different ethnicities. The powerful Aztec state extracted so much food and resources from the countryside, in the form of both labor and products of labor, families had to adjust their daily practices to meet these increased demands. Such restructuring had an impact on the preparation of family meals. Brumfiel (1991) demonstrates that women had to reschedule their food preparation tasks so they could meet household weaving quotas required by the state and still have dinner ready. Such oversight and control of household production by the state influenced the families' daily culinary practices as people tried to maintain their local, if relatively simple, diet. This is an example of a top-down impact on regional cuisines.

Wilk (2006) provides a riveting example of a nation engaged in the invention of itself through a new cuisine – in this circumstance, out of the ashes of colonialism. Similar to the historical European example of creating new tastes through changing foods and meal structures discussed in Chapter 2, the recent path of Belizean cuisine is instructive. Since its independence from England in 1964, the country has had to create itself out of its complex history of Native American residence (primarily Maya), arrival of Europeans in the form of explorers and pirates, importation of slaves by Europeans for the extraction of natural resources, as well as many years as a British colony. Wilk (2006) presents this circuitous local history and emphasizes the major impact of these multiple cultures and policies within every household. Today much of Belize's food is imported, even though they could produce more of their own food. Years of bad management, poor economic policy, and misinformation have halted most local production projects. The population is indebted to and unwillingly engaged in a range of different worlds outside Belize. But out of the recent burgeoning sense of nationalism has emerged a cuisine, as people awaken their own agency to craft a cuisine based on local products, notwithstanding these historical constraints.

The early postcolonial local foods were signature foods of poverty: wild plants, seafood, and fruit wine. In 1964, few traditional foods remained in the cuisine; restaurant foods were foreign products linked to the British Empire. Today restaurant food is a poly-culinary mix, based on Mexican, Caribbean, and U.S. ingredients. One of the most striking factors in this new cuisine creation was the migration of many of its residents to other countries and cities, where they were overcome with nostalgia. Once away from their homeland, residents realized what they missed about their country (Wilk 2006:169). They brought these food desires with them when they returned to Belize, specifically rice, beans, and fish dishes. Wilk points out that people in Belize have worked at creating their identity through this earlier cuisine, with the impetus of promoting tourism and other industries, as well as reforming and strengthening their identity. Their menus are clearly global, yet local "poverty" foods are now being fused with foreign ingredients into a hybrid but unique cuisine. Because of this shift, local food production is now expanding as most of the current population has grown up in an independent Belize. This is an example of a bottom-up cuisine shift in a global world.

Wilk's Belize study illustrates the tensions that arise from food globalization, as local people find themselves at times resisting and at other times reaffirming their local food traditions based on reevaluations of their cuisine while they are being bombarded by other food traditions. Regional foods participate in the redefinitions of identities as they jockey within the global economy (Hobsbawm and Ranger 1986; James 1997). Reinventing past traditions has become a self-conscious cuisine strategy in many places; the issue of authenticity in ingredients, dishes, and menus was discussed in forty-five contributions to the 2005 Oxford symposium focusing on *Authenticity in the Kitchen* (Hosking 2006). Similar reinvention trajectories have occurred in the past as well. The Romans, for example, reinvented, indigenized, and reactivated Greek culture through sculpture, design, architecture, and food (Foss 1994).

Archaeologically we should be able to recognize the results of both top-down policies as well as on-the-ground reinventions through the evidence of heirlooms, architecture, cooking styles, and the distribution of certain preparations and ingredients. The Japanese are a case in point. Rice has become a signature food that has actively participated in constructing the modern nation of Japan. The place of this food by the populace was fueled by the state (Ohnuki-Tierney 1993:5). A proper Japanese meal must include short-grained sticky rice. In its absence, the meal is only a snack (Ashkenazi 1991). How did rice become this symbolic icon? Why not nuts or fish, both have been important food ingredients for much longer than rice and, unlike rice, indigenous to the Japanese islands? Rice has been a state food since the unification of Japan in the sixteenth century, as it was first brought to Japan in the Yayoi period (between 300 BC and AD 250; Hosoya 2000). Early Japanese documents indicate that the emperor legitimated the centralization of control by mimicking rural harvest rituals in his new state rituals, referencing each farmhouse as he reified rice as a national food (Ohnuki-Tierney 1993:45; Smith 2006). These unifying rituals were filled with symbolism, referring to rice's productivity and fecundity. Linking its chthonic fruitfulness to the growth of the people and the nation became a naturalized metaphor, performed at rituals of aggrandizement that in turn became associated with the emperor but could also resonate within each village. This rice ritual, with its interweaving of meanings and politics, is analogous to the Inka Empire's employment of maize planting and harvest rituals as part of the annual cycle of rites of perpetuation, adopted to symbolize and validate imperial power while referring to each farmer's fields throughout the empire (Rowe 1946).

We go back 2,000 years in Japanese history to track the start of this nationalistic trajectory and note some indigenous tensions surrounding rice. Rice enters the islands' archaeological record at the time of the early formation of polities, during the Yayoi period (Hosoya 2000). Groups migrating to the Japanese islands from the mainland brought rice and paddy farming, augmenting the slash-and-burn farming style of the indigenous people. These indigenous people, the Jomon, were pushed to the extremities of the islands, where they continued hunting and gathering, with a cuisine primarily consisting of meat, nuts, and mixed grains (Ohnuki-Tierney 1993:33–35). Today, because of archaeological research, we know that the symbolic originators of the Japanese spirit, the Jomon, did not eat rice. This fact has caused tension in the nationalist rhetoric, however, owing to the primacy of rice in the modern state's consciousness (Habu 2004). Rice is not indigenous; it is indigenized. The Jomon cuisine focused on nuts and wild seed grains, and their descendants, the Ainu, claim bear meat as their emblematic food. Meat has remained the most highly valued food for the Ainu, whereas Japanese leaders and emperors promoted rice as their signature food, as can still be seen in the Asian food pyramid (Figure 7.2). The Ainu remain at odds with the continued expansion of the rice-eaters' nation, and they use their meat-oriented culinary tradition to help their resistance and survive as a minority within the Japanese state.

Early modern Japanese cultural self-definition was constructed in relation to China, reflected today in the islanders' preference for Japanese short-grain over Chinese/Indian long-grain rice varieties. This rice is central to Japanese national identity, especially as Japan has joined the global economy in the past two centuries. Even the rice paddy has become a sacred place of production "*our* ancestral land, *our* village, *our* region, and ultimately, *our* land, Japan ... *our* pristine past before modernity and foreign influences contaminated it" (Ohnuki-Tierney 1993:10, emphasis in the original). The preference for Japanese varieties of rice and the paddies that produce them has remained an agent in the construction of personhood and society throughout Japanese history (Smith 2006). Today, rice continues to be an agent in Japanese identity maintenance. When cheaper short-grain rice began to be imported from the United States in the late twentieth century, issues of authenticity entered the national debate aggressively (Ohnuki-Tierney 1993). The U.S.-grown rice is the same variety as that grown in Japan, but it is not grown on Japanese soil and thus is not proper, authentic food. Numerous policies to halt rice imports were implemented, but have been eroded with the Japanese recession. As discussed in Chapter 1, Japanese national identity is being re-enforced corporeally, through the taste, texture, and production of rice, as this signature food is a metaphor for the national landscape.

Culinary policies that fed on and encouraged culinary aspirations participated in the formation of the modern British state as well. The image of a meat-rich British cuisine, especially as opposed to the cheese eaters in France, became the stereotype as early as the fourteenth century and has been perpetuated in government policies ever since. Such cuisine promotion became especially important in nation building during the wars against France (Rogers 2004). Later, in the seventeenth century, with the rise of English Puritanism, the British nobility shifted from using food to using furniture, architecture, and the constructed landscape to assert cultural unity, while the French continued to focus on their elite cuisine both at home and in the newly introduced institution of public restaurants. This divergence has meant that *haute cuisine* (by definition) evolved in France rather than in England. The eighteenth-century French nationalistic concern to cook and eat complex dishes meant that French cuisine gained a world standing with which the British to this day cannot compete (sorry Delia Smith and Jamie Oliver).

The British Isles' culinary history, like their political history, is one of waves of arriving immigrants, ideas, and ingredients, the most recent surge coming from the distant territories of the British Empire (Rogers 2004). Meat has been highly valued since at least the Middle Ages. The English nobility prized meat above all other foods. With the expansion of the political machine beyond their shores, there was pressure among the common people at home to participate in the noble ideal of meals dominated by large roasts. If you are what you eat, it is no surprise that the burgeoning Industrial Revolution bourgeoisie wanted to eat like royalty. Ironically, radical acts of parliament were enacted to encourage the production of meat in the seventeenth century, and at the same time sumptuary laws were passed to control the eating of meat. The Scottish Highland Clearance laws gave landowners permission to drive people off lands that had been farmed since Neolithic times to make room for animals. Middle-class meat consumption then increased in part because there were more animals on the landscape. The Sunday roast became the ideal meal in English households until well after World War II, and for many families it still is, but now much of the meat sold in the United Kingdom comes from former colonies, such as New Zealand (Lupton 1996), illustrating again the power of gastropolitical emulation by both those who set the ideal (top-down) as well as the populace who buy into the ideal, perpetuating the Sunday roast, even if the meat comes from across the globe.

French-English tensions continue in competing European Union food policies. The 1997–2000 EU ban on British beef cut to the very core of British pride, exposing their signature food, beef, as being polluted by the mad cow disease that existed at some farms. Pursuant to this ban were extensive campaigns across the United Kingdom promoting the consumption of British beef. Meanwhile, the British press worried that joining the EU would mean that the British market would be swamped by "dodgy food, foul soft cheese and garlic breath" (Hardt-Mautner 1995:188).

The cultural manipulation of top-down political leadership in the construction of new societal identities, such as by the Aztecs, can be juxtaposed with bottom-up instigations of nation formation, as with the growth of the ideal beef on every table in England. Both societies recursively re-crafted their cultural heritage as some local food traditions were enhanced and others rejected within their cultural and political structures of the day. Some national cuisines have gone through a great deal of change over time, as in Italy, where we see constant additions to the core Neolithic diet, with noodles, tomatoes, and finally maize polenta now forming core Italian dishes. Other territories have stable culinary traditions, illustrated across the Anatolian plain where lamb, wheat, lentils, chickpeas, and yogurt have been the signature ingredients for 10,000 years. Of course, both regions grow and eat very old food traditions as well as newer, introduced crops. Both trajectories are outcomes of many local practices converging with larger political pressures across differing landscapes. Through the ebb and flow of local agricultural decisions and broader policymaking some culturally important foods are crafted into metaphors of the self and of the state, at times propagating nationalistic feelings, at other times channeling economic policies.

National cuisines are often fantasies conjured by policymakers to encourage a sense of identity throughout an imagined community. But if we look a bit closer, at the social meanings, the political reasons for their existence, and the ubiquity of their engagements, we can see how the dynamic between food traditions and policy provides a sense of how both bottom-up and top-down gastroforces could be active in our understandings about the past. Culinary strategies can activate a form of resilience, as in the case of Mexicans who are still able to enjoy their native crops; resistance, as with the Ainu and their meat consumption; or ambivalence, as in the new foods taken up by the Oglala Lakota (beef taco instead of buffalo) and the Samburu (maize instead of cow blood), both still claiming as their signature food something they are no longer consuming in substantial amounts now. Evidence of rapid, radical culinary shifts in the archaeological record may suggest a shift in food production and distribution as a consequence of external pressures. Slow shifts such as the uptake of the Neolithic package across Europe suggest a cognitively dissonant dance of the old and the new during this adoption, resistance occurring hand in hand with curiosity.

### Food at the Boundary: Culture Contact

> Anthropologists have known that at least since the work of Boas and his students that cultures are generally foreign in origin and local in pattern.
>
> Sahlins 1999:xi

Italian and Anatolian culinary histories highlight an important characteristic of culinary change. People react differently when they come in contact with others' traditions. As mentioned before, these situations create moments in which individuals must actively reassess their long-held values and ways of living. Although both Italians and Anatolians came in contact with many culinary traditions, through conquest, trade, and migration, they reacted differently to these contacts. What can these different contact histories tell us about identity construction and ontologies? Beliefs about the proper ways of being in the world, especially about preparing and eating food, reflect how communities see themselves as well as their control over their own identities. How much transformation occurs when communities interact with others illustrates both their cultural resilience and their power to engage in this cultural contact.

Cuisine transformations usually correlate with social or political upheaval (Macbeth and Lawry 1997:4; Powers and Powers 1984). I have discussed how groups give significance to salient foods and dishes and have seen how these become signature items even in the face of radical change (Appadurai 1981; Douglas 1984). What happens to group identities when groups are in sustained contact? Traditional foods are presented using unfamiliar etiquette; new ingredients alter common dishes, resurrecting the omnivore's dilemma on both sides. Changes in plants, animals, and vessels often occur before other material signs of this contact are manifest in the archaeological record, reminding us how important the culinary window is to studying meaning in past social and political worlds.

Colonial Encounters

> We [Algerians] can marry [French] Christians, but we cannot eat with them. We can eat with the Jews, but we cannot marry them.
>
> Jansen 2001:207

Colonial encounters bring to the fore issues of inclusion and exclusion that had been unspoken. The study of identity through colonial entanglements starkly points out the differential powers that operate at contact situations (Thomas 1991). In a colonial conjuncture, asymmetrical polities not only come in contact with each other but also when one group wrests control from the other, initiating deep political, economic, psychological, and social transformations. Less subtle than in the nationalism endeavor, colonialism is an overt act of people making subjects of other people. These encounters often accompany conquest. But even when colonial actions are not conquest situations, the asymmetries ripple across all aspects of social, political, economic, and religious life. These unequal processes have been occurring throughout human history: "[I]t is reasonable to assert both that contemporary foodways and identities around the world are in large measure the product of a long history of colonial encounters and that, reciprocally, food has been a consistently prominent material medium for the enactment of colonialism" (Dietler 2007:218–219). There is no uniform outcome to these aggressive meetings, nor is there a typical colonial trajectory that can be applied to all investigations. As many historical examples suggest, culinary traditions participate at the heart of the colonial entanglement. In these historical moments, what does it mean when some foods instigate resistance while others are avidly accepted? How do these ingredients, preparations, tools, and flavors participate in the colonial endeavor? We can look at the participation of foods in colonial situations for these tensions in cultural identity practices.

Most cuisines incorporate exotic foods that were introduced through colonialism; many of these dishes have even become signature foods. The chile pepper throughout China, the potato in Ireland, and the tomato in Italy all are outcomes of colonialism, brought from their homelands, adopted and indigenized into the heart of a cuisine (Buccini 2006). Clearly not all plants experience this globalization: what happened to maygrass (*Phalaris caroliniana* Walter), or lupine (*Lupinus mutabilis* L.), or mashua (*Tropaeolum tuberosum* Ruíz y Pavón)? They did not spread around the globe as important foods; these three plants have remained in their home territories and some, like the domestic maygrass, have stopped being produced and eaten altogether. This selective process of encounter and incorporation has created a world of creolized food (Dietler 2007:225). Dietler's example of selective appropriation along the French coast illustrates the asymmetrical resistance people have to many foods, in particular they did not take up Roman cooking whereas wine was accepted. Along the medieval Silk Road, people who came in contact with other culinary traditions were often curious and even desirous of the new commodities. However, colonial entanglements always have a sinister side, with forced acceptance of new foods and restrictions on old eating habits. Some cultural settings are very restrictive, with almost total control over food intake, and yet there is evidence of selectivity and choice operating in terms of preparation if not in terms of ingredients.

Many colonial encounters illustrate selectively adopted foods. In indigenous cultures any adopted foods were politically charged, as if eating the foods was incorporating the conquest. Although exchanges go both ways, it is often the subjected who end up tasting the bitterness of the colonial foods. Bread is an important food in Algeria, where it is salient in all communities, even now after the colonists have relinquished their full power. Because Algeria was a French colony, French Christians and Jews have settled there, bringing European foods into the cities and shops. This is highlighted most iconically in the baguette. More than different processing steps, shape, and taste differentiates French leavened bread from Arab flatbread. These two breads carry powerful political and colonial connotations (Jansen 2001). Ten percent of Algerians' income is spent on bread, both French and Algerian styles. Algerians have assimilated the dominant French ideology outwardly by purchasing and eating baguettes, but not inwardly (Jansen 2001). Their appreciation of French bread is tinged with resentment. Although they eat both types of bread, their practices around the breads differ. They save and reheat their homemade flat bread, eating every scrap, while they throw away the French bread if it is not consumed at the meal for which it was purchased. These acts are not linked to the cost of these loaves, as the French bread is more expensive and logically would be the type more likely to be saved as leftovers. This reaction to the colonizer is seen even more clearly at Algerian ceremonial meals where only homemade Arab bread is served, never baguettes (ibid.:204). Through situated consumption of these two breads, Algerians are negotiating their continued resistance to the colonizers while reaffirming their Algerian and Islamic identities (ibid.:206).

These colonial entanglements are multifaceted, with many different social and symbolic trajectories. To understand these in archaeological settings we should trace the encounter first through the impact on the colonized, who are usually the more severely impacted. Changes in food use and differing food values can reflect the dynamics between the conquered and the conquerors. As I suggested with regard to the expansive power of Chinese Han conquests, the colonizer can influence the local culinary traditions. The strength of the larger political influences as they come in contact with the resilience of the local culture speaks to the depth of the entanglements. It is our archaeological task to separate enforced foodways from "emulatory" practices. We can attempt to see these differences through the combination of foods processed and consumed by the different groups.

Enrique Rodríguez-Alegría (2005) illustrates the double side of this food entanglement in the American Spanish colonies. Finding local indigenous serving vessels along with the Spanish vessels in colonial houses, he suggests that despite the well-defined moral dictates and rules against Spaniards eating the same food as the Aztec natives, some of the colonizers not only ate with the Aztecs, they also ate "like Aztecs," incorporating indigenous foods and their presentation styles, reflected in the pottery, into their own culinary practices. In the range of reasons for such acceptance, Rodríguez-Alegría supports a show of respect for the indigenous elites by some Spanish, as the Spanish negotiated their social relationships in the larger Aztec society.

Such negotiations are seen in the multidimensional identities reformed after the Roman conquest of England. Archaeological data provide evidence of acceptance and emulation but also of rejection and resistance (van der Veen 2008). These tensions played out across many domains. Examples of these values are evident in culinary styles of spicing food. Differences between the conquerors and the conquered are evident at Romano-British settlements, where soldiers received cuts of meat that were better quality than what was available in the local fare (Crabtree 1990:163). Local leaders, propped up by the Roman Empire, found themselves having to perform Roman meals and eat Roman foods (M. Jones 2007). While this might have been resisted at first, the archaeological data reflect that some of these Roman foodways filtered into both the local landed gentry as well as the rural peasantry. This can be glimpsed in the evidence of foreign plant use and cooking habits at late Iron Age–early Roman settlements such as Silchester (Lodwick 2013a, 2013b) and across rural England (Ballannye 2006; Cramp et al. 2011; M. Jones 1997, 2007; Willcox 1977). At Silchester (Calleva Atrebatum in Hampshire), celery (*Apium graveolens* subsp. *Dulce* (Mill.) Schübl. & G. Martens), olive (*Olea europea* L.), and coriander (*Coriandrum sativum* L.) have been found in deposits dating to between AD 20 and 40, suggesting an early taste for these traded items (Lodwick 2013a, 2013b; van der Veen 2008). Other fruit and spices arrived during Roman rule, such as fig (*Ficus carica* L.) and apple (*Malus* sp.). After the departure of the Romans many of their herbs slowly disappeared from southern England, not returning until the late medieval times, as discussed in Chapter 5. This extinction of colonial culinary traditions reflects both the agency of value and taste as well as the power of identity within English cuisine. The Roman soldiers who settled slowly began to eat like the English.

We can trace this conquest and its impact on local identities in the changing meat use at one community, Wilconte, Oxfordshire (Hamshaw-Thomas 2000). From Roman texts and artifactual remains archaeologists know that this village was occupied for two hundred years, AD 47–260. Before the Romans arrived, the local populace ate mainly sheep and goat meat, with mutton stew being the main protein dish in their cuisine. We can assume that local residents enjoyed the flavor of mutton. The community's political, economic, and gustatory conditions changed with the Roman military occupation. Based on the evidence from their barracks, the Romans preferred beef and pork, which they procured as tribute. The local population continued to eat sheep and goat as evidenced in their rubbish pits, which contained almost 70 percent sheep bone with little evidence of cattle (Hamshaw-Thomas 2000:167). Hamshaw-Thomas suggests that the local farmers continued their culinary tradition but not their farming strategies. They had to pay their taxes in the animals the Romans requested. Likewise, at Silchester and Colchester (Camulodunum, in Essex), large numbers of pig bones have been uncovered in the central basilica sector of the Roman town, suggesting pig offerings were made to the deities. These faunal densities contrast with much lower proportions of pig bone in the deposits near the town defenses, where the local populace resided. These differences seem to be more than economic; as at Wilconte, they suggest that both the Roman military in Britannia as well as the local residents were maintaining their preferences for meat (Grant 2002).

As the Roman occupation dragged on, however, the ideals of Roman life – wearing togas and sandals, drinking wine, and eating imported fruits – began to percolate into the British landed gentry's *habitus* as part of the local politics and economic jockeying. This is seen most clearly at Fishbourne near Chichester (Sussex), a seat of the tribal leader Cogidumnus, who ruled the local tribe on behalf of the Roman emperors from his Roman-style villa. This Romanization, complete with arcades and banquets, began to influence British eating habits after the first generation of Roman residence and is marked at Wilconte by more cattle being consumed after his time (Jones 2007:227). Around AD 120, as Roman influence waned, Wilconte became less engaged in the trading networks that the Romans had operated, retreating into self-sufficient production. But things had changed permanently. Even after the Romans left, Wilconte's meat preferences remained Romanized, with the middens now containing 30 percent cattle remains while sheep and goat made up 55 percent. The adoption of beef into the local diet reflects the colonial influence on local production (forced) but also on taste (adopted). Were these Romanized meals unintentional fusions generated by enforced beef production, learned eating Roman culinary traditions, intentional links to the past, or forced consumption by the colonized that took the form of eating the colonizers' food?

Emulation as well as power dance throughout these shifting colonial cuisines. This imperial pressure on local culinary traditions is also visible in the Inka conquest evidence in the Jauja region of Perú, presented in Chapter 5. Based on macrobotanical data from that intermontane valley, maize production increased in the local diet when the residents were required to produce maize for the ruling Inka. After the defeat of the empire, maize remained common in the local fields and diets, much as beef did in post-Roman England (Hastorf 2001). Today both crops are highly valued in these modern states – beef in England and maize in Perú.

The fact that this colonizing entanglement works both ways is not often mentioned. British cuisine also influenced the Roman soldiers, who began to eat mutton stew and drink beer (Grant 2002). Such appropriation of indigenous cuisine is especially evident for those who budded off from the empire and remained in the country of conquest – ex-pats, like the French-speaking Christians living in Algeria today. Justin Lev-Tov (1999) presents evidence of this type of colonial entanglement, of acceptance interwoven with resistance, by the Frankish crusader immigrants who settled in a walled compound in Corinth, Greece, in the eleventh century. These immigrants were small-scale conquerors, ostensibly on their way to Jerusalem but basically settling down along the way. Studying the faunal remains, Lev-Tov identified several eating communities living within the Frankish compound. By comparing them with the indigenous community and finding differences in the consumption patterns, he ascertained the web of values and identities that the conquerors practiced. The two Frankish groups that he identified were (1) the elite Frankish lords along with the monks (together constituting the Crusaders) and (2) their Frankish servants. While all dwelt in the fortress, only the servants' rubbish was similar to the local Greek residents' food remains. These servants to the knights ate the local domestic animals: pigs, cattle, sheep, and goats. Perhaps the Frankish servants had local wives who prepared food for them, like the Uruk traders at the fringes of Mesopotamia (Stein 2012) or the Inuit marine hunters at the Russian colony of Fort Ross, California (Wake 1995)? These servants were not able to or concerned with maintaining their previous food traditions but "went native" and probably engaged with additional local cultural practices, clearly different from the elites of the Frankish community who ate their identity.

The Frankish monks and the upper-class ecclesiastical leaders continued their French food traditions. The monks and nobility ate wild, hunted animals, as did the European upper classes at the time (Grant 2002; Lev-Tov 1999; Super 1988). To determine the strength of boundary maintenance for the ecclesiastical elite, Lev-Tov (1999:94) also compared this Corinthian priory rubbish with that of the contemporaneous Augustinian Friars of Leicester, England. Again, both religious communities consumed meat with similar frequencies, reflecting the enforcement of a codified economic and social tradition in their meat consumption. At Corinth, the meat that the Frankish noblemen and clergy consumed was diverse, including terrestrial and marine foods, domestic animals (sheep, goat, cow, pig, and birds), and also fish, mollusks, and birds (including peacock, partridge, and great bustard). The clustered densities of wild animal taxa suggested to Lev-Tov that they were consumed in feasts at the monastery. These feasts would have allowed the ex-pat Corinthian elite to participate in their cuisine ideals, activating identity, nostalgia as well as euphoria. The faunal remains illustrate how the different foods subtly document the differing identities and self-identified groups within this Crusader community. This variability was due in part to the fact that the food was produced locally but also to the powerful position of the Crusaders across that region. The monks and priests clearly worked hard to maintain their Frankish identities through unwavering aesthetics and cuisines. Despite being conquerors, however, some members of the Frankish group were from the lower classes, who perhaps had begun to identify (and intermarry) with the local population.

These relationships with the locals are evident outside the compound. The Frankish impact on the local cuisine was not so much in the ingredients being consumed as in the style of dining and ways of eating. In the Byzantine era, mainland Greeks ate communally, sitting around a common dish and bringing food to their mouths with chunks of bread (a practice now better known for Anatolia, the Levant, and North and East Africa). Their consumption style became more individualized after the Crusader invasion. Even in the eleventh century, the elite Franks ate their food from individual plates and bowls (Vroom 2000). This influence is reflected in the changing ceramic serving assemblages throughout Greece at this time. Later, with the routing of the Franks by the Ottoman Empire, family meals reverted to communal serving bowls, suggesting that the articulation between these two communities, the Franks and the Greeks, was less potent than that between the Romans and the Britons, who left longer-lasting culinary influences in England. Additionally, the Greeks might have been relieved to be able to return to their native ways of communal eating, remembering these past meals even after several generations of conquest.

The colonization experiences of the Greeks and the British reveal not only how the conquered react to new political pressures but also the spectrum of cultural emulation. The permeable boundaries and shifting identities within these encounters provide a sense of the varied impacts within the colonial struggle. Did the Greeks take up other individuating constructs from the Franks? There is little evidence of it. It seems that the Franks and their individualistic propensities did not last in the region once the Crusaders left. The Greeks had not yet begun to envisage themselves as part of the Frankish world by the time the Franks departed, whereas the British tribal leaders seem to have appropriated more of the imperial Roman world during that longer occupation. This conclusion is also indicated in the roads, architecture, town structure, and clothing as well as in the cuisine shifts of the British nobility that lingered after the departure of the Roman legions.

Based on these examples, we can begin to follow the contexts of specific inculcations and how they are reassigned meaning within the British medieval world. Recall some of the examples mentioned earlier, including that of Richard Wilk (2006) on Belizean cuisine and Amanda Logan (2012) regarding the series of colonial waves in western Africa, discussed in Chapter 3. Both cogently illustrate the complex tensions and entanglements fomenting within the waves of colonial encounters. Types and tempos of cultural contact have become a rich and productive place not only to trace colonialism and group identity but also to see how values shift through recursive practice in these dynamic settings. Strategies we can identify archaeologically include the blending of cuisines, dishes, and ingredients; submersion through concealment; resilience of crops, flavors, and dishes; substitutions, as in the structural replacement of one item for another; and alternation, which is evident in small shifts within the general cuisine that suggest external influence, but without changing the core of the cuisine. Through historical and archaeological examples we learn how political, economic, social, and psychological conquests impacted local people, entering their homes and their cuisines. This process was not uniform, as Dietler (2007) points out for the Lattes of southern France, when the Romans came to trade. Acceptance of foreign cuisine was not uniform in any colonial setting; rather, it led to the emergence of a range of creolized foods. These histories of differential power and influence highlight the usefulness of food to archaeologists for revealing the dynamics of these larger forces, activated in everyday experiences, such as that clearly illustrated by the Algerians and their feelings about the baguette (Jansen 2001).

Immigration
Culinary traditions are put to the test when people move. Different immigrant histories are registered in cuisine transformations, reflecting not only the political and economic forces underlying such movements but also the level of integrity of a group's identity. For example, the common Near Eastern combination of fruit and meat can be traced back to Bronze Age, pre-Islamic consumption styles, reaffirming links to millennium-old living conditions with each meal, carried along in many migrations. As with the Anatolian cuisine mentioned earlier in the chapter, the signature recipes have endured a series of conquests and migrations across their territory. Their cuisine still centers on the signature foods of bulgur wheat, fruit, nuts, and lentils. Recent Iranian immigrants to London, for example, have been confronted by many new foods and ways of preparation. Yet

they maintain the flavor combinations of core ingredients, such as meals with apricots and lamb, which continue to re-create Iranian identities in a foreign land, both physically and emotionally (Harbottle 1997:177). They are able to maintain this culinary tradition because of global trade, which brings apricots to England regularly, and also because they have the economic capacity to purchase them. What if they could not buy apricots or were forced to eat only local cuisines? How much more would their identities change?

Nineteenth-century California received an onslaught of immigrants from around the world, because of the Gold Rush. When the Chinese first arrived, merchants began importing food items from China, enabling traditional food patterns to persist among the Chinese immigrants (Huelsbeck 1988). This culinary continuity encouraged the Chinese to retain their ethnic identity via language, clothing, and food, despite fairly constant antagonism from their Anglo neighbors (Naruta 2006; Voss 2008). In Oakland, California, contrasting yet contiguous ethnic identities are found in distinct midden deposits in the different neighborhoods (Felton et al. 1984). In Chinese-American deposits, pig bones constitute 50–100% of the large animal bones, reflecting the Chinese consumption of pork dishes. These frequencies are substantially higher than in contemporaneous Euro-American rubbish (Huelsbeck 1988). The Chinese district deposits also uniquely contain cat and pond turtle remains, neither of which was considered food by Anglo-Americans. Butchery and preparation styles also persisted, reflecting different ways of breaking and cutting the various carcasses. Tensions arose between these communities in Oakland as the more powerful Anglos periodically burned Chinese food shops and even relocated entire Chinese neighborhoods (Naruta 2006).

In the twentieth century, Italian immigrants moved to many U.S. cities, where they actively maintained their Italian cuisine by opening their own food stores and restaurants. This parallel story also illustrates conscious identity re-creation, thanks to energetic trade networks. Italian restaurants and delicatessens eventually spread to all North American cities.

Continuity is not always the norm for immigrants. Many immigrants shifted their diets when they settled in the United States and Canada. Scandinavian immigrants, for example, typically moved to the countryside to grow their own food. By moving to the center of the continent, they lost the marine component of their cuisine; further, they switched from a barley- to a wheat-based diet. Daily meals were significantly different for these Norwegian immigrants, much more so than for the Italian Americans, who worked hard to reproduce their homeland food traditions.

These two extremes suggest the ends of a spectrum with joining the encircling culture on one end or resisting and actively working to maintain their food identity on the other. Nowhere is this tension more clear than in elementary schools in the United States, where children feel the need to eat what others are eating in order to fit in. Many of us felt this pressure, even if we were not first-generation immigrants.

## Family and Household Identity

Probably the most intensive location of identity formation is within the family. This is the place for training, sharing, and forming social relationships, as well as forming one's sense of self (Fischler 1988:280). Understanding familial food culture provides insight into the social building blocks of most societies, whether large or small, aggregated or dispersed, hierarchical or egalitarian. Archaeology has experienced a renewed interest in this social unit and the relational world of people in small household groups (Carsten and Hugh-Jones 1995; Joyce and Gillespie 2000). Eating together demarcates family membership, with sharing being central (Appadurai 1981; Lupton 1996:25; Meigs 1987). Mealtimes are when these social units typically come together, making eating the activity that dominates and unites the household (Falk 1991, 1994; Fischler 1988). At family meals, eating preferences become habituated in unconscious acts, as children gain their membership by sharing certain foods and preparation practices. Females usually monitor the family's physical and emotional well-being through these acts of preparation and serving (March 1987).

The etiquette of food handling, bodily comportment, social skills, and table manners is taught at family meals (Lupton 1996:36). The emotional side of food sharing, whether self-contained with individual portions or open with communal bowls, expresses different but shared identities. Probably the most common topic of conversation when people are away from their family is about the food they normally eat. Nostalgia for childhood foods triggers strong emotions, out of desire, practice, and identity. It is through these memories that food participates in family maintenance so far from the physical home (Lupton 1996:37; Shack 1971; Sutton 2001).

Both Gillespie (2000) and LeCount (2008) note how the house anchors members in space and time through daily mealtimes. These crucial loci for identity tend to be less prominent in archaeological discussions, with more focus on civic ceremonies than on families. By reorienting our interests to emphasize family creation we can also reorient toward people's daily lives and their identity practices (Gillespie 2000; Hastorf 2003).

As I discussed in Chapter 2, the daily meal's locations of production – the kitchen, the hearth, or the table – are the locales of family *habitus* creation, where social relationships are most commonly renewed or renegotiated. Children realign their position within the family at each meal. Participants are informed about their place in the world by how food is distributed and the consumption actions expected (Appadurai 1981). People who share food tend to trust each other. One always feels closer to those with whom one has shared a meal. In Arab society, eating together creates fictive kin, and this kinship reverberates into other domains (Robertson Smith 1889).

Although the definition of a household varies, determining household membership based on those who eat together provides us with a useful definition. The associated activities, including food presentation and meal content, shift the discussion from the objects to the actors and their interaction with the objects. Some archaeologists have begun to move in this direction by focusing on the hearth (Isbell 1997; Jones 2007; King 2003, 2007). Sharing food around a hearth creates community. Hearths, stoves, or hobs can become the material representation of familial existence. This orientation places the emphasis on food sharing and the archaeology of cooking.

Anna Meigs (1987) noted that Highland New Guinea residents become family members not through birth or marriage, but through being fed by the same person. Kinship is created by postnatal food sharing. Immigrants can become kin through eating food produced on community lands and prepared by its members (Meigs 1987:121). This creation of family through food sharing can come about by close proximity to each other (Meigs 1988). In societies such as the Hua or the Arabs, eating together creates family membership, which is different from the western European concept of unchangeable family membership based on shared genes.

In the Western tradition, we are aware of a subtle ordinal scale of intimacy in inviting someone to share food. Mary Douglas created a sequence of family intimacy that begins with the sharing of a nonalcoholic drink and proceeds to an alcoholic drink, a snack, a quick meal, a sit-down dinner, a family meal, a birthday party meal, and finally a family feast. Participation even in the family feast, however, does not equate to family membership. Other ties must happen for that membership to occur.

We learn more about culinary membership and intra-family relations from the Culina of the Brazilian state of Acre in the westernmost Amazon Basin. Pollock (1985, 1992) describes a relational personhood and family construction that is reconfirmed through eating. Men provide households with the raw ingredients, focused around the white-lipped peccary (*Tayassu pecari*). Women then "tame" the foodstuffs through processing and cooking. Once the food is acculturated and civilized, it becomes edible. For the Culina, a family group that eats together maintains their social balance as well as corporeal harmony. Culina relational personhood is defined by specific food restrictions, as will be clarified in Chapter 8. For example, new parents must focus on eating good-smelling plants, such as wild fruit. To help the baby, they are prohibited from eating meals consisting of meat and most cultivated plants. Eating together performs and creates community. The Culina therefore enact a sense of civilized corporeality in their meals; the Culina's social axis is family membership.

Like the Hua, the Culina and their neighbors, the Wari' perpetuate the family through eating their recent dead. Their internal logic is filled with care, as this act of endocannibalism helps ensure the continuity of the family line (Conklin 1993, 1995; Pollock 1992; Sanday 1986). The reason for this consumption is to help the recently deceased family member transform into a white-lipped peccary, the signature food of the Culina, who can then return and feed the family. Family members see themselves in a recursive cycle in which individuals alternate between being a human (and eating peccary) and being a peccary (to be eaten by humans) (Conklin 1995:80; Pollock 1992:2). Consumption is the metaphor of life. As Conklin (1995:95) notes, "For Wari', however, the magic of existence lies in the commonality of human and animal identities, in the movements between the human and nonhuman worlds embodied in the recognition through cannibalism and human participation in both poles of the dynamic of eating and being eaten." This may seem unusual, but as archaeologists, it behooves us to consider these ontologies of creating membership through eating.

Family dining takes many different forms, but each one is informative about the social world of the participants. In some settings men and women do not eat the same food but eat together; in others they do not eat together but eat the same food. In India, for example, lower cast and elite families eat together around the hearth (Conklin 1988). This was true also in medieval Europe, where even the lord of a manor house ate daily meals with the servants, close to the hearth. Throughout Africa and the Near East, men and women eat separately.

Studying household food activities illustrates how food imbues families with social position and membership. In his study of familial gastropolitics of Tamil Brahmin families Appadurai (1981) emphasizes that behavior encodes social position, as seen in Mary Weismantel's example of the

Ecuadorian family meal cooked by the angry wife, described in Chapter 6. Social position determines who makes the decisions about meal preparation. Although men's decisions are rarely contested, the senior woman, based on seniority and affinity, typically organizes cooking tasks. A different structure operates for food presentation. Male precedence in India means that the elder male patrikin receive food before the matrikin, and old people before the younger ones. When families live together but have separate hearths, serving from the different hearths becomes even more complex. Tensions that arise as to what and where the in-laws and kin guests should eat are played out in what is to be served, in what sequence, and from whose larder. Food in these familial settings forcefully displays the multiple strategies of the female players. If there is tension between the senior mother-in-law and the daughter-in-law, the younger woman can resort to sabotaging the meal preparation through altering the spices, the serving order, or the contents of each plate. The family meal becomes a gastropolitical discourse about where one fits in the social world (Appadurai 1981:497).

Women's ability to constitute and structure family identity through food practices has been recorded in many settings. As with the Tamil women studied by Appadurai, pre-contact Iroquois women also controlled the distribution of the agricultural produce, both by what was brought into the household and through the meals they prepared (Brown 1975:249). Commensal hospitality was highly valued in Iroquois society. Notably different from the Tamil, among the Iroquois generosity reflected well on the females only, not on the men (ibid.:247). Iroquois elder women oversaw the preparation and serving of the meals. Stored food stuffs was a major form of wealth in the tribe (ibid.:250). Most powerfully, these women could withhold food from their male family members if they did not agree with their political opinions. Such an action would not be possible for Tamil women. For archaeologists, the size and structure of the daily meal helps define household size, moving us closer to discovering the composition and identity of past households. The performance of food presentation must for the most part remain in our imaginations, but one of my goals is to encourage you to realize how important in culinary culture, identity, and family relations this performance is.

To better reconstruct past meals I turn to the tools, containers, sources of heat, preparation surfaces, and spaces that are engaged in meal preparation. Any utensil that has a "distinct referent and transmits a clear message" may be emblematic of a group (Wiessner 1983:257). The capacity to express both household and community identity lies in the culinary equipment's everyday presence. Pottery expresses social identities as strongly as culinary traditions do, hinting at the form of institutionalized political power as it participates in local *habitus*. Bowls and jars in a household have value and history for the people who use them. Their production and circulation mark affiliation at a very fundamental level, associated with all who share the same type of cooking and presentation styles. Domestic cooking vessels participate in identity discussions because of their central place in routinized culinary tasks. Vessel forms usually conform to required tasks as they connect the people who use them with the tasks they perform (LeCount 2008). In the American Southwest, Mills (2004) and Turner and Lofgren (1996) offer evidence of changing family size by comparing the volumes of the cooking pots and the serving vessels. They estimate the typical number of people a cooking vessel can serve at one time, based on modern average portion sizes. They conclude that for more than a thousand years, between AD 500 and 1900, the average Hopi family size steadily increased (Turner and Lofgren 1996). By measuring the individual serving vessels in relation to the cooking pot volumes we learn that group-dining size grew from about 4 to 7 people over 1,400 years. These meal changes speak of changing family structure. Did grown children continue to live at home? Were more elders staying in the family unit? Did extended families increasingly eat together? Were more people being brought into the family, or did more children survive? These cooking vessel changes suggest that the sense of family identity shifted over time, which in turn unveils the social world of the Hopi villages, supporting the inference of the family unity's increasing importance within the larger society.

Ethnographic information helps us consider such questions. In Dangtalan, Philippines, Trostel (1994) found that only certain cooking vessels in a family's ceramic assemblage are closely correlated with household size. The vessels used to prepare the signature dish of meat and vegetables reflect the family's size and social standing (wealth) more than did the vessels used to cook rice, the other main ingredient in their meal. Rice pots are more or less the same volume across all families and statuses in the Dangtalan community. The fact that family size and social engagement can be selectively recorded in ceramic vessels might clarify the history of the Hopi eating community. Which of the Hopi vessels coincided with family size? Plotting vessel size ranges for *different* cooking and consumption vessels, especially in conjunction with isotope or organic residue evidence to record potential diets and meals, can clarify past family cuisines, family compositions, and relational identities, as Barbara Mills (1999, 2004, 2007) has found in the American Southwest.

## The Maya Culinary Tradition through Family Meals and Feasts

Pursuing the issues that have been raised in this chapter concerning identity formation and the power of recursive memory activation in meals,
signature dishes, and family creation, I present a detailed archaeological
example to illustrate that archaeologists can uncover community identities, praxis, and social entanglements through archaeological food patterns.
Identity taskscapes are materialized in the activities that feed a family. The
archaeology of the southern Maya (1800 BC–AD 1050) provides us with
especially detailed information about cooking practices and how they created both the family and the village community, evident by focusing on several meals. Mayan families who lived in moist climates typically lived on
and around raised housemounds. These mounds were arranged in small
clusters. People prepared their daily meals on and around these mounds
and workspaces (Morell-Hart 2011).

The ethnographic and archaeological evidence indicates that most
meals were composed of two dishes: boiled soups and steamed tamales.
The major staple was maize, usually with some meat added to one of the
dishes. Beans, squash, and a range of wild plant taxa were also important.
Daily food preparation involved boiling and toasting. Although maize
dominated most diets, the cuisine was diverse, resulting in regional variation in this maize-centric diet. Based on a stable isotope analysis from
Lamanai, Belize (500 BC–AD 100), in addition to other sites in the highlands and lowlands, maize constituted between 37 percent and 50 percent
of the Maya diet, increasing over time (White and Schwarcz 1989; Tykot
2002). Higher nitrogen values and wild animal bones regularly found in
middens suggest that the elite (larger house mounds) ate more meat and/or
seafood than did their neighbors.

Farmers had control over their own production and diet. In Belize, farmers ate a greater range of plants than did the elites who resided in the center
of the settlements, suggesting that farmers gathered wild forest plants as
they worked in their maize fields (*milpas*) (Gerry 1998). The same narrow
diet among the elite is also recorded later at Copan (in Honduras, AD
600–1000) in urban households, where men especially ate slightly more
maize-enriched diets than did women (Reed 1999).

In addition to the daily meal, private familial rituals that include food
offerings to the ancestors and the deities taking place in the house have a
long history among the Maya (Bayles 2001; McAnany 1995). The ceramic
and isotope data suggest that even the more modest families had ritual
meals and feasts. Cooking vessels and their sizes were similar across all

statuses, but their frequencies varied. The ceramic distributions suggest that each house cluster re-created its identity through honoring the individual lineage with these meals. The more modest households conducted these sacred feasts with maize-filled gourds and a few chocolate vessels. The most intricate decorated vessels used for serving chocolate are concentrated in elite houses.

There is also evidence for larger, more competitive political meals where alliances were negotiated and reconfirmed (LeCount 2001). Maya feasting images found on murals and cut stone suggest a wide range of feast dishes, adding meat wrapped in leaves or maize sheaves and steamed in earth ovens. Cacao beverages were heated in jars and then poured into ceramic tumblers for presentation (LeCount 2001:946). Ethnographer Evon Vogt (1976) notes that beverages are an essential part of any important social Maya transaction, with the use of these drinking vessels differentiating daily meals from special meals. Today, beverages are made from a variety of substances, but in the past, feast drinks were derived from chocolate (Joyce and Henderson 2007). Cacao (*Theobroma cacao* L.) is expensive today, as it was in the past, growing in quite specialized conditions that cannot be industrialized.

These ceramic "cacao" tumblers developed out of gourd cups. In the region today, gourd vessels filled with cacao or maize drinks are associated with fertility (Ventura 1996). Gourds symbolize wombs and breasts among some Maya groups, linking the fecundity of the people who are drinking to that of the earth. In some ways, gourds might be more chthonically significant for sacred offerings than ceramic serving bowls are. The elite Maya used ceramic vessels as well as gourd bowls in their offerings, recorded on paintings and carvings. The small ceramic vessels uncovered in excavations seem to have had a skeuomorphic link to these gourds. Gourd fragments have not been identified at Maya sites, nor have leaves that would have been used to wrap the tamales. Poor preservation has thus far prevented us from pursuing this macrobotanically, but future microbotanical analysis could find evidence of gourds and leaves. Differential preservation directs Maya scholars to be ceramic-centric in their food discussions, but these plant utensils should be thought about and included in food discussions as well.

To reveal the ceramic distribution at Xunantunich, a Late Classic Maya city in Belize, house mounds of both centrally located elite households as well as families living on the edge of the settlement were excavated. Lisa LeCount (2001) identified five major ceramic jar types, four for serving and one for boiling. She found fewer of the small ceramic bowls in the Maya "commoner" [*sic*] house mound clusters than in the centrally located, larger mounds, supporting the ethnographic evidence that the elite meals were served in ceramic bowls while others ate out of gourds or on leaves. Plates and platters are sparse at any of the house mounds, suggesting that they were for rare or otherwise very special dishes. Chocolate drinking vessels are present at all house clusters but are more numerous in the larger, elite structures. LeCount does not quantify the vessel differences between the households directly, but she does note variability in assemblage composition. This fairly redundant pattern strongly suggests a regular *chaîne opératoire* food preparation activity for these daily meals that spilled over into the feasts occasionally.

The spectacularly well-preserved Maya village of Joya de Cerén in El Salvador provides a closer view of how food creates family and community identities (Sheets 2002a, 2002b). Cerén was occupied in Classic times (AD 250-900), before Xunantunich became a large town. It was a farming village located in the fertile Zapotitán Valley in the far southern Maya cultural sphere. From the detailed excavations and the exquisitely preserved households covered by deep volcanic ash deposits, Payson Sheets and his colleagues have found no evidence of what LeCount calls "elites" and others call "lineages" that intermarried with other Maya centers (Sheets 2002a, 2002b). This was a small community of farmers who fed themselves with their own produce, periodically trading for ceramics, obsidian and jade tools, pigments, and marine shell. There is little evidence of the incursion of state power at this village, but they seem to have followed the Maya belief system.

The excellent preservation at Cerén provides a rare glimpse of how Maya farming families lived and worked, prepared their meals, and created community. After being built (and remodeled) and occupied for several hundred years, the settlement was rapidly abandoned in AD 660 when the Loma Caldera vent exploded and covered the area with 4–7 m thick ash layers. The research team has sampled four household clusters located near a plaza with two apparent ritual-civic buildings (nearest to household 1; Sheets 2002a:2). The typical Maya domestic layout is evident in these four sampled households (Figure 7.3), each of which includes two to three buildings, one that concentrated on food. The "storage" buildings can have one or two rooms, occasionally with detached corncribs. The "kitchens" are single-room structures with associated outside workspaces. The domiciles seem to have been rebuilt several times, adding benches and verandas. Shade and fruit trees of avocado (*Persea americana* Mill.), guava (*Psidium guajava* L.), cacao (*Theobroma cacao* L.), Mexican calabash (*Crescentia*

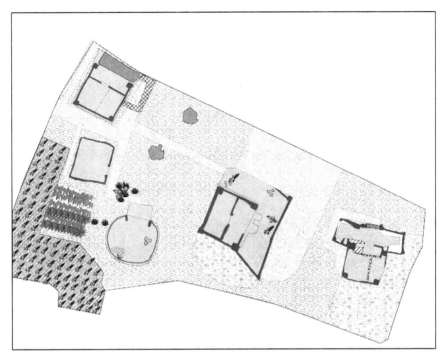

FIGURE 7.3. Plan of Household 1 with the two ceremonial-civic structures at Joya de Cerén, El Salvador (based on Sheets 2002:2, figure 1.1)

*alata* Kunth.), and hog plums (*Spondias* sp. L.) were scattered among the structures. Kitchen gardens, small *milpas*, and crop-drying areas are located around the buildings of each house compound. A mixed range of edibles was growing in the kitchen garden, just to the side of the round structure.

The botanical evidence from these excavations indicates what the farmers produced: maize, beans, chile peppers (*Capsicum annuum*), agave, manioc (*Manihot esculenta*), arrowroot (*Maranta arundinacea*), and the edible corm *malanga* (*Xanthosoma sagittifolium* (L.) Schott.) in addition to the tree crops (Lentz and Ramírez-Sosa 2002:38). Their house gardens contained a full range of food, including cherry (*Prunus*), starchy staples, spices, cacao, vegetables, and plants for making utensils, as well as herbs. From the food stores we learn that their outer fields were primarily maize, manioc and beans, and, to a lesser extent, cotton (*Gossypium hirsutum*), and squash (*Cucurbita moschata* and *C. pepo*) (Lentz and Ramírez-Sosa 2002:38–41; Sheets et al. 2012). The residents periodically hunted deer, peccary, turtle, and birds. They also ate domestic dogs and ducks (Brown 2002:155).

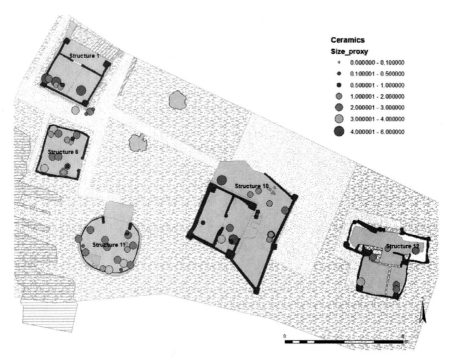

FIGURE 7.4. Household 1 Joya de Cerén, El Salvador, with ceramic vessel sizes plotted

All families farmed, storing their produce and equipment, preparing daily
meals in their kitchens. They seemed to eat in a range of different spots,
sometime in the kitchen sometimes on the porch. I focus on Household 1,
the subject of recent spatial analysis by a team at UC Berkeley (Farahani et
al. 2016; Hastorf et al. 2011). This compound contains three structures (1, 6,
and 11). Much of the surrounding work area has been excavated. Structures
1 and 6 are residential buildings, and Structure 11 is called the kitchen
(Beaudry-Corbett et al. 2002). These structures provide an unusually clear
view of the family's processing and eating practices (Sheets 2002b:50). All
of the artifacts across this household at the time of abandonment have been
plotted. What we learn from a quick look at this household is that food
was grown all around the house and that food was stored in most nooks
and crannies, in most structures, including the sleeping quarters (Str. 1),
if we can even designate a structure explicitly for that activity. We also see
discrete food preparation locations. Figure 7.4 begins this process by plotting the ceramics left across the household by size. This allows us to see
where food storage and processing occurred. Many of these jars and bowls
held plant food remains. Slightly distant from these buildings were a few

localized areas where domestic ash was dumped, but on the whole the well-trampled space in and around the structures was kept clean and tidy.

At the time of the volcanic eruption, Structure 1 held a range of tool and craft production items. This may be where the family slept. Braziers, scattered ceramic vessels, and food products support the suggestion that some meals were also cooked and eaten there. One jar held wild *Celtis* (hackberry) pits; another jar held beans (Lentz et al. 1996). Chile pepper strings were hung from the roof beams. These plants were clustered near the pots and braziers. Outside, by an exterior corner of the building, toward the storehouse, was a food-processing area with grinding stones, a *metate* and *mano*, along with a few ceramic vessels on a mat. This work location had a good view of the whole compound, placing the food preparers in a central position, like the earlier Natufian food preparers discussed in Chapter 4 (Wright 2000). This structure had evidence of a range of activities in and around it, mainly along the back wall, including food storage. Its veranda was remarkably clean; perhaps this was a sleeping area.

Structure 6 sits between structures 1 and 11. It contained more craft items than foodstuffs, including many stone tools. Food was also prepared there, as indicated by three *mano* grinding stones, two *metates*, six hammerstones, and some obsidian blades. Alan Farahani has completed analysis on the artifact distributions in this structure. The nearest neighbor analysis located three clusters of tools and food ingredients, suggesting three worksites within the structure (Figure 7.5). Botanicals especially cluster in these food preparation areas. (Lipid organic analysis should be completed on these grinding stones as well as the floor). Here we are seeing a family completing their daily tasks, talking, grinding, and cooking together within arms length.

Structure 11 is unique in that it is round (Figure 7.6). Called the kitchen by the excavators, the food preparation equipment clusters around the three-burner hearth and along the eastern side, where cooking probably occurred regularly (Beaudry-Corbett et al. 2002:51–52). This room also stored food staples, maize, beans, squash, and chile peppers. A series of storage items – gourds, a basket, and ceramic vessels – were within 2 m on either side of the hearth, within the cook's reach. Several of the ceramic pots in the room were encrusted with cooked food and external charring, as part of the cooking assemblage. Some of the serving gourds were decorated, as were many of the ceramics, including the cooking vessels (Beaudry-Corbett 2002:118). The small gourds could have been ladles or cups, used with the larger ceramic bowls, to serve the stews that were prepared there. Farther from the hearth, along the back wall, was a wooden shelf on which

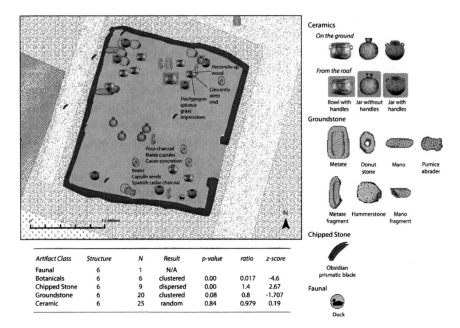

Ceramics

On the ground

From the roof

Bowl with   Jar without   Jar with
handles       handles      handles

Groundstone

Metate   Donut   Mano   Pumice
           stone            abrader

Metate   Hammerstone   Mano
fragment                    fragment

Chipped Stone

Obsidian
prismatic blade

Faunal

Duck

Nectandra sp.
wood

Crescentia
elata
rind

Trachypogon
spicatus
grass
impressions

Ficus charcoal
Maize cupules
Cacao concretion
Beans
Capulín seeds
Spanish cedar charcoal

N

| Artifact Class | Structure | N | Result | p-value | ratio | z-score |
|---|---|---|---|---|---|---|
| Faunal | 6 | 1 | N/A | | | |
| Botanicals | 6 | 6 | clustered | 0.00 | 0.017 | -4.6 |
| Chipped Stone | 6 | 9 | dispersed | 0.00 | 1.4 | 2.67 |
| Groundstone | 6 | 20 | clustered | 0.08 | 0.8 | -1.707 |
| Ceramic | 6 | 25 | random | 0.84 | 0.979 | 0.19 |

FIGURE 7.5. Structure 6 at household 1, Joya de Cerén nearest neighbor artifact distribution

serving and food storage vessels had been placed, including several vessels filled with squash and bean seeds. This building also had chile peppers hanging from the rafters. We can almost see the actions of the food preparers as they sat and tasted the cooking meal while flavoring it.

The artifact distributions inform us that food was regularly prepared throughout the entire household area, as indicated by the grinding stones both inside and outside the structures and the multiple hearths. A core Mayan food was ground maize, making grinding a full-time task. Cooking vessels seem to be more common in the round structure, but they were found in all structures. The evidence of several food preparation stations in Structure 6 suggests that multiple cooks may have worked simultaneously on dinner preparation in that structure. At all of these cooking stations the cooks could grab what they needed to prepare the meal as they sat around the hearth.

The family ate inside at portable braziers, where decorated serving vessels were found in structures 11 and 6, but people probably were also eating outside on the veranda of structure 1 just before the eruption. This location was particularly clean and likely had mats on the ground with a thatched *ramada* shade cover (Figure 7.7). The family gathered in the shade for the meal, with water basins set just inside. At the entrance a suspended ceramic vessel held cool water. Gourd bowls filled with stew could have been handed around, along with maize tamales that were prepared at the

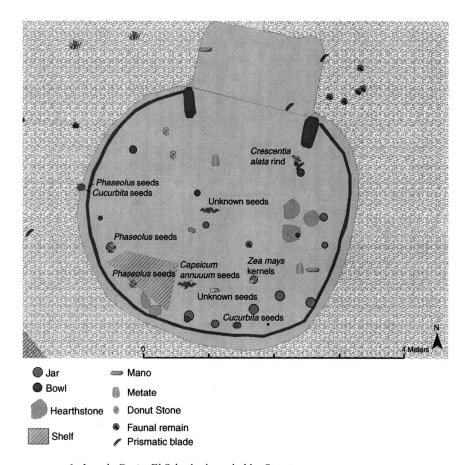

FIGURE 7.6. Joya de Cerén, El Salvador household 1, Structure 11

hearth. From this dining area, the family would have been able to look out across their courtyard, with a good view of other work areas and Structure 10, the community feasting house (Brown 2001).

The organic evidence does not enable us to separate meals from ritual offerings. No evidence for food offerings has been identified yet. We can envision a range of daily meals based on the artifact and botanical assemblages, which suggest that dishes and recipes varied, incorporating root crops, grains, and legumes, providing a balanced diet.

Determining how many people would have eaten together requires a ceramic volumetric analysis such as that completed by Barbara Mills (1999) with data from the American Southwest. Using volumes for two vessel types, Beaudry-Corbett (2002) determined that the Structure 6 domicile does not appear to be the locus of daily meal preparation and serving but of

FIGURE 7.7. A meal at Joya de Cerén, El Salvador (by Anna Harkey)

storing; rather, meal preparation probably occurred most often in Structure 11 or 1. Recent work by Anna Harkey and the members of the Berkeley team has attempted to determine the ceramic meal capacity more precisely by calculating the volume of individual ceramic vessels. The first problem is how to record vessel volume. Three methods were tested: summed volume of cylinders from vessel photographs, calculation of volume based on geometric shape (after Ericson and Stickel 1973), and estimating based on height and maximum diameter. Finally, the team completed volume calculations using computer aided design (CAD) software. Obviously, having access to complete vessels is best, but most archaeologists do not have this luxury. Erin Rodríguez tested the worthiness of the cylinder and geometric shape methods with Andean Nasca vessels housed in the Phoebe A. Hearst Anthropology Museum at the University of California Berkeley (Rodríguez and Hastorf 2013). From that project we concluded that the best way to estimate volume is to use a formula based on an ellipsoidal geometric shape, not the summed volume of cylinders or the height and maximum diameter method. Anna Harkey and colleagues built on those results with the Cerén ceramics, adding autocad equations. Being able to test the equations against true volumes of some of the vessels housed in the David J. Guzman National Museum of Anthropology, El Salvador, that Harkey measured with small beads, we now know that besides the actual measured volume, the autocad is the best volume estimator, being on average only 10 percent variance from the actual volume. With that strategy the team was able to gain better volumes from the images of the Cerén vessels provided by Beaudry-Corbett as well as taking additional photographs of vessels in El Salvador. The ceramic volumes by structure are plotted in Figure 7.4. Structure 11 has the most ceramics, but they tend to be smaller vessels than in Structure 1. Structure 6 also mainly has small vessels (1.8 L average). In Structure 1 we find fewer, larger vessels, suggesting water and food storage. From Anna Harkey's volume measurements, the 21 bowls that were properly measured average 3.8 L or 15.3 cups, suggesting a storage volume size. The bowl volume ranged from 2.5 cups (600 cc) to 23 cups (5,510 cc). Linda Brown (2001:380) reports that one of the smaller "serving" bowls holds around 855 cc (just under 4 cups) of liquid. The 17 measured small bowls we completed averaged 1.5 liters (6.3 cups), much like a family meal serving bowl that was shared around during a meal. The 57 larger "storage" vessels average 7 liters (30 cups). These volumes suggest that food was shared among the family members at meal times in bowls. The remaining ceramic vessels are for storage. Together, these three Household 1 structures contain a reasonable amount of storage in ceramic vessels for a family.

Each household at Joya de Cerén appears to oversee part of the community's activities. Household 2 was located next to the community sweathouse (the *temescal*). Household 4 seems to have specialized in processing agave for fiber and *pulque*, a fermented beverage. It is proposed that Household 1 oversaw the community feasting and women's building (Structures 10 and 12). These supra-household spaces achieve a sense of community practice. Seen in this light, these non-domestic buildings are a fascinating reflection of communal identity, emitting a sense of dispersed authority, alongside the family identity, lived out within their own structures.

South of Household 1 lie Structures 10 and 12 (Figure 7.3, 7.4). Structure 12 is thought to have housed ritual divination. Because of its special exotic objects and because it was kept especially clean with no evidence of food preparation, the excavators considered it might have been a special-use space, especially within the female domain. Between this supra-household community structure and Household 1 stands Structure 10. This structure (Structure 10) is also considered to be a ritual building. Based on its orientation and access directly to the Household 1 courtyard, Structure 10 seems to have been allied to or overseen by Household 1 (Brown 2001).

This curious building seems to have been a community building for feasting and ceremonial storage (Brown 2001; Brown and Gerstle 2002).

Building 10 is not a monument but a structure with an unusual layout. Unlike any other building unearthed at Cerén, it has three rooms. The north corridor just inside the entrance, with two hearths, was where food preparation and serving occurred. One hearth is at the entrance to the room and the other just inside (represented by stone clusters in Figure 7.3). Near these hearths is a group of large vessels along with a pair of grinding stones. A nearby shelf held additional food preparation items (Brown and Gerstle 2002:98). The three staple foods were found in this kitchen: maize, beans, and squash. Bones of dog and deer were present, two ethnographically known feasting meats. The eastern corridor is filled with ceramic vessels. Some were stacked inside one another, stored for future use (Figure 7.4). A digging stick with doughnut stone weights, some obsidian knives, and corncobs were present, similar to what might be found in a household storeroom, but more abundant. Stepping up into the next room moves one into more overtly sacred or at least restricted space. This painted room curated ritual paraphernalia, including a series of deer skulls, antlers, costume elements, and effigy jars, including one full of achiote (*Bixa orellana*) endocarps (used for red coloring) and another containing squash seeds and some ears of corn (Brown and Gerstle 2002:99). Interestingly, this innermost room held only a few utilitarian items, including bone tools along with a few jars and bowls. Thus, this room could have been a place for ritual preparation or even ritual experience. The costume pieces made from deer suggest that this building was used for white-tailed deer rituals. The final remodeling placed the preparation of the meals in the outermost rooms with ritual curation in the innermost rooms. Its eastern orientation resonates with the path of the sun and the rain deity of the east, *Chaahk* (ibid.).

According to Brown and Gerstle, the members of the family residing in Household 1 sponsored the periodic rituals occurring at Structure 10 and even prepared some of the food required for ceremonies. The largest cooking vessel on their hearth would have contained 64 helpings. A second large cooking vessel just outside of Structure 10 could have served 128 people, about half of Cerén's population (Brown 2001:380). Many of the community members, if not all, could have eaten at ceremonies held in and around Structure 10. Gourds could have been brought by all participants to ensure sufficient food serving. The evidence left at the time of the volcano suggests that the family was in the process of planning a feast – storing extra food and gathering ducks. We can envision friends and relations arriving early to help prepare the food in both Household 1 and Structure 10. Meanwhile, the ritual performers would check their paraphernalia and practice their dances inside. On the day of the feast, dances, songs, and stories would be performed around Structure 10, punctuated with drink and food, similar to Shalako at Zuni Pueblo today (personal experience 1980).

I hesitate to label this feast as having been competitive, as LeCount does for meals at the larger Maya center. At Joya de Cerén the evidence suggests a community or even a lineage meal rather than an aggrandizing one – a celebratory community feast, a Maya feast type noted by Vogt (1976). Unprecedented in Maya archaeology, Joya de Cerén's detailed data reveals all stages of food production; growth, storage, preparation, and consumption at the family and the community levels. Families were strong social entities in this farming world. They lived in discrete spaces, surrounded by shady kitchen gardens. The residents stored, prepared, and ate their meals in familial groups by their houses, never that far out of view of their neighbors. Periodically, a family or lineage hosted community or supra-community ceremonies, including feasting and possible use of the sweat-house. The feast appears to have been rich in meat, but with the full range of food staples, perhaps even from community fields. Neither a potluck nor a potlatch, these events incorporated food the community had placed in the communal store of the ceremonial building. At Joya de Cerén the populace participated in the reaffirmation of their identity, in this instance around the image of the white-tailed deer.

How did such feasts activate Maya identity? The Maya symbolism, found fairly consistently across the region and also at Joya de Cerén, is linked to the rain deity and the deer dance suggesting a shared ontology of fertility. These *communitas* activities would have accentuated participatory self-identity within the community and among the families. There is little evidence for gaining direct power from these events. Maize was clearly a signature food, although it was adorned with many other ingredients. Feast meals varied. The ingredients that are in Structure 10, especially the red condiment, would have made the meals prepared and served there stand out from daily fare. Joya de Cerén provides us with a rare look into the cuisine of a community, allowing us to pursue the ideas of group agency presented in this chapter.

## In Sum

At the beginning of this chapter I asked how we could investigate the intangible yet important social dimensions of group identity agency through cuisine. The modern, historical, and archaeological examples discussed here illustrate some of the many ways food has played a role in societal construction and group identity formation. Studying culinary traditions is perhaps the most sensitive way archaeological inquiry can unveil these multidimensional identities in the past. Tracing networks of action provides us with the potential to recognize the creation of groups through their culinary boundaries, their actions, and their *habitus*.

The fact that everyday practices transmit larger significances that define, reaffirm, and alter identity resonates at Joya de Cerén. Determining what can and cannot be eaten helps us delineate a group from its neighbors. Food taboos clearly have the power to determine membership. Anyone who has altered her or his diet based on a philosophical standpoint can attest to the sharp discursivity of this new affiliation out in the world. Everyday actions transpose eating practices into larger conceptual cultural worldviews from age-class membership to forbidden and signature foods. Daily household practices can embody cultural orders that ramify in the larger populace and back again to the hearth.

Meals are important ontological markers, syntagmatically linking them to society. The embodiment and agency of social identity is transmitted though the meal, displayed in the everyday items of table manners, ingredient combinations, and comportment, conveying membership through practices while satisfying the body. These are the realities of the people we study. Kitchens and kitchen gardens are where people lived and worked. Boundaries of culinary traditions become loci of social dissonance between groups. Food evidence from the American Southwest, Greece, England, the Andes and Mesoamerica demonstrate diverse ways people employ signature foods and food taboos to claim, negotiate, or resist group membership while distinguishing themselves from others. Culinary practices are therefore potent ways to position oneself in the world on both the largest and the smallest scale. Thinking about meal performances, we begin to see a more nuanced view of the creation of the family and the group as well as the strengths of their social valences beyond the kitchen.

CHAPTER 8

# The Creation of Personal Identity: Food, Body, and Personhood

*How people treat their bodies reveal the deepest dispositions of their habitus.*

Bourdieu 1984:190

*The modern individual's body is the product of the industrial revolution.*

Mintz 1996:78

Continuing an interest in and the agency of the social self, this chapter shifts focus on how food and culinary traditions participate in an individual's identity formation. Informed by Western philosophical tradition, the creation of personhood and the body has loomed large over many archaeological interpretations of the individual, channeling and at times blinkering our possibilities of learning about people in the past. While the body has received much discussion, this has not translated into food archaeology yet. I hope this chapter can stimulate such archaeological work, linking concepts of the body with food engagement. As we will see in the historical and ethnographic discussion that follows, there have been many ways of conceiving of the body and the self and these are reflected in a person's foodways. Food, of course, literally creates the body, so there is a regular and intimate link among the body, food, and personal identity. Here we seek the multiple possibilities of how individuals are formed through food's importance: economically, socially, in practice, and in embodiment. Individuals' haptic senses (touch), social relations, and memories craft their tastes and activities throughout life (Lalonde 1992). As Hamilakis (2002) reminds us, we engage with the world around us through all of our senses – taste, smell, hearing, touch, as well as sight – suggesting that "thinking through the body," as he calls it, is a viable means of engaging with the past. We must be careful, however, because many aspects of our own concept of an individual are constructs of the "modern Western cult of the individual" that should not be imposed on all other cultures we study (Insoll 2007:3). We can study individuals, especially from burials, but it is not easy to study individualism in prehistory, since we usually merge the many actions reflected in the deposited remains from which we collect our data.

I begin this discussion about the individual primarily with historical and ethnographic examples before adding prehistoric material. Thinking about the self through the body starts from how the conception of one's body impacts personhood, gender, and one's relationship with society. A focus on the body allows us to contemplate interactions with food and that all actions associated with its creation speak to the individual as channeled through the worldview of the actor. By engaging with several ontologies concerning the individual, the body and its bodily practices we can move closer to some lived selves in the past. Since a person must eat to stay alive, food is an essential part of any discussion of the body, making it an especially productive entry. Techniques of the body/personhood themes will lead us to embodiment, corporeality, memory, and the haptic qualities of life. Our sensory feelings and memories are created through the food and drink we consume (Hamilakis 2002:124). Acts of food preparation and eating are stored in the body in many ways, and some remain in the archaeological record, in muscle attachments, in bone, and in teeth. We can also seek bodily actions through the material with which past people engaged. The recurrence of these practices form bodily habits and memories that are recalled by the senses and molecularly engraved in the body. By discussing approaches to the body as it engages with food, we will consider the ways people might have conceived of themselves.

We eat our way through life, reforming ourselves with each bite and sip. A person's culinary culture is entwined with a person's identity. As archaeologists, we want to see what can be learned about individuals' places in their world through their food evidence and their cuisine, while remembering the impact of our own individualized, self-centered personhood. There are not many archaeological examples on this scale of culinary analysis outside of recent archaeological studies, leaving these rich questions open to further thought and investigation. Here I suggest that it will be productive to look for individuals through their actions – what they ate, what they did in their days, what they paid attention to. The frameworks presented here include the techniques of the body, embodiment, the modern individuated-bounded body, the open-fluid body, the partible body, and the permeable body.

## Body Concepts

As Mary Douglas (1970:16) pointed out, the body is an organ of communication. The act of incorporation through eating is at the heart of embodiment, activating our sensory world while creating memories that, in turn, circle back to create the self (Hamilakis 2002). In the modern (Western) world, where we are trained to focus on our own individual bodies and the creation of our own self-identities, scholars have been grappling with the constitution of the body in the theorizing of personhood and culture, often removed from the senses when they engage with bodily expressions. This is in part due to Platonic philosophy's sway on Western thought. Plato stressed that bodily pursuits such as eating and sensual pleasures get in the way of truth and knowledge, reifying the conceptualizing of the mind/body divide that continues today. Over the millennia there have been many critiques of this perspective, with sensualists, hedonists, and others bringing sensory existence to the fore. In anthropology, other epistemologies have been proposed, beginning with Douglas's (1966) productive anthropological discussion of bodily boundaries, which has been greatly expanded upon through a range of recent ethnographies. Some of these ideas are discussed in this chapter, including the more recent archaeological approaches applying this standpoint.

The mind/body divide's popularity was advanced in the Renaissance concept of *civilizing*, which promoted a process of individualization, seen both in society's breaking up into specializations and also in the concept of the individual being disarticulated from other individuals around them, already discussed in this book. Two orienting axes have developed within this debate that shed light on how archaeologists approach not only the past body and the past person but especially of their engagement with food in society. One of these axes concerns the construction of the body and how cultures conceive of individuals as either open or closed. In archaeology, the classical Cartesian ontology of the closed body, so long non-discursively accepted as universal, is gradually being discussed and even replaced by new orientations of the potency of the experience of "lived or open bodies" in the past, articulated by Butler (1990). A second orientation addresses a person's self-reflexive boundaries in the world. These two trajectories will be presented as they pertain directly to incorporation and individual identity.

The mind/body problem has been debated throughout Western scholarship, including Nietzsche, Marx, and Foucault (Csordas 1990, 1994; Shilling 2006; Turner 1994). Out of this debate *"constructivist" body* theories have arisen (Butler 1990, 1993; Lupton 1996). Foucault and Butler present the body as a constructed phenomenon, formed through acts, thoughts, participation, and perception, endlessly made and remade within the circumstances of life, adhering and contesting in a social world, never complete but always emergent (Butler 1990; Foucault 1979, 1980; Shilling 1993). The body, and one's concept of it, is partially a creation of society – malleable, formed within a larger framework of meaning that is contingent upon lived practices of comportment and language, created by activities, including drinking and eating, incorporation (taking things into the body) and inscription (putting things on the surface of the body) (Connerton 1989). This constructed body, created by cultural rules that control and regulate formations of personality, as well as flesh and bone, is only part of the essence of the biological body. These authors point out that our bodily aggregate has become camouflaged by these cultural regulations. This concept of embodiment is postmodern. Foucault (1979), like Elias (1939), traced the history of the socially constructed modern body by focusing on society's increasing discipline of the mind in the body, not on the body itself.

Connections between body and mind are particularly evident in daily practices and sensations (Falk 1994; Frank 1991). Elias (1939) and Bourdieu (1984) provide insights about the individual body and its socialization by applying the concept of *habitus* (also discussed earlier in Chapters 3 and 7). *Habitus* in Mauss's original sense is the learned actions, a culturally constituted system of cognitive and motivating structures operating within the person, impacting every aspect of bodily and mental techniques through conscious and unconscious engagement (Mauss 1973 [1934]). How people use their bodies reveals their deepest dispositions as well as their learned technologies, governing all forms of incorporation and action, choosing and modifying everything that the body ingests, digests, and assimilates, both physiologically and psychologically (Bourdieu 1984:177). How people stand, sit, walk, laugh, frown, place their arms, and how their eyes speak, all reflect their being. Through this relationship within the self, the person is created. This corporeal idea, along with Mauss's (1973 [1934]) "techniques of the body," allow us to dwell on the participatory aspects of body and personhood through every body's engagement with food. A food focus highlights not only the sensory aspects of an individual's lived life but also the physicality through the many aspects of food work, which includes walking, hoeing, picking, netting, shooting, grabbing, carrying, gutting, skinning, chopping, drying, cooking, grinding, pouring, trimming, stirring, tasting, smelling, serving, and eating. The techniques of gaining and preparing food do not have to loom large in all that we study, but the eating of food, along with its sensations, be it hot soup, sticky rice, or cold water, has been experienced by all. This individual embodiment of food techniques is crucial for us to remember and pursue archaeologically.

Foucault places the idea of the individual body at the center of modern Western ontology; we are now firmly individually oriented. Foucault focused on the outside world's impact on the body, inscribing tasks on the body, shifting the interpretive attention to the mind and its conception of the body, the "body" being controlled not by brute force but by cultural and self-surveillance (Shilling 1993:26). In so doing he removes the body itself from discussion. Society creates our social bodies through its traditions and rules, internalized, reproduced, preformed, and resisted through each individual's practices. We are created through this daily, repetitive work and practice, as Bourdieu noted, thereby internalizing larger societal power structures through what is considered acceptable practice. Like Elias and Mennell, with their historical models of increasing separation of people from their world around them, Foucault traces the history of the modern, industrialized constructed body, transforming from the medieval communal body. Through the process of industrialization and modernity the Western body has become disarticulated. This modern conception of the body gives little space for the influence of the haptic world, the impact of hormones, corporeal hunger, pain, tiredness, let alone sensory memory.

The constructed bodily view is distinct from those of Connerton (1989), Ingold (1993), Lave and Wenger (1991), and Sutton (2001), who write about the importance of bodily actions, bodily memory, and the techniques of the body. This *corporeal body* notion focuses on the importance of bodily actions, inscription, and incorporation but also on the interrelatedness of the tasks and activities that each person engages with. Considering the body in this way resonates in archaeological inquiry.

Archaeologists often study bodies excavated from graves and other bodily remains, especially researchers applying the *life course approach* to body studies. Agarwal and Glenncross's (2011) studies uncover how food and lifestyle are marked on individual bodies, providing us with an additional approach to lived lives through food. In their detailed study of burials from several time periods in medieval southern England, Agarwal and her colleagues learned that women worked just as hard as men did, but their diets throughout their adult life were not as good (Agarwal et al. 2004). These women clearly lived and experienced different lives than did their male relatives.

The dominant, unconscious prevalence of the modern, Western understanding of the contained body in most analyses has made it more difficult for archaeologists to conceive of other bodily ways of living in the past (Shilling 1993:10; Turner 1992). To learn about other ways individual people conceived of themselves, anthropologists have been studying societies that place the body's corporeality more centrally in their construction of the self. A person, in these different worldviews, can change as s/he interacts within the world. In some ways this is a cognitive approach, one that recognizes that bodies interact with the world around them, have bodily functions, have limits to their actions, and that these experiential actions will have an impact on how people engage with their own bodies (Mauss 1973 [1934]; Shilling 2006). This is central to the concept of embodiment.

Lambek (1998:105) nicely clarifies *embodiment* as the mind-in-body. This notion assumes that we live with mindful bodies and embodied minds. This orientation provides productive concepts for contemplating food-person-identity situations. Some non-Western concepts of embodiment assume that the body is unfinished at birth, becoming fully formed only through living (Connell 1987). Fullness is completed by the bodily activities that are enacted throughout life. *Techniques of the body* are a *habitus* in which daily practices form both the body and the mind through enacting culturally embodied techniques. These actions become engrained, inscribed, and remembered within the body, even as it changes over time. These bodily practices are channeled by social, sensory, economic, cultural, and emotional experiences. Through bodily performances a person is created as the culture around them is made and remade through these acts, recursively and actively interacting with the principles and ways of being with those around them. In this view, the senses, the physical and the gendered experiential body, participate actively in the formation of personhood and of society. Food is central in the study of the person because it is the most common material with which people engage, and in the most oft-used tasks. What and how a person eats alters one's body, making eating a fundamental gateway to learning about individuals and societies.

Another productive axis of body engagement that can enrich our pursuit of food and the individual has been expressed as a spectrum between discrete, *bounded, "closed" individual bodies* and fluid, *"open," partible "dividual" bodies* (Falk 1994; Strathern 1988). This spectrum of different, relational bodily perspectives allows us to trace how the body participates in identity formation, especially through food (Brück 2005; Busby 1997; Fowler 2004; Logan and Cruz 2014). This spectrum of how a body is formed in the world is never simply one-dimensional but is polysemic, making it an obstacle but also a benefit in archaeological inquiry. We can use this constant engagement with food to study many parts of this network of body-material interactions.

The open body concept operates in societies where the community is intimately manifested within each person, extending a person's identity throughout the community and the community's identity within each individual (Falk 1994). The relationship between self and community in this world is more fluid than what we are used to in Western society. In this open body ontology, one's actions continually make and remake society. This is illustrated most strikingly in the Hawai'ian example of the chief eating for the whole community. His large body is the community's body, renewing the self and the community with each meal. His body reflects the condition of his society for all to see.

The closed body ontology views bodies as separate, bounded, and contained. Each body has boundaries that match its identity, creating an entity distinct from others. In this body concept, the mouth becomes particularly important. It is the interface between inside and outside, between the self and the world (Falk 1994:28). Thus the incorporation of food becomes a focal point in one's definition of the body and of the self. The logical extension of this model is that one becomes what one eats, incorporation being the basis of identity (Fischler 1988:280). Once in the mouth, food is incorporated into the body. Gaining the properties of the food as the food envelopes the consumer into a culinary system. This Western idea of "you are what you eat" has been applied in many archaeological examples, including my own work with stable isotope geochemistry of Andean people (Hastorf 1991). Although appealing from our own vantage point, this concept of the body is not a universal one and did not operate in every group we study. As geochemistry has demonstrated more recently and as other body constructions also suggest, the individualized, closed body is only one way in which people have lived in their bodies and their societies in the past. The open body is also active; one is in fact not always what one eats.

Elias (1978) and Mennell (1991) are spoilers regarding the universality of the closed body concept. They propose, through their detailed historical accounts, that before the "civilizing" of Europe that occurred during the Middle Ages (increased separation from others), bodies were conceived of as more fluid and open. This transition from open to closed body was brought up in Chapter 2, when taste and table manners were discussed. Acquiring good taste was all about making distinctions about food, art, and manners vis-á-vis oneself, which included separation. In Europe before the sixteenth century, the psychophysical world was communal, not only among the residents but with their world around them. People were more outwardly emotional, expressing despondency and ecstasy as they ate together. Beings around them were truly part of their world, sleeping, eating, working, and defecating together. Medieval feasts lasted for days, with eating, sleeping, dancing, and vomiting occurring in the same setting (Ladurie 1978). People touched each other's food as they ate out of the same containers. They spit on the tables and threw bones onto the floors where they slept. Paintings from that time show that dogs joined in the feasts. Such communal sentiments between people are also reflected in the treatment of the dead; each family prepared and buried their dead on their own land. The family was the important entity.

As the European world became increasingly obsessed with the individual and the place of the individual within the world, interest in personal control grew. Whereas earlier bodies merged with the community, sleeping in a heap or taking bites off a shared piece of meat, the corporeal ideal shifted to that of separation and controlling both the body and the mind. This concept grew in a range of lived outcomes such as houses being divided into a series of rooms (Glassie 1975; Johnson 1993) and individual place settings at the table (Deetz 1977). Self-consciousness, hiding bodily functions, and serving individual portions at the dinner table all emanate from this civilizing (individualizing) process in European foodways (Elias 1978:137). These *techniques of the body* led to more closed bodies.

After the Renaissance in Europe, the clergy encouraged more atomization and separation, as reflected in the dead being taken away from the family and placed in church lands, eventually with names on burial markers identifying each person discretely (Gilchrist and Sloane 2005). Individuals became more significant as "communion and sociality" moved inside each individual person. This led to a sharper emphasis on the body's boundaries, an increasing concern about orifices and privacy, more acceptance of living alone, as well as more rules regarding the comportment of the body both in public and in private. With this management of external and internal bodily responses came an increasing concern about bodily actions and how food was presented and consumed. Meals became a place to remake these social rules, as instruction books regarding table manners proliferated across seventeenth-century Europe (Mennell 1985). The weeklong feasts of the past were curtailed as extravagant. Leaders sent out dicta to prohibit certain foods to be eaten. By the Victorian age in England, for example, overeating or eating food with one's hands was considered in very bad taste, almost obscene. Decorum surrounding food consumption was at its height, as the use of many utensils to keep food from touching the external body proliferated. Accompanying this bodily boundary and control was the shift in table manners, no longer allowing emotive scenes in public, especially at the table, as had occurred at feasts of old. In this process, self-control was no longer part of the seasonal cycle of community fasting and feasting. Control was increasingly internalized in each person's body and regulated individually throughout the year. This clearly set the stage for the Christian Reformation, as these self-regulated individuals were allowed to do more for themselves both physically and spiritually, including communicating with God.

Bordo (1987) traces this transition from one ontology to the other during the centuries of the European Renaissance as identity shifted from being located in the world, the landscape, to becoming located in the mind and specifically in the cranium (Fowler 2004:14). An example of this form of personal embodiment is the fasting of European women discussed in Chapter 6. These women tried to gain control over their lives by gaining control over their bodies, primarily through their control of food intake, outward appearance, and actions. Some of their bulimic tendencies were controversial, even verging on being heretical (Arnott 1991a; Mennell 1991:135–136). They were modern in their eating practices, insisting on individual rights separate from the church, their community, and their families. From our vantage point we see the emphasis on the individual as quite normal, from an earlier, medieval standpoint, this individual self-control was a radical concept and a major departure from the relational communal world. Through fasting they created socially informed bodies and selves within their historical moment. These actions embodied what contemporary power and control they could by separating themselves from those around. Would individuals have done this in Neolithic Europe, or among the Maya, where the social world was communal? Probably not. By asking such questions of our archaeological settings we can try to sense what people thought of themselves in their world, again asking where the boundaries of identity and self would have resided.

Some sociologists who study the modern body contrast this individual body view with the "other," the "dividual," wherein a person cannot be separated from, but only exists within, a society and its landscape. "This is characteristic of primitive society, in which the ritual sharing of food and its physical incorporation functions simultaneously as an act in which the partaker is incorporated or eaten into a community" (Falk 1994:15). Although this dichotomy can provide insights for archaeological investigations of nonwestern cuisines, applying only two models about the individual, the individual and the "dividual," to all peoples still remains overly simplistic as well as Western-ontology-centric (Cobb 2005). It is best to consider this as a spectrum, with the potential to have multiple aspects of these potential beings to fracture the universalization of the modern concept of the bounded individual and seek other worldviews of the self, the body, and the community, as well as of other ways of living and sharing within social groups. Being aware of the authority that Western concepts hold within our interpretations of the past, we need to remain vigilant as to our biases and be more aware of other potential ways of being in the past to improve our interpretations. Privileging how bodies interact with food can add to embodiment approaches as well as technology discussions. I turn now to the open body concepts to initiate this charge.

## The Open Body

Ethnographic fieldwork teaches archaeologists about different body ontologies that are analytically useful, especially in our research relating to food. Open body identities have been described as either changing with incorporation and interaction or fixed and stable from birth. The relational bodies are created through exchange and sharing. In many societies it is the feeding of people that brings them into existence (Falk 1994:21; Meigs 1988). For members of a community, this act of incorporation physically folds each person into the group. When you eat, you eat for and with the group, and the resulting existence reflects on the community's health as a whole (Fowler 2004:102). In this worldview an individual's gender is created through actions and exchanges, through techniques of the body. These practice-based strictures generate food-related protocols that define and create the community and its members (Strathern 1988; Meigs 1984). I trace these relational body ideas along two avenues, *permeable* and *partible* bodies. Both ontologies incorporate Strathern's concept of the relational, emergent social being, the "dividual."

### The Permeable Body

A permeable person is perpetually renewing himself or herself through eating, within the humoral belief system, discussed in Chapter 2. The permeable body concept carries the notion of the relational "dividual" body, which conceives of the body and therefore the person as being created through interpersonal relations and engagement with things in the environment (Strathern 1988). The body's engagement with the world constantly recalibrates it, remaining in balance by the intake and outflow of substances and with whom they interact. This means that the permeable body is continuously adjusting in its surroundings, both physically and socially (Busby 1997; Marriott 1976). Busby studied this corporeal concept in a South Indian Dravidian community, the Mukkuvar. In their worldview the permeable body creates a bounded yet open "dividual," formed in the womb by receiving of substances (Busby 1997:262). Shared substances form a person's body as well as define their position within their family, differentiating between male and female. The concept of the body is concrete: according to the Dravidians, you are born male or female. Males and females perform different tasks, reaffirming these gendered bodies through practice. But a person can become more masculine or more feminine through their food consumption, daily practices, and technologies of the body. Substances have fixed properties that influence the body into which they are incorporated.

In marriage, a man and a woman are brought together, creating a new being through cooperation, sharing, and exchange (Busby 1997:267). Men and women do not require a partner to create their own gender, but within marriage they define and balance their different traits as they create new permeable beings. This interactive dynamic spirals out into their family and society.

In this Dravidian world hot food makes people more masculine and aggressive whereas cooling, soft foods make people calm and feminine. A person can therefore alter their gender leanings by what they consume, shaping personality as well as orientation in their marriage and society. Food is at the core of permeable personhood formation because every meal eaten participates in reorienting and recreating the person, adjusting the body, mind, and soul. One's body is not internally divided into separate parts; it is made up of a range of substances that flow in and out of the body, reflecting its permeable nature. Gender and personhood participate in this formed yet permeable "dividual" body creation. One can eat oneself into becoming a person with particular traits, but it is a constant performance (similar to today's diets, proposing to help people eat into a "perfect body").

## The Partible Body

A partible person is formed of multiple components (Fowler 2004:33). In some societies, these parts can be divided up and even circulated because identity is connected not only to the body but also to the objects associated with that person. I discussed aspects of this phenomenon earlier with the concepts of gifts, heirlooms, and memorials in Chapter 2. Partibility is activated especially with the death of a person, when body parts and cultural heirlooms are distributed, each living relative getting a "piece" of the dead person.

A partible "dividual" therefore is a composite entity, a person made up of body parts, organs, fluids, soul, mind, and also of items given to (or belonging to) the person. The body is made up of many gendered parts that stream together (Strathern 1988). One's gender is created by what one does with one's parts (Busby 1997). Some of these parts can be given away to others; other substances are received (Fowler 2004:8–9; Marriott 1976; Strathern 1988). Through these activities a person is formed and reformed, connecting with a community of exchangers (Fowler 2004:36). Some substances do not remain part of a corporeal entity. In fact, some parts must be passed on, such as heirlooms, land, or named lineage trade items – the person holding them has only temporary rights to interactions with these partible substances, just as a body is only a temporary entity.

Food figures centrally in this web of partible personal identity as well. In Melanesia, to help children grow, a mother not only feeds them plant- and animal-derived foods but also saliva and blood, while a father gives semen to the baby regularly while the fetus grows in the woman's body. Family members, whether male or female, become united by way of shared partible essences as each person moves through his or her life activities. Each person exists because the other family members share substances. To better understand this form of open, partible body and food in Melanesia, we return to the study of food rules and personal identity formation of the Papua New Guinea Hua by Anna Meigs (1984, 1987), presented in Chapter 2. Each Hua person is created by what s/he gives and receives. For the Hua, to eat food produced by another person is to experience that person both physiologically and emotionally. One's food rules mirror one's age, gender, and reproductive status, making personal existence relational within the community and family, hence open. Whether the food is beneficial or harmful to a person depends on the consumer's relationship to the producer. These rules increase as people reach adulthood (Meigs 1988). Each person therefore has slightly different sets of food rules based on their age and place in the family.

Bodies are created through incorporation. Eating therefore creates personhood. An individual's identity changes over time, as does their relationship to their family members, which in turn dictates what they can eat. All living things, including people and food ingredients, carry a vital essence, *nu*, which is a limited good. Harvested food contains the spiritual essence of its producers as well as the ingredients' own *nu*. A Hua person grows because of the *nu* they are given by family members older then themselves via both food and personal bodily secretions. A child grows by gaining this essence from the food his/her parents give them. With adulthood and marriage, the cycle reverses and people start giving more of their *nu* away than receiving it, finally dying when they have given most of their *nu* to their offspring.

Parents give their blood and sweat to create children. This transference occurs during sexual intercourse as well. Every time a husband copulates with his wife, he loses some *nu*. This is especially important during pregnancy, when both parents want to give *nu* to the growing fetus. This parental transference continues throughout a child's life. Men continue to give saliva, sweat, and semen to their children up to adulthood; women give food. Because women basically have more *nu* than do men, owing to their ability to produce babies and to farm, men spend much of their lives worrying about losing this vital essence. As people age, they dry out (become less moist), a direct reflection of their decreasing *nu*. What little *nu* a person has when s/he dies should be consumed by kin of the same sex, to retain the *nu* along gendered family lines. This distribution of *nu* is done by matrikin eating the dead elder's body. The Hua partible self is therefore created through interpersonal exchange and consumption.

Besides gaining from adult bodies, *nu* is also generated by cultivation. Unlike in the industrial West, food is not considered to contain nourishment by virtue of the plant's chemical properties. The nourishment a person gains from Hua plants comes from the gardener's interaction with the plant, through planting, weeding and cultivating, harvesting, and processing. When the food is eaten, the consumer receives the crop producer's vital essence captured in the ingredients during food production and preparation. You are very much what you eat as well as becoming who gave you the food. Eating food produced or processed by one's enemies could cause weakness or illness, whereas food procured and prepared by one's mother provides sustenance and well-being. In this way personhood is distributed throughout activities. One becomes polluted when one consumes items that violate the boundaries of the family and the self. By interacting with food that is out of place the consumer becomes unclean, as when one eats in a restaurant. The more powerful and fertile the individual, the more restrictions there are on the foods that they can consume. Through these rules of preparation and consumption food plays a critical role in the construction of personhood in Hua society.

Plants and animals pass on their physical characteristics when they are consumed. Vitality gained from the produce is linked to the plant or animal's physical characteristics, similar to the humoral classification system described in Chapter 2. Important food characteristics include rates of growth, texture, moisture content, shape, smell, color, and size. Prepared food is perceived to have the same characteristics as the plants and animals that go into the dish. Exceeding the proper balance of *nu* in the body for one's age is another way one can become ill. When someone is out of balance, they should avoid or consume specific plants to realign the unbalanced characteristics, adjusting their *nu* intake. For example, men going into battle should eat sharp and scratchy things to make them fiercer. They should not eat anything that resembles women's anatomy, for this will make them soft and moist, or anything red, which, like menstrual blood, is polluting. Women about to give birth eat fast-growing things to help the baby grow quickly.

For the Hua, personal identity is based on exchange of essences between partible "dividuals." To be a member of the group is to eat food produced by another group member and thus to experience that person, binding the consumer to the producer in a dynamic and powerful web. For this reason, endocannibalism is part of the Hua food system. Eating one's kin helps the consumers retain all the vitality of *nu* in the family, operating like inheritance rules in Western society. A person in the Hua world is therefore partible, and their identity is created through this family exchange (Meigs 1988; Strathern 1988).

Given that movable parts are central to the concept of partible identity, the evidence from Neolithic Britain supports this type of identity operating as well. People in southern England were laid to rest in long barrow mounds. After burial in interior chambers, some of the human bones were removed and placed in other settings (Thomas 1999:151). Some were curated in causewayed enclosure ditches that had been constructed for large ceremonial gatherings. These enclosures were places of periodic ceremonies and feasting (Hill 1995). Such human bone curation and redeposition is suggested at the Hambledon Hill enclosure (Richards 2000). Stable isotope results from the ceremonially deposited bodies encountered in the ditches suggest that bones were brought in from communities scattered across the countryside, forming a broad community of the dead at these ceremonial locations. Richards (2000) compared these ditch results to values from four different chambered tombs in the region. Each of these tombs has a unique isotope value range, mimicked in some of the enclosure bones. These enclosures curated both the ancestral bones as well as feasting remains, which were placed systematically in pits, suggesting that both persons and animals could have been considered partible. This movement of buried bones to the ritual center suggests that bodies may have been considered partible in Neolithic Britain, especially in death (Fowler 2004:98).

These two perspectives of the open body model, the permeable and the partible body, illustrate how a range of relational "dividuals" inhabit societies. Both of these relational notions suggest that the body exists only with others through the giving and receiving of substances. They differ in their conception of how the person is formed, which in turn will reflect how people see themselves in their lives. There could be other ways of viewing the individual as well. Ideas raised by these ontologies about the formation of personhood can be brought to bear when investigating individuals in the past. We know that there is a wide range of cultural perceptions about the body from bounded, autonomous (closed), to the less-bounded and relational body, both permeable and partible, all enacted through the techniques of the body and maintained through food. With careful study, these viewpoints can be identified in past social practices and will help us track the "structuring principles" of personal identity in the past.

## Embodiment, Corporeality, and the Senses

Let us return to the concept of personhood as identified by Foucault and expanded on by Lupton, based on the experience of "lived bodies," to consider the notion of how a holistic view of the individual is formed through food (Ingold 2000). As people go about their daily tasks, they adhere to cultural rules and comportments through their own movements. Foucault (1980) calls these small actions, such as food preparation and consumption, the *technologies of self*. Habitual daily activities such as sleeping, eating, and talking become embedded in the body and the self, forming our bodies and minds. These activities have also been called *body technologies* (Fowler 2004), *techniques of the body* (Mauss 1973 [1934]), and embodiment (Csordas 1990). Some studies of these techniques of the body focus on food preparation and eating practices to elucidate how people are formed through their physical actions (Jansen 2001:208; Mauss 1973 [1934]). Social theorists have turned to this smaller scale to study the experiential, sensory aspects of social life (Bourdieu 1977; Csordas 1990; Lupton 1996). Both Csordas and Lupton echo Bourdieu's approach to the personal identity, "with a focus on collapsing the dualities of body-mind and sign-significance in the concept of *habitus*" (Csordas 1990:10–11).

> This principle is nothing other than the socially informed body, with its tastes and distastes, its compulsions and repulsions, with, in a word, all its senses, that is to say, not only the traditional five senses – which never escape the structuring action of social determinisms – but also the sense of necessity and the sense of duty, the sense of direction and the sense of reality. (Bourdieu 1977:124)

Bourdieu's emphasis on the body echoes Foucault's disciplined subjectified body through which society creates the individual by internalizing rules, language, and morals. Bourdieu (1979) expanded our interest in corporeality and experiential anthropology by studying the daily rhythms of people. Csordas (1990) takes this inquiry one step further with a more explicit guide to embodiment that privileges the haptic world, experienced throughout the day. His view of embodiment blends Bourdieu's *habitus* with a phenomenological approach of perception. Performance being at the core, where bodily activities interlace with the mind's configurations of them to form the self (Butler 1990, 1993). Eating is therefore an embodied practice as it creates the person on multiple levels through multiple sensory pathways.

Through engagement with the material world people become embodied members of society. While bodies are created through performance, they are also formed through consumption. Incorporation is the most common form of material engagement. Following this intellectual approach, anthropologist Alfred Gell (1998) proposed that objects also have a type of agency through their interactions with individuals, who in turn influence things. One's body and therefore one's self is created by the choices about what one eats, informed by the wider society and its expectations, as Anna Meigs (1984) so clearly articulated for the Hua. This interaction, of body acting on mind while mind is negotiating body, is called the corporeal realism of embodiment by Shilling (2006). Such recursive corporeal realism resonates with how the flavor principle structures people's food choices, which in turn directs people's future choices, as discussed in Chapter 2.

Some scholars focus their discussion of embodiment on perception and inscription (recorded memories) rather than incorporation (acts of bodily habit memories) (Connerton 1989). Most archaeological embodiment studies tend to focus on inscription – meaningful communication placed on things and bodies (e.g., Hamilakis et al. 2002; Joyce 1993, 1998). Although this approach has been productive, I seek here to reorient embodiment studies toward incorporation – individual embodiment created through eating. This is not as difficult archaeologically as it once was. Embodiment focuses on both incorporation and inscription through performative *techniques of the body* that people feel and viewers sense. Through these habitual body practices of enacting and remembering, individuals give their acts meaning. Individuals are linked to the world around them through such corporeal actions, where an object "is never perceived, without evoking … chains of associations that link this object with particular people, places or situations, all of which are responded to at a basic, emotional level" (Meredith 1990:208).

Although Meredith (1990) stresses the emotional side of individual beliefs and actions, the effect of these actions can produce material traces. He is also suggesting that aesthetics are a force in the construction of individual taste practices and embodiment, which has been applied to archaeological settings of planned depositions (Pollard 2001); why not bodies and how they engage with meals as well? In his discussion about such aesthetics, Pollard presents a series of Neolithic British deposits in enclosures and the potential ontological significance of the clusters. Like him, we can let the past remains direct us towards the aesthetics that were being enacted in the material remains and the bodies that we find. Like the ceramic evidence Tringham's team uncovered in the three different houses in Serbia, where each house portrays different aesthetics of meal practices and performances, they direct us to what was important for these residents. Such evidence provides us with the inscriptive and incorporative evidence of the processing and consumption of meals, but also in the deposition of its leftovers. Aesthetics can reflect the agency and embodiment of these remains and their engagement with those who cooked and cleaned up after the meal, being a permanent reminder of previous meals, as illustrated by the many very long-lived shell middens around the world.

Along these same embodiment, aesthetic lines, Hamilakis (2004), like Sutton (2001), makes a case for memories and therefore meanings being stimulated by taste and smell as much as by sight. He urges archaeologists to move beyond the privileging of sight and, to a lesser extent, sound in our reconstructions of the past and to consciously consider smell and taste in the discussion of eating (Csordas 1990; Kus 1992). Tasting food not only jogs the memory; it can connect us to a web of theoretical approaches to ritual, embodiment, and structured meaning, as well as other haptic experiences (Sutton 2001:159). Hamilakis (1996, 1999, 2002) takes this corporeal approach in the analysis of Bronze Age feasting. Wine, meat, cheese, and honey were the Cretan feast foods, served at Bronze Age palace banquets.

These foods became increasingly common in villas throughout the Bronze Age, suggesting their continued and expanding importance. Although these ingredients have not all been identified archaeologically (honey in particular), they can be sought for systematically with focused pollen and molecular analyses of ceramic and metal vessels and from specific places within the palaces where the feasts were likely to have occurred. Pursuing feast evidence in these villas and their distributions will help us fill in the network of interdependent activities.

Burial rites were accompanied by eating and drinking as well as music, dance, and sex (Hamilakis 2002:128). Hamilakis (1999:49) invites us to imagine the scent of expensive and aromatic foodstuffs as well as fragrant oils at these banquets; these aromas, mixed with that of moving bodies, would have been part of the memorable experience. He evokes a scene of tastes, fragrances, and bodily contacts that activated not only the identity of each person but also the economic and political jockeying for power that occurs at competitive feasts. Minoan society continued on with these expressive practices as the hosts manipulated gatherings to advance themselves through their generosity and gifting while the participants joined in the feasting, obliging themselves for later work. The impact of these sensory experiences should not be lost in our translations of past ceremonial events. These feasts were meant to be a bombardment of the senses, producing synesthesia and altered states of consciousness, making them memorable for many years afterwards. Can we add sensory phenomena such as aromas and touch to our archaeological descriptions, as people have begun to add music (Tringham personal communication)? Imagining how performative, incorporation, and embodied activities participated in past societies is not easy from basic artifactual quantitative data. It is our job to try to activate these in our studies of past people. As outlined in Chapter 4, there are a range of new analytical methods, detailed excavation recording, bio-geochemistry, and micro-oriented laboratory analyses that can help us learn about past movements within the landscape, work histories, meal consumption styles, health, food preparation, and even cuisine, seeking embodiment as well as types of personhood in the archaeological record.

## Relational Personhood, Gender, and Age

I now return to gender, age, and identity, aspects of personhood I brought up earlier in this chapter. Personhood usually refers to the condition of the outward person as they are presented to and interact with the world, rather than to the body and its actions, as discussed in the previous section on embodiment (Fowler 2004:7), let alone one's innermost feelings and thoughts, which we value so much in our own lives today. Personhood merges identity and social interaction, which are maintained through long-term relationships with people, places, and things. Gender, age, kin, and ethnicity are identities of the individual, reflexively created by how others see the individual. Food figures prominently in personhood, being an important "tactic" in identity practice (Jansen 2001:202). Culinary traditions connect people through eating together and sharing likes and dislikes. To initiate investigating personhood in the past I outline a few important characteristics that operate in gender construction before I turn to an archaeological example, at a Neolithic settlement where we attempt to uncover some dimensions of past individual identity through the food and consumption evidence found at the settlement.

Meals are important places to learn how gendered persons are created. In rural highland Ecuador, women serve cooked food to their families, creating membership as well as reaffirming their gendered position through this act of preparing the meal (Weismantel 1988). In Chapter 5 I discussed how the technologies of cooking and serving reaffirm familial power relations in Ecuador as they recreate the family members; who gets fed first and how much they receive denote who each person is, in a relational manner (Appadurai 1981; Douglas 1997. Mary Douglas (1997) pursues the metaphoric significance of daily interactions in the formation of a person, asking questions about personhood and gender maintenance in her English food study. There is deep personal and gendered significance in the British family meal, where food, especially cooked food, is used to negotiate interpersonal power. Sociologist Ellis (1983) reports that in England wife beating can sometimes occur after the presentation of a bad meal.

Bemba polygamous families in Zambia are hierarchically structured through food (Richards 1939). These families are segmented. Each wife grows, stores, and cooks food for her own family. Like communities feeding their chief, co-wives take turns feeding their husband. The husband and wife might eat the same food (although not together; women usually eat with their children); the husband probably has a more varied diet than his individual wives do because of the wives' varying circumstances, such as the number of children they support and their access to productive fields. The personal experiences of eating separately maintain men's and women's different relations, and the different presentations of each gender reflect their different spheres of power. The Banda of Ghana focus their discernment of the porridge and soup meals on their taste and texture, reflecting the body techniques and valuations of its preparation by women, which take up more time to make the dish smooth (Logan and Cruz 2014:214).

Mary Braithwaite (1982) illustrates similarly gendered meals in her study of Sudanese Azande ceramics used to prepare and serve food. Ingredients are stored in undecorated ceramics. As the ingredients move from raw to cooked, the ceramics become more decorated. The most decorated vessels are used to display and serve men's food in the men's houses. Women serve themselves and eat from much less decorated bowls. Here the vessels clearly speak to gender and status differences at each eating experience. Stored ingredients, while potent, are not as valued as cooked food, reflected in the less-ornate ceramic storage tradition. The cooked food prepared for men is presented in the most elegant vessels, while less elaborate bowls are for the women's meals, illustrating the lower status within the household. Gender is daily reenacted through these Azande meals.

Eating different meals within the same family solidifies relational identities especially when looking at particular foods that can be associated with age and gender. Food properties reflect gender-assigned differences among the Hua (Meigs 1988). As discussed earlier in this chapter, because *nu*-enriched women are fast growing and are filled with juicy, soft, moist essences, they eat hard, slow-growing foods to balance out the wetness and its associated pollution. Men, being hard, dry, and pure, have less *nu*. They eat more moist, fast-growing, *nu*-filled foods to maintain their nu balance. Hua men's and women's meals are therefore different, like the Azande's, but in terms of content, not form of presentation.

A very different relational gender dynamic is performed at South Indian Kerala fisher-folk meals, where Mukkuvar husbands and wives always eat their food together off the same plate (Busby 1997). Busby describes these couples as permeable "dividuals" in the sense that the husband and wife's identities are interdigitated. People are not considered adults until they marry, and once wed, they become progressively entwined with their partner. Their food consumption reflects this closeness: not only do they eat together; they eat from the same plate (Busby 1997:268). The couple therefore eats the same food at the same time throughout their adult lives, slowly becoming one entity in their community's and their own eyes. The Mukkuvar believe that this form of consumption creates open-joined bodies through the exchange of body fluids, including saliva, making eating a bodily act of union just as is sexual intercourse. Through these acts the married pair creates one body, considered to be a single entity. These two gendered halves form an important category in Kerala life. This close bond is considered to be stronger than the bond between mother and child. As Busby (1997:274) points out, however, "Men and women do not need each other to activate their own gender or gender capacities. Where they do need each other is in realizing the potential *power* of those capacities" (emphasis in the original). These two genders not only complement each other in techniques of the body by the different tasks each of them do throughout the day; they also strengthen each other as a united pair through sharing. Both participate in this permeable existence. These merged, permeable bodies join and balance each other as they operate in an opposite manner from Bemba couples, among whom the solitary, separate male is juxtaposed while being defined by his wives. Married gender is not being overtly negotiated in the Bemba or the Mukkuvar; both genders are reproduced through their incorporation practices but with very different senses of self and also of society.

Appadurai (1981:496), building on Marriott's (1976) discussion of the dual divisions in Hindu society, also sees this permeability operating within Indian society when it comes to an individual's social status. According to Appadurai, Hindu thought is the reverse of the Western notion that intimacy inversely correlates with rank. Unlike Europeans, Hindus define the individual as permeable. In that society, food exchanges among families sustain rank, age, and caste rather than abolish or mask them. Families and groups are served differentially at large social occasions, reinforcing and maintaining position within the hierarchy. This contrasts with the Western European view in which, according to Mary Douglas, food sharing acts to create intimacy wherein shared relationships are reinforced and differences are masked or even broken down in the privacy of the home meal.

Though people in Papua New Guinea and India both express gender and personhood through the food they eat, people are gendered differently. These practice-based strictures generate food-related protocols that define and create the community and its members (Strathern 1988; Meigs 1988). In India, one is born with a gender, which then becomes softened and blended with the other gender throughout married life. This permeable Hindu personhood is different from the more performative, even changeable genders of Melanesia (Busby 1997:269; Strathern 1988). For the Hua, gender, like age, is created by what people feed their children and what children consume, continually reaffirming or altering one's gender and position in the life cycle. A child has both male and female potential but becomes more female or male because of the essences they consume throughout their lives, provided by their mothers and fathers (Meigs 1984).

For both partible and permeable identities, Busby (1997) notes that sharing substances alters the overall strength of a person's gender as well as a person's age class (Fowler 2004). The Hua change what they eat with age. Modern Western societies also have eating patterns based on age and gender orientation, but we associate them with metabolic, bodily changes or social class instead of personal identity. We believe that babies, youth, adults, and the elderly have different diets based on metabolism and ability to taste. The elderly do not usually crave pizza, beer, and pop-tarts (or do they?), whereas some teenagers yearn for them. These accepted differences are based on concepts of the body and what is proper for people to eat at different stages of life. In societies where bodies are more interconnected, as we learned with the Hua, one's eating pattern is determined by one's age. In Douglas's ethnography of English meals, when sitting down to a Sunday roast, or at a North American Thanksgiving meal, everyone should eat the same thing. These eating patterns create distinct yet different set of individuals, as well as gendered beings. This setting is different from the African examples where eating is clearly divided by gender and daily tasks. From the examples presented here we learn that there are many ways gender is created through food practice, and therefore we must consider this when we address any gender question in archaeology.

Archaeologists have traced gender and age in the archaeological record (Conkey and Gero 1991; Gero and Conkey 1991; Joyce 2000b). Identifying different eating practices is a productive method for personhood investigations (Hastorf 1991; LeCount 2001). The agency of gender identity in food production and consumption has been lurking throughout this book. Our job as archaeologists is to recognize the active dimensions that determine personhood within the societies we study, including gender and hope that we can unravel evidence of these actions. Ethnographic examples stimulate us to look for the materializations of these identities in the archaeological record. It is helpful that food is one of the most common substances involved in creating persons, and central in gender and age identity formation, whether a person follows a closed, open, partible, or permeable body ontology.

Can we see different age-grade and/or gendered eating habits archaeologically through material distributions such as those laid out for the partible Hua's conceptions? Fortunately, personhood is often commemorated at death and recorded in burials, allowing us to get a sense of general personhood in the past before moving on to food identities. Joanna Brück (2001) suggests that the Middle Bronze Age British saw themselves as partible "dividuals," as did the Neolithic folk. Through their *technologies of self* the inhabitants created themselves through their engagement with their artifacts. After death, human body parts (partible bodies) were recycled. Some of these body parts were transformed and exchanged in a reciprocal process with other material objects. Brück illuminates this in her study of the social life of the deceased, in which bones were curated and circulated among the living. Breaking up and reusing bodies and their accompanying essences to maintain society resonates with the symbolic concept of food consumption and energy transfer seen in the Micronesian personhood creation. The same transformative activity of breaking up (crushing) and circulating parts was evident in other Bronze Age practices. Just as the grinding of wheat to be made into bread helped form new bodies through processing and consumption, ceramic sherds were ground to make temper that was then used to make new cooking pots. Both processes illustrate the recycling of parts into the future bodies in this society, perhaps also outlining how reused ancestral bones would help birth and fecundity (Brück 2005).

Studying changes through time in an individual's diet using stable isotopes is an increasingly important path in discussions about personhood. Investigating multiple tissues from the same individual provides a dietary life history: bone, skin, teeth, nails, and hair each record diets at different times during a person's life. Teeth begin to develop in the womb and continue up to the first few years of life; rib bone records the last seven to ten years of an individual's life, and hair near the scalp can track the last few months of life (Sealy et al. 1995; Turner et al. 2010). These results do not just indicate where a person lived and died; they direct us to an individual's sense of self and position in society as their diet shifted throughout their life (Cadwallader 2013; Schroeder et al. 2009). Schroeder and colleagues (2009) describe individual Barbadian slave histories using carbon, nitrogen, oxygen, and strontium stable isotope values. Their analyses of teeth and bones from the Newton slave cemetery enable them to trace who was born and remained at the plantation their whole lives and who arrived as a youth or an adult from Africa. They even propose the place of origin of the people who were brought from Africa, ranging from the Gold Coast to the Senegambia region. These different locations yield different staple crops – rice, sorghum-millet, and yams – that have unique isotopic signatures and thus different ratios in human bones. Newly arrived African slaves will have a very different relationship with the Barbarian cuisine than those born and raised there, even if they were "of the same rank." Tracking people's lives through their eating and drinking histories is an important means of situating the individual in their world.

Gendered and aged bodies are created by food. When archaeological data show that people of different sexes ate different foods throughout their lives, we can begin to discuss how these people lived their lives, as recorded in their consumption acts and their workloads.

Personal boundaries are an important facet of the constitution of the person. The known range of the self-in-the-world extends well beyond the Western notion of the well-defined individual. Chris Fowler (2004:35) calls this multiplicity between "dividual" and individual *facets of personhood*. Thus far I have discussed three facets of personhood, gender, age, and family. Each can be placed along the axes of permeable and partible personhood. Can we identify any of these different forms of personhood in the archaeological record? The most productive way to initiate this search for personhood is by tracking food *habitus* in all of its corporeal realms. Let's pursue some of these concepts in an archaeological example.

### The Individual: Techniques of the Body, Food Consumption, and Gender Identity at a Neolithic Anatolian Village

The level of detail from ongoing excavations of the Neolithic Anatolian settlement of Çatalhöyük offers an excellent opportunity to search for prehistoric embodiment and to distill how individuals might have conceived of themselves as well as lived (Hodder 2005a, 2005b, 2005c, 2006a, 2006b, 2014; Tringham and Stevanović 2012). I propose that the people of the Çatalhöyük community tended toward "dividual" personhood, both partible and permeable, with identity boundaries operating closer to the family's edge than the individual. Çatalhöyük houses reflect strong family boundedness and control of bodily comportment within their spaces, while the residents' treatment of the dead suggests corporeal fluidity between the living and the dead. In a manner reminiscent of Falk's (1994) concept of the open body, their boundaries probably crystallized beyond the individual on the family scale. Supporting evidence for this claim is done through presenting a brief overview of the architecture and food evidence. I document the corporeal concept with the evidence on work, disease, and body treatment. With these data I then turn to outline what I think their concept of embodiment and personhood was.

The Neolithic east mound, inhabited between 7400 and 6200 BC, was built and rebuilt with densely packed houses superimposed on previous houses. Repetitive practices are manifested in the architecture, with very similar homes being built throughout the aceramic and into the ceramic Neolithic levels, suggesting a remarkably consistent home life over many generations. The use life of a single home spanned about three generations, or about forty-five to ninety years. Walls were built on the previous foundations and replastered annually, if not seasonally (Matthews 2005). The memory of the previous home was actively present in the builders of the next building, clearly seen by the mimicked walls and hearths. Ovens were rebuilt multiple times within one home, with their location in the central room shifting slightly over the generations (Hastorf 2012; Tringham and Stevanović 2012). The rectangular houses consisted of a central room with smaller rooms hived off by partition walls. Dead individuals were buried below these central room floors, keeping the family close. The dead participated in the activities of the living and were regularly remembered as pits were reopened to add bodies to the earlier burials (Cessford 2007).

Food-related data sets include plants, phytoliths, stable isotopes, micromorphological traces of depositional activities, animal, fish, and bird bone, eggshell, microfauna, and organic molecules (Hodder 2005b). Other materials include evidence of baskets, clay cooking balls, ceramic vessels, lithic tools, mats, hearths, ovens, and storage areas. From the subfloor burials we learn about individual diets, workloads, and family size (Cessford 2007; Hodder 2006b; Pearson et al. 2015; Richards and Pearson 2005). The detailed spatial data furnish a picture of daily cooking and eating throughout the year (Atalay and Hastorf 2005, 2006).

The settlement was constraining yet rich with dense symbolic life. Movement within the house as well as across the roofscape was controlled. Mud-brick houses often shared exterior walls, creating densely packed neighborhoods. The tidiness of the interior spaces and the narrow openings between rooms channeled personal movement, as these spatial patterns were repeated over decades and centuries, suggesting that long-lived, stable, embodied domestic practices were enacted at the settlement. The interior spaces are small, averaging 5 m by 5m, and were well maintained, swept often, and kept clear of debris. As discussed in Chapter 4, the storage area was usually in one of the side rooms, separated from the central room (Figure 8.1). These small rooms were filled with permanent bins but also baskets and most likely netted bags. Detailed analysis of the floor soil micromorphology samples (Matthews 2005), flotation material (Cane et al. 2012), and organic compound analysis (Middleton et al. 2005) indicate that different sectors of the interior floor space received varying amounts and types of wear.

Interior activities were visible only to someone within the house due to the lack of windows. Many daily activities occurred on the flat rooftops, with recent evidence suggesting that at least some of the rooftops

(a)

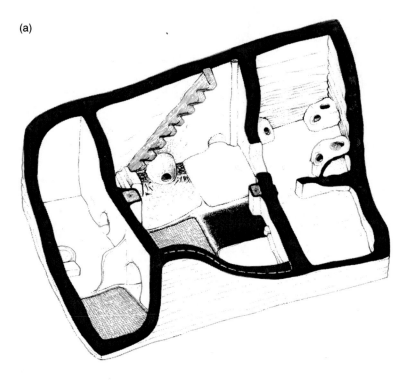

(b)

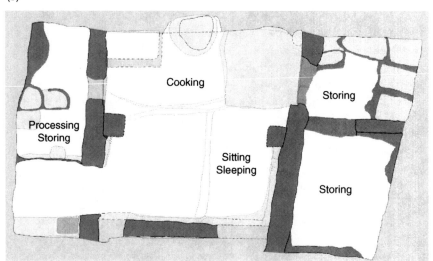

FIGURE 8.1. Building 5 at Çatalhöyük. (a) Isometric drawing by John Swogger; (b) Plan of phase B5.B. Used with permission of the Çatalhöyük Archaeological Research Project

contained small walled enclosures. The houses were accessed via a laby-
rinth of pathways, with individuals moving across many roofs; presumably
these paths were deeply inscribed in bodily memory. Public and private
life was clearly separate. Only away from the settlement could one have
freedom of movement and an unrestricted view. This dichotomy of sequestered family-communal space with its discrete, tidy, delimited workspaces
and the openness of the valley plain is central to our understanding of the
residents' personal embodiment. Individuals were formed by three domesticated worlds: small, dark interior communal rooms; open, visible rooftop
workspaces; and the expansive, diverse environment of the Konya plain
and nearby mountains, with the ability to hide or be seen throughout. Food
processing occurred outside the settlement, on the rooftops, and also in the
small, interior spaces.

The residents had a remarkably steady diet over the thousand years of
the site's occupation (Pearson et al. 2015; Richards et al. 2003; Richards
and Pearson 2005). Living by a river overlooking a broad marshy plain,
the residents hunted and fished, farmed on surrounding dry patches, and
hiked into the mountains to collect nuts, berries, wood, and wild game.
Meal ingredients were a combination of wild and domestic plants and animals. Food seemed to be categorized as raw/stored or processed/cooked,
with no requirements to keep different ingredients or sources separate
in storage or in the cooking pot (Twiss et al. 2009). The domestic foods
included wheat, barley, rye, chickpeas, lentils, sheep, and goats, dominated by emmer wheat, present in 25–84 percent of the flotation samples
(Fairbairn et al. 2005). Nuts and berries from the patchy forests were sparse
but present throughout the sequence and in every house. Marsh rhizomes
(*Bolboschoenus glaucus* (Lam.) S.G.Sm.) were ubiquitous and associated
with a range of uses, including food (Wollstonecroft et al. 2011). Along with
domestic and wild herbaceous plants, rounding out the cuisine was wild
(cattle/aurochs, wild boar, and deer) and domestic (goat and sheep) meat,
with eggs, birds, and fish. Meal ingredients shifted with the seasons. Food
storage was clearly important as indicated by the mud brick bins in every
building with a fairly regular capacity (Atalay and Hastorf 2006; Bogaard
et al. 2009). Overall, the diet of the Çatalhöyük residents was healthy.
The most common dietary ailment registered on their bodies was anemia
(Molleson et al. 2005).

Although the Çatalhöyük dietary ingredients remained stable for a thousand years, the cooking styles did not. Over time, the cooks shifted meal
preparation from toasting, roasting, and indirect boiling in wood, hide,
and wicker baskets with heated clay balls to toasting, roasting, and direct

boiling in ceramic vessels, gaining more control over cooking temperature with this shift. Çatalhöyük, a settlement made of clay, was occupied for 600 years before ceramic vessels were used, and the earliest pots were not for cooking but for storing grease. Only in the uppermost levels was there evidence of ceramic vessels on direct heat. Along with these new cooking technologies domestic foods increasingly entered the settlement. Cooks spent a great deal of time processing food for storage as well as daily meals. The increased control of heat allowed the meals to be cooked faster. More importantly, placing pots directly on the heat source allowed the cook to multitask, from which we can surmise that planning was increasingly important in the household daily cycle. After all, the residents had harnessed clay long before they used it to produce clay pots, so something was creating an interest in this item.

Within the 250 buildings that have been mapped at Çatalhöyük to date, 90 clay ovens and approximately 160 hearths have been identified. Ovens are substantial, domed clay features; hearths are smaller, open, and often ephemeral. Some hearths have a clay lip; only a scorched patch of floor marks others. Being both ubiquitous and relatively ephemeral, the hearths show greater variability in number and location within the rooms than the ovens. One or more hearths could have been in use within a household at any one time. Although some buildings had evidence of more than one oven, rebuilding rarely moved them, and only one of the ovens was in use at a time (Farid personal communication 2006). Ovens were rebuilt multiple times, however, with their locations early on shifting only slightly along the southern wall of the central room (Düring 2006:173; Farid 2007). In the lower levels of the site, ovens were built just below the roof opening at the entrance to the house. The cook could look into all rooms in the building, the sacred (more decorated and clean) northern area of the main room as well as the roof entrance. In the later houses, ovens were larger and were located in more prominent places within the building. In the earliest levels of the settlement, ovens were placed within the walls. Especially after level VII, ovens become not only larger; they are no longer recessed, moving into and taking up more of the central room space and therefore more prominent in the minds and lives of the inhabitants (Hastorf 2012). The more central ovens in the later buildings, away from the wall and entrance, suggest that the cook was increasingly prominent in family life and its *habitus*. Whoever was overseeing the oven was controlling heat, sustenance, and most likely storage.

The area around the oven was the hub of the house with the cook at its center. This shift occurred at the same time as ceramic bowls and jars used for boiling, storing, processing, and consuming liquids were added to the culinary equipment. Increasingly, people would have had to walk around the oven and the cook to get to other sectors of the home. The small, pinched clay female figures, often deposited in food activity contexts both bins and middens, provide additional evidence of the importance of the cook within the household. Whether for fertility, stability, or commensal power, they signify the potency of food production activities within the Çatalhöyük world.

There is little evidence of gender differentiation in the burial treatments, in diet, or in material status. Dietary parity is reflected in the human bone stable isotopic evidence and the tooth wear analysis (Andrews et al. 2005; Pearson et al. 2015:77; Richards and Pearson 2005). Richards and Pearson's stable isotope values from the burials indicate a mix of plants and animals in the diet, suggesting that some ingredients continued to be procured from the forests throughout the entire occupation sequence. Wendy Matthews (2005) has identified a coprolite from a midden that contained wild pistachios, acorns, and almond shells. Nevertheless, starchy domestic cereals were a regular part of the diet at Çatalhöyük, deduced from both the number of caries in the permanent teeth as well as the dental calculus evidence (46.5% presence, albeit mostly in small aggregations). Although everyone was omnivorous, some adults ate more meat or fish than did others, as seen in the higher-than-average nitrogen values, illustrated by two individuals in Figure 8.2. This might be because these inhabitants were regularly away from the settlement for weeks or months at a time, perhaps on trading or hunting journeys (Richards and Pearson 2005). Strontium analysis on these same individuals would be useful. Or it could be that they were given more meat toward the end of their lives (the isotopes record the last decade of life). The team's biological anthropologists note that the Çatalhöyük residents show no evidence of death by starvation, although they experienced occasional periods of stress (Andrews et al. 2005; Larsen et al. 2015). The stress markers were probably from disease or injury rather than prolonged lack of food, suggesting that dense as the settlement was, people produced enough food to keep everyone fed.

Both cooked and raw food was eaten whole or roughly cracked rather than finely ground. The grinding stones in the houses do not occur in numbers that would indicate daily food grinding, nor do the teeth (Baysal and Wright 2005). Thirty-six percent of the teeth are chipped and display evidence of self-cleaning, suggesting that harder foods such as dried fruit or meat were regular meal ingredients. Tooth wear was steady, initiating in the third year of life, including tool-processing wear as well as mastication (Boz 2005). Tooth grinding is linked to eating processed foods, whereas the

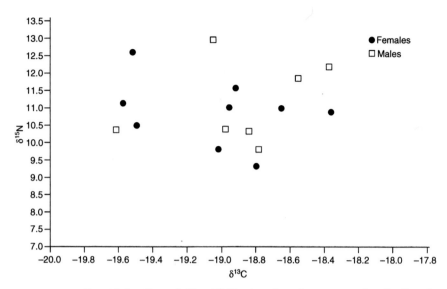

FIGURE 8.2. Adult collagen ∂¹³C and ∂¹⁵N values from the east mound at Çatalhöyük. Sex determinations from Molleson and Andrews (1997), Molleson et al. (1998, 1999), and Richards and Pearson (2005:317)

food-crushing evidence suggests whole nuts and grains were consumed regularly. Sheep (*Ovis* sp.) and goat (*Capra* sp.) were the most common meat sources. Cattle/aurochs (*Bos taurus/Bos primigenius*) were rarely eaten, with deer, wild horse, and boar even less commonly consumed (Pearson et al. 2015; Richards and Pearson 2005:315; Russell and Martin 2005, 2012; Twiss 2008, 2012). The fish and bird remains are scarce enough to suggest distaste for them, as the overall bone evidence suggests that together they contributed only a small but steady portion to the community's diet (Russell and Martin 2012).

Once within the homes they were surrounded by significant, meaningful material that linked spiritual realms with daily meals. We can see the occupants' gendered lives considering Brück's *technologies of self* through an analysis of food consumption at Çatalhöyük. Although presence of caries is generally the same in men and women, women have *more* teeth with caries and greater erosion of those teeth than do men (65.6% versus 34.3%; Molleson et al. 1996, 2005). This implies that the women ate starchy cereals and tubers more regularly than did the men. But this difference could also be due to pregnancy and lactation, one of the effects of which is to weaken women's teeth, further increasing the effect of starchy carbohydrates in their diet.

The evidence of caries at Çatalhöyük presents a slightly different view of the adult diet than the stable isotope data do. For the fifteen adults from buildings 1 and 5 that have stable carbon and nitrogen isotope values, there is no significant difference in the average food consumption between adult females and males (Richards and Pearson 2005; Figure 8.2). The gendered evidence suggested in the dental caries differences might reflect the timing of starch consumption throughout the day, week, or year, not the quantities. An additional interpretation is that these differences could be attributed to the activities in which women were engaged. Regular processing of reeds and hides (activities requiring the use of their teeth) to make baskets and bags would definitely have an impact beyond that of their diet. The differences between male and female teeth do not covary with the other dietary data, suggesting that the caries were created through pregnancy and work activities not eating habits. The differences in consumption were not great enough to suggest any gender or social hierarchical differences, but we do learn that these two sexes had different daily routines. We therefore see gender being activated and embodied through daily tasks at the settlement.

The inference of work equality is supported in the bone wear and muscle attachment evidence, which reflects life-long activity patterns. The muscle and ligament marks demonstrate that adult males and females had about the same body weight and activity levels, although the men were slightly taller and more uniform, suggesting women were moving in through marriage (Molleson et al. 2005; Larsen et al. 2015). Altogether, the notion that women were much heftier, as suggested by the clay figurines, does not hold up in the skeletal evidence. Their bodies confirm intensive, repetitive actions, especially carrying heavy loads and thrusting digging sticks or pounding, all of which are typical activities of farmers and gatherers. They also sat on their haunches a lot, probably on the matted floors around their ovens or on their roofs. With this background material on food and activity, let us turn to the question of self, identity, and personhood.

In a discussion about the residents' embodiment, Hodder (2006b) proposed that their concept of the body was open and somewhat permeable, which fits with the strong household boundedness mentioned earlier. His discussion is based on three adult males from an intensively studied sequence of two houses (Building 5 sits directly below building 1). These three men (B.2529, B.1378, B.1466) were buried below the platforms. I have added two females (B.2115, B.1424) also buried in Building 5 to this discussion of individual lives and taskscapes at Çatalhöyük to gain a more equitable view of adults individual living there. Four of these five adults were buried individually; one woman (B.1424) had a neonate next to her in her burial pit. The elder female (B.2115) showed evidence of considerable trauma and some degenerative pathology demonstrating a life of constant work (Larsen et al. 2015).

One man's cranium (B.1466) was removed after burial and replaced with another cranium. This activity is not unique to this settlement (it occurs throughout the greater Near East at this time), but here this practice is not common. Such flexibility of body parts indicates a partible body ontology at work in the community, at least for certain "ancestors." This activated partibility suggests that he was an important ancestor who was remembered through his cranium, curated elsewhere as well as remembering where his burial was within the house by the later added cranium. The Anatolian Neolithic residents appear to have engaged in a tradition built upon ancestral power, materialized in human and aurochs crania, which were circulated, displayed, and curated within their homes, reflecting a partible personhood of both animals and humans as well as a rich spiritual materiality. Plants interestingly enough tended to be hidden and undepicted. They had a very different relationship with the residents than did animals.

All five adults lived busy lives. Their musculature suggests that they each spent a great deal of time performing physical tasks, carrying heavy loads, using their hands, and squatting (Molleson et al. 2005). In their later years the two women and two of the men (B.2529 and B.1378) spent much of their time indoors. This is indicated by the black, amorphous, insoluble carbon-related anthracosis lining of their chest cavities (lungs), brought about by inhalation of smoke from open fires in poorly ventilated areas (Andrews et al. 2005:277). These four adults clearly spent years in and around the house interior, staying warm, tending the fires, and perhaps cooking. The other man (B.1466), the person with a different cranium, did not have this black lung condition, suggesting that he kept active and out of doors throughout his whole life. Toward the end of their lives the four individuals mainly ate soft, starchy foods, probably prepared separately from the younger house members, seen in the above-average amounts of plaque on their teeth (Boz 2005).

Of fifteen adults analyzed for collagen stable carbon and nitrogen isotopes, three adults have outlying dietary values from the last seven to ten years of their lives – including two of the men and one woman mentioned earlier (B.1466, B.1378, B.1424; Figure 8.2). These three individuals – the headless man who was across the countryside until death, an elder man housebound at the end of his life, and the younger birthing woman – ate slightly more meat (from cattle/aurochs) than the community average (Richards and Pearson 2005:316–317). Because it was primarily grilled, which was not a daily form of food preparation, Russell and Martin (2005) suggest that beef (aurochs) was a feasting dish. Eating aurochs is thought to have been a sacred act (Twiss 2012a). A range of questions can be offered about these people and their eating *habitus*. What were these feasting ceremonies like? Were these meat-rich meals staged away from the settlement, so non-family members could not partake, or did some specific people, such as these three buried in this building, have a status that provided them with extra food in addition to the house feasts, brought to them in their home from other families feasts, as an offering to their status? Did hunters eat more of their captured meat themselves, either raw or barbequed out in the marshes or on the plain while hunting? Did some women hunt with the men, suggested by B.1424's values? Were these three elders receiving more wild meat because of their status in the family and/or the community? Or did these three spend more time away from the settlement during their lives, hunting and consuming more meat? One conclusion that can be accepted is that B.1466, the active elder, was especially honored with extra meat during his life, by not remaining at home toward the end of his life, and by the unique curation and remembering of his cranium and body placement after his death. He indeed must have been an especially honored "ancestor" due to his actions that reflected in his eating habits during life. Was he the head of the community that gravitated to this particular building?

Through such detailed, multiple investigations individuals and their daily practices are brought into sharper focus. Burial locations and associated evidence provide us with a vision of tightly knit groups who cultivated fields, foraged, hunted, trapped, fished, and trekked widely to collect obsidian, mountain foods and supplies, carrying their produce back to the household, processing and storing it for the winter when it would be eaten around the warm ovens. For months they lived and worked near their ovens, the focal point of the house, where daylight entered only via the roof hole (Figure 8.1b). Adults appear to have performed parallel tasks and eaten similar diets, suggesting similar amounts of labor between the two sexes. Was age and tasks-completed more important than gender at this settlement? As they grew old, four of these people spent their last years mainly at home, breathing in the smoky air of the hearth, perhaps repairing tools, processing food, tending children, and resting, after years of hard work. The headless man, however, was the most honored, having completing tasks in the landscape up to the end. Some tasks might have been more respected, and therefore he was more honored at death, with his head continuing to participate in rituals of the living.

The smoky odor of those enclosed rooms would have mingled with the smell of the hanging herbs, drying fruit and meat, bins of seeds, baskets of nuts, skins full of syrup, and perhaps even milk. Something was probably always cooking on or drying by the oven, as people endlessly fed the fire with wood and dung during the snowy winter months, weaving, making baskets, singing and telling tales of earlier times, of the great aurochs hunts, nut harvests or the volcano eruptions depicted on some of the house walls. Were these elders identified in a single task-age-grade regardless of gender, like southwestern U.S. sodalities (Mills 2014) (or old folks homes)? Had they changed their societal position and identity into an elder (rather than a man or a woman) when they became housebound residents in these special buildings? The evidence suggests that this is so. Did the two housebound males become women in society's eyes, living by the oven, as suggested by their burials being similar to younger women's burials? Or was the one woman who consumed more beef marked as a male later in life due to her activities?

Partible individuals can take on traits and shift genders throughout their lives (Busby 1997). Recall the Hua of New Guinea, where postmenopausal women alter their genders, becoming males through age and tasks. Perhaps the Çatalhöyük men became women when they could no longer leave the house, focusing their days around the hearth. Or was there another category of person in this community, an elder living below the roof, on his/ her way to being an ancestor – those who lived below the platform? These elders ate differently than the younger family members did, further suggesting a partible ontology.

Çatalhöyük identity was closely tied to its ancestors. Although over time its residents may have increasingly enacted an individualized self, perhaps as part of the emergence of "private" household storage and curated property and murals, at the same time the residents were highly socialized in their redundant age-class activities. This settled world produced a regulated and relational personhood. Their homes speak of structure and order. They were bounded, being defined by fairly strict rules of movement that channeled their bodily comportment throughout their home activities. Long-term repetitive and controlled bodily practices suggest boundedness for these individuals, as we see in Bourdieu's Berber house dwellers (1979).

Burials, such as that of the active male elder (B.1466), illustrate how residents viewed individuals differently than in our Western, individuated identity tradition. Both men and women generally ate the same diet and performed tasks at the same level of intensity, suggesting parity in gender on some corporeal levels. It was acceptable, perhaps even honorable, to remove the head of an especially well-fed elder after death and make him whole with a different head. The head removal was an act of ancestral memorializing, but also a sign of partible personhood (Brück 2005; Hastorf 2003b; McAnany 1995; Parker Pearson 1999; Rowlands 1993). Portions of these individuals therefore belonged to the group and could be passed on, similar to what operates in the Melanesian relational model of personhood and heirlooms (Strathern 1971, 1988). This partible nature allowed some elders to carry on their social work even after they died. In this Neolithic example we find the concept of the body crosscutting a description of selfhood that is unlike ours today, expressed in their active lives, body treatment, as well as their food practices, dynamically changing with age.

## In Sum

In this chapter focusing on personhood and eating we have looked at how identity is formed through the consuming body. With a focus on the individual, our task is more difficult than that of ethnographers, who can see people enacting with each other as they eat. Sadly, for archaeologists, hindsight is not 20–20. Our own worldviews tend to color all that we see. In our culture, we tend to conceive of bounded individuals who can alter their identities slightly but who are fundamentally fixed. We are taught from an early age that the ego (the self-aware individual) is the only reality. For anthropologists and sociologists interested in selfhood and the mind/body, there are many ways of being, and this was surely so in the past. Personhood is still a complex of murky boundaries and interpersonal dynamics. There is still a spectrum of fluidity even within our own, highly individuated world. Today, some people happily share food from the same plate; others will not even taste the food if anyone else has touched the container holding it.

Several perspectives have been presented in this chapter concerning the body, embodiment, and personhood. These concepts overlap but also carry divergent aspects of how a person is positioned in the world. *Techniques* or *technologies of the body* bring an activity-based slant to food and cuisine studies, closer to what people did and therefore what they valued and were valued for. The bodies themselves are the result of these ontologies, but how do we know their place in the world? In juxtaposition to the Western, bounded self is the open, relational "dividual." An open person can be permeable or partible, reflecting different influences of their society on the relational self. Partible bodies can be subdivided in life and in death, can be reconfigured, and can reside in a number of places. This alternative way of interaction with others spills over into interactions with things, in that bodies and objects can be both reconfigured and reused. Heirlooms along with their histories become part of the personal body through wearing and exchange, becoming attached in memory and myth. Food, especially recipes, can also be exchanged and shared, linking people through experience and incorporation.

With *nu* being the ultimate valuable, the Hua view of the partible body stresses the use of bodily essences to grow children, calling upon the living world in this formation. Consumed food makes the body and the person. Çatalhöyük provides an archaeological example of this notion as heads are removed, used, and redeposited as heirloomed memorials of a group and its activities. These bodies are partible in that heads can be replaced to complete the whole. In medieval England, men had better diets than did women, suggesting a clear rank by gender even if their bodies were more open than today. Constraint and control exist for the Hua and for those from Çatalhöyük. These groups each had rules of comportment, incorporation, and movement within the community and landscape, determining where one can walk or work, but especially what one can eat.

In many ways the intellectual dominance of the individual, whole body is a Western preoccupation (Csordas 1994:6–7). The body is the central reality to us, yet this was not so for everyone. For some the family or the group was the central reality. We must be aware of these biases in our research and seek out other forms of personal identity in the archaeological record. We can sometimes see individuals via their material traces in tools and burials, but that does not mean that these items carried the same symbolic capital that they do in our world. Groups have developed a variety of ways they define and value the individual or the gendered person throughout life and death. Looking for evidence of the social (in)dividual in the practices surrounding food preparation and consumption, in the daily tasks carried out by people and in the relational evidence between them, will help us unveil past dynamics of personal identities.

CHAPTER 9

# Food Creates Society

My goal in this book is neither to seek nor to promote *a* theory of food archaeology, nor is it to outline the best methodologies. The study of food is a perspective, an approach, a constellation of questions about the past, a way of doing archaeology from a basal concept that centrally engages with both the materiality and the cognition about the world. Clearly, food inspires intellectual thought. It leads researchers to meditate broadly and deeply about social life. Issues surrounding food are present in many social theories as well as ethnographies, as I have tried to outline. Food has the uncanny ability to link the minutiae of everyday experience to broader cultural patterns, spiritual beliefs, personal dissonances, hegemonic structures, and political economic processes, structuring experience in ways that can be logical and illogical, that are conscious, rule bound, and beyond awareness. Food urges scholars from one side of the intellectual spectrum to read outside their comfort zone: symbolic archaeologists reading about isotope analysis and ancient historians reading about cognitive approaches. The beauty is that food studies require a holistic approach to the past that adopts current strategies to gain a fuller understanding of past lives and meanings of past bodily memories.

This book attempts to engage archaeologists who seek an understanding of the past through the cultural side of food procurement and eating practices. We often think about eating, as others have done throughout human history. The relationship between people and things is made more real through the study of food because of its corporeal, symbolic, and material aspects in addition to its emotional associations. Studying food is therefore robust, engaging with the materialization of sociality and identity, as it has the potential to engage with many intellectual trajectories. Archaeologists ask probing questions about life in the past, about social relations and exclusions, tensions and cohesions, personal and societal constructions, the family, the self, and the body, which can be productive through interactions with food. Individuals and groups construct themselves through their daily practices, entangled in and around all that is related to a cuisine. While food is central to biological, ecological, and economic systems, it is also significant as a symbol, a means of communicating condensed social content, occupying a large referential field in human existence. Our portal to these past activities traces the many steps and stages of food production and consumption, allowing us to look at life broadly and deeply and track the critical work of food in society.

I wanted to trace what is signified in material and mental worlds, reflected in both past and present culinary traditions discussing a few of the methods archaeologists can employ. Modern social and religious groups are wedded to certain cuisines, reconfirming their self-identified corporeal boundaries through these social lives of food, as introduced in the first chapter – through the shared tastes, forms of appetite, and bodily comportments (Barthes 1979; Douglas 1984). To track these different lived experiences we follow the artifacts through their uses in food preparation and consumption. These small but regular cuisine acts can be reconstructed through a range of data that are woven together to uncover past social values.

The book is organized roughly around a historical perspective of food approaches. I began by laying the groundwork for food investigation, presenting a series of broad approaches that can be materialized and studied archaeologically. Included is a range of ways to approach food that have not been commonly applied to archaeological issues but could perhaps give us insights and enable us to untangle the web of meanings that surround examples we study in the past. In particular, Chapter 2 illustrates how rules of edibility exist for everyone, including rules that sometimes operate on the unconscious level, specifically the omnivore's paradox, the Galenic theory, and the Humoral structure. Some basal social theories in food studies are discussed in Chapter 2, including gifting, taste, and flavor. All of these principles exist in our lives today and did so in the past. It is to our benefit that we engage with them in our work on food and specifically on food in the past. In Chapter 3 I make a case for the meal as an important entry into our thinking about the past as it is an important conceptual unit, even if it is not always identifiable in archaeological settings. This discussion is a call to think more about meals, about eating events, as these were the concentrated locations of food engagement.

Part II includes a range of current approaches archaeologists have been working with to reach better understandings of the past. Considering many of the tasks across the broad foodscape of any group brings daily life and long-term planning to the center of our thoughts and understandings. There is a case for this centrality of food in most of our studies about the past through the classic approaches of economic, political, and symbolic dynamics. Global trade, political hierarchy, bodily engagements, memory, and *habitus* all work together in our attempts to approach the past. Food choice directs many aspects of life, from what is edible and why to how that edibility was constructed within society. Food dictates the work patterns and taskscapes of most production and processing, informing us about seasonal cycles and labor investments as well as ingredient choice and even taste. Tracing presentations informs us about valuations in rituals and ceremonies; food for the gods is often not the same as food for humans, food for the brain is not always food for the stomach. Central in these gatherings is sharing, whether smoke, hallucinogens, meat or flowers, taking us to the primary social glue of the food gift.

Part III turns to the potentials in food studies, presenting what questions we can begin to address about the past. I enter this web of possibilities through the issue of identity, beginning with the large group and tacking to the individual. In the two chapters comprising this part I present a series of frameworks that open up our inquiries into the past by presenting modern food studies as ways to think about eating that can aid future inquiries. Colonialism and nationalism reverberate throughout our lives today, playing out in global trade, as in Mintz's discussion of slaves and sugar, but they also participate in individual meals, as in the potato becoming an essential Irish dish. Chapter 7 highlights these dynamics while making a case for the power of boundaries and identity in group maintenance. In Chapter 8 the focus is on the individual and the body – how corporeal reality constructs and is constructed through eating. Embodiment is being studied in archaeology as it is in our own world. Writing this chapter made me reassess how I sense and deal with my own body: How permeable or partible am I, how disconnected are my mind and body? How do I share food with others, and how does that food sharing or lack thereof create me? I realized that I am quite emotional when it comes to the techniques of the body; seeing others eat food I do not like physically disturbs me. This emotive-body link is a conduit we must consider in our archaeological investigations, even if we cannot always materialize it. Cooking also is highly charged – I find deep-frying an impossible task, whereas chopping vegetables I could do all day. These practices, so mundane for most people, link action to being and identity, again topics that can lead us closer to past lived lives as well those of today.

These webs of meaning are played out in the body, as discussed in Chapter 8. Regardless of how an individual senses her/his world, s/he is formed by her/his interactions with food. I have tried to illustrate how these social approaches to food can be viable when inquiring about specific circumstances in both present and past societies. Food is the social glue that brings people together and calms differences, which literally allows us to live another day. This surely participated in making people human. Sharing food is an activity wrapped up with life, memory, and emotion (Sutton 2001). It inscribes these memories onto our bodies while it is incorporated into them (Connerton 1989).

Food and drink are important symbolic media, being lubricants of communication in everyday ideological discourse and conduits for physical and psychological transformations. Even if not consciously seen as performance, how one eats is a declaration of placement in the world and personal identity, an affirmation of the self and group, or, equally, a rejection of group membership. Chapter 7 discusses how small social acts harken to larger social issues, no matter how mundane the circumstance (Douglas 1984). Consumption therefore is at the heart of identity construction, bringing people together while differentiating them from each other (Orlove 1994:106). Self-image is partly formed by how one's body moves through the world and how one perceives this. A person's *habitus* is built in part by their taste and eating patterns – what is considered good and how it is procured – as meals structure and punctuate the lives not only of the consumers but also of the cooks (Bourdieu 1977). These habitual food practices are not arbitrary; they link people to their past through mimicry during early training, repeating movements and practices that refer back to the *habitus* of a mother and beyond. They continue to structure the food practice structures, as knowledge is passed on and groups eat.

One goal of this book has been to weave the various theoretical warps applied in the study of food with the weft of archaeological data, presenting some interpretive possibilities with arguments from today. The unpacking of food tasks in Chapter 4 provides many possibilities for study. Both ethnographic and archaeological examples depict an array of productive approaches to think about eating. Although the larger discussion has concentrated around food and social life, the methods and approaches presented in Chapter 4 are also applicable to many other social archaeological topics and data sets. And there are more actions not mentioned or investigated here, more hidden activities that we must recall and add to our food studies: cleaning up, kitchen habits, vessel life histories, identifying steps in preparing a dish and a meal, to name a few.

Eating begins with the elements: land, water, plants, animals, fungi, bacteria, fire, and people. These constituents activate aesthetics, appetite, place, and memory, which at times are agents in their own right within society. Working together, these constituents reflexively join objects and people together, reflecting the dialectic of personal habits where objects craft people's actions and people manipulate material to work with them (Gell 1998). Food participates in this enactment and through its construction becomes culturally meaningful. Memories of past meals activate the anticipation of the next meal while binding people to the ingredients and their constructions (Barthes 1979; Douglas 1970; Mauss 1973 [1934]; Meigs 1988; Sutton 2001; Visser 1986). This transformation is completed through cultural acts, processing, cooking, and serving, remembered in recipes and "body techniques" of creation (Logan and Cruz 2014). Relationships, created through shared meal incorporation and memories, also define group and individual boundaries, delimiting situations in which food is (and is not) edible. These are the edges of practice that define membership and identity.

Canons of taste, discussed in Chapter 3, strongly direct a community's boundaries of acceptable action, forged by shared styles and consumption valuation (Veblen 1899). National, regional, and familial culinary traditions signal that ethnic boundaries are not arbitrary (Jones 1997:120). We can learn how shifts in the body technologies of cooking and serving practices also reflect realigned power relations (Appadurai 1981; Douglas 1985; Mauss 1973 [1934]; Weismantel 1988). Ethnographic and archaeological examples show that these political complexities can be made visible through weaving multiple data in the story of the meal. Chapter 6 discusses how multiple food identities can be created simultaneously in feasts of largesse (potlatches) that bestow status on the food presenters while creating debt, joy, and at times shame for the participants. The multiple political meanings layered in such experiences are what we hope to realize if not tease apart in our artifactual data as it is thought about contextually, through the relations of artifacts to each other. These discussions show how taste can be sought and found in archaeological material.

Culinary activities leave material traces, providing paths of meaning and agency, as they guide us to a fuller understanding of the questions we pose about the past, coordinated across data sets in webs of relations. Important aspects that we should seek in our data are the variations in the material, not forcing them to be normative. While archaeologists look for trends and large shifts, sometimes it is the subtle dimensions in food practices that define different groups of people. Such is the case of medieval England, where meal ingredients were shared by all, but different ages, classes, and genders ate different quantities and qualities of these items, seen not only in the analysis of stable isotopes by Muldner and Richards (2007) but also in the bone itself by Agarwal and colleagues (2004), presented in Chapter 8.

Long-standing food traditions have profound implications on current daily practices. What philosophers of science refer to as dialectical "tacking" between the big picture and the small is productive. We can concentrate on how the larger social and political domains affect the smaller food practices through material studies. Archaeologists only dig up small, individual objects. These quotidian activities imply larger cultural meanings if we can untangle them out of the data. The large scale is registered in the small through avenues like core flavors, perpetuated in cuisine enactments, like pasta, tomatoes and garlic. Each of these ingredients has a unique and very different adoption history in Italian cuisine and production on the landscape, reflecting a long history of change in taste and recipe. Core foods create and define cultural groups over the long term, but these are constantly in motion even if we sense they are timeless. These ingredients carry lots of baggage – of long histories of trade, of use and meaning shifts, of rejection and acceptance, and of gradual shifts in meaning and valuation, occurring with every cooked meal and every bite. Pasta is an indigenized food, the grain from the Near East and the processing originally coming from Asia. The history of the "Italian" tomato includes the conquest and colonization of Mexico, layered with color bias and beliefs by Europeans in its risqué and poisonous potency, its global history varied in the different places it traveled to (Brandes 1999). Garlic, domesticated in central Asia, spread east and west some 8,000 years ago to color all of the cuisines it touched (Zohary et al. 2013). The political, social, sensory, and economic stories of these three ingredients meeting up in a meal today in Italy could fill a book that would focus on cultural beliefs, sensory perceptions, colonial encounters, trade, nationalism, identity, flavor principles, cuisines, economics of taste, and embodiment.

Harnessing this broad-to-small tacking of memory activation, I turn to South America and the Inka Empire, with a case of community boundaries, hierarchy, and power illustrating consumption. The Inka imperial activities included presenting and eating specific feast meals with the recently conquered enemy to signal a successful conquest and submission. Part of this submission ceremony included the gifting by the Inka of two drinking cups (qeros) of gold or silver (traditionally they were made of wood) to the recently conquered leaders. The conquered ruler and the conquering Inka military general then simultaneously drank maize beer together in front of the populace. Drinking maize beer together signaled that the conquered group was now merged into the Inka Empire, underpinning the Inka's privilege and power over the local people while superficially showing generosity in the food sharing. Literally the conquered consumed the conquering through that act. From then on, the use of these two vessels at a gathering would re-inculcate the power of the Inka to that conquered populace. At the same time the *qeros*, according to Tom Cummins (2002:75, 78), represented the benevolent, peaceful, and productive aspects of the Inka state, the largesse of the earth and the transformative qualities of the alcoholic beverage. The beer vessels both hid and illustrated the power of the state, enacting and entrapping people through this shared consumption, reminding us of the conflict and compliance in many social acts.

I experienced the same hiding-while-seeing differential power in the central Andes in 1986. I was the director of a small archaeological excavation project near Jauja, Perú. At the end of each workweek, the whole team met in the laboratory's courtyard and I paid each local participant his or her week's wages in cash. As they came up and signed for their salary, I offered them a small glass of beer. I thought I was being friendly by this act of gifting beer. After the first person completed this money exchange, the next person requested a second glass. I went to our kitchen and brought back a second jam jar. They then poured out the beer into two glasses and we both drank together, arms entwined, after they received their money. This continued person after person, week after week. Only later, when I read about this symbolic drink-conquest by the Inka, did I see the link to power and performance in our weekly pay ritual, which had passed on through the colonial, republican, and modern eras, marking me as the empowered outsider. The Sausa were reminding themselves and me of our huge social and economic differences with every sip of beer. This was real food for thought.

The spatial distribution of food-related artifacts does inform us about social settings in the past, as presented in Chapter 4. Meals place the server center stage, allowing for endless invention within these settings (Weismantel 1988; Wiessner 1996:6). While we tend to think of meals as warm, relaxing moments, meals can be divisive and hierarchical, manipulating families, communities, and individuals into new positions and powers, causing insult, attack, and even war (Appadurai 1981; DeBoer 2001). New ceramic serving dishes suggest new community dynamics, if not new haptic experiences (Mills 2007). The new cooking and hearth locations documented at Çatalhöyük, mentioned in Chapter 8, reflect changing household interactions (Hastorf 2012). New cooking features speak to changing sensory experiences. On the other hand, evidence of unchanging food preparations speaks to a continuity of the family meal, informing us about the strength of the social rules and sanctions that were being inculcated into the newer members and maintained by the elders, the architecture reining in any deviant tendencies through bodily control and discipline, seen at Barnhill. Such unchanging forms of placement and comportment too must be actively created and are also a locus of agency within the *habitus* of the past and the social power of the meal setting.

Throughout the book I have stressed meals as good to think with about the past, not only analytically but sensorialy and ontologically. They loom large in ethnographic daily life and historical accounts. This does not mean that archaeologists often dig up meals. They tend to dig up palimpsests or fragments of meals, making this an uncommon unit of archaeological analysis. While the meal is perhaps not the most common analytical tool, I have been stressing it as a concept and an entity because it is so central in life, whether easily visible or not. This, in part, is a stumbling block on the way to our goal of getting closer to past understandings. If we can begin to include the agency of meals as a central tenet in our research, we are not only taking food seriously; we are also getting at common practices and concerns of the people who lived in the past. This therefore is a challenge, to seek meals in the archaeological record, and by doing so to get closer to people's practices and structuring structures while tracing the agency of their daily life.

Many scholars have demonstrated how the meal is a metaphor of the social unit, whether for the individual, the couple, the family, the community, the group, or the state. But it is also a metaphor for gender relations and political hierarchies as discussed in Chapters 6 and 7. Mary Douglas pursued these metaphors of daily acts, studying the formation of the person, the family, and the greater society through meals, through choice, and through agency. With meal preparation she asked about personhood and gender. She illustrated how individual acts reflect the greater society in decisions, enacted etiquette, and consumed "good" food. We can transform her substantial points into new platforms of archaeological inquiry with social theory.

In Chapter 8 I focus on the individual to better understand how personhood resonates out to the larger community through food practices. People can be seen as autonomous and individuated or fluidly merged with their family members, wives, husbands, age grades, or on the community level (Strathern 1988). Each node of the social web experiences food consumption differently. Some individuals eat uniquely distinct meals, as among the Bemba or the Hua; others eat what everyone else eats, as in England. These different incorporation tactics create a range of personal identities. Archaeological studies that address questions of such personal identity formation through meals can be applied in ceramic analyses, such as seen in Blitz (1993) and Mills (2001, 2007). These two scholars trace how changing ceramic vessel sizes and designs inform us about meal presentation. Barbara Mills suggests that the addition to the Hohokam repertory of larger, more-decorated food serving dishes reflected more-intensive, face-to-face social interactions, discussed in Chapter 4's section on meal presentation. These small adjustments reflect shifting views of the self and levels of interpersonal commitment that ripple through a community. It is by slippage in emulation and in tastes that people reposition their place in the world and their moral economies, whether through increasing their family size, altering their age classes, changing their gender, or expanding their social networks.

Such individuated engagements also operate on the regional level. In Chapter 6 we considered the politically driven culinary changes across the Mississippian society in the American Bottoms with Johannessen's (1993) data. She demonstrates shifts in ingredients and culinary styles as foreign crops were added to the production and cuisine. This was evident in the diversity of the serving dishes, in the placement of houses, and especially in the location of storage pits. All of these traits reflect an increasing interest in communal food sharing that crystallized in the later, central plazas of classic Cahokia times, a broad political directive that in turn entered every household across the valley. In these settings we see an intensification of community production accompanying an expansion in table manners (and rules), which she suggests reflected increased community concern over its own autonomy in the face of a growing regional political hegemony. Daily foodways were linked to regional political dynamics.

With such food examples we can glimpse a much larger and recursive picture of the relationship of communities to their society. They speak to how a society interacts with the environment, as food is at the ecotone in the debates about nature and nurture, nature and culture, and the domestic and the wild. The American Bottoms story is one of crop intensification, perhaps even reaching a maximum limit of crop yields during the height of Cahokia's power, shifting again as Cahokia's influence ebbed. Early agricultural evidence provides us particular insights into the changing boundaries of cultural life and food.

What was wild and how did a wild plant become food and then get brought into society and cultured (increasingly manipulated by people and finally domesticated) like maygrass or barley (e.g., Boyd 2001; Fuller et al. 2010; Hastorf 1998; Hodder 1990; Scott 2001; Smith 2007; Twiss 2001)?

Indigenous plants and animal foods can remain wild or they can be folded into human society. This requires a shift in perspective, landscape engagement, and agency by all parties. Reorienting our food studies from people to the foodstuffs helps us see the social boundaries and the connections between people and other life forms, defining differences and similarities, directing our gaze of social practice within and between all participating life forms (Kohn 2007; Rival 1998). Many societies do not register the difference between animals and themselves. To some extent pets fall into this category in urban Western lives, but in the Amazon, non-domesticated monkeys can be part of the family (Hugh-Jones 1996). The wild (natural) and domestic (cultural) spectrum for plants also carries this ambivalence. How people interact with the plants around them has much to say about social relations and feelings about these interactions. Plants can be kin and old friends (Rival 1998). The dialectical nature of these plant and animal categories keeps us in an active web of values and meanings.

Not only do we want to learn about the place of these different beings within society; we can use these differences to help us with the questions we ask about the past. Difference can become a prism for the definition of self and non-self, family and non-family, the wild and the domestic, the feast and the daily meal (Douglas 1972; Logan and Cruz 2014; Meigs 1988; Ohnuki-Tierney 1993).

Forging kinship through food sharing is essential in society. Both Meigs (1987) and Weismantel (1991, 1995) provide powerful modern examples of strong kin boundary formation through not eating with others, discussed in Chapters 6 and 7. In these societies children become members of their family by eating with them. Sharing food can be as important as similar bloodlines are in establishing kinship. Eating with others denotes kin, especially for those with permeable body concepts. In small communities, such as those we study archaeologically, eating together could be an important sign of community definition, kinship, or even selfhood, as discussed in Chapter 7 about the residents of Joya de Cerén eating as a community as well as eating as a family.

Analysis of Japanese imperial documents indicates that the early emperors mimicked the folk harvest rituals in the nascent state feasting rituals to entangle the population into legitimating and centralizing their power, evoking the supernatural powers of fecundity while drawing in each village and villager through their personal knowledge of their own hometown event (Ohnuki-Tierney 1993:45). These folk rituals revolved around rice, its production, and its fecundity. This chthonic fecundity was transferred to the growth of the people through the ritual feast, a natural result of rituals, and one that can slip easily into aggrandizement, enabling the emperor to marry rice's power with imperial power, linking the core food's potency to the state efficacy in the population's ontology. The Japanese plant-people-power resonances are almost identical to the Inka state's use of maize planting and harvest rituals that participated in their validation of imperial power across South America. Such manipulation of core symbolic foods seems to be a global phenomenon in many different guises.

The quotidian dinner vs. feast is perhaps the most prominent dichotomy highlighted within this subdiscipline, as outlined in Chapter 3. Food scholars define feasts and everyday meals by their contrasting traits. What do these categories mean, and can we only claim to find them archaeologically when we find big differences? Feasts, especially, are recognizable precisely because they are unlike ordinary meals – that is, by context and contrast. Yet even these definitions and their associated events are fluid. How much food is enough for a feast, and how different, how big, how extended, how diverse does the meal have to be to be called a feast? What do we need to encounter to enable us to label remains as representing a feast? And what created such a special meal and its setting to gain its extraordinary significance? These questions must be addressed in each historical setting we investigate. A well-studied meal can expose social stratification, history, and meaning, as I hinted at with pasta, tomatoes, and garlic earlier in this chapter. Although meals always have a political component, feasts can create cohesion and shared *communitas* while also reaffirming hierarchy, as my example of sharing beer in Perú illustrates. Are feasts more of the same (in terms of quantity or quality of presentation), or must they be filled with rare foods and recipes? These questions must be addressed in each investigation.

The archaeological examples presented in this book illustrate some of the vibrancy of feasts. We can view elite meals, such as that preserved forever in the tomb in Mawangdui, China, for a woman who wanted to party into the afterlife with her select, elegant friends (Pirazzoli-t'Serstevens 1991). The archaeological record also has examples of communal feasts, such as the potluck meals described by VanDerwarker (1999) and Pauketat and his colleagues (2002) for the Midwestern Mississippian agricultural peoples. These feasts suggest community gatherings, requiring detailed data collection and study to support the feast moniker. Then there are the huge feasts full of symbolically charged offerings, of exotic/rare foods and complex preparations. Examples of these memorable meals are depicted in Dietler's Gallic wine- and beer-drinking feasts, in Hamilakis's Cretan burial rituals with their honey and wine, at Çatalhöyük's auroch feasts, or the medieval feasts in Leicester with their swans and geese.

Colonial food activities can demonstrate the clash of culinary cultures, portraying political and social ruptures and differential power alignments more clearly than in indigenous hierarchical settings, whether in North America, Greece, or China. When people, their cuisines, tastes, and animals arrived in new situations, past eating patterns were discursively judged, rethought, and reconfigured, at times blending with the indigenous food patterns, at other times maintaining past food traditions despite the different ecological or economic food provisions locally available, or at times destroyed, with new foods conquering the dinner table. These cultural encounters are registered in cuisine changes, discussed by Lev-Tov (1999) and Vroom (2000) for Greece, where waves of conquerors passed through, influencing populations and their cuisines to varying degrees. In North America, Scott (2001) and Serjeantson (2000) illustrate a range of enslavements through the food to which the slaves had access. Remarkably, there was a wide variety of meat access, mainly thanks to local wildlife. We would learn even more from these studies if the authors had included a sense of what possum actually tasted like, or the smell of it boiling. What herbs might have been in the pot or on the skewer? We could gain a sense of the bodily experiences of slaves by thinking about how they sat, where they cooked, or where they ate. All of these aspects are important to us in comprehending our own world, and certainly they were also important to people in the past. Such material would enrich the faunal data reported in these publications, making their discussion about food more enchanting and embodied.

In another colonial setting, that of the English in North America, we can trace the strictures of identity as well as the importance of context and setting in their food strategies. Comparing the eating traditions of the English with those of the English immigrants in North America, we learn how diligent some families were on maintaining their eating traditions. We know that in medieval England, as the wilderness shrank, wild meat became a luxury, with harsh restrictions on hunting by the masses (Thomas 2007). In colonial North America, the wilderness was an accessible larder and even an obligatory place for meat procurement (Scott 2001). For some English immigrants, hunting remained highly valued and associated with the nobility, whereas for others, hunting became synonymous with the working class or even the slaves. Lev-Tov (1998) studied the subtle shifts in food valuation of English immigrants to Virginia. There the wealthy Calverts, residing in the European-based community of Annapolis, ate wild game, which tells us that they still identified with the upper classes of England (Lev-Tov 1998). On the other hand, the slaves on Louisiana plantations also ate wild game where that was the only accessible meat protein they could gather on their own time (Scott 2001). These two cuisines clearly were valued quite differently in the greater U.S. society of the time, as surely the animals' meanings were as different as were their preparations in these two kitchen settings.

Some of the most exciting stories have come from the greater attention given to contextual detail of the cooking regimes and the importance the subtle differences reveal about past community life. Karen Wright's (2000) work on Neolithic food preparation traces grinding tool locations through a series of phases, allowing us to see how the shifts in food preparation and meal consumption locations can reflect an increasingly bounded society in the Neolithic Levant, and probably in women's comportment as well. We learn not just about the walls and visibility at these settlements but also about the amount of physical work that grinding entailed, as it became an increasingly central and valued part of their food tradition. Such valuations had a high price, however: Neolithic bodies show increasingly more workloads on the joints.

Hard et al. (1996) and Sutton and Reinhard (1995) provide nuanced views of culinary traditions of seasonal meals. They identified annual and seasonal variation in meals not only in terms of ingredients but also in their preparations. Coprolites provided information on these seasonal recipes. Culinary traditions are further clarified in the ceramics, grinding stones, and the microfossils from these settlements, making their daily practices much clearer than any other study. We can now discuss how the inhabitants hunted, harvested, carried, stored, and prepared their food, collecting items throughout the year, as well as worrying about rodents and bugs stealing their stores. These detailed cuisine data reflect the embodiment of the occupants of this region, allowing us to envision daily practices, meals, and taskscapes.

Each ingredient in a cuisine carries social and political histories. This is why Mark Kulansky (1997) could write a whole book on cod, and Sidney Mintz on sugar (1985). When Mintz (1996) noted that the modern body is the product of the Industrial Revolution, he meant that each ingredient in every prepared or purchased meal has a long biological as well as cultural lineage. An entire history of power and cultural manipulation lurks within every globalized meal that we eat today (Mann 2011). Our bodies are engraved with worldwide food transport and the many activities performed to acquire that food, as invisible to us as is the archaeological past. We supermarket shoppers will not display the life-long burden of carrying or squatting, unlike those of the Neolithic or of the farm workers in central valley California. We now have the burden of sugar running through our veins and hearts, seen in the plethora of modern illnesses while others are squatting and sweating in the hot sun to harvest the tea, coffee, cocoa, and bananas for us in the same way that in the past all humans had to work, and work hard, for their food. Our cuisines may only partially mark our bodies, but they mark our minds. We too are embodied persons, eating the global carbon-rich economy. We owe it to ourselves and to our society to learn from the past regarding the embodied *dividual*. None of us is a complete entity; we are connected into the global system with every bite we take, we are all *dividuals* really, created by the transport and times we live in, even if we believe we are unique individuals.

When these histories and conditions are investigated, in the past or the present, we trace the lived lives etched in each body and its molecules. That is the beauty and the power of food studies – we can take the most mundane archaeological data (plant remains, for example) and, by placing them in their historical context and linking them to associated data such as isotope evidence from teeth, bone, and hair, we can view many dimensions of how these past plants participated in society in gender relations, economic networks, travel, work histories, group affiliations, techniques of the body, personhood, and taste. Through these palimpsests of data we can perceive agency in the lives of each member of a society, rich and poor, past and present.

What continues to be exciting is the increasing number of food studies in the archaeological literature. I have not presented all of this work, as the corpus grows, but its existence suggests an interest in this doorway into the past, and its productivity and resilience. The archaeological examples I have included in this book span the globe – England, Perú, Scotland, Jordan, China, Bolivia, California, Virginia, Japan, El Salvador, Anatolia, Italy, Arizona, Greece, Melanesia, Papua New Guinea, Ethiopia, and France, encompassing many habitats – dry and wet, temperate and tropical, forests and plains. This was intentional, to help us see that such intimate interactions are universal, although their meanings and contexts are not. Some of the archaeological projects presented here are especially valuable because they build on contextual, multiple data sets. We want to see the big picture as well as the small daily meal; we want to see the people carrying baskets of food, cooks boiling soups, or chile peppers hanging from the rafters as well as continental-wide trade. All are rich topics for us to think about.

Dancing through the ideas I have presented in this book is unwieldy because they span such a wide range of topics, regions, and approaches. One theme stands out in all of this, however, that is that the past is not as distant as we might assume. We keep the people we study at an arm's length at our peril (Cobb 2005). They are no odder than we are. Their different ways of being, whether open bodies or slaves, whether meat hunters or plant farmers, does not stop them from liking certain dishes better than others; it does not stop them from missing their mothers' cooking or the smells of home kitchens. How your body feels after eating well is not that different from everyone else. Just because my society prefers closed bodies in nuclear families does not make that the universal unmarked category. It is our job to be more encompassing in our archaeological work, and this includes noting the perspectives of others.

With a focus on food, archaeological research can bring us closer to past lives and gain a deeper understanding about being in the world both in the short term but also over the long run. That was my goal when I set out on this project. Approaching the past through food usually begins with something relatively small, even insignificant: the contents of a midden or the placement of a grinding stone in a building. But what begins as mundane recording can lead us toward fresh perspectives to old questions. My point is that such perspectives usually bring the lived experiences into closer focus. Food and the necessity for food have directed much in human lives, the pattern of daily life, the techniques of the body, and the associated significances.

Because food is at the heart of life and society, entangled with people and their daily *habitus*, it does not serve us to treat it as a given, to ignore it because of its essentialist qualities, or to forget the agency endowed in such things. A working hypothesis here is that by seeking the past through a culinary approach we learn more about the different ways of being both in the past and today. I have presented a range of social approaches to the study of food to illustrate how archaeology can apply anthropological food studies to societal questions. Likewise I hope that these archaeological inquiries can help us understand more fully the world we live in anthropologically. It is the meaning associated with these small acts – the elements of food consumption, the incorporation and embodiment – that we want to incorporate in our archaeological studies. Identifying and weaving together these small but crucial social acts opens up referential fields of cognition and meaning, enabling us to learn more about the way the world was lived in and thought about. Food practices in the past were undoubtedly as complex, multifaceted, and important as they are today. The study of food in the past is a challenge, but also a valuable entry to human existence. There is much to learn from thinking about eating.

# References

Abrams, Jr., H. Leon, 1987, The preference for animal protein and fat: A cross-cultural study. In *Food and evolution*, Marvin Harris and Eric B. Ross (eds.), Temple University Press, Philadelphia, pp. 207–223.

Adams, Vanessa, 2011, Frybread as identity: Consuming a discourse of survival and resistance in contemporary Native American society. BA senior honors thesis, Department of Anthropology, University of California Berkeley, on file in the Anthropology Library, UC Berkeley.

Adapon, Joy, 2008, *Culinary art and anthropology*, Oxford University Press, Oxford.

Agarwal, Sabrina C, M. Dumitriu, G.A. Tomlinson, and M.D. Grynpas, 2004, Medieval trabecular bone architecture: The influence of age, sex, and lifestyle, *American Journal of Physical Anthropology* 124(1):33–44.

Agarwal, Sabrina C. and Bonnie Glenncross (eds.), 2011, *Social bioarchaeology*, John Wiley and Sons, Oxford.

Albarella, Umberto and Dale Serjeantson, 2002, A passion for pork: Meat consumption at the British Late Neolithic site of Durrington Walls. In *Consuming passions and patterns of consumption*, Preston Miracle and Nicky Milner (eds.), MacDonald Institute of Archaeology Monograph, Cambridge, pp. 33–48.

Albion, Sara, 1997, *Recipes from Shantivan forest of peace*. Eternity Ink, Melbourne, Australia.

Alcock, Susan E., Carla Sinapoli, Katrinia Schreiber, and Terence D'Altroy (eds.), 2001, *Empires: Perspectives from archaeology and history*, Cambridge University Press, Cambridge.

Aldenderfer, Mark (ed.), 1993, *Domestic architecture, ethnicity and complimentarity in the south-central Andes*, University of Iowa Press, Iowa City.

Allen, Brigid (ed.), 1994, *Food: An Oxford anthropology*, Oxford University Press, Oxford.

Allen, Stuart Lee, 2002, *In the devil's garden*, Ballantine Books, New York.

Allison, Anne, 1997, Japanese mothers and obentos. In *Food and culture, a reader*, Carole Counihan and Penny van Esterik (eds.), Routledge, London, pp. 296–314.

Ambrose, Stanley, 1993, Isotopic analysis of paleodiets: Methodological and interpretive considerations, in *Investigations of ancient human tissue: Chemical analyses in anthropology*, M.K. Sandford (ed.), Gordon and Breach Science Publishers, Langhorne, pp. 59–130.

Ambrose, Stanley H., Brian M. Butler, Douglas B. Hanson, Rosalind L. Hunter-Anderson, and Harold W. Krueger, 1997, Stable isotopic analysis of human diet in the Marianas Archipelago, Western Pacific, *American Journal of Physical Anthropology* 104(3):343–361.

Ambrose, Stanley and M. Anne Katzenberg, 2000, *Biochemical approaches to paleoediet analysis*, Kluwer Academic/Plenum Publishers, New York.

Ambrose, S.H., J.E. Buikstra, and H.W. Krueger, 2003, Gender and status differences in diet at Mound 72, Cahokia, revealed by isotopic analysis of bone. *Journal of Anthropological Archaeology*, 22:217–226.

Ammerman, Albert J. and Luca L. Cavalli-Sforza, 1971, Measuring the rate of spread of early farming in Europe. *Man*, 6(4):674–688.

Anderson, Benedict R. and Richard O'Gorman, 1991, *Imagined communities: Reflections on the origin and spread of nationalism*, Verso, London.

Anderson, Eugene N., 1980, Heating and cooling foods in Hong Kong and Taiwan. *Social Science Information* 19(2):237–268.

1988, *The food of China*, Yale University Press, New Haven.

Anderson, J. 1971, A Solid Sufficiency: An Ethnography of Yeoman Foodways in Stuart England. PhD dissertation, Department of Anthropology, University of Pennsylvania Folklore and Folklife Department, Philadelphia, PA, UMI Ann Arbor.

Andrews, Jean, 1993, Diffusion of Mesoamerican food complex to Southeastern Europe. *Geographical Review*, 194–204.

Andrews, Peter, Theya Molleson, and Başak Boz, 2005, The human burials at Çatalhöyük. In *Inhabiting Çatalhöyük: Reports from the 1995–1999 seasons*, Ian Hodder (ed.), McDonald Institute Monographs and British Institute of Archaeology at Ankara, pp. 261–278.

Angier, Natalie, 2002, Cooking and how it slew the beast within, *New York Times*, May 28, D1.

Apicius, Caelius, 1958, *The Roman cookery book [De re coquinaria]*. Translated by Barbara Flower and Elisabeth Rosenbaum, Harrap, London.

Appadurai, Arjun, 1981, Gastro-politics in Hindu South Asia. *American Ethnologist* 8(3):494–511.

Appadurai, Arjun (ed.), 1986, *The social life of things: Commodities in cultural perspective*, Cambridge University Press, Cambridge.

Arendt, Hannah, 1998 [1958], *The human condition*, University of Chicago Press, Chicago.

Arnold, Bettina, 1999, Drinking the feast: Alcohol and the legitimation of power in Celtic Europe. *Cambridge Archaeological Journal* 9(1):71–93.

Arnold, Denise Y. and Juan de Dios Yapita, 1996, La papa, el amor y la violencia. La crisis ecológica y las batallas rituals en el linde entre Oruro y Norte de Potosí. In *Madre melliza y sus crías. Antología de la papa*, Denise Y. Arnold y Juan de Dios Yapita (eds.), ILCA and Hisbol, La Paz, pp. 311–371.

Arnold, Denise Y. and Christine A. Hastorf, 2008, *Heads of State: Icons, power and politics in the ancient and modern Andes*, Left Coast Press, Walnut Creek, CA.

Arnott, Margaret Louise, 1975, The breads of Mani. In *Gastronomy: The anthropology of food habits*, M.L. Arnott (ed.), Mouton Publishers, The Hague, pp. 297–307.

Arnott, Margaret Louise (ed.), 1975, *Gastronomy: The anthropology of food habits*, Mouton Publishers, The Hague.

Arnott, Sigrid, 1990, Gender, power and meat: Fasting women in the Middle Ages. In symposium Thinking about Eating, organized by Sissel Johannessen and Christine Hastorf, Annual Meetings of the Society for American Archaeology, Las Vegas.

1991a, Gender and power in the flesh: Fasting medieval women. In symposium Thinking about Eating, American Anthropological Association Annual Meeting, Chicago, Illinois, November 21.

1991b, Meat, gender and power in the Middle Ages. MS on file with the author.

Arriaza, B.O., 1996, Preparation of the dead in coastal Andean preceramic populations. In *Human mummies: A global survey of their status and the techniques of conservation*, K, Spindler, H. Wilfing, E. Rastbichler-Zissernig, D. zür Nedden, and H. Nuedurfer (eds.), Springer-Verlag, Berlin, pp. 131–140.

Arzigian, Connie, 1987, The emergence of horticultural economies in southwestern Wisconsin. In *Horticultural economies of the Eastern Woodlands*, W.F. Keegan (ed.), Southern Illinois Press, Carbondale, IL. pp. 217–242.

Ashkenazi, Michael, 1991, From *tachi soba* to *maorai*: Cultural implications of the Japanese meal. *Social Science Information* 30(2):287–304.

Ashmore, Wendy and Richard Wilk, 1988, Introduction: Household and community in the Mesoamerican Past, in *Household and community in the Mesoamerican past*, Wendy Ashmore and Richard Wilk (eds.), University of New Mexico Press, Albuquerque.

Atalay, Sonya and Christine A. Hastorf, 2005, Foodways at Çatalhöyük. In *Çatalhöyük perspectives: Themes from the 1995–1999 seasons*, Ian Hodder (ed.), McDonald Institute Press, Cambridge and the British Institute of Anatolian Archaeology, Cambridge, pp. 111–125.

2006, Food, meals and daily activities: The *habitus* of food practices at Neolithic Çatalhöyük. *American Antiquity* 71: 283–319.

Atchison, J. and R. Fullagar, 1998, Starch residues on pounding implements from Jinmium rock-shelter. In *A closer look: Recent Australian studies of stone tools*, R. Fullagar (ed.), Sydney University Archaeological Methods Series No. 6, Sydney, pp. 109–126.

Atkinson, Jane, 1987, *Wana shamanship*, Stanford University Press, Stanford.

Atran, Scott, 1985, The nature of folk botanical life forms. *American Anthropologist* 87:298–315.

'Azzām, 'Imām Abdullāh, 2004, *The ruling on meat slaughtered in the West*, www .kalamullah.com/Books/the-ruling-on-meat-slaughtered-in-the-west.pdf, 29-4-2013.

Babot, M del Pilar, 2003, Starch grain damage as an indicator of food processing. In *Phytolith and starch research in the Australian-Pacific-Asian regions: The state of the art*, Vol. 19, D.M. Hard and L.A. Wallis (eds.), Pandanus Books, Australian National University, Canberra.

Bakker, Egbert J., 2013, *The Meaning of Meat and the Structure of the Odyssey*. Cambridge, Cambridge University Press.

Balée, William L., 1994, *Footprints of the forest: Ka'apor ethnobotany – the historical ecology of plant utilization by an Amazonian people*, Columbia University Press, New York.

Ballanyne, Rachel M., 2006, *Narratives of food procurement and cultural identity in Roman Britain*, American Institute of Archaeology 107th Annual Meeting Abstracts. Montreal, Vol. 29:47, Oxbow Books, Oxford.

Bandy, Matthew, 2001, Population and history in the ancient Titicaca Basin. PhD Dissertation, Department of Anthropology, University of California-Berkeley, University Microfilms International, Ann Arbor.

2005, Energetic efficiency and political expediency in Titicaca Basin raised field agriculture. *Journal of Anthropological Archaeology* 24 (3):271–296.

Barker, Lewis (ed.), 1982a, *The psychology of human food selection*, Ellis Horwood Ltd Publishers, Chichester.

Barker, Lewis, 1982b, Geography and genetics as factors in the psychobiology of human food selection. In *The psychology of human food selection*, L. Barker (ed.), Ellis Horwood Ltd Publishers, Chichester, pp. 205–224.

Barlow, K. Renee, 2002, Predicting maize agriculture among the Fremont: An economic comparison of farming and foraging in the American Southwest, *American Antiquity* 67(1):65–88.

Barnett, H.G., 1938, The nature of the potlatch, *American Anthropologist* 40(3): 349–358.

Barrett, John, 1989, Food gender and metal: Quest of social reproduction. In *The Bronze Age – Iron Age transition in Europe*, Marie Louise Sorensen and Roger Thomas (eds.), British Archaeological Reports 483(ii), Oxford.

1994, *Fragments from antiquity*, Blackwell, Oxford.

Barth, Fredric, 1967, Economic spheres in Darfur. In *Themes in economic anthropology*, Raymond Firth (ed.), Tavistock, London, pp. 149–174.

Barthes, Roland, 1979 [1961], Towards a psychosociology of contemporary food consumption. In *Food and drink in history: Selections from the annales, economies, societes, civilizations, volume 5*, Robert Forster and Orest Ranum (eds.), Johns Hopkins University Press, Baltimore, pp. 166–173.

Bartram, William, 1928, *Travels of William Bartram, 1773–1778*, Marck Van Doren (ed.), Dover, New York.

Bass, George F., 1986, A Bronze Age Shipwreck at Ulu Burun (Kaş): 1984 Campaign. *American Journal of Archaeology*, pp. 269–296.

Bayles, Bryan, 2001, Scaling the world trees: Ethnobotanical insights into Maya spiked vessels. *Journal of Latin American Lore* 21(1):55–78.

Baysal, Adnan and Katherine I. Wright, 2005, Cooking, crafts and curation: Ground stone artefacts from Çatalhöyük (1995–99 Excavations). In *Changing materialities at Çatalhöyük: Reports from the 1995–99 seasons*, Ian Hodder (ed.), McDonald Institute Press, Cambridge and the British Institute of Anatolian Archaeology, Cambridge.

Beaudry, Mary, C., 1999, House and household: The archaeology of domestic life in early America. In *Old and new worlds*, G. Egan and R.L. Michael (eds.), Oxbow Books, Oxford, pp. 117–126

Beaudry-Corbett, Marilyn, 2002, Ceramics and their use at Cerén. In *Before the volcano erupted, the ancient Cerén village in Central America*, Payson Sheets (ed.), University of Texas Press, Austin, pp. 117–138.

Beaudry-Corbett, Marilyn, Scott E. Simmons, and David B. Tucker, 2002, Ancient home and garden: The view from Household 1 at Cerén. In *Before the volcano erupted, the ancient Cerén village in Central America*, Payson Sheets (ed.), University of Texas Press, Austin, pp. 44–57.

Becker, Sara K., 2013, *Labor and the rise of the Tiwanaku state (AD 500–1100): A bioarchaeological study of activity patterns*, Doctoral dissertation, Anthropology Department, University of North Carolina at Chapel Hill.

Beehr, Dana E. and Stanley H. Ambrose, 2007, Were they what they cooked? Stable isotopic analysis of Mississippian pottery residues. In *We are what we eat: Archaeology, food and identity*, Kathryn Twiss (ed.), Southern Illinois University Press, Carbondale, pp. 171–191.

Beidler, Lloyd M., 1982, Biological basis of food selection. In *Human food selection*, Lewis M. Barker (ed.), Ellis Horwood Ltd, Chichester, pp. 3–15.

Bell, Catherine, 1992, *Ritual theory, ritual practice*. Oxford University Press, Oxford.

Bell, David and Gill Valentine, 1997, *Consuming geographies: We are where we eat*. Routledge, London.

Bender, Barbara, 1978, Gatherer-hunter to farmer: A social perspective. *World Archaeology* 10:204–222.

Bentley, R.A., Chikhi, L. and Price, T.D., 2003, The Neolithic transition in Europe: Comparing broad scale genetic and local scale isotopic evidence. *Antiquity*, 77(295), pp.63–66.

Berdan, F., 1993, Trade and tribute in the Aztec Empire. In *Current topics in Aztec studies: Essays in honor of Dr. H.B. Nicholson*, Vol. 30, A. Cordy-Collins and D. Sharon (eds.), San Diego Museum of Man, San Diego, pp. 71–84.

Berlin, Brent, 1973, The relation of folk systematics to biological classification and nomenclature. *Annual Review of Ecology and Systematics* 4:259–271.

1992, *Ethnobiological classification: Principles of categorization of plants and animals in traditional societies*. Princeton University Press, Princeton.

Betanzos, Juan de, 1996, *Narrative of the Incas* translated and edited by Roland Hamilton and Dana Buchanan, University of Texas Press, Austin.

Bethel, P.H., R.P. Evershed, and L.J. Goad, 1993, The investigation of lipids in organic residues by gas chromatography / mass spectrometry: Applications to Palaeodietary studies. In *Prehistoric human bone-archaeology at the molecular level*, Joseph B. Lambert and Gisela Grupe (eds.), Springer-Verlag, New York, pp. 229–255.

Bianca D'Anna, Maria, 2012, Between inclusion and exclusion: Feasting and redistribution of meals at Late Chalcolithic Arslantepe (Malatya, Turkey), in *Between feasts and daily meals: Toward an archaeology of commensal spaces*, Susan Pollock (ed.), eTopoi, Special Volume 2: 97–123.

Bickle, P. and Whittle, A. eds., 2013. *The first farmers of central Europe: Diversity in LBK lifeways*. Oxbow Books.

Biers, William R. and Patrick E. McGovern (eds.), 1990, Organic contents of ancient vessels: materials analysis and archaeological investigation, Vol 7 MASCA Research Papers in *Science and Archaeology*, University of Pennsylvania, Philadelphia.

Binford, Lewis R., 1967, Smudge pits and hide smoking: The use of analogy in archaeological reasoning. *American Antiquity* 32:1–12.

1978, *Nunamiut ethnoarchaeology*. Academic Press, New York.

Bird, Robert McK., 1970, Maize and its cultural and natural environment in the sierra of Huanuco, Peru. Department of Geography, PhD, University of California, Berkeley.

Bird, Robert Mck., 1984, The Chupachu/Serrano cultural boundary – multifaceted and stable. In *Social and economic origins in the Andes*, D. Browman, R. Burger, and M. Rivera (eds.), British Archaeological Reports International 194, Oxford, pp. 79–95.

Black, Maggie, 1985, *Food and cooking in Medieval Britain: History and recipes*. English Heritage, Birmingham.

Blinman, Eric, 1989, Potluck in the protokiva: Ceramics and ceremonialism in Pueblo I villages. In *The architecture of social integration in prehistoric pueblos*, Michelle Hegmon and William D. Lipe (eds.), Crow Canyon Archaeological Center, Cortez, pp. 113–124.

Blitz, J.H. 1993, Big pots for big shots: Feasting and storage in a Mississippian community. *American Antiquity* 58(1):80–96.

Blom, F., 1932, *Commerce, trade, and monetary units of the Maya*. Publication 4, No. 14. MARI, New Orleans.

Bober, Phyllis Pray, 1999, *Art, culture, and cuisine, ancient and medieval gastronomy*. The University of Chicago Press, Chicago.

Bocquet-Appel, J.P., 2009, The demographic impact of the agricultural system in human history. *Current Anthropology*, 50(5), pp. 657–660.

Bocquet-Appel, J.P., Naji, S., Vander Linden, M. and Kozlowski, J., 2012, Understanding the rates of expansion of the farming system in Europe. *Journal of Archaeological Science*, 39(2), pp. 531–546.

Bogaard, Amy, 2004, Neolithic farming in central Europe: An archaeobotanical study of crop husbandry practices. London, Routledge.

Bogaard, Amy, Michael Charles, M., Katheryna C. Twiss, Andrew S. Fairbairn, Nurçan Yalman, Dragana Filipović, G.A. Demirergi, Fusun Ertuğ, Nerissa Russell, and J. Henecke, 2009, Private pantries and celebrated surplus: Storing and sharing food at Neolithic Çatalhöyük, Central Anatolia. *Antiquity*, 83(321), pp. 649–668.

Bogan, Arthur E., 1983, Evidence for faunal resources partitioning in an eastern N. American chiefdom. In *Animals and archaeology. Hunters and their prey*, T. Clutton-Brock and C. Grigson (eds.), British Archaeological Review, Oxford, pp. 305–324.

Bohrer, Vorsilla, 1991, Recently recognized cultivated and encouraged plants among the Hohokam. *The Kiva* 56(3):227–235.

Bonsall, C., C.T. Cook, R.E.M. Hedges, T.F.G. Higham, C. Pickard, and I. Radovanovic, 2004, Radiocarbon and stable isotope evidence of dietary change from the Mesolithic to the Middle Ages in the Iron Gates: New results from Lepenski Vir, *Radiocarbon* 46(1):P293–300.

Bordo, Susan, 1987, *The flight to objectivity: Essays on Cartesianism and culture*, State University of New York Press, Albany.

Borić, Dušan, 2003, 'Deep time' metaphor Mnemonic and apotropaic practices at Lepenski Vir. *Journal of social archaeology*, 3(1), pp. 46–74.

Borić, Dušan and T. Douglas Price, 2013, Strontium isotopes document greater human mobility at the start of the Balkan Neolithic. *Proceedings of the National Academy of Sciences*, 110(9), pp. 3298–3303.

Borić, D., Radović, M. and Stefanović, S., 2012, Mesolithic-Neolithic Transformations The Populations of the Danube Gorges. *Sickness, Hunger, War, and Religion*, p.25.

Boserup, Ester, 1965, *The conditions of agricultural growth: The economics of agrarian change under population pressure*, Aldine Pub. Co., Chicago.

Bottéro, Jean, 2004, *The oldest cuisine in the world*, University of Chicago Press, Chicago, translated by Teresa Lavender Fagan.

Bourdain, Anthony, 2001, *Kitchen confidential: Adventures in the culinary underbelly*. Harper Collins Publishers, New York.

Bourdieu, Pierre, 1977, *Outline of a Theory of Practice*, translated by R. Nice, Cambridge University Press, Cambridge.

1979, *Algeria 1960: The disenchantment of the world, the sense of honour and the Kabyle house or the world reversed: Essays*, translated by Richard Nice, Cambridge University Press, Cambridge.

1984, *Distinction: A social critique of the judgment of taste*. Routledge and Kegan Paul, London.

1990, *The logic of practice*, translated by Richard Nice, Polity Press, Cambridge.

Boyd, Brian, 2001, Ways of eating/ways of being in the Later Epipalaeolithic (Natufian) Levant. In *Thinking through the body: Archaeologies of corporeality*, Y. Hamilakis, Mark Pluciennik, and Sarah Tarlow (eds.), Kluwer Academic/Plenum Publishers, New York, pp. 137–152.

Boz, Başak, 2005, The oral health of Çatalhöyük. In *Inhabiting Çatalhöyük: Reports from the 1995–1999 seasons*, Ian Hodder (ed.), McDonald Institute Monographs and British Institute of Archaeology at Ankara, pp. 587–592.

Brace, Loring C., 1995, *The stages of human evolution*, Prentice Hall, Englewood Cliffs.

1999, Comment in Wrangham, R.W., Jones, J.H., Laden, G., Pilbeam, D. and Conklin-Brittain, N., 1999. The raw and the stolen. *Current Anthropology*, 40(5), pp. 577–579.

Bradley, Richard, 2000, *An archaeology of natural places*. Routledge, London.

Braidwood, Robert J., Jonathan D. Sauer, Hans Helbaek, Paul C. Mangelsdorf, Hugh C. Cutler, Carleton S. Coon, Ralph Linton, Julian Oppenheim Steward, and A. Leo, 1953, Did man once live by beer alone? *American Anthropologist* 55:515–526.

Braithwaite, Mary, 1982, Decoration as ritual symbol: A theoretical proposal and an ethnographic study in southern Sudan. In *Symbolic and structural archaeology*, Ian Hodder (ed.), Cambridge University Press, Cambridge, pp. 80–88.

Brandes, Stanley, 1990, Ritual eating and drinking in Tzintzuntzan: A contribution to the study of Mexican foodways, *Western Folklore* 49: 163–175.

1999, The perilous potato and the terrifying tomato. Consequences of cultivar diffusion, *Ethnology Monographs* 17:85–96.

Brandes, Stanley and Thor Anderson, 2011, Ratatouille: An animated account of cooking, taste, and human evolution, *Journal of Anthropology* 76(3):277–299.

Braudel, Fernand, 1972, *The Mediterranean and the Mediterranean world in the age of Philip II*, Harper and Row, New York.

1973, *Capitalism and material life, 1400–1800*, Harper and Row, New York.

Bray, Tamara L., 2003a, Inka pottery as culinary equipment: Food, feasting and gender in imperial state design, *Latin American Antiquity* 14(1):3–28.

Bray, Tamara L, 2003b, To dine splendidly: Imperial Inca pottery, commensal politics and the Inca state. In *The archaeology and politics of food and feasting in early states and empires*, Tamara L. Bray (ed.), Kluwer Academic/Plenum Publishers, New York, pp. 93–142.

Bray, Tamara and Anita Cook, 1999, The iconography of Andean Empires: A comparison of the Inca and Huari state ceramic assemblages. MS on file with the author.

Briggs, George and Doris H. Colloway, 1984, *Nutrition and physical fitness. 11th edition*, Rinehart and Winston, New York.

Brookfield, Harold, 1972 Intensification and disintensification in Pacific Agriculture, *Pacific Viewpoint* 13:30–48.

1984, Intensification revisited. *Pacific Viewpoint* 25:15–44.

Brown, C.H., 1985, Mode of subsistence and folk biological taxonomy. *Current Anthropology* 26(1):43–64.

Brown, Judith, 1975, Iroquois women: An ethnohistoric note. In *Toward an anthropology of women*, Rayna R. Reiter (ed.), Monthly Review Press, New York, pp. 235–251.

Brown, Linda A., 2001, Feasting in the periphery, the production of ritual feasting and village festivals at the Cerén site, El Salvador. In *Feasting*, Michael Dietler and Brian Hayden (eds.), Smithsonian Institution Press, Washington D.C., pp. 368–390.

Brown, Linda, A, 2002, Household and community animal use at Cerén. In *Before the volcano erupted, the ancient Cerén village in Central America*, Payson Sheets (ed.), University of Texas Press, Austin, pp. 151–158.

Brown, Linda A. and Andrea I. Gerstle, 2002, Structure 10: Feasting and village festivals. In *Before the volcano erupted, the ancient Cerén village in Central America*, Payson Sheets (ed.), University of Texas Press, Austin, pp. 97–103.

Brown, Linda K. and Kay Mussell, 1984, Ethnic and regional foodways in the United States: The performance of group identity. University of Tennessee Press, Knoxville.

Brück, Joanna, 2001, Body metaphors and technologies of transformation in the English middle and late Bronze Age. In *Bronze Age landscapes: Tradition and transformation*, J. Brück (ed.), Oxbow Books, Oxford, pp. 149–160.

2005, Homing instincts: Grounded identities and dividual selves in the British Bronze Age. In *The archaeology of plural and changing identities: Beyond identification*, Eleanor C Casella and Chris Fowler (eds.), Plenum, New York, pp. 125–160.

Brumfiel, Elizabeth M., 1991, Weaving and cooking: Women's production in Aztec Mexico. *In Engendering archaeology*, Joan Gero and Margaret Conkey (eds.), Basil Blackwell, Cambridge MA., pp. 224–251.

Brumfiel, Elizabeth M. and Timothy K. Earle (eds.), 1987, *Specialization, exchange and complex societies*, Cambridge University Press, Cambridge.

Buccini, Anthony F., 2006, Western Mediterranean Vegetable Stews and the Integration of Culinary Exotica. In Authenticity in the Kitchen. Proceedings of the Oxford Symposium on Food and Cookery 2005, Prospect Books, Totnes, England, pp. 132–45.

2011, Continuity in culinary aesthetics in the wesern Mediterranean Roman Garum and liquamen in the light of the local survival of fermented fiahs seasoning in Japan and the western Mediterranean. In *Cured, fermented and smoked foods: Proceedings of the Oxford Symposium on Food and Cookery 2010*, Helen Saberi (ed.), Prospect Books, Totnes, England, pp. 66–75.

Buchler, Justus, 1940, *The philosophy of Peirce*, Kegan Paul, Trench, Trubner and Co, Ltd., London.

Buikstra, Jane E. and George R. Milner, 1991, Isotopic and archaeological interpretations of diet in the central Mississippi Valley, *Journal of Archaeological Science* 18:319–329.

Busby, Cecilia, 1997, Permeable and partible persons: A comparative analysis of gender and the body in South India and Melanesia, *The Journal of the Royal Anthropological Institute* 3:261–278.

Bush, Leslie L., 2001, Boundary conditions: Botanical remains of the Oliver Phase, Central Indiana, A.D. 1200–1450. Department of Anthropology, Unpublished PhD dissertation, Indiana University.

Bush, Peter and Ezra B.W. Zubrow, 1986, The art and science of eating, *Science and Archaeology* 28:38–43.

Butler, Judith, 1990, *Gender trouble: Feminism and the subversion of identity*, Routledge, New York.

1993, *Bodies that matter*, Routledge, London.

Bynum, Caroline W., 1987, *Holy feast and holy fast: The religious significance of food to medieval women*, University of California Press, Berkeley.

1997, Fast, feast and flesh. In *Food and culture, a reader*, Carole Counihan and Penny van Esterik (eds.), Routledge, London, pp. 138–159.

Cadwallader, Lauren, 2013, Investigating 1500 Years of Dietary Change in the Lower Ica Valley, Peru Using an Isotopic Approach. PhD dissertation, Fitzwilliam College, University of Cambridge.

Cambridge Evening News, 2013, Winship Road, Milton, Cambridge, CB24 6BQ, UK.

Campbell, Ewan, 2000, The raw, the cooked and the burnt. *Archaeological Dialogues* 7(2):184–198.

Canclini N.G., 2001, *Consumers and citizens: Globalization and multicultural conflicts*, University of Minnesota Press, Minneapolis.

Cane, Rachel M., Rob Q. Cuthrell, Matthew P. Sayre, K. Elizabeth Soluri, and Christine A. Hastorf, 2012, The life of Building 3 through plant use: The macrobotanical evidence of Neolithic dwelling from the Berkeley Archaeology at Çatalhöyük (BACH) excavations 1997–2003. In *Last house on the hill: BACH Area Reports from Çatalhöyük, Turkey*, Ruth Tringham and Mirjana Stevanović (eds.), *Monumenta Archaeologica* 27, Cotsen Institute of Archaeology Press, UCLA, Los Angeles, pp. 269–295.

Caplan, Pat, 1993, Feasts, fasts, famine: Food for thought. *Berg Occasional Papers in Anthropology*, no. 2, New York University, Oxford, pp. 13–15.

Caplan, Pat (ed.), 1997a, *Food health and identity*, Routledge, London.

Caplan, Pat, 1997b, Approaches to the study of food, health and identity. In *Food health and identity*, Routledge, London, pp. 1–31.

Capparelli, Aylen, Soultana Maria Valamoti, and Michèle M. Wollstonecroft, 2011, After the harvest: Investigating the role of food processing in past human societies, *Archaeological Anthropological Science* 3:1–5.

Carsten, Janet and Stephen Hugh-Jones, 1995, *About the house*, Cambridge University Press, Cambridge.

Cassoli, Pier Francesco and Antonio Tagliacozzo, 1997, Butchering and cooking of birds in the palaeolithic site of Grotta Romanelli (Italy), *International Journal of Osteoarchaeology* 7(4):303–320.

Castells, Manuel, 1999, *The power of identity*, Blackwell, Oxford.

Cauvin, Jacques, 2000, *The Birth of the Gods and the Origins of Agriculture*. New Studies in Archaeology. New York: Cambridge University Press.

Cessford, Craig, 2005, Estimating the Neolithic population at Çatalhöyük. In *Inhabiting Çatalhöyük: Reports from the 1995–1999 seasons*, Ian Hodder (eds.), McDonald Institute Mongraphs and the British Institute of Anatolian Archaeology, Cambridge, pp. 323–326.

———— 2007, The north area. In *Excavating Çatalhöyük: South, north and KOPAL area report from the 1995–1999 seasons*, Ian Hodder (ed.), McDonald Institute Monographs and British Institute of Anatolian Archaeology at Ankara, Cambridge, pp. 345–531.

Chandler-Ezell, Karol, Deborah M. Pearsall, and James A. Zeidler, 2006, Root and tuber phytoliths and starch grains document manioc (*Manihot esculenta*) arrowroot (*Maranta arundinacea*) and llerén (*Calathea sp.*) at the Real Alto site, Ecuador, *Economic Botany* 60(2):103–120.

Chang, K.C., 1977a, Ancient China. In *Food in Chinese culture*, K.C. Chang (ed.), Yale University Press, New Haven, pp. 25–52.

Chang, K.C. (ed.), 1977b, *Food in Chinese culture*, Yale University Press, New Haven.

Chapman, G. and H. Maclean, 1993, "Junk food" and "healthy food" meanings of food in adolescent women's culture, *Journal of Nutrition Education* 25(3): 108–13.

Charles, M., G. Jones, and J.G. Hodgson, 1997, FIBS in archaeobotany: Functional interpretation of weed floras in relation to husbandry practices, *Journal of Archaeological Science* 24:1151–1161.

Charters, S., R.P. Evershed, L.J. Goad, P.W. Blinkhorn, and V. Denham, 1993, Quantification and distribution of lipid in archaeological ceramics: Implications for sampling potsherd for organic residue analysis, *Archaeometry* 35(2):211–223.

Chisholm, B.S., D.E. Nelson, and H.P. Schwarcz, 1982, Stable carbon ratios as a measure of marine versus terrestrial protein in ancient diets, *Science* 216:1131–1132.

Christakis, Kostas S., 1999, Pithoi and food storage in Neopalatial Crete: A domestic perspective. *World Archaeology*, 31(1), pp.1–20.

Claasen, Cheryl, 1991, Gender, shellfishing, and the shell mound archaic. In *Engendering archaeology. Women and prehistory*, Joan M. Gero and Margaret W. Conkey (eds.), Basil Blackwell, Cambridge, MA, pp. 276–300.

Clutton-Brock, J., 1999, *Domesticated animals*, 2nd edition. British Museum of Natural History, London.

Cobb, Charles R., 2003, Mississippian chiefdoms: How complex? *Annual Review of Anthropology* 32:63–84.

———— 2005, Archaeology and the "savage slot": Displacement and emplacement in the premodern world, *American Anthropologist* 107(4): 563–574.

Cobo, Bernabe, 1979, History of the Inca Empire: An Account of the Indian's Customs and Their Origin, Together with a Treatise on Inca Legend. University of Texas Press, Austin.

Codere, H., 1950, Fighting with property: A study of Kwakiutl Potlatching and Warfare 1792–1930, *Monographs of the American Ethnological Society*; 18, University of Washington Press, Seattle.

Cohen, M.N. and G.M.M. Crane-Kramer (eds.), 2007. *Ancient health: Skeletal indicators of agricultural and economic intensification. Bioarchaeological interpretations of the human past: Local, regional, and global perspectives*, University Press of Florida, Gainesville.

Collins, 1986, *English dictionary*, Collins, London.

Conkey, Margaret and Janet Spector, 1984, Archaeology and the study of gender. In *Advances in archaeological method and theory*, vol. 7, M. Schiffer (ed.), Academic Press, New York, pp. 1–38.

Conkey, Margaret W. and Joan M. Gero, 1991. Tensions, pluralities, and engendering archaeology: An introduction to women and prehistory. *Engendering archaeology: Women and prehistory*, Basil Blackwell, Cambridge MA, pp.3–30.

Conklin, Beth A., 1993, Hunting ancestor: Death and alliance in Wari' cannibalism, *Latin American Anthropology Review* 5(2):65–70.

1995, "Thus are our bodies, thus was our custom": Mortuary cannibalism in an Amazonian society, *American Ethnologist* 22(1):75–101.

Conklin, Harold, 1957, *Hanunoo agriculture: A report on an integral system of shifting cultivation in the Philippines*, Food and Agriculture Organization of the United Nations, Rome.

Conklin, George H., 1988, The influence of economic development on patterns of conjugal power and extended family residence in India. *Journal of Comparative Family Studies*, pp. 187–205.

Connell, R.W. 1987, *Gender and power: Society, the person and sexual politics*, Polity Press, Cambridge.

Connerton, Paul, 1989, *How societies remember*. Cambridge University Press, Cambridge.

Copley, M.S., R. Berstan, S.N. Dudd, G. Docherty, A.J. Mukherjee, V. Straker, S. Payne, and R.P. Evershed, 2003, *From the cover: Direct chemical evidence for widespread dairying in prehistoric Britain*. PNAS 100, 1524–1529.

Cordain, L., S.B. Eaton, J. Brand Miller, N. Mann, and K. Hill, 2002, The paradoxical nature of hunter-gatherer diets: Meat-based, yet non-atherogenic. *European Journal of Clinical Nutrition* 56(1):542–552.

Cornejo Happel, Claudia A., 2012, You are what you eat: Food as expression of social identity and intergroup relations in the colonial Andes, *Cincinnati Romance Review* 33:175–193.

Costin, Cathy L., 1986, From chiefdom to empire state: Ceramic economy among the prehistoric Wanka of Highland Peru. Ph.D. dissertation, Department of Anthropology, UCLA.

Costin, Cathy L. and Timothy K. Earle, 1989, Status distinction and legitimation of power as reflected in changing patterns of consumption in late prehispanic Peru, *American Antiquity* 54(4):691–714.

Counihan, Carole M., 1985, What does it mean to be fat, thin, and female in the United States: A review essay, *Food & Foodways* 1(1):77–94.

1997 (1984), Bread as world: Food habits and social relations in modernizing Sardinia. In *Food and Culture*, Carole Counihan and Penny Van Esterik (eds.), Routledge, London, pp. 283–295.

1999, *The anthropology of food and body*, Routledge, New York.

Counihan, Carole M. and Steven L. Kaplan (eds.), 1998, *Food and gender: Identity and power*. Harwood Academic Publishers, Netherlands.

Counihan, Carole M. and Penny Van Esterik (eds.), 2013, *Food and culture*, third edition, Routledge, London.

Coupland, G., Stewart, K. and Patton, K., 2010. Do you never get tired of salmon? Evidence for extreme salmon specialization at Prince Rupert harbour, British Columbia. *Journal of Anthropological Archaeology*, 29(2), pp. 189–207.

Courty, Marie-Agnès, Paul Goldberg, and Richard Macphail, 1989, *Soils and micromorphology in archaeology*, Cambridge University Press, Cambridge.

Coveney, John, 2000, *Food, morals and meaning; the pleasure and anxiety of eating*, Routledge, London.

Coy, Jennie P., 1975, Iron Age cookery. In *Archaeozoological studies*, A.T. Claeson (ed.), North Holland, Amsterdam, pp. 426–430.

Crabtree, Pam, 1990, Zooarchaeology and complex societies: Some uses of faunal analysis for the study of trade, social status, and ethnicity, *Archaeological Method and Theory* 2:155–205.

1996, Production and consumption in an early complex society: Animal use in Middle Saxon East Anglia, *World Archaeology* 28(1):58–75.

Crader, Diana C., 1990, Slave diet at Monticello, *American Antiquity* 55(4):690–717.

Craig, Oliver E., 2003, Dairying, dairy products and milk residues: Potential studies in European prehistory. In *Food culture and identity in the Neolithic and early Bronze Age*, M. Parker Pearson (ed.), BAR International Series 1117, Archaeopress, Oxford, pp. 89–96.

Craig, Oliver E., and M.J. Collins, 2000, An improved method for the immunological detection of mineral bound protein using hydrofluoric acid and direct capture, *Journal of Immunological Methods* 236:89–97.

Craig, Oliver E., V.J. Steele, A. Fischer, S. Hartz, S.H. Andersen, et al., 2011, Ancient lipids reveal continuity in culinary practices across the transition to agriculture in Northern Europe. Proc Natl Acad Sci USA 108(44): 17910–17915.

Cramp, Lucy, J.E. Richard, P. Evershed, and H. Eckardt, 2011, What was a mortarium used for? Organic residues and cultural change in Iron Age and Roman Britain, *Antiquity*, 85(330):1339–1352.

Crawford, Gary, 1992 The transitions to agriculture in Japan. In *Transitions to agriculture in prehistory*, A.B. Gebauer and T.D. Price (eds.), Prehistory Press, Madison, pp. 117–132.

Crawford, Gary W. and Chen Shen, 1998, The origins of rice agriculture: Recent progress in East Asia (Special Section: Rice Domestication), *Antiquity* 72(278):858–866.

Crosby, Jr., Alfred W., 2003. *The Columbian exchange: Biological and cultural consequences of 1492 (Vol. 2)*. Greenwood Publishing Group, Westport, Connecticut.

Crosswhite, Frank, 1981, Desert plants; habitat and agriculture in relation to the major pattern of cultural differentiation in the O'odham People of the Sonoran Desert, *Desert Plants* 3(2):47–76.

Crown, Patricia L., 2000, Women's role in changing cuisine. In *Women and men in the prehispanic Southwest*, Patricia L. Crown (ed.), School of American Research Advanced Seminar Series, Santa Fe, pp. 221–266.

Csordas, Thomas J., 1990, Embodiment as a paradigm for Anthropology, *Ethos* 18:5–46.

1994, Introduction. In *Embodiment and experience*, Thomas J. Csordas (ed.), Cambridge University Press, Cambridge, pp. 3–14.

Cummins, Thomas B.F., 2002, *Toasts with the Inca: Andean abstraction and colonial images in quero vessels*, University of Michigan Press, Ann Arbor.

Curtin, Deane W., 1992, Food/body/person. In *Cooking, eating, thinking: Transformative philosophies of food*, Deane W. Curtin and Lisa M. Heldke (eds.), Indiana University Press, Bloomington, pp. 3–22.

Cushing, Frank H., 1886, A study of Pueblo pottery as illustrative of Zuni culture growth. *Fourth Annual Report of the Bureau of Ethnology 1882–3*. Washington, DC.

Cutler, Hugh C. and M. Cárdenas, 1947, Chicha, a native South American beer, *Botanical Museum Leaflets*, Harvard University 13(3):33–60.

Daggett, R.H., 1972 [1888], Introduction. In *The legends and myths of Hawaii: The fables and folklore of a strange people* by David Kalakaua, Charles Tuttle Company, Vermont, pp. 1–15.

Dalby, A. 1996. *Siren feasts: A history of food and gastronomy in Greece*. Routledge, London.

D'Altroy, Terence N., 2001, Politics, resources, and blood in the Inka Empire. In Empires: Perspectives from archaeology and history, Susan Alcock, Terence N. D'Altroy, Kathleen Morrison and Carla M. Sinopoli (eds.). Cambridge University Press, Cambridge, pp. 201–26.

2002, *The Incas*, Blackwell, Oxford.

2014, *The Incas*. John Wiley & Sons, New York.

D'Altroy, Terence N. and Timothy K. Earle, 1985, Staple finance, wealth finance, and storage in the Inka Political economy, *Current Anthropology* 26:187–206.

D'Altroy, Terence N. and Christine A. Hastorf, 1984, The distribution and contents of Inca state store houses in the Xauxa region of Peru, *American Antiquity* 49(2):334–349.

D'Altroy, Terence N. and Christine A. Hastorf (eds.), 2001, *Empire and domestic economy*, Plenum Publ. Corp., New York.

D'Andrea, A.C., 1999, The dispersal of domesticated plants into north-eastern Japan. In *The prehistory of food, appetites for change*, Chris Gosden and Jon Hather (eds.), Routledge, London, pp. 166–183.

D'Andrea, A.C, Gary W. Crawford, M. Yoshizaki, and T. Kudo, 1995, Late Jomon cultigens in northeastern Japan. *Antiquity* 69:146–152.

D'Arms, John N., 2004, The culinary reality of Roman upper-class *convivia*, *Society for Comparative Study of Society and History* 46(3):450–428.

Damerow, Peter, 1996, Food production and social status as documented in proto-cuneiform texts. In *Food and the status quest*, Polly Wiessner and W. Schiefenhövel (eds.), Berghahn Books, Oxford, pp. 149–170.

DaSilva, Cara (ed.), 1996, *In memory's kitchen, a legacy from the women of Terezín*, Jason Aronson Inc., London.

David, Nick, Judy Sterner, and K. Gavua, 1988, Why pots are decorated, *Current Anthropology* 29:365–388.

Davis, C.M., 1928. Self selection of diet by newly weaned infants: An experimental study. *American Journal of Diseases of Children*, 36(4):651–679.

1939. Results of the self-selection of diets by young children. *Canadian Medical Association Journal*, 41(3):257.

Davidson, Adam, 2015, On money, *The New York Times Magazine*, August 30, pp. 22–26.

Davidson, Alan, 1999, *The Oxford companion to food*, Oxford University Press, Oxford.

DeBoer, Warren R., 1975, The archaeological evidence for manioc cultivation: A cautionary note, *American Antiquity* 40:419–433.

DeBoer, Warren, R., 2001, The big drink: Feast and forum in the Upper Amazon. In *Feasting*, Michael Dietler and Brian Hayden (eds.), Smithsonian Institution Press, Washington, DC, pp. 215–239.

deCerteau, Michel, 1989, *The practice of everyday life*, University of California Press, Berkeley.

deCerteau, Michel, L. Giard, and P. Mayol, 1998, *The practice of everyday life, vol. 2, living and cooking*, University of Minnesota Press, Minneapolis.

Deetz, James, 1977, *In small things forgotten: An archaeology of early American Life*, Doubleday, Garden City.

DeMarrais, Elizabeth, Chris Gosden, and Colin Renfew (eds.), 2004, *Rethinking materiality: The engagement of mind with the material world*, McDonald Institute for Archaeological Research, Cambridge.

DeMoulins, D., 2000, Abu Hureyra: Plant remains from the Neolithic. In *Village on the Euphrates, from foraging to farming at Abu Hureyra*, A.M.T. Moore, G.C. Hillman, and A.J. Legge (eds.), Oxford University Press, Oxford, pp. 399–422.

DeNiro, Michael J., 1987, Stable isotopes and archaeology, *American Scientist* 75:182–191.

DeNiro, Michael, J. and Sam Epstein, 1978, Influence of diet on the distribution of carbon isotopes in animals, *Geochimica and Cosmochimica Acta* 42:495–506.

DeNiro, Michael J. and Christine A. Hastorf, 1985, Alteration of $^{15}N/^{14}N$ and $^{13}C/^{12}C$ ratios of plant matter during the initial stages of diagenesis: Studies utilising archaeological specimens from Peru, *Geochimica and Cosmochimica Acta* 49:97–115.

DeNiro, Michael J. and Steve Weiner, 1988, Use of collagenase to purify collagen from prehistoric bones for stable isotopic analysis, *Geochimica et Cosmochimica Acta* 52(10):2425–2431.

Dennell, Robin, 1976, The economic importance of plant resources represented on archaeological sites, *Journal of Archaeological Science* 3:229–247.

1979, Prehistoric diet and nutrition: Some food for thought. *World Archaeology* 11(2):121–135.

Derrida, J., 1999, Hospitality, justice and responsibility: A dialogue with Jacques Derrida. In *Questioning ethics: Debates in contemporary philosophy*, Richard Kearney and Mark Dooley (eds.) Routledge, New York, pp. 65–83.

Descola, Phillipe, 1994, *In the society of Nature*. Cambridge University Press, Cambridge.

de Garine, Igor, 1997, Food preferences and taste in an African perspective: A word of caution. In *Food preferences and taste: Continuity and change 2*, Helen Macbeth (ed.), Berghahn Books, Providence, RI, pp. 187–207.

Dickson, C., 1996, Food, medicinal and other plants from the 15th century drains of Paisley Abbey, Scotland, *Vegetation History and Archaeobotany* 5:25–31.

Dietler, Michael, 1990, Driven by drink: The role of drinking in the political economy and the cast of early Iron Age France, *Journal of Anthropological Archaeology* 9:352–406.

1996, Feast and commensal politics in the political economy: Food power, and status in prehistoric Europe. In *Food and the status quest: An interdisciplinary perspective*, Polly Wiessner and W. Schiefenhövel (eds.), Berghahn Books, Providence, pp. 87–125.

1998, Consumption, agency, and cultural entanglement: Theoretical implications of Mediterranean colonial encounter. In *Studies in culture contact: Interaction, culture change, and archaeology*, James G. Cusick (ed.), Center for Archaeological Investigations, Southern Illinois University, Carbondale, pp. 288–315.

1999, Rituals of commensality and the politics of state formation in the "princely" societies of early Iron Age Europe. In *Les Princes de la protohistoire et l'emergence de'Etat*, P. Ruby (ed.), Actes de la Table Rondu internationale, Ecole Francaise de Rome, Paris, pp. 135–152.

2001, Theorizing the feast: Rituals of consumption, commensal politics, and power in African contexts. In *Feasts: Archaeological and ethnographic perspectives on food, politics and power*, M. Dietler and B. Hayden (eds.), Smithsonian Institution Press, Washington DC, pp. 65–114.

2007, Culinary encounters: Food, identity and colonialism. In *The archaeology of food and identity*, Kathleen Twiss (ed.), Southern Illinois University Press, Carbondale, pp. 218–242.

2010, *Archaeologies of colonialism, consumption, entanglement, and violence in ancient Mediterranean France*, University of California Press, Berkeley.

Dietler, Michael and Brian Hayden (eds.), 2001a, *Feasts: Archaeological and ethnographic perspectives on food, politics and power*, Smithsonian Institution Press, Washington, DC.

Dietler, Michael and Brian Hayden, 2001b, Digesting the feast – good to eat, good to drink, good to think: An introduction. In *Feasts: Archaeological and ethnographic perspectives on food, politics and power*, Michael Dietler and Brian Hayden (eds.), Smithsonian Institution Press, Washington, DC, pp. 1–22.

Dietler, Michael and Ingrid Herbich, 1998, Habitus, techniques, style: An integrated approach to the social understanding of material culture and boundaries. In *The archaeology of social boundaries*, Miriam Stark (ed.), Smithsonian Institution Press. Washington, DC, pp. 232–263.

Dietler, Michael and Ingrid Herbich, 2001, Feasts and labor mobilization. In *Feasts: Archaeological and ethnographic perspectives on food, politics and power*, Michael Dietler and Brian Hayden (eds.), Smithsonian Institution Press, Washington, DC, pp. 240–264.

Di Schino, June, 2011, Kimchi: Ferment at the heart of Korean cuisine, from local identity to global consumption, In *Cured, fermented and smoked foods: Proceedings of the Oxford Symposium on Food and Cookery 2010*, Helen Saberi (ed.), Totnes, England: Prospect Books, pp. 76–83.

Dobres, Marica-Anne, 2000, *Technology and social agency: Outlining a practice framework for archaeology*, Blackwell, Oxford.

Dobres, Marcia-Anne and John Robb, 2000, *Agency in archaeology*, Routledge, London.

Donnan, Christopher B. and Guillermo A. Cock (eds.), 1986, *The Pacatnamu papers*, vol. 1, Fowler Museum of Cultural History, University of California, Los Angeles.

(eds.), 1997, *The Pacatnamu papers*, vol. 2, Fowler Museum of Cultural History, University of California, Los Angeles.

Douglas, Mary, 1966, *Purity and danger: An analysis of concepts of pollution and taboo*, Routledge and Kegan Paul, London.

1970, *Natural symbols*, Random House, New York.

1971, Lele economy compared with the Bushong. In *Economic development and social change*, George Dalton (ed.), The Natural History Press, Garden City, pp. 62–87.

1975, *Implicit Meanings: Essays in Anthropology*, Routledge and Kegan Paul, London, Boston.

1982, Passive voice theories. In *Religious sociology. In the active voice*, M. Douglas (ed.), Routledge and Kegan Paul, London, pp. 1–10.

1984, Standard social uses of food: Introduction. In *Food in the social order, studies of food and festivities in three American communities*, M. Douglas (ed.), Russell Sage Foundation, New York, pp. 1–39.

1985, *Taboo, Magic, Witchcraft, and Religion*, Third Edition, Arthur C. Lehmann and James E. Myers (eds.), Mayfield Publishing Co., Mountain View, pp. 50–54.

1997 [1972], Deciphering a meal. In *Food and culture*, Carole Counihan and Penny Van Esterik (eds.), Routledge, New York, pp. 36–54.

Douglas, Mary and S. Ney, 1998, *Missing persons: A critique of personhood in the social sciences*, University of California Press, Berkeley.

Douglas, Mary and Michael Nicod, 1974, 'Taking the biscuit': The structure of British meals, *New Society* 30:744–747.

Drummond, J.C. and Anne Wilbraham, 1994 [1939], *The Englishman's food, five centuries of English diet*. Pimlico, London.

Dudd, Stephanie N. and Richard P. Evershed, 1998, Direct demonstration of milk as an element of archaeological economies, *Science* 282:1478–1481.

Dudd, S.N., Richard P. Evershed, and A.M. Gibson, 1999, Evidence for varying patterns of exploitation of animal products in different prehistoric pottery tradition based on lipids preserved in surface and absorbed residues, *Journal of Archaeological Science* 26:1473–1478.

Dudley, Robert, 2000, Evolutionary origins of human alcoholism in primate frugivory, *Quarterly Review of Biology* 75:3–15.

2014, *The drunken monkey: Why we drink and abuse alcohol*, University of California Press, Berkeley.

Dunne, Julie, Richard P. Evershed, Mélanie Salque, Lucy Cramp, Silvia Bruni, Kathleen Ryan, Stefano Biagetti, and Savino Di Lernia, 2012, First dairying in green Saharan Africa in the fifth millennium BC, *Nature* 486:390–394.

Düring, Belda S., 2006, Constructing communities: Clustered neighborhoods settlements of the central Anatolian Neolithic, CA 8500–5500 BC. Unpublished PhD dissertation, Department of Archaeology, University of Leiden, The Netherlands.

Durkheim, Emile, 1965 [1915], *The elementary forms of religious life*, Free Press, New York.

Earle, Timothy K., 1987, Specialization and the production of wealth: Hawaiian chiefdoms and the Inka Empire. In *Specialization, exchange and complex societies*, E. Brumfiel and T.K. Earle (eds.), Cambridge University Press, Cambridge, pp. 1–9.

    1997, *How chiefs came to power: The political economy of prehistory*, Stanford University Press, Stanford.

Earle, Timothy K. and Andrew Christenson (eds.), 1980, *Modeling change in prehistoric subsistence economies*, Academic Press, New York.

Earle, Timothy K and J.E. Ericson (eds.), 1977, *Exchange systems in prehistory*, Academic Press, New York.

Edwards, Kevin, 1991, Using space in cultural palynology: The value of the off-site pollen. In *Modeling ecological change*, D. Harris and K. Thomas (eds.), Institute of London, London, pp. 61–73.

Eichinger Ferro-Luzzi, G., 1980, Food avoidances during the puerperium and lactation in Tamilnadu. In *Food, ecology and culture*, J.R.K. Robson (ed.), Gordon and Breach, New York, pp. 109–118.

Eliade, Mircea, 1959, *Cosmos and history; the myth of the eternal return*. Translated from French by Willard R. Trask. Harper, New York.

Elias, Norbert, 1978 [1939], *The civilizing process, volume 1, The history of manners*, Basil Blackwell, Oxford.

Ellis, R., 1983, The way to a man's heart: Food in the violent home. In *The sociology of food and eating: Essays on the sociological significance of food*, Anne Murcott (ed.), Gower, Aldershot, Hants, pp. 164–171.

Engels, Friedrich, 1942, *The origin of the family, private property and the state, in the light of the researches of Lewis H. Morgan*, International Publishers, New York.

Erickson, Clark, 1987, The dating of raised-field agriculture in the Lake Titicaca basin, Peru. In *Pre-Hispanic agricultural fields in the Andean region*. Proceedings of the 45 Congreso Internacional de Americanistas, Denevan, W. Mathewson, K., and Knapp, G. (eds.), volume 359 (ii), International Series, British Archaeological Reports, Oxford, pp. 373–384.

    1988. Raised field agriculture in the Lake Titicaca basin, *Expedition* 30(3):8–16.

Ericson, Jon and Gary Stickel, 1973, A proposed classification system for ceramics. *World Archaeology* 4(3):357–367.

Ericson, Jonathon E., Michael West, Charles H. Sullivan, and Harold Krueger, 1989, The development of maize agriculture in the Viru Valley, Peru. In *The chemistry of prehistoric human bone*, T. Douglas Price (ed.), Cambridge University Press, Cambridge, pp. 68–104.

Etkin, Nina L., 2006, *Edible medicines*, University of Arizona, Tucson.

Eveleigh, David J., 1997, *Old cooking utensils*, Shire Publications Ltd, Risborough.

Evershed, R.P., 1993, Biomolecular archaeology of lipids, *World Archaeology* 25(1):74–93.

Evershed, R.P., C. Heron, C. Charles, and L.J. Goad, 1992, The survival of food residues: New methods of analysis interpretation and application. In *New developments in archaeological science*, M.A. Pollard (ed.), Proceedings of the British Academy 77:187–208, London.

Evershed, R.P., Carl Heron, and L. John Goad, 1990, Analysis of organic residues of archaeological origin by high-temperature gas chromatography and gas chromatography/mass spectrometry, *The Analyst* 115:1339–1342.

Evershed, Richard P., Sebastian Payne, Andrew G. Sherratt, Mark S. Copley, Jennifer Coolidge, Duska Urem-Kotsu, Kostas Kotsakis, Mehmet Özdogan, Aslý E. Özdogan, Olivier Nieuwenhuyse, Peter M.M.G. Akkermans, Douglass Bailey, Radian-Romus Andeescu, Stuart Campbell, Shahina Farid, Ian Hodder, Nurcan Yalman, Mihriban Özbaşaran, Erhan, Yossef Garfinkel, Thomas Levy, and Margie M. Burton, 2008, Earliest date for milk use in the Near East and southeastern Europe linked to cattle herding, *Nature* 455:528–532.

Evershed, Richard and Noreen Tuross, 1996, Proteinaceous material from potsherds and associated soils, *Journal of Archaeological Science* 23:429–436.

Fairbairn, Andrew, Julie Near, and Daniele Martinoli, 2005, Macrobotanical investigations of the north, south and KOPAL area excavations at Çatalhöyük east. In *Inhabiting Çatalhöyük: Reports from the 1995–1999 seasons*, Çatalhöyük Project, Ian Hodder (ed.), McDonald Institute Monographs/British Institute of Archaeology at Ankara, Cambridge, pp. 137–202.

Fairbairn, Andrew S., and Ehud Weiss (eds.), 2009, From Foragers to Farmers: Papers in honour of Gordon C. Hillman, Oxford, UK; Oakville, CT: Oxbow Books.

Fajans, Jane 1988, The transformative value of food: A review essay, *Food and Foodways* 3:143–166.

Falk, Pasi, 1991, *Homo culinarius*: Towards an historical anthropology of taste. *Social Science Information* 4:757–790.

1994, *The consuming body*, Sage, London.

Farahani, Alan, Katherine Chiou, Anna Harkey, Christine A. Hastorf, David L. Lentz, and Payson D. Sheets, 2016, Exploring plantscapes at the ancient Maya Village of Joya de Cerén, El Salvador, Antiquity.

Farb, Peter and George Armelagos, 1980, *Consuming passions: The anthropology of eating*, Washington Square Press, New York.

Farid, Shahina, 2007, Introduction to the South Area excavations. In *Excavating Çatalhöyük: South, North and KOPAL area reports from the 1995–1999 seasons*, Çatalhöyük Project, Ian Hodder (ed.), McDonald Institute Monographs/British Institute of Archaeology at Ankara, Cambridge, pp. 41–58.

Fausto, Carlos, 2007, Feasting on people, *Current Anthropology* 48(4):497–530.

Felton, David L., Frank Lortie, and Peter D. Schulz, 1984, The Chinese laundry on second street: Papers on archaeology at the Woodland Opera house site. California Archaeological Reports, No. 24, California, Department of Parks and Recreation, Sacramento.

Fenton, Alexander and T.M. Owen (eds.), 1981, *Food in perspective*, John Donald Publishers, Ltd, Edinburgh.

Fiddes, Nick, 1991, *Meat, a natural symbol*, Routledge, London, New York.

1995, The Omnivore's Paradox. In *Food choice and the consumer*, David W. Marshall (ed.), Chapman and Hall, London, pp. 131–151.

Finucane, Brian, Patricia Maita Agurto, and William H. Isbell, 2006, Human and animal diet at Conchopata, Peru: Stable isotope evidence for maize agriculture and animal management practices during the Middle Horizon, *Journal of Archaeological Science* 33(2):1766–1776.

Fischer, Anders, Jesper Olsen, Mike Richards, Jan Heinemeier, Arny E. Sveinbjörnsdóttir, and Pia Bennike, 2007, Coast-inland mobility and diet in the Danish Mesolithic and Neolithic: Evidence from stable isotope values of humans and dogs, *Journal of Archaeological Science* 34:2125–2150.

Fischler, Claude, 1980, Food habits, social change and the nature/culture dilemma, *Social Science Information* 19(6):937–953.

1988, Food, self and identity, *Social Science Information* 27(2):275–292.

Fish, Suzanne K., 1994, Archaeological palynology in gardens and fields. In *Archaeology of garden and field*, N. Miller and K. Gleason (eds.), University of Pennsylvania Press, Philadelphia, pp. 44–69.

Fish, Suzanne K, Paul R. Fish, and John H. Madsen, 1990, Analyzing regional agriculture: A Hohokam example. In *The archaeology of regions*, S.K. Fish and S.A. Kowalewski (eds.), Smithsonian Institution Press, Washington, DC, pp. 189–218.

Fish, Suzanne K., Paul Fish, C. Miksicek, and John Madson, 1985, Prehistoric agave cultivation in southern Arizona, *Desert Plants* 7(100):107–112.

Fisher, Len, 2011, Fermented, cured and smoked: The science and savour of dry-fermented sausages. In *Cured, fermented and smoked foods: Proceedings of the Oxford Symposium on Food and Cookery 2010*, edited by Helen Saberi (ed.), rospect Books, Totnes, England, pp. 102–105.

Fitchen, Janet M., 1988, Hunger, malnutrition and poverty in the contemporary United States: Some observations on their social and cultural context, *Food and Foodways* 2:309–333.

Flannery, Kent V., 1968, The Olmec and the Valley of Oaxaca: A model for inter-regional interaction in formative times. In *Dumbarton Oaks Conference on the Olmec*, E.P. Benson (ed.), Dumbarton Oakes, Washington DC, pp. 79–110.

1972, The cultural evolution of civilizations. *Annual Review of Ecology and Systematics*, 3 Annual Reviews: 399–426.

1973a, Prehistory and human ecology of the Valley of Oaxaca, Museum of Anthropology, University of Michigan, *Memoirs of the Museum of Anthropology*, No. 7, University of Michigan, Ann Arbor.

1973, The origins of agriculture, *Annual Reviews of Anthropology*, 2:271–310.

Forson, P.W. and C. Counihan, 2013, *Taking food public: Redefining foodways in a changing world*. Routledge, London.

Forster, R. and O. Ranum, 1979, *Food and drink in history*, Johns Hopkins University Press, Baltimore.

Foss, Pedar William, 1994, Kitchens and dining rooms at Pompeii: The spatial and social relationship of cooking to eating in the Roman household. PhD dissertation, Department of Classical Art and Archaeology, University of Michigan, Ann Arbor.

Foucault, Michel, 1979, *Discipline and punishment. The birth of the prison*. Penguin Books, Harmondsworth.

1980, Body/Power. In *Michel Foucault: Power/Knowledge selected interviews and other writings 1972–1977*, Colin Gordon (ed.), Harvester Press, Brighton, pp. 55–62.

1988, Technologies of the self. In *Technologies of the self: A seminar with Michel Foucault*, L.H. Martin, H. Gutman, and P.H. Hutton (eds.), Tavistock,London, pp. 16–49.

Fowler, Brenda, 2002, The last meal of the Ice Man. www.pbs.org.wgbh/nova/icemummies/iceman.htm/

Fowler, Catherine, 1995, Some notes on ethnographic subsistence systems on Mojavean environments in the Great Basin, *Journal of Ethnobiology* 151(1):99–117.

Fowler, Chris, 2004, *The archaeology of personhood*, Routledge, London.

Fox, Rachel Sarah, 2012, Feasting practices and changes in Greek society from the Late Bronze age to early Iron Age, *British Archaeological Reports International Series* 2345, Oxford.

Frake, Charles, 1969, The ethnographic study of cognitive systems. In *Cognitive anthropology: Readings Stephen A. Tyler (ed.)*, Holt, Rinehart, and Winston, New York, pp. 28–41.

Frank, Arthur, 1991, For a sociology of the body: An analytical review. In *The body: Social process and cultural theory*, Mike Featherstone, Mike Hepworth, and Brian S. Turner (eds.), Sage, London, pp. 36–102.

Franklin, Maria, 2001, The archaeological dimensions of soul food: Interpreting race, culture, and Afro-Virginian identity. In *Race and the archaeology of identity*, Charles E. Orser, Jr. (ed.), University of Utah Press, Salt Lake City, pp. 88–107.

Frazer, J.G., 1959 [1890] *The golden bough, a study in magic and religion*. Macmillan, New York.

Freeman, Michael, 1977, Sung. In *Food in Chinese culture*, K.C. Chang (ed.), Yale University Press, New Haven, pp. 143–193.

Friedman, Jonathan and Michael Rowlands, 1978, Notes toward an epigenetic model of the evolution of "civilization". In *The evolution of social systems*, J. Friedman and M.J. Rowlands (eds.), Duckworth, London, pp. 201–278.

Friesen, T. Max, 2001, A zooarchaeological signature for meat storage: Rethinking the drying utility index, *American Antiquity* 66(2):315–331.

Frink, Lisa, 2007, Storage and status in precolonial and colonial coastal western Alaska, *Current Anthropology* 48(3):349–374.

Frison, George C., 1970, *The Genrock Buffalo Jump*, 48 CO304. Plains Anthropologist Memoir No. 7, Plains Anthropologist Corp, Lincoln.

1974, *The Casper site: A Hell Gap Bison Kill on the high plains*. Academic Press, New York.

1983, Stone circles, stone-filled fire pits, grinding stone and high plains archaeology. In *From microcosm to macrocosm: Advances in tipi ring investigation and interpretation*, L. Davis (ed.), Plains Anthropologist Memoir No. 19, Plains Anthropologist Corp, Lincoln, pp. 81–91.

Froehle, A.W., C.M. Kellner, and M.J. Scheoninger, 2010, FOCUS: Effect of diet and protein source on carbon stable isotope ratios in collagen: Follow up to Warinner and Tuross (2009), *Journal of Archaeological Science* 37:2662–2670.

Fuller, Dorian Q., 2001, Harappan seeds and agriculture: Some considerations, *Antiquity* 75:410–414.

Fuller, Dorian Q. and Mike Rowlands, 2011, Ingestion and food technologies: Maintaining differences over the long-term in West, South and East Asia. In *Interweaving worlds: Systematic interactions in Eurasia, 7th to 1st millennia BC*, J. Bennet, S. Sherratt, and T.C. Wilkinson (eds.), Oxbow Books Ltd., Oxford, pp. 37–60.

Fuller, Dorian Q. and Chris Stevens, 2009, Agriculture and the development of complex societies: An archaeobotanical agenda. In *From foragers to farmers: Papers in honour of Gordon C. Hillman*, Andrew Fairbairn and Ehud Weiss (eds.), Oxbow, Exeter, pp. 37–57.

Fuller, Dorian Q., Chris Stevens, and Meriel McClatchie, 2008, Routine activities, tertiary refuse and labor organization: Social inference from everyday archaeobotany. In *Ancient plants and people. Contemporary trends in archaeobotany*, Marco Madella and Manon Savard (eds.), University of Arizona Press, Tucson, pp. 174–217.

Fuller, Dorian Q., Robin G. Allaby, and Chris Stevens, 2010, Domestication as innovation: The entanglement of techniques, technology and chance in the domestication of cereal crops, *World Archaeology* 42(1):13–28.

Galaty, J., 1989, Cattle and cognition: Aspects of Maasai practical reasoning. In *Domesticated animals from early times*, J. Clutton-Brock (ed.), University of Texas Press, Austin, pp. 215–230.

Gamerith, Anni, 1981, The privileged position of farinaceous foods in Austria. In *Food in perspective*, A. Fenton and T.M. Owen (eds.), John Donald Publishers Ltd, Edinburgh, pp. 83–117.

Garb, J.L. and A.J. Stunkard, 1974, Taste aversions in man, *American Journal of Psychiatry* 131:1204–1207.

Garcilaso de la Vega, El Inca, 1966 [1609], *Royal commentaries of the Incas and general history of Peru*, translated by Harold V. Livermore, University of Texas Press, Austin.

Garnsey, Peter, 1988, *Famine and food supply in the Graeco-Roman World*, Cambridge University Press, Cambridge.

1999, *Food and society in Classical Antiquity*, Cambridge University Press, Cambridge.

Garnsey, Peter and Ian Morris, 1989, Risk and the polis: The evolution of institutionalized responses to food supply problems in the ancient Greek state. In *Bad year economics*, Paul Halstead and John O'Shea (eds.), Cambridge University Press, Cambridge, pp. 98–105.

Gasco, Jan and Barbara Voorhies, 1989, The ultimate tribute: The role of the Soconusco as an Aztec tributary. In *Ancient trade and tribute: Economies of the Soconusco region of Mesoamerica*, B. Voorhies (ed.), University of Utah Press, Salt Lake City, pp. 48–94.

Gasser, Robert E. and Scott M. Kwiatkowski, 1991a, Regional signatures of Hohokam plant use, *The Kiva* 56(3):207–226.

1991b, Food for thought: Recognizing patterns in Hohokam subsistence. In *Exploring the Hohokam; prehistoric desert peoples of the American Southwest*, George J. Gumerman (ed.), Amerind Foundation Publication, Dragoon, pp. 417–459.

Gebauer, A.B. and T.D. Price (eds.), 1992, *Transitions to agriculture in prehistory*, Prehistory Press, Madison.

Geertz, Clifford, 1973, *The interpretation of culture*, Basic Books, New York.

Gell, Alfred, 1998, *Art and agency: An anthropological theory*, Oxford University Press, Oxford.

Gentry, Howard S., 1982, *Agaves of continental North America*, University of Arizona Press, Tuscon.

Gerhardt, Klaus, Scott Searles, and William Biers, 1990, Corinthian figure vases: Non-destruction extraction and gas chromatography-mass spectroscopy. In *Organic contents of ancient vessels: Materials analysis and archaeological investigation*, William Biers and Patrick McGovern (eds.), MASCA Research Papers in Science and Archaeology, Vol. 7, University of Pennsylvania Museum of Archaeology and Anthropology, Philadelphia, pp. 41–50.

Gero, Joan M., 1990, Pottery, power and parties! At Queyash, Peru, *Archaeology* March–April:52–55.

    1992, Feasts and females: Gender ideology and political meals in the Andes, *Norwegian Archaeological Review* 25:15–30.

Gero, Joan and Margaret W. Conkey (eds.), 1991, *Engendering archaeology: Women and prehistory*, Basil Blackwell, Cambridge MA.

Gero, Joan and Christine A. Hastorf, 1991, Political meals in the Andes. Symposium in the Society for American Archaeology, New Orleans.

Gerritsen, Fokke, 2000, Of calories and culture, introduction to a special section, *Archaeological Dialogues* 7(2):169–172.

Gerry, John, 1998, Bone isotope ratios and their bearing on elite privilege among the classic Maya, *Geoarchaeology* 12(1):41–69.

Gibbins, D.J.L., 1991, The Roman wreck of c. AD 200 at Plemmirio, near Siracusa (Sicily): Third interim report: The domestic assemblage 2: Kitchen and table pottery, glass, and fishing weights. *International Journal of Nautical Archaeology* 20(3):227–246.

Giddens, Anthony, 1979 *Central problems in social theory: Action, structure and contradiction in social analysis*. MacMillan, London.

Giddens, Anthony and Philip Cassell (ed.), 1993, *The Giddens reader*, Macmillan Press, London.

Gidney, Louisa, 2000, Economic trends, craft specialization and social status: Bone assemblages from Leicester. In *Animal bones, human societies*, Peter Rowley-Conwy (ed.), Oxbow Books, Oxford, pp. 170–178.

Gifford, Diane P., 1980, Ethnoarchaeological contributions to the taphonomy of human sites. In *Fossils in the making*, A.K. Behrensmeyer and A.P. Hill (eds.), University of Chicago Press, Chicago, pp. 93–106.

Gifford, Diane P. and A. Behrensmeyer, 1977, Observed formation and burial of a recent human occupation site in Kenya, *Quaternary Research* 8:245–266.

Gifford-Gonzalez, Diane P., 1991, Bones are not enough: Analogues, knowledge and interpretive strategies in zooarchaeology, *Journal of Anthropological Archaeology* 10:215–254.

    1993, Gaps in the zooarchaeological analysis of butchery: Is gender an issue? In *From Bones to Behavior: Ethnoarchaeological and Experimental Contributions to the Interpretation of Faunal Remains*, J. Hudson (ed.), Occasional Papers,

No. 21, Center for Archaeological Investigations, Southern Illinois University, pp. 181–199.

Gilchrist, Roberta and Barney Sloane, 2005, *Requiem: The medieval monastic cemetery in Britain*, Museum of London Archaeology Service, London.

Gillespie, Susan D., 2000, Maya "nested houses" the ritual construction of place. In *Beyond kinship: Social and material reproduction in house societies*, R.A. Joyce and S.D. Gillespie (eds.), University of Pennsylvania Press, Philadelphia, pp. 135–160,

Giorgi, John, 1997, Diet in late Medieval and Early Modern London: The archaeobotanical evidence. In *The age of transition, the archaeology of English Culture 1400–1600*, David Gaimster and Paru Stamper (eds.), The Society for Medieval Archaeology Monograph 15, Oxbow Monograph, Oxbow Publishers, Oxford, pp. 197–213.

Glassie, Henry, 1975, *Folk housing in Middle Virginia: A structural analysis of historic artifacts*. University of Tennessee Press, Knoxville.

Glob, Peter V., 1969, *The bog people*, Faber and Faber, London.

Godelier, Maruice, 1974, On the definition of a social formation: The example of the Incas, *Critique of Anthropology* 1(1):63–73.

Goette, Susan, Michele Williams, Sissel Johannessen, and Christine A. Hastorf, 1994, Toward reconstructing ancient maize: Experiments in processing and charring, *Journal of Ethnobiology* 14(1):1–21.

Goldfrank, Walter, 2005, Fresh demand: The consumption of Chilean produce. In *The cultural politics of food and eating*, J. Watson and M. Caldwell (eds.), Blackwell Publishers, Oxford, pp. 42–53.

Goldstein, David J., 2007, Forests and fires: A paleoethnobotanical assessment of the impact of Middle Sicán pyrotechnology on the dry tropical forests of the La Leche River Valley, Lambayeque, Peru (950–1050 CE). PhD dissertation, Department of Anthropology, Southern Illinois University.

González Turmo, Isabel, 1997, The pathways of taste. In *Food preferences and taste*, H. Macbeth (ed.), Berghahn Books, Oxford, pp. 115–126.

Goodman, Melissa, 2003, Anthropogenic landscapes in the Andes: A multidisciplinary approach to precolumbian agricultural terraces and their sustainable use. Unpublished PhD dissertation, Department of Archaeology, Cambridge University, Cambridge.

Goody, Jack, 1982, *Cooking, cuisine, and class. A study in comparative sociology*, Cambridge University Press, Cambridge.

Gosden, Chris, 1999, Introduction. In *The prehistory of food, appetites for change*, C. Gosden and J. Hather (eds.), Routledge, London, pp. 1–9.

2005, What do objects want? *Journal of Archaeological Method and Theory* 12(3):193–211.

Gosden, Chris and Jon Hather (eds.), 1999, *The prehistory of food, appetites for change*, Routledge, London.

Gose, Peter, 1991, House rethatching in an Andean annual cycle: Practice, meaning and contradiction. *American Ethnologist* 18(1):39–66.

1994, *Deathly waters and hungry mountains: Agrarian ritual and class formation in an Andean town*, University of Toronto Press, Toronto.

Gozzini Giacosa, Ilaria, 1992, *A taste of Ancient Rome*, The University of Chicago Press, Chicago.

Graeber, David, 2001, *Toward an anthropological theory of value*, Palgrave, New York.

Grainger, Sally, 2006, *Cooking Apicius: Roman recipes for today*. Prospect Books, London.

Grant, Annie, 1984, Animal husbandry. In *Danebury, an Iron Age Hillfort in Hamsphire*, vol 2, Barry Cunliffe (ed.), Council for British Archaeology, London, pp. 496–548.

1988, Animal resources. In *The countryside of Medieval England*, Grenville Astill and Annie Grant (eds.), Basil Blackwell, Oxford, pp. 149–187.

2002, Food, status and society hierarchy. In *Consuming passions and patterns of consumption*, Preston Miracle and Nicky Milner (eds.), MacDonald Institute of Archaeology Monograph, Cambridge, pp. 17–24.

Greig, James, 1983, Plant foods in the past: A review of the evidence from northern Europe, *Journal of Plant Foods* 5:179–214.

1988, Plant resources. In *The Countryside of Medieval England*, Basil Blackwell, Oxford, pp. 108–127.

1990, Plant and parasite remains from 16th century pits 22, 41 and 56, pp. 139–149. In *Excavations at 5–8 Fore Street*, I. Burrow (ed.), Taunton, 1979. Proceedings of the Somerset Archaeological Natural History Society 132 (for 1988), pp. 95–164.

1996, Archaeobotanical and historical records compared – a new look at the taphonomy of edible and other useful plants from the 11th to the 18th centuries A.D, *Circaea* 12(2):211–247.

Gremillion, K.J. (ed.), 1997, *Plants and landscapes*, University of Alabama Press, Tuscaloosa.

Gremillion, Kristen J., 2011, *Ancestral appetites: Food in prehistory*, Cambridge University Press, Cambridge.

Grigson, Catherine, 2007, Culture, ecology and pigs from the 5th to the 3rd millennium BC around the Fertile Crescent. In *Pigs and Humans, 10,000 years of interaction*, U. Albarella, K. Dobney, A. Ervynck, and P. Rowley-Conwy (eds.), Oxford University Press, Oxford, pp. 83–108.

Grivetti, Louis Evan, 1978, Culture, diet and nutrition: Selected themes and topics, *Biosceince* 28(3):171–177.

Grocock, C.W. and Grainger, S. (eds.), 2006, *Apicius*. Prospect Books, London.

Gudeman, Stephen, 1986, *Economics as culture: Models and metaphors of livelihood*, Routledge & K. Paul, Boston.

Gumerman IV, George, 1991, Subsistence and complex societies: Diet between economic groups at Pacatnamu, Peru. Unpublished Ph.D dissertation, Department of Anthropology, University of California, Los Angeles.

1994a, Corn for the dead: The significance of *Zea mays* in Moche burial offerings. In *Corn and culture in the prehistoric New World*, S. Johannessen and C.A. Hastorf (eds.), Minnesota Anthropology Series, Westview Press, Boulder, pp. 399–410.

1994b, Feeding specialists: The effect of specialization on subsistence variation. In *Paleonutrition: The diet and health of prehistoric Americans*, Kristin D. Sobolik (ed.), Center for Archaeological Investigations, Occasional Paper 22, pp. 80–97.

1997, Food and complex societies, *Journal of Archaeological Method and Theory* 4(2):105–139.

2002, Llama power and empowered fishermen: Food and power at Pacatnamu, Peru. In *The dynamics of power*, Maria O'Donovan (ed.), Center for Archaeological Investigations, Occasional Paper No. 30, The Board of Trustees, Southern Illinois University, Carbondale, pp. 238–256.

2010, Big hearths and big pots: Moche feasting on the north coast of Peru. In *Inside ancient kitchens: New directions in the study of daily meals and feasting events*, Elizabeth A. Klarich (ed.), University of Colorado Press, Boulder, pp. 111–132.

Guss, David, M., 1989, *To weave and sing, art, symbol and narrative in the South American rain forest*. University of California Press, Berkeley.

Haaland, R., 2007, Porridge and pot, bread and oven: Food ways and symbolism in Africa and the Near East from the Neolithic to present, *Cambridge Archaeological Journal* 17(2):165–182.

Habu, Junko, 2004, *Ancient Jomon of Japan*, Cambridge University Press, Cambridge.

Hagen, Ann, 1992, *A handbook of Anglo-Saxon food, processing and consumption*, Anglo-Saxon Publications, Chippenham.

1995, *The second handbook of Anglo-Saxon food, production and distribution*, Anglo-Saxon Publications, Chippenham.

Hagstrum, Melissa, 1989, Technological continuity and change: Ceramic ethnoarchaeology in the Peruvian Andes. PhD dissertation, Department of Anthropology, UCLA.

Hall, S. and P. DeGuay (eds.), 1996, *Questions of cultural identity*, Sage, London.

Halstead, Paul and John O'Shea (eds.), 1989, *Bad year economics*, Cambridge University Press, Cambridge.

Hamilakis, Yannis, 1996, Wine, oil and the dialectics of power in Bronze Age Crete: A review of the evidence, *Oxford Journal of Archaeology* 15(1):1–32.

1999, Food technologies/technologies of the body: The social context of wine and oil production and consumption in Bronze Age Crete, *World Archaeology* 31(1):38–54.

2002, The past as oral history: Towards an archaeology of the senses. In *Thinking through the body: Archaeologies of corporeality*, Yannis Hamilakis, Mark Pluciennik, and Sarah Tarlow (eds.), Kluwer Academic/Plenum Publishers, New York, pp. 121–136.

2004, *Sensory archaeology*, Cambridge University Press, Cambridge.

Hamilakis, Yannis, Mark Pluciennik, and Sarah Tarlow (eds.), 2002, *Thinking through the body: Archaeologies of corporeality*, Kluwer Academic/Plenum Publishers, New York.

Hamshaw-Thomas, John, 2000, When in Britain do as the Britons: Dietary identity in early Roman Britain. In *Animal bones, human societies*, Peter Rowley-Conwy (ed.), Oxbow Books, Oxford, pp. 166–169.

Harbottle, Lynn, 1997, Taste and embodiment, the food preferences of Iranians in Britain. In *Food preferences and taste*, H. Macbeth (ed.), Berghahn Books, Oxford, pp. 175–185.

Hard, Robert, Raymond Mauldin, and Gerry Raymond, 1996, Mano size, stable carbon isotope ratios and macrobotanical remains as multiple lines of evidence of maize dependence in the American Southwest, *Journal of Archaeological Method and Theory* 3(4):253–318.

Hardt-Mautner, G., 1995, 'How does one become a good European?': The British press and European integration. *Discourse and Society* 6(2):177–207.

Harris, David (ed.), 1996, *The origins and spread of agriculture and pastoralism in Eurasia*. Smithsonian Institution Press, Washington, DC.

Harris, David and Gordon Hillman (eds.), 1989, *Foraging and farming: The evolution of plant exploitation*, Unwin Hyman, London.

Harris, Marvin, 1977, *Cannibals and kings*, Random House, New York.

1985, *Good to eat, riddles of food and culture*. Allen and Unwin, London.

Harris, Marvin and Eric Ross (eds.), 1987, *Food and evolution*, Temple University Press, Philadelphia.

Hastorf, Albert H., 1959, They saw a game, *Journal of American Psychology* 49:129–134.

Hastorf, Christine A., 1980, Changing resource use in subsistence agricultural groups of the prehistoric Mimbres River Valley, New Mexico. In *Modeling change in prehistoric subsistence economies*, T. Earle and A.L. Christenson (eds.), Academic Press, New York, pp. 79–120.

1987, Archaeological evidence of coca (*Erythroxylum coca*) in the Upper Mantaro Valley, Peru, *Economic Botany* 41(2):292–301.

Hastorf, Christine A., 1988, The use of paleoethnobotanical data in prehistoric studies of crop production, processing, and consumption. In *Current paleoethnobotany: Analytical methods and cultural interpretations of archaeological plant remains*, C.A. Hastorf and V.S. Popper (eds.), University of Chicago Press, Chicago, pp. 119–144.

Hastorf, Christine A., 1990, The effect of the Inka state on Sausa agricultural production and crop consumption, *American Antiquity* 55(2):262–290.

1991, Gender, space and food in prehistory. In *Engendering archaeology: Women and prehistory*, Joan Gero and Margaret Conkey (eds.), Basil Blackwell Press, Cambridge AM, pp. 132–159.

1993, *Agriculture and the onset of political inequality before the Inka*, Cambridge University Press, Cambridge.

1998, The cultural life of early domestic plant use, *Antiquity* 72:773–782.

1999, *Cultural implications of crop introductions in Andean prehistory, the prehistory of food, appetites for change*, C. Gosden and J. Hather (eds.), Routledge, London, pp. 35–58.

2001a, Agricultural production and consumption. In *Empire and domestic economy*, T.N. D'Altroy and C.A. Hastorf (eds.), Plenum Publishing Corp., New York, pp. 155–178.

2001b, Making the invisible visible: The hidden jewels of archaeology. In *Fleeting identities: Perishable material culture in archaeological research*, Penelope B. Drooker (ed.), Occasional paper/Center for Archaeological Investigations, Southern Illinois University, Carbondale, pp. 27–42.

2003a, Andean luxury foods: Special food for the ancestors, the deities and the elite, *Antiquity* 77:110–119.

2003b, Community with the ancestors: Ceremonies and social memory in the Middle Formative at Chiripa, Bolivia, *Journal of Anthropological Archaeology* 22:305–332.

2012, The *habitus* of cooking practices at Neolithic Çatalhöyük – What was the place of the cook? In *The menial art of cooking*, Enrique Rodríguez-Alegría and Sarah Graff (eds.) University of Colorado Press, Boulder, pp. 65–86.

Hastorf, Christine A., Harriet Beaubien, Marilyn Beaudry-Corbett, Linda Brown, Katie Chiou, Rob Cuthrell, Alan Farahani, Anna Harkey, Brian McKee, Shanti Morell-Hart, Annelise Morris, Peter Nelson, Scott Simmons, Payson Sheets, Christine Simmons, and Jillian Swift, 2011, GIS Modeling at the Site of La Joya de Cerén, 2011. In *Forum: La Joya de Cerén*, El Salvador, an update on the database, 76th Annual Meeting of the Society for American Archaeology in Sacramento, CA, March 30.

Hastorf, Christine A. and Michael DeNiro, 1985, Reconstruction of prehistoric plant production and cooking practices by a new isotopic method, *Nature* 315:429–491.

Hastorf, Christine A. and Sissel Johannessen, 1993, Pre-Hispanic political change and the role of maize in the central Andes of Peru, *American Anthropologist* 95(1):115–138.

Hawkes, John G., 1990, *The potato: Evolution, biodiversity and genetic resources*, Smithsonian Institution Press, Washington, DC.

Hawkes, Kristen, Kim Hill, and James F. O'Connell, 1982, Why hunters gather: Optimal foraging and the Aché of Eastern Paraguay, *American Ethnologist* 9(2):379–398

Hawkes, Kristen and James O'Connell, 1992, On optimal foraging models and subsistence transitions, *Current Anthropology* 33(1):63–66.

Hayden, Brian, 1990, Nimrods, piscators, pluckers, and planters: The emergence of food production, *Journal of Anthropological Archaeology* 9:31–69.

1992, Models of domestication. In *Transitions to agriculture in prehistory*, Anne Brigitte Gebauer and T. Douglas Price (eds.), Prehistory Press, Santa Fe, pp. 273–299.

Hayden Brian, 1996, Feasting in prehistoric and traditional societies. In *Food and the status quest: An interdisciplinary perspective*, P. Wiessner and W. Schiefenhövel (eds.), Berghahn Books, Providence, pp. 127–146.

2001, Fabulous feasts: A prolegomenon to the importance of feasting. In *Feasts: Archaeological and ethnographic perspectives on food, politics and power*, M. Dietler and B. Hayden (eds.), Smithsonian Institution Press, Washington, DC, pp. 23–64.

Hayden, Brian and Suzanne Villeneuve, 2011, A century of feasting studies, *Annual Review of Anthropology* 40:433–449.

Heaton, T.H.E., J.C. Vogel, G. von la Chevallerie, and G. Collett, 1986, Climatic influence on the isotopic composition of bone nitrogen, *Nature* 322:822–823.

Hedges, R.E.M. and L.M. Reynard, 2007, Nitrogen isotopes and trophic level of humans in archaeology, *Journal of Archaeological Science* 34:1240–1251.

Hegmon, Michelle, Scott G. Ortman, and Jeanette L. Mobley-Tanaka, 1997, The changing multiple dimensions of women's status in the prehistoric American

Southwest. Paper presented at the 96th Annual Meeting of the American Anthropological Association, Washington, DC.

Helbaek, Hans, 1964, First impressions of the Çatal Hüyük plant husbandry. *Anatolian Studies*, 14:121–123.

Helms, Mary W., 1979, *Ancient Panama: Chiefs in search of power*, University of Texas Press, Austin.

Hellwig, Maren, 1997, Plant remains from two cesspits (15th and 16th century) and a pond (13th century) from Göttingen, southern Lower Saxony, Germany. *Vegetation History and Archaeobotany*, 6(2), pp. 105–116.

Hendon, Julia A., 1996, Archaeological approaches to the organization of domestic labor: Household practice and domestic relations, *Annual Review of Anthropology* 25:45–61.

2000, Having and holding: Storage, memory, knowledge and social relations, *American Anthropologist* 102(1):42–53.

Henry, Amanda G., Holly F. Hudson, and Dolores R. Piperno, 2009, Changes in starch grain morphologies from cooking, *Journal of Archaeological Science* 36:915–922.

Henshilwood, Christopher, Peter Nilssen, and John Parkington, 1994, Mussel drying and food storage in the late Holocene, SW Cape, South Africa, *Journal of Field Archaeology* 21(1):103–109.

Hesse, Brian, 1990, Pig lovers and pig haters: Patterns of Palestinian pork production, *Journal of Ethnobiology* 10(2):195–225.

Higgs, Eric (ed.), 1972, *Papers in economic prehistory*, Cambridge University Press, Cambridge.

Hill, J.D., 1995, *Ritual and rubbish in the Iron Age of Wessex*, British Archaeological Reports British Series 242, Tempus Reparatum, Oxford.

Hillman, Gordon C., 1984, Interpretation of archaeological plant remains: The application of ethnographic models from Turkey. In *Plants and ancient man: Studies in paleoethnobotany*, W. Van Zeist and W.A. Casparie (eds.), Balkema, Rotterdam, pp. 1–42.

1986, Plant foods in ancient diet: The archaeological role of palaeofaeces in general and lindow man's gut contents in particular. In *Lindow Man: The body in the bog*, I.M. Stead, J.B. Bourke, and D. Brothwell (eds.), British Museum Publications, London, pp. 105–115.

2000, Abu Hureyra I: The Epipalaeolithic. In *Village on the Euphrates, from foraging to farming at Abu Hureyra*, A.M.T. Moore, G.C. Hillman, and A.J. Legge (eds.), Oxford University Press, Oxford, pp. 327–398.

Hillman, Gordon C., Susan Colledge, and David Harris, 1989, Plant-food economy during the Epipaleolithic period at Tell Abu Hureyra, Syria: Dietary diversity, seasonality and modes of exploitation. In *Foraging and farming*, D. Harris and G.C. Hillman (eds.), Unwin Hyman, London, pp. 240–268.

Hobsbawm, Eric J. and Terence Ranger (eds.), 1986, *The invention of tradition*, Cambridge University Press, Cambridge.

Hodder, Ian, 1982, *Symbols in action*, Cambridge University Press, Cambridge.

1986, *Reading the past*, Cambridge University Press, Cambridge.

1987, The meaning of discard: Ash, and space in Baringo. In *Method and theory for activity area research*, S. Kent (ed.), Columbia University Press, New York, pp. 424–448.

1990, *The domestication of Europe: Structure and contingency in Neolithic societies*, Basil Blackwell, Oxford.

2005a, *Inhabiting Çatalhöyük: Reports from the 1995–99 seasons*, McDonald Institute for Archaeological Research / British Institute of Archaeology at Ankara Monograph.

2005b, *Changing materialities at Çatalhöyük: Reports from the 1995–99 seasons*, McDonald Institute for Archaeological Research / British Institute of Archaeology at Ankara Monograph.

2005c, *Çatalhöyük perspectives: Themes from the 1995–99 seasons*, McDonald Institute for Archaeological Research / British Institute of Archaeology at Ankara Monograph.

2006a, *Excavating Çatalhöyük: South, North and KOPAL Area reports from the 1995–99 seasons*, McDonald Institute for Archaeological Research / British Institute of Archaeology at Ankara Monograph.

2006b, *The leopard's tale*, Thames and Hudson, London.

Hodder, Ian (ed.), 2014, *Integrating Çatalhöyük: Themes from the 2000–2008 seasons*, volume 10, Cotsen Institute, Los Angeles.

Hodder, Ian and Craig Cessford, 2004, Daily practice and social memory at Çatalhöyük, *American Antiquity* 69:17–40.

Hoffman, Brian W., Jessica M.C. Cpiltz, and Megan A. Partlow, 2000, Heads or tails: The zooarchaeology of Aleut salmon storage on Unimak Island, Alaska, *Journal of Archaeological Science* 27(8):699–708.

Holden, Tim, 2000, The use of henbane as a hallucinogen in Neolithic ritual sites. *Antiquity* 74(283):49–53.

Holtzman, Jon D., 2006, Food and memory, *Annual Review of Anthropology* 35:361–378.

2009, *Uncertain tastes, memory, ambivalence, and the politics of eating in Samburu, Northern Kenya*, University of California Press, Berkeley.

Homer, 1935, *The Iliad and the Odyssey*, Walter Leaf, New York.

Hosking, Richard, 2006, Authenticity in the Kitchen: Proceedings of the Oxford Symposium on Food and Cookery 2005. Oxford Symposium, Prospect Books, Totnes, Devon.

Hosoya, Leo Aoi, 2000, Sacred commonness: An archaeobotanical view to the social complexity in prehistoric Japan. PhD dissertation, Department of Archaeology, University of Cambridge.

Huang, Roy, 1969, Fiscal administration during the Ming Dynasty. In *Chinese government in Ming Times*, Charles O. Hucker (ed.), Columbia University Press, New York, pp. 73–128.

Hubert, Annie, 1997, Choices of food and cuisine. In *Food preference and taste*, H. Macbeth (ed.), Berghahn Books, Providence, pp. 167–174.

Huelsbeck, David R., 1988, Are inferences of ethnicity and state from faunal remains reliable and efficient? Paper at the Society for Historical Archaeology Meetings, Reno, Nevada.

Hugh-Jones, Christine, 1979, *From the milk river*, Cambridge University Press, Cambridge.

Hugh-Jones, Stephen, 1995a, Coca, beer, cigars and yagé: Meals and anti-meals in an Amerindian community. In *Consuming habits: Drugs in history and anthropology*, Jordan Goodman, Paul E. Lovejoy, and Andrew Sherratt (eds.), Routledge, London, pp. 47–66.

1995a, Inside-out and back-to-front: The androgynous house in northwest Amazonia. In *About the house*, J. Carsten and S. Hugh-Jones (eds.), Cambridge University Press, Cambridge, pp. 226–252.

1996, Bonnes raisons ou mauvaise conscience? De l'ambivalence de ertains Amazoniens envers la consommation de viande. (Good reasons or bad conscience? or Why some Indian people of Amazonia are ambivalent about eating meat), *Terrain* 26:123–148.

2001, The gender of some Amazonian gifts; an experiment within an experiment. In *Gender in Amazonia and Melanesia; an exploration of the comparative method*, T. Gregor and D. Tuzin (eds.), University of California Press, Berkeley, pp. 245–278.

Hunn, Eugene, 1976, Toward a perceptual model of folk biological classification, *American Ethnologist* 3:508–524.

Huss-Ashmore, Rebecca and M. Glantz, 1993, Intra-household variation in diets of Swazi women and children, *American Journal of Physical Anthropology* Supplement 16:112.

Huss-Ashmore, Rebecca, A.H. Goodman, et al., 1982, Nutritional Inference from paleopathology, *Advances in Archaeological Method and Theory* 5:395–474.

Huss-Ashmore, Rebecca and Susan L. Johnston, 1997, Wild plants as famine foods. In *Food preference and taste: Continuity and change*, Helen Macbeth (ed.), Berghahn Books, Providence, pp. 83–100.

Ingold, Tim, 1983, The significance of storage. *Man (NS)* 18:553–571.

1986, *The appropriation of nature*, Manchester University Press, Manchester.

1987, *What is an animal*, Allen & Unwin, London.

1993, The temporality of the landscape. *World archaeology*, 25(2), pp. 152–174.

2000, *The perception of the environment*, Routledge, London.

Insoll, Timothy, 2007, Introduction Configuring Identities in Archaeology. In *The archaeology of identities: A reader*, Routledge, New York, pp. 1–18.

Isbell, William, 1997, *Mummies and mortuary monuments: Post processual prehistory of central Andean social organization*, University of Texas Press, Austin.

Jackson, S. and S. Moores (eds.), 1995, *The politics of domestic consumption*, Prentice Hall, London.

James, Alison, 1997, How British is British food? In *Food, health, and identity*, P. Caplan (ed.), Routledge, London, pp. 71–86.

Janik, Liliana, 2003, Changing paradigms: Food as metaphor for cultural identity among prehistoric fisher-gatherer-hunter communities of Northern Europe. In *Food culture and identity in the Neolithic and Early Bronze Age*, M. Parker Pearson (ed.), BAR International Series 1117, Archaeopress, Oxford, pp. 113–124.

Jansen, Willy, 1997, Gender identity and the rituals of food in a Jordanian community, *Food and Foodways* 7(2):87–117.

2001, French bread and Algerian wine: Conflicting identities in French Algeria. In *Food, drink and identity*, P. Scholliers (ed.), Berg, Oxford, pp. 195–218.

Jennings, Justin, K. Antrobus, S. Atencio, E. Glavich, R. Johnson, G. Loffler, and C. Lau, 2005, Drinking beer in a blissful mood: Alcohol production, operational chains and feasting in the Ancient world, *Current Anthropology* 46(2):275–303.

Jochim, Michael A., 1976, *Hunter-gatherer subsistence and settlement: A predictive model*, Academic Press, New York.

Johannessen, Sissel, 1988, Plant remains and culture change: Are paleoethnobotanical data better than it seems? In *Current Palaeoethnobotany: Analytical methods and cultural interpretations of archaeological plant remains*, Christine A. Hastorf and Virginia Popper (eds.), University of Chicago Press, Chicago, pp. 145–166.

1993, Food, dishes, and society. In *Foraging and farming in the eastern woodlands*, C.M. Scarry (ed.), University of Florida Press, Gainesville, pp. 182–205.

Johannessen, Sissel and Christine A. Hastorf, 1989, Corn and culture in central Andean prehistory, *Science* 244:690–692.

1990, A history of Andean fuel use (A.D. 500 to the present) in the Mantaro Valley, Peru, *Journal of Ethnobiology* 10(1):61–90.

Johannessen, Sissel, Ronald C. Schirmer, and Leslie L. Bush, 2002, People and plants at cultural boundaries. In symposium: The power of multiple data analysis: A symposium in honor of Deborah M. Pearsall, 67th Annual meeting of the society for American Archaeology, Denver March 22.

Johns, Timothy and Isao Kubo, 1988, A survey of traditional methods employed for the detoxification of plant foods, *Journal of Ethnobiology* 8(1):81–129.

Johnson, Greg, 1982, Organizational structure and scalar stress. In *Theory and explanation in archaeology: The Southampton Conference*, Colin Renfrew, Michael Rowlands, and Barbara A. Segraves-Whallon (eds.), Academic Press, New York, pp. 389–421.

Johnson, Matthew, 1993, *Housing culture: Traditional architecture in an English landscape*, University College London Press, London.

Jones, Andrew, 1996, Food for thought: Material culture and the transformation in food use from the Mesolithic to Neolithic. In *The Early Prehistory of Scotland*, Tony Pollard and Alex Morrison (eds.), Edinburgh University Press, Edinburgh, pp. 291–300.

1999, The world on a plate: Ceramics, food technology and cosmology in Neolithic Orkney, *World Archaeology* 31(1):55–77.

2002, *Archaeological theory and scientific practice*, Cambridge University Press, Cambridge.

Jones, Glenn A., 2008, "Quite the Choicest Protein Dish": The Costs of Consuming Seafood in American Restaurants, 1850–2006. In *Oceans Past*, David Starkey, Paul Holm, and Micheala Barnard (eds.), Earthscan, London and Sterling, pp. 47–75.

Jones, Glynis, 1983, The ethnoarchaeology of crop processing: Seeds of a middle-range methodology, *Archaeological Review from Cambridge* 2(2):17–26.

1984, Interpretation of archaeological plant remains: Ethnographic models. In *Plants and Ancient Man: Studies in Paleoethnobotany*, W. Van Zeist and W.A. Casparie (eds.), Balkema, Rotterdam, pp. 43–59.

1987, A statistical approach to the archaeological identification of crop processing, *Journal of Archaeological Science* 14:311–323.

Jones, Glynis and Paul Halstead, 1995, Maslins, mixtures, and monocrops: On the interpretation of archaeobotanical crop samples of heterogeneous composition, *Journal of Archaeological Science* 22:103–114.

Jones, Glynis, Kenneth Wardle, Paul Halstead, and Diana Wardle, 1986, Crop storage at Assiros, *Scientific American* 254(3):96–103.

Jones, Martin, 1985, Archaeobotany beyond subsistence reconstruction. In *Beyond domestication in prehistoric Europe*, Graeme W.W. Barker and Clive Gamble (eds.), Academic Press, New York, pp. 107–128.

2007, *Feast: Why humans share food*, Oxford University Press, Oxford.

Jones, Michael Owen, 2000, What's disgusting, why, and what does it matter? *Journal of Folklore Research* 37(1):53–71.

Jones, Rhys, 1977, The Tasmanian paradox. In *Stone tools as cultural markers: Change, evolution and complexity*, R.V.S. Wright (ed.), Humanities Press, Canberra, pp. 189–204.

Jones, Siân, 1997, *The archaeology of ethnicity*, Routledge, London.

Jones O'Day, Sharyn and Patrick Kirch, 2003, New archaeological insights into food and status: A case study from pre-contact Hawaii, *World Archaeology* 34(3):494–497.

Jordan, Peter, 2003, *Material culture and sacred landscape: The anthropology of the Siberian Khanty*. Rowman and Littlefield, London.

Joyce, Rosemary, 1993, Women's work: Images of production and reproduction in pre-hispanic southern Central Maya monuments, *Current Anthropology* 34(3):255–266.

1998, Performing the body in prehispanic Mesoamerica, *RES* 33:147–165.

2000a, Heirloom and houses, materiality and social memory. In *Beyond kinship: Social and material reproduction in house Societies*, R.A. Joyce and S.D. Gillespie (eds.), University of Pennsylvania Press, Philadelphia, pp. 189–212.

2000b, Girling the girl and boying the boy: The production of adulthood in ancient Mesoamerica. *World Archaeology* 31(3):473–483.

2003, Concrete memories: Fragments of the past in the classic Maya present (5000–1000 AD). In *Archaeologies of Memory*, R.M. Van Dyke and S.E. Alcock (eds.), Blackwell, Malden, pp. 104–126.

Joyce, Rosemary A. and Susan D. Gillespie (eds.), 2000, *Beyond kinship: Social and material reproduction in House Societies*, University of Pennsylvania Press, Philadelphia.

Joyce, Rosemary A. and John S. Henderson, 2007, From feasting to cuisine: Implications of archaeological research in an early Honduran village. *American Anthropologist* 109(4):642–653.

Junker, Laura, 2001, The evolution of ritual feasting systems in prehispanic Philippine Chiefdoms. In *Feasts: Archaeological and ethnographic perspectives on food, politics and power*, M. Dietler and B. Hayden (eds.), Smithsonian Institution Press, Washington, DC, pp. 267–310.

Kahn, Miriam, 1986, *Always hungry, never greedy*, Cambridge University Press, Cambridge.

1988, Men are taro, they cannot be rice, political aspects of food choices in Wamira, PNH, *Food & Foodways* 3(1):41–58.

Katz, Solomon, 1982, Food, behavior and biocultural evolution. In *The psychology of human food selection*, Lewis Barker (ed.), Ellis Horwood Ltd, Chichester, pp. 171–188.

Katz, Solomon and Mary Voigt, 1986, Bread and beer: The early use of cereals in the human diet, *Expedition* 28(2):23–34.

Kealhofer, Lisa, Robin Torrence, and Richard Fullagar, 1999, Integrating phytoliths within use-wear/residue studies of stone tools, *Journal of Archaeological Science* 26:527–546.

Keene, Arthur, 1981, *Prehistoric foraging in a temperate forest*, Academic Press, New York.

Kelertas, Kristina A., 1997, Agricultural food systems and social inequality: The archaeobotany of Late Neolithic and Early Bronze Age Thy, Denmark. PhD dissertation, Archaeology Program, University of California, Los Angeles.

Kelly, Lucretia, S., 2001, A case of ritual feasting at the Cahokia site. In *Feasts: Archaeological and ethnographic perspectives on food, politics and power*, M. Dietler and B. Hayden (eds.), Smithsonian Institution Press, Washington, DC, pp. 334–367.

Kempe, Margery, 2001, *The book of Margery Kempe*, Lynn Staley (trans and ed.), Norton, New York.

Kent, Susan, 1999, The archaeological visibility of storage: Delimiting storage from trash areas, *American Antiquity* 64:79–94.

Khare, R.S., 1976, *The Hindu hearth and home*, Carolina Academic Press, Durham.
    1980, Food as nutrition and culture: Notes towards an anthropological methodology, *Social Science Information* 19(3):519–542.

Khare, R.S. and M.S. Rao (eds.), 1986, *Food, society, and culture: Aspects in South Asian Food Systems*, Academic Press, Durham.

Kieschnick, John, 2005, Buddhist vegetarianism in China. In *Of tripod and palate; food, politics and religion in traditional China*, Roel Sterckx (ed.), Palgrave Macmillan, New York, pp. 186–212.

King, Stacie M., 2003, Social practices and social organization in ancient coastal Oaxacan households. PhD dissertation, Department of Anthropology, University of California-Berkeley.
    2007, The spatial organization of food sharing in Early Postclassic households: An application of soil chemistry in Ancient Oaxaca, Mexico, *Journal of Archaeological Science*:1–16.

Kiple, Kenneth F. and Kriemhild Conee Ornelas, 2000, *The Cambridge world history of food*, Cambridge University Press, Cambridge.

Kirch, Patrick V., G. Asner, O.A. Chadwick, J. Field, T. Ladefoged, C. Leef, C. Puleston, S. Tuljapurkar, and P.M. Vitousek, 2012, Building and testing models of long-term agricultural intensification and population dynamics: A case study from the Leeward Kohala Field System, Hawai'i, *Ecological Modelling* 227(2012):18–28.

Kirch, Patrick V. and Marshall Sahlins, 1992, *Anahulu: The anthropology of history in the Kingdom of Hawaii*, University of Chicago Press, Chicago.

Klarich, Elizabeth A., 2010, Behind the scenes and into the kitchen: New directions for the study of prehistoric meals. In *Inside ancient kitchens: New directions in the study of daily meals and feasts*, E. Klarich (ed.), University Press of Colorado, Boulder, pp. 1–15.

Knudson, Kelly, T. Douglas, Jane Buikstra, and Deborah Blom, 2001, Tiwanaku residential mobility as determined by strontium and lead isotopes. Paper presented at 66th annual meeting of the Society for American Archaeology, New Orleans, LA.

Knudson, Kelly J., Arthur E. Aufderheide, and Jane E. Buikstra, 2007, Seasonality and paleodiet in the Chiribaya polity of Southern Peru, *Journal of Archaeological Science* 34(3):451–462.

Koch, Elizabeth, 1998, *Neolithic bog pots from Zealand, Møn, Lolland, and Falster*, Nordiske Fortidsminder, Copenhagen.

Kohn, Eduardo, 2007, How dogs dream: Amazonian natures and the politics of transspecies engagement, *American Ethnologist* 34(1):3–24.

Kolata, A. and C. Ortloff, 1996, Tiwanaku raised-field agriculture in the Lake Titicaca basin of Bolivia. In *Tiwanaku and its hinterland: Archaeology and paleoecology of an Andean civilization*, Alan Kolata (ed.), Smithsonian Institution Press, Washington, DC, pp. 109–152.

Kroeber, Theodora, 1967, *Ishi*, University of California Press, Berkeley.

Krondl, M. and D. Lau, 1982, Social determinants in human food selection. In *Human food selection*, Lewis Barker (ed.), Ellis Horwood Ltd, Chichester, pp. 139–151.

Kubiak-Martens, L., 2002, New evidence for the use of root foods in pre-agrarian subsistence recovered from the late Mesolithic site at Halsskov, Denmark. *Vegetation History and Archaeobotany*, 11(1–2), pp. 23–32.

Kurlansky, Mark, 1997, *Cod: A biography of the fish that changed the world*, Vintage, London.

    2002, *Choice cuts: A savory selection of food writing from around the world and throughout history*, Ballantine Books, New York.

Kus, Susan, 1992, Toward an archaeology of body and soul. In *Representations in archaeology*, J.-C. Gardin and C. Peebles (eds.), Indiana University Press, Bloomington, pp. 168–177.

Küster, Hansjörg, 2000, Trading in tastes. In *The Cambridge World History of Food*, Kenneth F. Kiple and Kriemhild Coneé Ornelas (eds.), Cambridge University Press, Cambridge, pp. 431–437.

LaBianca, Oystein, 1991, Food systems research: An overview and case study from Madava Plains Jordan. *Food & Foodways* 4(3–4):221–235.

Ladurie, Emmanuel Le Roy, 1978, *Montaillou: Cathars and catholics in a French village, 1294–1324*, translated from the French by Barbara Bray, Scholar Press, London.

Lalonde, Marc P., 1992, Deciphering a meal again, or the Anthropology of taste, *Social Science Information* 31(1):69–86.

Lambeck, Michael, 1998, Body and mind in mind, body and mind in body: Some anthropological interventions in a long conversion. In *Bodies and persons*, Michael Lambeck and Andrew Strathern (eds.), Cambridge University Press, Cambridge, pp. 103–123.

Lambert, Joseph B. and Gisela Grupe (eds.), 1993, *Prehistoric human bone – Archaeology at the molecular level*, Springer-Verlag, New York.

Lappé, Francis Moore and Joseph Collins, 1997, Beyond the myths of hunger: What can we do? In *Food and culture: A reader*, Carole Counihan and Penny Van Esterik (eds.), Roultedge, London, pp. 402–411.

Larsen, Clark S., 1997, *Bioarchaeology: Interpreting behavior from the human skeleton*, Cambridge University Press, Cambridge.

Larsen, Clark S. (ed.), 2001, *Bioarchaeology of Spanish Florida: The impact of colonialism*, University Press of Florida, Gainesville.

Larsen, Clark S., Simon W. Hillson, Başak Boz, M.A. Pilloud, J.W. Sadvari, S.C. Agarwal, B. Glencross, Patrick D. Beauchesne, J. Pearson, C.B. Ruff, and E.M. Garofalo, 2015, Bioarchaeology of Neolithic Çatalhöyük: Lives and lifestyles of an early farming society in transition. *Journal of World Prehistory*, 28(1):27–68.

Latour, Bruno, 1993, *We have never been modern*, Harvard University Press, Cambridge, MA.

2005, Reassembling the social-an introduction to actor-network-theory. In *Reassembling the Social: An introduction to actor-network-theory*, Oxford University Press, Oxford.

Laurioux, Bruno, 1985, Spices in the medieval diet: A new approach, *Food and Foodways* 1:43–76.

Lave, Jean and E. Wenger, 1991, *Situated learning: Legitimate peripheral participation*, Cambridge University Press, Cambridge.

Leach, Edmund, 1954, *Political systems of highland Burma: A study of Kachin social structure*, Harvard University Press, Cambridge, MA.

1964, Anthropological aspects of language: Animal categories and verbal abuse. In *New directions in the study of language*, E.H. Lenneberg (ed.), MIT Press, Cambridge, MA, pp. 23–64.

Leach, Helen M., 1999, Food processing technology: Its role in inhibiting or promoting change in staple foods. *In The prehistory of food*, C. Gosden and J. Hather (eds.), Routledge, London, pp. 129–138.

Lechtman, Heather, 1977, Style in technology: Some early thoughts. In *Styles, organization, and dynamics of technology*, H. Lechtman and R. Merill (eds.), West Publishing Co., St. Paul, pp. 3–20.

LeCount, Lisa, 2001, Like water for chocolate: Feasting and political ritual among the Late Classic Maya at Xunantunich, Belize, *American Anthropologist* 103(4):935–953.

2008, Mount Maloney People? Domestic Pots, Everyday Practice and the Social Formation of the Xunantunich Polity. MS on file with the author.

Leechman, Douglas, 1951, Bone grease, *American Antiquity* 16(4):355–356.

Lee, Richard B., 1984, *The Dobe!Kung*, Holt, Rinehart and Winston, New York.

Lehrer, A., 1972, Cooking vocabularies and the culinary triangle of Lévi-Strauss. *Anthropological Linguistics* 14:155–171.

Lentz, David, M.P. Beaudry-Corbett, M.L. Reyna de Aguilar, and L. Kaplan, 1996, Foodstuffs, forests, fields and shelter: A paleoethnobotanical analysis of vessel contents from the Cerén site, El Salvador, *Latin American Antiquity* 7:247–262.

Lentz, David and Carlos R. Ramírez-Sosa, 2002, Ceren plant resources: Abundance and diversity. In *Before the volcano erupted, the ancient Cerén village in Central America*, Payson Sheets (ed.), University of Texas Press, Austin, pp. 33–42.

Leone, Mark and Constance Crosby, 1987, Epilogue: Middle-range theory in historical archaeology. In *Consumer choice in historical archaeology*, Suzanne M. Spencer-Wood (ed.), Plenum Press, New York, pp. 397–410.

Leopold, A.C. and R. Ardrey, 1972, Toxic substances in plants and the food habits of early man, *Science* 176:512–513.

Lev-Tov, Justin S., 1998, Zooarchaeology and social relations in Annapolis, Maryland. In *Annapolis pasts*, Paul A. Shackel, Paul R. Mullins, and Mark S. Warner (eds.), The University of Tennessee Press, Knoxville, pp. 119–146.

Lev-Tov, Justin, 1999, The influences of religion, social structure and ethnicity on diet: An example from Frankish Corinth. In *Palaeodiet in the Aegean*, S.J. Waughan and W.D.E. Coulson (eds.), Oxbow Books, Oxford, pp. 85–98.

Lev-Tov, Justin and Kevin McGeough, 2007, Feasting at Late Bronze Age Hazor as political and religious identity expression. In *We are what we eat: Archaeology, food and identity*, Kathryn Twiss (ed.), Southern Illinois University Press, Carbondale, pp. 85–111.

Lévi-Strauss, Claude, 1966, The culinary triangle, *Partisan Review* 33:586–595.

1968a, L'Origine des manières de table. In *Mythologiques IV*, Seuil, Paris.

1968b, *Structural anthropology*, vol. 1, Penguin Press, Harmondsworth, Allen Lane, London.

1970, *The raw and the cooked: Introduction to a science of mythology*, translated from the French by John and Doreen Weightman. Jonathan Cape Ltd., London.

1978, *The origin of table manners, introduction to a science of mythology*, translated from the French by John and Doreen Weightman, Cape Ltd., London.

1982, *The way of the mask*, University of Washington Press, Seattle.

Lewis, Gilbert, 1980, *Day of shining red*, Cambridge University Press, Cambridge.

Lightfoot, Kent, A. Martinez, and A.M. Schiff, 1998. Daily practice and material culture in pluralistic social settings: An archaeological study of culture change and persistence from Fort Ross, California, *American Antiquity*:199–222.

Lillie, Malcolm C. and Michael Richards, 2000, Stable isotope analysis and dental evidence of diet at the mesolithic–neolithic transition in Ukraine, *Journal of Archaeological Science* 27(10):965–972.

Livarda, Alexandra, 2011, Spicing up life in northwestern Europe: Exotic food plant imports in the Roman and medieval world. *Vegetation History and Archaeobotany*, 20(2):143–164.

Livarda, Alexandra and Van der Veen, Marikje, 2008, Social access and dispersal of condiments in North-West Europe from the Roman to the medieval period. *Vegetation History and Archaeobotany*, 17(1):201–209.

Livarda, Alexandra and Hector Orengo, 2015, Reconstructing the Roman London flavourscape: New insights into the exotic food plant trade using network and spatial analyses. *Journal of Archaeological Science*, 55:244–252.

Lock, Margaret, 1993, Cultivating the body: Anthropology and epistemologies of bodily practice and knowledge, *Annual Review of Anthropology* 22:133–155.

Lodwick, Lisa, 2013a, Condiments before Claudius: New plant foods at the Late Iron Age oppidum at Silchester, UK, *Vegetation History and Archaeobotany*:1–7.

2013b, Cultivating Calleva: Archaeobotanical evidence for food consumption and production at Late Iron Age and Roman Silchester. PhD dissertation, Archaeology, University of Oxford.

Logan, Amanda L., 2012, A History of food without history: Food, trade, and environment in West-Central Ghana in the second millennium AD. PhD dissertation, Anthropology Department, University of Michigan.

Logan, Amanda L. and M. Dores Cruz, 2014, Gendered taskscapes; food, farming and craft production in Banda, Ghana in the eighteenth to twenty-first centuries, *African Archaeological Review* 31:203–231.

Logan, Amanda, Christine Hastorf, and Deborah Pearsall, 2012, "Let's Drink Together": Early ceremonial use of maize in the Titicaca basin, *Latin American Antiquity* 23(3):235–258.

Lopinot, Neal, 1997, Cahokian food production reconsidered. In *Cahokia: Domination and ideology in the Mississippian World*, Timothy R. Pauketat and Thomas E. Emerson (eds.), University of Nebraska Press, Lincoln, pp. 52–68.

Lupton, Deborah, 1996, *Food the body and the self*, Sage Publications, London.

Lyons, Diane and A. Catherine D'Andrea, 2003, Griddles, ovens and the origins of agriculture: An ethnoarchaeological study of bread baking in highland Ethiopia, *American Anthropologist* 105(3):515–530.

Macbeth, Helen (ed.), 1997, *Food preferences and taste: Continuity and change*. Berghahn Books, Oxford and Providence.

Macbeth, Helen M. and Alex Green, 1997, French Italian border food. In *Food preferences and taste: Continuity and change*, vol. 2, Helen M. Macbeth (ed.), Berghahn Books, Oxford and Providence, RI, pp. 139–154.

Macbeth, Helen and Sue Lawry, 1997, Food preferences and taste: An introduction. In *Food preferences and taste: Continuity and change*, H. Macbeth (ed.), Berghahn Books, Oxford and Providence, pp. 1–13,

MacLean, Rachel and Timothy Insoll, 1998, The social context of food technology in Iron Age Gao, Mali, *World Archaeology* 31(1):78–92.

Malinowski, Branislaw, 1935, *Coral gardens and their magic, Part I*, American Book Co., New York.

Mann, Charles C., 2011, *1493: Uncovering the New World Columbus created*, Knopf, New York.

March, Kathryn S., 1987, Hospitality, women and the efficacy of beer, *Food & Foodways* 1(4):351–388.

Marriott, M., 1976, Hindu transactions; diversity within dualism. In *Transaction and meaning: Directions in the anthropology of exchange and symbolic behavior*, Bruce Kapferer (ed.), Institute for the Study of Human Issues, Philadelphia, pp. 109–137.

Marx, Karl, 1939 [1867], *Capital, vol. 1*, International Publishers, New York.

Masson, Marilyn, 1999, Animal resource manipulation in ritual and domestic contexts at Post Classic Maya communities, *World Archaeology* 31(1):93–120.

Matthews, Wendy, 2005, Micromorphology and microstratigraphic traces of uses and concepts of space. In *Inhabiting Çatalhöyük: Reports from the 1995–1999 seasons*, Ian Hodder (eds.), McDonald Institute and the British Institute of Anatolian Archaeology, Cambridge, pp. 355–398.

Matthews, Wendy, C. French, T. Lawrence, D.F. Cutler, and M.K. Jones, 1997, Micromorphological traces of site formation processes and human activities, *World Archaeology* 29(2):281–308.

Mauss, Marcel, 1973 [1934], Techniques of the body, *Economy and Society* 2:70–88. 1980 [1925], *The gift: Forms and function of exchange in archaic societies*. London: Routledge and Kegan Paul.

Mays, Simon A., 1997, Carbon stable isotope ratios in medieval and later human skeletons from northern England, *Journal of Archaeological Science* 24:561–567.

McAnany, Patricia, 1992 Agricultural tasks and tools: Patterns of stone tool discard near prehistoric Maya residences bordering Pulltrouser Swamp, Belize. In *Gardens of prehistory: The archaeology of settlement agriculture in Greater Mesoamerica*, T. Killion (ed.), University of Alabama Press, Tuscaloosa, Alabama, pp. 184–214.

McAnany, Patricia A., 1995, *Living with the ancestors, kinship to kingship in ancient Maya society*, University of Texas Press, Austin.

McAnany Patricia A., 1998. Obscured by the forest: Property and ancestors in lowland Maya society. In *Property in Economic Context*, R.C. Hunt and A. Gilman (eds.), University Press, Lanham, pp. 73–87.

McGee, Harold, 2004, *On food and cooking: The science and lore of the kitchen*, Scribner, New York.

McGhee, R., 1977, Ivory for the Sea Woman: The symbolic attributes of a prehistoric technology, *Canadian Journal of Archaeology* 1:141–159.

McGuire, Randal, 1982, The study of ethnicity in historical archaeology, *Journal of Anthropological Archaeology* 1:159–178.

McIntosh, Wm. Alex, 1994, *Sociologies of food and nutrition*, Plenum Press, New York.

Mead, Margaret, 1964, *Food habits research. National Academy of Science*, National Research Council, Publ. 1225, Washington, DC.

Meigs, Anna S., 1984, *Food, sex, and pollution: A New Guinea religion*, Rutgers University Press, New Brunswick.

  1987, Blood kin and food kin. In *Conformity and conflict*, James Spradley and David McCurdy (eds.), Little Brown, Boston, pp. 117–124.

  1988, Food as a cultural construction, *Food & Foodways* 2:341–357.

Meiggs, David C. and R. Alexander Bentley, 2003, Strontium isotope pilot study. In symposium Recent Research at Çatalhöyük, UK Archaeological Science Conference, Oxford, April 2–6.

Mellaart, James, 1963. Excavations at Çatal Hüyük, 1962: Second preliminary report. *Anatolian Studies*, pp. 43–103.

Mennell, Stephen, 1985, *All manners of food: Eating and taste in England and France from the Middle Ages to the present*, Basil Blackwell, Oxford.

  1991, On the civilizing of appetite. In *The body: Social process and cultural theory*, M. Featherstone, M. Hepworth, and B.S. Turner (eds.), Sage, London, pp. 126–156.

  1997, On the civilizing of appetite. In *Food and culture*, Carole Counihan and Penny Van Esterik (eds.), Routledge, London, pp. 315–337.

Mennell, Stephen, Anne Murcott, and Anneke Hivan Olterloo, 1992, *The sociology of food: Eating, diet, and culture*, Newbury Park, London.

Meredith, Jeremy, 1990, The Aesthetic artefact: An exploration of emotional response and taste in archaeology, *Archaeological Review from Cambridge* 9(2):208–217.

Messer, Ellen, 1997, Three centuries of changing European taste for the potato. In *Food preferences and taste*, H. Macbeth (ed.), Berghahn Books, Oxford, pp. 101–113.

Methany, Karen and Mary Beaudry (eds.), 2015, *Archaeology of food encyclopedia*, Rowman and Littlefield, Lanham.

Meyer-Renschhausen, Elizabeth, 1991, The porridge debate: Grain, nutrition and forgotten food preparation techniques, *Food & Foodways* 5(1–2):95–120.

Meyers, Albert, 1975, Algunos problemas en la clasificación del estilo Incaico, *Pumpapunko* 8:7–25.

Middleton, William D., T. Douglas Price, and David C. Meiggs, 2005, Chemical analysis of floor sediments for the identification of anthropogenic activity residues. In *Inhabiting Çatalhöyük: Reports from the 1995–1999 seasons*, Ian Hodder (eds.), McDonald Institute and the British Institute of Anatolian Archaeology, Cambridge, pp. 399–412.

Miksicek, Charles, 1987, Formation processes of the archaeobotanical record, *Advances in Archaeological Method and Theory* 10:211–247.

Miller, Daniel, 1985, *Artefacts as categories: A study of ceramic variability in central India*. Cambridge University Press, Cambridge.

Miller, Daniel (ed.), 1998a, *Material cultures: Why some things matter*, University of Chicago Press, Chicago.

Miller, Daniel, 1998b, *A theory of shopping*, Polity Press, Cambridge.

2005, *Materiality*, Duke University Press, Durham.

Miller, George R., 1979, An introduction to the ethnoarchaeology of the Andean camelids. Unpublished PhD dissertation, Department of Anthropology, University of California-Berkeley.

Miller, George R. and Richard L. Burger, 1995, Our father the cayman, our dinner the llama: Animal utilization at Chavín de Huántar, Peru, *American Antiquity* 60(3):421–458.

Miller, Naomi, 1989, What mean these seeds: A comparative approach to archaeological seed analysis, *Historical Archaeology* 23:50–59.

Miller, Naomi and K. Gleason (eds.), 1994, *Archaeology of garden and field*, University of Pennsylvania Press, Philadelphia.

Mills, Barbara J., 1999, Ceramics and the social context of food consumption in the N. Southwest. In *Pottery and people: A dynamic interaction*, J.M. Skibo and G.M. Feinman (eds.), University of Utah Press, Salt Lake City, pp. 99–114.

2004, Identity, feasting and the archaeology of the greater southwest. In *Identity, feasting and the archaeology of the greater southwest*, Barbara Mills (ed.), University Press of Colorado, Boulder, pp. 1–23.

2007, Performing the feast: Visual display and suprahousehold commensalism in the Puebloan Southwest, *American Antiquity* 72(2):210–239.

2014, Relational networks and religious sodalities at Çatalhöyük. In *Religion at Work in a Neolithic Society: Vital Matters*, I. Hodder, (ed.), Cambridge University Press, Cambridge. pp. 159–86.

Milner, G.R., 1984. Social and temporal implications of variation among American Bottom Mississippian populations, *American Antiquity* 49:468–488.

Milner, Nicky and Preston Miracle, 2002, Introduction: Patterning data and consuming theory. In *Consuming passions and patterns of consumption*, P. Miracle and N. Milner (eds.), MacDonald Institute Monographs, Cambridge, pp. 1–5.

Milner, N., O.E. Craig, G.N. Bailey, K. Pedersen, and S.H. Andersen, 2004, Something fishy in the Neolithic? A re-evaluation of stable isotope analysis of Mesolithic and Neolithic coastal populations, *Antiquity*:9–22.

Milton, Katherine, 1987, Primate diets and gut morphology: Implications for hominid evolution. In *Food and evolution, toward a theory of human food habits*, M. Harris and E.B. Ross (eds.), Temple University Press, Philadelphia, pp. 93–115.

Minnis, Paul E., 1989, Prehistoric diet in the northern Southwest: Macroplant remains from Four Corners feces, *American Antiquity* 54:543–563.

1991, Famine foods of the northern American desert borderlands in historical context, *Journal of Ethnobiology* 11(2):231–257.

Mintz, Sidney, 1985, *Sweetness and power, the place of sugar in modern history*. Penguin Books, New York.

Mintz, Sidney (ed.), 1987, Symposium review on sweetness and power, *Food & Foodways* 2:107–197, special edition.

Mintz, Sidney, 1996, *Tasting food, tasting freedom*, Beacon Press, Boston.

2011, The absent third: The place of fermentation in a thinkable world food system. In *Cured, fermented and smoked foods: Proceedings of the Oxford Symposium on Food and Cookery 2010*, Helen Saberi (ed.), Totnes, England: Prospect Books, pp. 13–50.

Miracle, Preston T., 2002, Mesolithic meals from Mesolithic middens. In *Consuming passions and patterns of consumption*, P.T. Miracle and N. Milner (eds.), McDonald Institute for Archaeological Research, Cambridge, pp. 65–88.

Miracle, Preston T. and N. Milner, 2002, *Consuming passions and patterns of consumption*, McDonald Institute for Archaeological Research, Cambridge, pp. 65–88.

Molleson, Theya and Peter Andrews, 1997, The human remains, Çatalhöyük Archive Report 1997, http://catal.arch.cam.ac.uk/catal/archive_reps.html.

Molleson, Theya, Peter Andrews, Başak Boz, Jo Sofaer-Derevenski, and Jessica Pearson, 1998, Human remains up to 1998, Çatalhöyük Archive Report 1998, http://catal.arch.cam.ac.uk/catal/archive_reps.html.

Molleson, Theya, Peter Andrews, and Başak Boz, 1999, Report on human remains recovered from the South Area, together with a summary of material from the BACH area and the KOPAL trench, Çatalhöyük Archive Report 1999, http://catal.arch.cam.ac.uk/catal/archive_reps.html.

Molleson, Theya, Peter Andrews, and Başak Boz, 2005, Reconstruction of the Neolithic people of Çatalhöyük. In *Inhabiting Çatalhöyük: Reports from the 1995–1999 seasons*, Ian Hodder (ed.), McDonald Institute and the British Institute of Anatolian Archaeology, Cambridge, pp. 279–300.

Molleson, Theya, Başak Boz, Kathryn Nudd, and Berna Alpagut, 1996, *Dietary indications in the dentitions from Çatalhöyük*, T.C. Kultur Bakanliği and Anilitar ve Muzeler Genel (eds.), Mudurlugu XI Arkeometri Sonucari Toplantisi, T.C Kultur Bakanligi, Ankara, pp. 141–150.

Monaghan, John, 1996, The Mesoamerican community as "Great House", *Ethnology* 35(3):181–194.

Moore, Henrietta, 1986, Space, text and gender: An anthropological study of the Marakwet of Kenya. Cambridge University Press, Cambridge.

1994, *A passion for difference: Essays in anthropology and gender.* Indiana University Press, Bloomington.

1999, Gender, symbolism and praxis. *In Those who play with fire gender, fertility and transformation in East and Southern Africa,* H. Moore, T. Sanders, and B. Kaare (eds.), The Athlone Press, London, pp. 3–27.

Moore, Jerry, 1996, *Architecture and power in the ancient Andes: The archaeology of public buildings.* Cambridge University Press, Cambridge.

Moore, Jerry D., 2004, *Visions of culture: An introduction to anthropological theories and theorists,* 2nd ed., AltaMira Press, Walnut Creek.

2005, *Cultural landscapes in the prehispanic Andes: Archaeologies of place,* University Press of Florida, Gainesville.

Moore, Katherine M., 1989, Hunting and the origins of herding in Peru. PhD dissertation, Department of Anthropology, University of Michigan, Ann Arbor, Ann Arbor, University Microfilms.

Moore, Katherine, Maria Bruno, Kathryn Killackey, José Capriles, and Christine A. Hastorf, 2006, Integrated contextual approaches to understanding past activities using plant and animal remains from formative sites in the Titicaca Basin, Bolivia. In symposium Quantitative integration of Zooarchaeological and archaeobotanical Data: A consideration of methods and Case studies, Organizers: T. Peres & A. Vanderwarker, at the 71st Annual Meeting of the Society for American Archaeology, April 29, San Juan Puerto Rico.

Morell-Hart, Shanti, 2011, Paradigms and syntagms of ethnobotanical practice in Pre-Hispanic Northwestern Honduras. PhD dissertation, Department of Anthropology, University of California Berkeley.

Moseley, Michael and Kent Day (eds.), 1982, *Chanchan: Andean desert city,* University of New Mexico Press, Albuquerque.

Moss, Madonna L., 1993, Shellfish, gender, and status on the Northwest Coast: Reconciling archeological, ethnographic, and ethnohistorical records of the tlingit, *American Anthropologist* 95(3):631–652.

Muldner, Gundula and Michael P. Richards, 2005, Fast or feast: Reconstructing diet in later medieval England by stable isotope analysis, *Journal of Archaeological Science* 32(1):39–48.

2007, Diet and diversity at later Medieval fishergate: The isotopic evidence, *American Journal of Physical Anthropology* 134:162–174.

Muller, Jon, 1997, *Mississippian political economy,* Plenum, New York.

Mukherjee, A.J., M.S. Copley, R. Berstan, and R.P. Evershed, 2005, Interpretation of d13C values of fatty acids in relation to animal husbandry, food processing and consumption in prehistory. In *The zooarchaeology of fats, oils, milk and dairying,* J. Mulville and A.K. Outram (eds.), Oxbow Books, Oxford.

Mulville, J. and A.K. Outram (eds.), 2005, *The zooarchaeology of fats, oils, milk and dairying,* Oxbow Books, Oxford.

Murcott, Anne, 1982, On the social significance of the 'cooked dinner' in south Wales, *Social Science Information* 21:677–695.

1993, Talk of good food: An empirical study of women's conceptualizations, *Food & Foodways* 5(3):305–330.

1987, Sociological and social anthropological approaches to food and eating. In *World Review of Nutrition and Dietetics* 53, G.H. Boure (ed.), Karger, Basel, pp. 1–40.

Murdock, George P. and Caterina Provost, 1973, Measurement of cultural complexity, *Ethnology* 12(4):379–392.

Murra, John V., 1960, Rite and crop in the Inca state. In *Culture in history*, S. Diamond (ed.), Columbia University Press, New York, pp. 393–407.

1980, *The economic organization of the Inka state*, JAI Press, Greenwich.

Murray, M. and Margaret Schoeninger, 1988, Diet, status, and complex social structure in Iron Age Central Europe: Some contributions of bone chemistry. In *Tribe and polity in late prehistoric Europe*, D. Gibson and M. Geselowitz (eds.), Plenum Press, London, pp. 155–176.

Nabhan, G.P., 2005, *Why some like it hot: Food, genes and cultural diversity*. Island Press, Washington, DC.

Naruta, Anna Noel, 2006, Creating whiteness in California: Racialization processes, land, and policy in the context of California's Chinese Exclusion Movements, 1850 to 1910. PhD dissertation, Department of Anthropology, University of California, Berkeley.

Neitschmann, Bernard, 1973, *Between land and water: The subsistence ecology of the Miskito Indians, Eastern Nicaragua*. Seminar Press, New York.

Norconk, Marilyn A., 1987, Analysis of the UMARP burials, 1983 field season: Paleopathology report. In *Archaeological Field Research in the Upper Mantaro, Peru, 1982–1983 Investigations of Inka Expansion and Exchange*, Monograph 28, T. Earle, T. D'Altroy, C.A. Hastorf, C. Scott, C. Costin, G. Russell, and E. Sandefur (eds.), Institute of Archaeology, University of California, Los Angeles, pp. 124–133.

Nystrom, Pia and Susan Cox, 2003, The use of dental microwear to infer diet and subsistence patterns in past human populations: A preliminary study. In *Food culture and identity in the Neolithic and Early Bronze Age*, M. Parker Pearson (ed.), BAR International Series 1117, Archaeopress, Oxford, pp. 59–67.

O'Connell, James, Kristen Hawkes, and Nicholas Blurton-Jones, 1988, Hadza hunting, butchering and bone transport practices and their archaeological implications, *Journal of Anthropological Research* 44:113–161.

Ohnuki-Tierney, Emiko, 1993, *Rice as self: Japanese identities through time*, Princeton University Press, Princeton.

Orlove, Benjamin, 1994, Beyond consumption. In *Consumption and identity*, J. Friedman (ed.), Harwood Academic Publishers, Chur, pp. 119–146.

Ortner, Sherry, 1973, On key symbols, *American Anthropologist* 75(5):1338–1346.

O'Shea, John, 1981, Coping with scarcity: Exchange and social storage, *Economic Archaeology*, A. Sheridan and G. Bailey (eds.), British Archaeological Reports, International Series 96:167–183.

Outram, A.K., 2001, A new approach to identifying bone marrow and grease exploitation: Why the "indeterminate" fragments should not be ignored. *Journal of Archaeological Science*, 28(4):401–410.

Overing, Joanna, 1989, The aesthetics of production: The sense of community among the Cubeo and Piaroa, *Dialectical Anthropology* 14(3):159–175.

Owen, Bruce D. and Marilyn A. Norconk, 1987, Analysis of the human burials, 1977–1983 field seasons: Demographic profiles and burial practices. In *Archaeological Field Research in the Upper Mantaro, Peru, 1982–1983 Investigations of Inka Expansion and Exchange*, Monograph 28, T. Earle, T.

D'Altroy, C.A. Hastorf, C. Scott, C. Costin, G. Russell, E. Sandefur (eds.), Institute of Archaeology, University of California, Los Angeles, pp. 107–123.

Özdoğan, Mehmet, 2002, Redefining the Neolithic in Anatolia: A critical overview. *The Dawn of Farming in the Near East, Ex Oriente, Berlin*, pp. 153–158.

Panter-Brick, Catherine, 1996, Food and household status in Nepal. In *Food and the status quest: An interdisciplinary perspective*, P. Wiessner and W. Schiefenhövel (eds.), Berghahn Books, Oxford, pp. 253–262.

Paoli, U.E., 1963, *Rome: Its people, life and customs.* Longman, London.

Parker Pearson, Mike, 1999, *The archaeology of death and burial*, Texas A & M University anthropology series, no. 3.

    2003, Food, identity and culture: An introduction and overview. In *Food culture and identity in the Neolithic and Early Bronze Age*, M. Parker Pearson (ed.), BAR International Series 1117, Archaeopress, Oxford, pp. 1–30.

Parker Pearson, Mike (ed.), 2003, *Food culture and identity in the Neolithic and Early Bronze Age*, BAR International Series 1117, Archaeopress, Oxford.

Parker Pearson, Mike and Colin Richards (eds.), 1994, *Architecture and order: Approaches to social space*, Routledge, London.

Parsons, Jeffrey R. and Mary H. Parsons, 1990, Maguey utilization in highland central Mexico: An archaeological ethnography. Anthropological Papers No. 82, Museum of Anthropology, University of Michigan, Ann Arbor.

Passariello, Phyllis, 1990, Anomolies, analogy, and sacred profanities: Mary Douglas on food and culture, 1957–1989, *Food & Foodways* 4(1):53–71.

Pauketat, T., 2002. A fourth-generation synthesis of Cahokia and Mississippianization, *Midcontinental Journal of Archaeology* 27:149–170.

Pauketat, Timothy R., 1994, *The ascent of chiefs: Cahokia and Mississippian politics in native North America*, University of Alabama Press, Tuscaloosa.

Pauketat, Timothy R., Lucretia S. Kelly, Gayle J. Fritz, Neal H. Lopinot, Scott, and Eve Hargrave, 2002, The residues of feasting and public ritual at early Cahokia, *American Antiquity* 67(2):257–279.

Pauketat, Timothy R. and Neal H. Lopinot, 1997, Cahokian population dynamics. In *Cahokia: Domination and ideology in the Mississippian world*, T.R. Pauketat and T.E. Emerson (eds.), University of Nebraska Press, Lincoln, pp. 103–123.

Pearsall, Deborah M., 2015, *Paleoethnobotany: A handbook of procedures.* Left Coast Press, Walnut Creek.

Pearsall, Deborah and Dolores Piperno, 1998, *Origins of agriculture in the lowland neotropics*, Academic Press, San Diego.

Pearson, Jessica, H. Buitenhuis, R.E.M. Hedges, L. Martin, N. Russell, and K.C. Twiss, 2007, New light on early caprine herding strategies from isotope analysis: A case from Neolithic Anatolia, *Journal or Archaeological Science* 34:2170–2179.

Pearson, Jessica A., Amy Bogaard, Mike Charles, Simon W. Hillson, Clark Spencer Larsen, Nerissa Russell, and Katheryn Twiss, 2015, Stale carbon and nitrogen isotope analysis at Neolithich Çatalhöyük: Evidence for human and animal diet and their relationship to households, *Journal of Archaeological Science* 57:69–79.

Perry, Charles, 2011, Dried, rotted: Food preservation in central Asia and Siberia. In *Cured, fermented and smoked foods: Proceedings of the Oxford Symposium on*

*Food and Cookery 2010*, edited by Helen Saberi (ed.), Prospect Books, Totnes, England, pp. 240–247.

Perry, Linda, 2004, Starch analyses reveal the relationship between tool type and function: An example from the Orinoco valley of Venezuela, *Journal of Archaeological Science* 31:1069–1081.

Phillips Jr., David A. and Lynne Sebastian, 2004, Large-scale feasting and politics. In *Identity, feasting, and the archaeology of the greater southwest*, B.J. Mills (ed.), University Press of Colorado, Boulder, pp. 233–258.

Piperno, Dolores R. and Irene Holst, 1998, The presence of starch grains on prehistoric stone tools from the humid neotropics: Indications of early tuber use and agriculture in Panama, *Journal of Archaeological Science* 25:765–776.

Pirazzoli-t'Serstevens, Michéle, 1991, The art of dining in the Han period: Food vessels from Tomb no. 1 at Mawangdui, *Food & Foodways* 4 (3–4):209–219.

Pliner, P. and C. Stallberg-White, 2000, "Pass the ketchup, please" familiar flavors increase children's willingness to taste novel foods, *Appetite* 34 (1):95–103.

Politis, Gustavo G., 1999. Plant exploitation among the Nukak hunter-gatherers of Amazonia: Between ecology and ideology. In *The prehistory of food*, Chris Gosden and Jon Hather (eds.), Routledge, London, pp. 99–125.

Politis, Gustavo G. and Nicholas J. Saunders, 2002, Archaeological correlates if ideological activity: Food taboos and spirit-animals in an Amazonian hunter-gatherer society. In *Consuming passions and patterns of consumption*, Preston Miracle and Nicky Milner (eds.), MacDonald Institute of Archaeology Monograph, Cambridge, pp. 113–130.

Pollard, Joshua, 2001, The aesthetics of depositional practice, *World Arcaehology* 33(2):315–333.

Pollock, Donald K., 1985, Food and sexual identity among the Culina. *Food and Foodways*, 1(1–2):25–41.

    1992, Culina shamanism; gender, power, and knowledge. In *Portals of power: Shamanism in South America*, J.M. Langdon and Gerhard Baer (eds.), University of New Mexico Press, Albuquerque, pp. 25–40.

Pollock, Susan, 2012, Towards an archaeology of commensal spaces. An Introduction, eTopoi. In Between feasts and daily meals: Toward an archaeology of commensal spaces, Susan Pollock (ed.), *Journal for Ancient Studies*, Special Volume 2, pp. 1–20. http://journal.topoi.org/index.php/etopoi/article/view/61

Pollan, Michael, 1991, *Second nature*, The Atlantic Monthly Press, New York.

    2001, *The botany of desire: A plant's eye view of the world*, Random House, New York.

    2006, *The omnivore's dilemma, a natural history of four meals*, The Penguin Press, New York.

Polyani, Karl, 1957, *The economy as instituted process in trade and market in the early empires*, K. Polanyi, C.M. Arensberg, and H.W. Pearson (eds.), The Free Press, Glencoe, pp. 243–269.

Potter, James, 2000, Pots, parties, and politics: Communal feasting in the American Southwest, *American Antiquity* 65(3):471–492.

Potter James M. and Scott G. Ortman, 2004, Community and cuisine in the prehispanic American Southwest. In *Identity, feasting, and the archaeology of the greater southwest*, B.J. Mills (ed.), University Press of Colorado, Boulder, pp. 173–191.

Powers, William K. and Marla M.N. Powers, 1984, Metaphysical aspects of an Oglala food system. In *Food in the social order: Studies of food and festivities in three American communities*, Mary Douglas (ed.), Russell Sage Foundation, New York, pp. 40–96.

Price, T. Douglas, 1996, The first farmers of southern Scandinavia. In *The origins and spread of agriculture and pastoralism in Eurasia*, D.R. Harris (ed.), UCL Press, London, pp. 346–362.

    1989, The reconstruction of Mesolithic diets. In *The Mesolithic in Europe*, C. Bonsall (ed.), John Donald, Edinburgh, pp. 48–59.

Price, T. Douglas (ed.), 1989, *The chemistry of prehistoric human bone*. Cambridge University Press, Cambridge.

Proust, Marcel, 1934, *Remembrance of things past (La recherché du temps perdu)*, *Remembrance of things past*. Translated by C.K. Scott-Moncrieff, New York, Random House.

Radcliffe-Brown A.R., 1922, *The Andaman Islanders, a study in social anthropology*, Cambridge University Press, Cambridge.

Ramírez, Susan E., 2005, *To feed and be fed*, Stanford University Press, Stanford.

Rappaport, Roy, 1968, *Pigs for the ancestors*, Yale University Press, New Haven.

Rasteiro, R., Bouttier, P.A., Sousa, V.C. and Chikhi, L., 2012, Investigating sex-biased migration during the Neolithic transition in Europe, using an explicit spatial simulation framework. *Proceedings of the Royal Society of London B: Biological Sciences*, p.rspb20112323.

Rathje, William, 1977, *Le project du garbage. Historical archaeology and the importance of material things*, Leland Ferguson (ed.), Society for Historical Archaeology, Columbia, pp. 36–42.

Reagan, Albert B., 1930, Notes on the Indians of the Fort Apache region. Anthropological papers of the American Museum of Natural History 31(5), The Trustees, New York.

Reed, David Millard, 1999, Cuisine from Hun-Nal-Ye. In *Reconstructing ancient Mayan diet*, C.D. White (ed.), University of Utah Press, Salt Lake City, pp. 183–196.

Reinheard, Karl J., Donny L. Hamilton, Richard Hevly, 1991, Use of pollen concentration in palaepharmacology: Coprolite evidence of medicinal plants, *Journal of Ethnobiology* 11(1):117–132.

Reinhard, Karl J., 1993, The utility of pollen concentration in coprolite analysis: Expanding upon Dean's comments, *Journal of Ethnobiology* 13(1):114–128.

Reinhard, Karl J., and V.M. Bryant Jr., 1992, Coprolite analysis: A biological perspective in archaeology. In *Archaeological method and theory*, M.B. Schiffer (ed.), University of Arizona Press, Tucson, pp. 245–288.

Renfrew, Colin and Ezra B.W. Zubrow (eds.), 1994, *The ancient mind: Elements of cognitive archaeology*, Cambridge University Press, Cambridge.

Richards, Audrey, 1932, *Hunger and work in a savage tribe*, George Routledge and Sons, London.

Richards, Audrey I, 1939, *Land, labour, and diet in northern Rhodesia, an economic study of the Bemba tribe*, Oxford University Press, London.

Richards, Colin and Julian Thomas, 1984, Ritual activity and structured deposition in Later Neolithic Wessex. In *Neolithic studies: A review of some current research*, R. Bradley and J. Gardiner (eds.), British Archaeological Reports, Oxford, British Series 133, pp. 189–218.

Richards, Michael P., 2000, Human consumption of plant foods in the British Neolithic: Direct evidence from bone stable isotopes. In *Plants in Neolithic Britain and beyond*, Neolithic studies groups seminar papers 5, A. Fairbairn (ed.), Oxbow Books, Oxford, pp. 123–135.

Richards, Michael P., B.T. Fuller, and R.E.M. Hedges, 2001, Sulphur isotopic variation in ancient bone collagen from Europe: Implications for human palaeodiet, residence mobility, and modern pollutant studies, *Earth and Planetary Science Letters* 191:185–190.

Richards, Michael P. and Richard E.M. Hedges, 1999, Stable isotope evidence for similarities in the types of marine foods used by Late Mesolithic humans at sites along the Atlantic coast of Europe, *Journal of Archaeological Science* 26:717–722.

Richards, Michael P. and Jessica A. Pearson, 2005, Stable isotope evidence of diet at Çatalhöyük. In *Inhabiting Çatalhöyük: Reports from the 1995–1999 seasons*, Ian Hodder (ed.), McDonald Institute and the British Institute of Anatolian Archaeology, Cambridge, pp. 313–322.

Richards, Michael P., Jessica A. Pearson, Theya I. Molleson, Nerissa. Russell, and Louise Martin, 2003, Stable isotope evidence of diet at Neolithic Çatalhöyük, Turkey, *Journal of Archaeological Science* 30:67–76

Richards, Michael P., T. Douglas Price, and Eva Koch, 2003, Mesolithic and Neolithic subsistence in Denmark: New stable isotope data, *Current Anthropology* 44(2):288–295.

Richards, Michael P, Rick J. Schulting, and Robert E. M. Hedges, 2003, Sharp shift in diet at onset of Neolithic, *Nature* 425:366.

Riddervold, Astri, 1990, *Lutefisk, rakefisk and herring in Norwegian tradition*, Novus Press, Oslo.

Rival, Laura (ed.), 1998, *The social life of trees, anthropological perspectives on tree symbolism*, Berg, Oxford.

Robb, John, 1998, Time and biography: Osteobiography of the Italian Neolithic life span. In *Thinking through the body: Archaeologies of corporeality*, Y. Hamilakis, M. Pluciennik, and S. Tarlow (eds.), Kluwer Academic/Plenum Publishers, New York, pp. 153–171.

2004, The extended artefact and the monumental economy: A methodology for material agency. In *Rethinking materiality: The engagement of mind with the material world*, E. DeMarrais, C. Gosden, and C. Renfrew (eds.), McDonald Institute for Archaeological Research, Cambridge, pp. 131–139.

2007, *The early Mediterranean village: Agency, material culture, and social change in Neolithic Italy*, Cambridge University Press, Cambridge.

Roberts, Neil, Peter Boyer, and Jamie Merrick, 2007, The KOPAL on-site and off-site excavations and sampling. In *Excavating Çatalhöyük: South, North and KOPAL area reports from the 1995–1999 seasons*, Ian Hodder (ed.), McDonald

Institute Monographs and British Institute of Archaeology at Ankara, pp. 553–588.

Robertson Smith, W., 1889, *Lectures on the religion of the Semites*, 1st Series. Adam and Charles Black, Edinburgh.

Robins, G.V., K.D. Sales, D. Oduwole, T. Holden, and G.C. Hillman, 1986, Postscript: Last minute results from ESR spectroscopy concerning and cooking of Lundow Man's last meal. In *Lundow Man: The body in the bog*, I. Stead, J. Bourke, and D.R. Brothwell (eds.), British Museum Publications, London, pp. 140–142.

Roddick, Andrew and Christine A. Hastorf, 2010, Tradition brought to the surface: Continuity, innovation and change in the Late Formative Period, Taraco Peninsula, Bolivia, *Cambridge Archaeological Journal* 20:157–178.

Rodríguez, Erin Christine and Christine A. Hastorf, 2013, Calculating ceramic vessel volume: An assessment of methods, *Antiquity* 87(338):1182–1190.

Rodríguez-Alegría, Enrique, 2005, Eating like an Indian: Negotiating social relations in the Spanish Colonies, *Current Anthropology* 46(4):551–573.

Rodríguez-Alegría, Enrique and Sarah Graff (eds.), 2012, *The Menial Art of Cooking*, Boulder, University of Colorado Press.

Roe, Daphne A. and Stephen V. Beck, 2000, Pellagra. In *The Cambridge World History of Food*, Kenneth F. Kiple and Kriemhild C. Ornelas (eds.), Cambridge University Press, Cambridge, pp. 960–967.

Rogers, Ben, 2004, *Beef and Liberty*, roast beef, John Bull and the English Nation, Vintage, London.

Rolls, Edmund T. and Batbara Rolls, 1982, Brain mechanisms involved in feeding. In *Human food selection*, Lewis Barker (ed.), Ellis Horwood Ltd, Chichester, pp. 33–62.

Rosen, Arlene Miller, 2005, Phytolith indicators of plant and land use at Çatalhöyük. In *Inhabiting Çatalhöyük: Reports from the 1995–1999 seasons*, Ian Hodder (ed.), McDonald Institute and the British Institute of Anatolian Archaeology, Cambridge, pp. 203–212.

Rosen, Arlene Miller and Stephen Weiner, 1994, Identifying ancient irrigation: A new method using opaline phytoliths from emmer wheat, *Journal of Archaeological Science* 21:125–132.

Rottländer, R.C.A. and H. Schlichtherle, 1979, Food identification of samples from archaeological sites, *Archaeo-Physika* 10:260–267.

Rovane, Carol, 2006, Why do individuals matter? *Daedalus* 135(4):49–59.

Rowe, John H., 1946, Inca culture at the time of the Spanish conquest. In *Handbook of South American Indians*, vol 2, Julian Steward (ed.), Bureau of American Ethnology, Bulletin 143, Washington, DC, pp. 183–330.

Rowlands, Michael, 1993, The role of memory in the transmission of culture, *World Archaeology* 25(2):141–151.

Rowley-Conwy, Peter, 1984. The laziness of the short-distance hunter: The origins of agriculture in western Denmark, *Journal of Anthropological Archaeology* 3:300–324.

Rowley-Conwy, Peter and Marek Zvelebil, 1989, Saving it for later: Storage by prehistoric hunter-gatherers in Europe. In *Bad year economics*, Paul Halstead and John O'Shea (eds.), Cambridge University Press, Cambridge, pp. 40–67.

Rozin, Elizabeth, 1973, *The flavor principle cookbook*. Hawthorn, New York.

1982, The structure of cuisine. In *Human food selection*, Lewis Barker (ed.), Ellis Horwood Ltd, Chichester, pp. 189–203.

Rozin, Elizabeth and Paul Rozin, 1981, Culinary themes and variations, *Natural History* 90(2):6–14.

Rozin, Paul, 1976, The selection of food by rats, humans and other animals. In *Advances in the study of behavior, vol. 6*, J. Rosenblatt, R.A. Hinde, C. Beer, and E. Shaw (eds.), Academic Press, New York, pp. 21–76.

1982, Human food selection: The interaction of biology, culture and individual experience. In *The psychobiology of human food selection*, L.M. Barker (ed.), Ellis Horwood Ltd, Chichester, pp. 225–254.

1987, Psychobiological perspectives on food preferences and avoidances. In *Food and evolution*, M. Harris and E.B. Ross (eds.), Temple University Press, Philadelphia, pp. 181–205.

Rozin, Paul and April E. Fallon, 1987, A perspective on disgust, *Psychological Review* 94(1):23–41.

Rozin, Paul, Jonathan Haidt, Clark McCauley, and Sumio Imada, 1997, Disgust: Preadaptation and the cultural evolution of a food-based emotion. In *Food preferences and taste*, Helen MacBeth (ed.), Berghahn Books, Oxford, pp. 65–82.

Rudebeck, Elisabeth, 2000, Tilling nature, harvesting culture, *Acta Archaeologica Lundensia*, Series in 8, No 32, University of Lund, Almquist & Wiksel Intl., Stockholm, Sweden.

Rumold, Claudia Ursula, 2010, Illuminating women's work and the advent of plant cultivation in the Highland Titicaca basin of South America: New evidence from grinding tool and starch grain analyses. PhD dissertation, Department of Anthropology, University of California Santa Barbara.

Russell, Glenn S., 1988, The impact of Inka policy on the domestic economy of the Wanka, Peru: Stone tool production and use. PhD dissertation, Department of Anthropology, UCLA.

Russell, Nerissa, 1999, Symbolic dimensions of animals and meat at Opovo, Yugoslavia. In *Material symbols: Culture and economy in prehistory*, J.E. Robb (ed.), Southern Illinois University, Center for Archaeological Investigations, Occasional Papers, No. 26. Center for Archaeological Investigations, Southern Illinois University at Carbondale, pp. 153–172.

Russell, Nerissa and Louise Martin, 2005, Çatalhöyük mammal remains. In *Inhabiting Çatalhöyük: Reports from the 1995–1999 seasons*. Çatalhöyük Project, Ian Hodder (ed.), McDonald Institute Monographs/British Institute of Archaeology at Ankara, Cambridge, pp. 33–98.

2012, Cooking meat and bones at Neolithic Çatalhöyük, Turkey. In *The menial art of cooking*, Enrique Rodríguez-Alegría and Sarah Graff (eds.), University of Colorado Press, Boulder, pp. 87–98.

Sabban, Françoise, 1986, Court cuisine in the fourteenth-century Imperial China: Some culinary aspects of Hu Sihui's *Yinshan Zhengyoa, Food & Foodways* 1(2):161–196.

2000, China. In *The Cambridge world history of food*, Kenneth F. Kiple and Kriemhild Coneé Ornelas (eds.), Cambridge University Press, Cambridge, pp. 1165–1175.

Sahlins, Marshall, 1972, *Stone Age economics*, Aldine, Chicago.

1976, *Culture and practical reason*, University of Chicago Press, Chicago.

1999, Two or three things that I know about culture. *Journal of the Royal Anthropological Institute*, pp. 399–421.

Sallaberger, Walther, 2012, Home-made bread, municipal mutton, royal wine. Establishing social relations during the preparation and consumption of food in religious festivals at Late Bronze age Emar, between feasts and daily meals. *Toward an Archaeology of commensal spaces*, Susan Pollock ed., eTOPOI, special volume 2:157–177. http://journal.topoi.org/index.php/etopoi/article/view/33/100

Sallares, J. Robert, 1991, *The ecology of the Ancient Greek world*, Duckworth, London.

Samuel, Delwen, 1993, Ancient Egyptian cereal processing: Beyond the artistic record, *Cambridge Archaeological Journal* 3(2):276–283.

1994, An archaeological study of baking and bread in New Kingdom Egypt. PhD dissertation, Department of Archaeology, Cambridge University.

1996a, Approaches to the archaeology of food, *Petits Propos Culinaires* 54:12–21.

1996b, Bread in New Kingdom Egypt: An archaeological approach to the cultural context of food. In Symposium Eating up old paradigms: A discussion of archaeological food, organized by Christine Hastorf and Sissel Johannessen, 61st Annual Meeting of the Society for American Archaeology, New Orleans, LA.

1999, Bread making and social interactions at the Amarna Workmen's village, Egypt, *World Archaeology* 31(1):121–144.

Sanday, Peggy, 1986, *Divine hunger*, Cambridge University Press, Cambridge.

Sandefur, Elsie, 2001, Animal husbandry and meat consumption. In *Empire and Domestic Economy*, T.N. D'Altroy and C.A. Hastorf (eds.), Plenum Publishing Corp., New York, pp. 179–202.

Sandford, Mary K. (ed.), 1993, *Investigations of ancient tissue*, Gordon and Breach Science Publishers, Amsterdam.

Saul H., M. Madella, A. Fischer, A. Glykou, S. Hartz, et al., 2013, Phytoliths in Pottery Reveal the Use of Spice in European Prehistoric Cuisine. PLoS ONE 8(8): e70583. doi:10.1371/journal.pone.0070583

Saussure, F., de, 1966, *Course in general linguistics*, translated by Wade Baskin, P. Owen, London.

Scarry, C. Margaret, 1993a, Variability in Mississippian crop production strategies. In *Foraging and farming in the eastern Woodlands*, University of Florida Press, Gainesville, pp. 78–90.

Scarry, C. Margaret (ed.), 1993b, *Foraging and farming in the eastern woodlands*, University of Florida Press, Gainesville.

Scarry, C. Margaret, 1994, Variability in late prehistoric corn from the lower southeast. In *Corn and Culture in the Prehistoric New World*, S. Johannessen and C.A. Hastorf (eds.), Minnesota Anthropology Series, Westview Press, Boulder, pp. 347–367.

Schafer, E.F., 1977, T'ang. In *Food in Chinese culture, anthropological and historical perspectives*, K.C. Chang (ed.), Yale University Press, New Haven.

Schirmer, Ronald C., 2002, Plant-use systems and late prehistoric culture change in the Red Wing locality. Unpublished Ph.D dissertation, Department of Anthropology, University of Minnesota.

Schlosser, Eric, 2001, *Fast food nation: The dark side of the all-American meal*, Houghton Mifflin, Boston.

Schneider, David Murray, 1975, The American kin universe: A genealogical study, *University of Chicago Studies in Anthropology*, no. 3, Chicago.

Schoeninger, Margaret J., 1979, *Dietary reconstruction at Chalcatzingo, a formative period site in Morelos, Mexico*. Technical reports no. 9, Museum of Anthropology, University of Michigan, Ann Arbor.

Schoeninger, Margaret, Michael DeNiro, and Henry Tauber, 1983, Stable nitrogen isotope ratios of bone collagen reflect marine and terrestrial components of prehistoric human diet, *Science* 220:1381–1383.

Scholliers, Peter, 2001, Meals, food narratives, and sentiments of belonging in past and present. In *Food, drink and identity, cooking, eating and drinking in Europe since the Middle Ages*, Peter Scholliers (ed.), Berg, Oxford, pp. 3–22.

Schroeder, H., T.C. O'Connell, J.A. Evans, K.A. Shuler, and R.E.M. Hedges, 2009, Trans-Atlantic slavery: Isotopic evidence for forced migration to Barbados, *American Journal of Physical Anthropology* 139:547–557.

Schultes, Richard Evans and Robert F. Raffauf, 1992, *Vine of the soul: Medicine men, their plants and rituals in the Columbian Amazon*, Synergetic Press, Oracle.

Schultz, Peter D. and Sherri Gust, 1983, Faunal remains and social status in the 19th Century Sacramento, *Historical Archaeology* 17(1):44–53.

Scott, Elizabeth, 2001, Food and inter-social relations at Nina Plantation, *American Anthropologist* 103(3):671–691.

Scott, Susan L. and H. Edwin Jackson, 1998, Early Caffo Ritual and patterns of animal use: An analysis of faunal remains from the Crenshaw site (3MI6), southern Arkansas, *The Arkansas Archaeologist* 37:1–27.

Sealy, J., R. Armstrong, and C. Schrire, 1995, Beyond lifetime averages: Tracing life-histories through isotopic analysis of different calcified tissues from archaeological human skeletons, *Antiquity* 69:290–300.

Serjeantson, Dale, 2000, Good to eat and good to think with: Classifying animals from complex sites. In *Animal bones, humans societies*, P. Rowley-Conway (ed.), Oxbow, Oxford, pp. 179–189.

Shack, Dorothy N., 1969, Nutritional processes and personality development among the Gurage of Ethiopia, *Ethnology* 8(3):292–300.

Shack, William A., 1971, Hunger, anxiety, and ritual; deprivation and spirit possession among the Gurage of Ethiopia, *Man* 6(1):30–43.

Shafer, H. 1983, The lithic artifacts of the Pulltrouser area: Settlement and fields. In *Pulltrouser Swamp: Ancient Maya habitat, agriculture, and settlement in Northern Belize*, L. Turner III and P. Harrison (eds.), University of Texas, Austin, pp. 212–245.

Shanks, Michael and Chris Tilley, 1982, Ideology, symbolic power and ritual communication: A reinterpretation of Neolithic mortuary practices. In *Symbolic and structural archaeology*, Ian Hodder (ed.), Cambridge University Press, Cambridge, pp. 129–154.

Sheets, Payson (ed.), 2002a, Introduction. In *Before the volcano erupted, the ancient Cerén village in Central America*, Payson Sheets (ed.), University of Texas Press, Austin, pp. 1–8.

(ed.), 2002b, *Before the volcano erupted, the ancient Cerén village in Central America*, University of Texas Press, Austin.

Sheets, Payson, David L. Lentz, Dolores Piperno, John Jones, Christine Dixon, G. Maloof, and A. Hood, 2012, Ancient manioc agricultural south of the Cerén village, El Salvador, *Latin American Antiquity* 23:259–281.

Sherratt, Andrew, 1983, The secondary exploitation of animals in the Old World, *World Archaeology* 15:90–104.

1991, Sacred and profane substances: The ritual use of narcotics in Later Neolithic Europe. In *Sacred and profane*, P. Garwood, D. Jennings, R. Skeates, and J. Toms (eds.), Monograph 32, Oxford University Committee for Archaeology, Oxford, pp. 50–64.

1995, Introduction: Peculiar substances. In *Consuming habits: Drugs in history and anthropology*, Jordan Goodman, Paul E. Lovejoy, and Andrew Sherratt (eds.), Routledge, London, pp. 1–10.

Sherratt, S., 2004, Feasting in Homeric epic. In *The Mycenaean feast*, J. Wright (ed.), American School of Classical Studies, Princeton, pp. 181–213.

Shilling, Chris, 1993, *The body and social theory*, Sage, London.

2006, Discussion: Past bodies. Leverhulme Research Programme, Royal Anthropological Institute Symposium, Cambridge, January 13.

Shimada, Melody and Izumi Shimada, 1985, Prehistoric llama breeding and herding on the north coast of Peru. *American Antiquity*, pp. 3–26.

Sigurdsson, V., G. Foxall, and H. Saevarsson, 2010, In-store experimental approach to pricing and consumer behavior, *Journal of Organizational Behavior Management* 30(3):234–246.

Sillar, B., 2009, The social agency of things? Animism and materiality in the Andes. *Cambridge Archaeological Journal*, 19(03):367–377.

Simmel, Geog, 1992 [1910], The sociology of a meal (auf deutsch Soziologie der Mahlzeit), translated by Michael Symons, *Food & Foodways* 5(4):345–351.

Simoons, Frederick J., 1991, *Food in China. A cultural and historical inquiry*. CRC Press, Boca Raton.

1994, *Eat not this flesh. Food avoidances from prehistory to present*, 2nd Edition, University of Wisconsin Press, Madison.

Simon, Mary L., 2000, Regional Variations in Plant Use Strategies in the Midwest During the Late Woodland. In *Late Woodland societies: Tradition and transformation across the midcontinent*. Thomas Emerson, Dale L. Mclrath, and Andrew C. Fortier (eds.).pp 37–75. University of Nebraska Press, Lincoln.

Singelton, Teresa, 1985, *The archaeology of slavery and plantation life*. Academic Press, New York.

Skoglund, P., H. Malmström, M. Raghavan, J. Storå, P. Hall, E. Willerslev, et al., 2012, Origins and genetic legacy of Neolithic farmers and hunter-gatherers in Europe, *Science* 336(6080):466–469.

Smith, Adam, 1999 (1776), *The wealth of nations*, Penguin, London.

Smith, Bruce D., 2007, Niche construction and the behavioral context of plant and animal domestication, *Evolutionary Anthropology* 16(5):188–199.

Smith, C., W. Denevan and P. Hamilton, 1968, Ancient ridged fields in the region of Lake Titicaca, *Geographical Journal* 134:353–366.

Smith, Michael, 1987, Household possessions and wealth in agrarian states: Implications for archaeology, *Journal of Anthropological Archaeology* 6(4):297–335.

Smith, Monica, 2006, The archaeology of food preference, *American Anthropologist* 108(3):480–493.

Sobolik, Kristen D., 1988, Diet change in the lower Pecos: Analysis of Baker Cave coprolites, *Bulletin of the Texas Archaeological Society* 59:111–127.

Speth, John, 2000, Boiling vs. baking and roasting: A taphonomic approach to the recognition of cooking techniques in small mammals. In *Animal bones, human societies*, Peter A. Rowley-Conwy (ed.), Oxbow, Oxford, pp. 89–105.

Spielmann, Katherine A., 1989, A Review: Dietary restrictions on hunter-gatherer women and the implications for fertility and infant mortality, *Human Ecology* 17(3):321–345.

2002, Feasting, Craft Specialization, and the Ritual Mode of Production in Small-Scale Societies. *American Anthropologist*, 104(1), pp. 195–207.

2004, Communal feasting, ceramics and exchange. In *Identity, feasting, and the archaeology of the greater southwest*, Barbara J. Mills (ed.), University Press of Colorado, Boulder, pp. 210–232.

Spindler, Konrad, 1994, *The man in the ice: The discovery of a 5,000 year-old body reveals the secrets of the Stone Age*, translated by E. Osers, Harmony Books, New York.

Staal, Fritz, 1975, The meaninglessness of ritual, *Numen* 26(1):9.

Stagg, D.J., 1979, A *calendar of new forest documents 1244–1334*, Hampshire County Council, Winchester.

Stahl, Ann B., 1984, Hominid dietary selection before fire, *Current Anthropology* 25:151–168.

1989, Plant-food processing: Implications for dietary quality. In *Foraging and farming: The evolution of plant exploitation*, David R. Harris and Gordon C. Hillman (eds.), Unwin Hyman, London, pp. 171–194.

2002, Colonial entanglements and the practices of taste: An alternative to logocentric approaches, *American Anthropologist* 104(3):827–845.

2014, Intersections of craft and cuisine: Implications for what and how we study, *African Archaeological Review* 31:383–393.

Stahl, Peter, 1999, Structural density of domesticated South American camelid skeletal elements and the archaeological investigation of prehistoric Andean ch'arki, *Journal of Archaeological Science* 26:1347–1368.

Stein, Gil J., 2012, Food preparation, social context, and ethnicity in a Prehistoric Mesopotamian colony. In *The Menial Art of Cooking*, Enrique Rodríguez-Alegria and Sarah Graff (eds.), University of Colorado Press, Boulder, pp. 47–63.

Stephens, David W. and John R. Krebs, 1986, *Foraging theory*, Princeton University Press, Princeton.

Steponaitis, Vincas, 1983, *Ceramics, chronology, and community patterns: An archaeological study at Moundville*, Academic Press, New York.

Sterckx, Roel, 2005, Food and philosophy in early China. In *Of tripod and palate; food, politics and religion in traditional China*, Roel Sterckx (ed.), Palgrave Macmillan, New York, pp. 34–61.

Steward, Julian, 1955, *Theory of culture change*, University of Illinois Press, Urbana.

Stokes, Paul R.G., 2000, The butcher, the cook and the archaeologist. In *Taphonomy and interpretation*, J.P. Huntley and S. Stallibrass (eds.), Oxbow, Oxford, pp. 65–70.

Strathern, Andrew, 1971, *The rope of Moka*, Cambridge University Press, Cambridge.

Strathern, Marilyn, 1988, *The gender and the gift: Problems with women and problems with society in Melanesia*, University of California Press, Berkeley.

Super, John C., 1988, *Food, conquest and colonization in 16th Century Spanish America*. University of New Mexico Press, Albuquerque.

Susanne, C., R. Hauspie, Y. Lepage, M. Vercauteren, 1987, Nutrition and growth in applied nutritional principles in health and disease. In *World review of nutrition and dietetics*, volume 53, G.H. Bourne (ed.), Karger, Basel, pp. 69–170.

Sutton, David E., 2001, *Remembrance of repasts. An anthropology of food and memory*, Berg, New York.

Sutton, Mark Q. and Karl J. Reinhard, 1995, Cluster analysis of the coprolites from Antelope House: Implications for Anasazi diet and cuisine, *Journal of Archaeological Science* 22:741–750.

Swanton, John R., 1911, *The Indians of the lower Mississippi Valley*, Bulletin 43, Bureau of American Ethnology, Smithsonian Institution, Washington, DC.

Tambiah, S.J., 1969, Animals are good to think and good to prohibit, *Ethnology* 5:423–459.

Taube, Karl, 1985, The classic Maya maize god: A reappraisal. In *Fifth Palenque round table 1983*, vol. 7, Virginia M. Fields (ed.), Pre-Columbian Art Research Institute, San Francisco, pp. 171–181.

1989, The maize tamale in classic Maya diet, epigraphy and art, *American Antiquity* 54(1):31–51.

Tauber, Henry, 1981, 13C evidence for dietary habits of prehistoric man in Denmark, *Nature* 292:332–333.

1983, 14C dating of human beings in relation to dietary habits, *PACT* 8:365–375.

Thomas, Julian, 1991, *Rethinking the Neolithic*, Cambridge University Press, Cambridge.

1999, *Understanding the Neolithic*, Routledge, London.

2004, *Archaeology and Modernity*, Routledge, London.

Thomas, Kenneth D. (ed.), 1993, Biomolecular archaeology. *World archaeology* 25(1).

(ed.), 1999, Food technology in its social context: Production, processing and storage, *World Archaeology* 31(1):38–54.

Thomas, Nicholas, 1991, *Entangled objects: Exchange: Material culture and colonialism in the Pacific*, Harvard University Press, Cambridge, MA.

Thomas, Richard M., 2007, They were what they ate: Maintaining social boundaries through the consumption of food in medieval England. In *We are what we eat: Archaeology, food and identity*, Kathryn Twiss (ed.), Southern Illinois University Press, Carbondale, pp. 130–151.

Tomka, Steve A., 1994, Quinoa and camelids on the Bolivian Altiplano: An ethnoarchaeological approach to agro-pastoral subsistence production with an emphasis on agro-pastoral transhumance. PhD dissertation, Department of Anthropology, University of Texas, Austin.

Thompson, Eric P., 1971, The moral economy of the English crowd in the eighteenth century, *Past and Present* 50:76–136.

Tozzer, A.M., 1941, *Landa's relación de las cosas de Yucatán: A translation*, Papers Peabody Museum, Harvard University, Cambridge, MA.

Tringham, Ruth, 1991, Households with faces: The challenge of gender in prehistoric architectural remains. In *Engendering archaeology: Women in prehistory*, Joan Gero and Margaret Conkey (eds.), Basil Blackwell Publishers, Cambridge, MA., pp. 93–131.

Tringham, Ruth, N. Brukner, T. Kaiser, K. Borojevic, L. Bukvic, P. Steli, N. Russell, M. Stevanovic, and B. Voytek, 1992, Excavations at Opovo, 1985–1987: Socioeconomic change in the Balkan Neolithic, *Journal of Field Archaeology* 19:351–386.

Tringham, Ruth and Mirjana Stevanović (eds.), 2012, *Last house on the hill: BACH Area reports from Çatalhöyük, Turkey*. Monumenta Archaeologica 27, Cotsen Institute of Archaeology Press, UCLA, Los Angeles.

Trostel, B., 1994, Household pots and possessions: An ethnoarchaeological study of material goods and wealth. In *Kalinga ethnoarchaeology*, W. Longarce and J. Skibo (eds.), Smithsonian Institution Press, Washington, DC, pp. 209–224.

Turkon, Paula, 2002, Exposing the elusive elite: Status variation and domestic activities in the Malpaso Valley, Mexico. PhD dissertation, Department of Anthropology, Arizona State University.

Turner, Bethany L., John D. Kingston, and George J. Armelagos, 2010, Variation in dietary histories among the immigrants of Machu Picchu: Carbon and nitrogen isotope evidence, *Chungara* 42:515–534.

Turner, Brian S., 1991, Recent developments in the theory of the body. In *The body: Social process and cultural theory*, Mike Featherstone, Mike Hepworth, and Brian S. Turner (eds.), Sage, London, pp. 1–35.

1992, *Regulating bodies: Essays in medical sociology*, Routledge, London.

1994, Introduction. In *The consuming body by Pasi Falk*, Sage, London, pp. vii–xvii.

Turner, C.G. and L. Lofgren, 1966, Household size of prehistoric Western Puelbo Indians, *Southwestern Journal of Anthropology* 22:117–132.

Turner, Nancy J. and Harriet V. Kuhnlein, 1983, Camas (*Camassia* spp.) and riceroot (Fritillaria spp.): Two lilaceous "root" foods of the Northwest Coast Indians, *Ecology of Food and Nutrition* 13:199–219.

Turner, Victor, 1966, *The ritual process. Structure and anti-structure*. Aldine, Chicago.

Twiss, Katheryn C., 2007, Home is where the hearth is: Food and identity in the Neolithic Levant. In *We are what we eat: Archaeology, food and identity*, Katheryn C. Twiss (ed.), Southern Illinois University Press, Carbondale, pp. 50–68.

2008, Transformations in an Early Agricultural Society: Feasting in the southern Levantine pre-pottery Neolithic, *Journal of Anthropological Archaeology* 27(4):418–442.

2012, The complexities of home cooking: Public feasts and private meals inside the Çatalhöyük House, in eTopoi, Susan Pollock (ed.), Between Feasts and Daily Meals: Toward an Archaeology of Commensal Spaces, *Journal for Ancient Studies*, Special Volume 2, pp. 53–73. http://journal.topoi.org

Twiss, Katheryn C, Amy Bogaard, Mike Charles, J. Henecke, Nerissa Russell, Louise Martin, and Glynis Jones, 2009. Plants and animals together, *Current Anthropology* 50(6):885–895.

Tykot, R.H., N.J. van der Merwe, and N. Hammond, 1996, Stable isotope analysis of bone collagen, bone apatite, and tooth enamel in the reconstruction of human diet: A case study from Cuello, Belize, archaeological chemistry, *ACS Symposium Series* 625:355–365.

Tykot, Robert H., 2002, Contribution of stable isotope analysis to understanding dietary variation among the Maya, *Archaeological Chemistry Symposium Series*, v. 831, Archaeological Chemistry Symposium Publications, pp. 1–19.

Uberoi, J.P. Singh, 1962, *Politics of the Kula Ring: An analysis of the findings of Bronislaw Malinowski*. Manchester University Press.

Urton, Gary, 2012, Mathematics and Accounting in the Andes before and after the Spanish Conquest. In *Alternative forms of knowing (in) mathematics*, Swapna Mukhopadhyay and Wolff-Michael Roth (eds.) New directions in mathematics and science education vol. 24, pp. 17–32, Sense Publishers, Rotterdam, Boston, Taipei.

*U.S. News and World Report*, 2005, http://health.usnews.com/usnews/health/articles/050328/28sugar.b.htm, March 28.

Valamoti, S.M., 2004, Plants and people in Late Neolithic and Early Bronze Age northern Greece: An archaeobotanical investigation (Vol. 1258). British Archaeological Reports Limited, Oxford.

van der Veen, Marijke (ed.), 2003, Luxury foods. *World Archaeology* 34(3).

Van der Veen, Marijke, 2008, Food as embodied material culture: Diversity and change in plant food consumption in Roman Britain, *Journal of Roman Archaeology* 21:83–110.

van der Veen, Marijke, 2014, Arable farming, horticulture and food: Expansion, innovation and diversity in Roman Britain. In *The Oxford handbook of Roman Britain*, Millett, Martin, Louise Revell, and Alison Moore (eds.), Oxford University Press, Oxford, pp. 1–20.

van der Veen, Marijke, G. Andre, and Keith H. Steinkraus, 1970, Nutritive value and wholesomeness of fermented foods, *Journal of Agriculture and Food Chemistry* 18(4):576–578.

VanDerwarker, Amber M., 1999, Feasting and status at Toqua Site, *Southeastern Archaeology* 18(1):24–34.

Veblen, Thorstein, 1899, *The theory of the leisure class*, Macmillan, New York.

Velik, Susan C., 1977, Bone fragments and bone grease manufacturing: A review of their archaeological use and potential, *Plains Anthropologist* 22:169–182.

Ventris, Michael and John Chadwick, 1973, *Documents in Mycenaean Greek*, Cambridge University Press, Cambridge.

Ventura, Carol, 1996, The symbolism of Jakaltek Maya tree gourd vessels and corn drinks in Guatemala, *Journal of Ethnobiology* 16(2):169–183.

Visser, Margaret, 1986, *Much depends on dinner*, Grove Press, New York.
   1991, *The rituals of dinner, the origin, evolution eccentricities and meaning of table manners*, Viking, Penguin Books, Ltd, London.

Vogt, Evon, 1976, *Tortillas for the gods: A symbolic analysis of Zinacanteco rituals*, Harvard University Press, Cambridge, MA.

Voss, Barb L., 2008, Between the household and the world system: Social collectivity and community agency in Overseas Chinese archaeology. *Historical Archaeology*: 37–52.

Vroom, Joanita, 2000, Byzantine, garlic and Turkish delight, dining habits and cultural change in central Greece from Byzantine to Ottoman times. *Archaeological Dialogues* 7(2):199–216.

Wagner, Gayle E., 1987, Uses of plants by the Fort Ancient Indians. PhD thesis, Anthropology Department, Washington University, St. Louis, MO.

Wake, Thomas A., 1995, Mammal remains at Fort Ross: A study of ethnicity and culture change. PhD dissertation, Department of Anthropology, University of California, Berkeley, UMI publications, Ann Arbor, MI.

Walker, William H., 1995 Ceremonial trash. In *Expanding archaeology*, J.M. Skibo, W.H. Walker, and A.E. Nielson (eds.), University of Utah Press, Salt Lake City, pp. 67–79.

Walker, William H. and Lisa J. Lucero, 2000, *The depositional history of ritual and power agency in archaeology*, Routledge, London, pp. 130–147.

Wandsnider, Luann, 1997, The roasted and the boiled: Food composition and heat treatment with special emphasis on pit-hearth cooking, *Journal of Anthropological Archaeology* 16:1–48.

Wapnish, P. and B. Hesse, 1988, Urbanization and the organization of animal production at Tell Jemmeh in the Middle Bronze Age Levant, *Journal of Near Eastern Studies* 47(2):81–94.

1991, Faunal remains from Tell Dan: Perspective on animal production at a village, urban, and ritual center, *Archaeozoologia* 4:9–86.

Warde, Alan, 1997, *Consumption, food and taste*, Sage, London.

Watson, James L., 2005, China's Big Mac attack. In *The cultural politics of food and eating*, J. Watson and M. Caldwell (eds.), Blackwell Publishers, Oxford, pp. 70–79.

Weber, Max, 1992, *The Protestant ethic and the sprit of capitalism*. Routledge, London.

Weiner, Annette, B., 1992, *Inalienable possessions: The paradox of keeping-while-giving*, University of California Press, Berkeley.

Weismantel, Mary, 1988, *Food, gender and poverty*, Waveland Press, Prospect Heights.

1989, The children cry for bread: Hegemony and the transformation of consumption. In *The social economy of consumption*, B. Orlove and H. Rutz (eds.), Monographs in Economic Anthropology, No 6, Society for Economic Anthropology Publications, University Press of America, Lanham, pp. 105–124.

1991, Tasty meals and bitter gifts: Consumption and production in the Ecuadorian Andes. *Food & Foodways* 5(1–2):79–94.

1995, Making kin: Kinship theory and Zumbagua adoptions, *American Ethnologist* 22(4):685–709.

2004, Feasting on enemies in the Inca state. Andean Foodways Conference, Precolumbian Society, Washington, DC, September 18.

Wellhausen, E.J., L.M. Roberts, and E. Hernandez X, 1952, *Races of maize in Mexico: Their origin, characteristics and distribution*, The Bussey Foundation, Harvard University, Cambridge, MA.

Welch, Paul D. and C. Margaret Scarry, 1995, Status-related variation in foodways in the Moundville Chiefdom, *American Antiquity* 60(3):397–419.

Wendrich, Willeke, 2005 Specialist report on the Catalhöyük basketry. In *Changing materialities at Çatalhöyük: Reports from the 1995–1999 seasons*, Çatalhöyük

*Project Vol.* 5, Ian Hodder (ed.), McDonald Institute Monographs/British Institute of Archaeology at Ankara, Cambridge, pp. 333–338.

Wesson, Cameron B., 1999, Chiefly power and food storage in southeastern North America, *World Archaeology* 31(1):145–164.

Wetterstrom, Wilma, 1978, Cognitive systems, food patterns and paleoethnobotany. In *The nature and status of ethnobotany*, Richard I. Ford, (ed.), Museum of Anthropology, Anthropological papers, no. 67, University of Michigan, Ann Arbor, pp. 81–95.

Wheaton, B., 1983, *Savoring the past: The French kitchen and table from 1300 to 1789*, University of Pennsylvania Press, Philadelphia.

White, Christine D. and Henry P. Schwarcz, 1989, Ancient Maya diet: As inferred from isotopic and elemental analysis of human bone, *Journal of Archaeological Science* 16:451–474.

White, R. and H. Page (eds.), 1992, *Organic residues and archaeology: Their identification and analysis*, UKIC Archaeology Section, London.

White, T.E., 1953, Observations on the butchering technique of some aboriginal peoples No. 2, *American Antiquity* 19(2):160–164.

Whittle, Alasdair, 1996, *Europe in the Neolithic; the creation of new worlds*, Cambridge University Press, Cambridge.

Widgren, Mats, 2007, Pre-colonial landseque capital: A global perspective. In *Rethinking environmental history: World system history and global environmental change*, A. Hornborg, J.R. McNeill, and J.M. Alier (eds.), Roman Altamira,Walnut Creek.

Wiessner, Polly, 1981, Measuring the impact of social ties on nutritional status among the !Kung San, *Social Science Information* 20(4/5):641–678.

    1983, Style and social information in Kalahari San projectile points, *American Antiquity* 48:253–276.

    1996, Introduction: Food, status, culture and nature. In *Food and the status quest: An interdisciplinary perspective*, Polly Wiessner and Wulf Schiefenhövel (eds.), Berghahn Books, Oxford, pp. 1–18.

    2001, Of feasting and value: Enga feasts in a historical perspective. In *Feasts: Archaeological and ethnographic perspectives on food, politics and power*, M. Dietler and B. Hayden (eds.), Smithsonian Institution Press, Washington, DC, pp. 115–143.

Wiessner, Polly and Wulf Schiefenhövel (eds.), 1996, *Food and the status quest: An interdisciplinary perspective*, Berghahn Books, Oxford.

Wilk, Richard R., 1999, "Real Belizean food": Building local identity in the transnational Caribbean, *American Anthropologist* 101(2):244–255.

    2006, *Home cooking in the global village: Caribbean food from buccaneers to ecotourists*, Berg, London.

Wilk, Richard R. and L. Barbosa, 2012. *Rice and beans: A unique dish in a hundred places.* Berg, London.

Wilk, Richard R. and William Rathje, 1982, Household archaeology. Archaeology of the household: Building a prehistory of domestic life, *American Behavioral Scientist* 25(6):617–640.

Wilkie, Laurie A., 1996, House gardens and female identity of Crooked Island. In symposium Eating up old paradigms: A discussion of archaeological food, organized by Christine Hastorf and Sissel Johannessen, 61st Annual Meeting of the Society for American Archaeology, New Orleans, LA.

2001, *Lucrecia's well: An archaeological glimpse of an African-American midwife's household*, University of South Alabama Center for Archaeological Studies, Mobile.

Wilkins, John, n.d. Public (and private) eating in Greece, 450–3000 BC. MS on file with the author.

Wilkins, John, David Harvey, and Harvey Dobson (eds.), 1995, *Food in antiquity*, University of Exeter, Exeter.

Williams-Dean, Glenna, 1986, Pollen analysis of human coprolites. In *Archaeological investigations at Antelope House*, D.P. Morris (ed.), National Park Service, U.S. Dept. of the Interior, Washington, DC, pp. 189–205.

Williams-Dean, Glenna and Vaughn M. Bryant Jr., 1975, Pollen analysis of human coprolites from Antelope House. *The Kiva*, pp. 97–111.

Willcox, George H., 1977, Exotic plants from Roman waterlogged sites in London, *Journal of Archaeological Science* 4(3):269–282.

Wills, W.H. and Patricia L. Crown, 2004, Commensal politics in the prehispanic Southwest. In *Identity, feasting, and the archaeology of the greater southwest*, Barbara J. Mills (ed.), University Press of Colorado, Boulder, pp. 153–172,

Wilson, Anne C., 1973, *Food and drink in Britain*, Constable, London.

Wilson, Bee, 2012, *Consider the fork*, Penguin Books Ltd, London.

Wilson, Christine S., 1979, Food, custom and nurture: An annotated bibliography on sociocultural and biocultural aspects of nutrition, *Journal of Nutrition Education* 11(4):211–264, supplement 1.

Wilson, Thomas M. (ed.), 2005, *Drinking cultures: Alcohol and identity*, Berg, Oxford.

Wing, Elizabeth S. and Jane C. Wheeler (eds.), 1988, *Economic prehistory of the central Andes*. British Archaeological Reports International series #427, Oxford.

Winter, Marcus, 1976, The archaeological household cluster in the valley of Oaxaca, Mexico. In *The Early Mesoamerican village*, Kent V. Flannery (ed.), Academic Press, New York, pp. 25–31.

Winterhalder, Bruce, 1986, Optimal foraging simulation studies for diet choice in a stochastic environment, *Journal of Ethnobiology* 6(1):205–223.

Winterhalder, Bruce and Carol Goland, 1993, On population, foraging efficiency and plant domestication, *Current Anthropology* 34(5):710–715.

1997, An evolutionary ecology perspective on diet choice: Risk and plant domestication. In *People, plants, and landscapes: Studies in paleoethnobotany*, Kristen J. Gremillion (ed.), University of Alabama Press, Tuscaloosa, pp. 123–160.

Wittfogel, Karl, 1957, *Oriental despotism; a comparative study of total power*, Yale University Press, New Haven.

Wood, Jacqui, 2001, *Prehistoric cooking*, Tempus Publications, Charleston.

Woodward, Colin, 2004, *The lobster coast: Rebels, rusticators, and the struggle for a forgotten frontier*, Penguin Group, New York.

Wollstonecroft, Michèle, P.R. Ellis, Gordon C. Hillman, and Dorian Q Fuller, 2008, Advancements in plant food processing in the Near Eastern Epipalaeolithic and implications for improved edibility and nutrient bioaccessibility: An experimental assessment of sea club-rush (*Bolboschoenus maritimus* (L.) Palla), *Vegetation History and Archaeobotany* 17(suppl 1):S19–S27.

Wollstonecroft, Michèle and Aylan Erkal, 1999, Summary of plant processing experiments at Çatalhöyük. MS on file with the author.

Wollstonecroft Michèle, Zdenda Hroudova, Gordon C. Hillman, Dorian Q Fuller, 2011, *Bolboschoenus glaucus*, a new species in the flora of the ancient Near East, *Vegetation History and Archaeobotany* 20(5):459–470.

Wrangham, Richard W., 2009, *Catching fire: How cooking made us human*, Basic Books, New York.

Wrangham, Richard W., N. James, Holland Jones, Gregory Laden, David Pilbeam, and Nancy Lou Conklin-Brittain, 1999, The raw and the stolen: Cooking and the ecology of human origins, *Current Anthropology* 40(5):567–594.

Wright, Henry T., 1977, Recent research on the origin of the state. *Annual Review of Anthropology*, 6, pp. 379–397.

Wright, Henry T., Richard Redding, and Susan Pollack, 1989, Monitoring inter-annual variability: An example from the period of early state development in Southwest Iran. In *Bad year economics*, P. Halstead and J. O'Shea (ed.), Cambridge University Press, Cambridge, pp. 106–113.

Wright, Jr., Herb E., 1993, Environmental determinism in Near Eastern prehistory, *Current Anthropology* 34(4):458–469.

Wright, James C. (ed.), 2004, *The Mycenaean Feast, American School of Classical Studies at Athens*, Oxbow Books, Oxford.

Wright, Katherine, 2000, The social origins of cooking and dining in early villages of Western Asia. *Proceedings of the Prehistoric Society* 66:89–121.

Yellen, John, 1977, *Archaeological approaches to the present: Models for reconstructing the past.* Academic Press, New York.

Yen, Douglas E., 1980, Food crops. In *South Pacific agriculture: Choices and constraints*, R.G., Ward and A. Proctor (eds.), Agricultural Development Bank, Manila.

Yentsch, Ann, 1991, The symbolic divisions of pottery: Sex related attributes of English and Anglo-American household pots. In *The archaeology of inequality*, Randall Hall McGuire and Robert Paynter (eds.), Blackwell, Cambridge, MA, pp. 192–230.

1994, A *Chesapeake family and their slaves: A study in historical archaeology*, Cambridge University Press, Cambridge.

Ying-Shih Yü, 1977, Han China. In *Food in Chinese culture*, K.C. Chang (ed.), Yale University Press, New Haven, pp. 55–83.

Young, Michael, 1971 *Fighting with food: Leadership, values and social control in a Massim society*, Cambridge University Press, Cambridge.

1986, The worst disease: The cultural definition of hunger in Kalauana. In *Shared wealth and symbol: Food, culture and society in Oceania and Southeast Asia*, L. Anderson (ed.), Cambridge University Press, Cambridge, pp. 111–126.

Zeder, Melinda, 1991, *Feeding cities: Specialized animal economy in the ancient Near East.* Smithsonian Institution Press, Washington, DC.

Zeder, Melinda, Daniel Bradley, Eve Emshwiller, and Bruce D. Smith (eds.), 2006, *Documenting domestication new genetic and archaeological paradigms*, University of California Press, Berkeley.

Zohary, Daniel, Maria Hopf, and Ehud Weiss, 2013, *Domestication of plants in the Old World*, 4th edition. Oxford University Press, Oxford.

Zvelebil, Marek, 1995, Plant use in the Mesolithic and its role in the transition to farming, *Proceedings of the Prehistoric Society* 60:35–74.

    2000, Fat is a feminist issue: On ideology, diet and health in hunter-gatherer societies. In *Gender and material culture in archaeological perspective*, Moira Donald and Linda Hurcombe (eds.), St. Martin's Press, New York, pp. 209–221.

# Index

abstinence, 190
acceptance, 249
achiote, 270
acorn, 117
acorns, 116, 171, 205
aesthetics, 30, 227
affiliation, 225
Africa, 67, 118, 122, 148, 171, 253, 257
African. *See* Africa
Agarwal and Glenncross, 277
agave, 106, 121, 235, 236, 237, 263
agency, 2, 3, 7, 8, 14, 15, 29, 45, 57, 73, 92,
    106, 122, 129, 132, 142, 160, 164, 192, 200,
    219, 237, 241, 249, 271, 272, 273, 288,
    289, 294
agent, 2, 8, 54, 146, 243
agents, 7
agribusiness, 210
agriculture, 207
Agua Fria River, 236
Ainu, 242, 245
Alan Farahani, 265
Alaska, 99
Algeria, 57, 247
Algerians, 253
*algorrobo*, 137
alienated, 144
alkaloids, 120
alliance building feasts, 199, 208
alliance feast, 203
almonds, 114
*Amaranthus*, 236, 245
Amarna, 234
Amazon, 93
ambivalence, 196, 245
American South, 166

American Southwest, 92, 103, 104, 106, 121,
    130, 187, 199, 235, 259
American Spanish colonies, 248
Americas, 95
Anatolia, 71, 73, 86, 116, 245
*anatrepho*, 4
ancestors, 93, 117
ancestral power. *See* power
Ancestral Pueblo, 76
Ancestral Puebloan, 130, 235
ancestral stories, 196
Andean, 47, 61, 134, 146, 161, 279
Andes, 93, 96, 124, 187, 193, *See* Andean
animal bones, 85
Anna Harkey, 268
Annapolis, 166
Antelope House, 64, 65, 66
anthracosis, 304
apatite. *See* stable isotopes
Apicius, 172, 180
Apollonius, 175
Appadurai, 9, 64, 70, 129, 182, 191, 203, 205,
    257, 258, 293, 326
appetite, 6, 31
apples, 116, 249
apricots, 254
Arab flatbread, 247
Arabian Peninsula, 122
Arabs, 150, 256
archaeobotanical. *See* archaeobotany
archaeobotanicals, 125, 150
archaeobotany, 121
archaeological record, 92
Archaic, 96
Arizona, 136, 236
Arkansas, 139

Arnott, 189, 191
arrowroot, 106, 263
arsenical bronze, 163
Ashanti, 67
Asia, 238
Asia Minor, 172
Asıklıhöyük, 86
Assiros, 112
Atchison and Fullagar, 106
Athenaeus, 172
Athenians. See Athens
Athens, 170, 172, 174, 177
attached specialists, 167
Attica, 171, 172, 173
Augustinian Friars, 251
aurochs, 299
Australia, 185
Austria, 76
authenticity, 241, 243
authority, 195, 198
autobiography, 189
autocad, 268
aversion, 69
avocado, 137, 262
*ayni*, 198
Ayurvedic, 50
Ayurvedic medicine, 50
Azande, 292
Aztec, 240, 244, 248

baguette, 247, 253
bakeries, 168
baking, 73, 93
Banda, 63, 291
Barasana, 62, 235
Barbadian, 295
barbaric, 203
barley, 105, 114, 116, 121, 132, 171, 176, 299
barley cakes, 171
Barnhill, 116, 132
Barthes, 7, 13, 24, 52, 328
baskets, 91, 133, 297
beans, 64, 192, 205, 207, 209, 260, 263, 265, 270
bear meat, 242
beef, 116, 165, 244, 250
Beehr and Ambrose, 212
beer, 147, 166, 203
belief system, 208
Belize, 63, 240, 253
Belizeans. See Belize

Bemba, 25, 59, 61, 65, 291, 293
Bender, 169
Berber, 57, 191, 306
Binford, 99
bins, 116
birds, 263, 299
black pepper, 147, 150
Black Sea, 170, 171, 173, 176
blackberry, 209
blanching, 96
Blinman, 199
Blitz, 133
blood and body of Christ, 190
blowfish, 23
blueberry, 209
boar, 114
bodily memories, 11
body, 35, 135, 191, 273, 275, 277
body and blood of Christ, 189
*body technologies*, 287
Boeotia, 78
Bogaard, 90
boiling, 98, 299
bone tools, 91
bone wear, 92
Boserup, 145
boundaries, 229, 230, 252
boundary maintenance, 251
Bourdieu, 21, 30, 31, 57, 67, 68, 93, 217, 276, 287, 306
bourgeoisie, 244
bowls, 270
Brace, 92
Brahma Kumaris, 50
Brahmin, 257
Braithwaite, 292
Braudel, 152
Brazil, 256
bread, 75, 93, 146, 166, 172, 227, 233, 247
bread wheat, 201
breweries, 168
Brian Hayden, 194
brining, 95, 96
Britain, 75, 76, 286
British, 289, 294, *See* England
British Empire, 152
British Isles, 116
Britons, 252
Bronze Age, 75, 90, 112, 136, 138, 200, 201, 253, 289, 294
Brown, 269

Brown and Gerstle, 270
Brück, 294
Brumfiel, 92
buffalo, 72
burials, 297, 301, 306
Busby, 283, 292, 294
butchering, 98
butchering marks, 98
butchers, 167
butchery, 92, 254
Butler, 275
Bynum, 189
Byzantine, 78, 252

cacao, 261, 262
Cahokia, 205, 209, 210, 211, 213, 215
cairns, 112
cake, 8
*Calathea*, 106
caldrons, 203
California, 77, 254
*calla*, 96
camas root, 121
cannibalism, 257
canning, 91
canons of taste, 232
Canton, 38
Canyon de Chelly, 66
carbohydrates, 302
cardamom, 151
Caribbean, 148, 164, 166
caribou, 99
caries, 301, 302
carrying loads, 92
Cartesian ontology, 275
cat, 254
Catalan, 227
Çatalhöyük, 86, 101, 113, 115, 296, 308
Catherine of Siena, 191
Catholic, 139
cattle, 114, 165, 250
celebratory feasts, 197
celery, 249
Celtic, 29, 200, 203
*Celtis*, 265
Celts, 80, 176, 203
Central American, 51
ceramic, 130, *See* ceramics
ceramics, 78, 91, 116, 292
*ch'arki*. *See* jerky
*Chaahk*, 270

chaff, 101
*chaîne opératoire*, 15, 59, 60, 77, 81, 83, 95, 101, 123, 124, 140, 219, 224, 262
Charles, 90
cheese, 172
*Chenopodium*, 86, 116, 235
cherry, 263
chert, 210
chestnuts, 171
*chicha*, 212, *See* maize beer
chickpeas, 245, 299
chile heads, 52
chile peppers, 23, 24, 38, 51, 52, 156, 235, 247, 263, 265
Chimu, 113, 143, 154
Chimur, 161, 163, 164, 166, 170
China, 35, 48, 68, 71, 163, 247
Chinese, 254, *See* China
Chiripa, 198
*cholla*, 236
Chowtaw, 206
Christian, 189, 190, 191, 233, 247
Christianity. *See* Christian
Christmas, 61, 215
Christmas pudding, 41
*chunky*, 206
*chuño*, 96
citrus, 152
civilized, 257
civilizing, 32, 34, 35, 275, 279
civilizing of the appetite, 31
*civilizing* process, 31
Claasen, 187
class, 8
Classical, 177
Classical Greece, 173
Classical Greek, 48
clay cooking balls, 297
climate change, 77
closed body, 275, 278
coca, 156, 160, 235
Cochabamba, 125
cocoa, 148
codes of behavior, 196
coffee, 72, 148
cognitive dissonance, 23, 25, 169, 245
Colchester, 250
collagen. *See* stable isotopes
collecting, 84
collection, 187
collective memory, 9, 223

Colombia, 184, 235
colonial culinary traditions. *See* colonialism
colonial encounters, 29, 30, 246
colonial entanglements, 247
Colonial North American, 164
colonialism, 247, 253
colonization, 240, 252
Columbian Exchange, 148
comfort food', 79
commensal, 4, *See* alliance building
commodity, 160, *See* Marx
commodity fetishism, 144
communal identity, 269
communion, 190
communities of practice, 66
community, 169, 183, 271
competitive, 200, 271
competitive feasts, 203, 290
comportment, 31, 224, 228, 230, 255, 296, 306
Conibo-Shipibo, 202
Connerton, 60, 277
conquests, 79, 246, 253
*constructivist*, 275
consuming. *See* consumption
consumption, 21, 83, 85, 134, 144, 160, 187, 257, 271, 286, 289, 294
consumption etiquette. *See* etiquette
contamination, 228
control, 169
convent, 191
cook, 192
cookbooks, 180
cooked, 91, 95
cooking, 92, 117, 122, 131, 133, 192, 216, 257, 265, 289
cooking pots, 210
cooking vessel volumes, 259
Copan, 260
copper, 210
coprolites, 64, 135
core flavors, 10, 36, 51, 54
core food, 37, 53
core ingredients, 158
coriander, 249
Corinth, 251
corn, 207, 270
corn syrup, 148
cornbread, 207
corporeal body, 277
corporeality, 274
Cortez, 107

cotton, 263
cows, 72, 90, 214, 233
Crader, 98
cranium, 304
Crenshaw, 139
Crete, 112, 289
crop preferences, 88
crop production strategies, 90
crop valuation, 101
crops, 191
Crown, 92, 104, 187
Crusader invasion. *See* Frankish
Csordas, 287
cuisine, 5, 6, 14, 36, 67, 70, 71, 72, 78, 79, 80, 81, 86, 92, 109, 158, 161, 166, 177, 240, 241, 243, 249, 253, 254, 271
cuisine rupture, 71
cuisines, 14, 15, 51
Culina, 256
culinary clashes. *See* colonialism
culinary communities, 231
culinary encounters, 31
culinary rules, 30
culinary traditions, 32, 224, *See* table manners
*culinary triangle*, 42
culling, 85
cultural construction, 118
Cummins, 315
cuneiform, 168
curdling, 96
curiosity, 245
cutlery, 78
cutting, 119

D'Altroy, 112, 160
daily meals, 208
Damerow, 168
dancing, 196
Dangtalan, 259
Danish. *See* Denmark
Danube Gorges, 74, 186, *See* Mesolithic
David J. Guzman National Museum of Anthropology, 268
dead, 117, 196, 296
debts, 195, 200
deer, 114, 117, 184, 207, 212, 214, 215, 263, 270, 271, 299
Deetz, 131
deities, 196, 229
Delwin Samuel, 234
Democratic, 170

Denmark, 75, 76, 135, 136, 187
dental calculus, 301
deprivation, 189
Derrida, 200
desire, 152, 196
desire economy, 148
detoxify, 118, 120
Deuteronomy, 228
diacritical, 203
diastase, 97, 125
diet, 72
Dietler, 180, 203, 204, 247, 253
Dietler and Hayden, 198, 199, 204
digestibility, 120
digestion, 120
dining patterns, 78
discard, 138
disgust, 6, 11
dishes, 3, 5
display feast. *See* competitive feast
*distinctive authority*, 30
distributing, 192
dividual, 292, 296
*dividual body*, 278
dogs, 207, 263, 270
domestic contexts, 90
Douglas, 22, 31, 42, 46, 55, 57, 59, 61, 62, 63,
    64, 98, 129, 134, 138, 183, 228, 229, 256,
    275, 291, 293
Dravidian, 283
dried, 91
drink, 196
drink-conquest, 315
drought, 173
Drummond and Wilbraham, 179
drunken competition, 202
drying, 91, 92, 93, 95
Drying Utility Index, 99
ducks, 263, 270

Earl of Huntingdon, 214
Earle, 160
Early Intermediate Period, 137
earthovens, 121
Eastern agricultural complex, 205
eastern U.S., 204
eating, 2, 60, 83, 134, 190, 216
*ecological storage*, 108
economic capital, 143, 179
economic debt, 200
economic power, 161

economics, 10, 11, 14, 15, 93, 142, 200
Economics of Desire. *See* desire economy
Ecuador, 146, 191, 194, 291
edibility, 95
edible, 46, 91, 257
efficiency, 167
eggs, 299
Egypt, 170
El Salvador, 262
Elias, 31, 34, 129, 130, 152, 276, 279
elite, 167
elite cuisine. *See* cuisine
Ellis, 291
emancipation, 166
embodied practices, 203
embodiment, 11, 22, 272, 273, 274, 278, 281,
    287, 289, 296, 299, 303
emigration, 173
empowering, 197
empowerment, 183, 189, 191
emulation, 30, 39, 76, 79, 146, 149, 152, 153,
    203, 244, 249, 250
enchantment, 9
endocannibalism, 257, 286
energetics, 145
Engels, 142, 143
England, 61, 147, 148, 152, 160, 170, 187, 189,
    215, 233, 244, 277, 308
English, 214, *See* England
English Puritanism. *See* England
Enlightenment, 143
entrepreneurial feast. *See* celebratory
    feasts
Erin Rodriguez, 268
Ethiopia, 121, 122
etiquette, 192, 196, 255
Etruscan, 146, 148
Eucharist, 190
euergetism. *See* generosity
euphoria, 252
Eurasia, 149, 236
Euro-American, 254
Europe, 32, 47, 52, 73, 74, 76, 78, 116,
    130, 136, 146, 147, 186, 189, 194, 213,
    230, 279
Europeans, 149, 256, *See* Europe
European Renaissance, 227
exchange, 27
exchange networks, 167
exclusion, 246
experimentation, 64

*facets of personhood*, 296
Fajans, 8, 12, 118
Falk, 296
family, 255
family construction. *See* family
family feast. *See* feast
family politics, 192
famine, 172
famine foods, 171
farming, 74, 92, 191, 271
fast food, 69, 188
fasting, 189, 190
fasting women. *See* women
fasts, 189
fatty acids. *See lipids*
faunal analysis, 165
faunal remains, 251
feast consumption. *See* consumption
feast types, 197
feasting, 189, 208, *See* feasts
feasts, 9, 29, 34, 129, 150, 160, 162, 167, 183,
    194, 202, 207, 213, 214, 235, 251, 260, 271,
    286, 289, 305
female saints, 190
feminist, 189
feminist politics, 191
fermentation, 93
fermented, 91
Fertile Crescent, 74
fertility, 191, 271
festival foods, 152
festive landscape, 216
festive revolution', 202
fig, 249
finger millet, 121
fire, 92
fish, 116, 172, 207, 212, 214, 299, 301
fish and chips, 178
fish paste. *See garum*
fish processing, 99
Fish, S., 106
Fishbourne, 250
Fishergate monastery, 215
Five Dynasties, 37
Flavor Principle, 25, 36, 51, 61, 151, 288
flavors, 93
flotation, 88
food, 191, 200
food abstention, 191
food advertising, 227
food agency. *See* agency

food crises, 171–173
food distribution. *See* provisioning
food gifting, 207
food insecurity, 169
food of incarceration, 72
food pyramid, 61, 238
food resources, 169
food rules, 230
food selection, 19, 21
food stability, 174
Food stress, 175
food surplus, 161
food tradition, 5
food trucks, 133
foodscape, 214
foodways, 14, 149
foragers, 59
formal hospitality. *See* alliance building
Fort Ross, 77, 80, 251
Foss, 133
Foucault, 177, 275, 276, 277, 287
Fourth of July barbeque, 198
Fowler, 296
France, 243, 253
Frankish, 251, 252
Franks, 78, *See* Frankish
freeze-drying, 93, 96
freezing, 91
French, 7, 227, 247, 251
French colony, 247
French Revolution, 227
Freud, 186
Friedman and Rowlands, 169
Friesen, 99, 112
fruit, 100
fuel, 103, 104, 118
Fuller and Rowlands, 236

Galenic, 51
Galenic Theory. *See* humoral
game birds, 214
Gamerith, 76, 105
Garcilaso de la Vega, 162
Garnsey, 142, 173, 179
*garum*, 97, 172, 181
gas chromatography, 128
Gasser and Kwaitkowski, 236, *See* Ancient
    Puebloan
gastropolitical, 213
gastropolitics, 9, 16, 146, 182, 183, 192, 193,
    194, 216, 244, 257, 258

gathering, 92
GC/MS, 115, 116, 132, 137
Gell, 8, 288
gender, 8, 16, 124, 183, 192, 290, 296, 301
gender inequality. *See* gender
gender politics, 191
gender relations, 118
gender status, 186
generosity, 174, 200
gentry, 166
geophagy, 26
geophyte, 121
Gerhardt, 137
Germany, 74
Ghana, 291
Giddens, 58
Gidney, 214
Gifford-Gonzalez, 98, 99
gifts, 3, 15, 27, 192, 200, 201, 229, 284
gifting. *See* gifts
Gila and Salt Rivers, 236
Gila River, 236
Gillespie, 255
ginger, 150
giving-while-keeping, 110
Glassie, 131
Glenn Jones, 204
glucose, 196
goats, 90, 167, 299
gold, 163
Gold Coast, 295
Gold Rush, 254
Goodenough Island, 9, 110, 116, 188
Goody, 69, 91, 95
goose, 215
gourd, 207, 235, 261
grain distribution. *See* distribution
grain processing, 101
grapes, 171
*gravloks*, 108
grease extraction, 99
Great Lakes, 206, 208
Greece, 130, 251
Greeks, 50, 52, 80, 137, 144, 170, 171, 172, 176, 203, 252
griddle, 121, 122
grinding, 92, 93, 102, 103
grinding stones, 102, 104, 265
ground maize. *See* maize
ground stone, 104
gruel, 75

guava, 262, 263
Gumerman, 164, 231
gut contents, 135

habituation, 64
*habitus*, 21, 22, 57, 58, 67, 71, 73, 77, 79, 80, 81, 223, 225, 227, 231, 250, 256, 259, 272, 273, 276, 278, 288, 296, 300, 327, 351
halal meat, 228
Hallstatt, 203
hallucinogenic plants, 163
Hambledon Hill, 286
hamburger, 178, 180
Hamilakis, 273, 289
Hamshaw-Thomas, 249
Han, 35, 37, 38, 50, 163, 248
hand-cleaning, 101
hanging, 91
haptic, 196, 277, 288, 289
Harbottle, 71
hare, 214
Harris, 145
harvest festivals, 198
harvest rituals, 242
Harvesting, 84
haute cuisine, 36, 38, 40, 69, 70, 240, 243
Hawai'i, 185, 194, 279
Hayden and Dietler, 197
hazelnuts, 116, 205
hearth power. *See* power
hearths, 79, 102, 256, 265, 297, 300
Heating, 95
Hebraic kosher animal processing, 228
heirlooms, 9, 173, 284, 307, 308
Hellenistic, 203
Hendon, 109
Henshilwood, 100
herd management, 85
herders, 167
herding, 86
herding strategies, 86
heretic, 191
heretical, 190
hickory nuts, 205
hierarchical societies, 169
hierarchy, 194
Highland Clearance, 244
Hillman, 100
Himalayan Mountains, 28
Hindu, 293
hoard, 169

hoarding, 174
Hodder, 139
hog plums, 263
Hohokam. *See* Ancient Puebloan
holiness, 189
Holst, 106
holy, 191
Holy fasting. *See* fasting
homegrown, 188
Homer, 52
hominy, 128
honey, 116
honoring the dead, 195
Hopi, 259
hormones, 277
horsemeat, 23, 230
hospitality, 195
host, 200
hosting, 173, 198
households, 34, 255
Hu Sihui, 49
Hua, 19, 22, 256, 257, 284, 285, 286, 288, 292,
    293, 294, 306, 308
Hugh-Jones, 235
human physiology, 121
humoral, 47, 48, 49, 50, 54
Hungary, 75
hunger, 188, 277
hunter-gatherers, 111
hunters, 207
hunting, 84, 98

Iceland, 108
ICP, 115
*identification*, 220
identity, 3, 6, 7, 8, 9, 10, 13, 14, 15, 16, 19, 46,
    78, 88, 92, 109, 122, 135, 148, 189, 207,
    208, 220, 238, 243, 249, 251, 252, 253, 255,
    257, 271, 273, 275, 278, 284, 287, 294
identity construction. *See* identity
imagined communities, 69, 238
impure food, 187
inclusion, 246
incorporated practice, 60
incorporation, 2, 15, 40, 46, 48, 50, 190, 275,
    277, 289, 308
indebtedness, 201
India, 129, 145, 194, 237, 257, 258, 293
Indian, 283
indigenous cultivated crops, 208
*individual body*, 278

individualized presentation, 131
individuated-bounded body, 274
individuation, 16
inequality, 147, 153, 161, 169, 170
infanticide, 173
Ingold, 108, 109, 277
ingredients, 78, 93
Inka, 88, 112, 124, 157, 158, 160, 161, 162, 169,
    177, 193, 242, 250, 314
Inka Empire, 181
input, 145, 152
inscription, 276, 277, 288
insecurity. *See* food insecurity
intensification, 202, 207
Inuit, 251
inulin, 121
Iran, 71
Iranian, 253
Ireland, 123, 247
Irish, 76, *See* Ireland
Iron Age, 29, 135, 136, 147, 203
Iroquois, 258
Ishi, 117
Islam, 78
Italian, 73, 254
Italy, 52, 107, 136, 244, 245, 247

Japan, 237, 242
jars, 270
Jauja, 88, 250, 315
jerky, 95, 99
Jewish, 8, 78
Jews, 247
Johannessen, 209
John Stuart Mill, 180
Jomon, 242
Jones, A., 116, 117, 132
Jones, G., 89, 100, 112
Joya de Cerén, 56, 135, 139, 262, 271
jugglers, 196
Junín Puna, 85
Jutland. *See* Denmark

Kabyle, 57
Kahn, M., 185, 186, 187
*kapu*. *See* taboo
Kashrut. *See* Kosher
Kelertas, 201
Kelly, 212
*keng* meat stew, 37, 39
Kerala, 292

*kero*, 127
*kimchee*, 93, 97
kin-based system, 162
kitchens, 103, 272
kneading, 93
Knossos, 112
knotweed, 205
Konya plain, 299
Koreans, 93
Kosher food rules, 228
Küçükköy, 113
Kur River Basin, 167

labor, 92, 170, 202
labor mobilization, 162
labor taxation, 162
lactic acid, 97
Lady Dai, 38, 135
Lamanai, 260
lamb, 245, 254
Lambek, 278
*landesque capital*, 85
landscape storage. *See* storage
largesse, 195
Late Intermediate Period, 134
Late Neolithic, 201
Late Uruk, 166
Late Woodland, 208, 209
Latin America, 49, 62
latrines, 150
Lattes, 253
Lave and Wenger, 277
Leach, H., 123
least-cost, 152
leaves, 133
LeCount, 255, 261
legumes, 86, 88, 171
Leicester, 214
lentils, 113, 245, 299
Lepinski Vir, 74, 186
Levant, 89, 90, 102, 104, 229
Lévi-Strauss, 42, 44, 46, 56, 83, 92, 95, 97, 119
Leviticus, 228
Lev-Tov, 166, 251
Libya, 172
Lidwina, 190
lineage meal, 271
lipids, 97, 115, 128, 131, 135, 137
lithics, 91, 115, 160, 297
little barley, 205, 235, 236
lived lives, 58

loans, 201
lobster, 204
Logan, 63, 253
London, 253
*longue durée*, 46
Los Angeles, 197
Louisiana, 165
lower classes, 188
lower-class cuisines, 165
*lúcuma*, 137
Lupton, 229, 287
lutefisk, 73, 97, 119
Lyons and D'Andrea, 121, 122

Macbeth and Green, 227
macrobotanical data
    macrobotanicals, 88
macrobotanicals, 86
*madeleine* cookie, 3
maize, 23, 64, 86, 88, 104, 105, 116, 128, 137,
    156, 158, 160, 193, 205, 209, 210, 212, 235,
    242, 245, 250, 260, 263, 270
maize beer, 124, 163
*malanga*, 263
Malyan. *See* Tal-e-Malyan
mammals, 207
manioc, 93, 106, 137, 235, 263
Maori, 123
Margery Kempe, 189
marinating, 96
marriage, 191
Marriott, 293
marrow, 99
Marx, 122, 143, 144, 147, 169, 177, 275
Marxist, 103, *See* Marx
*masa*, 105
maslins, 172
material correlates, 93
materiality, 5, 7
materialize membership, 230
mats, 297
Matthews, 301
Mauss, 21, 27, 42, 229, 276
Maya, 260, 281
maygrass, 205, 212, 235
meal/meals, 3, 5, 7, 8, 9, 15, 42, 52, 55, 59,
    68, 80, 91, 93, 103, 104, 135, 138, 139,
    158, 166, 172, 182, 183, 187, 192, 194, 200,
    203, 204, 207, 242, 244, 253, 255, 258,
    260, 272, 289, 290, 291
meal grammars, 62

mealtimes, 255
meaning, 63, 95, 118
means of food production, 143
means of production, 169
meat, 8, 37, 39, 44, 46, 61, 90, 98, 99, 100,
       116, 121, 138, 147, 160, 163, 167, 172, 186,
       190, 192, 208, 214, 242, 243, 244, 249,
       257, 301
Meat, 244
Meat Drying Index, 99
meat hunger, 26
meat production. *See* production
Medieval, 32, 169, 189, 214, 253, 277, 308
medieval Europe, 257
Mediterranean, 51, 147, 171
Meigs, 19, 22, 25, 256, 284, 288
Melanesia, 110, 284, 293, 307
membership, 229
memories, 255, 273, *See* memory
memory, 3, 7, 11, 28, 51, 60, 107, 109, 165,
       194, 198, 260, 274, 277, 289
Mennell, 31, 33, 34, 41, 129, 179, 279
Meredith, 289
Mesa Verde, 65
Mesoamerica, 105
Mesolithic, 73, 74, 75, 76, 77, 78, 79,
       186, 187
Mesopotamia, 70, 71, 166, 251
mesquite, 236
metal vessels, 203
*metaphor of self*, 219
Mexican calabash, 262
Mexico, 63, 71, 92, 106, 107, 240
Michael Dietler, 194
Michelle Obama, 238
microbotanicals, 106
micromorphology, 86, 114, 297
Micronesia, 184
micro-organisms, 96
midden, 138, 149
Middle Ages, 149, 189, *See* Medieval
Middle Eastern, 122
middle-class, 166
middlemen, 167
military service, 193
milk, 90, 116, 132
milk vetch, 235, 236
millet, 171, 295
milling. *See* mill
milling stations, 102
Mills, 130, 259
Milton, 59

Ming, 38
Minnesota church dinners. *See* potluck
Minnis, 65
Minoan, 290
Mintz, 147, 164
Mississippi, 199, 204, 208
Mississippi Valley, 209
Mississippian, 205, 206, 208, 209
mixed grains, 242
mnemonics, 117
Monaghan, 234
Monks Mound, 213
Monticello, 98
moral, 109
moral authority, 162
moral commitments, 169
moral economy, 169, 170, 175
Morell-Hart, 63
mortality counts, 90
mortars, 102
Moss, 187
mounds, 206, 210
muesli, 68, 105
Mukkuvar, 283, 292
mummified, 96
Mund, 209
muscle attachments, 92
Musculoskeletal Stress Markers, 92
music, 196
musicians, 196
mussel harvesting, 100
mutton stew, 249
myths, 196

Nasca, 268
national dishes, 227
nationalism, 237
Natufian, 105, 265
Nautufian, 102
Near East, 102, 257
Near Eastern, 74, 253
Neolithic, 13, 20, 53, 71, 74, 75, 76, 77, 79,
       86, 101, 102, 103, 105, 111, 113, 116, 117,
       122, 123, 131, 132, 133, 186, 244, 245, 281,
       286, 289, 294, 296, 304, 307, 325, 327,
       333, 336, 338, 341, 343, 349, 351, 353,
       354, 355, 357, 358, 360, 364, 366, 367,
       370, 372, 374, 375, 377, 378, 381
Nepal, 28
Netherlands, 190
New England, 204
New Mexico, 124

New Zealand, 123
Nietzsche, 275
nitrogenous, 86
nixtamalization, 107
nomadic herders, 167
noodles, 37, 146, 245
Norman, 215
North America, 49, 71, 76, 121, 147, 205
North American, 99, 146
North American natives. *See* Native American
North American Plains, 71, 97
Norway, 108, 111
Norwegian, 254
nostalgia, 252, 255
nouvelle cuisine, 34
*nu*, 285, 292, 308
Nukak, 184
nutmeg, 150
nutrients, 120
nutrition, 26
nuts, 242

Oakland, 254
oats, 171
Oaxaca, 234
obligation, 196, 200
*Odyssey. See* Homer
Oglala, 76, 80, 164, 245
Oglala Lakota, 71
Ohio, 209
Ohnuki-Tierney, 219, 223
oil, 116
Olive oil, 172, 249
olives, 116, 171
omnivore, 25
omnivore's dilemma, 246
omnivore's paradox, 24, 80, 135, 153
omnivorous, 135
onion, 116
ontologies of the individual, 274
open body, 275, 278, 282
open-fluid body, 274
opium poppy, 150
opossum, 165
Opovo, 131
*Oriental Despotism. See* Wittfogel
origin myths, 206
Orkney, 116, 117
ortolan, 182
Osteoarthritis, 92
Ottoman, 78

Ottoman Empire, 252
Ötze, 136
output, 145
ovens, 121, 122, 133, 297, 300
overt competition, 197

Paca, 88
Pacatnamu, 154, 157, 164, 168, 177
Pacific Northwest, 121, 187, 200
pain, 277
Paleolithic, 13, 76
Palestine, 140
Panama, 106
Papua New Guinea, 19, 22, 185, 191, 197, 233, 256, 282, 284, 293
paradigm, 63
paradigmatic, 73
parching, 91, 92, 96, 101
parliamentary acts, 244
partible, 286, 287, 295, 304, 307
partible body, 274, 283
Passover, 234
pasta, 73
patron-client. *See* alliance building
patron-role. *See* alliance building
Pauketat, 208, 212
Payson Sheets, 262
peace, 195
peanut, 137
Pearsall, 106
peas, 114
peccary, 263
*pellagra*, 107, 211
Peloponnesian war, 170
performative giveaways. *See* potlatch
permeable, 293, 303
permeable body, 49, 51, 274, 282
personhood, 4, 15, 24, 92, 210, 220, 243, 273, 278, 287, 294, 306, 307
Perú, 86, 112, 153, 163, 166, 231, 233, 250
Phoebe A. Hearst Anthropology Museum, 268
phytolith, 89, 114
pickling, 95, 96
pigs, 90, 165, 197, 214, 233, 250, 254
pine pitch, 116
Piperno, 106
*pithoi*, 112
pits, 112, 214
place settings, 34
plantain, 236
plantations, 165

plastered bins, 113
Plato, 275
plazas, 207
*poi*, 184
poisonous, 171
political, 14
political control, 194
political economy, 197
political ideology, 193
political meals, 190
politics, 192
Pollan, 148
Pollard, 289
pollen, 86
Pollock, 200, 256
Polynesia, 121, 184
Pomo, 80
Pompeii, 133, 135
pork, 116, 197, 229, 230
porridge, 171, 172
post-Pleistocene, 77
potatoes, 86, 88, 123, 192, 233, 247
potlatch, 208, 271, *See* alliance building
potluck, 129, 198, 208, 214, 271
Potter and Ortman, 199
pounding, 91, 102
power, 8, 30, 71, 98, 113, 143, 169, 188, 191,
     192, 196, 200, 202, 211, 213
PPNA, 102
PPNB, 102, 103
*practical*, 108
practical knowledge, 11
practices, 7, 57, 68
praxis, 58, 219, 260
prayer, 233
pregnancy, 302
preparation, 2, 15, 60, 64, 81, 92, 124, 125, 187,
     254, 255, 265, 271, 286, 287, 299
presentation, 81, 83, 129, 196
prestige, 161, 166, 170, 195, 196, 197
prestige economy, 161
Price, 76
priests, 190
processing, 83, 91, 257, 289
processing methods, 92
procurement, 84
production, 77, 83, 84, 85, 86, 90, 92, 118,
     122, 133, 144, 162, 170, 294
  agricultural production, 86, 88
  crop production, 87
production intensification, 89

Proust, 3
provisioning, 163
psychological, 186
puffer fish, 23
*pukka-pukka*, 117
pulses, 172
pure, 188
purity, 31, 42, 187, 228, 234
Pyrenees, 227

*qero*, 314
*qolqa*, 112, 175, 177
Quechua, 95, 198
querns, 93
quinoa. *See Chenopodium*
*quipu*, 162

rabbits, 117, 124
raccoon, 165
Radcliffe-Brown, 145
*rakefisk*, 108
rank, 168
Rapapport, 197
*Ratatouille*, 79
raw, 91, 93, 95
raw food, 228
Real Alto, 106
recipes, 3, 9, 12, 39, 49, 60, 78, 203, 213, 224,
     227, 232, 308
reciprocity, 161, 162, 174
redistributive, 200
reduction, 119
reformation, 190
rejection, 249
relational personhood, 256, *See* personhood
religious elite, 167
Renaissance, 275
Republican, 170
resentment, 248
resilience, 245, 248
resistance, 245, 247, 249
restrictions. *See* taboo
rhizome, 299
Rhône Valley, 203, 204
rice, 36, 37, 38, 69, 242, 295
Rich Neck Plantation, 165
Richards, 25, 286
Richards and Pearson, 301
Rio Grande, 41
risk, 173
risk aversion, 110, 174

risk management, 107
ritual games, 206
rituals, 139, 260
roasting, 95, 98, 299
Robertson Smith, 229
Robin Hood, 182
Rodríguez-Alegría, 248
rolling, 105
Romans, 133, 150, 170, 180, 189, 247, 250, 252
Roman conquest, 248
Roman Empire, 142, 175
Rome, 171, 172, 173
root, 121, 123
Rosen, 89, 113
rotted, 91, 95
Rotting, 95, 97
Rowley-Conwy, 77
Rozin, 22, 68
Rozin, E., 10, 51, 52
Rozin, P., 24, 25
rubbish, 138
rubbish disposal, 83
ruminant mammals, 229
rupture, 227
Russian, 77
rye, 171, 299

sacred, 96
saffron, 151
Sahlins, 27
saint, 191
saintliness, 190
Sallaberger, 200
Salt, 173
Salt River, 236
salting, 96
Samburu, 71, 245
Santa Cruz River, 236
Sardinia, 233
satiation, 13
sauce, 172
sauerkraut, 97
Sausa, 134, 160, 162, 177, 315
Saussure, 63
Scandinavian, 73, 254
Scholliers, 220
Schroeder, 295
Scotland, 132
Scott, 165, 166
Seafood, 172
seashells, 210

security, 108
sediment analysis, 86
seed cakes, 212
seed harvests, 100
selective appropriation, 247
self-definition, 108
semiotics, 133
Semitic rituals, 229
Senegambia, 295
senses, 21, 273
sensory, 9
sensory traditions, 6
sensual pleasure, 196
sentient, 44
separation, 119
serotonin, 196
servers, 192
serving, 83, 131, 132, 133, 255, *See* presentation
serving vessels, 209
sex, 196
sexual favors, 190
Shalako, 271
shaming, 197
Shang, 49
sheep, 90, 167, 214, 299
shelf-life, 91
shell mounds, 289
shellfish, 187
shelling, 91
Sherpa, 28
Sherratt, 2, 116
Shilling, 288
Shiriah law, 228
shredding, 91
sieving, 101
signature dishes, 259, 260
signature foods, 232, 244, 257, 271
signifying units, 52
Silchester, 249, 250
Silk Road, 247
Silk Trade Road, 50
silos, 112
silver, 160, 163
singing, 196
slave owners, 204
slavery, 147
slaves, 156, 164, 165, 168, 177, 188, 204, 295
Smith, Adam, 143
smoke, 237
smoked, 91
smoking, 91, 95, 96

snack, 242
social agency, 8
social control, 195
social exclusion, 183
social fact, 2
social memory, 9, 17
social power. *See* power
*social storage*, 109
society, 243
solidarity, 195
solidarity feast, 198
Solon's rule, 174
sorghum, 122, 295
soup, 260
South African Cape, 100
South America. *See* Andes
soybean, 36
space, 139
Spain, 107, 172
Spanish, 157, 248
Spanish inquisition, 78
specialists, 161
Speth, 124
spice trade, 181
spices, 149, 160, 214, 249
Spielmann, 41, 185
spirituality, 189
squash, 137, 205, 207, 209, 260, 263, 270
squirrel, 165
St. Louis, 205
stable isotopes, 74, 79, 97, 125, 128, 135, 136,
    211, 214, 260, 286, 295, 301
stable isotopic. *See* stable isotopes
Stahl, A., 120
staple, 172
staple distribution, 167
staple finance, 159, 160, 162
staple food production, 161
staple production, 160, 168, *See* production
starch grains, 106, 107, 121, 128
starvation, 188, 191
state, 170
state farms, 162, 168
status, 107, 161, 168, 187
stewing, 91
sticky rice, 237
Stirling phase, 210
stirring, 92
stone ground, 105
storage, 2, 60, 64, 78, 80, 81, 83, 91, 96, 97,
    98, 99, 100, 102, 103, 107, 108, 109, 110,
111, 112, 114, 116, 117, 122, 125, 131, 132,
    133, 162, 163, 172, 209, 213, 262, 265, 269,
    270, 271, 297, 299, 300, 306, 330, 337,
    344, 352, 353, 354, 356, 357, 366, 371,
    377, 381
    storing, 93
storage pits, 207, 210
storage vessels, 109, 116
storytelling, 196
Strathern, 282
stratification, 196
Strontium, 301
structural, 50
structuralism, 42, 146
structuralist, 47
structuration, 58, *See* structuring structures
structuring structure, 43, 73, 93
Stylistic competition, 203
subaltern, 189
subsistence, 108
suffering, 191
sugar, 148, 160
sugar cane, 147
sumac, 209
Sumer, 177
Sumerian, 168
sumptuary laws, 33, 153, 244
sumpweed, 205, 212
Sunday roast, 244
sunflower, 205, 209
surplus, 160, 161, 163, 168, 169, 202, 207, 210
surplus production, 162, 197, 208
Sutton, 277, 289
swan, 212, 215
Sweden, 75
sweet, 148
Switzerland, 238
symbolic, 93
symbolic capital, 143, 161, 179, 198. *See* value
symbolic codes, 6
symbols, 196
syntagm, 63
syntagmatic, 73
Syria, 130

T'ang, 38
table manners, 32, 34, 39, 78, 129, 130, 255, 272
taboo, 22, 23, 46, 184
Tal-e Malyan, 167
tamales, 260
*tambo*, 112

Tamil, 191, *See* Brahmin
*tannur*, 122
tansy mustard, 235
taphonomy, 138, 139, 140
tapir, 184
*tapu. See* taboo
task, 93
taskscape/s, 58, 60, 83, 98, 260
taste, 6, 10, 14, 15, 25, 29, 35, 39, 67, 78, 80, 249
taste aversions, 24
taxation, 168
techniques of the body, 7, 15, 44, 274, 276, 280, 287, 289, 293, 296
technologies of self, 287, 294, 302
*technologies of the body*, 307
technology, 122
teeth, 301
teff, 121, 122
Tell Jemmeh, 90
temperature, 120
temples, 167
tending, 84
Tenochtitlan, 240
tepary beans, 236
Terezín, 9
Thanksgiving, 11, 225, 294
theory of action, 58
theory of feasting, 194
Thomas Jefferson, 98
threshing, 92, 93, 101
Thule, 47
Thy, 201
Tiwanaku, 158
Tlingit, 187, 188
toasting, 122, 196, 299
tobacco, 148, 207, 209
Tohono O'odam, 236
tomatoes, 23, 73, 230, 245, 247
tooth-wear, 301
Torah, 229
Tories, 170
tortillas, 105
toxic molecules, 95
toxins, 120
trace element analysis, 135
traction, 90
trade, 173, *See* exchange
trade hub, 210
traditional dishes, 79
transformation, 9
tribute, 195, 208

Tringham, 131, 289
Trobriand Islands, 28, 233
*trophe*, 4
Trostel, 259
tubers, 121
*Tuchungkee*, 206
*tunta*, 97
turkey, 215
Turkish, 96
Turner and Lofgren, 259
turtle, 254, 263

Ukraine, 76
unattached specialists, 167
Unimak Island, 99
United States, 7, 52, 148, 170, 198, 238, 254, 255
unleavened bread, 8
Upper Mantaro, 157, *See* Upper Mantaro Valley
Upper Mantaro region, 134
Upper Mantaro Valley, 86, 112, 125, 140, 157, 162
upper Ohio, 208
Uruk, 168, 169, 170, 177, 251
U.S. government, 72
utensils, 91, 93, 118, 133, 140, 192, 196

Valley of Mexico, 211
valuations. *See* value
value/s, 10, 22, 63, 88, 89, 93, 107, 118, 121, 138, 139, 146, 152, 192, 194, 228, 238, 249, 251, 253
VanDerwarker, 208
Veblen, 42
Vedic. *See* Ayurvedic
Venice, 150
venison, 116, 207
vertical solidarity. *See* alliance building
vessel volume, 267
vessels, 200, 297
Victorian, 215
Vilcanota Valley, 163
Virginia, 165
Virú Valley, 137
Vix krater, 200
Vlasac, 186
Vroom, 78, 130

Wamira, 185, 186, 188, 191
Wandsnider, 95, 120, 124
Wanka I, 88

Wanka II, 88, 125, 193
Wanka III, 88, 193
*wanlla*, 146
war, 173, 195
Wari, 158, 257
Warren DeBoer, 202
water, 85
waterlogged conditions, 150
wealth, 113
wealth finance, 160, 169
*Wealth of Nations. See* Smith, Adam
weapon of the weak, 189
weed taxa, 90
Weiner, 28
Weiner, S., 89
Weismantel, 67, 70, 146, 191
Wendrich, 113
whales, 182
wheat, 36, 38, 105, 114, 116, 121, 171, 176, 180, 245, 299
wheat flour, 168
white bread. *See* bread
white-lipped peccary, 257
Whittle, 75
Wiesmantel, 192
Wilconte, 249
wild boar, 299
wild game, 165
wild plants, 171
Wilk, 63, 240, 253
wine, 116, 137, 139, 146, 148, 171, 172, 176, 203

winnowing, 91, 92, 93, 101
Wisconsin, 208
Wittfogel, 85, 143, 161
women, 186, 189
women's work, 104
wooden basins, 133
Woodland, 205
wool, 90
woven mats, 114
Wrangham, 92
Wright, K., 102

Xunantunich, 261

yams, 116, 233, 295
Yanamarca, 88
Yangtze, 38
Yellen, 99
Yemen, 122
yield, 145
*yin* and *yang*, 49
yogurt, 245
York monastery, 214
Young, 9, 197

Zambia, 61
Zeder, 167
Zhou, 35, 36, 39
Zumbagua, 191
Zuni Pueblo, 271
Zvelibil, 185

CPSIA information can be obtained
at www.ICGtesting.com
Printed in the USA
LVOW10*0235150717

541464LV00011B/314/P